PLANETARY MODERNISMS

MODERNIST
LATITUDES

MODERNIST LATITUDES

JESSICA BERMAN AND PAUL SAINT-AMOUR, EDITORS

Modernist Latitudes aims to capture the energy and ferment of modernist studies by continuing to open up the range of forms, locations, temporalities, and theoretical approaches encompassed by the field. The series celebrates the growing latitude ("scope for freedom of action or thought") that this broadening affords scholars of modernism, whether they are investigating little-known works or revisiting canonical ones. Modernist Latitudes will pay particular attention to the texts and contexts of those latitudes (Africa, Latin America, Australia, Asia, Southern Europe, and even the rural United States) that have long been misrecognized as ancillary to the canonical modernisms of the global North.

Barry McCrea, *In the Company of Strangers: Family and Narrative in Dickens, Conan Doyle, Joyce, and Proust*, 2011

Jessica Berman, *Modernist Commitments: Ethics, Politics, and Transnational Modernism*, 2011

Jennifer Scappettone, *Killing the Moonlight: Modernism in Venice*, 2014

Nico Israel, *Spirals: The Whirled Image in Twentieth-Century Literature and Art*, 2015

Carrie J. Noland, *Voices of Negritude in Modernist Print: Aesthetic Subjectivity, Diaspora, and the Lyric Regime*, 2015

PLANETARY MODERNISMS

PROVOCATIONS ON MODERNITY ACROSS TIME

SUSAN STANFORD FRIEDMAN

COLUMBIA UNIVERSITY PRESS

NEW YORK

Columbia University Press
Publishers Since 1893
New York   Chichester, West Sussex
cup.columbia.edu
Copyright © 2015 Columbia University Press
Paperback edition, 2018
All rights reserved

Library of Congress Cataloging-in-Publication Data
Friedman, Susan Stanford.
Planetary modernisms : provocations on modernity across time / Susan Stanford Friedman.
  pages cm.—(Modernist latitudes)
Includes bibliographical references and index.
ISBN 978-0-231-17090-1 (cloth : alk. paper)
ISBN 978-0-231-17091-8 (pbk. : alk. paper)
ISBN 978-0-231-53947-0 (e-book)
1. Modernism (Literature) 2. Modernism (Aesthetics)
3. Civilization, Modern. 4. Cosmopolitanism.
5. Postcolonialism. I. Title.
PN56.M54F75 2015
809'.9112—dc23
2014044880

Columbia University Press books are printed on permanent and durable acid-free paper.

Cover design: Matt Roeser
Book design: Lisa Hamm

For

Owen Friedman Weber
2008–2012
Ever curious, ever laughing, ever tender, ever brave
Everlastingly cherished

and

Dylan Friedman Weber
Ever loving older brother

CONTENTS

Preface ix

Introduction 1

PART I
RETHINKING MODERNIST STUDIES

1. Definitional Excursions 19

2. Planetarity 47

PART II
RETHINKING MODERNITY, SCALING SPACE AND TIME

3. Stories of Modernity: Planetary Scale in the *Longue Durée* 83

4. Figures of Modernity: Relational Keywords 143

PART III
RETHINKING MODERNISM, READING MODERNISMS

5. Modernity's Modernisms: Aesthetic Scale and Pre-1500 Modernisms 183

6. Circulating Modernisms: Collages of Empire in Fictions
of the Long Twentieth Century   215

7. Diasporic Modernisms: Journeys "Home" in Long Poems
of Aimé Césaire and Theresa Hak Kyung Cha   283

Conclusion. A Debate with Myself   311

Notes 345

Bibliography 403

Index 433

PREFACE

Planetary Modernisms: Provocations on Modernity Across Time proposes a paradigm shift to reorient the way we think about *modernity* and the aesthetic *modernisms* that contribute to its creation. Challenging the familiar story that the West invented modernity in the post-1500 period of Europe's "rise," the book enlarges the scale of space and time to argue for a fully planetary approach to modernity. Within this larger frame, modernity is a planetary phenomenon across the millennia and is understood as multiple, polycentric, and recurrent instances of transformational rupture and rapid change across the full spectrum of political, economic, cultural, technological, demographic, and military arenas of interlocking societies and civilizations. Not reducible to utopic progress or dystopic devastation, modernity in the full scope of geohistory often incorporates both ends of the spectrum, with uneven effects on different groups of people and areas of the world. As a bang/clash of contradiction, modernity often results from violent conquest and imperial expansions that produce hybridic and regenerative mixtures of peoples, cultures, goods, and ideas. Out of the vortex comes change that takes shape in vast networks of relational circulation around the globe.

In some ways, the planetary turn in modernist studies is a phenomenon of the twenty-first century, enabled as a new way of reading geohistory and its aesthetic manifestations by the new modernities of an ever-more interconnected and digital age. What our new modernity of today helps us see is that an additive approach cannot fully accomplish a planetary turn in the field. To assume "Western modernity" (itself an ideological construct with real consequences) as the baseline, point of origin, and measure of all other concurrent and subsequent modernities does not sufficiently rethink the framework of modernist studies. *Planetary Modernisms*, in contrast, challenges the center/periphery and diffusionist frameworks that still prevail in the field across the disciplines. It draws on the many impressive studies that characterize the transnational turn in modernist studies but provocatively asks for an even more radical epistemological shift, one that can incorporate the geo-histories and cultures of the planet *before* 1500, the conventional benchmark for the emergent rise of Western modernity.

In its efforts to do so, *Planetary Modernisms* travels far afield in space and time to test the usefulness of a more expansive framework. It compares, for example, the sedentary modernity of the Tang Dynasty with the mobile modernity of the Mongol Empire. It refuses the conventional approach to modernism as a definable aesthetic style, movement, or period of the late nineteenth and early twentieth centuries. Instead, it regards *modernism* as the aesthetic dimension of any given modernity and tests the usability of such a view with scalar reductions, snapshot examinations, and collaged readings of aesthetic modernities *before* 1500 and in the long twentieth century: in chapter 5, the Tang Dynasty poetry of Du Fu, the ceramic innovations of the Abbasid Empire, and the ongoing improvisational phenomenon of Kabir in the wake of Tamerlane's conquest of northern India; and in chapters 6 and 7, the interlocking modernisms in the wake of empire in the fictions and poetry of Joseph Conrad / Tayeb Salih, E. M. Forster / Arundhati Roy, Rabindranath Tagore / Swanakumari Devi / Virginia Woolf, and Aimé Césaire / Theresa Hak Kyung Cha.

Planetary Modernisms has a long history of its own, filled with the landscapes of many different regions of the world where I learned so much from others as I presented my work, including especially Argentina, Britain, China, Hong Kong, India, Italy, Lebanon, the Netherlands, Portugal, the United Arab Emirates, and Taiwan, as well as the United States and Canada. The book grew not only out of my earlier work on modernists including H.D., James Joyce, Sigmund Freud, and Woolf but also out of the convictions of a transnational/locational feminist theory forged in *Mappings:*

Feminism and the Cultural Geographies of Encounter (1998), which posits the existence of circulating networks of locational feminisms open to ideas from elsewhere but attuned to perspectives of the local.

Naming all the many scholars, students, fellowships, and institutional affiliations to whom I am indebted for their help in bringing *Planetary Modernisms* into print feels like an impossible task. Edward Friedman merits the first thanks for introducing me to world history and for his own capacity to shift assumed paradigms in startlingly fresh and prescient ways. Cassandra Laity, as the Modernist Studies Association coeditor of *Modernism/Modernity*, encouraged me to continue experimenting with alternative modes of critical writing by publishing "Definitional Excursions" in 2001 and two subsequent essays. Jessica Berman and Paul Saint-Amour, editors of the Modernist Latitudes series, have offered invaluable and generous advice on shaping the book's full contours, along with the astute suggestions of Philip Leventhal, my editor at Columbia University Press.

Stimulating and often downright heated exchanges with Eric Hayot have helped immeasurably in honing my arguments, and the work, constructive criticism, and encouragement of Jay Clayton, Wai Chee Dimock, Rita Felski, B. Venkat Mani, Tejumola Olaniyan, R. Radhakrishnan, V. Naranaya Rao, Ken Seigneurie, Shu-mei Shih, and Rebecca L. Walkowitz have greatly improved the book. Many others whose work and conversation have contributed significantly include Houston A. Baker Jr., Christopher Bush, Marina Camboni, Pamela Caughie, Michael Coyle, Melba Cuddy-Keane, Kevin Dettmar, Laura Doyle, Rachel Blau DuPlessis, Fan Ming-ju, Guillermina De Ferrari, Christine Froula, Christopher GoGwilt, Margaret Homans, Paul Jay, Priya Joshi, Mary Layoun, Satya Mohanty, Adalaide Morris, Rob Nixon, Jahan Ramazani, Brian Richardson, Stephen Ross, Irene Ramalho Santos, Nirvana Tanoukhi, Andrew Thacker, Jennifer Wicke, Laura Winkiel, Mark Wollaeger, and Stephen Yao. Friends, colleagues, and former colleagues in other disciplines have helped me broaden and deepen my forays into their fields—especially Noel Carroll, John Dower, Ken George, Linda Gordon, Liu Dong, Nicole Huang, David Morgan, Judith Walzer Leavitt, Lewis Leavitt, Kirin Narayan, James C. Scott, Thongchai Winichakul, Anna L. Tsing, Neil Whitehead, and André Wink. To my students at the University of Wisconsin–Madison, I am especially grateful for the chance to test out my ideas and learn from their projects. Graduate student assistants who have been especially helpful include Anupam Basu, Jack Dudley, Elizabeth Evans, Alainya Kavaloski, and Elizabeth Schewe. Final thanks go to the anonymous readers, who took the time to do in-depth critical readings, offering numerous substantive suggestions that I have attempted to address.

The Institute for Research in the Humanities at the University of Wisconsin–Madison provided the interdisciplinary matrix out of which *Planetary Modernisms* emerged. Fellowships from the ACLS, the Feminist Scholar program of the UW-Madison Center for Research on Gender and Women, and the UW-Madison Graduate School also provided the time for expansive research. As a senior fellow at the Institute from 1994 through 1999 and as director of the IRH since 2007, I learned firsthand the powerful effects of interdisciplinary community in learning to address better what is at stake in one's research and how to reach a wider audience outside one's inner circle of specialists. The Institute also served as the first home of the Border and Transcultural Studies Research Circle (1996–2006), where I first heard articulated the multiple formations of modernity in different times, places, and disciplines. At the Institute, I learned to trust the potential of creative symbiosis and serendipity in producing new ways of seeing human experience and meaning making across time, space, medium, and discipline.

PLANETARY MODERNISMS

INTRODUCTION

> Modernity is back with a vengeance. People are reflecting anew on the protean meanings of the modern, on its ambiguous legacies and current realities. . . . Yet this return is also a beginning, as scholars tackle well-worn ideas and calcified debates from new angles. As a result, our view of modernity is changing dramatically. The modern is not what it used to be.
>
> —Rita Felski, "New Cultural Theories of Modernity"

> It is so important, if one is to have a bit of freedom from the constraints of the field, to attempt to explore the limits of the theoretical culture: to provide the means for knowing what one is doing and for freeing oneself from the naiveté associated with the lack of consciousness of one's bounds.
>
> —Pierre Bourdieu, *The Field of Cultural Production*

The twenty-first century opens with a sense of urgency. Once again, "things fall apart; the centre cannot hold."[1] Once again, modernity is "at large."[2] The forms of globalization closing off the old century and opening the new have expanded global networks and accelerated mobilities of all kinds—from money to people, from drones to popular culture. It is by now a truism but true nonetheless that 9/11 shook the foundations of the world in ways that will continue to unfold for decades, spawning new modernities in an ever-more interconnected world. Once again, the rise of new global conflicts and new world orders has unsettled familiar modes of thinking and reconstituted the world along new lines of power, new modes of resistance, and new modes of meaning making that collide and blend with the old. New technologies of transnationalism both serve and bypass the nation-state as the new cosmopolitanism contests the new communalism. The modernities of today—from China to Iran, Brazil to Nigeria, from Turkey to the nations of the Arab Spring—compel a rethinking of the modernities of the past. The digital revolution has ruptured old ways of knowing, transformed everyday life, and ushered in an age of big data with staggering potentials for panoptical surveillance, instantaneous communication, and virtual communities from the local to the global. "Modernity is now (and has been for some time) everywhere, and the discourse of postmodernity seems only an episode (if a significant one) within a certain transformation of Western modernity itself," Andreas Huyssen wrote at the opening of the twenty-first century.[3] "The modern is not what it used to be," Rita Felski suggests; it "is back with a vengeance."[4] Once again, modernity is reinvented. The New is Now. Once again.

Planetary Modernisms: Provocations on Modernity Across Time is about expanding the frameworks of modernist studies, about freeing ourselves from the assumptions that govern the field and opening our work to a radical rethinking of modernity and modernism suitable for the new modernities of the twenty-first century. In this sense, the book is a series of provocations that bring to modernist studies the spirit of epistemological rupture long associated with modernism itself. The book challenges the tendency of all new fields to institutionalize knowledge, to settle down into a fixed terrain of questions and approaches, to close off new ideas beyond the "limits of the theoretical culture" (to echo Pierre Bourdieu). The intent is to provoke questions, not to settle them—to map new ways of thinking rather than to set new boundaries of thought.

Planetary Modernisms is not a manifesto. It does not assert axioms to work within and live by as scholars, students, and readers. Instead, it asks that we shake the ground upon which we stand, that we circle around the questions of modernism/modernity, seeing them from multiple perspectives, examining their different effects, opening up possibilities for new ways of thinking. Its aim is to keep alive the contradictions in the field, affirming that this tension is dynamic and open to productive interrogation.

The meanings of modernity and modernism are perpetually unsettled, unsettling. And herein lies the potential of the field. *To provoke* means to unsettle, also possibly to annoy. It is my hope that *Planetary Modernisms* unsettles settled ways of thinking and that any annoyance it produces can become productive for new kinds of work in the field that go well beyond what I can myself produce or even imagine. *Planetary Modernisms* intends to open doors others may go through.

Why? What's wrong with the doors we already have, the frameworks within which we work? Too much provocation can turn into an end in itself, a stance of perpetual critique that does not endear the humanities to a wider public. Yet *Planetary Modernisms* does emerge from a strongly ethical standpoint that begins in critique but moves beyond the gadfly position to offer new ways of thinking about modernity and modernism. Its aim is to open up the possibility for new knowledge that matters—not only for our understanding of the past but also for how we shape our futures. As a field in general, modernist studies is insufficiently planetary to fulfill the promise of what Douglas Mao and Rebecca L. Walkowitz have termed "the transnational turn" in the field.[5] Whether adhering to a canonical modernism, a Jamesonian "singular modernity," the modernity of a Wallersteinian "world-system," or a Deleuzian "minor" or "alternative" modernity, the field has insufficiently challenged the prevailing "Western" framework within which studies of modernity and modernism are conducted.[6] By "the West" and "Western" here and throughout *Planetary Modernisms*, I refer not to a fixed geographical area of the earth but rather to an *idea* that places certain peoples and cultures at the center of a diffusionist, linear human history, whether for praise as the signifier of civilization or for condemnation as the sign of oppression.[7] *Planetary Modernisms* argues that this idea of the West—what Shu-mei Shih calls a "symbolic construct"—is thoroughly entangled with the *idea* of modernity as an invention of the West, as a product of the West's exceptionalism, and as the kind of nonconscious ideology to which Ella Shohat and Robert Stam allude in the resonant pun of their title: *Unthinking Eurocentrism*.[8] *Planetary Modernisms* aims to "unthink" the West's idea of itself as the Ur-modernity by rethinking modernity on a planetary scale.

What drives *Planetary Modernisms* is a commitment to a planetary modernist studies, by which I mean the imperative to develop a framework for the field that encompasses the world across time, in the *longue durée* of human history. Positing "other," "alternative," or "minor" modernities have been important for unthinking Euro/American centrisms, cracking open the door to the West's exclusivity, but such categories are insufficient because they leave the West as the measure by which all other modernities are understood. It is not enough to add alternative modernities to the Western instance of modernity. In Kuhnian terms, the various notions of other modernities are the anomalies to a Weberian concept of modernity that have begun to pile up, the exceptions that taken together are harbingers of a major paradigm shift that will supplant the Western idea of modernity.[9] The shift that *Planetary Modernisms* asks for is a fundamental rethinking of modernity that posits it as a geohistorical condition that is multiple, contradictory, interconnected, polycentric, and recurrent for millennia and across the globe. Modernity, I argue, takes various forms—thus, the *plural*; it happens again and again—thus, *recurrence*; it is constituted through many interconnected centers—thus, *global, relational*. In all its various forms in geohistory, modernity produces heightened, often extreme and accelerating change that spreads through the various domains of society—from the technological and commercial to the political and philosophical; from the aesthetic and cultural to the epistemological and linguistic. Modernity can signal rebellion or capitulation—thus, *contradictory*. Modernity can enslave or free, shatter or exhilarate, displace or replace, dismantle or reassemble—thus, *utopian* and *dystopian* at once. Modernity is itself rupture: a paradigm shift, a geohistorical transformation on a large scale.

Like the modernity of which it is a part, modernism is also multiple, polycentric, relational, and recurrent. Modernism, as I use the term in *Planetary Modernisms*, is not a single aesthetic period, a movement, or a style. Instead, the creative expressivities in all media constitute the modernisms of given modernities—on a planetary scale, across time, in the *longue durée*. *Planetary Modernisms* treats modernism as the aesthetic domain of modernity—it helps create that modernity; it reflects it; it responds to it; it challenges it; it reformulates it. We need no longer debate, I suggest, whether modernism starts with Baudelaire's *Les fleurs du mal*, Picasso's *Les demoiselles d'Avignon*, Stravinsky's *The Rite of Spring*, Stein's *Tender Buttons*, Marinetti's futurism, H.D.'s imagism, Eliot's *The Waste Land*, or Joyce's *Ulysses*; whether Paris, London, Berlin, Rome, or New York is the generative center of modernism. Instead, we ought first turn to the specificities of a given modernity and then ask what creative forms it produced—in the Tang Dynasty, for example, or the Abbasid Caliphate, Al-Andalus, the Songhay Empire, Renaissance Florence, Enlightenment Paris, colonial Calcutta, or imperial London.

To constitute modernism—even pluralized modernisms—so broadly goes against the prevailing views of the field. It opens an institutional can of worms. Across the disciplines in the humanities as they have become institutionalized in the past century, periodization has been foundational for the study of literature, the arts, history, and philosophy. Modernism as a distinctive "period" and aesthetic style following romanticism, realism, and naturalism "makes sense"; it's teachable and allows for an orderly curriculum, recognizable hiring and promotion practices, and professional societies and publications. Yet *Planetary Modernisms* challenges such periodization, as practical as it may seem. It argues that such limitations in the field shut the door on effective globalization of modernist studies by institutionally reifying the West as the center, the Rest as periphery, a structure of knowledge that is misleading and potentially pernicious in its long-term effects. *Planetary Modernisms* does not resolve the institutional problems that an expanding modernist studies engenders. Instead, the book attempts to open up the field of debate about what constitutes modernity and modernism, to raise the issues that ought to drive the institutional changes that are bound to come as knowledge production and higher education undergo dramatic transformations in the future. Nonetheless, the burden is on me to provide a compelling case for such an expansion of modernism's commonly accepted, even if a bit porous and contentious, boundaries. Fortunately, I am not alone.

Planetary Modernisms, many years in the making, is part of the work of a community of scholars challenging canonical modernist studies, pushing the field in new directions by focusing on other modernisms in non-Western parts of the world, engaging in what I regard as the planetary turn, echoing with a difference Paul Jay's *Global Matters: The Transnational Turn in Literary Studies*.[10] Affected by the new globalization of the late twentieth century and general calls for transnationalizing literary studies, studies of non-Western modernisms in the late nineteenth and early twentieth centuries have provided in-depth examinations of how these modernisms wrestle with and maintain considerable independence from Euro/American modernisms—to name an influential few, Simon Gikandi's *Writing in Limbo: Modernism and Caribbean Literature*, Priya Joshi's *In Another Country: Colonialism, Culture, and the English Novel in India*, Fernando J. Rosenberg's *The Avant-Garde and Geopolitics in Latin America*, and Shu-mei Shih's *The Lure of the Modern: Writing Modernism in Semicolonial China, 1917–1937*.[11] Edited collections and special journal issues—*Geomodernisms, Geographies of Modernism, Translocal Modernisms, Modernism, The Oxford Handbook of Global Modernisms, The Oxford Handbook of Modernisms, Modernism/Modernity*, and *Literary Compass: The Global Circulation Project*—combine theory with studies of specific non-Western modernisms and of intertextual, circulatory networks and encounters.[12] Comparative books like Jessica Berman's *Modernist Commitments*, Christopher GoGwilt's *The Passage of Literature*, Charles W. Pollard's *New World Modernisms*, Jahan Ramazani's *Transnational Poetics*, and Gayle Rogers's *Modernism and the New Spain* recast modernism's internationalism on a transcontinental landscape of multiply located agencies in the long twentieth century.[13]

Underlying these studies of global modernisms, including *Planetary Modernisms*, is the pervasive influence of postcolonial studies, the new world literature studies, and the anthropology of traveling cultures. The rise of postcolonial studies after the publication of Edward W. Said's formative *Orientalism* in 1978, the recovery of such earlier postcolonial thinkers as Aimé Césaire and Frantz Fanon, and the blend of post/colonial issues with poststructuralist, race, and feminist theories in the work of people like Gayatri Chakravorty Spivak, Homi K. Bhabha, Dipesh Chakrabarty, Anne McClintock, and R. Radhakrishnan profoundly affected the transnationalizing of modernist studies, developing a framework for new examinations of Western imperial power on a global terrain and the cultural productions of emergent nation-states and their colonial pasts in Asia, Africa, and the Caribbean in the wake of World War II.[14] The revitalization of world literature studies challenged comparative literature's Europeanist origins, insisting on attention to literatures produced outside of or in relation to "the West," to be read either in the original or in translation. Comparatists such as Emily Apter, David Damrosch, Wai Chee Dimock, Eric Hayot, Djelal Kadir, Françoise Lionnet, Haun Saussy, and Shu-mei Shih (among many others) have dramatically changed the literary archives of comparative studies, influencing the global expansion of modernist studies.[15] Anthropologists of circulating peoples and cultures such as Arjun Appadurai, James Clifford, Renato Resaldo, and Anna L. Tsing provided modernist studies with theoretical frameworks for thinking through the global migrations, hybridizations, and indigenizations of ideas and people confronting the dislocations and relocations of modernity in their art.[16] The new transnational modernist studies in no sense displaces these fields, each of which retains its own particular emphases, concerns, and methods. But in drawing on them, a globalized modernist studies blends in a new way the issues of post/colonialism, world literature, and hybridized cultures on mobile, global landscapes of interchange. *Planetary Modernisms* is unthinkable without this expansive, interdisciplinary arena of transformative thought.

What *Planetary Modernisms* contributes to this growing body of work on global modernisms and cultural globalism more generally is twofold: first, an articulation in the broadest possible sense of the paradigm shift that undergirds this work and, second, an extension of the logic of that shift to consider modernities and their modernisms over the millennia. I argue that the planetary turn in a modernist studies confined within conventional periodization reinstates the modernisms of the West as the powerful center to the rest's weak periphery, as the origin point with which all others must engage and through which they must be understood. To fulfill the promise of the planetary turn, I suggest, we must rethink *modernity* and *modernism* outside the long twentieth century, outside the post-1500 temporal frame commonly understood as the *period* of the *modern* in its stages from early to late. I use the term *planetary* to invoke this greater expanse of time and space, to signal my attempt to break away from periodization altogether.[17] *Planetarity*, I write in chapter 2, is an epistemology, not an ontology. The *planetary* contains resonances that are suggestive for the approaches I develop for rethinking modernity throughout *Planetary Modernisms*. Although I continue to use the more common *transnational* and *global*, I privilege *planetary* because it bypasses the overdetermined associations of the other terms: *transnational* suggests the ongoing tension between nation-states and globalized postnational political formations; *global* invokes the endlessly debated pros and cons of contemporary globalization. *Planetary*, on the other hand, echoes the spatial turn in cultural theory of the twenty-first century. It is cosmic and grounded at the same time, indicating a place and time that can be both expansive and local. *Planetary* also gestures at a world beyond the human, even beyond the Earth, by invoking the systems and networks of inner and outer space that are both patterned and random. *Planetary* suggests the Earth as a place of matter and climate, life and the passage of time, and an array of species of which the human is only one. Although the focus in *Planetary Modernisms* is solidly on the modernity of human societies, I like that *planetary* opens up the possibility of thinking about nonhuman modernities or the interconnections of the human and nonhuman in rethinking modernity and modernism—new directions for others to follow. *Planetary* has an open-ended edge that *transnational* and *global* lack. What could it possibly mean? What doors of thought could it open?

As an epistemology, *planetary* also suggests the importance of scale in rethinking modernity and modernism, especially in unthinking Euro/Americancentrism. *Planetary Modernisms* suggests that the fluidity of scale—from small to large to small—is essential for the revisionist project of the book. To remain locked into the conventional periodizations of modernity (e.g., early, middle, and late modernity) and modernism (e.g., late nineteenth through early twentieth centuries) results in a center/periphery and diffusionist model that undermines transnational or global revisionisms. There is no doubt that the so-called rise of the West happens during this period, with a tremendous (though not exclusive) concentration of global power centered in first Europe and then the United States. To rethink the West's modernity, however, requires a larger scale of history, one that goes back before the West's rise and forward into the twenty-first century, when the West's economic, political, and military hegemonic power shows many signs of cracking up or retreating in the face of new global forces, conflicts, and technologies.

To develop a flexible approach to spatio/temporal scale, I adapt Fernand Braudel's concept of the *longue durée* in *The Mediterranean and the Mediterranean World in the Age of Phillip II* as well as Immanuel Wallerstein's use of Braudel in his influential book, *The Modern World-System*.[18] *Planetary Modernisms* argues, however, that Braudel's and Wallerstein's *longue durée* going back to about 1500 isn't nearly long enough and that their spatial reach (which largely ignores Asia) isn't nearly broad enough.

To rethink modernity, *Planetary Modernisms* zooms out into a longer *durée* and a wider planetary reach and then zooms in on selected instances of rapid, radical, and transformational change from the Tang Dynasty and the Mongol Empire through the twenty-first century. This broad spatio/temporal scale sets the stage for small-scale examinations of specific modernist creativities that are interpreted in the context of their specific modernities. This scope and flexibility of scale is critical to the project of *Planetary Modernisms*.

The work of world historians like Janet Abu-Lughod, J. M. Blaut, Andé Gunder Frank, John Hobson, Stephen K. Sanderson, and Jane Burbank and Frederick Cooper has been inspirational for *Planetary Modernisms*.[19] Once a relative backwater in the discipline of history, world history has emerged as a large-scale approach more suited to a networked and globalized world than the highly focused, national, or local histories that have dominated (and still dominate) the discipline. On large landscapes of time and space, these geohistorians provide a broader context for the "rise of the West," one that emphasizes the contributions of earlier world systems to Europe's growing hegemony, challenges theories of European exceptionalism, and supplants the linear diffusionism and center/periphery models with broad-scale concepts of global interculturalism and circulation over the millennia. In the context of their archives, Europe becomes something of a latecomer to the world system, able to dominate by the nineteenth century for a complex of reasons, including its adaptation of knowledge and technology from the Mongol and Islamic empires and its ability to enter the world market as a major player for the first time after the relatively rapid conquest of the Americas and the enslavement of Africans. For Frank, the West's rise has been a detour in world history, a blip between the earlier dominance of China and its rise in the twenty-first century. William H. McNeill, the author of the influential *The Rise of the West* (1963), recognizes the significance of this longer and more global *durée* in his 1990 critique of his earlier work for exhibiting "residual Eurocentrism," for not taking into account the dominance and contributions of earlier civilizations.[20] "The fluctuating growth of this sort of world system," he writes, "with shifting centers and a great multiplicity of peoples and cultures caught within it, seems to me now to be a part of world history that largely escaped my attention when writing *The Rise of the West*" (316). He still agrees with his earlier proposition—that "reaction to contacts with strangers was the major motor of historical change"—but the new world history with its millennial archives provides the perspective to address the limitations of his earlier Eurocentrism.

McNeill's epistemological journey is one that *Planetary Modernisms* advocates, drawing on the vast archives of the world historians to disturb often unacknowledged assumptions in modernist studies. In doing so, *Planetary Modernisms* addresses questions the world historians themselves seldom explore—namely, the debates about the meanings of the term *modernity*. World history, I suggest, provides a framework for formulating a planetary approach to questions of modernity: where, when, what, why, how. I focus largely on the cultural dimensions of multiple, polycentric, and recurrent modernities, aspects that are largely missing from their more economically, politically, technologically, and demographically oriented approaches. I also bring major tools of my original trade—literary studies—to bear on their archives—namely, an analysis of narrative and figural patterns in the discourses about modernity. What are the prevailing *stories* about modernity, I ask. How are they told, and to what effect? What are the *figures*—images, metonyms, metaphors, symbols—that characterize modernity, and how are they deployed? How might other stories and figures help us retheorize a planetary approach to modernity?

Planetary Modernisms has a three-part structure, each part rethinking the meanings of modernity and modernism from a different angle. Part 1, "Rethinking Modernist Studies," addresses the problems and possibilities of the interdisciplinary field in general. Chapter 1, "Definitional Excursions," travels the difficult landscape of terminological usage, and chapter 2, "Planetarity," provides a roadmap for a planetary modernist studies. Moving experimentally through the labyrinthine maze of definitional debate, chapter 1 examines the multiple and often directly opposite meanings that *modernity* and *modernism* have acquired within and across the disciplines. Rather than escape the labyrinth, it asks that we confront the definitional monster head on. Interrogate the dissonance, it suggests, and we find at its center the contradictory core of modernity itself, a bang/clash never to be stilled.

Contradiction by itself, however, is never fully satisfactory—everything is contradictory, in the end; where do we go from there? So chapter 2 moves beyond the definitional problematic, turns to the significance of the slash in *modernity/modernism*, and relies upon Wallace Stevens's "Thirteen Ways of Looking at a Blackbird" to propose thirteen ways of developing a planetary epistemology for modernist studies.[21] Defying the conclusion of chapter 1, chapter 2 aphoristically proposes a provisional definition of modernity and axioms of issues that just *might* have the flexibility and scope to be useful. It does so with no illusions of stilling the debate or quelling the anxiety caused by a newly expansive and still expanding field. To allay this anxiety, the chapter offers four modes for reading modernism planetarily, each strategy with its own particular, manageable focus and archive: *re-vision* of aesthetic works in the conventional time/space of modernism for traces of the global, *recovery* of works outside these boundaries in the specificity of their own time and place, tracking the global *circulation* of aesthetic modernisms on a transnational landscape, and *collaging* modernisms in different times and places for the insight radical juxtaposition can produce.

Part 2, "Rethinking Modernity, Scaling Space and Time," draws on narrative theory and the suggestive possibilities of figural language to rethink modernity across large-scale time and space. Chapter 3, "Stories of Modernity: Planetary Scale in the *Longue Durée*," argues that the "now" of modernity has a geohistory, has a place in time, through time. It examines different stories of pre-1500 modernity—pairing the sedentary Tang Dynasty and the nomadic Mongol Empire—to break open the ideological metanarrative of Western modernity as originary and singular, then to call for a multiplicity of stories of modernity throughout world history. Chapter 4, "Figures of Modernity: Relational Keywords," returns to the definitional problematic explored in chapter 1 and suggests an approach based in a combination of metaphorical keywords such as *rupture, vortex, mobility, acceleration, system, network, circulation,* and *heterotopia* as ways to construct a relational definition of modernity that can accommodate a planetary *longue durée*.

Part 3, "Rethinking Modernism, Reading Modernisms," turns from modernity as a geohistorical condition to the aesthetic expressivities it spawns: its modernisms. The accelerating ruptures of particular modernities, it argues, encompass particular innovative representational forms, modernisms that engage with and probe the contradictory meanings of their modernities. This section, with its small-scale readings of texts and artifacts, tests the utility of the planetary framework presented in part 2 for producing new insights into aesthetic modernity. Chapter 5, "Modernity's

Modernisms: Aesthetic Scale and Pre-1500 Modernisms," makes the general case for linking modernism to modernity in all geohistories and zooms in on three instances of modernist breakthrough: Du Fu as a poet of Tang Dynasty modernity; the story of the cobalt-blue glaze and ceramic painting in the Abbasid Caliphate; and Kabir as an iconoclastic poet-singer in the wake of Tamerlane's conquest of northern India, initiating an inventive improvisational tradition that continues today.

Chapter 6, "Circulating Modernisms: Collages of Empire in Fictions of the Long Twentieth Century," reduces the scale of time and text by examining three pairs of writers caught up within the logic and structures of empire, specifically the British Empire in Africa and India—Joseph Conrad and Tayeb Salih; E. M. Forster and Arundhati Roy; Virginia Woolf and the siblings Tagore, brother Rabindranath, and sister Swarnakumari Devi. Demonstrating the centrality of postcolonial studies for modernist studies in the long twentieth century, this collage of pairs shows the mutually constitutive nature of different modernities in the recent colonial and postcolonial eras and also demonstrates a complex pattern of circulation and affiliation among writers that encourages a rethinking of binary approaches to transnational modernity and modernism. Chapter 7, "Diasporic Modernisms: Journeys 'Home' in the Long Poems of Aimé Césaire and Theresa Hak Kyung Cha," juxtaposes two poets typically read in relation to their African/French/Caribbean or Korean/Asian American contexts. This cultural collage reveals a specifically diasporic modernity in which "make it new" involves a return home to the underworld of abjection in the history of their peoples and an aesthetic process of gender-inflected regeneration. In doing so, it places notions of modernist exile and expatriatism within the broader framework of diasporic trauma, travail, and rebirth into a newly constituted homeland of the imagination.

With their focus on the modernities of the long twentieth century, chapters 6 and 7 foreground the centrality of empire for the production of interconnected but distinctive transcontinental modernisms during the period conventionally associated with modernism. In so doing, the chapters argue that a planetary modernist studies necessarily draws upon colonial and postcolonial geohistories—that is, the period of early-twentieth-century imperial power (European, American, Turkish, Russian, Japanese), its dissolution in the context of world war, and the emergence of new nation-states in Africa and Asia. At the same time, the readings uncover ways in which gender, sexuality, race, caste, and class often interrupt simple oppositional readings of imperial modernities to create unexpected lines of affiliation across post/colonial difference.

Planetary Modernisms's conclusion, "A Debate with Myself," resists the standard genre of synthesis and summation by performing a return to the book's beginnings in the dialogical field of debate in modernist studies about the meanings of *modernity* and *modernism* and what the scope of our inquiry should or can be. As a standalone essay, this staged debate, I insist, not only structures the field but also rages inside my own head, reflecting the anxiety of our own, twenty-first-century modernity and gesturing at the very real difficulties of institutionalizing the new ways of thinking about modernity/modernism that the book promotes. In the end, however, taking into account the challenges such a project engenders, *Planetary Modernisms* takes sides in the debate and affirms the political and epistemological generativity of a planetary modernist studies.

Planetary Modernisms is, for the most part, not written in conventional academic prose. It experiments with alternate forms of argumentation—using stories, juxtapositions, metaphors, metonymies, parataxes, aphorisms, oralities, charts, collages, maps, and so forth. Sometimes, chapters don't look like chapters; paragraphs don't exhibit the principles of development and evidence; sentences don't follow the rules. The logical progression of a Ciceronian argument seldom structures an oftentimes more dialogic or associational procession of ideas and examples. To experiment with academic prose in this book was not a deliberate plan: it just happened, it evolved, and it was damnably difficult to do. It began in the late 1990s as I entered the labyrinth of definitional debate. I had just published *Mappings: Feminism and the Cultural Geographies of Encounter* (1998), in which I mapped the developing intersectional and transnational debates of feminist theory. As I read widely in modernist studies, I thought I could do the same: map the positions of various divisions within the field. But I was caught in the vertigo of the definitional maze, in the often absolute dissonance of meaning in the terms people used. That's when the experiments began: the stories, the parataxes, the morals, the detours, the figures of binaries and circles, and so forth—all as indirect mechanisms for getting out of the labyrinth, making sense of its hidden patterns. They helped me think differently; they suggested an alternative to arguing a single thesis by proposing travels through many lines of thought. The result was "Definitional Excursions," first published in *Modernism/Modernity* in 2001 and reproduced here with some modification as chapter 1 to capture the early-twenty-first-century moment of its intervention and to serve as the still necessary foundation of the arguments to come in later chapters. Of course I was aware that these experiments mirrored the representational crises of the early-twentieth-century Anglo-American and European modernism about which I had been writing since the 1970s. Citing Yeats in chapter 2, I ask, "How can we know the dancer from the dance?"[22]

Like "Definitional Excursions," *Planetary Modernisms* grew in pieces as the early twenty-first century unfolded in all its own revolutionary modernities. Although I kept trying to come up with a "plan," I had no clear map of how I could ever put together into a coherent whole the disparate research I was doing—from delving into the manuscripts of Forster's *Passage to India* to reading about the Mongol Empire, tracing the circulations of ceramic innovation, uncovering the story of Shakespeare's sister in the Tagore family, or learning from the large-scale histories of world systems. There were countless opportunities for articles, conference papers, and lectures—each pulling me this way and that.[23] There were detours into other fields I could not resist—migration/diaspora studies, cosmopolitanism, narrative theory, world literature, comparatism, Muslim feminisms, and religious studies. Each of these diversions delayed "the book" but then made its way into its unfolding formulation of a planetary modernist studies. *Planetary Modernisms* is layered through time, like the skins of an onion, pungent with past meanderings.

How to make it all cohere? (Pace Ezra Pound.) It just happened, organically. In a flash, Stevens's cubist poem and cubism more generally came to me as a way of organizing my disparate thoughts. The invitation to do a keynote address for the Modernist Studies Association conference in Montréal in 2009 resulted in "Planetarity: Musing Modernist Studies," published in *Modernism/Modernity* in 2010 as a synthesis of the work I had been doing for ten years. Appearing as chapter 2 in *Planetary Modernisms*, it represents my recognition that the book as a whole must present the "object" of *modernity/modernism* from as many angles as possible, with as many methods as possible, with as many archives as possible: the principle that governs the chapters that follow.

As the chapters took shape, each gradually acquired a different experimental form. Chapter 2 invokes only to resist the manifesto form so important in Anglo/European modernism of the early twentieth century. Its aphoristic style serves as an overture for the more extended arguments to come in later chapters. Chapter 3, engaging diachronically with a millennial *longue durée*, does so through telling stories of modernity and using narrative theory to unravel the metanarrative of Western modernity. Chapter 4 focuses synchronically on words as a figural rather than narrative epistemology for rethinking *modernity*. Each section opens with keywords—their denotative definitions, synonyms, and antonyms—then moves into reflections on modernity focalized through its images and metaphors, each illustrated by brief examples taken from different times and continents. Chapter 5 zooms in onto three sharply focused, historically contextualized snapshots of unrelated modernisms before the emergence of European modernities; taken together, they test the usefulness of positing modernism as the aesthetic dimension of any modernity rather than as a specific period, movement, or style tied to a single modernity. Chapter 6 focuses on fictions of modernity read as a form of collage. Its form—a collage of paired collages—borrows from early-twentieth-century European art, where sharp juxtapositions of fragments produce new relational perceptions, where the eye circulates, moving back and forth to read the whole. Chapter 7 turns to poetry, specifically two modernist long poems, reading them as a woven collage whose shuttle back and forth between the two performs a paratactic comparison that produces a new theory of a diasporic modernism. The conclusion takes the form of a stylized debate organized oppositionally around thirteen issues, echoing in form the blackbirds of chapter 2. *On the one hand; on the other hand*: each side exists inside my head and outside in the field. Resisting the conventions of a conclusion, it reproduces the dialogics of an expansive modernist studies that perpetually questions itself.

The modernities of today's world remind us that modernity is still Now, everywhere present in our lives, but they also compel us to look beyond the present to both the past and the future. *Planetary Modernisms* begins with the ethical imperative to get outside a purely Western framework to rethink the modernities of the past. It resists the presentism of our Now to bring the planetary perspectives of world history, of literature, of the arts, of the knowledge produced in the humanities to bear on the meanings of modernity for our future.

PART I
RETHINKING MODERNIST STUDIES

ONE
DEFINITIONAL EXCURSIONS

What is *modernity*? What is or was *modernism*? Why is the energetic, expanding, multidisciplinary field of modernist studies so filled with contestation over the very ground of study? Definitional activities are fictionalizing processes, however much they sound like rational categorization. As such, I will begin with three stories, allegorized but rooted in my own experience in an evolving field.[1]

STORY 1: WHERE HAVE ALL THE REBELS GONE?

Imagine a young woman starting graduate school in 1965 in an American land-grant university. Remember the suburban dream of the 1950s for middle-class (white) girls: the penny loafers and saddle shoes, the poodle skirts and prom chiffon, the cheerleaders and Elvis screamers, college for the MRS degree, the station wagon and four kids. No books. No art. No ideas. No passion. Conformity was the name of the game. Conformity and materialism. Then. The first butts of the Berkeley Free Speech Movement. Fuck. Shit. Sex. Pot. Buttons. Pierced ears. Long hair. Unisex style. Civil Rights. Vietnam. Pigs. Feminism. Gay Rights. Welfare Rights. Union Rights. What was "modernism" to a graduate student in English and American literature in the heady days of the 1960s? Modernism was rebellion. Modernism was "make it new."[2] Modernism was resistance, rupture. To its progenitors. To its students. Modernism was the antidote to the poison of tradition, obligation.

STORY 2: WHAT DOES A CYBERPUNK REALLY WANT?

Picture an aging scholar in 1995, past the half-century mark, entering into her first graduate seminar on modernism in a land-grant university. "What was modernism?" she asks. A circle of eyes and silences. A couple to the side shift uncomfortably. She has cropped purple hair and kohled eyes. He wears fishnet stockings and thick buckled Pilgrim heels. A tidy tail of silky golden hair flows down his back. So thin in black, so pale in whiteface, they are their own shadows. They know "what modernism was." Modernism was elitism. Modernism was the Establishment. "High Culture" lifting its skirts against the taint of the "low," the masses, the popular. Modernism was the supreme fiction, the master narrative, the great white hope. To its pomo descendents, modernism is the enemy. Postmodernism is the antidote to the poison of tradition, obligation.

STORY 3: WHAT'S A POOR STUDENT TO DO?

Listen in on an exchange between two scholars, the one graying and the other balding in the wisdom of their seniorities—she a cultural critic, he a social scientist. Children of the 1960s, teachers of the 1990s. It is 1995; their manuscripts pass back and forth through snail mail. "What was modernism?" they ask, both acknowledging it as a historical phenomenon but neither willing to assert that it is fully over and done with. For both, modernism both was and is. But *what* was modernism? She knows. It is the (illusory) break with the past, a willed forgetting of tradition, continuity, order. It is the embrace of chaos. It is the crisis of representation, fragmentation, alienation. It is indeterminacy, the rupture of certainty—material and symbolic. It is the poetics of modernity—change—and the aesthetic inscriptions thereof. (Pace cyberpunks, for whom modernism no longer "is" as it recedes into the deadness of postmodernism's past.)

He knows too. Modernism is state planning. Modernism is totalization, centralized system. Modernism is the Enlightenment's rational schemata.

"Progress"—"Science"—"Reason"—"Truth." Modernism is the ideology of post-Renaissance modernity—conquest—and the inscriptions thereof. (Pace cyborgs, modernism still lives in the danger of ever-forming centralized hegemonies and utopian totalitarianisms.)

Moral of the Stories

Just what *is* modernism in an exchange where the word means not just different things but precisely opposite things?

∞ ∞ ∞

The opposition of meanings produced over time (from story 1 to story 2) morphs into a binary of oppositions existing across space (story 3). In toto, the stories represent a conjuncture of temporal and spatial oppositions. So. Let's move from storytelling to another kind of conjuncture: parataxis—the juxtaposition of things without providing connectives. *Parataxis*: a common aesthetic strategy in modernist writing and art, developed to disrupt and fragment conventional sequencing, causality, and perspective. *Parataxis*: the opposite of *hypotaxis* in linguistics, thus the opposite of hierarchical relationships of syntactic units. *Parataxis*: a mechanism of the "dream work" in Freud's grammar for the unconscious processes of disguised expression of the forbidden, indicating unresolved or conflicting desires.

PARATAXIS 1

- "Modernism . . . is the one art that responds to the scenario of our chaos."[3]
- "'Who says modernity says organization,' it has been remarked."[4]

PARATAXIS 2

- "We have seen that the creators of modernist works are negative demystifiers: they unmask absolutism, rationalism, idealism—and all illusions."[5]

- "But I do not think we shall begin to understand modernism unless we look at the way it was seemingly compelled, over and over, at moments it knew were both testing ground and breaking point, to set itself... the task of Enlightenment, or the task of bourgeois philosophy, in its ruthless, world-breaking and world-making mode."[6]

PARATAXIS 3

- "Indeed Modernism would seem to be the point at which the idea of the radical and innovating arts, the experimental, technical, aesthetic ideal that had been growing forward from Romanticism, reaches formal crisis—in which myth, structure and organization in a traditional sense collapse, and not only for formal reasons. The crisis is a crisis of culture."[7]
- "What is 'high modernism' then? It is best conceived as a strong, one might say muscle-bound, version of the beliefs in scientific and technical progress associated with the process of industrialization in Western Europe and North America from roughly 1830 until the First World War. At its center was a supreme self-confidence about continued linear progress, the development of scientific and technical knowledge, the expansion of production, the rational design of social order, the growing satisfaction of human needs, and, not least, an increasing control over nature (including human nature) commensurate with scientific understanding of natural laws. *High* modernism is thus a particularly comprehensive vision of how the benefits of technical and scientific progress might be applied—usually through the state—in every field of human activity."[8]

PARATAXIS 4

- "To be modern is to find ourselves in an environment that promises adventure, power, joy, growth, transformation of ourselves and the world—and, at the same time, that threatens to destroy everything

we have, everything we know, everything we are.... To be modern is to be part of a universe in which, as Marx said, 'all that is solid melts into air.' "[9]
- "The paramount figure in modernism is that of the static and abstract model separated from the dynamic ebb and flow of reality. This figure is that of the Cartesian 'I,' of the abstract natural rights of the French Revolution, of Kantian reason, of the unsuccessful blueprints of the worst of orthodox Marxism, of city grids, of Corbusier's *machine à habiter*, of Habermas's ideal speech situation."[10]

PARATAXIS 5

- "Intrinsic to the condition of modernity.... has been a rejection by and within those [Enlightenment] narratives of what seem to have been the strongest pillars of their history: Anthropomorphism, Humanism, and Truth.... In France, such rethinking has involved, above all, a reincorporation and reconceptualization of that which has been the master narratives' own 'non-knowledge,' what has eluded them, what has engulfed them. This other-than-themselves is almost always a 'space' of some kind... coded as *feminine*, as *woman*."[11]
- "I will use the term modern to designate any science that legitimates itself with reference to a metadiscourse... making an explicit appeal to some grand narrative, such as the dialectics of Spirit, the hermeneutics of meaning, the emancipation of the rational or working subject, or the creation of wealth...: this is the Enlightenment narrative, in which the hero of knowledge works toward a good ethico-political end—universal peace...."[12]

PARATAXIS 6

- "If it is possible to talk about 'modernism' as the major movement in Western literature (and art in general) of the first half of the twentieth century, I would argue that it is also possible to talk about 'modernist form,' a shorthand term used to designate that cluster of stylistic practices . . . : (1) aesthetic self-consciousness; (2) simultaneity, juxtaposition, or 'montage' [and] . . . 'fragmentation'; (3) paradox, ambiguity, and uncertainty; and (4) . . . the demise of the integrated or unified subject. . . . I would add . . . : abstraction and highly conscious artifice, taking us behind familiar reality, breaking away from familiar functions of language and conventions of form . . . the shock, the violation of expected continuities, the element of de-creation and crisis. . . . "[13]

- " . . . certain schematic differences . . . "

Modernism	Postmodernism
Romanticism/Symbolism	Pataphysics/Dadaism
Form (conjunctive, closed)	Antiform (disjunctive, open)
Purpose	Play
Design	Chance
Hierarchy	Anarchy
Mastery/Logos	Exhaustion/Silence
Art Object/Finished Work	Process/Performance/Happening
Creation/Totalization	Decreation/Deconstruction
Synthesis	Antithesis
Presence	Absence
Centering	Dispersal
Genre/Boundary	Text/Intertext . . .
Hypotaxis	Parataxis . . .
Signified	Signifier
Narrative/*Grande Histoire*	Antinarrative/*Petite Histoire*
Master Code	Idiolect
Genital/Phallic	Polymorphous/Androgynous
Origin/Cause	Difference-Differance/Trace . . .
Metaphysics	Irony
Determinacy	Indeterminacy
Transcendence	Immanence[14]

PARATAXIS 7

- "Modernity, therefore, not only entails a ruthless break with any or all preceding historical conditions, but is characterized by a never-ending process of internal ruptures and fragmentations within itself."[15]
- "The belief 'in linear progress, absolute truths, and rational planning of ideal social orders' under standardized conditions of knowledge and production was particularly strong. The modernism that resulted was, as a result, 'positivist, technocratic, and rationalistic' at the same time as it was imposed as the work of an elite avant-garde of planners, artists, architects, critics, and other guardians of high taste."[16]

Moral 1

As terms in an evolving scholarly discourse, *modernity* and *modernism* constitute a critical Tower of Babel, a cacophony of categories that become increasingly useless the more inconsistently they are used. We can regard them as a parody of critical discourse in which everyone keeps talking at the same time in a language without common meanings. When terms mean radically different or contradictory things to people, then their use appears to threaten the project of scholarship/teaching altogether.

Moral 2

As contradictory terms resisting consensual definition, *modernity* and *modernism* form a fertile terrain for interrogation, providing ever more sites for examination with each new meaning spawned. As parody of rational discourse, their contradictions highlight the production of meaning possible by attention to what will not be tamed, by what refuses consistency and homogenization. Their use ensures the open-ended ongoingness of the scholarly/pedagogical project whose first task is to sustain the continuation of interrogation, to ensure, in short, its own perpetuation.

∞ ∞ ∞

Modernisms is one thing, but *modernism* as absolute contradiction is quite another. Definitions spawn plurality in the very act of attempting to herd meaning inside consensual boundaries. Definitions mean to fence in, to fix, and to stabilize. But they often end up being fluid, in a destabilized state of ongoing formation, deformation, and reformation that serves the changing needs of the moment. They reflect the standpoint of their makers. They emerge out of the spatio/temporal context of their production. They serve different needs and interests. They accomplish different kinds of cultural work. They change dramatically over time and through space. Definitions wear the mask of synchronic abstraction, but they are always subject to diachronic histories and spatial geographies of continuity, change, and difference. I have no expectation, therefore, of determining or discovering a fixed meaning for terms like *modernity* and *modernism*. I expect differences.

But opposition of meanings is something else. It goes beyond difference, beyond resistance to totalizing metanarratives, beyond the provisional, strategic, fluid, permeable, and situationally adaptable meanings that characterize the most useful definitional exercises. I don't seek fixity or plurality. I seek instead to confront directly the contradictory status of meanings.[17]

∞ ∞ ∞

The stories began with the problematic of *modernism* but drew us inexorably into a web of words—*modernism* and its siblings *modern, modernity,* and *modernization*. Not only does the meaning of the concept deny fixity; so do its grammatical and semantic aspects. The root word *modern* is both noun and adjective, whether signifying descriptively or normatively. The different suffixes herd the word into different grammatical functions that carry semantic weight. The *-ity* of *modernity* limits the word *modern* to a noun—a status as a thing or condition that is distinguishable from other things or conditions. The *-ism* of *modernism* turns the noun *modern* into an advocacy, a promotion, a movement presumably centered around a systematic philosophy, politics, ideology, or aesthetics. The *-ization* of *modernization* signifies a process, an evolution or revolution from one condition to another, with modernity as the condition achieved by modernization.[18]

And what about the cousins of the siblings—*premodern, postmodern, postmodernity, postmodernism*? How do *pre-* and *post-* inflect the root meanings? To what extent are these categories distinctly separate when they appear to merely qualify *modern, modernity,* and *modernism*?[19] In what way is the entire family of terms dependent on their variously implied or invoked antonyms—*traditional, classical, ancient, feudal, agrarian, past*?

Once upon a time, literary and art critics used *modernism*—especially with the orthographic marker of the capital, Modernism, or the intensifying adjective *high*, as in high modernism—to delineate movements in the arts based in loose affiliations or parallel developments. In contrast, social theorists, historians, and social scientists used *modern, modernity*, and *modernization* to refer to historical periods, conditions, and processes. But now, such disciplinary boundaries have ceased to function, as people appropriate all forms of the root concept to serve their different purposes.

Symptomatically and provocatively, the interdisciplinary journal *Modernism/Modernity* yokes two of these terms, as if the slash between them signaled their interchangeability on the one hand yet their permanent separation on the other. The slash is a bar that forever connects and disconnects (like the Saussurian/Lacanian bar between signifier/signified). This is yet another contradiction that demands attention. Is there a slash/bar separating and conjoining *modern/modernity/modernism/modernization* with all its cognates and antonyms as well?

A PSYCHOANALYTIC DETOUR

The family romance of squabbling siblings and cousins invites a psychoanalysis of definitional debate. The dissonance of meanings—particularly the opposition of meanings—opens the possibility of a psychodynamic reading that looks for the irrational and covert processes of repression, return, and transference in modernist studies across the disciplines as these processes reflect unresolved complexes within modernity itself.

The scene of analysis for Freud is a psychodynamic one, a stage onto which the analysand and the analyst transfer repressed desires and complexes long since seemingly forgotten. Transference (and countertransference) in analysis involves the repetition of what cannot be consciously remembered, the reenactment of repressed patterns not yet consciously faced. Freud's clinical practice involved the deliberate incitement of the transference so that the drama of repetition could become the grounds for analysis itself.[20]

The terminological quagmire of modernist studies may be the result of a transferential process in which people become caught in a repetition of the unresolved contradictions present and largely repressed in modernity itself. The stories and parataxes of this chapter deliberately stage this dissonant drama to shift the focus from the debate about signifieds for the disputed terms to an analysis of what produces the dissonance in the first place. I am adapting and blending Julia Kristeva's notion of the "textual unconscious," Fredric Jameson's concept of the "political unconscious," and Shoshana Felman's psychoanalytic interpretations of contentious critical literatures on Edgar Allan Poe and Henry James's *The Turn of the Screw*.[21] Particularly heated and unresolvable debates about literary meaning, Felman argues, can be read as transferential scenes of resistance and repetition. Such scenes, often confrontational and even bitter, have an "unconscious" that can be read psychoanalytically as a "case history" that brings to light hidden complexes repressed and unresolved in the original literary texts. Adapting Jameson's notion of the political unconscious for this scenario allows for a reading of how oppositional views encrypt a politics not immediately evident or intended.

Similarly, multidisciplinary modernist studies spawns terminological debates that reenact contradictions already present within the terms and the phenomena to which they allude. What then is hidden within the proliferation of meanings for *modernity* and *modernism*? How might the dissonances and oppositions constitute fault lines inviting interpretation in and of themselves? What might such fault lines tell us about the contradictory and complex-ridden meanings and politics of the phenomena to which terms refer as they change and vary in different historical moments and spatial locations?

PATHWAYS IN THE WANDERLAND OF MODERNIST STUDIES

How to enter into and perhaps emerge out of the maze of contestation and opposition in modernist studies? I suggest two routes for definitional excursion—the first, grammatical and philosophical; the second, political and cultural. They engage the issue of oppositional meanings in complementary ways. Without resolving anything, they open up different routes to the contradiction of meaning, different ways of negotiating definitional debate, each necessary in its own way. Without resolving or silencing it, they clarify what is at stake in the debate and why interrogating what produces it can loosen fixed loyalties to partial meanings.

GRAMMATICAL/PHILOSOPHICAL ROUTE

This pathway starts with the recognition of the difference between nominal and relational modes of definition—that is, regarding the terms (the siblings *modern/modernity/modernism*) as *nouns* with a specific, definable content (however debated) and viewing them as *adjectives* implying comparison to some other condition of being.[22] The difference between these approaches to definitional tasks accounts for some of the opposition in modernist studies but not all. Contradiction exists not only between the modes but within each mode as well.[23]

Nominal Mode: The Noun

In nominal terms, the words *modern*, *modernity*, and *modernism* signify a specific content: a set of characteristics with particular material conditions and spatio/temporal locations. This is not to say, however, that there is always agreement about this specific content. But for those working within or seeking a nominal framework, the definitional project centers on fixing the categories to a set of meanings to which others might be persuaded. Whether canonical or revisionist, such projects assume the nominal status of modernism or modernity: it is a noun, with a specific meaning, albeit subject to disagreement about its potential explanatory power.

Nominal discussions of *modern/modernity/modernism* tend to be very field specific, with definitional dissonance and even outright contradiction developing as a result of disciplinary boundaries and considerable isolation of disciplinary discourses from one another. The most radical disjuncture of nominal meanings exists in the chasm between the social sciences and the humanities. Social theorists, political scientists, sociologists, and anthropologists tend to follow the lead of historians of Europe, who typically periodize their field into the subfields of classical, medieval, early modern, and modern, thus defining *modern* as the initial break with medieval institutions and outlooks that evolved over time. Within this context, *modernity* signifies a specific set of historical conditions developing in the West, including the Industrial Revolution, conquest of and expansion economically and politically into other continents, the transition to urban culture, the rise of the nation-state, and growing power of the bourgeoisie.[24] Consistent with this periodization, philosophers often regard the theories of reason in Locke, Kant, and Hegel as the embodiment of a distinctly modern secularism and humanism. For political scientists, modernity often involves the development of specific kinds of political systems away from feudalism and toward limited monarchies, democracies, and various autocracies; for economists, types of markets, capital, or labor; for anthropologists, the eradication or (forced) assimilation of traditional cultures through conquest or encroachment by nation-states, market systems, more "advanced" technologies, or hegemonic cultural groups. Postcolonial theorists often link modernity with imperialism and the national struggles for emergence within the contradictory conditions of hybridization and continued dependence on the colonial power. And so forth.[25]

In the humanities, on the other hand, modernity and modernism are most often associated with the radical *rupture* from rather than the supreme embodiment of post-Renaissance Enlightenment humanism and accompanying formations in the West. Artists and writers, within this view, constitute an avant-garde of change, seeing sooner and more searchingly the profound significance and future effects of epistemological, ontological, political, technological, demographic, cultural, and aesthetic transformations. The dating, location, and forms of rupture associated with a modernist style sometimes overlap, sometimes vary considerably. Critics of modernist poetry often identify a poetics of fragmentation, parataxis, image, and idiosyncratic rhythms and sound patterns. Art historians often focus on the rupture from realism in the heightening attention to form, especially pure geometric shapes and planes. Architectural historians often look to the stark, functionalist minimalism of Bauhaus design or cityscape towers as the expression of modernity and its aesthetic in the age of the machine. For music historians, the embrace of primitivism and atonality in a composer like Igor Stravinsky might constitute modernism. Media critics look to the radical effects of the new mechanical means of reproduction—photography, radio, cinema, television—for the sights and sounds of modernity. And so forth.[26]

However debated, modernism in the context of the humanities is most often understood as the loosely affiliated movements and individuals in the arts and literature that reflect and contribute to the conditions and consciousness of modernity in Europe, Britain, and the United States.[27] Periodization, however much it varies among different subfields, differs sharply from that proposed by social theorists and historians. Moreover, the epitome of modernity for those in the social sciences is precisely what modernity dismantles for those in the humanities.

At first glance, this definitional divide seems arbitrary, produced through the accident of disciplinary location and isolationism in the academy and thus not particularly interesting for definitional interrogation. However, several factors challenge such a view.

First, the opposition between the social sciences and the humanities cannot be so easily dismissed as arbitrary or insignificant because some fields like cultural anthropology, history, geography, political theory, media studies, ethnic studies, gender and women's studies, and postcolonial studies are multidisciplinary or interdisciplinary. They exist on the liminal threshold between the two divisions, equally engaging in questions of representation, theory, social organization, power relations, and empirical as well as imaginative formations. Consequently, the oppositional meanings of *modern/modernity/modernism* often coexist within certain disciplines, fields, and institutional units in the academy.

Second, with the relegitimation of interdisciplinarity, the borders between disciplines and divisions of knowledge have become increasingly porous in the past forty years. Such cross-disciplinary work with modernity produces rich hybridities but also some confusion. For example, in his collection *Modernist Anthropology*, Marc Manganaro (who holds an appointment in a literature department) brings together anthropologists and literary critics to examine the interplay between literary modernism and modernist anthropology in the first half of the twentieth century. The result is an exciting interdisciplinary examination of the intermingling of aesthetic and ethnographic projects in the period. But the term *modernism* slips and slides between oppositional meanings—from rational ordering sought in Boasian or Malinowskian anthropology to anarchistic disordering found in avant-garde art and poetics. This oscillation is never directly confronted anywhere in the volume and is even reproduced in many individual essays. The collection intensifies rather than illuminates the definitional problems evident in an uninterrogated mixing of social theory's and aesthetics' meanings of *modernism*.[28]

To take another example, the geographer David Harvey begins his influential book *The Condition of Postmodernity* with an invocation to Baudelaire's notion of modern life as "the transient, the fleeting, the contingent," cites the literary critic Marshall Berman on modernism and modernity in *All That Is Solid Melts Into Air*, and then quotes Yeats's paradigmatic modernist lines in "The Second Coming": "Things fall apart; the centre cannot hold; / Mere anarchy is loosed upon the world" (10). Harvey appears to be firmly entrenched in the conventional literary meanings of *modernism* as disruption. But then he goes on to discuss postmodernism as a break from modernism, whose meaning has shifted to be the Enlightenment project of the "development of rational forms of social organization and rational modes of thought" (12). Having at first associated modernism with formalist ruptures of epistemology, ontology, and representation, he goes on to cite Ihab Hassan's famous schematic chart asserting postmodernism's absolute break with modernism's Cartesian subject and Enlightenment reason (42–44). In his splendid book, influential across the disciplines in modernist studies, Harvey slides back and forth between "anarchy" and "organization" as the defining modes of modernism with only occasional allusion to the tension between these meanings.

Third, the insistence on arbitrary disciplinary difference obscures what is shared across the social sciences and humanities—namely, the emphasis on rupture from the past, debate about the politics of modernity/modernism, and a pervasive Eurocentrism. Just what "past" modernity abandons differs, but transformative change is a constant component of definition. Social theorists and art critics alike argue fiercely among themselves about the value of modernity and modernism in debates that are more similar than different across the methodological divides. Is modernity or modernism liberating or oppressive, revolutionary or elitist, progressive or regressive, something to be reinforced or dismantled? Do its ideas and ideals require the oppression or exclusion of some for the benefit of others? Or do they open doors for ever-expanding, ever-more inclusive conditions of freedom and plenty? The questions are similar, whether addressed to issues of revolution and slavery or avant-garde art and mass culture. Some defend modernity/modernism; others attack it. Underlying all these nominal debates is the problematic assumption that modernity/modernism originated in the West and is either forced upon or imitated in diluted form by the Rest. Given these similarities, the dissonance in the core meanings of *modernity* and *modernism* is deafening.

A nominal approach to defining *modernity/modernism* presumes the possibility of consensual agreement about the meanings of the terms as nouns with a specific content: a set of characteristics existing within discernable boundaries of meaning, space, and time. However, a closer look reveals little consensus either across disciplines or within them. This capacity of the nominal approach to spawn diverse and even opposite meanings undermines the naming function of nouns. If what a noun signifies cannot be consistently named, of what use is it as a category?

Relational Mode: The Adjective

A relational approach to the meaning of *modernity/modernism* looks for the latent structure rather than the manifest contents of the root term. Instead of locating modernity in the specific time of the post-Renaissance or post-Enlightenment West, a relational definition stresses the condition or sensibility of radical disruption and accelerating change wherever and whenever such a phenomenon appears, particularly if it manifests widely.[29] What is modern or modernist gains its meaning through negation, as a rebellion against what once was or was presumed to be. Just as adjectives such as *tall* or *big* have meaning only in reference to other adjectives like *short* or *small*, the relational meaning for *modern* (and its siblings) exists within a comparative binary in which the opposite is *traditional*. Neither term has a fixed or universal meaning in and of itself but rather acquires meaning only in relation to its implied opposite. Where tradition signals the unfolding of the future within the continuous pathways of the past, modernity calls for perpetual subversion of the past as the precondition of the future.

Relationally speaking, modernity is the insistence upon the Now—the present and its future as resistance to the past, especially the immediate past. It establishes a cult of the new that constructs retrospectively a sense of tradition from which it declares independence. Paradoxically, such a tradition—or, the awareness of it as "tradition"—might come into existence only at the moment of rebellion against it. As Jürgen Habermas argues in "Modernity Versus Postmodernity," modernity requires "a cult of the new": "Modernity revolts against the normalizing functions of tradition; modernity lives on the experience of rebelling against all that is normative."[30] Such resistance is embedded in the manifestoes of early-twentieth-century Anglo-American aesthetic modernism. "Make it new" is Pound's definitive rallying cry. "DIE in the Past / LIVE in the Future" declares Mina Loy in her "Aphorisms on Futurism." "Our vortex is not afraid of the Past: it has forgotten it's existence," intone the vorticists of *Blast*. "*FIRE*," shouts the collective editorial voice of the Harlem Renaissance little magazine *Fire!*: "*melting steel and iron bars, poking livid tongues between stone apertures and burning wooden opposition with a cackling chuckle of contempt.*"[31]

Precisely because a relational definition does not seek the fixity of nominal definitions, modernity need no longer reside solely in a specific set of institutional, ideological, or aesthetic characteristics emergent in the post-Renaissance West, radiating globally along the pathways of empire and postcoloniality, and appearing as pale copies of Western genius. Instead, a particularized modernity located in space and time could potentially emerge wherever and whenever the winds of radical disruption blew, the conditions of rapid change flared up, or the reflexive consciousness of newness spread—whether these were eagerly sought or resisted, whether imposed from without or developed within.

But the relational approach to defining *modern/modernity/modernism* raises as many questions as it appears to resolve. First, there is the impossibility of perpetual disruption or revolution as change becomes institutionalized. What begin as multiple acts of rebellion against prevailing hegemonies become through their very success a newly codified, often commodified system. Margins become centers with the proliferation and dissemination of rupture. In intellectual and aesthetic realms, for example, outsiders become insiders; pariahs become icons; the rebels become the Establishment. The new science of the Enlightenment that overturned the symbolic order based on religious faith itself became the hegemonic norm based in a faith in reason. The avant-garde artists initially greeted with hoots of derision—the impressionists, postimpressionists, cubists, abstract expressionists—are now the great masters whose works are mainstays of museums and sell for fabulous sums. Rejected, banned, ridiculed, and often unread in the beginning, figures such as Freud and Joyce are for many the supreme avatars of the age, essential reading in any history of ideas and literature. As Raymond Williams argues, the antibourgeois origins of modernism are lost as modernism is canonized in the post–World War II era.[32] As the principle of disruption, the more widespread modernity becomes, the more codified and authoritative it becomes, thus undermining its character as the spirit of explosive rebellion and change. Institutionalized, the avant-garde of rupture becomes the new establishment to be revoked in the making of new avant-gardes. The very success of modernity (and its modernist expressivities) evident in its institutionalization accomplishes its demise—the imperative of postmodernity, or, as I will argue in chapter 4, the inevitability of new modernities.

Second, for all its insistence on the new, a relational modernity is inevitably part of a generational dynamic. Modernity rebels against its parental precursors only to be rebelled against by its inheritors—yet another form of the family romance. It occupies an uneasy location between the *pre*modern that it disrupts and the *post*modern that disrupts it. Never fully stable, it exists in the middle of a prepositional chain, defined by its coming *after* the traditional and *before* the postmodern.

Third, this chain of prepositions in generational succession challenges the relational assumption of freedom from history. The (self)consciousness of modernity—the sense of radical rupture from the immediate past—refuses the principle of historical continuity and evolution in its insistence on origin, newness, and revolution. Indeed, it denies its own production as a historical formation. History produces change as well as continuity; the new cultural and institutional formations of modernity are themselves the product of historical process.

Moreover, the relational notion of modernity tends to resist just the immediate past, often leapfrogging the prior generation in a reinvocation of a more distant past as an inspiration of rebellion. To justify this rejection, inaccurate or heuristic readings or even demonizations of one's recent precursors are common, much as the modernists (inaccurately) condemned the Victorian realists to epistemological and psychological naiveté, much as the postmodernists (inaccurately) reduce the modernists to mere makers of Enlightenment grand narratives. As Paul de Man suggests in echoing

Nietzsche, modernity involves a form of "ruthless forgetting," the "*desire to wipe out whatever came earlier*," not the actual erasure of the past.³³ As such, the relational consciousness of modernity is based in historical illusionism—an insistence on "making it new" as a manifesto that refuses to acknowledge the presence of the past in the present and future. The more modernity protests its absolute newness, the more it suppresses its rootedness in history. And the more that history is repressed, the more it returns in symbolic forms to haunt and disrupt the illusionary and ideological mythology of the new.

A relational approach to defining *modernity/modernism* presumes the possibility of consensual agreement about the meanings of the terms as the structural principle of radical rupture—wherever, whenever, and in whatever forms it might occur. Freed from the fixity a noun suggests, the relational definition appears to garner more agreement across and within disciplines. However, a closer look reveals a pattern of contradiction just as the nominal approach does. Like the noun *modernity*, the adjectival form slips and slides between meanings rooted in the possibility and impossibility of "making it new." If the adjectival form of *modernity* signifies both revolution and evolution, both the break from history and its return, of what descriptive use is it?

∞ ∞ ∞

Both nominal and relational meanings of *modernity* and *modernism* end in contradiction, signaling a phenomenon that signifies both the formation of hegemonies and their dissolution, the production of grand narratives and their dismantling. As noun and adjective, *modernity* is a term at war with itself, a term that unravels its own definition, a term that codifies the principle of indeterminacy and in so doing opposes its own commitment to perpetual change.

In sum, the grammatical/philosophical approach to a definitional project confirms the partial and misleading nature of any definition that focuses on only the nominal or only the relational meanings of modernity. Modernity is not solely a fixed set of characteristics that might have appeared in a given space and time, such as the European Enlightenment or the twentieth-century avant-garde in the arts. Nor is modernity exclusively the principle of rupture. Modernity is best grasped as a set of meanings that encompasses both the specificities of nouns and the relational structures of comparative adjectives. Additionally, this combined approach suggests that meaning does not lie exclusively with either the formation of hegemonies or their dismantling. Instead, modernity encompasses both centripetal and centrifugal forces in contradiction and constant interplay. I pose this neither as a concept of historical stages nor as a utopian dialectic. Rather, I insist upon a meaning produced liminally, a dialogic that pits the contradictory processes of formation and deformation against each other, each as necessary to the other.

POLITICAL/CULTURAL ROUTE

The grammatical/philosophical excursions lack historical and geographical contextualization, lack reflexivity about the production and consumption of meaning, and lack attention to issues of power and the institutionalization of knowledge in the definitional project itself. Definitions don't come into being or function in an abstract cosmos of pure reason or arbitrary signification. (Pace linguists and philosophers: decontextualized definitions have their place, but it is only a partial one in the arena of contestation.) The textual unconscious of definitional debate is also a political unconscious. More issues must be posed under a broadly defined umbrella of cultural studies in historical, global, and comparative contexts.

We need to ask: Who is producing a given set of meanings for *modernity/modernism*? For what audience? From what position or standpoint in space and time? For what purpose and with what effect? What cultural work do these meanings perform? In what way was and is modernity a set of cultural formations with diverse parts and functions, manifesting differently in various temporal and spatial situations, with different effects? How do power relations condition the production, dissemination, and reception of contested meanings? In short, how do questions of power and politics shape both the concept of modernity and the historical phenomena to which the term refers? These are questions upon which a cultural studies approach to definitional power relations focuses.[34]

Modernist studies tends to produce three distinct configurations in the politics of definition: the binary, the circle, and the metonym. Recognizing all three helps expose the flows of power in the institutionalization of knowledge.

The Binary

The definitional act itself typically depends upon a binary of inclusion and exclusion. Depending on who does the defining, certain phenomena belong to the category of *modernity* or *modernism*. Other phenomena do not. By definition. Definitional acts establish territories, map terrains, and determine centers, margins, and areas "beyond the pale." Attempts to establish permeable borderlands instead of fixed boundaries and liminal spaces of considerable intermixing between differences diffuse to some extent the territorial imperative of definition but cannot ultimately eliminate the function of categories to demarcate some phenomena in opposition to others that do not belong. As Toni Morrison writes about canon formation (a type of definitional act in literary, art, and religious history), "Canon building is Empire building. Canon defense is national defense. Canon debate, whatever the terrain, nature and range . . . is the clash of cultures. And *all* of the interests are vested."[35]

Take, for example, the conventional social theory concept of modernity as the invention of the West, as reflected in this assertion by a leading sociologist of modernity, Anthony Giddens:

> When we speak of modernity, however, we refer to institutional transformations that have their origins in the West. How far is modernity distinctively Western? . . . [T]wo distinct organisational complexes are of particular significance in the development of modernity: the *nation-state* and *systematic capitalist production*. Both have their roots in specific characteristics of European history and have few parallels in prior periods or in other cultural settings. If, in close conjunction with one another, they have since swept across the world, this is above all because of the power they have generated. . . . Is modernity distinctively a Western project in terms of the ways of life fostered by these two great transformative agencies? To this query, the blunt answer must be "yes."[36]

To what extent does this definition reflect the Western standpoint of Giddens and social theorists like him—not only as products themselves of the

West but also as specialists in Western societies and history? Without a sufficient knowledge base in the civilizations of Asia, Africa, and the non-Anglo Americas, is it any surprise that the definitional binary of inclusion/exclusion is profoundly Eurocentric, all the more so when the approach is more nominal than relational? (No.) Such Eurocentrism is pervasive in the field whether the writer is celebrating (like Habermas) or critiquing (like Harvey) Western modernity. Left intact is a center/periphery model of globalization in which the West invents and exports while the periphery assimilates and copies. Left unexamined is the degree to which the production of Western forms of modernity resulted from the heightened interaction Western societies had with non-Western others—with the Other of the Western imaginary and with the real, heterogenous, multiplicitous others outside the West. Also left unexplored is the production of different modernities through the histories of non-Western peoples.

Listen to the difference between Giddens's binarist logic and that evident in Sanjay Subrahmanyam's view, which originates in his standpoint and knowledge base outside the West, foregrounds intercultural contact among civilizations as constitutive of modernity, and assumes multiple nodal points for the modern around the globe:

> I have tried to argue that modernity is historically a global and *conjunctural* phenomenon, not a virus that spreads from one place to another. It is located in a series of historical processes that brought hitherto relatively isolated societies into contact, and we must seek its roots in a set of diverse phenomena—the Mongol dream of world conquest, European voyages of exploration, activities of Indian textile traders in the diaspora ... and so forth.[37]

Subrahmanyam's notion still establishes an inside/outside for modernity, but the center is not by definition Western and singular. Rather, it is scattered, interactive, and multiple. His approach invites a rethinking of the times and places of modernity. Where else might accelerated societal change brought about by a combination of new technologies, knowledge revolutions, state formations, and expanding intercultural contacts contribute to radical questioning and dismantling of traditional ontologies, epistemologies, and institutional structures? What about the Tang Dynasty in China, with its great metropolis as the cultural/political center of a vast empire? Or Mughal India, in which the cultural, economic, and religious riches of different peoples clashed and blended? Or Timbuktu, a large city of learning linked to the mercantile hub of the vast Songhai Empire in West Africa at about the same time the cities of Europe were, relatively speaking, backwaters to the great centers of learning and trade in Asia, Africa, the Middle East?

The Circle

The approaches of Giddens and Subrahmanyam to defining modernity—however different their politics—exhibit the familiar problem of the hermeneutic circle as well as the binary of inclusion and exclusion.[38] Defining historical periods and conditions or movements in the arts and writing depends upon a circular process. Definers often identify the characteristics of *modernity* and *modernism* by describing the qualities of the phenomena that they have already assumed to exist within the boundaries of the category. Put differently, definitional mapping relies upon prior assumptions of where the boundary belongs, assumptions that reflect the preexisting beliefs or standpoint of the mapmaker. Such circularity has a politics—all the interests are vested, as Morrison says.

Take for example the literary history of modernism. Periodization, canonization, and the naming of the defining characteristics of modernism are all based on a pool of tenets, people, and/or events whose selection depends upon preexisting notions of the period. Thus, Hugh Kenner declares that expatriate internationalism is a central defining characteristic of high modernism and uses writers like Pound, Eliot, and Joyce to demonstrate his assertions. On this basis, he asserts that Williams, Faulkner, and Woolf are "provincial" or "regional" writers, not modernists. But if he had included these writers in his pool of modernists to begin with, his generalizations about modernism would have been different. So might his concept of the internationalism of modernism if his pool had included writers from Africa, South America, and Asia.[39]

The case of the Harlem Renaissance in modernist studies is even more striking. Until recently, the literature, arts, and music of African Americans centered in Harlem in the 1920s and 1930s have been missing from conventional maps of modernism. Not even represented with an occasional token figure, as female modernists like Woolf and Stein sometimes are. Simply not there. Picasso's primitivism, Fitzgerald's Jazz Age, Eliot's apelike Sweeney, Sherwood Anderson's "dark laughter," Faulkner's racially divided South—all exist on the terrain of canonical modernist studies. But not the primary producers of jazz, not the black artists turning to an imaginary (or real) Africa, not the blues singers and the folk leaving the rural South for the urban North in the Great Migration, not the soldiers returning from a brutal war to demand more freedoms. Their linguistic and rhythmic experimentation, intertexutal "signifyin'," Africanist mythmaking, parodic mimicry, revolutionary fervor, and self-identification with the New do not seem to qualify them for literary modernism in most histories of the movement, even though these same histories frequently list formalist experimentation, citation, mythic analogues, irony, and self-reflexivity as definitional markers. Since the Harlem Renaissance was largely absent from the pool of texts out of which literary historians generated definitional characterizations of modernism, the particular formulations of modernity produced by African Americans were also missing.[40]

The Metonym

Another form the politics of definition takes is the identification of certain figures or qualities to stand for the whole. This metonymic substitution of the part for the whole is widespread in the establishment of the reigning characteristics of the historical condition of modernity or the aesthetic constellation of modernism. To some, Locke or Rousseau are supreme embodiments of Enlightenment modernity; to others, Joyce is the defining icon of modernism. Similarly, some might characterize Western modernity in terms of the rise of the bourgeoisie, democracy, and science; others might define modernism in terms of utopian social planning or the poetics of disruption. Common to all such definitional generalizations is the heuristic tendency to characterize the whole in terms of what the historian retrospectively believes to be its most influential or significant components. In this way, categories like modernity and modernism govern or contain different cultural formations, absorbing their specificities within the definitional boundaries of the privileged metonymic part. And such categorical discipline returns us to the locational question of who is producing these metonymic histories. Who and what has been left out? For what purposes? With what effects?

The pluralist move to multiple modernities—multiple nodal points in space and time for the production of different modernities—attempts to circumvent the reductionistic politics of metonymic approaches. In the 1990s, two special issues of *Daedalus*—"Early Modernities" (1998) and "Multiple Modernities" (2000)—led the way in departing from metonymic practices in the definition of modernity. The editors of "Early Modernities," Shmuel N. Eisenstadt and Wolfgang Schluchter, argue for new research into "multiple modernities." A broadly comparative and global perspective is needed, one that takes into account not the "convergence" into a single modern civilization but rather the "divergence" of different modern formations.[41] In the same issue, Björn Wittrock argues for the "multiplicity of modernities" against the widespread assumption in the "social and human sciences" that "modernization is a process of the global diffusion of Western civilization and its key institutions." What has been a "peculiarly European path to modernity" is assumed to be the definitional model of modernity itself, a view that posits a single origin for and homogeneity of modernity. For both "champions and critics of modernity," "modernization [has] seemed synonymous with Westernization" without sufficient interrogation of "the identification of modernity with the development and diffusion of the cultural program of one specific civilization."[42] Since those early *Daedalus* issues appeared, the assertion of modernity and modernism in the plural has become commonplace, as I discuss in chapter 4.

The move from singularist to pluralist definitions of modernity, however, does not guarantee an escape from metonymic practice. Genuine pluralism is notoriously hard to achieve because the move from the singular to the plural all too often obscures the covert continuation of a model, ideal type, yardstick, or point of reference to which divergent others are silently compared. Eisenstadt and Schluchter, for example, assert the need to recognize multiple modernities, but they do so within a framework that justifies the use of a Western model for modernity. The power of metonymic thinking along with their resistance to it coexist uneasily in their definition of their comparative method:

> These are deviances not from a norm but from an ideal type used only for heuristic purposes. . . . The European constellation in the early modern

and Enlightenment period serves as an ideal type to measure deviances, to identify differences encountered in other civilizations. But this is only a beginning. Contrary to the assumptions of many historical and sociological studies that the development of the West should constitute the major yardstick according to which the dynamics of other civilizations are measured, it is the basic assumption of our approach that each civilization has developed distinct institutional formations and cultural foundations and that the specific characteristics of these civilizations should be analyzed not only in terms of their approximation to the West but also in their own terms.

(8)

Assertions of "yardsticks" and multiplicities conflict. Difference as "deviance" from an "ideal type" does not live up to the stated intention to understand each modernity in its own terms. The epistemological tendency to substitute the part for the whole—the single instance for the diversity of instances—can potentially overwhelm a theoretical or definitional exercise, no matter the good intentions to avoid it.

∞ ∞ ∞

The tendency of binarist, circular, and metonymic definitional acts to reproduce the play of power relations within institutions of knowledge might lead some to affirm the need for epistemological anarchy—the elimination of all such periodizing categories. However, the problematic of definitional history should not, in my view, result in its abandonment. Rather, as Jameson writes, "The problem of periodization and its categories, which are certainly in crisis today . . . seem to be as indispensable as they are unsatisfactory for any kind of work in cultural study."[43] Without historical categories, we would face an infinity of singularities, an approach to knowledge that requires some form of selection that is no more politically neutral than the heuristic construction of historical narratives. Without some definitional categories, the politics of choice would be driven further underground, rendered even less visible.

Given our need for definitional categories, however imperfect they are, what, then, does the political/cultural route have to offer? I regard the binarist, circular, and metonymic problems inherent in definitional acts not as dead ends but rather as opportunities for interrogation that lead right into the heart of the dialogic meanings of *modernity* and *modernism*. They insist upon a recognition of how such terms are themselves historical constructions—with their own story of development, function, and effect, all of which invite interpretation and critique. Different configurations of modernity reflect the different positionalities of their producers, serve different interests, and have different effects. It is this that returns us to the question of politics—how power relations inform not only the cultural artifacts of modernity but also the subsequent readings of them.

The notion of multiple modernities, for example, has been used in parts of Asia to justify the continuation of certain power structures and elites and a resistance to democracy as a "foreign" importation not suited to "Asian values."[44] Such arguments, based as they are on the pluralization of modernity, often ignore the longstanding history of democratic formations in parts of Asia. Moreover, the use of the concept of multiple modernities to justify the status quo and resistance to change in places like China, Singapore, Indonesia, or Iran ignores the way in which powerful ideas about modernity can travel from one part of the world to another.[45] Such "traveling theories" (to invoke Edward Said) inevitably transplant, indigenize, and divergently evolve in different locations at varying points of time to produce a genuine multiplicity of modernities.[46] Thus in Western contexts, the concept of multiple modernities may help critique Eurocentric definitional practices, while in non-Western parts of the world, the insistence on multiple modernities can be appropriated for the justification of local configurations of power. The political/cultural route for the definition of *modernity* and *modernism* requires sensitivity to the different uses to which definitions can be put and cannot provide fixed terrains of meaning. Contradictions abound.

BANGCLASH

In a Nietzschean (or perhaps Fanonian) mood, Amiri Baraka writes in "Return of the Native" :

> Harlem is vicious
> modernism. BangClash.
> Vicious the way its made.
> Can you stand such beauty.
> So violent and transforming.[47]

Whether the BangClash of definitional contestation produces such transformative beauty is doubtful. But this excursion—through the byways of story, parataxis, hypertextual detour, aphorism, and collage—has an endpoint. In this chapter, I have resisted the desire to come up with my own, yet another definition of *modernity* and *modernism* for others to argue about or ignore. (Resistance is never easy. The magnetic slide toward fixed meaning feels irresistible at times, and I will succumb to it in subsequent chapters.) Instead, in this chapter, I have attempted to shift attention to the processes and patterns of definitional contestation.

In these terms, there is a conclusion of sorts to be made. Definitional dissonance matters. The fact of not only diverse but downright opposite meanings signifies. These differences should not be ignored as accidental or arbitrary, the ordinary product of disciplinary background or semantic disagreement. Nor should they be tamed within the deceptive inclusiveness of pluralism. In practice, the pluralization of *modernity* and *modernism* runs the risk of covertly reinstating a center/periphery pattern in which a hegemonic norm is covertly privileged over marginal variations.[48] Instead, the BangClash should be confronted directly.

The grammatical/philosophical and political/cultural routes I explored suggest that the oppositional meanings of *modernity/modernism* point to the contradictory dialogic running through the historical and expressive formations of the phenomena to which the terms allude. Order and disruption are symbiotically necessary to each other for each to have its distinctive meaning. The center comes into being as it dissipates. Modernity's grand narratives institute their own radical dismantling. The lifeblood of modernity's chaos is its order. The impulse to order is the product of chaos. Modernism requires tradition to "make it new." Tradition comes into being only as it is rebelled against. Definitional excursions into the meanings of *modernity* and *modernism* begin and end in reading the specificities of these contradictions.

TWO
PLANETARITY

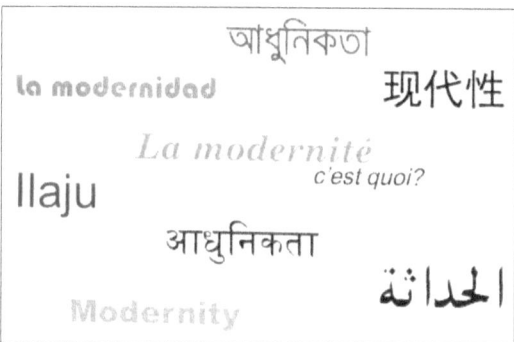

La modernité, c'est quoi?[1] Modernity, what is it? Imagine a polylogue of reflections on this question.

Modernity is Europe's Enlightenment, the break from religious hegemonies and the spread of science, technology, and cosmopolitan ideals of freedom and democracy.

Ilaju ti awon oyibo mu wa si ile awon enia dudu, imunisin and imuleru lo da, ati awon orile ede ti ko too rara; orile ede tori jakujaku rederede ranran, opolopo ijoba l'onkuna lotun losi.

Modernity is Europe's brutal colonialism built on the systematic enslavement of Africans, arbitrary and imposed nation-state boundaries, and the formation of modern African identities amid the legacies of corruption and failed states. Translated from Yoruba.

(*above*) Anupam Basu, *Scripts of Modernity*. Source: Courtesy of Anupam Basu.

আধুনিকতা মানে বাংলার নবজাগরণ ।
বাঙালির আত্মবিশ্লেষন। আত্মউপলব্ধি ।
শুধু বাঙালি হিসেবে নয়, ভারতবাসী হিসেবে
ব্রিটিশ সাম্রাজ্যবাদের বিরুধ্যে রুখে দাড়ানো ।

    Modernity is Bengal's Renaissance, its self-critique and self-realization that emerges in the nineteenth century out of its struggle against British colonialism, not only as Bengalis but as Indians. Translated from Bengali.

La modernidad en Latinoamerica es el mestizaje, producto de una mezcla excepcional de culturas colonizadoras y colonizadas; un mestizaje atrapado entre la hegemonía europea y la norteamericana.

    Modernity is Latin America's *métissage*, its particular mixture of colonizing and colonized cultures, caught between European and North American hegemonies. Translated from Spanish.

现代性是中国迈向未来的必经之途，是文明古国彻底摆脱了封建主义的落后和西方列强的凌辱，并重树五千年历史的荣耀，在新的世纪里主导全球。

    Modernity is China's project for the future, moving beyond the backwardness of the past and the humiliations of foreign domination, reasserting the centrality of its five-thousand year civilization as a moral, global force. Translated from Chinese.

الحداثة في العالم العربي هي تجديد لكل قديم متبلور بالثقافة الدينية، والإنسانية العربية، والنهضة العلمية، ومنطق الإجتهاد، والتغيير الإبداعي عوضاً عن التمسك بالتراث الراكد.

    Modernity is the Arab world's rebirth of the old informed by religious discourse, Arab humanism, scientific progress, the rationalism of *ijtihad*, and creative transformation rather than conformity to a stagnant *turath* (heritage). Translated from Arabic.

आधुनिकता भारतीय स्वतंत्रता है, ब्रिटिश राज से जन्मी, विभाजन के लहु में नहायी, विश्व के वृहदतम प्रजातंल व तकनीकी महाशक्ती में विकिसत होती ।
मार्डनिटि
आधुनिकता

Modernity is Indian Independence, born of British rule, bathed in the blood of Partition, and growing as the world's largest democracy and a technological powerhouse. Translated from Hindi.

Modernity, of course, has no single meaning, not even in one location. This polylogue—constructed collaboratively with colleagues at the University of Wisconsin–Madison—voices particular views shaped by different planetary positionalities.[2] Globally and locally, modernity appears infinitely expandable. Listening to these diverse voices, reading their scripts, I despair—especially for the new scholar just entering the field of dreams, a Tower of Babel with too many levels to climb, but also for the older scholar, trained in the old modernist studies: vertigo out on a limb, whirled up into a vortex of the new. Yet I also rejoice. Change is what drew me to modernism in the beginning. Why should it ossify? Why should the fluid freeze over, the undecidable become decided?

All that is solid melts into air.[3] We know that. Why should we want a stability for the field that the modernists themselves rebelled against? Caught in the polylogue, we are in the thick of things. We inhabit at the level of scholarship and teaching what it is we study. As W. B. Yeats asks, "How can we know the dancer from the dance?"[4] We are participating in what we study, and we should not be apologetic about it. This is a planetary epistemology of modernity, of modernism.

THE NEW MODERNIST STUDIES: EXPANSION AND CONTAINMENT

In their 2008 overview of the "new" modernist studies in *PMLA* Douglas Mao and Rebecca L. Walkowitz characterize the field's expansions along three major axes—the temporal, horizontal, and vertical, by which they mean the growing historical and geographical reach of modernist studies as well as the dissolution of divisions between high and low art and culture.⁵ Jennifer Wicke has dubbed the field's making itself new a form of rebranding, a commodification of the field that ensures our own complicity in the logic of globalization.⁶ In *Disciplining Modernism*, Pamela L. Caughie asks whether modernism can or should be contained and, if so, what would be the ethics/politics of such "disciplining"?⁷ Have the field's boundaries become so boundless as to incorporate everything and thus lose all definitional cogency or analytic utility? Does this rebranding exhibit imperial ambitions to colonize other fields? Or is this new planetary reach an unraveling of foundational hierarchies?

Modernism, like modernity, exceeds definitional and disciplinary limitations. Yet these terms require some set of meanings to provide any functional use. The conjunction of the need for limits and their failure to contain characterizes modernist studies today, recapitulating the logic of modernism/modernity itself. As Garry Leonard suggests, modernism/modernity is like the internal combustion engine: both exhibit an endlessly recurring dynamic of explosion and containment. The logic of modernity follows the hydraulics of pressure and explosive release, containment and then movement.⁸

BEYOND ANXIETY AND THE COMFORT ZONE

There is a palpable anxiety pervading modernist studies, according to Stephen Ross, a metacritical angst about the nature of the field that manifests in uncanny attempts to define modernism and "make it new," thereby creating an ethically unjustifiable need for ourselves as a professorial elite.⁹ But a retreat into the comfort zone of a modernist studies based on late-nineteenth and early-twentieth-century "high modernist" experimentation in Europe and the United States is neither desirable nor possible. The cat is already out of the bag. And yet the danger of an expansionist modernism lapsing into meaninglessness or colonizing gestures is real.

To navigate between these extremes, I advocate a *transformational* planetary epistemology rather than a merely expansionist or additive one, one that builds on the far-reaching implications of the linkage of modernism with modernity. This link, reflected in the title of the Modernist Studies

Association's journal, *Modernism/Modernity*, might seem so obvious by now as to be unworthy of note. But it wasn't always so. In the early days of the field, modernism was understood primarily in formalist terms as a loose affiliation of movements coalescing around certain aesthetic rebellions, styles, and philosophical principles and resisting the aesthetics of immediate precursors in the arts and literature of so-called high culture.[10] Curiously, the substantive link between modernism and modernity appeared in Malcolm Bradbury and James McFarlane's introduction to their 1976 volume, *Modernism*. They wrote:

> Modernism is the one art that responds to the scenario of our chaos. It is the art consequent on Heisenberg's "Uncertainty principle," of the destruction of civilization and reason in the First World War, of the world changed and reinterrupted by Marx, Freud, and Darwin, of capitalism and constant industrial acceleration, of existential exposure to meaninglessness or absurdity.[11]

In spite of their book's limited canon, the seed was sown for a radical departure from aestheticism as the definitional foundation for modernism.

Modernism, for many, became a reflection of and engagement with a wide spectrum of historical changes, including intensified and alienating urbanization; the cataclysms of world war and technological progress run amok; the rise and fall of European empires; changing gender, class, and race relations; and technological inventions that radically changed the nature of everyday life, work, mobility, and communication. Once modernity became the defining cause of aesthetic engagements with it, the door opened to thinking about the specific conditions of modernity for different genders, races, sexualities, nations, and so forth. Modernity became modernities, a pluralization that spawned a plurality of modernisms and the circulations among them.

To resist the definitional expansions in modernist studies is to fight modernism's constitutive link with modernity. Could it be that the anxieties about the geohistorical and generic expansion of modernist studies represents an uncanny desire to reestablish a particular early-twentieth-century Western aesthetic style as the sine qua non of modernism? What is the ethics of that interminably repeated comfort zone? How are we to break the hold of the old modernist mold? That is the question, if we want to foster a planetary modernist studies.

Thirteen ways of looking at a blackbird.[12] Thirteen ways of looking at the interconnections of modernism slash modernity. The point of Wallace Stevens's iconic poem—like the point of cubism—is epistemological: that seeing is multifaceted, that what is seen must be seen from multiple points of view. Hold it up. Walk around it. Mull on its multiplicities. Listen to others who hold it up, walk around it, mull on its multiplicities. Resist fixity, finality, single perspectives.

BLACKBIRD ONE: THE SLASH—MODERNISM/MODERNITY

Selena Beckman-Harned, *Thirteen Blackbirds*.
Source: Courtesy of Selena Beckman-Harned.

Interrogate the slash! A planetary epistemology in modernist studies begins by looking at the meanings embedded in that slash between modernism/modernity. The slash both connects and separates: the paradox of all borders. Many regularly assume that modernism mirrors, reflects, reacts, or responds to modernity—as if the historical condition of modernity precedes the aesthetic response to it, as if modernism comes belatedly as the avant-garde of dissolving epistemological and political hegemonies. I want to suggest, however, a simultaneity of effects and practices. I think we should stop positing modernism as modernity's self-reflexive other, its symptomatic reaction formation, its oppositional consciousness.

Instead, I suggest we regard modernism in its different geohistorical locations and periods as a powerful domain *within* a particular modernity, not something outside of it, caused by it, or responding belatedly to it. From this perspective, modernism is a force effecting change as much as it intersects other domains of change. Thus, I am suggesting that we treat modernism as the domain of creative expressivity *within* modernity's dynamic of rapid change, a domain that interacts with the other arenas of rupture such as technology, trade, migration, state formation, societal institutions, and so forth.

The slash between modernity/modernism implies a simultaneity but also a distinction, a connection but also a separation. Modernism is a part of modernity, a part that is centered in modernity's aesthetic dimension, which is distinct from other dimensions but not separate from them. Though interlocked with institutional or economic forces, for example, modernism's expressive domain is a product of particularly human agencies in the media of the creative, the aesthetic, and the representational. Focused on the contradictions of the slash, this approach opens doorways to seeing how the aesthetic interacts with other arenas of change. It also empowers a planetary approach to modernism that breaks the Anglo-European hold on the field. Every modernity has its distinctive modernism.

BLACKBIRD TWO: A CONFESSION

Ken Mowatt, Wegyat Legend, Raven Stealing the Sun
Source: Legacy Art Galleries, University of Victoria.

I must confess, however, to some anxieties that I have not yet resolved. The power of those early concepts of modernism as the crisis of aesthetic representation, with a repudiation of nineteenth-century realism, remains very strong within me. It is one thing to claim, as I do in chapter 6, that texts like Tayeb Salih's *Season of Migration to the North* (1966) and Arundhati Roy's *The God of Small Things* (1997) are "modernist," defining a postcolonial modernism both interlocked with yet distinct from Euro/American modernism.[13] The formalist experimentalism of these texts makes them philosophically, psychologically, and aesthetically attuned to writers like Conrad, Joyce, Woolf, and Faulkner, however different their modernities. It's another thing entirely for me to make such a claim about a novel like *Brick Lane* (2003), Monica Ali's predominantly realist novel of Bangladeshi migration to London. *Brick Lane* deliberately echoes *Ulysses* and *Mrs. Dalloway*, embeds epistolary narratives from London and Bangladesh, and deals centrally with what the migration scholar Nikos Papastergiadis calls "the restless trajectories of modernity," the dialogic and contrapuntal psychologies characterizing the "turbulence of migration."[14] But is *Brick Lane* a "modernist novel"?

I'm caught in a conundrum of my own making—my insistence on a planetary approach to modernism alongside my anxiety at the implications of its scope. This is a confession. I find it hard to call a novel like *Brick Lane* "modernist." But I think this is my problem, not the problem of the more capacious understanding of modernism as the expressive domain of modernity I proposed earlier. I think the struggles within the field are embedded in my psyche. The anxiety is there, but I'm not proud of it. It needs to be worked through, as a holdover from the past. That's what it means to leave the comfort zone.

BLACKBIRD THREE: EUROCENTRISM'S HOLD

Pistoxenos Painter. Apollo and his raven on a white-ground bowl, c. 480 BCE.
Source: Delphi Archaeological Museum.

A planetary epistemology of modernism/modernity must break the mold of Eurocentrism. "*Eurocentrism*," writes Aamir Mufti, is "an *epistemological* problem."[15] Epistemology signifies ways of knowing and embeds the political questions of who is doing the knowing, for whom knowledge is produced, how knowledge is deployed, and who benefits from that deployment. Eurocentrism, of course, is not the only centrism on earth—all societies construct narratives of their own centrality, exceptionalism, and worldview through which others are seen and against which they are measured. But in modernist studies, Eurocentrism is the dominant centrism to confront because the West's narrative of itself is the story of its own invention of modernity and because the field of modernist studies itself began in the West as a study of Western modernities and modernisms. A planetary modernist studies begins with "provincializing Europe," to invoke Dipesh Chakrabarty's resonant phrase.[16] Add to this an awareness that the concept of "the West" is itself deeply centric, repressing the heterogeneities and peripheries *within* Europe and North America and ignoring the degree to which the West has never been and is not "one." Eurocentric "structures of historical knowledge," as Mufti writes, normalize and *make* normative the idea of Europe as "the scene of the birth of the modern." . . . It is the social and cultural *force* of this idea of Europe in intellectual life . . . that I am referring to here as Eurocentrism. . . . Humanistic culture is saturated with this informal developmentalism—a "first in the West, and then elsewhere" structure of global time . . . in which cultural objects from non-Western societies can be grasped only with reference to the categories of European cultural history, as pale or partial reflections of the latter, to be seen ultimately as coming late, lagging behind, and lacking originality.[17]

The old mold of modernist studies narrates just such a tale of informal developmentalism—"we" did it first in the West (although the origin dates and locations differ radically, from Baudelaire to imagism, from the impressionists to the cubists), and then "they" did it elsewhere: derivative and belated.

The power of the field's originary narratives of modernism is a wonder to behold.

BLACKBIRD FOUR: THE END OF THE NOMINAL AND THE RISE OF THE RELATIONAL

Lynnette Shelley. *Three Ravens*. 2009. Mixed media on Canson pastel paper. *Source*: http://www.lynetteshelley.com.

How can we challenge these Eurocentric originary narratives, explode radically out of their forces of containment—to invoke Leonard's combustion metaphor? The first step is to set aside the nominal definition of modernity as it has so commonly been constructed:

Modernity is: [fill in the blanks]
a.
b.
c.

To recall the example cited in chapter 1, Anthony Giddens, a progressive doyen of sociological modernity studies, defines modernity as a specific historical development characterized by the rise of the nation-state, panoptic bureaucracies, and capitalism as developed in the West from the eighteenth century and spread to many parts of the world by the twentieth century. In his view, globalization is the diffusion of Western modernity to the rest of the world. He is not alone.[18]

A planetary epistemology of modernity, in contrast, needs to be relational, delineating not a nominal set of characteristics (e.g., "big" = x, y, and z), but rather defining one thing in relation to another (e.g., "big" is not "small"). It focuses on the dynamics of change, the self-consciousness of change, or even the illusion of change—a "before" and "after," an "old" and a "new." As Bruno Latour writes, "Modernity comes in as many versions as there are thinkers or journalists, yet all its definitions point, in one way or another, to the passage of time. The adjective 'modern' designates a new regime, an acceleration, a rupture, a revolution in time."[19] This relational, adjectival approach to modernity is more suited than a nominal definition to planetarity because it enables recognition of a spatial dimension to modernity's temporality, an interactional set of relations throughout the globe that may also manifest differently in particular places and times. It provides a comparative framework that balances the commensurable—what different modernities share—with the incommensurable—how they are different.

Of course, the relational dynamic of old and new is fraught with contradictions. In chapter 1, I suggested that modernity's relational structure is a temporal narrative that invents the "before" as "tradition." Tradition is itself a construct of modernity, coming into being at the moment of its loss, a process both celebrated and lamented. Modernity in relational terms contains within it a struggle—often a violent one—between modernizers and traditionalists—evident, for example, in *both* the United States and the Middle East today. It also contains a palimpsestic layering of new over old, one that often involves a misrecognition of powerful continuities—a misrecognition constitutive of modernity. For some, such misrecognition involves a haunting of the old in the new, a return of the repressed occasioned by the ruthless forgetting of the past that Nietzsche and de Man theorized as constitutive of modernity.[20] For others, it represents illusory thinking based in what Latour describes as the needs of the moderns "to invent the Great Divide" between themselves and the premoderns, between the human and the nonhuman.

In facing the question of how new is "the new" and how much must we forget to think of it as "the new," we also bump squarely into a major difficulty with the relational approach. Where the nominal definition provides the comfort of relative stability (modernity = a, b, and c), the relational approach opens us up to the difficult question whether anything is "not modern" and thus whether any expressive form is "not modernist." Is there a historical period that is not undergoing rapid change across a spectrum of social indicators? Are there texts that are not engaged with that change? For any text that I might name, would someone rise up to defend its particular form of engagement with a particular modernity? Milton's *Paradise Lost* for example? Willa Cather's *Oh Pioneers!*? Norman Mailer's *The Naked and the Dead*? For *modernity/modernism* to have utility as analytic categories, even relationally defined, must we identify the *not modern, not modernist*?

BLACKBIRD FIVE: AN EXPERIMENT, BOUND TO CREATE RESISTANCE

Although I still struggle with these questions, let me briefly share an experiment: an attempt to draw a verbal map of modernity relationally defined as a set of conditions—dare I say structures?—open to a vast array of distinctive articulations across the *longue durée* of history.[21]

Mark Graver. *Blackbird V*. 2008. Acrylic resist etching. 300x300mm. *Source*: Wharepuke Print Studio.

MODERNITY AS MATRIX OF CONVERGING CHANGES

Vortex of Change
technological, commercial, political
cultural, religious, aesthetic
familial, sexual
uneven
unequal

Radical Ruptures
shattering breaks
movement, mobility
acceleration, speed
collisions
fluidity
dynamism
freedom/unfreedom

Hybridity Heightened
encounters
contact zones
mixing, mimesis
convergence, conjuncture
transaction, translation
juxtaposition
innovation

Phenomenology of the New and the Now
utopic/dystopic
exhilaration, alienation
disorientation, defamiliarization, despair
nostalgia
the Other elsewhere and within
epistemological flexibility
ruthless forgetting
haunting
invention of tradition

Striking, you might say, how much that map exhibits a modernist poetics drawn from the early twentieth century in the West. In fact, Satya P. Mohanty challenged my chart on just those grounds, saying that it represents an imposition of an aesthetic perspective onto modernity instead of the philosophical one, featuring individualism, which he prefers, or the socioeconomic one Giddens delineates. He may be right.[22] Perhaps all relational definitions slide into the nominal, incorporating willy-nilly some presupposed characteristics. As I struggle with this problem, I acknowledge that I am what I study, formed by my background in literary studies—this is epistemologically true. I cut my critical teeth on manifesto modernism—perhaps my efforts to move outside of my epistemological frame end up repeating it. On the other hand, for the word *modernity* to mean anything at all, we need to think about what is put into relation with what and how that relationship takes on different forms at different geohistorical locations. Perhaps the modernist poetics of the early twentieth century in the West presciently articulated a logic at work in other times and places.

BLACKBIRD SIX: THE MULTIPLE, POLYCENTRIC, AND RECURRENT

Blackbirds.
Source: Clipart.

A relational epistemology allows us to see the globe afresh, to see that modernity which is not one, to see modernity in its multiple and diverse forms in the geohistory of the world. In step with the rapidly proliferating rhetorics of plural modernities, I ask, here, for an approach diametrically opposed to that of Fredric Jameson in *A Singular Modernity*, in which he argues that "Everyone knows the formula by now. . . . you talk about 'alternate' or 'alternative' modernities. . . . But this is to overlook the other fundamental meaning of modernity which is that of a worldwide capitalism. . . . I believe that the only satisfactory semantic meaning of modernity lies in its association with capitalism."[23] Such a reductionist view limits the nominalist definition, even more radically than Giddens does, to a set of one: capitalism. Jameson's notion of singularity impoverishes what needs to be a complex approach to the overdeterminations of history and the enmeshments of different systems of power in understanding modernity.

The profusion of terms for modernity's plural formations belie the singularity Jameson seeks. As chapter 4 examines in more detail, the field abounds in such adjectives for modernity or modernities as *multiple*, *polycentric, early, at large, alternative, other, peripheral, divergent, discrepant, uneven, conjunctural,* and *recurrent.*[24] Each term is its own keyword, with different nuances, particularly in what it suggests about the relation to Western modernities. I like how they suggest a spatial approach to modernity, a necessity for globalizing a concept that has been predominantly temporal. I like how they assume an uneven temporality for the emergence of different modernities. Some arise at the same time, such as the modernities of colonizer and colonized in the *fin de siècle* of Britain, Egypt, and India. Some arise at different times, such as the early modernities of India in the fourteenth and fifteenth centuries or the postcolonial modernities of Africa after 1960. I like how the term *polycentric* posits each modernity as its own center, with others as their peripheries. I also like how the terms *uneven* and *discrepant* invite analysis of unequal power and privilege, both between differently located modernities and within a single location. I do object to the way such terms as *alternative, other, peripheral,* and even *divergent* reinstate Western modernity as the center, with all the "other" modernities as marginal or derivative. In sum, I like terms that suggest the fluidity and multiplicity of modernities, terms that refuse to use one modernity as the measure of all others.

I have been probing the potential of yet another term, *recurrent* modernities, because it suggests that human history cycles unevenly through periods of relative stasis and then explosive kinesis; between retrenchment and expansion, continuity and change, consolidation and risk; between inward and outward mobilities.[25] The concept of recurrent modernities requires a scalar approach to a capacious historical archive, the *longue durée* of world historians or what Wai Chee Dimock calls "deep time."[26] Different points of the globe flare up at different times as nodal points of transformational change across a wide spectrum of societal domains, each taking a particular form in its geohistorical location—from long-ago world systems to today's globalization. As Dilip Parameshwar Gaonkar writes, "*everywhere, at every national/cultural site, modernity is not one but many, modernity is not new but old and familiar; modernity is incomplete and necessarily so.*"[27]

BLACKBIRD SEVEN: CONQUEST, COLONIALITY, AND WORLD SYSTEMS

U.S. Air Force Blackbird.
Source: http://www
.militaryfactory.com.

"There is no modernity without coloniality," Walter D. Mignolo writes.[28] He is speaking specifically of European and Latin American modernities formed constitutively through conquest since 1500. He regards them as distinctive modernities, but ones thoroughly enmeshed, formed through interaction with one another through conquest or through colonial and postcolonial relations. "We have come to understand colonialism and conquest as the very condition of possibility for modernity and for aesthetic modernism," writes Andreas Huyssen of Euro/American modernism.[29] Have we all come to this understanding, I wonder, or do post/colonial modernities and modernisms remain at the periphery of the field?

More fundamentally, do other, even earlier empires combine periods of violent conquest with rapid technological change, world systems of trade and cultural exchange, the bang/clash of different peoples and their worldviews, and new representational practices in the arts and other expressive domains? Yes, I think they do. For starters, the Roman Empire; Tang Dynasty China; the Muslim Empire centered especially in the commercial and cultural capitals of Baghdad, Al-Andalus, and Timbuktu; the Mughal Empire in India; and the largest land empire in human history, the Mongol Empire all encompassed these phenomena I am calling modernity *before* the modernities of the post-1500 world system, as I discuss in more detail in chapter 3. All produced explosively creative mixtures of peoples and cultural practices.[30] Putting the formation of Western modernity within that *longue durée* does not diminish its global power, but it does change the exceptionalist, diffusionist, and hierarchical originary myths of modernity that have dominated the field.

Recognizing the violence and conquest that are so often a constitutive part of recurrent modernities helps prevent discourses of modernity's fluidity, multidirectionality, and reciprocal exchange from sliding into a utopian rhetoric of happy hybridity. To counter this tendency, I keep reminding myself that the massive ruptures of modernity across a spectrum of social formations are most likely to occur during periods of rapid, often brutal conquest that cause wide-scale material, psychological, spiritual, representational, and epistemological dislocation.

And yet, with the dislocations of imperial or hegemonic dominance come creative relocations. With suffering also come the transformative agencies of the human imagination. Recurrent modernities, I believe, are neither pure defeat nor pure progress. They are geohistorical moments of dynamic kinesis that put in dialectic the dystopic with the utopic, slaveries with freedoms, destructions with creations. At the center of these contradictions lie the self-reflexive and representational domains of modernity, the arena of all modernisms.

Just think of jazz: Remember that Paul Gilroy argues that the first modern subjects of the Enlightenment period were the Africans torn from their homes, enslaved in the New World—alienated, exiled, transplanted, and infinitely creative.[31] And in that new world, their descendants blended European and African musics to create creolized musical forms that have themselves transformed, traveled, and transplanted throughout the planet.

BLACKBIRD EIGHT: CIRCULATIONS, NETWORKS, AND TRANSLATIONS

Erin McKean. Photograph. 2010. *Source:* Courtesy of Erin McKean.

Polycentric, recurrent modernities and their modernisms develop not in isolation but always relationally through encounters with other societies and civilizations, encounters that are transcultural, not unidirectional. "Les contacts entre les cultures," Édouard Glissant writes, "c'est là une donnée de la modernité" ("Contact among cultures is one of the givens of modernity").[32]

Historians of the global ecumene like André Gunder Frank trace large-scale patterns of encounter through commerce, war, technology, migrations of people, and cultural practices.[33] Anthropologists like James Clifford and Arjun Appadurai trace traveling cultures, intercultural networks, and the processes of cultural translation and transculturation, asserting that distinctive cultures form through hybridic interaction with others.[34] In *The Hybrid Muse* and *A Transnational Poetics*

Jahan Ramazani adapts these concepts of circulating cultures to propose a planetary poetics of modernism that is "both discretely located and thoroughly enmeshed, networked, cross-racialized."³⁵ As Laura Doyle and Laura Winkiel argue in *Geomodernisms*, thinking "in terms of interconnected modernisms" "breaks open" the term *modernism* into something they call "geomoderisms," a landscape of interlocking engagements with "cultural and political discourses of global modernity."³⁶ In "Modernism, Geopolitics, Globalization," Melba Cuddy-Keane brings the "interactivity and interdependency" of "cultural globalization" to modernist studies, insisting on the multidirectional, kinetic, and impure fluidity of "disjunctive global flows."³⁷ Peter Brooker and Andrew Thacker modify Raymond Williams's question "when was modernism?" to "*where* was modernism?," suggesting that the answer lies in how transnational modernist practices "travel and migrate across nations and are, in turn, transformed by encounters with indigenous national cultures."³⁸ Regenia Gagnier's Global Circulation Project is a vast online dialogue among scholars around the world on the circulations of different Anglophone modernisms.³⁹

The borderlands of contact zones create creolizations on all sides through patterns of imitation, adaptation, transculturation, and cultural translation. "I call creolization the meeting," Glissant writes, "the interference, shock, harmonies, and disharmonies between the cultures of the world, in the realized totality of the world."⁴⁰ Beyond *creolization*, dozens of keywords in English are being used—and presumably in other languages— for these processes, each with different resonances for the practices and politics of intercultural encounter. Sometimes these words are utopic, sometimes dystopic, and sometimes complexly mixed or relatively neutral. *Contamination*, for example, suggests pollution or victimization, in contrast to *adaptation*, which incorporates agency. *Theft* invokes crime; *translation* connotes a more benign exchange. The vast array of English keywords for interculturalism can be sorted into distinctive rhetorics based on the main arenas of the rapid change associated with modernity: the biological, the corporeal, the commercial, the political, the technological, the cultural, and the representational.

> **Biological**: adaptation, adoption, androgyny, bastardization, circulation, contamination, dilution, erosion, friction, grafting, hybridization,

miscegenation, mongrelization, metamorphosis, mutation, naturalization, pollution, selection, transplantation, transmutation.

Corporeal: absorption, anthropophagy, cannibalization, engulfment, incorporation, ingestion.

Commercial: borrowing, circulation, commerce, debt, endebtedness, exchange, incorporation, importation, lending, merger, theft, traffic.

Political: accommodation, affiliation, alliance, appropriation, coalition, collaboration, compromise, co-optation, cosmopolitanism, encounter, engagement, influence, impact, imposition, interference, interpellation, interpenetration, intervention, mediation, negotiation, penetration, realignment, subsumption, subversion.

Cultural: acculturation, adaptation, anthropophagy, assimilation, blending, cannibalization, clashing, collision, deculturation, differentiation, encounter, friction, homogenization, hybridization, indigenization, interchange, interculturality, intermingling, intermixing, localization, mixing, nativization, naturalization, syncretism, transculturation, vernacularization.

Representational: copy, cutting and pasting, distortion, echo, elaboration, differentiation, influence, imitation, improvisation, intertextuality, mimesis, mimicry, morphing, parody, pidgin, reception, recombination, refiguration, refraction, reframing, reinvention, remaking, reversal, re-vision, rewriting, signifying, transcodification, translation, transposition, vernacularization, vampirization, versioning.[41]

Models of planetary cultural traffic, mimesis, and translation need to supplant older concepts of modernist internationalism, which are typically based on binaries of Self-Other, modern-traditional, civilized-savage, high art–primitive art. The appropriation model in particular regards the modernists of the West as cosmopolitan producers of culture who cite or steal the traditions of the Rest to break out of the repressive, clichéd, or narrow representational conventions of the West. Whether used in praise or critique of the West's

Figure 2.10 Pablo Picasso, *Les demoiselles d'Avignon*. 1907.

Source: The Museum of Modern Art, New York. © The Estate of Pablo Picasso / Artists Rights Society (ARS), New York.

modernism, the appropriation model recapitulates the logic of imperialism, with the Rest providing the raw material transmuted into modernist art in the West. As Ramazani argues, "Criticism that reduces high modernist . . . 'appropriations' to orientalist theft or primitivist exoticism may risk circumscribing instead of opening up possibilities for global and transnational analysis."[42] Picasso's *Les demoiselles d'Avignon* (1907), with its incorporation of African masks into three of the five faces of the prostitutes in the painting, is often invoked as the iconic example of this appropriation model.[43]

Figure 2.11 Pablo Picasso, detail, *Les demoiselles d'Avignon*. 1907.

Source: The Museum of Modern Art, New York. © The Estate of Pablo Picasso / Artists Rights Society (ARS), New York.

Figure 2.12 Mbuya mask, Pende, Congo. Nineteenth century. Painted wood, fiber, and cloth.

Source: EO.1959.15.18, collection MRAC Tervuren; photo R. Asselberghs, MRAC Tervuren ©. Musée Royal de l'Afrique Centrale, Tervuren, Belgium.

As Simon Gikandi has argued, such discussions often refuse to grant African art the position of aesthetic or formal innovation, instead reducing it to the fetishistic and psychological.[44] In contrast to the appropriation model, a planetary approach to cultural circulation would stress how the agencies of African artists producing and being collected in Africa in the late nineteenth century were part of a colonial modernity, constituting a colonial modernism that Picasso and the cubists indigenized, that is, made native to Parisian modernism. The creative agencies of modernities outside the West circulated into the West as transformative influences. Who, we must ask, is derivative of whom?

Take for another example the Ukiyo-e, or Floating World woodblocks from Japan, absorbed into Paris in the 1880s as *Japonisme* swept the West while Japan itself modernized in the Meiji period. As a form of "low" or popular art, the Ukiyo-e had been produced since the seventeenth century

Figure 2.13 Pablo Picasso, detail, *Les demoiselles d'Avignon*. 1907.

Source: The Museum of Modern Art, New York. © The Estate of Pablo Picasso / Artists Rights Society (ARS), New York.

Figure 2.14 Hongwe or Ngare, Republic of Congo. Nineteenth century. Semi-hardwood polychromed (black, white, red), height: 35.5cm.

Source: Formerly collections of Aristide Courtois (before 1930), Charles Ratton, and Museum of Modern Art, New York. Musée Barbier-Mueller, Geneva. Photo Studio Ferrazzini Bouchet.

in Edo, a little sea of commercial and aesthetic modernity within Japan's feudal state. Van Gogh called the Ukiyo-e "savage" and freely translated their bold aesthetics of cropped edges, radical designs, and color patterns to make his palette and frame "modern."[45] Mary Cassatt indigenized the Ukiyo-e as well, adapting formalist qualities, as in *The Boating Party* (1894), along with their fascination with interiors, fabrics, material culture, and moments of intimacy. She did not regard the Ukiyo-e artists as "savage" but rather promoted their artistry by collecting Ukiyo-e and displaying her favorite, Utamaro, side by side with her *Suite of Ten* (1890–1891) in her own house.

Again, I ask, who is derivative of whom? And how does seeing Japanese popular art as the source of aesthetic innovation indigenized in France change our understanding of modernism?[46]

Figure 2.15 Utagawa Hiroshige, *Plum Estate, Kameido*, from the series *One Hundred Famous Views of Edo*. 1857. Woodblock print.

Source: Brooklyn Museum. Gift of Anna Ferris.

Figure 2.16 Vincent van Gogh, *Flowering Plum Tree (After Hiroshige)*. 1887.

Source: Van Gogh Museum Amsterdam (Vincent van Gogh Foundation).

Figure 2.17 Vincent van Gogh, *The Sower*. 1888.

Source: Van Gogh Museum, Amsterdam (Vincent van Gogh Foundation).

Figure 2.18 Mary Cassatt, *The Boating Party*. 1893/1894. Oil on canvas.

Source: Chester Dale Collection, National Gallery of Art, Washington, D.C.

PLANETARITY • 69

Figure 2.19 Kitagawa Utamaro (1753–1806). *Midnight: Mother and Sleepy Child*. 1790. Polychrome woodblock print; ink and color on paper. H. 14 3/8in. (36.5 cm); W. 9 5/8 in. (24.4cm).

Source: Rogers Fund, 1922 (JP1278). The Metropolitan Museum of Art, New York, New York, U.S.A. Image copyright © The Metropolitan Museum of Art/Art Resource, NY.

Figure 2.20 Mary Cassatt, *The Bath* (1890/91). Drypoint, aquatint, and softground etching. 436x300 mm (sheet).

Source: Mr. and Mrs. Martin A. Ryerson Collection, 1932. 1287, The Art Institute of Chicago. Photography © The Art Institute of Chicago.

BLACKBIRD NINE: PLURAL POETICS

Lynn Simmons, *Blackbirds Fly*. 2000. Steel rod, wood beam, charred wood pieces. c. 7′ × 1′ × 8′. *Source*: www.lynnsimmons.com/objects.html

A planetary aesthetics of modernism needs to be transformative rather than merely additive. It is worthwhile to identify texts—visual, verbal, auditory—outside the West that exhibit the aesthetics of so-called high modernism, but a fully planetary approach should aim to detect the different forms that representational ruptures take in connection with different modernities. We need to let go of the familiar laundry list of aesthetic properties drawn from the Western culture capitals of the early twentieth century as *the* definitional core of modernism. I'm attached to that list, as I have confessed. But we need to provincialize it, that is to see "high" or "avant-garde" modernism as *one* articulation of a particularly situated modernism—an important modernism but not the measure by which all others are judged and to which all others must be compared. Instead, we must look across the planet, through deep time, and vertically within each location to identify sites of the slash—modernity/modernism—and then focus our attention on the nature of the particular modernity in question, explore the shapes and forms of creative expressivities engaging that modernity, and ask what cultural and political work those aesthetic practices perform as an important domain within it.

Let me be clear: I am not suggesting we abandon consideration of the aesthetic, the formal, particularly the creative agencies of expressive culture that put into question the representational conventions of their time and place. I want to avoid the familiar polarization of aesthetics and politics that privileges one over the other. Rather, I hope that we can be open to different kinds of aesthetic innovation linked to different modernities around the world and through time. In this regard, the aesthetic is always imbricated in the political, the historical. And vice versa. Not a single set of formalist characteristics, but rather the formal per se, however it might articulate the modern.

Take, for example, the experimental blend of high and low culture as aesthetic markers of an African diasporic modernity in the Harlem Renaissance. Langston Hughes's *Montage of a Dream Deferred* weds the blues aesthetic and jazz's syncopated rhythms to the lyric sequence form of the twentieth-century long poem and the dialectical principles of cinematic montage:

Dream Boogie

Good morning, daddy!
Ain't you heard
The boogie-woogie rumble
Of a dream deferred?

Listen closely:
You'll hear their feet

>   Beating out and beating out a—
>   . . . .
>   *You think*
>   *It's a happy beat?*
>   . . . .
>   Sure,
>   I'm happy!
>   Take it away!
>
>   *Hey, pop!*
>   *Re-bop!*
>   *Mop!*
>
>   *Y-e-a-h!*⁴⁷

Take the particular intertextuality of postcolonial modernisms. The global citational strategies of Pound and Eliot are reinvented in the dialogic engagement of the colonized with the colonizer, through denaturalizing mimicries or indigenizing transplantations, as in Tayeb Salih's or Arundhati Roy's rewriting of *Heart of Darkness*. As chapter 6 argues more fully, Roy's play with Conrad's title—"Dark of Heartness tiptoed into the Heart of Darkness"—does more than mimic in a colonial register. It relocates the "darkness" of all states (colonizing, colonized, and postcolonial) from the purely geopolitical to the interpenetrations of public and private, institutional and personal, thereby fostering a rereading of Marlow's lie to the Intended.⁴⁸ Postcolonial intertextualities are not derivative; they innovate, in a different register, breaking with other and often multiple conventions.

A planetary modernist poetics must be plural, opening up the concept of formal ruptures to a wide array of representational engagements with modernity. "Rather than privilege the radically new in Western avant-gardist fashion," writes Huyssen, "we may want to focus on the complexity of repetition and rewriting, *bricolage* and translation," or the layering of high and low, realism and experiment, "thus expanding our notion of innovation."⁴⁹ In Latin America, Mary Louise Pratt argues, European avant-gardism developed alongside other experimentalisms with rural, frontier, and ethnographic aesthetics blending orality, popular forms, realism, the vernacular, and the supernatural—as in the modernist magic realism of Gabriel García Márquez.[50]

BLACKBIRD TEN: PLURAL LANGUAGES

Blackbirds of 1928.
Music score cover.
Source: Clipart.

How can modernist studies be planetary if it is monolingual, if it operates within the lingua franca of any given era, if it reproduces the linguistic hegemonies of modernity's imperial legacies, if, for example, it remains within the confines of global English today?

"Le dit de la Relation," Glissant writes, "est multilingue. Par-delà les impositions des puissances économiques et des pressions culturelles, ils s'oppose en droit au totalitanisme des visées, monolingues" ("Relation is spoken multilingually. Going beyond the impositions of economic forces and cultural pressures, Relation rightfully opposes totalitarianism of any monolingual intent").[51] Even more than multilingualism, however, Glissant advocates a "worldness" in which "we write . . . in the presence of all the world's languages, all of them, leaving none out of consideration":

> If we say that we write, henceforth, in the presence of all the world's languages . . . if we rediscover the fact that we can change through exchange with others, without losing ourselves . . . then we are able to glimpse what I would like to call worldness, which is our common condition today.[52]

Modernity's polylogue is a vast archive of hundreds of languages beyond the ken of any individual. But Glissant's "worldness"—his concept of "planetary consciousness"—asks not for the impossible linguistically but rather for a transformative epistemology: that we write with the consciousness of the diversity of languages and cultures and the richness that these differences bring. In this sense, the multilingual archipelago of the Caribbean is

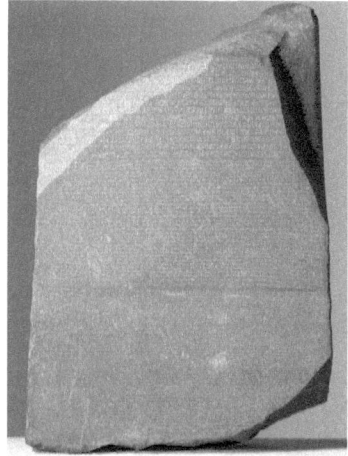

Figure 2.23 Rosetta Stone, Egypt. 196 BCE.
Source: © The Trustees of the British Museum.

Figure 2.24 Chengde Imperial Palace Stele, Qing Dynasty, China. Eighteenth Century. Inscriptions in Manchu, Tibetan, Chinese, and Mongol.
Source: Chengde Travel, http://www.cncn.com.

his model for "worldness." Creolization, for Glissant, is not the synthesis or fusion of difference into a monolingual sameness, not a global homogenization. Instead, *creolité* represents the principle of linguistic differences in mixture: the contact zones of encounter, linkages, interconnections—a poetics of multilingual relation based in the continual play of multiple vernaculars.[53]

Translation has a central role to play in the multilingual globalization of modernist studies. Translation involves a paradox of the commensurable and incommensurable, as Emily Apter argues in *The Translation Zone*. Equivalence from one language to another, one culture to another, is not possible, but the existence of world systems for thousands of years has necessitated the continual presence of translation, evident in the ancient Rosetta Stone in Egyptian hieroglyphics, Egyptian Demotic, and Greek from 196 BCE., and in the more recent Chengde Imperial Stele in Manchu, Tibetan, Chinese, and Mongol from China's Qing Dynasty in the eighteenth century.

Planetary cultural circulations, networks, and enmeshments of the global and local all depend upon translation, broadly understood from the linguistic to the cultural. Indeed, linguistic translation is essentially a practice of intercultural encounter and border thinking, the basis upon which other cultural traffic depends. Translation is a form of adaptation, transplantation, indigenization—from one culture to another. The multidirectional traveling of modernities and their modernisms is fundamentally a translational practice.

On a planetary scale, the multitude of vernaculars coexists with the singularity of a lingua franca, a common language that enables the cultural flows of the global ecumene—from Aramaic, Latin, Sanskrit, and Chinese to Arabic, French, and English. The coexistence is a dynamic and tense one, with the vernaculars perpetually under threat, with the native speakers of the common language privileged above all others.[54] Translation in a planetary modernist studies today ought to be reciprocal and multidirectional. But it is too much of a one-way street, with the rest of the world translating English texts into other languages, with many fewer works being translated into English, and with English translation too often serving as the mediation between two other languages.[55] Challenging modernity's complicity with colonialism in the formation of a planetary modernist studies requires studying, reading, and empowering the vernaculars.

Every modernity plays out linguistically in a dialectic of the vernacular and the cosmopolitan. The linguistic cosmopolitanism of *Ulysses*, *The Cantos*, or *The Waste Land* is famously citational, absorbing languages from elsewhere into English. Make no mistake, however. The opposition between vernacular and lingua franca or cosmopolitanism does not reproduce the binary of traditional/modern. The vernacular has often signaled a modernity of a different kind, a resistance to the hegemony of the language of elites of all kinds as part of widespread societal change.[56] Chaucer's Middle English and Dante's Italian were harbingers of the Renaissance, breaking with the dominance of Latin. Women, at times denied access to the languages of "high literature," wrote and read in the vernacular, helping local spoken languages develop literary cultures: for example, Lady Murasaki in the early eleventh century broke with the dominance of Chinese in high culture by writing *The Tale of Genji* in Japanese.[57] In medieval Al-Andalus, a new poetic form arose called the Muwashshahāt counterpointing the parallel love laments of a man speaking in classical Arabic and a woman speaking in the vernacular, as Maria Rosa Menocal shows.[58] In fifteenth-century Orissa, a group of low-caste (*sudra*) poet-saints challenged the Sanskrit-educated elite in producing revolutionary poems in Oriya, the local vernacular, according to Satya P. Mohanty. One of these, Balaram Das, writes an explicitly feminist narrative in the vernacular that advocates gender and caste equality.[59] As I will discuss in chapter 6, Rabindranath Tagore conflates the association of the vernacular with modernity and women writers in *The Broken Nest* by having a woman's anonymously published, fresh, modern writing in the vernacular take literary Calcutta by storm for its break with the artifice of convention-ridden Bengali poetics.[60] The vernacular, as Amit Chaudhuri writes, is "the idiom of modernity."[61]

BLACKBIRD ELEVEN: ANXIETY'S RETURN

The Blackbirds, *Anatomy of Melancholy*. 2006. Album cover, Blackdog Records. *Source:* Courtesy of Blackdog Records.

I sense doubt in your faces; I feel doubt in my own. Ten ways of seeing that blackbird have produced an archive of modernisms that is staggering in its global and temporal reach. That way paralysis lies. What's a poor scholar to do? This is too much. That's just going too far. Don't we need to discipline the proliferation of modernisms and their interconnections? Can't we just globalize modernism within a single and identifiable historical period—let's say, 1890 through 1950, as the Modernist Studies Association's website proclaims, or 1840 through 1950, if we want to include the French? *Genug*, enough already!

Ah, that old comfort zone again, the return of what is so hard to repress in modernist studies. I suggest, however, that we return instead to the full significance of the slash: modernism/modernity. If modernism is constitutively linked to modernity as the creative and expressive domain within it, then we are bound to recognize that particular modernisms take shape within different modernities and can potentially end up looking very different from one another. That slash has consequences.

BLACKBIRD TWELVE: THE ARCHIVES OF PLANETARY MODERNISMS AND HOW TO READ THEM

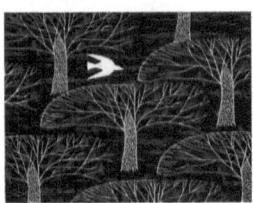

Whitney Sherman, "Blackbirds." © 2010. Screen print with cast paper appliqué. *Source*: http://www.whitneysherman.com.

To work within a planetary framework, no single scholar need do it all. Instead, we can recognize the foundational meaning of collaboration in the project of scholarship—we share a common project, however our views, methods, and languages differ. We can each locate ourselves in a manageable way among the multiplicity of critical practices in modernist studies. We can find our own place on the critical map of the field, one that suits our particular interests and knowledge base. As navigational guide, I suggest one or more of four main critical practices, each distinctive but also blendable: Re-vision, Recovery, Circulation, Collage.[62]

Re-vision is the act of looking again, of defamiliarizing the familiar archive by looking anew through a different lens, asking new questions of "high modernism": Picasso, Pound, Joyce, Woolf, Eliot, and so forth. What are the traces of other modernities within the texts of European and Anglo-American "high modernism"? Where are the footprints of the planetary in the local formations of the West? What is the ghost in the machine? Scores of scholars since Simon Gikandi's pathbreaking *Maps of Englishness* have learned to read coloniality in the modernisms of Europe and the United States.[63] But the planetary not only incorporates Western empires but also exceeds them. The planetary of what Dimock calls "deep time"—a transcontinental spatiality as well as *longue durée*—needs to be reread in the modernisms of the West.[64]

Recovery is the act of digging, creating an archaeology of new archives—other modernities outside the familiar Western ones and thus other forms of creative expressivities. New books on other modernisms are proliferating, working with modernisms contemporaneous with or in different timeframes from Western modernisms. In his translation of *Kalapurnodaymau/ The Sound of the Kiss* from the Telegu of the sixteenth century, V. Narayana Rao, for example, claims an early modernism for Pingali Suranna, citing his invention of the novel-in-verse genre for Telegu literature, his radical disruption of literary conventions, and his psychologizing of the human mind. Rao also translates a more recent Indian modernism: *Kanyasulkam/ Girls for Sale*, an 1892 Telegu play using parody, masquerade, and satire to attack both the colonial government and the gender system within Indian culture.[65] Multilingual scholars are the avant-garde of such recoveries, locating buried and forgotten texts in the global archive of languages, but scholars working in translation are also essential to bring knowledge of these modernisms into the *lingua franca* of the field.[66]

Circulation is the archive of mobility, calling for the act of seeing linkages, networks, conjunctures, creolizations, intertextualities, travels, and transplantations connecting modernisms from different parts of the planet. Often the pathways are the routes born of colonialism: passages to India or Africa or the Caribbean by Western writers like Forster or Conrad; passages to the colonizers' metropole by writers like Jean Rhys, Mulk Raj Anand, or Tayeb Salih. How is that relationality experienced, reflected upon, represented? What is the interplay of roots and routes in those circulations across the globe? Unlike a center/periphery model, circulation stresses the interactive and dynamic, assuming multiple agencies, centers, and conjunctures around the world.

Collage is the archive of radical juxtaposition, the scholar's act of paratactic cutting and pasting. It establishes a montage of differences where the putting side by side illuminates those differences at the same time that it spotlights commonalities. Ideally, collage is a nonhierarchical act of comparison, a joining that illuminates both commensurabilities and incommensurabilities. Take, for example, from different parts of the world and different decades, Aimé Césaire's *Notebook for a Return to the Native Land* and Theresa Hak Kyung Cha's *Dictée*. Voila! What comes into focus, as I will show in chapter 7, is a diasporic modernism based in the instabilities of colonial exile and the imaginative recreation of lost homes: for Césaire, Negritude reuniting the diasporas of slavery with black Africa; for Cha, the maternal body as route to a syncretic phenomenology of home and homeland. Both invoking the rhythm of *aller/retour*.

Re-vision, Recovery, Circulation, Collage: Four strategies for reading particular modernisms within a planetary epistemology. This is manageable. We can each find our place on the map without vertigo, paralysis. We don't need to try to do it all. We can change our epistemological framework and locate our specific method within it, as one part of a large, fluid, mobile project to which all of us are contributing differently. Planetarity: modernist studies as a living, breathing organism.

BLACKBIRD THIRTEEN: THE PLANET IN PLANETARITY

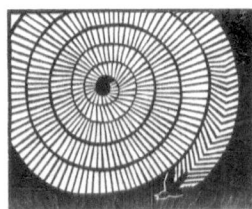

Michael Spafford, *The Planet* (1975), no. 9, from the series *Thirteen Ways of Looking at a Blackbird*. Source: Courtesy of Michael Spafford.

Planetarity in its very name invokes the Earth in deep time. Does the planet have its own modernities, crises distinct from those of the human species? The critical practices of re-vision, recovery, circulation, and collage can examine the meanings of the nonhuman world for the human and the interactions of human modernities with the Earth as a planet in the cosmos. The Earth moves in a scale of time almost unimaginable in human terms, although we attempt to name its ages and periodize its changes, often cataclysmic ones. How might we conceptualize modernity anew in the context of the Earth's and many of its species' indifference to the human? Conversely, what are the effects of human modernities on the Earth and the nonhuman, a question that discussions of rapid climate change and the Anthropocene attempt to address? Turning to literatures of modernity, can we, for example, re-vision Eliot's waste land in the context of ecological disasters and read the human mind as an objective correlative for a landscape scarred by war? How do the rivers of *Heart of Darkness*, *Season of Migration to the North*, and *The God of Small Things* both shape and exceed the human stories upon them? "Time passes," Woolf famously writes in *To the Lighthouse*, with human modernities a mere parenthesis within nature's own geohistory.[67] Are we humans, in short, utterly significant or insignificant in relation to the planet?

Perhaps more answerable is to examine the intersection of human modernities with the earth's nonhuman species, diversities, and cosmic rhythms. Ursula K. Heise calls for an "'eco-cosmopolitanism,' or environmental world citizenship," that frees the term cosmopolitanism from early-twentieth-century modernist "connotations of social privilege and leisure travel."⁶⁸ In dismissing what he sees as the inflated, heroic posturing of (Western) human modernity in *We Have Never Been Modern*, Latour looks to the "testimony" of the nonhuman world of things and the interpenetration of nature and culture. Glissant's poetics of relation includes a call to recognize the "relational interdependence of all lands, of the whole Earth," and the particularly harsh consequences of the "politics of ecology" for the poor.⁶⁹ He asks for an "aesthetics of the earth" that is not "anachronistic or naïve: reactionary or sterile" (150) but rather an "aesthetics of rupture and connection," of "disruption and intrusion" that can encompass "the half-starved dust of Africas," "the mud of flooded Asias," "in epidemics, masked forms of exploitation, flies buzz-bombing the skeleton skins of children," "in city sewers," and so forth (151). In what way do our human modernities Other the Earth, he wonders.

PLANETARITY

Akira Studios, *Guardian of the Blackbirds*. Source: © 2004 all rights reserved. Photo by Larry Blount.

Planetarity as I use the term is an epistemology, not an ontology. On a human scale, the "worldness" the term invokes—to echo Glissant—means a polylogue of languages, cultures, viewpoints, standpoints on modernism/modernity. It requires attention to modes of local and translocal meaning making and translation, to processes and practices of perception and expression on a global scale. It is not nominalist, fundamentalist: it doesn't name a singular modernism/modernity, thereby privileging one over all others. It must, by its very "worldness," encompass multitudes on a global grid of relational networks. And that means encompassing contradictions, tensions, oppositions, asymmetries. Like rooted and situated cosmopolitanisms, planetarity suggests a capacity to engage simultaneously with local and global modernities. It embraces the generative energies and synergies of modernism's Tower of Babel. In that, it is utopian. Not very quotidian, I know; not down and dirty in the trenches of reading, teaching, conferencing, publishing. But nonetheless planetarity is a vision that can percolate through the practices of everyday professional life.

Planetarity is not a threat; it's an opportunity. It means leaving the comfort zone for the contact zone.

PART II
RETHINKING MODERNITY, SCALING SPACE AND TIME

THREE
STORIES OF MODERNITY

Planetary Scale in the *Longue Durée*

Then and now, modernity is never one.
—Andreas Huyssen, "Geographies of Modernism in a Globalizing World"

One can provincialize Western modernity only by thinking through and against its self-understandings, which are frequently cast in universalist idioms. To think through and against means to think with a difference—a difference that would destabilize the universalist idioms, historicize the contexts, and pluralize the experiences of modernity.
—Dilip Parameshwar Gaonkar, "On Alternative Modernities"

If the question of modernity . . . can be historically and theoretically disentangled from the question of Western desires and designs for domination, and if its diverse cultural roots can be unearthed, then we can begin to talk of a new global modernity that celebrates and underscores difference rather than forced assimilation.
—Abbas Milani, *Lost Wisdom: Rethinking Modernity in Iran*

The story of modernity narrates an obsession with time: the modern forms as a rupture from the past, an escape into a continuous present, an eternal Now. The storytellers of modernity track its location in time, through time, against time. Rooted in the very notion of the modern and the kinetic drive of its stories is the logic of then and now.[1]

But what about modernity's here and there? How might attention to its *here-and-there* revise its *then-and-now*? How, in short, can we reconfigure the narrative chronotopes of modernity—the relational mediations of time *and* space in stories of modernity—so as to avoid the privileging of time over space? And why is it imperative that we do so? Fredric Jameson famously requires: "Always historicize!" I have suggested in response: "Always spatialize!"[2] Spatialization is a compensatory gesture, but ultimately modernist studies needs to engage in what I have been calling the *geohistory* of modernity: narratives of modernity's sweep across the globe and through time. Greatly enlarging the spatio/temporal scale, we need to "think through and against its self-understandings" to "provincialize Western modernity" as Dilip Parameshwar Gaonkar asks us to do. Moving fluidly back and forth between large and small scales, we need to examine the geohistorical stories told about modernity to disentangle it from what Abbas Milani calls "Western desires and designs for domination." Only then can we hope to fulfill the promise of Andreas Huyssen's claim, "Then and now, modernity is never one," and Gaonkar's assertion, "In short, modernity is not one, but many."[3]

SPATIALIZATION AND PERIODIZATION

In 1967, Michel Foucault presciently observed: "The great obsession of the nineteenth century was, as we know, history. . . . The present epoch will perhaps be above all an epoch of space."[4] Some twenty years later, the geographer Edward W. Soja asked that we "see spatiality with the same acute depth of vision that comes with a focus on *durée*."[5] In the globalization of the late-twentieth- and early-twenty-first centuries, the geographical imagination has taken root. The drive to internationalize, transnationalize, and globalize has both swept mainstream culture and the academy, constituting a significant dimension of the knowledge revolution initiated by the new technologies of the digital.

The new modernist studies has participated in this widespread "transnational turn," as Douglas Mao and Rebecca L. Walkowitz have called it.[6] Indeed, the global reach of the field is now staggering, and for some, it has been spiraling out of control, as chapter 2 acknowledges. *The Oxford Handbook of Modernisms* (2011), edited by Peter Brooker, Andrzej Gąsiorek, Deborah Longworth, and Andrew Thacker, includes some three hundred pages on modernisms outside the conventional Anglo-American and European orbits, with chapters on locations from Scotland to Japan, Scandinavia to Africa. *The Oxford Handbook of Global Modernisms*, edited by Mark Wollaeger with Matt Eatough, spotlights a number of little-known modernisms, from the Balkans to Vietnam and Turkey, while adding to European, African, Latin American, and Asian modernisms that have already spawned numerous individual and comparative studies.[7] The spatial and temporal borders of the field have become ever more porous as it globalizes and engages fundamentally with the implications of pluralization: the phenomenon of multiple modernities and their accompanying modernisms.[8]

∞ ∞ ∞

So, why am I not satisfied?
The problem begins with the period.
Periodization.

∞ ∞ ∞

Periodization has been particularly limiting in modernist studies because periodization reinforces the ideological construction of "the West" and "Western society and culture" as the defining center of world history. Eric Hayot complains about the "near-total dominance of the concept of periodization in literary studies, a dominance that amounts to a collective failure of the imagination and will on the part of the literary profession."[9] I agree with him, but see the problem as broader than the literary profession alone. In chapter 1, I moved out of the definitional morass of *modernism/modernity* by agreeing with Jameson that some sort of provisional periodization, however flawed, is better than none. But here, where I focus more fully on theorizing a planetary framework for modernist studies, I emphasize that even a strategic periodization has its dangers. As modernist studies has become ever more capacious in what it includes under its expanding umbrella, there has been a concomitant return of the repressed periodization, the charismatic pull of the "original" meaning of modernity as a post-1500 or post-Enlightenment phenomenon in the West that produces aesthetic modernism located in the culture capitals of Europe and the United States from the mid- to late-nineteenth century through the 1940s. This particular metropolitan modernism and its experimental forms across the arts and literature retain a hold on the epistemologies and institutional formations of the field that reinstates a conventional historical periodization. David James and Urmila Seshagiri, for example, criticize the "transnational turn" in modernist studies and remain "stubbornly in conflict with the critical rhetoric of transhistorical extension":

> What distinguishes our approach is its defense of returning to the logic of periodization. Such an approach not only offers a rubric for reading contemporary literature's relationship to modernism but also generates a retrospective understanding of modernism as a moment as well as a movement. That movement, we contend, should still be understood in historically conditioned and culturally specific clusters of artistic achievements between the late nineteenth and mid-twentieth centuries.[10]

Their "stubborn" return to the "logic of periodization" is self-consciously retrogressive. But even those more sympathetic to the transnational turn can end up reinstating the logic of periodization. The pluralization of modernism with rhetorics of "other," "alternative," or "peripheral," for example, subtly reconfirms the hierarchy of modernisms with the "original," "major," or "center" modernism of metropolitan Europe and the United States as the measure by which all others are understood. Even the ambitiously broad *Oxford Handbook of Modernisms* belies its own stated goal for seeing modernism "in globalizing and thus transnational terms."[11] Its final section, "National and Transnational Modernisms," includes fourteen chapters on modernisms outside Europe, England, and the United States (starting with Scottish, Welsh, and Irish and ending with Chinese and Japanese modernisms). But the three opening essays in the first section, entitled "Frameworks," develop their theoretical paradigms out of an entirely conventional archive, as do the more specialized sections on modernist contexts, media, aesthetic form, and metropolitan movements. The modernisms without geographical markers remain the default position. They signify modernism per se while the geographically located modernisms outside the unspecified center remain "other" to the bulk of the volume. In modernist studies, the center *can* hold, things do not fall apart. Not yet.

This reinstatement of the original periodization inhibits planetary thinking about modernism/modernity in the context of deep time, deep history, or the *longue durée*. No doubt, the conventional spatio/temporal boundaries of modernist studies facilitate logically packaged syllabi, curricula, and job descriptions. Without attempting to solve the institutional dilemmas of a planetary modernist studies, I nonetheless suggest that probing the epistemological frameworks of modernism/modernity is a necessary first step to prevent the magnetic pull back into the origins of the field. Such fundamental rethinking will help realign the field for the present and future; institutional transformations are likely to follow epistemological ones, as indeed they have already begun to do in the context of twenty-first century globalization. To begin this rethinking, I start with the problems inherent in periodization itself, problems that play out with special intensity around categories of modernity and modernism.

PROBLEM 1

Historical periodization enfolds a presumption of spatial location within the borders of a given time period. As a result, generalizations about historical periods typically contain covert assumptions about space that privilege one location over others. Whose period? Where is it located? Who and where are left out or peripheralized? What are the politics underlying a period's implied geography?

The prevailing periodization in the discipline of history, for example, names a progression of periods from the ancient to the classical, medieval, early modern, and modern, designations that have deeply informed the study of the arts, literature, and philosophy as well. This periodization typically appears without geographical locators, as if these periods were universal when they actually reference a place that came to be known as "the West."[12] Appearing to be a geographical region, the "West" functions as an ideological construction based upon the standard periodization of history in which modernity is the teleological endpoint (and postmodernity its deconstruction). As the geographer J. M. Blaut points out, the succession of periods from ancient to modern assumes a northwesterly shift in civilizational centers—beginning in the ancient near east (Mesopotamia, Canaan, Israel), then moving to classical Greece (especially Athens in the fifth century BCE) and later Rome and its empire, on through the passage of time to Christian medieval Europe radiating from papal Rome, then north and westward through Italy's Renaissance and on to France, the Netherlands, and Britain in the early modern period, and finally to the modernity of the Enlightenment and the Industrial Revolution led by France and Britain.[13] The U.S. conquest of its "west" and the rise of U.S. global power in the twentieth century completes the movement of European modernity ever northwestward. Blaut calls this dominant view "tunnel history," a "matter of looking back or down in this European tunnel of time and trying to decide what happened where, when, and why" (5). Developed since the eighteenth century, this linear periodization, with its covert European and eventually North American geography, rationalized Western imperialism and led to the formation of the *idea* of the West. As a function of historical periodization, this idea of the West is complicit with the *idea* of modernity as an invention of the West and the endpoint of history *in* the West.

PROBLEM 2

Naming a period bookends time. That is, periodization presumes beginning and ending points and constitutes a form of cutting up the past that invites endless debate and diversity on how and where to make the cuts. As Marshall Brown writes, "Periods are entities we love to hate. Yet we cannot do without them. . . . Consequently, the uses to which we put periods depend crucially on how we delimit them. . . . The art lies in the cutting."[14] Where Brown focuses on the "art" of cutting, I question its politics, particularly its spatial politics. For *when* a period is said to start and end contains a covert assumption about *where* it begins and concludes and also where it is and where it is not.

The prevailing periodizations of modernism evident in various mission statements of modernist studies associations are a case in point. In spite of the transnational turn in modernist studies, modernism (especially "canonical" modernism) is still often understood as a loose affiliation of aesthetic movements that began at the end of the nineteenth and unfolded in the first half of the twentieth century, a view reflected on the website of the U.S.-based Modernist Studies Association (MSA):

> The Modernist Studies Association is devoted to the study of the arts in their social, political, cultural, and intellectual contexts *from the later nineteenth- through the mid-twentieth century.* The organization aims to develop an international and interdisciplinary forum to promote exchange among scholars in this revitalized and rapidly changing field.[15]

MSA's temporal borders, roughly the 1890s to the 1940s, reflect an Anglo-American and English-language bias that marginalizes even the "canonical" modernisms located outside those temporal and spatial boundaries. However, such field-defining critics of modernism as Malcolm Bradbury and James McFarlane, Marshall Berman, Astradur Eiysteinsson, Peter Nicholls, and Pericles Lewis draw on a wider archive of European continental modernisms and consequently define an earlier beginning in the mid-nineteenth century, especially with the Charles Baudelaire of *Les fleurs du mal* in the 1840s–1850s and the cosmopolitan *flâneur* of his essay "The Painter of Modern Life" (1863).[16] For those drawing on the culture capitals of continental Europe, the artists and writers based in Paris in the 1870s and after—e.g., the impressionists and symbolists—initiated the transformational aesthetics that evolved into twentieth-century modernism. The periodization of modernism is more expansive on the website of the European Network for Avant-Garde and Modernism Studies (EAM), which "devotes itself to the study of the avant-garde and modernism *in Europe within a global setting, throughout the nineteenth and twentieth centuries.*"[17] EAM's bookends for "the avant-garde and modernism" (1800–2000) express a curious ambiguity about location even as they encompass a full two hundred years. Grammatically speaking, does "within a global setting" modify "Europe" or "the avant-garde and modernism"? Ambiguities and differences aside, the main point stands: periodization in modernist studies, like periodization in history, establishes beginnings and endpoints that enfold assumptions about a delimited geographical location.

While the different beginnings of modernism often reflect a linguistic focus (English versus continental European languages), the endpoint of modernism is more contentious and raises more angst and institutional confusion about what the workable temporal boundaries of modernist studies should be. The Modernist Studies Association's announced endpoint for modernism—the mid-twentieth century—is conventionally accepted in the field, assumed in descriptive overviews, many course syllabi, and most job descriptions for advertised positions in modernist studies. How, people wonder, can modernist studies have coherence as a field or a meaningful definition as a period if modernism is ongoing, still unfolding? Isn't there or shouldn't there be a clear distinction between "modern" and "postmodern" or between "modern" and "contemporary" periods? Wouldn't the field be more manageable if we could see it as part of the past, distinct from our present?

No doubt about it: the conventional is convenient. But it is also pernicious. This periodization assumes the centrality of Europe and Anglo-American modernism, thereby cutting off the agencies of writers, artists, philosophers, and other cultural producers in the emergent postcolonial world just as their new modernities are being formed. India's independence from Britain and the wrenching murder and displacement of millions in Partition that gave birth to two postcolonial nation-states happen in 1947–1948. One after another of the colonies in the Caribbean and in Africa acquire liberation from official colonial rule in the 1950s and 1960s. The 1950s are the period of Frantz Fanon's brilliant indigenizations of European psychoanalysis to dissect the psychopathologies of colonial racism for both whites and blacks, thus defining anew a modern sensibility.[18] New culture capitals formed in the wake of independence from colonial rule, and loose affiliations of exiled and diasporic writers articulated the new modernities of postcolonial nations. Beirut in the 1960s, for example, was one such lively center, where the exiled Sudanese writer Tayeb Salih published *Season of Migration to the North* (1966), now regarded as a classic of postcolonial modernism. The rise of postcolonial studies in the academy with the formation of subaltern studies in India and the pervasive influence of Edward W. Said's 1978 classic *Orientalism* has been instrumental in drawing the spatio/temporal boundaries of modernity anew.[19] As Gaonkar writes, "to announce the general end of modernity even as an epoch . . . seems premature, if not patently ethnocentric, at a time when non-Western people everywhere begin to engage critically their own hybrid modernities" (14).

Declaring the end of modernism by 1950 is like trying to hear one hand clapping. The modernisms of emergent modernities are that other hand that enables us to hear any clapping at all. Colonialism is constitutive of Western modernity and was essential to its formation from the sixteenth through the twentieth centuries. As Walter D. Mignolo argues, "Coloniality . . . is the hidden face of modernity and its very condition of possibility."[20] As a consequence, we must not close the curtain on modernism before the creative agencies in the colonies and newly emergent nations have their chance to perform. Their nationalist movements and liberations from the political dimensions of colonial rule are central to the story of their modernities. Therefore, the creative forces within those modernities—the writers, the artists, the musicians, the dancers, the philosophers, the critics, and so forth—are engaged in producing modernisms that accompany their own particular twentieth-century modernities. To call their postliberation arts "postmodern"—as they often are—is to miss the point entirely. Multiple modernities create multiple modernisms. Multiple modernisms require respatializing modernism and thus rethinking the unexamined assumptions that shape conventional periodizations of modernism.

PROBLEM 3

Periodization tends toward nominal rather than relational modes of definition, a distinction I discussed in chapters 1 and 2. A nominalist periodization requires characterizing the period's defining qualities—designating what makes, for example, the early modern period different from the late medieval period, or the early modern from the modern. The nominal approach to modernity treats the concept as a noun with a fixed and determinable set of characteristics: Modernity = (1) . . . ; (2) . . . ; (3) . . . ; etc. Many historians and social theorists—across the political spectrum from "right" to "left"—identify the distinctiveness of modernity with a series of static nouns including such formations as the nation-state, capitalism, industrialization, bureaucracy, democracy, citizenship and civic life, secularism, science, the bourgeois subject and family, and so forth. They typically generalize certain historical phenomena observed in the West from the early modern period through the twentieth century into a series of interlocking universal principles that are said to define modernity for all places, all times, and all peoples. This periodization defines in universal terms what developed as localized and particular in the West, thus reproducing the imperializing gestures of Western modernity itself. Taking what happened in Europe after 1492 (or a woefully homogenized representation of it) as the benchmark for modernity, this approach finds other arguably modern phenomena elsewhere to be peripheral, derivative, belated, or imitative: in short, pale copies of the West resulting from the West's conquest and colonization of the Rest. What happened in the West (Europe and its extension into the United States) is assumed to be the absolute point of origin, invention, and innovation.

Never mind that these characteristics vary significantly from scholar to scholar or that they function tautologically within a hermeneutic circle predetermined by the particular historical archive out of which definitions emerge—I have already addressed these problems in chapter 1. The point I want to explore here is the ways in which nominal definitions of modernity (and modernism) have been complicit with both triumphalist and critical narratives of European exceptionalism and what is known iconically as "the rise of the West." These narratives are profoundly Eurocentric, telling the story of modernity with Europe at the center and the rest of the world at its periphery. Such stories define a specifically located Western modernity as if it were modernity in general, as if it were universal, constituting the teleological endpoint of human history.

By way of example, let's return to Anthony Giddens, cited in chapters 1 and 2 for his influential articulations of mainstream, neo-Weberian definitions of modernity. In *The Consequences of Modernity*, Giddens emphasizes the plotline of periodization with stark simplicity:

> What is modernity? As a first approximation, let us simply say the following: "modernity" refers to modes of social life or organization which emerged in Europe from about the seventeenth century onwards and which subsequently became more or less worldwide in their influence. This associates modernity with a time period and with an initial geographical location, but for the moment leaves *its major characteristics safely stowed away in a black box*.[21]

Giddens doesn't leave the "major characteristics" of modernity stowed away in his black box for long, identifying them quickly with what he regards as European inventions in "modes of social life or organization": the nation-state, industrial capitalism, state bureaucracy, and the bourgeois subject. He concludes the book with a brief coda entitled "Is Modernity a Western Project?"—to which his "blunt answer" is "yes" (174–175). Giddens's "black box" is a Eurocentric box, a boxed-in way of thinking that is circular in its reasoning, stuck in its story of Europe's rise, ideological in its assertion of the West as a series of "firsts," nonempirical in its ignorance of history outside the West and before 1500. He is not alone.[22]

∞ ∞ ∞

How do we get outside the "black box"?
Paradigm Shift.

∞ ∞ ∞

MODERNITY: THE QUESTION OF SCALE

To fulfill the transnational turn in modernist studies, I ask that we resist the charismatic pull of periodization that covertly privileges a Western geographical center, thus marginalizing its peripheries. An additive approach to existing periodizations won't work; we need a radical shift in the frameworks for thinking about modernity. We need to begin by abandoning the notion of modernity as a *period*, instead considering modernity as a loosely configured set of conditions that share a core meaning of accelerated change but articulate differently on the global map of human history. This approach calls for a significant enlargement of spatio/temporal scale to consider the meanings of modernity in comparative world history across millennia. It requires a capacious archive of global modernities through time as the basis from which to generalize about the category of modernity. Without that planetary scale in the *longue durée*, we run the risk of reproducing Western modernity as the default position, the measure of all others. The large scale of different recurrent global modernities helps us see what is commensurable across time and space. But it also requires an attention to particularity, to difference—what makes one modernity unlike as well as like another. Without the small scale of localized, even textualized particularities, we run the risk of creating a new, homogenizing universal. The small scale helps us see what is incommensurable in different modernities through time; it enables the contributions of full historical and geographical contextualization and specificity. Consequently, we need a fluid approach to spatio/temporal scale, one that can move flexibly back and forth between large and small, between large-scale structural patterns that distance helps us see and the small-scale particularities that nearness brings into visibility. Fluid, moving scales create bird's-eye and ground-level views that can inform and complement each other.

As a historical concept, scalar thinking is largely diachronic, involving differing spans of time measured in years, decades, centuries, or millennia or being defined as events, periods, eras, or ages.[23] As a major figure in the French Annales School of historiography, Fernand Braudel rejected the history of the *courte durée* (short span) in favor of the broad-scale history of the *longue durée* and has been an influential model for enlarging the temporal scale of modernist studies. Rather than focusing on events, his method in *The Mediterranean and the Mediterranean World in the Age of Phillip II* established a wide-scale view of environmental, socioeconomic, and cultural forces combining to define the history of a region and its relationship to other regions. The *longue durée* in his work fostered attention to space in a way that event-based chronological narrative often did not. As a temporal scale, the *longue durée* fundamentally changes the way we think about modernity, fostering the possibility of multiple modernities across time and throughout the globe.[24]

As a geographical concept, scale is largely synchronic, addressing the significance of space at one time on the map of human history. Eric Sheppard and Robert B. McMaster's *Scale and Geographical Inquiry* distinguishes between the scalar thinking of two subfields—cartography and human geography—both of which enable extending the spatial scales of modernity.[25] In cartography, scale involves a relational mode of thinking that establishes a ratio between the material world and its representation, whereby the map (whatever its form) is a condensed symbolic form of the world it reproduces. As an instance of scale, the map also establishes epistemological borders: the space of the world represented and, by implication, the space of the world beyond the borders of the map. In conventional maps of modernism, for example, the cartographic scale is relatively small, with the metropoles of the West as its epicenters, the culture capitals of modernism identified in Malcolm Bradbury and James McFarlane's still influential *Modernism*.[26] Enlarging the cartographical scale of modernism would change the borders of the maps significantly. Rather than the triangle of London-Paris-New York, for example, the map might bring into focus the spatial connection between Paris and sub-Saharan Africa, particularly locations ruled by France. Picasso's Paris, where he sees the African masks he implants into *Les demoiselles d'Avignon* in 1909, might be mapped in conjunction with the parts of Africa where the masks originated and amassed as part of the commercial and military modernizing systems of the French, British, and Portuguese empires. Or the aesthetic modernities of major metropolitan culture capitals of the colonial world in the early twentieth century—e.g., Calcutta, Alexandria, Rio de Janeiro, Kingston, Mexico City, and Shanghai—might be mapped for their interrelations with their various colonizing cities (in Europe, the United States, Turkey, Japan) as well as with one another or others in their region.

Cartographic scale can also involve different ratios of representation in maps that contain other maps, insets that enlarge a small area on the bigger map. Adapting cartography's scalar thinking, maps of modernities can represent the relation between the big picture and the small, between the larger world system and particularized locales. We can, for example, see the large-scale map of British imperialism linking the colonizing and colonized modernities of London, Jamaica, Nairobi, Cairo, Calcutta, and Shanghai at the end of the nineteenth century. We can also enlarge the small-scale map of the Bengal Renaissance in Calcutta into an "inset," to demonstrate a particularized modernity on the larger map of the whole.

In human geography, scale involves two modes of spatialization: vertical and horizontal. The vertical mode, often referred to as "nesting," is the more conventional, moving from near to far (or vice versa) and embedding notions of hierarchy or different levels of power. Vertically speaking, any given local modernity is embedded within ever-larger units of social organization—from family, to neighborhood, district, region, nation, hemisphere, and so forth, a principle that Joyce captures in *A Portrait of the Artist as a Young Man* when young Stephen looks at what he had written in his geography book:

> Stephen Dedalus
> Class of Elements
> Clongowes Wood College
> Sallins
> County Kildare
> Ireland
> Europe
> The World
> The Universe[27]

The horizontal mode of human geography focuses on networks connecting different sites within a larger system of relationships.[28] Horizontally speaking, networks link mutually constitutive, though typically different and asymmetrical modernities and the circulations among them—how, for example, the early-twentieth-century colonial modernities of Ireland, India, the Congo, and Jim Crow America function as nodal points linking texts like Rudyard Kipling's *Kim*, Rabindranath Tagore's *Gora*, Joseph Conrad's *Heart of Darkness*, and James Weldon Johnson's *Autobiography of an Ex-Coloured Man*.

Scalar thinking about modernity in both temporal and spatial terms allows for the flexibility to zoom in, zoom out—back and forth from big to small, from the *longue durée* across the globe, to the particularities of distinctive periods and places, to the variations within localized periods, and to the "worlds" created in forms of expressive/symbolic culture—the modernisms of different modernities. Fluid scalar thinking is essential for breaking out of the Eurocentric box.

GLOBAL MODERNITIES OF THE *LONGUE DURÉE* BEFORE 1500

How long does the *longue durée* need to be to establish the spatial scale necessary for a planetary approach to modernity? Immanuel Wallerstein's influential world-systems analysis, first presented in 1974 and synopsized in his *World-Systems Analysis: An Introduction* in 2004, has been pathbreaking in its enlargement of the temporal and spatial scales for thinking about modernity.[29] Adapting Braudel's concept of the *longue durée*, Wallerstein advocates an "unthinking" of disciplinary "boxes" that arose as a component of modernity in favor of a "holistic social science" that fosters an integrated "world-system" approach to some five hundred years of global history (*Introduction*, x–xi, 1–15, 19). For Wallerstein, the scale of the "world-system" is transnational, beyond the nation-state, requiring the "substitution of a unit of analysis called the 'world-system' for the standard unit of analysis, which was the national state" (16). The hyphen in "world-system" underlines

> that we are talking not about systems, economies, empires *of the* (whole) world, but about systems, economies, empires *that are* a world (but quite possibly, and indeed usually, not encompassing the whole globe). . . . It [the hyphen] says that in 'world-systems' we are dealing with a spatial/temporal zone which cuts across many political and cultural units, one that represents an integrated zone of activity and institutions which obey certain systemic rules.
>
> (16–17).

Having begun his career as an Africanist, Wallerstein identifies with the have-nots of the world-system and regards his world-system theory as an anti-Eurocentric sociology of the *longue durée*. As a theory of modernity, Wallerstein features the post-1500 world-system dominated by the West through its unprecedented accumulation of capital enabled by the competition of the new nation-states of Europe. Invented in Europe, he claims, capitalism allowed the West to establish itself as the permanent center with other regions of the world constituting its peripheries and semiperipheries, which compete with one another in their struggles against the dominant center. The peripheries constitute the have-nots in the world-system and suffer the most from the "unequal exchange" capitalism produces, while the semiperipheries are more fluid, typically attempting to join the core or falling into the periphery. Cyclical patterns of expansion and contraction characterize the modern world-system over time, but in his reading of history, the post-1500 dominance of the West as the core of this integrated world-system has been the defining feature of modernity (28–31).

Wallerstein's approach to modernity in the *longue durée* has been widely influential, impacting, for example, the new world literature studies, as evidenced in the work of Pascale Casanova and Franco Moretti.[30] A number of world historians, however, have challenged Wallerstein on a variety of grounds—e.g., his assertion that capitalism did not exist before 1500; his ignorance or discounting of Asia, both before 1500 and in the late-twentieth and twenty-first centuries; his reductionistic emphasis on economics; and his peripheralization of culture, politics, slavery, imperial conquest, gender, disease, and other game changers in world history.[31] As André Gunder Frank writes in critiquing Wallerstein, "we must question the supposed *European* origin of the world system. Whenever the system really began to exist, it can hardly have done so in Europe, which remained quite marginal" until much later.[32]

In my view, Wallerstein's *longue durée* isn't nearly long enough: his world-system exhibits just the kind of periodization that is insufficiently global because it privileges the West and predetermines the story of modernity as the rise of Europe to dominance of the world system. World historians like Frank, J. M. Blaut, Marshall G. S. Hodgson, Janet Abu-Lughod, John Hobson, and George Makdisi work on a much larger scale—across the globe and in what Wai Chee Dimock calls "deep time."[33] In so doing, they identify major routes of conquest, trade, and intercultural exchange that fundamentally challenge the factual inaccuracies and ideological drive that underlie the story of modernity as an invention of the West in the post-1500 period. In particular, they disagree with Wallerstein's notion that capitalism appears first in post-1500 Europe, but more generally they enlarge the spatio/temporal scale of human history to encompass transcontinental and transoceanic world systems of commercial, military, and cultural connectivities over two to three millennia.[34] In her pioneering *Before European Hegemony: The World System, AD 1250–1350*, for example, Abu-Lughod places the relatively backward European region within a world system dominated by western, southern, southeastern, and eastern parts of Asia. The undeniably growing and ultimately hegemonic power of Europe from about the sixteenth through the twentieth centuries, she argues, is rooted in and develops out of the world system that preceded it, one in which the

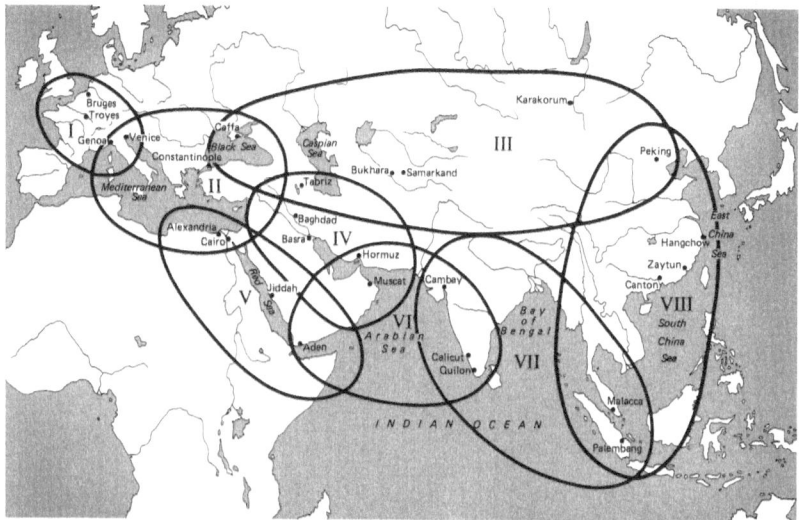

Figure 3.1 The Eight Circuits of the Thirteenth-Century World System.

Source: *Before European Hegemony: The World System, AD 1250–1350*, by Janet L. Abu-Lughod (1989), figure 1, from p. 34. By permission of Oxford University Press, USA.

Islamic empire was central, proving to be a major conduit for the ideas and commercial systems that fed European modernity.

In *ReOrient: Global Economy in the Asian Age*, Frank shows how the tremendous economic and cultural wealth variously concentrated in India, China, and the Islamic empire dominated the world system until about 1800, with Europe's rise dependent on the discoveries it adapted from elsewhere along with its conquest of the Americas, which provided vast resources, especially silver, that allowed it to compete aggressively in world markets for the first time. In Frank's view, Europe's post-1800 global dominance will be eclipsed by the reassertion of Asian power, especially China, in the twenty-first century.

As Makdisi has shown in *The Rise of Humanism in Classical Islam and the Christian West*, the European rediscovery of ancient Greece and Rome depended upon the libraries and the scholarship of the Islamic empires centered in Baghdad, Cairo, and Spain. Hobson develops the concept of

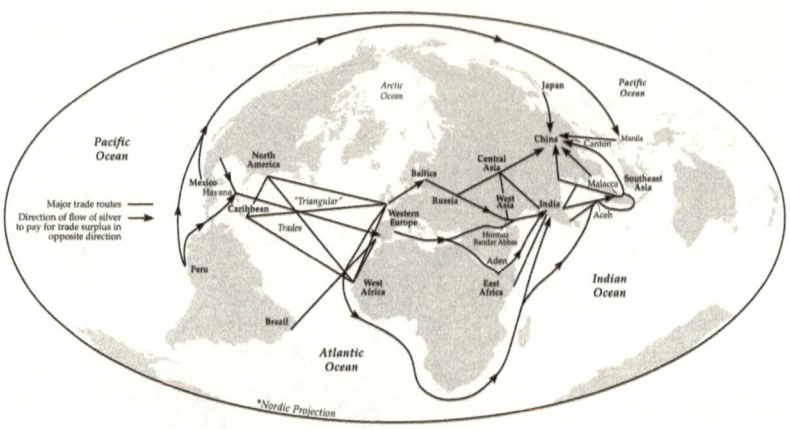

Figure 3.2 Major Circumglobal Trade Routes, 1400–1800.

Source: From *ReOrient: Global Economy in the Asian Age*, by André Gunder Frank, p. 65. © 1999 by André Gunder Frank. Reprinted by permission of the University of California Press.

the "oriental West" in *The Eastern Origins of Western Civilisation*, reaching back to global civilizations from 500 to 1900. These world historians and many others working within the scalar framework of a longer *durée* and broader planetary reach than Wallerstein's have split open the "black box" of Eurocentrism and inspire new ways of conceptualizing modernity.

Following in their wake, drawing heavily from their work, I turn now to stories of two very different kinds of centers in the world system before 1500: the Tang-Song empires of China from roughly the seventh through the thirteenth centuries and the Mongol empire from the thirteenth through the fourteenth centuries. These Asian empires—the first based in a sedentary society, the second, in a nomadic one—were engines of innovation and rapid change across a wide spectrum of societal domains—from the economic, political, and technological to the cultural, intellectual, and aesthetic. They were not, of course, the only significant innovators in the pre-1500 world system—the far-flung Islamic empire of the Abbasid Dynasty centered in Baghdad was a particularly influential one during this period; an instance of its significance is a story I will tell in chapter 5. I focus, however, on the Tang-Song and Mongol empires in particular because their radically different societies each exhibit in its distinctive way many of the characteristics that are commonly believed to have been created by post-1500 European modernity. I use these stories to provoke a rethinking of what constitutes "modernity," to suggest that "modernity is not one but many," and to lay the foundation for a narratologically informed reading of the hegemonic story of Western modernity. Taken together, these stories provide some grounds for conceptualizing modernity anew in chapter 4.

STORY 1: "MODERN" INNOVATIONS IN THE TANG-SONG EMPIRES, 618–1279 CE

The Chinese dynasties of the Tang (618–907) and the Song (960–1279) both emerged out of periods of political disintegration to produce highly complex and innovative economic, political, social, and cultural societies characterized by major changes: recurrent disruptions and reformations of the social order. They were imperial and cosmopolitan, extending the boundaries of China and centralizing power in the state, though continuous warfare and rebellions plagued both dynasties, which, like empires in general, experienced continuously expanding and contracting border areas. Intensified commercialization linked rural areas and cities to the great land- and sea-based trading routes of the world system connecting Asia to the Middle East, Africa, and Europe. The completion of the Grand Canal by 618—still the longest canal on the planet—linked the commercial, agricultural, and cultural systems of northern and southern China and led to an unprecedented growth in population and power. Major agricultural advances with the plough, harness, seed preparation, and irrigation led to a population explosion, producing the greatest concentration of people in large cities and suburbs on the planet, a demographic dominance that continues in the twenty-first century.

Literacy and book production increased in the cities among the rising middle classes, resulting in a flourishing of the arts, entertainments, and new poetic forms, as I will discuss in chapter 5. As a major break with Confucian culture, Buddhism and Taoism spread, bringing with them a somewhat less hierarchical family structure and gender relations. Elite women in particular had relatively more autonomy, as the Tang borrowed gender practices from the steppe cultures, including greater freedom, higher levels

Figure 3.3 Woman (on right) and Man Playing Polo. Tang Dynasty Tomb Figures. Eighth century. Earthenware, traces of polychrome decoration, 15 1/8 x 12 1/2 x 5 3/16 in. (38.4 x 31.8 x 13.2 cm).

Source: Norton Museum of Art, West Palm Beach, Florida, Purchase, R. H. Norton Trust, 62.13–62.14.

of education, the option of wearing tunics and boots, riding horses, and playing polo.[35]

Empress Wu, or Wu Zetian (624–705), the only woman in Chinese history to hold the title of emperor, is credited with many innovations, including instituting the national examination system for mandarins and other civil servants of the empire, a partial meritocracy that rewarded talent and challenged privilege by birth. Ruthless within the court and bureaucracy (though no more so than other emperors), she nonetheless managed to maintain a relatively peaceful reign, avoiding wars, welcoming ambassadors from far and wide, increasing land cultivation, ordering the production of farming textbooks, and instituting policies that allowed peasants to retain a greater proportion of their produce, thus enhancing general prosperity. Supporting the spread of Buddhism, Emperor Wu, as she called herself, challenged many Confucian values, including patriarchal ones, and promoted a greater valuation of women, overseeing the production of biographies of famous women and requiring children to mourn their mothers as well as their fathers. Even Mary Anderson, who is highly critical in *Hidden Power* of Wu's terror within the court, notes that under Wu's reign "military expenses were reduced, taxes cut, salaries of deserving officials raised, retirees given a viable pension, and vast royal lands near the capital turned over to husbandry."[36]

Chang'an, in northwestern China, was the Tang Dynasty's major capital, the largest city in the world with about two million people, and the gateway to the northern land-based Silk Road to West Asia and Europe. Major innovations in technology, agriculture, commerce, navigation, and education accompanied the establishment of a large state bureaucracy. Mark Edward Lewis's *China's Cosmopolitan Empire: The Tang Dynasty* provides a litany of what he calls "transformational innovations" in reviewing the changes developed during the Tang (101): new transregional and transnational trade; new commerce outside official markets; new agricultural technology and practices; new forms of paper credit and promissory notes; new laws and legal reforms; new weakening of the aristocracy; new autonomy for elite women; new national exams; new literacy in the urban middle classes; new wood block printing and use of paper for books, government documents, even toilet paper; new poetic and prose forms; new city gardens as artificial constructs of "nature"; new religious pluralism blending Confucian and Taoist practices with Buddhism; and a new embrace of the foreign and foreigners in their midst, a significant break with their Han predecessors.[37]

Practices that began in the late Tang Dynasty, Lewis, argues, were fulfilled through more innovations in the Song.[38] In *The Eastern Origins of Western Civilisation*, John M. Hobson stresses the empirical basis for claiming China as the most innovative and advanced civilization of the time, accomplishing what he details as an "industrial revolution," a "green revolution," a "navigational revolution," and a "military revolution." His litany of the new—innovations of the Song—include the invention of paper currency; expansions of steel, iron, and smelting production; energy through the substitution of coke for charcoal and the use of water mills; advances in textile manufacturing, including water-powered spinning machines; a tax system based on cash, which expanded participation in the market economy; the invention of the compass; shipbuilding of the world's largest ships; the invention of gunpowder and its use in warfare, including the gun, cannon, bombs, grenades, and rockets; and the development of the world's largest navy.[39]

The Silk Road of the Sea began in the port city Quanzhou, today a little-known city in Fujuan Province south of Shanghai but once the world's largest port city for hundreds of years, starting during the Tang Dynasty and rising to its height during the Song and Yuan Dynasties (960–1367). Quanzhou's eighth-century Luoyang Bridge was made of stone, using a floating technology; it was the first bridge in history to span the sea. A great shipbuilding center, Quanzhou led the world during the Song Dynasty in innovative design. The skeleton of a Quanzhou vessel from the late Song period (c. 1127–1279)—114 feet long by thirty-two feet wide—is preserved in the city's museum, starkly revealing the engineering feat that kept sections of the hull enclosed from the others to minimize risk. By the fourteenth century, the world's largest ships sailed from Quanzhou, bringing home commodities and animals from West Asia and Africa. Marco Polo is said to have left China from Quanzhou, and a huge, wall-size scroll from the fourteenth century shows a harbor with hundreds of masts and a variety of ships from many parts of the world. Quanzhou was once a cosmopolitan mixture of Chinese Arabs, Jews, Christians, Persians, Buddhists, and Taoists formed through commerce. The substantial remains of the Great Mosque of Quanzhou, built from 1009 to 1310, reflect the especially large

Figure 3.4 Great Mosque, Quanzho, China. Built 1009–1310.

Source: Photo by Susan Stanford Friedman, 2001.

Arab presence going back to missionary-traders sent by Mohammed in 618 CE and the vast trading empire of the Abbasid Caliphate centered in Baghdad.[40] Today's modern, bustling city of millions has adopted the characteristic Islamic arch as its signature architecture, a visual reminder of the city's powerful role in the world system of the Tang-Song period.

Against this landscape of innovative change during the Tang-Song Dynasties, such vital phenomena in the West after 1500 as the rise of print culture, industrialized production, military use of gunpowder, expanding bureaucracies of a central state system, currency and market changes, a lessening of religious conflict, a flourishing of the arts, and so forth no longer look so unique. How can they be the basis for defining "modernity" as an invention of the West?

STORY 2: NOMADIC "MODERNIZATIONS" AND THE MONGOL EMPIRE, 1206–C. 1400 CE

China of the Tang and Song Dynasties may have been the most populous, wealthy, and technologically advanced civilization of the time, but the story of their innovations is inseparable from the stories of the nomadic steppe peoples at their western borders. As Lewis writes, "the Tang ruling house was—both genealogically and culturally—a product of the frontier 'barbarian' culture that dominated northern China in the fifth and sixth centuries" (1). The earliest dynasties of the Tang spoke Turkic languages in the courts, relied heavily on the seminomadic Uighurs and Khitans to the west and northwest, and intermarried extensively with "the barbarians." "For at least two centuries," Lewis writes, "the Tang dynasty's embrace of foreign peoples and cultures is a defining element of Chinese civilization."[41] This conjunction of the highly advanced and the nomadic flies in the face of conventional periodization, thereby helping to rethink radically what we mean by "modernity."

Stories abound about periods of human civilizations—whether as myth or religion, narrative or science. The more "scientific" the story, the more it narrates a linear progression of successively more complex social organizations—from earliest upright *Homo sapiens*; on to hunters and gatherers; then to nomadic peoples; the Neolithic Revolution and the development of sedentary agricultural societies; urbanization and stratification of sedentary civilizations; expanding empires and tributary subject peoples; modernity, the nation-state, and the Industrial Revolution; late modernity and transnational globalization. Survivors of the older civilizational forms—the hunter/gatherers, the nomads—appear as "primitive" vestiges of earlier stages of human development. Or so the story goes for many. The new world historians are an exception, challenging conventional linear periodizations that envision European modernity and its diffusion as the telos of human history.

The new theories about the significance of nomads, especially the pastoral nomads of Central Asia, for the development of sedentary civilizations on the Eurasian continent suggest that nomadic conquests, empires, and trade enabled the rise of the sedentary societies by providing the technologies of mobility fostering the transcontinental transfer of goods, people, ideas, practices, and technologies produced by settled peoples.[42] The sedentary and nomadic steppe societies (many of them Turkic) had a symbiotic relationship based in trade necessary for both. In the first and second millennia, the steppe nomads expanded in all directions, using their superior breeding with horses and mounted warfare (cavalry, stirrups, compound bows) to invade the weakened empires of the Romans in the fifth century (the Huns); the Chinese in the seventh-eighth and eleventh-twelfth centuries; the Byzantines and Persians in the eleventh century (the Seljuks); central Europe, West Asia, and East Asia in the thirteenth and fourteenth centuries (the Mongols), and South Asia in the fifteenth and sixteenth centuries (the Mughals).[43] As Anatoly Khazanov points out, the nomads adapted to the new lands they inhabited, often becoming sedentary themselves, but they also influenced them greatly, a transcultural exchange that produced the hybridities familiar to contemporary global circulations. The knights of medieval Europe, for example, adapted the armor, saber, and regalia of Turkic nomads, including the iron stirrups that the nomads had themselves borrowed from the northern Koreans and greatly improved.[44] In the East, the Tang brought horses and camels from the steppes in large numbers (reflected in their signature ceramics and paintings of horses and camels), and fads in Tang cities based on Turkic clothing styles, food, banners, and totems were common.[45] As "bridge" societies, the nomads greatly intensified intercivilizational, transcontinental encounters. Through initial conquest, some integration with sedentary societies, and the maintenance of safe trading routes, they created a vast, land-based world system, an early form of globalization that brought different societies, technologies, religions, and ways of thought into sharp encounter—sometimes violent, sometimes peaceful, but always productive of rapid change and new ways of doing things. Or so the story goes now.

The Eurasian nomads were masters of speed, mobility, and adaptability in the formation of a world system from the 500s through 1400s—none more so than the Mongol Empire of Genghis Khan (c. 1155–1227) and his descendants in the thirteenth-fourteenth centuries (1206–c. 1400).[46] "The Mongol army led by Genghis Khan subjected more lands and people in twenty-five years than the Romans did in four hundred," writes the anthropologist Jack Weatherford in his revisionist history *Genghis Khan and the Making of the Modern World*.[47] In 1206, Temujin, a Mongol descended from a minor chieftain, completed his campaign to unite the various peoples of the steppes under his rule and declared himself the Genghis Khan (great leader) of the new Yeke Mongol Ulus, or the Great Mongol Nation. By his death in 1227, the Mongol Empire reached far east into Korea and northern China and far west into the Muslim lands of West Asia. Europe largely survived the Mongol onslaught by luck: the death of Ogodei Khan (Genghis Khan's son) in 1241 resulted in the abandonment of the Mongol campaign in central Europe, which had reached the doorsteps of Vienna. Subsequent khans were more interested in conquering the far wealthier China than the relatively poor nations of Europe. By 1260, the descendants of Genghis Khan ruled a vast military and commercial empire that included most of the Asian continent. Rulership of the empire was a family affair, divided into four khanates ruled by the sons and heirs of Genghis Khan: the Golden Horde of Russia, the Il-Khanate of Persia, the Chagatai Khangate of Mongolia, and Kah-balik/Yuan Dynasty China. Khubilai Khan (Genghis Khan's grandson) held the title of Great Khan and based himself in the wealthiest part of the empire, Khanbalik (Beijing), China, where Mongol rule initiated the Yuan Dynasty (1271–1368) and where Marco Polo claimed to work in his service from 1275–1292 (Bentley, 114).

The Mongol Empire, as Jane Burbank and Frederick Cooper describe it in *Empires in World History*, achieved a flexible hybridity based on the blending of nomadic and sedentary practices:

Figure 3.5 The Mongol Empires, c. 1300.
Source: Courtesy of the University of Wisconsin Cartography Lab.

The Mongol rulers drew strength from Eurasian political principles while continuing to adopt management strategies from the conquered. The Mongol way of rule, rather than a single formal empire, fostered connections between east and west, transformed culture, demographics, statecraft, and commerce and provoked new aspirations in the widening world. . . . Mongol sovereignty in the khanates was distinguished by its adaptability to local circumstances, including religion, artistic expression, science, and comforts, but also by tenacious adherence to particular elements in the Eurasian repertoire of power.

(106–107)

And that "repertoire of power" was based supremely in the Mongol institution of the army, in which all Mongol males had to serve.

In what sense, then, was the Mongol Empire "modern"? The Mongols don't appear to be modern at all.[48] They were originally nomads, not one of the "great civilizations" of Afro-Eurasia linked by trade, not the creators of a great metropole like the Tang's Chang'an or the Abbasid's Baghdad.

Figure 3.6 The Mongol Cavalry in Rashad al-Din's *Jami al-Tawarikh / History of the World*, thirteenth-century Persian manuscript.
Source: Bibliothèque nationale de France.

The Mongols were not even initially literate, living on the harsh steppes of Central Asia and surviving through hunting and herding. In the national imaginaries and histories of the peoples they conquered, the Mongols lived on as quintessential barbarians, ruthless murderers and destroyers, people without "culture," demonstrating the vulnerability of settled and civilized peoples to the savage and uncivilized. The Mongol Empire does not seem to be a likely candidate for a pre-1500, non-European modernity.

But a closer look at the Mongol Empire of the thirteenth and fourteenth centuries tells a different story. That the Mongol armies murdered and plundered with astounding speed and efficiency all those who refused to accept the rule of the Great Khan is unquestioned, as David Morgan details in *The Mongols* (49–73).[49]

But in areas of government, commerce, technology, science, religion, law, and culture, the Mongols also introduced concepts and practices into the world system that have been associated with a much later European modernity but in fact predated and no doubt directly or indirectly influenced the later modernity of the West. As Weatherford writes, "In nearly every country touched by the Mongols, the initial destruction and shock of conquest by an unknown and barbaric tribe yielded quickly to an unprecedented rise in cultural communication, expanded trade, and improved civilization" (xxiii). By the fourteenth century, the Pax Mongolica, as it was called, had transformed the world system linking Asia, Africa, and Europe.[50] "Where should one begin the study of *modern* history?" asks Arthur Waldron. "The soundest answer is probably with the Mongols."[51]

The rule of law, the supremacy of the state over religion, and religious freedom are three principles (not necessarily practices) of Western modernity that the Mongols initially instituted hundreds of years earlier throughout their empire. Genghis Khan, for example, refused to establish a state religion and declared religious freedom for all; he made no attempt to impose his own worship of the Mongol eternal deity in the heavens on others. Co-existing with Mongolian animism, the religions of Buddhism, Christianity, Islam, Judaism, and Manichaeism flourished throughout the empire and even within his family and their descendants. He established the concept of universal law, the Great Yasa (Law) of the empire that would override all local laws, and he appointed a supreme judge to oversee it. The first universal law he enacted was a ban against the kidnapping or stealing of women into marriage. He legitimated all children, whether born of wives or concubines. He outlawed slavery and the use of torture or disfigurement in criminal cases and warfare. He declared diplomatic immunity for envoys and ambassadors. Most significantly for the later formation of the modern state, Genghis Khan declared that the khan (ruler), including himself, was fully subject to the law and not above it. The concept of the divine right of monarchy would continue to dominate in Europe for many centuries before the West became as "modern" in its concept of the law as the Mongols.[52]

Many of Genghis Khan's laws arose out of his own suffering, represented a radical break from Mongolian tribal customs, and anticipated the transition from feudalism to capitalism in post-1500 Europe. He came from a relatively poor family of the "black" rather than the more privileged "white" lineage; his father stole his mother from her first husband; his clan abandoned his mother and children at the death of his father by poison; he was enslaved and tortured as a youth; his new wife was kidnapped and raped; his first son was most likely the product of that rape. It was the theft of his wife that started him on the path of conquest and astute political alliances that led first to his conquest of the Mongolian tribes and later to his conquests east and west of Mongolia. His resentment of elite lineages was the apparent motivation of what became one of his signature policies: the eradication of inherited aristocratic lineages and the institution of a meritocracy with advancement based on ability and loyalty instead of kinship ties. Moreover, for peoples who resisted the advance of his armies, he killed the aristocratic classes outright, lowered the taxes, and protected all other classes who would swear loyalty to him, opening up opportunities for the talented and ambitious. He was well known for his promotion of people to leadership positions in the army and administration of the empire on the basis of ability instead of family ties. Möngke Khan, Genghis Khan's grandson, who ruled from 1251 to 1259, strengthened these policies with widespread reforms aimed at reducing corruption among officials and equalizing the burdens of taxation among the subject peoples of the expanding empire.[53]

The difficulties of managing such a vast commercial and political empire led the Mongols to disseminate and standardize the inventions of others as well as to develop innovative mechanisms for the communication of information and goods.[54] Morgan stresses the pragmatism and adaptability of Mongol rule in the different khanates (94); Burbank and Cooper note the hybridic forms of governance. "Mongol sovereignty in the khanates," they write, "was distinguished by its adaptability to local circumstances, including religion, artistic expression, science, and comforts, but also by its tenacious adherence to particular elements in the Eurasian repertoire of power," particularly its armies (107). Shared engineering and maritime technology from throughout the empire improved irrigation, water systems for transport, and oceangoing ships. Genghis Khan created a relay postal service that linked all sectors of the empire with unprecedented speed; he then made free-trade zones and ensured the safety of trade routes to foster the expansion of trade. Adapting Chinese paper technology, he authorized paper currency backed up by silver and gold reserves; his grandson Möngke Khan realized the importance of a stabilized, standardized paper currency and created a Department of Monetary Affairs to control the issue of paper money and prevent inflation (Weatherford, 176).[55] A combination passport and credit card was established to facilitate the passage of government administrators throughout the empire.

Other monetary policies included principles for the orderly and fair distribution of captured wealth to the Mongol army and their families, as well as the concept of "shares," by which people in one part of the empire held rights to goods and income from another part of the empire. Rather than hoard wealth as rulers in Europe and lands conquered by the Mongols did, the khans put the wealth back into circulation through widespread distributions. During Khubilai Khan's rule, laws were enacted to allow and regulate bankruptcy, necessary because of the spread of the concept and practices of credit.[56] In opening new markets and trade routes, the Mongols were especially adept at taking local products and creating an international market for them, understanding "that items that were commonplace and taken for granted in one place were exotic and potentially marketable in another" (Weatherford, 225). They also fostered the manufacture of specialized products for niche markets, setting up factories in China, for example, to carve ivory images of the Madonna and Child for export to Europe.

For a nomadic culture that began as nonliterate, Genghis Khan and subsequent Mongol rulers moved quickly to expand the use of writing and print culture in general. Genghis Khan ordered the invention of a Mongolian script for use by a wide spectrum of people in the empire; he even attempted to create a single alphabetic script of forty-one letters into which all languages could be put. His grandson Khubilai Khan adapted the moveable type invented by the Chinese in the twelfth century for use throughout the empire, substituting efficient alphabetic type for the unwieldy use of thousands of Chinese characters. Literacy and publication increased dramatically during the Mongol rule, which encouraged the rise of print culture, often considered a hallmark of modernity and the formation of nation-states. Khubilai Khan established a government printing press to disseminate decisions and laws throughout the empire and fostered the rise of a wide variety of publications: religious books, novels, histories, medical treatises, songs, poetry, agricultural pamphlets, mathematical theory, and so forth (Weatherford, 233). He also established in China the principle (if not the reality) of universal education, establishing schools for peasants as well as elites.

Mongol support for the creation, dissemination, and application of knowledge was systematic and organized, often connected to governmental agencies that anticipated the development of the panoptic bureaucracies that Foucault associates with the rise of disciplinary knowledge in the West in the eighteenth through the twentieth centuries. Genghis Khan established a census procedure for the empire based on the decimal system, a means of registration that was perfected, expanded, and used as the basis for a progressive poll tax throughout the Mongol period (Burbank and Cooper, 107). The inflow of plundered goods from conquered peoples was meticulously enumerated so as to ensure systematic distribution, one based on the nomadic principles of dividing the kill from the collective hunt. His son Ogodei Khan established standardized weights and measures to facilitate trade and the collection of information. Khubilai Khan's Academy for Calendrical Studies standardized the calendar throughout the empire, fostered and disseminated astronomical devices and knowledge, and mass produced calendars and almanacs for widespread distribution.

From the beginning, the khans of the Mongol Empire exhibited a self-consciously cosmic concept of themselves as "world" rulers, leading them

Figure 3.7 Nasir ad-Din Tusi (1201–1274) at his famed observatory near Maragheh, founded during the reign of Hulegu Khan of the Il-khanate. Fifteenth-century Persian manuscript.

Source: University Library, Istanbul.

to oversee the production of histories that came to reflect the world system of the empire. Tchingis Qaghan—the name Temujin chose upon being proclaimed emperor in 1206—actually means "oceanic sovereign," according to Jean-Paul Roux, who claims that Genghis Khan determined to make the Mongols "masters of the world" (25). Khubilai Khan adapted the imperial Han tradition to "emphasize his status as a universal ruler" (Burbank and Cooper, 107). As the Great Khan, Khubilai Khan brought geographers to China to produce the world's most sophisticated maps, including terrestrial globes and flat maps that included Europe, Africa, Asia, and the adjacent Pacific islands (the Americas remained unknown to the Mongols).[57]

The Mongol belief in their cosmic rule stimulated an interest in history beginning with Genghis Khan's successor, his son Ogodei (d. 1241), who ordered the compilation of *The Secret History of the Mongols* in about 1228 (Morgan, 9).[58] As Morgan explains, the Mongols' "official history," called the *Atlan Debter* ("Golden Book"), was kept in the Mongol court, taboo for non-Mongols to see. Khubilai Khan set up the National History Office in the 1260s, and Persians under the rule of Il-Khans established a historiographical tradition with scores of histories reflecting the Mongol belief in its global rule, including Juzwani's *History of the Mongols* and Jawayni's encyclopedic *History of the World Conqueror*, based on Juwayni's extensive information gathering in travels throughout many parts of the empire (Morgan, 16–17). At the end of the thirteenth century, the Il-Khan Ghazan commissioned Rashid al-Din, a Jewish convert to Islam and chief minister of the empire, to oversee many scholars and translators contributing to the monumental *Collection of Histories*, which included histories of China, India, the Turks, the Jews, the pre-Islamic Persians, Muhammad and the caliphs, and the Franks (Morgan, 11–19). With access to the *Atlan Debter*, Rashid al-Din declared in his introduction that "the Mongol Empire marked a new era in world history." As Morgan claims, the extraordinary *Collection of Histories* deserves "the title of a world history" (18).[59]

At the center of Mongol innovation was the flexible adaptation of knowledge systems and technologies from different parts of the world that they melded, transported, and indigenized throughout the empire. The Mongols were masters of cultural translation. It is particularly telling that the only permanent structures Genghis Khan created were bridges.[60] But his heirs in the Khanates drew on, patronized, and developed to extraordinary heights the arts, literatures, and architectures of the settled lands they ruled, especially Persia and China (Burbank and Cooper, 110–111). The Mongol Empire created a "knowledge revolution" avant la lettre, one based on mastery of communication, transportation, and movement. German miners were transported to China to start up the Chinese mining industry, for example. The Mongol army borrowed Chinese gunpowder and developed an array of firepower (grenades, cannon, nepenthe, etc.) that easily defeated the walled cities of West Asia and Eastern Europe. Weatherford claims they also brought the Indian zero and Arabic mathematics, especially algebra, to China (231–232). Genghis Khan and later khans particularly valued the work of professionals, helping construct the concept of a professional class by exempting doctors, lawyers, teachers, scholars, and undertakers from taxation. As Weatherford puts it:

> The Mongols made culture portable. It was not enough merely to exchange goods, because whole systems of knowledge had to also be transported in order to use many of the new products. Drugs, for example, were not profitable items of trade unless there was adequate knowledge of how to use them. Toward this objective, the Mongol court imported Persian and Arab doctors into China, and they exported Chinese doctors to the Middle East. Every form of knowledge carried new possibilities for merchandising.
>
> (229)

Weatherford doesn't mention whether the significant transfer of knowledgeable people was voluntary or forced migration, but the effect was to greatly intensify and accelerate the transfer of technology and the knowledge of how to use it.[61]

The rise of every empire has its fall. What ended the Mongol rule? Surely a combination of causes, including difficulties of succession, the strain of increasingly different khanate societies held together by difficult family relations and rivalries. But the precipitousness of the fall lies in precisely what enabled the rapidity of its rise. The movement of goods, ideas, technology, and people that gave the Mongol Empire its special character also brought the bubonic plague. The very extent, speed, and efficiency of movement throughout the commercial and governmental arteries of the empire in the fourteenth century facilitated the spread of disease-carrying fleas from the newly conquered south of China to the rest of the Mongol world. The pandemic shut down the empire within decades of its early spread in 1338. Trade slowed to a trickle as societies walled themselves off from outsiders. The different parts of the empire devolved into separate parts where the sudden lack of wealth from trade and inner dissension in the ruling families led to rapid decline. Growth slowed in Europe, cut off from the great riches of the east. When Columbus set sail in 1492, he carried with him Marco Polo's account of the fabulous wealth of Cathay in the court of Khubilai Khan (Weatherford, 254). He didn't know that Khubilai Khan's Yuan Dynasty had dissolved and that China was now ruled by the Ming Dynasty, which had burned all the plans for its huge ships, halted its maritime expansion, and officially cut off contact with the world (Frank, *ReOrient*, 108). He didn't know that the New World he found on his way to Cathay would succumb to European diseases and conquest, leading to a relatively sudden influx of capital (silver and gold) that funded the rise of Europe.[62]

Nonetheless, the Mongol Empire greatly affected the European Renaissance. In 1620, the English scientist Francis Bacon named three technological innovations that he claimed to have changed the nature of the world: printing, gunpowder, and the compass. The Mongols had introduced all three into Europe (Weatherford, 236). What he did not mention because they hardly yet existed in Europe's early modern period, riven as it was by religious wars, was the "innovation" of tolerance for diversities of culture, language, and religion—an idea not widely prevalent in the West for another century or so (and then never fully actualized).

∞ ∞ ∞

Where is "modernity" in 1254?

∞ ∞ ∞

The Roman Catholic Inquisition officially began in 1231, after which Rome appointed Inquisition judges to investigate and stamp out heresy. Those excommunicated from the Church for failure to accept Church doctrine were burned at the stake. The Spanish Inquisition began in 1480 in the court of Queen Isabella and King Ferdinand, causing thousands of Jews to flee west to the Americas, south to Africa, east to West Asia, and north to more tolerant countries like Holland. The burning of heretics, massacres of religious minorities, and fierce religious wars dominated the European continent and Britain through the seventeenth century.

In 1253, a Franciscan monk, William of Rubruck, arrived as an envoy from Paris in the Mongol court, which was at that time largely Christian, with a mixture of Assyrian, Armenian, and Orthodox. Rubruck considered these Christians heretics because they did not acknowledge the authority of the Roman pope. Finally granted an audience with Möngke Khan (a grandson of Genghis Khan who ruled from 1251 to 1259), Rubruck asserted that "he knew the word of God and had come to spread it" (Weatherford, 172). A vigorous theological discussion ensued in the court, and Möngke Khan decided to sponsor a contest of rival religions, appointing a panel of judges to oversee the debate. Three judges—a Christian, a Muslim, and a Buddhist—presided over three teams of religious scholars who debated such questions as God's nature, good versus evil, whether God created evil, reincarnation, and life after death. No team managed to convince any other team, and the debate dissolved into heavy drinking, the Christians singing and the Muslims reciting the Koran. A few days later Möngke Khan summoned Rubruck to discharge him and to send a message to his king about Mongol beliefs and tolerance. "We Mongols believe in one God, by Whom we live and Whom we die and toward Him we have an upright heart," Möngke Khan told Rubruck. "Just as God gave different fingers to the hand so has He given different ways to men. To you God has given the Scriptures and you Christians do not observe them" (Weatherford, 174).[63]

No one was burned at the stake for religious beliefs or identity in the Mongol Empire. No one was tortured as an official procedure to determine heresy. The Mongols did not allow hangings or beheadings to become public entertainment. About the same time as the debate in Mongolia, Rubruck's sponsor, King Louis IX of France, burned some twelve thousand handwritten and illuminated Jewish books. For his piety, including his destruction of these books, the Church canonized him as Saint Louis.[64]

This episode in the complex history of the Mongol Empire is a story that ends on a utopian note of religious tolerance, a tolerance that did not appear in Europe until after a European modernity began to develop. But I want to resist the argument about origins and priority (e.g., the Mongols were tolerant/modern before the Europeans), a trap into which the metanarrative of European modernity so often falls. I also resist the urge to equate modernity with linear or utopian progress. The Mongols, it should be remembered, killed all those in their path who refused to accept their rule.

Modernity, whatever its forms, intermixes the utopian and dystopian, brings both exhilaration and suffering. I suggest even more provocatively that modernity seems constitutively related to empire, not to the post-Westphalian nation-state as is so often assumed. Empire, in one form or another, has been the prevailing large-scale unit of human social organization since Mesopotamia, including in the recent era of nation-states, as the European, American, Russian, Turkish, Chinese, and Japanese imperial projects since 1500 attest. It is a mistake, I believe, to assume that the formation of nation-states after Westphalia supplanted empires as a sign of modernity and as a new and superior stage of state formation. Nation-states from the eighteenth century through the present have drawn heavily on their expanding power in other parts of the world—whether contiguous or far away—for the production of their wealth and power. In *Empires in World History*, Burbank and Cooper suggest that empires and nation-states differ in their main challenges: empires need to manage vast diversities; nation-states create a sense of a unified, national identity. Additionally, empires experience recurrent expansion and contraction of their porous borders whereas nation-states establish and enforce fixed borders that have increasingly controlled border crossing and citizen/alien categories of identity (1–11). What I would add to this formulation is that in the so-called age of nation-states, empires continue to wax and wane as geographical extensions of the nation-states they enhance. Through their empires or imperial aspirations, nation-states continue to manage diversity (as the British Empire did with dire effects during the Raj and its breakup) at the same time that they formulate exclusionary national imaginaries based on binaries of us and them, insiders and outsiders. Empires in the age of nation-states and in the newly transnational formations of the twenty-first century differ from the pre-1500 empires, but empires have not withered on the vine as nation-states gained in power. Conquest and the competition among what Laura Doyle calls the "interlocked" and overlapping empires of human history—both before and after the rise of nation-states—might well be the single strongest factor in the production of the rapid change, epistemological ruptures, and societal interconnectivities associated with modernities of all kinds.[65]

THE STORY OF "MODERNITY" IN "THE WEST"

These stories of modernities in the *longue durée*—the one based in sedentary, the other in nomadic societies—are not meant to establish new origin points for modernity, nor are they meant to supplant, belittle, or ignore the significance of Western modernity. Rather, my intent has been to unsettle, even to shock us into rethinking the most fundamental categories of modernity. They have helped to establish, I hope, a global landscape in a longer *durée* that brings into focus the ideological drive behind the story of modernity as the invention of the West and as a single period with a nominal set of characteristics typically including formations such as the nation-state, capitalism, secularism, democracy, individualism, and so forth. There is a seductive tale of heroic proportions that underlies both conservative and critical stories about what is iconically known as "the rise of the West," a phrase that William H. McNeill coined as the title of his field-defining book *The Rise of the West* (1963) and that is reconstituted in such titles as *The Genius of the West* (Louis Rougier), *The Triumph of the West* (J. M. Roberts), *The European Miracle* (Eric L. Jones), and *The Uniqueness of Western Civilization* (Ricardo Duchesne).[66]

The *donné* of this tale is to explain the West's increasing dominance of the world system after about 1500, in a succession of historical periods from early to late modernity that begin with the Age of Discoveries, move through the Enlightenment, the Industrial Revolution, and European and American imperialisms, and end with contemporary globalization. The basic plot (story/fabula/*histoire*) that structures the various manifestations of the tale (discourse/*sjužet*/*discours*) features Europe as the active protagonist of an agonistic world history in which others are passive recipients, peripheral foils, or antagonists doomed to defeat and imitation—the acted upon rather than the actors of history across the spectrum from the economic, political, and technological to the philosophical and cultural.[67]

Sometimes the tales are originary, focused on the dilemma of how modernity arose sui generis in the West; at other times, they narrate modernity's unfolding from early to late. Central themes of the story revolve around Europe's exceptionalism, and figural elements and narrative patterns variously emphasize linear progression, cyclic repetition, organicism, mechanism, evolution, or revolution. Whether narrated from the political "right" or "left," the story of modernity is typically cast as heroic or demonic, as triumphalist or viral. For sure, narrators in between complicate the story, seeing the geocharacters of history as tragically flawed, the plot as complexly gray. As with all stories, storytellers matter: differing narrative points of view establish differing ethical resonances. But the basic plot, the metanarrative of modernity as the story of the West as it dominates the Rest from about 1500 to the present, remains.

This widespread metanarrative (story) is starkly evident in three succinct versions (discourse) that I cite here for illustrative purposes:

> In the late fifteenth and early sixteenth century, there came into existence what we may call a European world-economy. It was not an empire yet it was as spacious as a grand empire and shared some features with it. But it was different, and new. It was a kind of social system the world has not really known before and which is the distinctive feature of the modern world-system.
>
> —Immanuel Wallerstein, *The Modern World-System* (1974)[68]

> The West obviously differs from all other civilizations that have ever existed in that it has had an overwhelming impact on all other civilizations that have existed since 1500. It also inaugurated the processes of modernization and industrialization that have become worldwide, and as a result societies in all other civilizations have been attempting to catch up with the West in wealth and modernity.
>
> —Samuel Huntington, *The Clash of Civilizations and the Remaking of World Order* (1996)[69]

The underlying premise of this chapter is that "the West" is a *historical*, not a geographical, construct. By "western" we mean the type of society discussed in this series: a society that is developed, industrialized, urbanized, capitalist, secular, and modern. Such societies arose at a particular historical period—roughly, during the sixteenth century, after the Middle Ages and the break-up of feudalism. They were the result of a specific set of historical processes—economic, political, social and cultural. Nowadays, any society, wherever it exists on a geographical map, which shares these characteristics, can be said to belong to "the West." The meaning of this term is therefore virtually identical to that of the word "modern." Its "formations" are what we have been tracing in the earlier chapters in this book.

—Stuart Hall and Bram Gieben, *Formations of Modernity* (1992)[70]

I deliberately emphasize here the narratological elements of the prevailing concept of modernity to complement the empirically based arguments of comparative world historians like Blaut, Frank, and Hobson. They, among others, argue that the idea of modernity arose in the West in the nineteenth and twentieth centuries as an explanation of and rationalization for Europe's and then the United States' growing world domination. The invention of this idea, they argue, was especially entangled with the development of modern disciplinary knowledge, itself inseparable from European imperialism and the production of the very concepts of "the West" or "Western civilization." Whether as philosophical idea, historical periodization, sociological theory, or popular culture, the notion of modernity as a product and defining quality of the post-1500 West envisions world history from the point of view of the West. As an idea, "modernity" contains a story that both its defenders and attackers tell about the West from inside Western frameworks of thought. It is a widely influential story whose telos reflects and serves the interests of the powerful region that narrates it whether the narrator is celebratory or critical. Although this modernity presumes to be universal, its genesis and operational function are parochial. While the critiques of these world historians marshal empirical evidence for alternative histories of modernity as a product of the global eucumene in the *longue durée*, I focus below on the narratological dimensions of the prevailing story of modernity.

STORY SETTING

The story of modernity posits "the West" as narrative setting. The West appears to be a place identifiable as a location in time-space where the action of history occurs. It also functions as a directional term, implying a standpoint from which the global map is drawn, establishing a binary of East/West that rhetorically suppresses north/south. As Martin Bernal, Blaut, and Hobson (among others) point out, the West is in actuality not a place in space but a relational construct dependent on its opposite, the East, for its meaning.[71] "The West" connotes an imagined history of origins and evolution that developed as an idea in the eighteenth and nineteenth centuries in conjunction with the European empires and the accompanying rise of Oriental studies.

Although this idea is spatial, the West itself is difficult to locate geographically. Europe and Asia are constituted rhetorically as distinct continents, West and East, but they are part of the same land mass, with no geographical feature definitively separating them. Europe often appears as a metonym for the West, as if Europe's boundaries were not themselves constantly in motion, as if its separation from Asia were self-evident, as if North America were simply an extension of Europe instead of countries formed by people from all over the world, including the Americas. Russia, whose landmass reaches from Poland to the Pacific Ocean, has at times claimed to be part of Europe (at least west of the Ural Mountains); Turkey sees itself as part of both Europe and Asia, split by the Bosporus. The establishment of the Greenwich Prime Meridian and Greenwich Mean Time in 1884 at Britain's Royal Observatory marks England as the spatio/temporal reference point for the Earth, defining Greenwich as the center of the West and ground zero from which to measure distance from itself, a standpoint reflected in terms like the "Far East" and "Near East." Indicating at least rhetorical resistance to GMP and GMT as vestiges of imperial Britain, "West Asia" is for many a term of choice, supplanting the "Near" or "Middle East."[72]

The ideological underpinnings of the idea of "the West" become even clearer as the spatial term connotes the political, economic, technological, and cultural dimensions associated with modernity. In the post–World War II period, the rise of democratic Japan as an economic and technological powerhouse has at times provided it with an ambiguous membership in the West, but not China, whose economy has now overtaken Japan as theory second largest in the world and will no doubt soon surpass the United

States. Israel is part of the West, but Palestine is not. Modern countries are Western, but modernizing countries are not. Countries dominated by descendants of European settlers are modern (e.g., Australia), but neighbors are not (e.g., Indonesia).

Attempting to avoid the ideological baggage of the East/West binary, global theory increasingly divides the world into the Global North and Global South. Although rhetorically spatial, these terms are as geographically imprecise and ideologically weighted as East/West. Akin to the West, the Global North signifies modern global hegemony; the Global South (which includes many countries north of the equator) indicates the subaltern, that is, the unmodern or still modernizing Rest—a binary construction that continues to place the West at the controlling center of the plot.

The continuing dominance of the 1569 Mercator projection of the three-dimensional globe in two-dimensional maps of the world attests to the ongoing power of the Western "setting" for the metanarrative of modernity. As Hobson points out,

> This map is found everywhere—from world atlases to school walls to airline booking agencies and boardrooms. Crucially, the actual landmass of the southern hemisphere is exactly twice that of the northern hemisphere. And yet on the Mercator, the landmass of the North occupies two-thirds of the map while the landmass of the South represents only a third. Thus while Scandinavia is about a third the size of India, they are accorded the same amount of space on the map. Moreover on the Mercator, Greenland appears almost twice the size of China, even though the latter is almost four times the size of the former.
>
> (6)

A two-dimensional surface map necessarily reflects a geographical standpoint; no projection of the Earth is an "objective" scalar representation. But more recent projections such as the 1974 Peters projection have attempted to reflect actual surface areas, causing great controversy because of their radical difference from the familiar Mercator Projection (Hobson, 6).

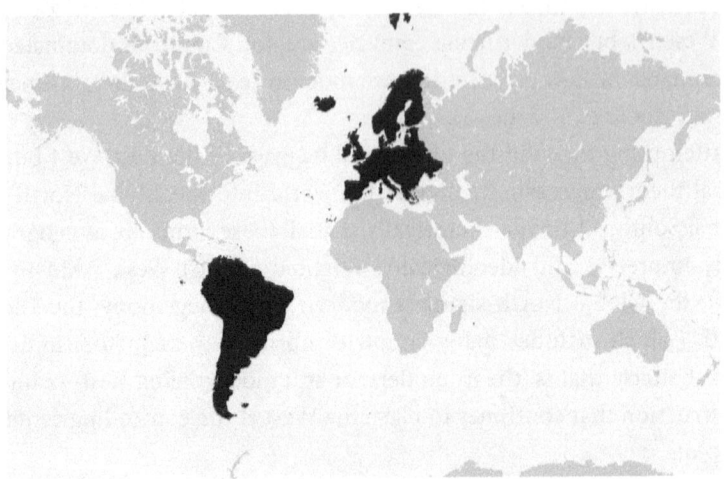

Figure 3.8 Contemporary world map based on the fifteenth-century Mercator projection.

Source: Courtesy of the University of Wisconsin Cartography Lab.

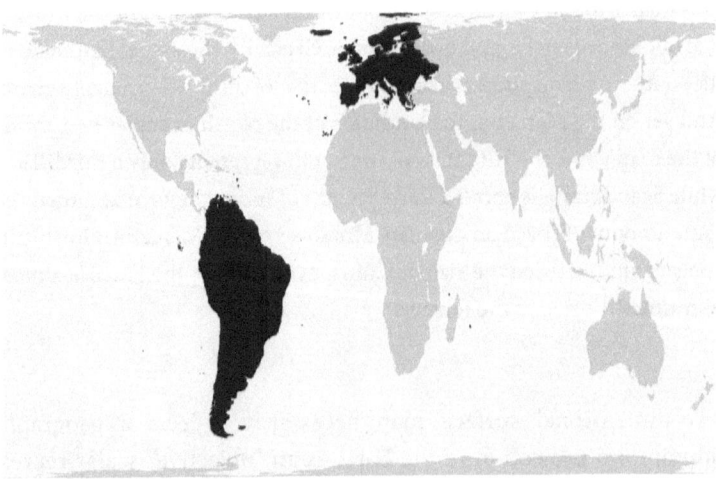

Figure 3.9 World map based on the Peters projection, 1974.

Source: Courtesy of the University of Wisconsin Cartography Lab.

STORY THEME

If the spatial setting of the West's story of modernity reflects a Western narrative point of view, so does the story's main theme: European exceptionalism, the belief that qualities internal to Europe account for its invention of modernity and rise to global power. Often with intellectual roots in Marx or Weber,[73] this theme emphasizes the dynamism of the West in contrast to the stagnation of the East while debating whether Europe's unique internal processes are primarily political, economic, religious, cultural, environmental, technological, racial, or some combination thereof. As a historical geographer, Blaut launches what is perhaps the most systematic attack on the assumption of European exceptionalism in the historiography of modernity, although his book rests on earlier influential works such as Hodgson's essays in world history collected in *Rethinking World History* (1993), Samir Amin's *Eurocentrism* (1988), and Janet Abu-Lughod's *Before European Hegemony* (1989).[74] Summarizing nearly two hundred years of historiography across the political spectrum, Blaut writes:

> The myth of the European miracle is the doctrine that the rise of Europe resulted, essentially, from historical forces generated within Europe itself; that Europe's rise above other civilizations, in terms of level of development or rate of development or both, began before the dawn of the modern era, before 1492; that the post-1492 modernization of Europe came about essentially because of the working out of these older internal forces, not because of the inflowing of wealth and innovations from non-Europe; and that the post-1492 history of the non-European (colonial) world was essentially an outflowing of modernization from Europe. The core of the myth is the set of arguments about ancient and medieval Europe that allow the claim to be made, as truth, that Europe in 1492 was more modernized, or was modernizing more rapidly, than the rest of the world.[75]

In the work of mainstream historians like Eric L. Jones and neo-Marxists like Immanuel Wallerstein, Blaut finds an operative framework that reflects and rationalizes "the colonizer's model of the world" as it evolved from the early nineteenth century through the late twentieth century. Eurocentrism, he argues, is "a belief system" (41) that arose alongside European imperialism and still pervades academic circles and Western culture in general. Its "classical" form in the nineteenth century ran the gamut of those justifying European colonialism based on the innate superiority of Western civilization to those like Marx, who attacked colonialism but nonetheless remained attached to the notion of European exceptionalism. In the twentieth century, Eurocentrism has evolved to incorporate not only the justifications of the West as the beacon of dynamic modernity in a dark world of stagnant traditionalism but also the neo-Marxist schools of dependency theory and Wallersteinian world-systems theory.

STORY STRUCTURES

As the story/discourse distinction suggests, variations on the theme of European exceptionalism abound, but underlying these versions are three related narrative structures that figure consistently in the dominant story of modernity: diffusionist, binarist, and relational. The diffusionist story of Western modernity is an originary narrative, positing the West as the source of a modernity that spreads throughout the rest of the world. Diffusionism, Blaut argues, "is a theory about the way cultural processes tend to move over the surface of the world as a whole" (1). European diffusionism is linear and assumes what Blaut calls a "core" and "periphery," the "outflowing of modernization from Europe" and its "inflowing" elsewhere as a form of influence locating agency in the source rather than its point of reception (17, 59).

Eurocentric diffusionism also operates on binarisms like modernity/tradition, innovation/imitation, change/stasis, progressivism/backwardness, rationality/irrationality. Blaut writes:

> Europeans are seen as the "makers of history." Europe eternally advances, progresses, modernizes. The rest of the world advances more sluggishly, or stagnates: it is "traditional society." Therefore, the world has a permanent geographical center and a permanent periphery: an Inside and an Outside. Inside leads. Outside lags. Inside innovates; Outside imitates.
>
> (1)

The dynamic West	The unchanging East
Inventive, ingenious, proactive	Imitative, ignorant, passive
Rational	Irrational
Scientific	Superstitious, ritualistic
Disciplined, ordered, self-controlled, sane, sensible	Lazy, chaotic/erratic, spontaneous, insane, emotional
Mind-oriented	Body-oriented, exotic and alluring
Paternal, independent, functional	Childlike, dependent, dysfunctional
Free, democratic, tolerant, honest	Enslaved, despotic, intolerant, corrupt
Civilised	Savage/barbaric
Morally and economically progressive	Morally regressive and economically stagnant

Figure 3.10 The orientalist and patriarchal construction of the "West" versus the "East."

Source: From *The Eastern Origins of Western Civilisation*, by John M. Hobson, © Cambridge University Press, p. 8. Reprinted with the permission of Cambridge University Press.

For Hobson, the binarisms that structure the Eurocentric story of modernity are also fundamentally patriarchal and racist; they depend on the feminization and racialization of the "East" as Other.[76]

The relational narrative structure in the story of European exceptionalist modernity emphasizes the interaction of the West and the Rest in the production of modernity. Wallerstein's world-system analysis, for example, is a relational story of unequal exchange among parts of the world. In defining the "modern world-system" not as the whole world but as a system that functions *as a world*, he emphasizes the relational inequality of the capitalist world economy in which the West's modernity has drawn its power from its dominance of the Rest. For all his abhorrence of Eurocentrism, Wallerstein's relational story maintains the fiction of the West as the driving force, the protagonist to which all others must react. "The world in which we are now living," Wallerstein writes, "the modern world-system, had its origins in the sixteenth century.... It is and has always been a *capitalist* world-economy... the system [that] gives priority to the *endless* accumulation of capital" (*Introduction*, 23–24). It is the "imperative of the endless accumulation of capital," he explains, that has generated "the need for constant technological exchange, a constant expansion of frontiers—geographical, psychological, intellectual, scientific" (2). And it is this imperative that has led the West to forge a system of "unequal exchange" with the rest of the world, a system made up of three interrelating parts: core, periphery, and semiperiphery. Narratologically speaking, Wallerstein's "discourse" differs from other European exceptionalist accounts, but his originary narrative about capitalism and the structural narrative patterns of core/periphery/semiperiphery in the modern world-system repeat the "story" embedded in such clearly Eurocentric discourses as the Mercator global projection, the Greenwich Prime Meridian, and Greenwich Mean Time: that post-1500 Europe is the center by which other social orders are determined and the measure by which all others are understood.

NARRATIVE POINT OF VIEW

Narrative point of view matters to the particular discourse of any given story, affecting the reliability of narrators and the ethical cast of the tale, among other things. McNeill makes this point as he revisits *The Rise of the West* some twenty-five years after its publication. He criticizes what he has come to consider the "subconscious" perspective of the book, which reflects the hegemony of the United States and its "post-war imperial mood" after World War II. He was writing, he says, "history from the *point of view* of the winners," looking at Eurasia "from a naively Western *viewpoint*," misunderstanding the effects of the global ecumene on the later rise of Europe (305; emphasis added). Reviewing what he subsequently learned about the explosively innovative and powerful societies of the Chinese, Muslims, and Mongolians before 1500, he concludes: "The fluctuating growth of this sort of world system, with shifting centers and a great multiplicity of peoples and cultures caught within it, seems to me now to be a part of world history that largely escaped my attention when writing *The Rise of Europe*" (316).

Where McNeill self-consciously notes the heuristic effects of narrative point of view on history writing and later shifts his perspective in the light of his greater exposure to history outside the West, Wallerstein and Samuel Huntington show little reflexivity about point of view as a factor in the stories they tell. Politically speaking, they couldn't be more different as narrators. Huntington's *Foreign Affairs* essay entitled "The Clash of Civilizations?" (1993) and his subsequent book *The Clash of Civilizations and the Remaking of World Order* (1996) treat transcivilizational interactions as the major threat facing modernity.[77] His work is a wake-up call to the West, a jeremiad against what he perceives as the softening of American will and the growing decadence of American society. The West faces, he claims, a fundamental threat to its hegemony from the Rest—his 1993 article is most likely the source of the widely used pairing of the West and the Rest: "The futures of the United States and of the West depend upon Americans reaffirming their commitment to Western civilization. Domestically this means rejecting the divisive siren calls of multiculturalism. Internationally it means rejecting the elusive and illusory calls to identify the United States with Asia" (*Clash*, 307). Immigration into the West is a major threat because immigrants refuse to assimilate (305). On the global landscape, he takes a segregationist view, imagining a kind of geopolitical apartheid, with the West holding onto its imperial power but not trying to universalize Western values. "Those who do not recognize fundamental divides," he warns, "are doomed to be frustrated by them" (309). The cornerstone of Huntington's belief in the West's uniqueness and superiority is his insistence that the West invented modernity:

> The West differs from other civilizations not in the way it has developed but in the distinctive character of its values and institutions. These include most notably its Christianity, pluralism, individualism, and rule of law, which made it possible for the West to invent modernity, expand throughout the world, and become the envy of other societies. In their ensemble these characteristics are peculiar to the West. . . . They make Western civilization unique, and Western civilization is valuable not because it is universal but because it *is* unique. The principal responsibility of Western leaders, consequently, is not to attempt to reshape other civilizations in the image of the West, which is beyond their declining

power, but to preserve, protect, and renew the unique qualities of Western civilization. Because it is the most powerful Western country, that responsibility falls overwhelmingly on the United States of America.

(311)

Wallerstein eschews the tone of the jeremiad and adopts the mantle of Eurocentric critique in "Eurocentrism and Its Avatars" (1997), an essay defending his concept of the modern world-system against the charges that his theory of capitalist modernity is Eurocentric.[78] He asserts that only one critique of Eurocentrism escapes reproducing what it challenges—namely, his own approach. His narrative point of view comes starkly into focus as he relies upon the rhetoric of disease:

> What happened in the Western world is that, for a specific set of reasons that were momentary—or conjunctural, or accidental—the *anti-toxins* were less available or less efficacious, and *the virus spread rapidly*, and then proved itself invulnerable to later attempts at reversing its effects. The European world-economy of the sixteenth-century became irremediably capitalist.... The fact that capitalism had this kind of breakthrough in the European arena, and then expanded to cover the globe, does not however mean that this was inevitable, or desirable, or in any sense progressive. In my view, it was none of these. And an anti-Eurocentric point of view must start by asserting this.
>
> ("Eurocentrism," 105; emphasis added)

As a mirror opposite of Huntington, Wallerstein sees the West as the source of pollution or disease, not the potential victim of it. But like Huntington, Wallerstein retells the metanarrative in crediting Europe with the rise of capitalism, which serves as metonym for modernity itself in his work. For those world historians like Frank, who find capitalism and other early modernities preexisting its rise in sixteenth-century Europe, Wallerstein has little respect. The production of modernity for Wallerstein is the story of the West's growing capitalist exploitation of the Rest, a demonization of the West that is itself a form of Eurocentrism. He embodies what Ella Shohat and Robert Stam characterize as the Eurocentrism of the left:

Nor do we believe in the inverted European narcissism that posits Europe as the source of all social evils in the world. Such an approach remains Eurocentric . . . and also exempts Third World patriarchal elites from all responsibility. Such "victimology" reduces non-European life to a pathological response to Western penetration. It merely turns colonialist claims upside down. Rather than saying that "we" (that is, the West) have brought "them" civilization, it claims instead that everywhere "we" have brought diabolical evil, and everywhere "their" enfeebled societies have succumbed to "our" insidious influence. The vision remains Promethean, but here Prometheus has brought not fire but the Holocaust, reproducing what Barbara Christian calls the "West's outlandish claim to have invented everything, including Evil."[79]

To one narrator (Huntington), the story of the West's rise is good, to another (Wallerstein), it's evil. Huntington advocates geopolitical separation in defense of the West; Wallerstein argues for the inevitability of an unequal integration of the Western core with its peripheries and semi-peripheries. But as much as they differ theoretically and politically, both narrators tell a story of modernity with striking structural similarities.

∞ ∞ ∞

Modernity is the Manifest Destiny of the West.
Manifestly, the destiny of the Rest is to copy the West.

∞ ∞ ∞

READER RESPONSE TO STORIES OF WESTERN MODERNITY

What effects—psychological, philosophical, political—does the West's hegemonic story of modernity have on those who hear it, read it, or see it? Do they internalize it, retell it, adapt it, or resist it? Reader response, or reception studies, is a branch of narrative theory focused on narratees, those to whom the story is addressed or those who actually absorb it in some form. Some narratees are embedded in the "discourse" of the "story" itself as characters or implied readers or viewers, others exist outside the world of the narrative as receivers of it, and still others are simultaneously constructed within the narrative as observers of it in their own time/space. Narratees are both individual and collective, generating responses that can be personal and idiosyncratic or communal and widely disseminated. How might these concepts of reader response help us understand the ideological effects of the West's metanarrative of modernity?

To those living within the West, the story potentially enhances their sense of power and centrality—whether narrators praise, condemn, or complexly analyze the significance of the West's modernity. To those living outside the West, the story potentially deflates their sense of worth, dignity, and empowerment—whether narrators praise, condemn, or complexly analyze the significance of the West's modernity. For both narratee locations, the story tends to fix the West as center to the Rest's periphery, suppressing the multiplicity of standpoints and the way in which any location on the globe serves as its own center, with others as its periphery. Huntington's sense of superiority and entitlement might be politically repugnant in contrast to Wallerstein's advocacy for the "Global South," but the effects of their parallel stories of Western modernity are potentially similar: creating or reinforcing in their readers an unshakeable conviction of the modern West as the controlling measure of the nonmodern Rest, fated to imitate and catch up.

One's geographical location inside or outside the West does not, however, automatically determine responses to the metanarrative of Western modernity. Some absorb the story in toto, subject to and reproducer of the story's telos, whether they approve (e.g., Huntington) or disapprove (e.g., Wallerstein) of Western modernity. Others consume the story only to retell it in new ways, reshaping its meanings fundamentally to emphasize the agency of the narratee as narrator. Still others draw on archives outside the West to tell counterstories that displace it altogether. Many responses, of course, combine these elements in complex, often contradictory ways.

Three stories illustrate these patterns of response to the metanarrative of Western modernity, patterns we might provisionally call internalization, cannibalization, and translation.

Story 1: Internalization: Shanghai, 2001

I was in Shanghai in 2001, sitting at a round banquet table with some faculty and graduate students from Fudan University and talking about recent changes in Shanghai. Since 1992, the city had experienced what is probably the most rapid urban transformation in history. With the exception of the historic Bund area at the riverfront and one of the old foreign concession areas left standing for tourists, Shanghai had been entirely demolished. Everywhere were now tall buildings—for business, for living, for schools, and for markets and shops. The number of highways crisscrossing the city, with elaborate ramping systems and elevated roads, outpaced even Los Angeles, and a new high-speed monorail—the fastest train in the world—dashed high above the highways in a blur of twinkling neon lights, looking like a people mover out of a science-fiction movie.

Suddenly, one of the graduate students—a tall, thin reed of a woman with an intense expression—burst into impassioned speech, her voice cracking with tears. She said that China was losing its soul to rampant commercialization. She said "Westernization" was leading to "money-means-all." It wasn't Starbucks and McDonalds that she worried about. What angered her was that Westernization had torn down all Shanghai's neighborhoods. And there was more: She said that she loved the music of Beethoven and Brahms but she couldn't understand Chinese music. She said Plato and Aristotle and Hobbes and Locke were important to study. But where in her political science courses was there study of any Chinese political philosophers? Why couldn't China modernize the way Japan had—building what was then the world's second most powerful economy but holding on to its difference, especially its cultural identity as distinct from the rest of the world? I looked around the table of stunned faces. No one said a word.

I decided I would try to defuse the situation by sharing some of my own culture shock in Shanghai—my sense of a city built like a space station—especially Pudong, Shanghai's new skyline across the river that had been fields a mere ten years ago. Shanghai made Manhattan feel provincial, caught in a time warp one hundred years out of date—with its streets of Korean and Italian grocers, its coffee shops and bakeries and pizzerias, its little neighborhoods and parks, and men playing checkers in Washington Square Park.

Figure 3.11 Pudong, Shanghai, China. 2000.

Source: Photo by Pin-chia Feng.

Figure 3.12 Vesuvio Bakery, New York City.

Source: Photo © Greg Gawlowski.

I said to her that I hadn't seen anything in "the West" like Shanghai. It seemed like a futuristic city, like nothing in the United States, like nothing in Europe—especially Europe, in which the past seems always to be around the next corner, in every preserved building, like the ancient columns that poke up among the trees and traffic of modern Rome. I told her what returning to Hong Kong had been like, to the neighborhood where I had lived in 1970. Most of Hong Kong's open markets were gone. Driving down the main streets, I didn't see any stores where people could buy food, although I have been told that little stores still exist in the side streets. I visited some prized public housing, a tall complex whose interiors contained what used to be in the open: wet markets now on the first floor; dry, on the second; and community organizations on the third. On the nearby mainland, the green paddy fields of rice just outside the city were still there, but sprouting up all over were scores of huge apartment buildings, connected by roads through the green fields, with no other kinds of buildings in sight. From my view inside one of the apartments, I could see scores of other apartment towers. Each building housed some five thousand people. Each contained its own school, restaurants, community organizations, swimming pool, and gymnasiums. Vertical villages in the sky.[80]

Nothing like it in "the West," I told the graduate student in Shanghai. Nothing. Why call this new way of living I was seeing in Shanghai and Hong Kong "Westernization"? She couldn't answer and didn't believe me anyway. It is true, I told her, that skyscrapers first appeared in the West, but now, the two tallest buildings in the world are in Taiwan and Malaysia.[81] And Paris still won't sanction a single skyscraper. No effect. I then tried a new line of questions. People who study the culture of everyday life have said, I reminded her, that one of the most profound changes of the past thirty-five years has been the way people listen to music—walking around with earphones, tuned into a private world of beat and lyric. At one time, music was largely a communal experience, but now people can opt for privacy. I asked her: Where did this "modern" form of musical experience come from? "The West," she replied. No, I said. The Walkman came from Japan. The Sony Corporation has led the world in the creation and marketing of electronics for everyday use. The new age of globalization is unthinkable without the innovations of Asia, I said. The formation of today's "modernity" cannot be reduced to the formulaic phrase, "the Westernization of the non-Western world."

None of what I said changed the mind of the passionate graduate student from Shanghai. "The West," a place she had never been, remained on her horizon as a monolithic place to be desired and despised, longed for and feared. She remained convinced that Shanghai's modernization was an imitation of the West, especially of the United States, thus participating in a metonymic chain of fixed associations: urbanization = modernization = Westernization = Americanization.[82] "Be careful that by modernization you don't mean Westernization," Stephen K. Sanderson and Thomas D. Hall write.[83] Easier said than done, I discovered in Shanghai. That chain of associations has been widely internalized, attesting to the ideological force of the metanarrative of Western modernity across the globe.

Story 2: Cannibalization: Brazil, 1920s

"Cannibalism alone unites us. Socially. Economically. Philosophically." So opens "Manifesto Antropófago," the playfully serious manifesto that appeared to acclaim in 1928 by the Brazilian modernist poet and novelist Oswald de Andrade. "Need for the cannibalistic vaccine," he insists. "To maintain our equilibrium, against meridian religions. And against outside inquisitions. . . . Cannibalism. Down with the vegetable elites. . . . those who came here weren't crusaders. They were fugitives from a civilization we are eating, because we are strong and vindictive like the Jabuti."[84] He made anthropophagy the centerpiece of his modernist poetics, influencing a group of Brazilian artists and intellectuals who were determined to enter the arena of modernism on their own terms, not just as imitators of European movements. As Vicky Unruh writes, "Manifesto Antropófago" and his earlier "Manifesto da Poesia Pau-Brasil" (1924) emerged out of a Latin American culture of manifestos that shared rebellions against social and artistic conventions, late-nineteenth-century Spanish American *modernismo*, and European intellectual and aesthetic traditions and vanguards.[85] Oswald de Andrade's manifesto became widely influential as a model for a Latin American cannibalization of European modernity as an act of agency to claim a hybrid modernity of its own.

"Topi or not topi, that is the question," Oswald de Andrade writes, "eating" Hamlet's quandary by invoking his cannibal ancestors, the Tupinamba Indians, who at times ate captured Europeans as a mark of respect and as an effort to gain their power. "Cannibalism," he continues.

"Absorption of the sacred enemy. The human adventure" (38, 43). As John King writes, "For Oswald de Andrade, Brazilian artists should similarly take on the powers of the colonizers, through ingestion, producing in this way an artistic practice that was very much their own."[86] The cultural practice of eating human flesh, particularly the bodies of enemies, involves a symbolic dialogic of making the outside inside. By consuming the other, one both has power over the other and incorporates the other's power into oneself. Difference becomes sameness in the act of eating—as one *corpus* is incorporated into another *corpus*. In cultural terms, the consumption of one culture by another involves the ingestion of the foreign and its digestion (so to speak) into hybrid forms that combine elements of each in a new mix. Anthropophagy, as Fernando J. Rosenberg argues, posed "a radical challenge to the metaphysic of origins" by representing the Latin American artist as "an innocent but savvy savage [who] would swallow and digest for his own benefit whatever is or stands for Western or modern . . . although the act of incorporation would purge it of its foreignness."[87]

Cannibalism as a trope for creativity emphasizes the agency of the local in its ability to devour the influences from afar. It also deliberately plays with the binary of civilized/savage that had structured Europe's early encounters with the inhabitants of the so-called New World during Europe's Age of Discovery. The "primitive" ingests the "civilized" and transforms it by blending it with popular cultural forms of Brazil, becoming in the process a new modernity. In promoting anthropophagy, Oswald de Andrade ironizes the metanarrative of Western modernity, in which the "civilized" swallows up the "primitive." He reverses the Western story of modernist "primitivism" in which the agency to produce art is located only in the Western appropriation of the primitive. Who swallows whom? Where does power lie? Oswald de Andrade asks. Anthropophagy turns the metanarrative of Western modernity on its head. Its story cannibalizes Western modernity to affirm itself as a hybridized point of creative origin.

Story 3: Translation: Goa, 1500s; Leiden, 1700s

The anthropologist Anna L. Tsing retells a story she finds in Richard Grove's *Green Imperialism: Colonial Expansion, Tropical Island Edens, and the Origin of Environmentalism, 1600–1860*:

It is the sixteenth century and the Portuguese are in Goa. A Jewish-Portuguese physician, trained, like other Europeans at the time, in Arab theories of medicine, decides to make his medical science more empirically accurate by tapping sources of local knowledge. Malayali doctors teach him their classification of pharmaceutical plants, which he publishes to great acclaim in Europe. After the Portuguese are kicked out of the area, a Dutchman is inspired to repeat the process. This time Ezhava of the toddy-tapper caste provides the plants and knowledge for publication. Finally, the great classifier Linnaeus reads these books in Leiden in the eighteenth century and unself-consciously adopts South Indian botanical classification into his universalist botanical logic.[88]

For Tsing, this story raises questions first of translation and then more broadly of the West's claims to originality. Written translation from one language into another, Tsing argues, involves a "rewriting of the text in which new meanings are always forged by the interaction.... Meaning arises from the slippages and supplements of the confrontation" (253). In such rewritings, she postulates, "there are no originals, but only a heterogeneous continuum of translations, a continual process of rewriting in which meaning—as well as claims of original and purity—are made" (253). Challenging the older model of translation in which the original language embodies a purity that the target language can never match, Tsing sees translation as the "continuous processes" of intercultural "transition," of transculturation as an intermixing of different agencies who absorb and remake the knowledges of others.

"Where is *Western* knowledge in this story?" Tsing asks (255). The chain of translations from India to Europe that lie behind Linnaeus's classificatory science challenges the story of pure origins, of Linnaeus as "a European original" who creates a "universal" science. The cross-cultural translations out of which his own "translation" emerges are not even between the West and its Other but rather between Arab and Hindu theories of medical botany, she points out. The people involved did not represent the elites of their respective cultures. Theirs was an encounter of "marginals": "The Jewish-Portuguese gathered low-caste, non-Brahminical knowledge, already marginal in its homeland" (256). Tsing narrates these complex global encounters between marginals as a series of translations that foster a rethinking of the historical narratives of Western science and by extension the movement of environmentalism typically credited with Western origins.

Where is Western modernity—specifically the modernity of botanical science—in the story that Tsing retells? Linnaeus's classificatory botanical system has surely been foundational for Western biological science, itself a vital component of Western modernity. But like Western modernity more broadly, Linnaeus's system is not a point of pure origin, not created sui generis as an instance of Western exceptionalism and then disseminated to the rest of the world. Rather, his contribution depends upon transcontinental exchanges fostered by the global ecumene and its empires, including the differently centered modernities of the globe. The point of the story is not to substitute Indian pharmaceutical knowledge for Linnaeus as the origin of biological science but rather to see the cultural translations engendered by traveling cultures in the global modernities of the *longue durée* as essential for the production of any given modernity.

Internalization, cannibalization, translation: three different stories of reader response to the metanarrative of Western modernity as the innovative center that the margins are always already destined to imitate. *Internalization* of the metanarrative obscures the agency of non-Western others, thus misrepresenting or suppressing the innovative agencies of their societies. *Cannibalization* and *translation* resist the narrative of unidirectional influence and tell counterstories that begin with an assumption of the "others'" agency. *Cannibalization* narrates the others' power to consume, transform, and thereby gain power over the center. *Translation* denies the center altogether; while acknowledging differences in power, it suggests that all cultural productions result from a continuing process of intercultural translation across the space/time of human history. As Tsing later argues in *Friction: An Ethnography of Global Connection*, "Cultures are continually co-produced in the interactions I call 'friction': the awkward, unequal, unstable, and creative qualities of interconnections across difference."[89]

And yet, *internalization* contains a story of a powerful psychical reality engendered by the dominating metanarrative of Western modernity, one not fully captured in the counterstories of *cannibalization* and *translation* that Oswald de Andrade and Anna L. Tsing tell. The Shanghai student's angst-ridden cri de coeur taps into an experiential reality born of the inequalities of geopolitical power and the pervasive effects of the West's story of its invention of modernity and mission to spread it around the globe. Postcolonial theorists have variously addressed this experiential dimension of global relations—from Frantz Fanon's diagnosis of the psychopathology of colonialism and Partha Chatterjee's exploration of the colonial subject's ambivalence toward Western modernity to Homi K. Bhabha's notion of "colonial mimicry."[90] As Chatterjee writes, "Ours is the modernity of the once-colonized. The same historical process that has taught us the value of modernity has also made us the victims of modernity. Our attitude to modernity, therefore, cannot but be deeply ambiguous."[91] For Chatterjee, the once-colonized are caught in the problematic of the "nationalist thinking" learned from the West: "how does one accept what is valuable in another's culture without losing one's own cultural identity?"[92] Although Bhabha's concept of colonial mimicry emphasizes how the colonized's imitation of the colonizer denaturalizes the assumption of Western superiority, still, his approach puts the colonized in the position of the imitator, not the originator of modernity. As Dipesh Chakrabarty writes (citing Meaghan Morris), "'The modern' will then continue to be understood . . . 'as a *known history*, something which has *already happened elsewhere*, and which is to be reproduced mechanically or otherwise, with a local context.' This can only leave us with a task of reproducing . . . 'the project of positive unoriginality.'"[93]

The experience of modernity outside the West as "belated," "derivative," or "imitative" leaves the West in place as the site of innovation and suggests that the Rest can be at best a diluted, pale, or secondary version of the "original" modernity. R. Radhakrishnan calls this "the ignominy of derivativeness," finding "epistemological derivativeness . . . particularly offensive and demeaning, since it was at the level of epistemology that colonization achieved its lasting psychic effect."[94] He seeks a new way of thinking about modernity that does not privilege the West: "If postcoloniality has to find a way out of the curse of 'derivativeness,' it can do so only on the basis of a double strategy: redeem itself specifically from the mark of derivativeness by signifying on modernity and the West in a certain way, and engage itself in the multilateral demonstration that there is nothing that is not derivative." He asks, "why does Europe have to be the floating signifier [of modernity] in this entire process of the utopianization of the political-cultural imagination? Why not Asia, why not Africa? . . . If it is indeed the case that there is nothing that is not derivative, why should postcoloniality alone be made to carry derivativeness as a stigma?" (788). Radhakrishnan's questions challenge the dominant story of modernity by suggesting that we become resisting readers, refusing the phenomenological stigma of the derivative and telling counterstories about modernity by radically shifting its epistemological framework as well as its spatial/temporal scale.[95]

CONCLUSION

This chapter is intentionally speculative, by no means definitive. I have provocatively suggested that to fulfill the much-vaunted transnational turn in modernist studies—to expand the geographical scope of the field and prevent its repeated collapse back into the comfort zone of early-twentieth-century Anglo-American and European modernism—we must rethink modernity in profound ways, rupturing familiar pathways of thought. Refusing the conventional association of modernity with a "period" of history, abandoning the desire to define modernity in nominal terms, scalar thinking allows for moving back and forth from the sweep of centuries to specific moments in time and space. In particular, enlarging the spatio/temporal scales to incorporate the last two millennia potentially produces the epistemological shock necessary for rethinking modernity. While Wallerstein's world-system in the *longue durée* has been an important first step, I have argued, we need a longer *durée* than his five hundred years to recognize how, in Gaonkar's words, "modernity is not one, but many."

I have drawn heavily on the *longue durée* work of world historians, retelling, for example, their stories of the Tang/Song Dynasties and the Mongol Empire—the one primarily sedentary; the other, nomadic—to throw into doubt the familiar claims of the West's sui generis invention of modernity, to "provincialize Europe," to echo Gaonkar (and Chakrabarty) once again. Those stories of what I call pre-1500 modernities laid the groundwork for an analysis of the story components of the West's metanarrative of its invention of modernity as the telos of history.

This master narrative—told in celebration and critique alike—remains the ground upon which conventional modernist studies has stood. It has been my intent that seeing its story components—its setting, its themes, its structures, its narrative points of view, and the reader responses it has spawned—potentially lessens the hold of its ideological force by exposing its construction *as a story* that poses as a useful analytic category arbitrarily defined and thus necessarily to be maintained. Using stories to "think through its own self-understandings," I have aimed to disrupt the strong attachment to modernity as conventionally defined and to open up new possibilities for rethinking modernity on a global and transhistorical scale. Doing so, however, does not go far enough. It still leaves untheorized what we mean when we say *modernity* or when we call a particular time/space like the Tang Dynasty or the Mongol Empire a kind of *modernity*. To answer that question, I turn in the next chapter away from stories and toward figures—that is, toward tropic keywords for figuring out the shared meanings of multiple modernities articulated through their differences.

FOUR
FIGURES OF MODERNITY

Relational Keywords

Essential to the idea of modernity is the belief that everything is destined to be speeded up, dissolved, displaced, transformed, reshaped.

—Stuart Hall and Bram Gieben, *Formations of Modernity*

There is a point at which Relation is no longer expressed through a procession of trajectories, itineraries succeeding or thwarting one another, but explodes by itself and with itself, like a network, inscribed in the self-sufficient totality of the world.

—Édouard Glissant, *Poetics of Relation*

If criticism is to be alert to both globalization and to any particular . . . text in its literal meaning of a woven thing . . . [we] might look to . . . enmeshment models, attuned to the "growing *extensity*, *intensity*, and *velocity* of global interactions" and the "deepening enmeshment of the local and global."

—Jahan Ramazani, *A Transnational Poetics*

The stories of different modernities in the *longue durée* in chapter 3 present an opportunity to figure out how they might be related and what they have in common. In this chapter, I turn from *stories* to *figures* of modernity, that is, to figurations that take the form of tropic keywords. Freely adapting Raymond Williams's *Keywords*, I identify a network of word-images I consider keywords for a relational concept of modernity.[1] These keywords, for which I provide their commonly understood definitions, synonyms, and antonyms, establish provisional characteristics that different modernities through time and across space might share, however various their geohistorical articulations, however fluid their categorical boundaries. Such figuring invokes, of course, the definitional problematic of modernity reviewed in earlier chapters: how to stabilize the meaning of the concept sufficiently to foster useful analytic thought without fixing it so rigidly that its limits reinstate the metanarrative of Western modernity or any other form of centric thought. Without some principle of inside/outside, the category qua category collapses into uselessness. To mean anything, *modernity* presumes the *not-modern* at the other end of the spectrum, even if we recognize there may be many points in between.

The dictionaries, to which I turn to begin discussion of each keyword-image, fix meanings of words, even as they track the etymology and evolution of usages, as the *OED* is dedicated to doing. The terms *modern*, *modernity*, and *modernism* in English are rooted in sixth-century usages of the Latin *modernus*, meaning "just now" or "today," the *OED* reports. English usages of *modern* and *modernity* appear in the fifteenth and sixteenth centuries, echoing the French *moderne* and the Italian *moderno* and meaning simply "the present," what exists "now." Moral resonances appear in such seventeenth-century usages as "The women of this Modern Age had need . . . of amendment," in Jonathan Swift's eighteenth-century excoriation of these "quaint modernisms," or even Henry Fielding's justification of his attempt to "modernize the language."[2] In short, the earliest usages of words like *modern*, *modernity*, *modernism*, and *modernization* in English gestured at the figure of the new, the now, the present, the contemporary.

But what does the concept of *modernity* mean beyond the *contemporary* and the *now*, beyond its temporal marker of the NOW, not the past and not the future? And how can we come to some consensual meanings for the term? In chapter 1, I distinguished between nominal and relational modes of definition, resisted a fixed definition of modernity, and advocated instead an interrogation of the radical dissonances in various uses of the terms *modernity*, *modernism*, and *modern*. In chapter 2, I aphoristically characterized modernity in its multiple forms through the use of an experimental chart of fragmentary phrases under the rubrics of Vortex, Rupture,

Hybridity, and the Phenomenology of the New and the Now. In chapter 3, I attacked the nominal definition of modernity as a historical period and told stories of different modernities, to break open the concept of a singular modernity into plural modernities. Here, in chapter 4, I attempt to *figure* out what these diverse modernities have in common—synchronically rather than diachronically. I do so by turning to a network of *figures* of modernity, looking particularly at spatialized tropes embedded in keywords, to delineate provisionally the concepts that underlie specific manifestations of modernity in different times and places. To test the usefulness of these keyword-images, I draw selectively on examples in varying scales, taken from a planetary *longue durée* for illustrative purposes.

Although these keywords for modernity begin in nominal definition, they move through the words' synonyms and antonyms toward a relational mode of definition that resists fixity and works comparatively. Nominal definition, it should be recalled, posits a set of characteristics that a concept exhibits (e.g., modernity = a., b., c.) whereas relational definition describes one thing in (dis)connection with another (e.g., modernity = a. vs. b.). Relational definition is inherently a comparative mode of thinking that fosters the production of general concepts essential for analytic thought.

The idea of multiple modernities rests upon an assumption of comparability based in the dynamic tension between commensurability and incommensurability—that is, in/commensurability, where the slash both connects and separates.[3] Multiple modernities share elements while being historically and spatially specific: thus, their in/commensurability. Fredric Jameson's singular modernity removes itself from the necessity of comparison; Immanuel Wallerstein's diffusionist vision of a single modernity that spreads like a virus throughout the world implies comparative modernities, but with Western modernity as the core standard against which the peripheries and semiperipheries are measured.[4] If we avoid privileging a singular or core modernity, comparison of different modernities for their in/commensurabilities is potentially more productive—*if* the spatio/temporal scale of our archive is sufficiently large to include a substantial variety of instances of modernity across time and throughout space. By identifying what different modernities share, we produce not a single *metanarrative* of modernity but rather a general *concept* that takes particular forms within spatially and historically specific *stories* of modernity.

Such a concept partakes of what Gayatri Chakravorty Spivak has famously called "strategic essentialism," which I here adapt to mean the delineation (drawing/figuring) of a category versatile enough to enable analytic thought or "theory."[5] I also borrow a synchronic, spatialized mode of thought that Michel Foucault believes especially suited to our "present epoch," which I (not he) consider yet another articulation of modernity. "We are in the epoch of simultaneity," he writes in "Of Other Spaces": "We are at a moment, I believe, when our experience of the world is less that of a long life developing through time than that of a network that connects points and intersects with its own skein."[6] This chapter maps a network of keyword-images that, taken together, propose a relational concept of modernity flexible enough to encompass a multiplicity of distinctive modernities while containing enough precision to be useful analytically.

RELATIONAL KEYWORDS OF MODERNITY

Multiple

Rupture : Conjuncture : Vortex

Speed : Acceleration : Velocity

Network : System

Circulation : Route : Contact

Divergence : Discrepance : Fissure

Utopia : Dystopia : Heterotopia

MODERNITY WHICH IS NOT ONE

Multiple: Manifold, many, shared by many.
Synonyms: collective, common, conjoint, conjunct, diverse, heterogeneous, legion,
mutual, polymorphic, shared, united, varied . . .
Antonyms: one, single, singular, sole . . .[7]

The first principle of modernity as concept is to recognize its inherent multiplicity and heterogeneity. Modernity embodies not a universal sameness of nominal characteristics but rather a diversity held together by certain shared qualities through time and space. As noted in chapter 3, Dilip Parameshwar Gaonkar writes, "modernity is not one, but many."[8] But *how* is this "many" conceptualized? Pioneering critiques of the metanarrative of Western modernity have often visualized modernities with the spatial rhetorics inherent in Gaonkar's term *alternative*, using such geographically weighted terms as *marginal, peripheral, uneven, polycentric, conjunctural, disjunctive, divergent, high, low,* and *vernacular* modernities. Even *multiple, minor,* and *other* modernities have spatial overtones. Occasionally, temporal rhetorics enter the picture, as in *early* modernity, or in referencing the other stages of modernity, as in *middle* or *late* modernity. The concept of *discrepant* modernities originates in sound imagery, suggesting discordant, unharmonious, or conflicting modernities; *vernacular* invokes spoken language. But overwhelmingly, the starting point for thinking globally about multiple modernities is spatial, as if different modernities could be imagined on vertical/horizontal axes or located on a global map.

This spatialized pluralization of modernity has its critics, of course, Jameson in *A Singular Modernity* preeminent among them. "Talk about 'alternate' or 'alternative' modernities," Jameson believes, allows people to avoid asking "serious political and economic, systemic questions" by focusing on the "cultural":

> Everyone knows the formula by now: this means that there can be a modernity for everybody which is different from the standard or hegemonic Anglo-Saxon model. Whatever you dislike about the latter, including the subaltern position it leaves you in, can be effaced by the reassuring and "cultural" notion that you can fashion your own modernity differently, so that there can be a Latin-American kind, or an Indian kind or an African kind, and so forth. Or you can follow Samuel Huntington's lead and recast all this in terms of essentially religious varieties of culture: a Greek or Russian Orthodox modernity, a Confucian modernity, and so on to a Toynbeean number. But this is to overlook the other fundamental meaning of modernity which is that of a worldwide capitalism itself. The standardization projected by capitalist globalization in this third or late

stage of the system casts considerable doubt on all these pious hopes for cultural variety in a future world colonized by a universal market order.[9]

Jameson's reductionistic economism is evident in his disdain for "cultural" explanations, his characterization of multiple modernities as "pious hopes," and his colonialist dismissal of Latin American or Indian or African modernities.

Jameson is not alone in attacking the concept of multiple modernities as a way to develop global understanding, though his scornful dismissal and what some might call "vulgar Marxism" is not characteristic of more thoughtful critiques. In advocating for more humanities attention to Wallerstein's sociohistorical work, Bruce Robbins, for example, argues that the term "alternative modernities" has functioned as "a slogan that has had all the success in the transnational zone of the humanities that world-systems theory itself has not."[10] Timothy Mitchell objects that "the language of alternative modernities can imply an almost infinite play of possibilities, with no rigorous sense of what, if anything, gives imperial modernity its phenomenal power of replication and expansion."[11] Nirvana Tanoukhi recognizes that as an analytic framework, "alternative modernity" has "proved immensely fertile," but she worries that it can also disguise "a real dissonance between an academic thesis that celebrates the periphery's specificity, and a local outlook that experiences 'specificity' as a mark of inferiority," or as a "symptom (or even the cause) of permanent economic troubles."[12] Alluding to a familiar definitional anxiety, Frederick Cooper worries that the multiplication of modernities illustrates the "vanishing analytic utility of the term in the plural." "As the modernities proliferate," he concludes, "the capacity to distinguish modernity from anything else is diminished."[13]

There is no doubt that the various discourses of multiple modernities can be deployed for nefarious purposes. Governments in China, Singapore, and Iran, for example, have appealed directly to the concept of an alternate modernity of their own in a global landscape of multiple modernities to justify their particular brand of authoritarianism, as I discussed in chapter 1. It is misleading as well to separate the cultural from the political and economic, as to some extent Gaonkar does in his introduction to *Alternative Modernities*. He makes a sharp distinction between "societal modernization" and "cultural modernity," which he defines as "the aesthetic wing" or the "other modernity" that arises in reaction against modernization (1–2). In my view, the cultural, political, and economic are dynamically intersecting systems that are articulated in and through one another, not separately or necessarily antagonistically. Modernisms are, I have argued, the expressive domains of any given modernities, not a gadfly to them.

However, my concern here is to sort through the implications of these variously spatialized rhetorics of multiple modernities. Which ones end up reinstating the metanarrative of Western modernity, and which ones break through to a new kind of planetary thinking about global modernities? Which ones reconfirm the centrality of Europe, and which provincialize it, as Dipesh Chakrabarty aims to do in *Provincializing Europe*?[14]

∞ ∞ ∞

> How to fulfill the promise of the plural: that is the question.
> Look to the geography of adjectives.

∞ ∞ ∞

Adjectives modifying modernity or even pluralized modernities are potentially just that—words that modify, that is, qualify the main noun, which remains in place. They are also frequently geographical grammars that spatialize modernity. Modifiers like *alternative, other, minor, marginal, peripheral,* and even *early* do not effectively challenge the metanarrative of Western modernity. They maintain it; indeed, they need it to make any sense whatsoever. Alternative to what standard of measure? Minor to what major? Peripheral to what core? Margin to what center? Early to what later period? And so forth. These terms operate out of the core/periphery binary that underlies Wallerstein's Eurocentric world-systems theory. The existence of a periphery, an Outside, always presumes a core, an Inside. The logic of the Western colonialist diffusionism that J. M. Blaut sees at the heart of the ideological formation of the *idea* of the West as the inventor of modernity operates as well with adjectives like *alternative* or *minor*. While aimed at critique of Western hegemony, such adjectives end up confirming it.

In his introduction to *Alternative Modernities*, Gaonkar exhibits the logic of a Wallersteinian core/periphery as much as he resists Wallerstein's dismissal of cultural dimensions of modernity and as much as he insists on alternative, multiple, and hybridized modernities in the postcolonial period and globalized present. For him, Western modernity came first, and alternative modernities are in some sense always already reactive to it:

> Born in and of the West some centuries ago under relatively specific sociohistorical conditions, modernity is now everywhere. It has arrived not suddenly but slowly, bit by bit, over the longue durée—awakened by contact; transported through commerce, administered by empires, bearing colonial inscriptions; propelled by nationalism; and now increasingly steered by global media, migration, and capital. And it continues to "arrive and emerge," as always in opportunistic fragments accompanied by utopic rhetorics, but no longer from the West alone, although the West remains the major clearinghouse of global modernity.
>
> (1)

Echoing Chakrabarty, Gaonkar argues that "One can provincialize Western modernity only by thinking through and against its self-understandings, which are frequently cast in universalist idioms" (15). Like Homi K. Bhabha's concept of colonial mimicry, provincializing Western modernity involves thinking through and against it "with a difference—a difference that would destabilize the universalist idioms, historicize the contexts, and pluralize the experiences of modernity" (Chakrabarty, 15). For Gaonkar, alternative modernities are the construct of the present as variations on a Western genealogy. They "cannot escape the legacy of Western discourse on modernity. Whoever elects to think in terms of alternative modernities (irrespective of one's location) must think with and also against the tradition of reflection that stretches from Marx and Weber through Baudelaire and Benjamin to Habermas, Foucault, and many other Western (born or trained) thinkers" (Gaonkar, 14–15).

In positing a prior genealogy of Western modernity with which all others must engage, Gaonkar remains caught within the ideological system he would challenge. His critique is entangled in what R. Radhakrishnan calls the "curse" of derivativeness, the psychology of belatedness, as discussed in chapter 3. Without large-scale world history, without a globalized *longue durée* before 1500, Gaonkar grants Western modernity an originary status that recapitulates the master story the West tells about itself. So too for the story he tells of modernism and its recent alternative modernisms. For him, modernism—that is, the "cultural modernity" that resists modernization—begins with Baudelaire, who "was the first to offer a poetics of civil society" in the metropolitan center of the West: Paris (5). Baudelaire represents Gaonkar's ground zero for modernism, recapitulating such master narratives of modernist studies as Peter Nicholls's *Modernisms: A Literary Guide*, which also identifies the beginnings of modernism in Baudelaire. Gaonkar's plural modernisms are more global than Nicholls, for whom the locus of modernism is the European continent, with some scant attention to London, Ireland, and the United States and a single chapter focused on women modernists called "At a Tangent: Other Modernisms."[15] But the logic of core/periphery, of origin/derivation, operates as fully in Gaonkar's formulation of alternative modernities as it does in Nicholls's more conventional and limited account of pluralized modernisms.

The adjective *minor* has perhaps more currency than *alternative* as a descriptor for other modernities, in part because the term has a strong history rooted in the work of Gilles Deleuze and Félix Guattari on "minority literature" and adapted for postcolonial and transnational studies, as evident in such influential volumes as *The Nature and Context of Minority Discourse*, edited by Abdul R. JanMohamed and David Lloyd, and *Minor Transnationalism*, edited by Françoise Lionnet and Shu-mei Shih.[16] *Minor* in this framework is based fundamentally in a critique of Western hegemony (whether explicitly "modern" or not), from the shared standpoint of those the West dominates—ethnic minorities, post/colonial subjects, and/or the Third World specifically. As JanMohamed and Lloyd define it, "minority discourse" means "a theoretical articulation of the political and cultural structures that connect different minority cultures in their subjugation and opposition to the dominant culture. This definition is based on the principle that minority groups, despite all the diversity and specificity of their cultures, share the common experience of domination and exclusion by the majority" (ix). Their use of the term *minor* not only relies on a post-1500 spatio/temporal scale (like Wallerstein) but also stretches the signifier beyond useful limits. Just as feminists have challenged the use of the term *minority* to signify women, who outnumber men, just as racial minorities in the United States have resisted the term *minority* for people of color, who, globally speaking, outnumber whites, so *minority discourse* as JanMohamed and Lloyd deploy it ends up suppressing historical realities. So too *minor modernities* continually signals the ongoing hegemony of the *major*, that is Western, modernity.

Perhaps to avoid the problems of JanMohamed and Lloyd's formulation, Lionnet and Shih further develop this concept of *minor* to focus on the relations among minor locations, not always their relationship to the center. "We study the *center* and the *margin*," they write, "but rarely examine the relationships among different *margins*" (2, my emphasis). Using Deleuze and Guattari's concept of the *rhizome* in *A Thousand Plateaus* and Édouard Glissant's notion of relationality in *Poetics of Relation*, Lionnet and Shih move beyond the transnational binaries of above/below and global/local to focus on "minor-to-minor networks that circumvent the major altogether" (8). "Critiquing the center, when it stands as an end in itself," they write, "seems only to enhance it; the center remains the focus and the main object of study" (3). Although they don't address modernity directly, their focus on transnational minor-to-minor networks represents a sharp departure from Gaonkar's belief that study of alternative modernities must begin in an examination of their engagement with Western modernity. The adjective *minor* in Lionnet and Shih's work clearly signals their desire to keep analysis of hegemonic power fully in play. However, the adjective *minor* is inevitably haunted by its binary opposite *major*, thus perpetuating the vertical structures of *center/margin* they intend to supplant with horizontal, global networks.

If adjectives like *alternative, minor, other, peripheral,* and *marginal* reinforce the metanarrative of Western modernity even when their intent is explicitly to undermine it, what about adjectives like *multiple, conjunctural, divergent, discrepant, uneven, polycentric, multinodal,* and *recurrent*? In my view, each of these latter adjectives avoids the problems of *alternative, minor, marginal,* and so forth—but in different ways. *Multiple* modernities is a neutral term. Like the pluralization of modernity (or modernism), *multiple* simply indicates that there is more than one modernity—presumably, modernities that are "site specific" (Gaonkar, 17) and time specific. By itself, *multiple* says nothing about the spatio/temporal locations of these multiple modernities and nothing about the distinctions, linkages, or power relations among them. As such, *multiple modernities* contains the same potential problem as the term *pluralism*—the danger of overlooking or decontextualizing differences, of obscuring how power works among them.

Related adjectives begin to address the problems of *multiple*'s seeming neutrality. *Divergent* suggests distinctiveness, difference among modernities; *conjunctural* connotes relations or intersections among them—but still, no particular indication of the nature of those differences and relations, particularly the dynamics and distributions of power. *Discrepant* and *uneven*, however, connote differential, asymmetrical power relations among different modernities—some more privileged, others less advantaged. *Discrepant* modernities, for example, might describe the different nature, power, and prestige of London's and Calcutta's modernities at the height of the Raj, yet their metropolitan modernities are co-constitutive, emergent out of the asymmetrical power relations of empire that affect each differently.

Polycentric and *multinodal* suggest power linkages differently. The globe, these adjectives suggest, has multiple centers or nodes of power, not one. Positing different cores existing synchronically within a single time period fundamentally rewrites the diffusionist metanarrative of Western modernity, along with a Wallersteinian core/periphery/semiperiphery model. *Recurrent* modernities signifies a multiplicity over time, also a pattern of historical repetition with a difference. *Recurrent* suggests little about global synchronicity or about relational power among coexisting modernities. Rather, it connotes a return to periods of heightened change, different in their specifics for each instance but sharing some structural similarities.

All of these adjectives signifying multiplicity are potentially useful for challenging Western modernity as the universal form of modernity. Some adjectives, however, are more useful than others. Just as words like *female pilot* or *male nurse* fail to change the gender assumptions of the unmarked default positions of *pilot* or *nurse*, adjectives like *alternative, other, minor, marginal*, and *peripheral* budge the singular story of modernity, but they do so without significantly displacing the originary centrality of the Western *core*. Adjectives like *multiple, recurrent, polycentric, uneven*, and so forth potentially decenter the Western metanarrative, make Western modernity one among many interrelated globally. But none of these adjectives are sufficient in themselves. They are only adjectives, after all.

∞ ∞ ∞

How to *figure* recurrent global modernities: that is the question.
Look to relational keyword-images.

∞ ∞ ∞

RUPTURE : CONJUNCTURE : VORTEX

Rupture: Break, burst.
Synonyms: break, bust, cleave, cleft, crack, disrupt, disunite, divide, erupt, puncture, rend, rip, separate, sever, shatter, snap, split, sunder, tear . . .
Antonyms: close, complete, join, make whole, mend, unite . . .

Conjuncture: Combination of circumstances or events usually producing a crisis.
Synonyms: boiling point, breaking point, clutch, crisis, crossroads, crunch, emergency, extremity, flashpoint, head, tinderbox, zero hour . . .
Antonyms: detachment, disconnection, disunion, division, isolation, separation . . .

Vortex: Eddy; whirling mass of water, air, or fire; any activity, situation, or way of life regarded as irresistibly engulfing.
Synonyms: cyclone, gyre, maelstrom, spiral, whirlwind . . .
Antonyms: calmness, serenity, smoothness, stasis . . .

Modernity involves a powerful vortex of geohistorical conditions that coalesce to produce sharp ruptures from the past that range widely across various sectors of a given society and open up new futures. The velocity, acceleration, and dynamism of change across a wide spectrum of societal dimensions are key components of modernity—change that interweaves the economic, political, technological, cultural, familial, aesthetic, epistemological, and symbolic. Such changes engulf, break the fabric of the usual or normal, potentially take the form of crisis. Their form is experienced relationally, contrasting the present with the past. They often result from the intensification of intercultural contact zones, whether produced through conquest, vast migrations of people (voluntary or forced), or relatively peaceful commercial traffic and technological or cultural exchange. Indeed, heightened hybridizations, jarring juxtapositions, and increasingly porous borders both characterize modernity and help bring it into being. Modernity in these terms appears in multiple forms—as a period or epoch; a condition of life or of the social order; a project, cause, or idea; a subjectivity or phenomenology; a pattern of representations.

Modernity has a self-reflexive, experiential dimension. It generates an awareness of change that produces a gamut of sensations from exhilaration, hope, and embrace of the new to nostalgia, displacement, and despair—a range that depends in part on the configurations of power and the utopic versus dystopic directions of change. The speed and scope of widespread transformation often leads to what Marshall Berman calls (citing Marx) the sensation that "all that is solid melts into air" and what I called the phenomenology of the new and the now in chapter 2.[17] People enmeshed in modernity, Berman writes, "are moved at once by a will to change—to transform themselves and their world—and by a terror of disorientation and disintegration, of life falling apart" (13). The realm of expressive/symbolic culture—the verbal, visual, aural, kinetic, graphic, performative, ritual, philosophical, and architectural arts—constitutes the prime arena for representing this self-reflexive dimension of modernity as its modernisms.

Consider, for example, Bimala, the dis/loyal wife swept into the fervor of the anticolonial nationalism of early-twentieth-century Bengal in Rabindranath Tagore's *Home and the World* (1916). She voices the experience of modernity as a simultaneous conjuncture of conditions that make for a vortex of rupture: "The new epoch came in like a flood, breaking down the dykes and sweeping all our prudence and fear before it. We had no time even to think about, or understand, what had happened, or what was about to happen."[18] She refers, significantly, not to the British rulers bringing "modernity" to "backward" Bengal but rather to the rupture of both colonizing and colonized social orders, from the economic and political to the domestic and cultural domains—all encapsulated in her leaving the *zenana* to participate in the Swadeshi movement, simultaneously enthralled by its charismatic leader and inspired by the vision of a free Indian nation reliant on its own indigenous goods. The mantra of this pre-Gandhian movement—*Bande Martaram*/Hail Mother—crystallizes the anticolonial image of Mother India and encapsulates in Tagore's novel India's contradictory modernity in the early twentieth century, one that blended British and Indian forms of nationalism, economics, activism, and feminism.

Modernity, as a relational temporal logic, has a complex and contradictory relationship to its seeming opposite—the past, often constituted as "tradition." Modernity and tradition are relational concepts that modernity produces to cut itself off from the past, to distinguish the "now" from the "then." As Rita Felski writes, "To be modern is to reject the dead weight of tradition, to respond to the siren call of the new and the now. It is to see oneself as a creature of contingency and flux, no longer beholden to the scripts of the past."[19] However, as she points out, this insistence on the new and the now often covers over the continuities with the past, the repetitions of both macro- and microlevel histories (69–70). Even Pound's famous dictum in the title of his 1934 book—*Make It New*—is not a repudiation of the past but rather a call to reinvent the past anew, in the "now," as Eric Hayot points out.[20] As I discussed in chapter 1, Paul de Man goes even further (invoking Nietzsche) to suggest that modernity fosters "a ruthless forgetting" of the past: "Modernity exists in the form of a desire to wipe out whatever came earlier."[21] The past that is repressed, that will not be remembered, comes back to haunt and trouble the present. Buried within the radical ruptures from the past are hidden continuities—all the things that refuse to change or cannot change, often having to do with uneven distributions of power and violent histories. In my view, however, "tradition" is a constitutive part of modernity, invented and named at the moment those who perceive it regard themselves as being cut off from it. Modernity invents tradition, suppresses its own continuities with the past, and often produces nostalgia for what has seemingly been lost.[22]

Modernity's dislocating break with the past also engenders a radical reaction in the opposite direction. As a result, periods of modernity often contain tremendous battles between "modernizers" and "traditionalists," those who promote the modern and those who want to restore an imagined and often idealized past. Indeed, the struggle between modernizing and traditionalizing forces within a given society is itself a defining characteristic of modernity. The conflict over the education of girls in Afghanistan—pitting the "traditionalist" Taliban and the "modernizing" reform movements against each other—is an instance of Afghanistan's particular modernity, which is entwined with the global politics of the late twentieth century and permeated with a long history of multiple imperial conquests. In this sense, past-oriented traditionalism is as much a feature of modernity as modernization. As Chakrabarty suggests in his discussion of elite Bengalis of late-nineteenth-century Calcutta, the modernity of such writers as Bankim Chandra Chatterjee and Rabindranath Tagore combines their urbanized colonial existence with their evocations of the pastoral Bengal village as the "image of Mother Bengal" representing "a land of bounty," accompanied by the "idea of a Bengali 'folk'" that contrasts with the artificiality of Calcutta.[23]

Traditionalism, moreover, can be mobilized for different purposes—to resist changes that take away the privileges of some in opening up possibilities for others, to challenge the new inequities of modernization, or to enable survival of those whom modernity marginalizes. Faced with economic, political, and economic annihilation in the name of modernity, indigenous peoples, for example, often insist upon their "traditions" (whether understood as fixed or ever-changing) as the foundation of their resistance, survival, and healing, as the novels of such writers as Leslie Marmon Silko, Louise Erdrich, and Linda Hogan suggest.[24] The Maroons of eastern Jamaica, to cite another example, showcase their "traditions" of eighteenth-century ambush dances for non-Jamaican audiences as an instance of their will to survive as Maroons through their entrance into the global economy of tourism.[25] The recognition of, need for, and deployment of "tradition" is often a defining component of any given modernity.

Given these complex mixtures of contesting modernities, the notion of postcolonial modernities as purely derivative of Western modernity contains an implicit and misleading binary that sets up the West as modern and the Rest as traditional, struggling to reject its traditionalism in favor of becoming modern, which by a subtle metonymic slide is the equivalent of becoming Western. While there is no doubt that many colonial subjects experience the humiliations and ambivalence of this modernity/tradition opposition, this phenomenological dimension of modernity reflects the ideological force of the diffusionist metanarrative and obscures both the traditionalisms within the West and the indigenous modernities outside the West. Instead, we need to look for the interplay of "modernity" and "tradition" *within* each location, that is, within both the West and the regions outside the West, as a feature of modernity itself. We need, in short, to examine how "tradition" is deployed within a particular modernity as one of its key features.

SPEED : ACCELERATION : VELOCITY

Speed:	Rate of motion, often fast.
Synonyms:	acceleration, hurry, hustle, liveliness, momentum, quickness, rapidity, rush, swiftness, urgency, velocity . . .
Antonyms:	motionlessness, slowness, stasis . . .
Acceleration:	Increasing speed.
Synonyms:	hastening, hurrying, intensification, quickening, speeding up, spurring, stepping up, stimulation . . .
Antonyms:	deceleration, retardation, slowing down . . .
Velocity:	Swiftness.
Synonyms:	alacrity, celerity, dispatch, fleetness, hurry, hustle, impetus, momentum, pace, quickness, rapidity . . .
Antonyms:	slowness, sluggishness . . .

The speed of change—the acceleration and velocity of mobility—is, I posit, at the definitional core of the concept of modernity uniting the disparate modernities through time and across space.²⁶ Modernity *revs* the engine of ongoing change. It heightens, intensifies, accelerates ordinary movement. It turns evolution into revolution, change into rupture. The speed of modernity shatters, induces the phenomenology of the new. The intensity of change—the sheer rapidity of civilizational transformations—distinguishes the *modern* from periods of ordinary evolution. The intensity of intercultural mixing enabled by speeding mobilities of all kinds produces jarring effects, defamiliarizes, calls into question the inevitability of the way things are. It loosens fixities, opens new pathways of possibility. It disorients and displaces. Such speed often produces vertigo: for some, a sensation of new freedoms; for others, a feeling of the world split open.

Such accelerating change often comes on the heels of violence, like the swift armies of the Mongols that wrought such destruction and then brought about Pax Mongolica and an unprecedented level of exchange to the Afro-Eurasian world. And such change creates its opposite as a constitutive part of modernity: the drive to invent "tradition" to compensate for loss, a nostalgic desire for a return to imagined or idealized homelands of stability, the need for certainty in the face of indeterminacy and too-rapid change.

Heightened mobilities of all kinds are markers for the emergence of a particular modernity or network of polycentric modernities. Glissant's "poetics of relation" presume a "speeding up of relationships" in modernity, especially as "speed becomes concentrated" in cities from New York to Lagos, an intensification that "explodes" (*Poetics*, 141). In *Modernity at Large*, Arjun Appadurai writes that "the sheer speed, scale, and volume of . . . these flows are now so great that the disjunctures have become central to the politics of global culture."²⁷ In *The Turbulence of Migration*, Nikos Papastergiadis tracks "the restless trajectories of modernity," arguing that global migration is constitutive of modernity and that the "flows of cultural change" should be examined "from at least two perspectives: the movement of people, and the circulation of symbols."²⁸ Stuart Hall and Bram Gieben identify modernity with acceleration of restless movement:

> It sometimes seems that what is quintessentially "modern" is not so much any one period or any particular form of social organization so much as the fact that a society becomes seized with and pervaded by this idea of ceaseless development, progress and dynamic change; by the restless

forward movement of time and history; by what some theorists call the compression of time and space.... It is the shift—materially and culturally—into this new conception of social life which is the real transition to modernity.[29]

It is no accident, I believe, that new technologies of movement for goods, people, money, militaries, information, knowledge, and the arts are typically associated with various modernities in the *longue durée*. Witnessing ever-faster means for human mobility on show at the Paris Exhibition of 1900, Henry Adams metaphorizes the new harnessing of nature's vast energy into machines in the figure of the *dynamo*, with its power to combust and explode.[30] In *The Speed Handbook: Velocity, Pleasure, Modernism*, Enda Duffy focuses his study of the epistemology of speed in a particular case—the modernism of late European imperialism. Taking his cue from the futurists' fascination with the racing car, Duffy writes that "much modernism is about human movement," as "speed itself becomes the very narrative heft of much modernist artistic production" (10). He finds in the early-twentieth-century phenomenology of speed a "gyrating dynamism" and suggests that speed itself has "its incitements, its rules, its practices, and its terrors improvised for it in a few years—the modernist moment."[31]

Like many, Adams, Duffy, Appadurai, and Papastergiadis link their arguments about modernity and speed specifically to the twentieth century. But in *Tracking Modernity: India's Railway and the Culture of Mobility*, Marian Aguiar turns to nineteenth-century colonial modernity in India, suggesting that the increased mobility of trains enabled both British rule and rising Indian nationalism.[32] Zygmunt Bauman broadens the temporal frame for modernity's speeding mobilities even further. In *Culture as Praxis*, he writes that

> Modern history has been marked by the constant progress of the means of transportation, and so the volume of mobility. Transport and travel was the field of particularly radical and rapid change.... The mark of modernity is increased volume and range of mobility and so, inevitably, the weakening of the hold of locality and the local networks of interaction.[33]

I suggest that we enlarge the spatio/temporal scale even further to include all those periods of human history in which accelerating velocities intensified the disjunctives of rapid change. In the world history of recurrent modernities, relatively sudden advances in the technologies of movement have affected a broad spectrum of societal domains. Accelerating physical movements across land and water often stimulated intensified commercial and/or military contact, resulting in a particularized form of modernity: for example, the domestication of horses (also camels, elephants, etc.); the invention of the wheel; paved or caravan roadways; boats, canals, moveable sails; railroads; clipper and steam ships; and trams, subways, buses, cars, trucks, airplanes, jets, and spaceships. Evolving technologies of energy that allowed for the harnessing of fire, water, wind, electricity, petroleum, and the atom sharply increased human mobilities.

Less tangible technologies of movement have had no less wide-scale influence in producing strikingly rapid societal change. The Dutch, for example, whose modernity never involved an industrial revolution, innovated banking and financial systems such as stock and futures markets that made the Netherlands sudden leaders in a new commercial world system in the seventeenth century. The British development of insurance allowed shipping to increase exponentially in the seventeenth and eighteenth centuries, because of reduced risk. And the computer technologies of the late twentieth century made for instantaneous transfers of money globally and the creation of wealth through finance rather than manufacture.

New technologies of representation and communication have accelerated the speed of traveling ideas and knowledge revolutions. The creation of different modes of symbolic representation, for example, sped the flow of cultural and commercial traffic—from pictographic and alphabetic systems to kipu and wampum; from moveable type to the typewriter and computer; from print culture to the photograph, telegraph, telephone, radio, motion pictures, television, and the Internet. The digital revolution has produced informational matrices that operate through cyberspace at scarcely imaginable speeds.

These technologies are nodal points in polycentric and recurrent modernities, contributing to the acceleration of change often by intensifying the circulation of peoples, goods, money, militaries, cultural practices, information, and ideas. And they are always entangled with distributions of power, often violent, sometimes peaceful, typically a mixture of the utopic and dystopic in their short- and long-term effects. My point is not to identify modernity with any one of these technologies, nor to define the good and bad effects of them, but rather to shift the emphasis in thinking about modernity away from specific institutions like capitalism or the nation-state, away from specific locations like the West, and away from nominally defined historical periods like the Industrial Revolution or the Enlightenment. Instead, I suggest we look to spatio/temporal intensifications or breakthroughs in movement, mobility, and the speed of change across the *longue durée*.

NETWORK : SYSTEM

Network: A system of connections.
Synonyms: chain, circuitry, complex, contacts, conjuncture, crisscross, ecumene, enmeshment, fabric, grid, grill, interaction, interconnection, intersection, interweaving, labyrinth, linkage, matrix, maze, mesh, net, nexus, nodal, polycentrism, rhizome, structure, weaving, web, wiring . . .
Antonyms: delinkage, disconnection, fragmentation, isolation, simple, disunity . . .

System: A group of interacting, interrelated, or interdependent elements forming a complex whole.
Synonyms: arrangement, classification, combination, complex, fixed order, interaction, organization, philosophy, scheme, setup, structure, theory, totality . . .
Antonyms: disorder, fragmentation, separation . . .

Modernity is constituted through networks, geographies of connection, and systems of interaction and linkage. The global ecumene has developed ever larger and more complex systems of enmeshment through space in the *longue durée* of human history. Polycentric and recurrent modernities within that ecumene flare up as the pace of change accelerates, often through a multiplication of contact zones, arenas where different cultures collide, clash, and blend as a result of wars, conquest, technological advances, and increased trade. In "Cartographies of Connection," Kären Wigen notes that attention to "large-scale movements and processes" in the "global circulation of people and ideas, money and microbes, social movements and institutional responses" necessitates an understanding of networks, what she calls "a geography of interaction."[34] "Contact among cultures is one of the givens of modernity," Glissant writes. Large-scale patterns of encounter produce an "accelerated evolution," an "aesthetics of rupture and connection," and "new zones of relational community" in contacts that are often brutal, explosive, and lethal in the concentrated speed of "creolization," which he defines as the interference, shock, harmonies, and disharmonies between the cultures of the world, in the realized totality of the world" (*Poetics*, 151, 141, 142).

Such networks exist as patterns of encounter that are simultaneously rhizomatic and systemic. Rethinking modernity as a feature of a heightened global ecumene requires a blend of network theory and systems theory. Although networks contain systems and systems involve networks, network theory and systems theory enable rethinking modernity somewhat differently. Network theory, as George P. Landow reviews it, relies on a series of keywords that recur in theorists from Barthes, Foucault, and Bakhtin to Derrida and Deleuze and Guattari—words with strongly figural weight such as *link* (*liaisons*), *web* (*toile*), *network* (*rèseau*), *interwoven* (*s'y tissent*), *rhizome, node, path*, and *matrix*.[35] Albert-László Barabási writes in *Linked* that "Networks are present everywhere. All we need is an eye for them." He begins with the early network of Christian communities that Paul established across the Mediterranean and ends with the Internet.[36] Manuel Castells, in contrast, argues that the rapid innovations of the Information Revolution have created a complex, relatively nonhierarchical "network society" based on information diffusion that supplants the technological mobilities produced by the steam engine and electricity of the Industrial Revolution.[37] In the humanities, the Deleuzian/Guattarian *rhizome* has been particularly influential, suggesting connections that are random, fragmented, nonhierarchical, decentered, or subterranean, especially as

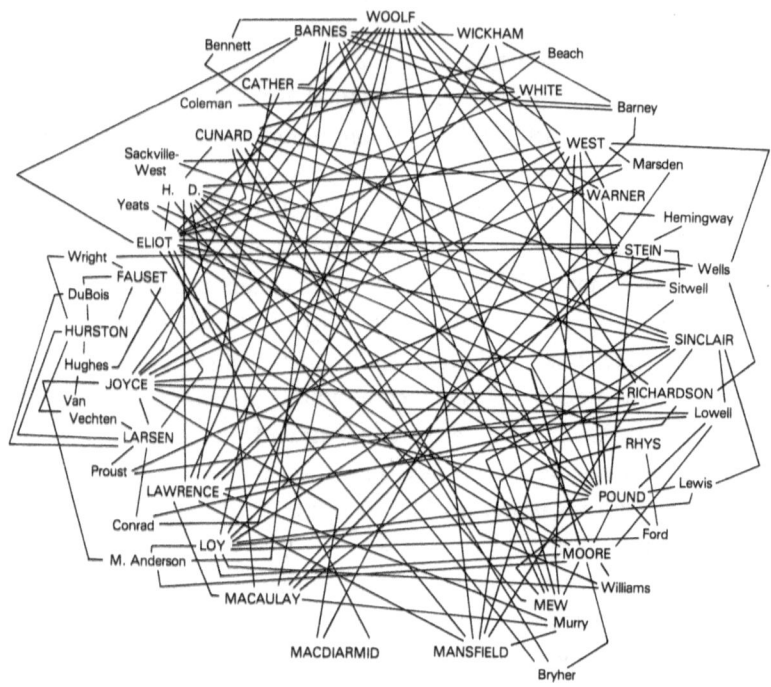

Figure 4.1 "A Tangled Mesh of Modernisms."

Source: From the introduction to *The Gender of Modernism*, by Bonnie Kime Scott, p. 10; used courtesy of Indiana University Press.

they accompany the ruptures of global modernities.[38] Bonnie Kime Scott's modernist map of early-twentieth-century European and Anglo-American connectivities captures the rhizomatic quality of the network:

However, the network geographies that enable such encounters are also part of an interlocking world system with different centers of heightened exchange. Networks, I would suggest in contrast to Deleuze and Guattari, are often polycentric and hierarchical—benefiting some, leaving out others.[39] There are systemic and structural factors of commerce, empire, interstate relations, religion, technology, language, and other cultural forms that affect the global connections of polycentric modernities at any given point in time. Niklas Luhmann, the German social theorist whose work is foundational in social systems theory, deemphasizes human agencies (so central to network theory) and approaches any social formation (from religion, to social movements, the arts, etc.) as part of a complex set of structured processes by which different systems influence one another.[40] Wallerstein's world-system theory, with its logic of core/periphery/semiperiphery, is a form of systems theory that emphasizes structural hierarchies and inequalities.

Modernity—with its heightened mobilities and accelerating ruptures—incorporates both the fragmentary and the systemic. As both network and system, modernity is the matrix of culture squared, exponentially intensified by forces of rapid change, be they military, commercial, technological, cultural, or demographic. In *Culture as Praxis*, Bauman distinguishes between concepts of culture as a "matrix" versus culture as a self-enclosed "system," complete unto itself (xx–xxix). Anticipating, perhaps, Pierre Bourdieu's concept of the *habitus*, Bauman's cultural matrix posits multiple centers and systems within the matrix interacting with one another. The matrix implies an image of dynamism and mobility; it assumes a network of moving parts and intersections of different arcs or trajectories. Some of the specialized meanings of the term *matrix* are suggestive. In biology, a matrix is the liminal substance between cells that links them together. The matrix of a computer is a circuit of component parts that act as relays for translating one code into another.[41] Any given modernity is a dynamic network of interactive centers and relational mobilities; its speed of change turns the matrix of culture into an accelerating vortex.

In spatial terms, the systemic and random networks of transformative change are located in both nodal and mobile areas of the global ecumene. For many, the city is a quintessential *modern* phenomenon, with urbanization (even in its earliest forms in Mesopotamia, Egypt, and the Indus Valley) often regarded as synonymous with *modernization*. Metropolitan centers are crossroads where the outflows and inflows of ideas, peoples, and goods produce the vortex effect of transformative change across a spectrum of commercial, technological, political, cultural, and aesthetic practices. Great cosmopolitan cities are conjunctural points within a larger network, but what enables their dynamism are the technologies of movement that connect them. In the *longue durée*, what André Gunder Frank calls "pivot" or "fulcral" cities linked continents and civilizations through the centuries and played key roles in periods of heightened change—cities like Istanbul, Alexandria, and Baghdad linking Venice as the gateway to Europe and Chang'an as an entry into China during the heyday of the Silk Road, for example. On a smaller temporal scale, cities on all continents—from Rio de Janeiro to Lisbon, from Toledo to Baghdad, from Lagos to London, from Beirut to Paris, from Timbuktu to Cairo—have risen relatively quickly to become cosmopolitan cauldrons of intense interculturalism linked through global networks of various kinds.

Major cities, however, are not the only places where wide-scale change can suddenly take hold in polycentric networks and systems of power relations. The case of the Mongol Empire provides a forceful counterexample, along with earlier and later instances of conquering nomadic peoples from the Eurasian steppes. Cities and steppes are different, indeed contrasting locations within global networks, constituting different modernities. To them, I would add the archipelagos, oceans, land-based waterways, and roadways as constitutive of networked modernities—each facilitating enhanced mobility in different ways. Glissant's articulation of an archipelagic modernity asks us to think about global modernities as "islands" linked by lines of movement among them. Archipelagos are what he calls "composite" or "creolized cultures" fostered by the waterways that connect rather than being rooted or atavistic cultures focused on a unique genesis or filiation.[42] Glissant's model for archipelagic modernity is the Caribbean, a crossroads of conquest, genocide, enslavement, commerce, and hybridity out of which he extrapolates a relational way of thinking about the globe.[43] There are other such archipelagoes, however, that have functioned centrally in stories of modernity: the some 17,508 islands of the Indonesian archipelago as a major nodal point in the global network of modernities, critical for the global trade in spices, for example.

Where Glissant focuses on islands, the new oceanic studies looks at vast waterways as enablers of mobility and the production of rapid change and epistemological ruptures, much as Paul Gilroy did in *The Black Atlantic*.[44] Oceanic studies also examines the patterns of oceanic worlds in general, the cultures of a given oceanic world, and the relations between different oceanic worlds. Basins such as the Indian Ocean and connectors like the Strait of Malacca are now the focus for a new, water-based examination of the global interconnections of commercial and cultural traffic. As Wigen writes in noting the difference between land-based and water-based studies, "the ocean is a crossroads, a site of interaction—a space of passage, rather than a place to settle and control" (139).

Land-based mobility systems—riverways, roadways, canals, railways—are also locations that enable new networks, intensified interculturalisms, and different modernities, especially when they connect different environmental and cultural centers, as did China's completion of the Grand Canal in the seventh century, enabling Tang modernity. In the fifteenth century, the Saharan caravans bringing iron, gold, ivory, metals, and salt from West Africa to Europe, Cairo, East Africa, Middle East, South Asia, and China produced great wealth and rapid change for the Songhay Empire (c. 1460–1500), especially under the reign of Askia the Great (1493–1538), who fostered the great intellectual/religious center of Timbuktu and the nearby trade cities of Goa and Jenne. He brought innovations in governmental bureaucracy, advancement by merit, tax collection, judicial systems, and the military to produce the largest and wealthiest empire in sub-Saharan Africa to date. The historian Basil Davidson identifies these changes as "modern," contrasting the literate, Islamic, globally networked centers of the Songhay Empire with the rule of the prior dynasty and with the practices of the rural countryside.[45]

In short, recurrent and polycentric modernities in the *longue durée* take shape as part of larger networks and systems of exchange that are transregional and often transcontinental in scale. The great metropolitan centers of human history constitute vital nodal points where rapid change can result from a vortex of converging factors. But rethinking any given modernity as part of a large-scale networking system requires thinking beyond the world's great cities to a range of other distinctive sites producing and produced by intensive flare-ups of accelerating change, including the nomadic, archipelagic, oceanic, and land-based waterways and roadways.

CIRCULATION : ROUTE : CONTACT

Circulation: Distribution.
Synonyms: circuit, currency, diffusion, dispersal, dispersion, dissemination, dissipation, expansion, mingle, movement, propagation, scattering,

	spread, transculturation, translation, transmission, translation, travel...
Antonyms:	fixity, immobility, stasis...
Route:	Road, course, way for travel.
Synonyms:	beat, beeline, byway, circuit, detour, direction, flyway, highway, itinerary, journey, line, orbit, passage, path, tack, track, trail...
Antonyms:	random movement, rooted...
Contact:	Coming together, connection, communication, touch.
Synonyms:	association, commerce, communion, intercourse, junction, link, meeting, network...
Antonyms:	apartness, disconnection, isolation, noncommunication, separation...

Networks are not just points on a grid; they are also lines connecting points, lines that create relationality through their mobilities from point to point, their contact zones and borderlands of interculturalism and transculturation. Systems are circuits, specifically a structure of circuitry through which energy, things, people, and knowledge move and disperse. Although circulation is not necessarily "modern," modernity always involves circulation of some sort—the routes of mobility, travel, translation, and transmission. Circulation breaks isolation, follows routes that create contact zones of connection and transculturation. Accelerated circulation is a constitutive component of modernity.

As figure, *circulation* suggests movement *around*, *through*, and *across* as the opposite of stasis. *Diffusion, dissemination* imply pervasive orderly *infusion, permeation*; *dispersion, scattering* conjure more fragmentary, even chaotic *spreading*. Whether orderly, as in the circulatory system of the body, or scattered and rhizomatic, as in the travels of microbes, *circulation* links one thing to another and another and another. In cultural terms, *circulation* is both agent and effect of the global ecumene, a process of interculturalism that has been variously theorized. Civilizational historians like David Wilkinson argue that wide-scale circulations characterize human history as a long-term, continuously unfolding process of exchange and contact. Wilkinson argues that "a criterion for defining and bounding a civilization [should be] based on transactions and connectedness rather than cultural similarity." For him, such connections include war as well as trade, for the "antagonistic bonding" of conflict "*always* integrates."⁴⁶ The influential anthropologist James Clifford proposes an ethnography of global circulation that stresses movement and hybridization as part of the ongoing processes of culture itself. He notes that his essays in *Routes* begin "with this assumption of movement, arguing that travels and contacts are crucial sites for an unfinished modernity."⁴⁷ Focusing especially on Latin America, Mary Louise Pratt and Walter Mignolo propose "contact zones" in the context of colonialism, zones that produce different ways of knowing as a product of often violent contact and oppression.⁴⁸

Theorists who focus on culture and aesthetics have drawn heavily on concepts of heightened circulation. For Homi K. Bhabha in *The Location of Culture*, colonial and postcolonial contact creates the interstitial, the third space of a hybridic in-between. Edward W. Said theorizes the "transplantation" of ideas from one cultural/political context to another as a form of "translation" that emphasizes the agency of adaptation.⁴⁹ David Damrosch develops a concept of global circulation to address the mobilities of literature from its time/space of origin; Wai Chee Dimock charts traveling literatures through "deep time" across continents. Jahan Ramazani tracks a "transnational poetics" as legacies of imperial circuits and postcolonial agencies, one in which poetries travel and indigenize in patterns of enmeshment. B. Venkat Mani coins the term *bibliomigrancy* to track the global circuits of print culture embodying complex patterns of translation, publication, and reception, and Rebecca L. Walkowitz designates literatures in a globalized world as "born translated," that is, written with circulation as constitutive of its linguistic and aesthetic forms.⁵⁰

The keywords in English of transcultural circulation and transculturation discussed in chapter 2 provide an extensive vocabulary whose nuanced differences provide a window into the myriad ways that cultures interact with material, intellectual, and cultural practices circulating though routes of intercultural contact. They operate ever more intensely during times of accelerating change.

The global circulation of commodities provides a particularly telling instance of modernities constituted through heightened exchange, adaptation, translation, and indigenization. As part symptom and part cause of the interconnected modernities of Europe and the Americas, Asia, and Africa after 1500, the circulations of foods, plants, and stimulants such as sugar, bananas, tobacco, chocolate, coffee, tea, and tulips were vital components of the new commercialism and consumption, as Europe newly entered the world market system as a major player, funded in large part by the conquests that produced the wealth of gold, silver, slaves, and land.[51] The travels and indigenization of three foods native to the Andes and long cultivated in what is now Bolivia and Peru provide a case in point—the white potato, the tomato, and the chili pepper. Mountainous regions often twelve thousand feet above sea level with little arable land on steep hillsides were the origin point for the plant species of pepper, tomato, and potato that made their way east, west, and north, after contact with the Spanish conquistadors, to become foods that symbolize the cuisine and national character of entirely different peoples. What is more Irish than the potato, more Italian than the tomato, more Indian (or Thai) than the chili pepper? These foods are entry points for a study of culture, economics, politics, and national imaginaries. But their relatively recent origin in the Andes, at a time when European modernity began to develop, is largely forgotten as they have become indigenized, nativized, localized, even vernacularized.

The circulations and indigenizations of the white potato in particular embody some of the divergent modernities of the post-1500 ecumene. As the Spanish destroyed the Incan empire, they brought the Andean potato (distinct from the orange sweet potato) back to Spain in 1570. Europeans and North Americans were slow to adopt the potato, deeming it food fit only for the poor because of its association with the deadly nightshade family. Eventually, however, as Larry Zuckerman explains in *The Potato: How the Humble Spud Rescued the Western World*, the potato enriched the diets of the poor from Ireland to Poland and Russia. He argues that the potato industry became a more valuable commodity than even the Andean metals, worth $100 billion by his book's publication in 1998. He even suggests that "the humble spud rescued the western world" by introducing a hardy plant that could grow in poor soil, provide good sustenance for the poor (to whom the potato was initially consigned), and help prevent scurvy for populations without access to fruit for much of the year, if at all.[52]

The Irish were the first Europeans to develop the potato as a field crop in the seventeenth century, and they turned it into a staple in the eighteenth century. English colonization of Ireland left the land-hungry Irish peasants increasingly dependent on the potato as their main food crop. With the deadly combination of British policies, absentee landlordism, and the potato blight of the 1840s, the Great Famine of 1845–1852 led to the loss of nearly one-third of the island's population through starvation and migration. The historical trauma of the famine in turn contributed to Irish resistance to British colonial power and the founding of the Irish Free State in 1922. Whether in feast or famine, the potato is so quintessentially Irish that the white potato's common name today is the Irish potato. The travels of the potato encapsulate the story of European modernity in all of its dimensions, including the unevenness of modernity in colonial relations as well as within Europe itself.

While circulation and transculturalism characterize global human history in toto, modernity accelerates their pace and scope in the global ecumene through heightened contact zones of the technological and commercial, the cultural and aesthetic. I emphasized the Mongol Empire in chapter 3 in part because its rapidly introduced transcontinental systems of relay and exchange so epitomize large-scale circulations as constitutive of the accelerating change characteristic of modernity. Although Appadurai in *Modernity at Large* argues that "today's world involves interactions of a new order and intensity" that differ from the "large-scale interactions for many [prior] centuries," his concept of late-twentieth-century global "cultural traffic" aptly describes a model of intensified circulations in realms from the material to the representational—from goods and people to ideas and the imagination—as a key component of any given modernity (27–38). In my view, these instances of circulation embody the role that broad-scale geographies of intercultural contact zones play in the formation of systemic and rhizomatic networks of recurrent and polycentric modernities long before the late-twentieth-century "modernity at large" that Appadurai theorizes.

Modernity intensifies cultural transplantation, adaptation, indigenization, translation—broadly speaking, all forms of transculturation. The more radical the juxtapositions of difference, the more possibilities of sudden breakthroughs, of innovations and transformative changes that speed up the ordinary processes of interculturalism. Such juxtapositions defamiliarize the normative and break open the possibilities for wide-scale change.

DIVERGENCE : DISCREPANCE : FISSURE

Divergence:	Branching out, difference.
Synonyms:	aberration, alternate, deflection, departure, detour, deviation, digression, discrepancy, disparity, dissimilarity, diversity, parting, separation, unevenness, unlikeness, variation . . .
Antonyms:	convergence, likeness, similarity . . .
Discrepance:	difference, disparity.
Synonyms:	at variance, conflicting, contradictory, contrary, discordant, disparate, dissonant, incompatible, incongruent, inconsistent, varying . . .
Antonyms:	alike, concurring, consistent, harmonious . . .
Fissure:	cleavage, gap, narrow opening.
Synonyms:	breach, cleft, crack, crevice, gash, hole, rift, rupture . . .
Antonyms:	whole . . .

Modernity is divergent, discrepant, fissured—through time, across space; over various locations, in the same place. Modernity affects different peoples differently, unevenly. Modernity contains overlapping, contesting modernities. No matter its claims of universalism, modernity is never the same, uniform, or whole. It diverges from itself in its very constitution. Not only the result of accelerating ruptures, modernity emerges from ruptures within: its fissures crack open the contradictions of expanding and contracting possibilities of rapid change. Just think of the slaveowner and the slave—they are part of the same modernity but are situated differently within it. The slaveowner known as Schoolteacher in Toni Morrison's

Beloved "scientifically" lists his slave Sethe's characteristics, human on one side, animal on the other; Sethe later kills her own baby at the sight of the slave catcher rather than have her beloved child grow up to be dehumanized as she herself was when Schoolteacher and his men "stole" her milk.[53] Hosna, the village woman in Tayeb Salih's *Season of Migration to the North*, attempts to claim "modern" womanhood for herself, only to die for it, as I will discuss at greater length in chapter 6.[54] Women are often held hostage to modernity, functioning as the embodiment of "tradition" as men try to grasp the benefits of modernity for themselves. Modernity might enhance the prospects of elites and retard those whom the society marginalizes. The effects of modernity are uneven. The world split open can produce new freedoms, new slaveries, new lives, new deaths, all at once or in sequence.

The disparities within and across different modernities have everything to do with shifting structures of power and how people are positioned within them. Some gain and others lose as societies undergo accelerating change, reflecting modernity's inherently contradictory core. Breaking free from European colonial powers in the eighteenth and nineteenth centuries in the Americas produced hemispheric modernities North and South, differentially. In the United States, the westward expansion of European Americans in the great land grabs of the nineteenth century, for example, represented a "manifest destiny" from coast to coast for the new nation. It brought Irish immigrants fleeing the Great Famine; Scandinavians and Germans to the Midwest farmlands and cities; Chinese workers for the building of the transcontinental railroads and the cities of the West Coast; Jews, Eastern Europeans, and Italians to the metropolitan centers of the East Coast. In the cities, prairies, and factories, women moved into labor forces and public arenas, demanding a voice. Great land-grant universities were founded, an expansion of higher education that laid the foundation for twentieth-century American economic and cultural global dominance.

Technologically, economically, demographically, culturally—nineteenth-century U.S. modernity produced explosive change. It also brought more disease and death to indigenous peoples and a devastating loss of their lands; the Mexican-American War of 1848 made second-class citizens of Mexican Americans overnight in the conquest of the American Southwest. The convulsions of the Civil War and the end of Reconstruction brought emancipation but economic and political reenslavement for many African

Americans. The Chinese Exclusion Acts cemented racially driven nativism that structured immigration policies until 1965. North-South-East-West: the modernity of the emergent national power was not one. We still live with the legacies of its divergent modernities, its unevenness and disparities, in the twenty-first century.

With its wars of independence from European colonial powers and its waves of immigrants, Latin America is part of the same global modernity as North America, but this hemispheric modernity is highly divergent, as the title of Julio Ramos's *Divergent Modernities: Culture and Politics in Nineteenth-Century Latin America* emphasizes.[55] José David Saldívar's introduction to *Divergent Modernities* argues for a Latin American "subaltern modernity" based on the "uneven modernization" of a Latin America caught in a triangulated relationship between European and North American dominance in cultural, intellectual, economic, technological, and political arenas. Ramos centers much of his argument on José Martí (1853–1895), the great Cuban writer and anti-imperialist national hero whose work challenges the mass media domination of North American culture at the same time that he resists Spain's cultural hegemony, arguing for a third space of Latin American intellectual culture.[56] Writing more broadly about Latin American avant-gardes, Fernando J. Rosenberg argues for an even more complex triangulation, one negotiating between European, North American, and Latin American cultures, layering the mestizo, African, and indigenous cultures. According to Rosenberg, Latin American avant-gardes in the early twentieth century rejected the high culture and primitivism of Europe and the U.S. modernists and created a new cosmopolitanism that drew on the different racial history of Latin American modernity, one in which indigenous populations survived in greater numbers than in North America, in spite of losing the Incan and Aztec empires and some 80 percent of their populations at initial contact with the Europeans. Brazilians like Oswald de Andrade, the author of the "*Manifesto Antropofágo*" discussed in chapter 3, created a hybridic blend of divergent modernities that mixed high and low culture and used indigenous culture to upend the modernities of Europe and the United States.[57]

Globally speaking, divergent modernities are often competing modernities—interconnected, overlaid, and often discordant. As Laura Doyle points out in her afterword to *The Oxford Handbook of Global*

Modernisms, "any model that focuses solely on the singular 'rise' of Anglo-European empire" has missed how contemporaneous imperial modernities are "mutually produced, highly contingent, and interactive," as the interrelations of the European, Ottoman, Mughal, and Qing empires in the post-1500 period attest.[58] Interlocking modernities are often discrepant, disparate—both with one another and within themselves.

Take for example the intersecting modernities of the Ottoman, Austro-Hungarian, and Russian Empires at the beginning of the twentieth century, as each was breaking apart in a series of interlocked events: the Balkan Wars, the Young Turks' attacks on the sultanate, World War I, the Russian Revolution, the founding of new nation-states in the wake of Versailles, the Allied and Greek postwar invasion of Turkey, and the Turkish War of Independence, which culminated in the founding of the Republic of Turkey in 1922, led by the secular nationalist and reformer Mustafa Kemal Atatürk. Turkish modernity, to focus on one region, encapsulates effectively the capacity of a single modernity to contain many divergent and uneven modernities within. In the space of a few years Turkey experienced the final loss of the Ottoman Empire, the Armenian Genocide of 1915–1916 led by the anti-imperial Young Turks, the ethnic cleansing in the so-called exchange of populations of 1923 (when Turkey expelled all its ethnic Greeks and Greece expelled all its ethnic Turks), Greece's attempt to reestablish Greater Greece by invading Turkey, and Ataturk's modernization campaign in education, religion, politics, family and women's rights, and general cultural life.

Discrepant modernities are nothing if not riven with contradictions.

UTOPIA : DYSTOPIA : HETEROTOPIA

Utopia: A real or imaginary society, place, or state considered to be ideal or perfect.
Synonyms: Paradise—Arcadia, bliss, dreamland, Elysian Fields, Garden of Eden, heaven, never-never land, perfection, pie-in-the-sky, Promised Land, Shangri-La, wonderland . . .
Antonyms: Dystopia . . .

Dystopia: A real or imaginary society, place, or state characterized by human misery, squalor, and oppression, where everything is as bad as it can be.
Synonyms: Hell . . .
Antonyms: Utopia . . .

Heterotopia: An "other" place, the site of otherness, crisis, deviance, contradiction, the incompatible.[59]

Utopia is no-where, no(t)here. But the utopian impulse—the vision or hope or yearning for the ideal—is everywhere in human experience and particularly intense in periods of rapid change. Dystopia is also no-where, no(t)here. But the dystopic dimension of human misery is everywhere and particularly intense in periods of rapid change. The accelerated ruptures of modernity produce heightened utopian and dystopian phenomenologies.

Modernity is a charged word, a verbal/figural icon that produces often passionate political advocates and detractors. For Habermasians, the promising project of modernity is still ongoing: the utopian hope of ever-expanding freedoms and opportunities, ever-lessening violence and irrationality. For Wallersteinians, the viral project of modernity is still ongoing: the dystopic despair of ever-expanding exploitations and restrictions, ever-lessening peace and rationality. The pros and cons of modernity debates are themselves ongoing, caught, as I argued in chapter 1, in the transferential trap of modernity's own contradictions. The point, I believe, is not to take sides in this unending contestation about the ethics and politics of modernity but rather to interrogate the debate for how it reveals the contradictory nature of radical societal rupture and its heterogeneous, discrepant effects.

In chapter 3, I paired the massive changes wrought by the sedentary Tang/Song and the nomadic Mongol empires, showing how each modernity incorporated the extremes of violence and the flowering of peace and human creativity—the dystopic and the utopic. The swift Mongol conquest of Baghdad in 1258 included the catastrophic dumping of the Grand Library's books into the Tigris, but it also brought about the Pax Mongolica, the new flowering of Persian culture, and the integration of Persia into the vast world system of the transcontinental empire. The European

Enlightenment produced transformative ideas of freedom that took hold even more fiercely in the colonies at the same time that it developed a science rationalizing the institutions of chattel slavery on a massive scale. Does the utopic require the dystopic in order to exist as an impulse? Must some one, some group of people, even some species always be left out of the dream of the ideal? Or is the utopian principle infinitely expandable, to the full planet, to the cosmos?

Modernity's heterotopias are those places set aside, set outside the regular sites of a society, but mirroring back the fundamental contradictions inherent in periods of intensified change. For Michel Foucault, heterotopias are "countersites" as disparate as cemeteries and prisons, fairgrounds and brothels, libraries and theaters, colonies and ships. Whether sites of crisis or deviation, of the sacred or profane, of "accumulating time" or separate spaces, heterotopias are full of "contradiction" and "superimposed meanings" for Foucault (24–27).

Adapting his concept, I suggest that any given modernity contains many heterotopic sites that contain competing utopic and dystopic effects. Take, for example, the building of dams—from the Aswan Dam in Egypt to the Hoover Dam in the United States, from the Sardar Sarovar and Narmada dams in India to the Three Gorges Dam in China. As countersites, these dams reflect back on the underlying tensions and structures of the societies that produce them. As spatial sites that symbolize "modernity," they superimpose the contradictory meanings of "progress"— control of flooding, irrigation, electricity, increased food production; massive displacement of peoples, negative environmental impacts, destruction of religious, archaeological, and cultural sites. About the Narmada dam projects, for example, Arundhati Roy writes in 1999:

> Big Dams haven't really lived up to their role as monuments to Modern Civilization. . . . Big Dams are to a nation's "development" what nuclear bombs are to its military arsenal. They're both weapons of mass destruction. They're both weapons governments use to control their own people. . . . They're both malignant indications of civilization turning upon itself. They represent the severing of the link, not just the link—the *understanding*—between human beings and the planet they live on.[60]

The "Judgement of the Supreme Court of India" counters in 2000:

> The argument in favour of the Sardar Sarovar Project is that the benefits are so large that they substantially outweigh the costs of the immediate human and environmental disruption. Without the dam, the long term costs for people would be much greater and lack of an income source for future generations would put increasing pressure on the environment.[61]

The progressive environmental historian Ramachandra Guha believes that Roy's "Manichaean" essay damages the Indian environmentalist movement, and the scholar and activist Gail Omvedt attacks Roy's complete condemnation of the dams.[62]

My point is neither to take sides nor to evade taking sides on this or other dam projects—I do not have the knowledge to make an informed judgment. Instead, I regard the debates about dam projects as quintessentially *modern*. They reflect modernity's production of heterotopic sites that bring into bold relief the contradictory utopian and dystopian dimensions of modernity itself—any modernity.

In their most apocalyptic forms, the clashing of utopic and dystopic aspects of modernity collide, expanding and contracting like the combustion engine to which modernity has been compared. The geohistories of utopic/dystopic modernity are not singular or linear. Instead, they are multiple and explosively present in the Now, pregnant with contradiction, like Walter Benjamin's figure, the Angel of History, apocalyptically projected into his "Theses on the Philosophy of History" shortly before his suicide in the face of the impending Holocaust:

> His face is turned toward the past. Where we perceive a chain of events, he sees one single catastrophe which keeps piling wreckage upon wreckage and hurls it in front of his feet. The angel would like to stay, awaken the dead, and make whole what has been smashed. But a storm is blowing from Paradise; it has got caught in his wings with such violence that the angel can no longer close them. This storm irresistibly propels him into the future to which his back is turned, while the pile of debris before him grows skyward. This storm is what we call progress.[63]

CONCLUSION

The *figures* of modernity, I have suggested in this chapter, complement the *stories* of modernity narrated in chapter 3. Like those stories, this network of keyword-images aims to rethink modernity outside its familiar Eurocentric boxes, to locate some common denominators in the multiplicity of different modernities across the globe in the *longue durée*. I began with the figure of the *multiple*, examining the many adjectives—from *other*, *alternative*, and *minor* to *polycentric*, *uneven*, and *recurrent*—used to characterize multiplicity, gauging which most effectively challenge the metanarrative of Western modernity. I examined the trope of *rupture*—and its correlates in *conjuncture* and *vortex*—to emphasize modernity's connection with a certain *kind* of change, one that tears apart the familiar, the expected, the "old" ways of doing things or understanding the world. Human societies change all the time. To have any meaning at all, modernity's change has to differ from ongoing societal evolution. *Rupture* conveys the radical nature of change, its abrupt conjuncture of forces across societal domains converging to form a dizzying vortex of transformations, its emplacement of new paradigms of thought, behavior, and structure. Modernity's *speed* of change, the swift *velocity* of transformation, the *acceleration* of ongoing change, are tropes of mobility. They signify a change in the pace of change, a technology of ever-faster movement, a phenomenology of *hurry up*. Modernity has its foot on the gas; it revs the engine of change. Its opposite is coasting, periods of consolidation, of gradual absorption of the new, adjustments made to the old.

All societies establish *networks* and *systems* of relation and engage in *routes* of *circulation* and *contact* both within and outside themselves. What is distinctive about modernity's networks and circulations is their very intensity and scope. The ordinary patterns of relations are shattered, replaced by new modes of relations—perhaps by the suddenness of conquest or the heightened hybridities of new borderlands, whether violent or peaceful. Rapidly changing forms of mobility, urbanization, transportation, and traveling transform societal networks and connect societies with ever-larger world systems of exchange. All societies are *divergent*, *fissured*, but modernity introduces greater extremes of *discrepance*, creating explosive divisions and societal transformations with colliding *utopic* and *dystopic* dimensions.

Defined comparatively, through its figures and tropes, modernity is, then, at least partly a question of degree: the intensification, heightening, scope, and range of patterns already incipient in societies as complex sets of relations across the domains of human organization and experience. As such, it is inherently a relational concept, not a nominal one. I return to the image of modernity as the internal combustion engine, borrowed from Garry Leonard and explored in chapter 2 as the logic of endlessly recurring building up of pressure, explosive release, containment, and then movement.[64] In this sense, modernity is also a question of scale. Zoom out: an instance of modernity might be centuries long—like the Tang Dynasty, the Mongol Empire, the European "rise." Zoom in: an instant of modernity might be the digital age of the twenty-first century as a radical break from the early-twentieth-century print culture as the tail end of the Gutenberg revolution.

Rethinking modernity through its keyword-images and across its multiple formations in time and space produces a category of thought that is fluid, flexible. In *Liquid Modernity*, Zygmunt Bauman proposes "fluidity" and "liquidity" as "fitting metaphors when we wish to grasp the nature of the present, in many ways *novel*, phase in the history of modernity."[65] I suggest that such fluidity is essential to break through the rigidities of a modernity conceived as the invention of the West. Fluids move, taking their shape from the time/space they move through—likewise, modernity in all its recurrent multiplicities.

PART III

RETHINKING MODERNISM, READING MODERNISMS

FIVE
MODERNITY'S MODERNISMS
Aesthetic Scale and Pre-1500 Modernisms

To include China among the global modernisms, to discover a global modernism at all, requires abandoning the temporal logic that has until now structured the field (and which has served as a screen for its geographic centrisms). Whether modernism as a concept can survive such a breach, or rather, what kind of modernism will emerge from that breaching, is one of the questions that remains before us.

—Eric Hayot, "Chinese Modernism, Mimetic Desire, and European Time"

Emerging in a multiplicity of languages, locations, cultures, and social temporalities . . . modernism's local situations and commitments modulate the possible global meanings of modernism and modernity even as they remind us of the political challenges to which they respond.

—Jessica Berman, *Modernist Commitments: Ethics, Politics, and Modernism*

We can consider the question of scale . . . from the grand geographical scale of the world to the admittedly small physical scale of an individual text. . . . [This] allows for the scaling back and forth between the world and the text as well as along the intermediary scales . . . excavating and activating the historically specific set of relationalities across time and space.

—Shu-mei Shih, "Comparison as Relation"

"Interrogate the slash!" I wrote in chapter 2. It's time to examine more closely what the connection/disconnection between modernism and modernity signifies. It's time to move from considerations of planetary modernities in the *longue durée* to understanding what such a transformational paradigm shift means for modernism, for the aesthetic dimensions of any given modernity or relational network of linked modernities. There are those who would deny the connection altogether.[1] As an aesthetic period category akin to romanticism, realism, or naturalism, modernism was named after the fact—not by the artists, writers, and thinkers themselves but by the critics and scholars who came afterward and saw a loose affiliation of aesthetic styles and principles based in what has been called "the crisis in representation."[2] As an aesthetic style, modernism initially meant a constellation of related practices that ruptured conventional forms, defamiliarized representational epistemologies, and experimented with visual, verbal, aural, and kinetic meaning making—for example, the multiperspectivism and simultaneity of cubism; the absurdist juxtapositions of Dada; the nonlinear chronologies and shifting interior monologues or free indirect discourse of Woolf or Faulkner; the symptomatic representations giving form to the subject split between conscious and unconscious thought and desire in Joyce; the paratactic poetics, citational intertextuality, and mythic methods of Eliot's *The Waste Land* and Pound's *Cantos*; the deconstruction of narrative and sentence in Stein; the atonal dissonances of Stravinsky; the stark lines of Bauhaus; the flowing lines of Isadora Duncan; and so forth.

As modernism's umbrella broadened beyond the strictly aesthetic to the philosophical and political, the term came to incorporate everything from Nietzsche, Freud, and Benjamin to the "new woman," the "new Negro," and the rise of popular culture from arcades to cinema, blues, and jazz. But even this expanded modernism, as a period term centered in the aesthetic and philosophical, has been resolutely limited in space (the West) and time (c. 1890s–1940s), thus provoking a plethora of studies asking "What was modernism?" or asserting "What modernism was."[3] In the face of the field's more recent spatio/temporal expansions, the term "high modernism" often appears as a substitute for the older term "modernism," signifying a core meaning with an originary and canonical status. With the proliferation of modernisms, the singular "high modernism" reassuringly affirms that the designation of a certain aesthetic style still retains a privileged position within the field. Whether intended or not, the term *high* exists in opposition to *low* and *middle*, inevitably invoking a scale of value—the more "experimental" the form, the "higher" the modernism and the higher its cultural capital in the landscapes of pluralized modernisms.

I have argued, in contrast, that modernism cannot be separated from the modernity of which it is a part. Modernism without modernity is aesthetics without history, without place. As Malcolm Bradbury and James McFarlane wrote in 1976 about early-twentieth-century Anglo-American and European modernism, "Modernism is then the art of modernization"; it is the "art that responds to the scenario of our chaos."[4] Broaden the geohistorical scale of their assertion, and the consequence is transformational for the concept of modernism. The attempt to posit a "republic of letters" as a world apart, with its own centers and peripheries, as Pascale Casanova does in *The Republic of Letters*, assumes an autonomy for the aesthetic realm that it does not in fact have.[5] Even the mantra "art for art's sake" is an aesthetic with a history, firmly rooted in its own time and place, having ideological force. The production, reception, medium, genre, and formal embodiment of all aesthetic expressivities exist and travel within larger cultural, political, and geohistorical fields. Texts not only have contexts, but contextuality is itself a constitutive component of textuality and form, not separable from it. What Rachel Blau DuPlessis terms "social philology" can be read within the text's very form and language, whatever the aesthetic medium.[6] These fundamental principles of the aesthetic as a cultural practice in the symbolic/representational realm establish the connection between modernity as the broad geohistorical condition and modernism as the aesthetic dimension within it.

CONNECTION: MODERNITY/MODERNISM

The slash in modernism/modernity signifies connection. And there are consequences for that connection. Once modernity is unmoored from its conventional nominal definition (the metanarrative of Western modernity), then it follows that modernism too must be set adrift from its original association with a specific aesthetic style. Multiple and recurrent modernities contain multiple and recurrent modernisms with a diversity of aesthetic styles. Any given "modernism" is the domain of the aesthetic that shapes, gives form to, and responds to the modernity of which it is a part. Modernism is an active agent within modernity, making its particular contribution to the vortex of accelerating mobilities. Like *modernity, modernism* needs to be delineated in predominantly relational terms to be genuinely planetary. How do the aesthetic expressivities of a particular modernity participate in the vortex of accelerating mobilities across societal domains? What symbolic modes are spawned in its midst? In what ways does it give representational form to the ruptures of modernity? Answering these questions involves a willingness to accept a wide diversity of aesthetic forms for planetary modernisms in the *longue durée*.

Recognizing the possibility of diverse aesthetic styles in the many modernisms of geohistory does not mean the marginalization of the particular aesthetics of so-called high modernism. The revolutionary poetics and disruptive forms of early-twentieth-century Anglo-American and European modernism remain crucially important to the field and influential for writers and artists in many parts of the world. What I ask for, then, is that we stop using this particular modernism as the default position for modernism per se, that we stop universalizing it to stand in for modernism itself and as the measure of all other modernisms. Instead of modifiers like "high," we should use spatio/temporal modifiers to indicate its geohistorical location. Such modifiers can vary significantly in scale. For example, locators can be as broad as continental modernism from the 1880s through the 1940s or as narrow as late-nineteenth-century modernism of the Bengal Renaissance or twentieth-century colonial modernism in Ireland. The point is to acknowledge that modernism experiments with many aesthetic forms through time and across space.

The diverse styles of various modernisms exist within a single as well as across different spatio/temporal locations. Resisting the charismatic pull of the field's early definitions of aesthetic modernism involves recognizing that variation. Within early-twentieth-century Anglo-American literary modernism, for example, styles that diverge significantly from so-called high modernism are now regularly considered part of, and sometimes even canonical within, modernism. Joseph Conrad and Henry James, to cite two instances, were not included in the critical canons of modernism during the 1960s and 1970s; rather, their novels were typically read as instances of realism, the style that preceded the modernism born of the chaos of World War I. Today, Conrad has been (re)claimed for modernism, with *Heart of Darkness* and *The Secret Agent* having canonical status, and James increasingly appears in studies of Anglo-American modernism. D. H. Lawrence and E. M. Forster were not considered experimental enough to be "real" modernist writers, though they lived and wrote within the milieu of British modernism. Today, their renderings of class, race, sexuality, and colonialism make them canonical figures within modernist studies—not as stylistic experimentalists (though their departures from nineteenth-century British realism are significant) but for their engagements with key issues of early-twentieth-century modernity. "New Woman" and "New Negro" modernisms, Black Atlantic modernisms, vernacular modernisms, pulp modernisms, camp modernisms, red modernisms—all these and more are now recognized as distinctive aesthetic styles of early-twentieth-century Anglo-American literary modernism. As Douglas Mao and Rebecca L. Walkowitz note, the "new modernist studies" has expanded along "vertical axes" from high to popular culture as well as along the "horizontal axes" of the "transnational turn."[7] Given the new receptivity to diverse aesthetic styles within early-twentieth-century Anglo-American modernism, it follows that a single aesthetic style (e.g., "high modernism") should not function as the definitive yardstick for modernisms from other spatio/temporal locations.

Giving up that single yardstick also involves recognizing a hybridic blending of aesthetic styles from the smallest scale of a single "text" to the larger scale of aesthetic affiliations and movements. Joyce's *Ulysses*, for example, combines elements of realism, naturalism, and avant-garde experimentalism along with its "mythic method" indigenizing Homeric epic, multilingualism, and global intertextualities. The novels of postcolonial writers like G. V. Desani, Tayeb Salih, Salman Rushdie, and Arundhati Roy should not be read as belated or derivative versions of Joyce, Conrad, or Woolf in their use of fragmented chronologies, multiple (un)reliable narrators, open-endedness, linguistic play, and irony. Their postcolonial modernisms create distinctive aesthetic styles that reflect their positioning within the hybrid modernities of postcoloniality—drawing on, resisting, reversioning, and repurposing the precursor texts from Britain but also blending these with revisionings of textual traditions from Indian or Arab cultures. The aesthetic form of Roy's *The God of Small Things*, for example, actively combines and recasts elements of the *Mahabharata*, Mulk Raj Anand, Rushdie, Conrad, Forster, Joyce, and Woolf. Postcolonial modernism is less a "writing back" to Empire as a purely resistant discourse than it is creative adaptations that articulate the particular modernities of their position in a relational imperial system.

DISCONNECTION: MODERNISM/MODERNITY

The slash in modernism/modernity also signifies disconnection. That is, the separation the slash delineates warns against an absolute conflation of modernity and the aesthetic domain within it. It reminds us to look for what is distinctive about the realm of the aesthetic in its myriad forms as it participates in the phenomenon of any given modernity. Broadly speaking, the aesthetic is a mode of imaginative/creative meaning making, giving representational form to the experiential, self-reflexive, and visionary. The aesthetic operates within the realm of the symbolic even as it creates material forms—some more or less tangible, others more or less performative. Though enmeshed in the commercial, political, technological, and other realms of human society, the aesthetic is also different from them, in part because its primary *donné* is the making of representational forms (whatever function such forms have within a society). Take for instance the modernity of the nineteenth-century whaling industry—a boon to the world's energy needs, a disaster for the whales themselves, a factor in the geopolitical competition of states (as oil is today). A novel about whaling— Herman Melville's *Moby-Dick*, for example—is entangled in the economics, technology, and geopolitics of whaling, but it differs categorically from them because it operates in the realm of the imaginary, symbolic, literary, and linguistic. Its particular modernism—its heteroglossic ruptures of conventional narrative, hybrid blend of genres, and philosophical/political/ scientific/ecological engagements—renders the fissures in the world system of industrial modernity as well as the phenomenological and imaginative dimensions of it. Even as we examine the novel's contextuality, we need to consider its aesthetic form.

Another distinctive element of the aesthetic is that it enables small-scale analysis nested within large-scale frameworks—what Shu-mei Shih in the epigraph to this chapter calls scaling back and forth between the world and the text, "excavating and activating the historically specific set of relationalities across time and space." In part, this is because aesthetic "texts"—in whatever material or medial form—function as relational networks that change through time. The "language" of their form and medium exists in intertextual relationship with others in that form, with other media, and with geohistorical discourses and conditions. Texts, in other words, are small-scale networks that exist within larger-scale networks that are both textual and contextual. As I discussed in chapter 3, geographical scale involves vertical nesting from small to large—for example, the vertical chain Stephen Dedalus creates starting with himself and ending with the universe. As a novel first published in 1916 in serial form in *The Egoist*, *A Portrait of the Artist as a Young Man* exists in the ever-increasing scales of the Irish revival, the early-twentieth-century modernist novel, the colonial novel in English, the genres of the *Bildungsroman* and *Künstlerroman*, and so forth. Each of these scalar levels are themselves networked with spatio/temporal particularities such as the historical conditions of colonialism or the rise of individualism. The horizontal relationships of a text like *Portrait* link the novel to other *Künstlerromane* of the period such as D. H. Lawrence's *Sons and Lovers*, Dorothy Richardson's *Pilgrimage*, or H.D.'s *HERmione*, as well as to other colonial novels of the time such as Rabindranath Tagore's *Gora* or *The Home and the World*. As a nodal point of early-twentieth-century modernism, Joyce can be connected to literatures and arts of linked modernities in locations as diverse as China, Egypt, India, Turkey, the United States, the Caribbean, Argentina, Mexico, and so forth. Such spatial networks can be small scale (e.g., the Irish revival) or ever wider in scale (e.g., national, regional, continental, oceanic).

MODERNISMS BEFORE WESTERN MODERNITY

"How temporally flexible is modernism, either as a concept or as a scholarly field?" Eric Hayot asks.[8] Although the urge to restrict the term *modernism* to a single historical period and location remains strong, the approach

I am urging suggests that diverse modernisms accompany different modernities, including those modernities before the European. It already violates the desire for a linear literary history to suggest that texts like *Moby-Dick*, conventionally associated with American romanticism and transcendentalism, are modernist. But even more radically to suggest that modernities before Western ones produced their own modernisms really goes against the grain of periodizing methodologies in literature and the arts. But I want to test the usefulness of this claim anyway. I want to suggest that all modernities have some sort of aesthetic dimension, some form of creative meaning making that engages substantively and formalistically with the epistemological ruptures characterizing modernity along with the vortex of other rapid changes. I want to call that aesthetic dimension a particular *modernism* whose spatio/temporal and cultural specificity can be named at the same time that its parallels with other modernisms can be identified.

This approach to identifying multiple and recurrent modernisms throughout the *longue durée* differs from one that identifies other modernisms based on their aesthetic similarity to early-twentieth-century Anglo-American and European aesthetic experimentation. To use the familiar modernism of the West as the formalist benchmark by which all others are measured reproduces the Eurocentrism that notions of multiple modernisms attempt to undermine. Instead, I urge that we look for aesthetic movements or specific instances that innovatively engage with the specific modernities of their space/time/culture, particularly for those whose forms as well as content push against or reinvent inherited conventions.

For examples of pre-1500 non-Western modernisms, I spotlight selected aesthetic productions of three, distinct modernities, each one of which illustrates a different form of creativity in the midst of empire: the poetry of Du Fu, writing in the midst of a chaotic civil war during the eighth century of the Tang Dynasty; the cobalt-blue ceramics of Basra, produced out of the commercial circulations of the Abbasid Empire, from the eighth century to the fourteenth; and the performance poetry of Kabir, first sung in the fifteenth century in the wake of Tamerlane's conquest of and religious conversions in northern India and continuing into the twenty-first century. What links them to the others and to post-1500 modernisms is *not* a single aesthetic style or philosophical sensibility but instead a creative rupture of conventional forms that accompanies the specific modernities of their time and place.

To establish the link between these different modernities and their accompanying modernisms, I consider them as aesthetic manifestations of their geohistorical location but also note their continuing circulation in world culture. In doing so, I necessarily depend on the expertise of scholars in the field. For Basra ceramics, I draw on the visual, linguistic, and contextual knowledge of art historians who have traced the formation and travels of innovative glazes originating in eighth-century Iraq. In the case of Du Fu and Kabir, I rely on contemporary English translations, fully aware of the controversies that surround the use of translation, including its problems and possibilities.[9] I engage, however, not in the "distant reading" Franco Moretti advocates in his sociological approach to world literature but rather in the "close reading" focused on the scale of the poetic or aesthetic text itself as it represents the geohistorical modernity of its creation or later reception. Close readings of the poem-in-translation are inherently limited; for some, close reading a poem-in-translation is oxymoronic. The linguistic and cultural/historical knowledge of area studies would no doubt produce much more nuanced and expansively knowledgeable readings.[10] Nonetheless, these poems-in-translation, read with the assistance of critics working in the original, point toward the sensibilities and aesthetics of modernist rupture. Moreover, the theoretical contributions of these selected case studies are significant. They demonstrate in verbal, visual, and performative texts how the innovative aesthetic forms of pre-1500 modernities might contribute to the case I am making for understanding modernism as the aesthetic domain of any given modernity.

DU FU AND TANG DYNASTY MODERNITY

The wide-scale societal transformations in economic, political, agricultural, family, and religious life during the Tang Dynasty (618–907 CE)—discussed in chapter 3—produced just such a confluence of aesthetic modernity—what I am calling Tang modernism. In *China's Cosmopolitan Empire: The Tang Dynasty*, Mark Edward Lewis devotes a chapter to the cultural domain of writing, describing the new poetic and prose forms, especially in the eighth century, the "golden age" of the "High Tang" poets like Li Bo (701–762) and Du Fu (712–770), recognized for centuries as China's greatest poets.[11] Later Chinese anthologies and even later translations of Tang poets established them as "masters," constituting the "classics" of Chinese poetry. But in their own times, they were "modern." Breaking with the rigid conventions of court poetry, Tang poets of the new urban culture (women as well as men) forged a more direct poetics of the personal and philosophical, with a highly self-conscious projection of the poet's self-reflexive subjectivity, vocation, oeuvre, responsibility, and even ownership of work. Li Bo, born in Sichuan to a probable Turkic family, developed a poetic persona characterized by "innovation and excess, a shocking violation of decorum" that Lewis likens to Bryon (254). He was the first poet, according to David Hinton, to import *tz'u*, the popular wine-house song form of courtesans originally from central Asia, into "serious" poetry, a practice that later became widespread in poetry of the Song Dynasty.[12]

Writing as highly educated courtesans, as women of elite households, or as Buddhist nuns, women poets flourished in the Tang Dynasty, in part, David Young reflects, because "the Tang Dynasty happens to have been a time when women had greater freedom of choice and social mobility than was the case both earlier and later."[13] Xue Tao (c. 768–831), among the best known and anthologized of these women poets, was born in Chang'an, the Tang capital, and grew up in Chengdu, Sichuan, a site of perpetual rebellion and violence and the place where Du Fu lived at the end of his life. Educated and promoted by her father as a child prodigy, Xue Tao achieved wide acclaim as a highly connected courtesan poet, a reputation that continued after her retirement as a Taoist nun. She broke conventional gender boundaries, writing in a wide array of poetic genres and tones, from intimate to public; some ninety of her poems are extant, with five times that number in circulation during her lifetime and later lost over the centuries.[14]

New Tang prose forms also developed, including short stories and critical essays, including highly self-conscious explorations of aesthetics and poetics. The early-twentieth-century Chinese modernist Lu Xun argued that "the Tang classical short stories now called *chuanqi* ('transmissions of the remarkable') were the first examples of self-conscious fiction in China" (Lewis, 258). Ezra Pound's translations of and essays on the High Tang poets helped spark a new revolution in poetics in early-twentieth-century London.[15] And Lewis's conclusion about Tang poetry might easily characterize the rise of literary culture in Europe and America in the "modern" period:

> All the new forms of writing were linked to the emergence of a distinctive urban culture, which provided both new settings where writing was pursued and new themes for literary treatment. The emergence of this new urban culture shifted the literary center of gravity away from the courts.... The rise of a more urban, mercantile society also facilitated the emergence of new private or semiprivate spaces as both setting and subject of literature.... Most important, all these developments converged in a new model of the writer and his place in society.... The Tang literary world translated individual character and literary genius into socially celebrated attributes.
>
> (270–271)

To some extent, Lewis's account relies on Western poetics (e.g., Byron, Pound, etc.) as familiar touchstones for characterizing the modernity of the new poetry and prose of Tang writers. But a closer look at his discussion, and at the poetry itself, shows that the parallels he suggests do not reside in specific poetic forms—*Childe Harold* and the *Cantos* differ dramatically from Tang poetry—but rather in how the conditions of the rapidly changing Tang society fostered the development of a self-reflexive, urban concept of artistic vocation and subjectivity linked to rising mercantilism and imperial conquest, concepts of authorship typically thought to have been created first in the West after 1500. He suggests, in other words, that the similarities of historical modernities in each space/time produced dramatically new poetic practices. A further structural parallel is that like Pound, Eliot, and H.D., the new Tang poetry invoked much older poetic forms as a way of breaking with the ornate, conventional poetics of their immediate predecessors (Lewis, 247–249), a practice reflected in its conventional characterization as "neoclassical."

Du Fu, often admired as China's greatest poet, is a case in point. As David Young explains, he is known

> for his technical brilliance, a fluent mastery of traditional forms combined with an originality that gives rise to apparently effortless innovation.... His poetry is more autobiographical, and honest about his failings, than any poet's had managed before. He documented his own life in great detail, placing it in the contexts of both historical change

and day-to-day life, in the capital and in provincial villages throughout the empire.[16]

David Hinton notes that Du Fu "was the first poet to write extensively about real, immediate social concerns," typically bringing the public and private domains into conjunction, breaking with the traditional requirement for "thematic unity."[17]

Most significant for my argument is that Du Fu's new poetics developed out of his direct experiences with one of the most chaotic and devastating periods in the Tang Dynasty: the An Lushan Rebellion (755–763 CE), a war started by a Tang general of Turkic and Iranian descent that caused a loss of some 33 to 36 million people, making it one of the most deadly wars in human history (Lewis, 40–44). While leery of imposing Western periodization on Chinese history, Lewis nonetheless argues that the changes resulting from the rebellion ushered in "early modern China":

> The Tang dynasty's abandonment of key economic, military, and social institutions after the An Lushan rebellion, its reconfiguration of the empire's cultural geography, the expansion of trade relations with the outside world, and the invention of new artistic forms to deal with this changing world were the initial steps that began to distinguish later imperial China from what had come before.
>
> (2)

Du Fu suffered terribly during the rebellion, losing his son to the famine, fleeing with his wife and two children, captured by the rebels, and then exiled (Young, 78–79). He was born and educated near Chang'an, the great capital city, but after 755 he lived the life of a refugee, wandering with his family in search of a patron and safety, living for brief periods in the Central Plains, Sichuan, and the Yangtze River regions. Of his 1,400 extant poems, 1,100 of them were written during or after the rebellion and reflect the chaos and suffering of the times, as Eva Shan Chou stresses in *Reconsidering Tu Fu: Literary Greatness and Cultural Context*.[18] "War horses are north of the passes, / I lean on the railing, tears flowing," he writes metonymically in "Climbing Yueh-yang Tower" (Chou, 113). His experiences of

Tang modernity generated the poetics associated with him, a poetics that I term an instance of Tang modernism.

Here is one poem, written in the new, autobiographical vein, constructing a poet's subjectivity in the midst of the chaos, entangling, as Hinton argues, public and private sorrows. The translation is Stephen Owen's:

> Weeping over battle, many new ghosts,
> In sorrow reciting poems, an old man alone.
> A tumult of clouds sinks downward in sunset,
> Hard-pressed, the snow dances in whirlwinds.
> Ladle cast down, no green lees in the cup,
> The brazier lingers on, fire seems crimson.
> From several provinces, now news has ceased,
> I sit here in sorrow tracing words in the air.[19]

Here, Du Fu reinvents the longstanding practice in Chinese poetry of using metonyms of the natural world—"tumult of clouds," "sunset," "snow dances in whirlwinds"—to signify emotional/philosophical states of mind. What he adds to this use of what Eliot would much later call "the objective correlative" is the figure of the self-conscious poet—the "old man alone" who weeps over battle and the dead and dying. Left without news, uncertain about what has happened, he sits "in sorrow tracing words in the air." Without the solace of "green lees in the cup," his words are mere traces in the air, joining the tumult of clouds in the setting sun. The "ladle cast down" and the lingering brazier—its crimson fire suggesting the blood of war and the dying of the sun at sunset—are human objects paralleling the natural world as correlatives for the poet's lonely despair. Yet the lingering fire that survives—not definitively but seeming "crimson"—invokes the color of life and good fortune, transitioning into his "tracing words in the air" as the act of creative self-reflection that insists on his presence and survival. The modern aesthetics of the poem are inseparable from the modernity of the mid-eighth-century Tang Dynasty, from the violent historical conditions in which the poet is trapped. The poem encapsulates a modern sensibility caught in the chaos of the world split open, where the center cannot hold.

Demonstrating what Eva Shan Chou terms Du Fu's poetics of "juxtaposition" (107–196), "Spring Prospect" opens at the grand level of the state, moves through the subjectivity of the poet's suffering, and ends with the irony of self-mockery:

> The state has fallen, mountains and rivers endure,
> Spring in the city, grasses and trees grow thick,
> I am moved by the times, flowers bring on tears,
> My sorrow at separation, birds startle the heart.
> Beacon fires have burned for three months on end,
> A letter from home would be worth its weight in gold.
> My white hairs even shorter now from tugging
> Soon will not take even a hatpin.
>
> (Chou, 114–115)

Du Fu breaks with the Chinese poetic convention of solace from the endurance of nature, the return of spring, to reflect on how "flowers bring on tears," "birds startle the heart." The fires of war still signal messages, their presence contrasting with the absence of letters from home. The poem ends jarringly with the poet's ironic self-reflection, viewing from outside his baldness that worry has produced. From "the state has fallen" to "not . . . even a hatpin" builds the short poem around different economies of scale, juxtaposing the big with the little, reverberating back and forth to ironize the vulnerable state and the poet's pate.

Where this poem focuses on the poet alone in the landscape of his words, another Du Fu poem addresses more directly the political situation that inspires his satiric irony, based in sharp juxtapositions of the natural and imperial worlds filtered through the poet's angry consciousness. "Five Hundred Words About My Journey from the Capital to Feng-Hsien" was written just before the An Lushan Rebellion broke out. To quote from it in part from David Young's translation:

> Year's end, the grasses withered
> a great wind scouring the high ridges
> in bitter cold at midnight I set out
> along the Imperial highway

sharp frost, my belt snaps
my fingers are too stiff to tie it

around dawn I pass
the emperor's favorite winter palace
in the Li Hills by the hot springs
. . . .
the hot baths here
are just for important people
nothing for common folks

the silk the courtiers wear
was woven by poor women
soldiers beat their husbands
demanding tribute

of course our emperor is generous
he only wants the best for us
I suppose we have to blame his ministers
when government is bad

plenty of good people at the court
must be worried
especially when they see the palace gold plate
carted off by royal relations
women like goddesses
are dancing inside
all silk and perfume
guests in sable furs
music of pipes and fiddles
camel-pad broth being served
with frosted oranges and pungent tangerines

behind those red gates
meat and wine are left to spoil

outside lie the bones
of people who starved and froze
luxury and misery a few feet apart!

my heart aches to think about it.[20]

"Luxury and misery a few feet apart": in the lines of the poem as well as the world they represent. The poor women who weave jar up against the women like goddesses, "all silk and perfume." The material culture of imperial wealth inside—its aromas, food, exotic tastes, warm water, music, and silks—contrasts with the poverty outside, signified by the withered grasses, high winds, and bitter cold of the highway: the path of the wandering poet and those with whom he identifies as the frozen and starving. The poem's juxtapositions, based in the poet's transposed images of inside and outside, reproduce a binary world of pleasure and suffering that construct the poet's aching subjectivity. The poem encapsulates the radical divisions of a world about to split open: the modernity of the poet's own place and time.

No doubt Du Fu's poem prefigures the later innovative poetries that events engender in the early twentieth century in Europe, especially World War I. But I am not designating Du Fu's poetry "modernist" because it reminds me stylistically of Eliot, Pound, H.D., or Yeats. Rather, I am suggesting that the recurrent nature of violent modernities throughout the *longue durée* of global history set the scene for repeated aesthetic breakthroughs, for poets abandoning the conventions of their immediate predecessors and seeking new forms to represent the historical ruptures that dislocate their lives, the scenario of *their* chaos. For reasons akin to those of the early-twentieth-century poets, Du Fu develops a poetics capable of representing the interpenetration of historical and personal catastrophe, blending the scales of history from national to individual trauma. For him, the watershed was the An Lushan Rebellion. For early-twentieth-century Anglo-American poets it was World War I. Each was a distinctive modernity in its own space/time, although they shared the traumatic ruptures large-scale imperial wars produce in the personal lives of small-scale individuals.

BASRA'S COBALT-BLUE GLAZE AND ABBASID MODERNITY

If imperial wars split apart the lives of people caught up in them, as Du Fu's innovative poetry suggests, empires can also create vast connections across different peoples and cultures, as the conditions of the Pax Mongolica discussed in chapter 3 demonstrate.[21] The story of cobalt blue provides an instance of a ceramic modernism developed in the heart of an imperial modernity with a genius for transcontinental commercialism. Cobalt blue is a global color, a richly intense and distinctive blue known worldwide as the blue of blue-and-white Chinese porcelain, Delft pottery, Portuguese *azulejo* tiles, and the willow pattern of English china. But where does it come from? The simple answer is Basra, the port city in Iraq, but the story of its origins and circulations is a parable of a breakthrough aesthetic technology formed in conjunction with other technological advances that intensified the intercultural contact of competing empires, the Tang and the Abbasid. The story continues with the travels of cobalt blue through the time/space of global modernities from the eighth century to the present. I use the story as a case study of an aesthetic modernism in the medium of ceramics that emerges suddenly in the midst of Abbasid modernity in the ninth century, affects commercial, technological, and aesthetic arenas of the world system, and subsequently takes on new forms as it indigenizes in other locations of later modernities through the centuries.

The story of cobalt blue begins in the "golden age" of the Arab-Islamic Empire during the Abbasid Caliphate, which ruled from 750 to 1258 CE. Wresting power from the Umayyad Caliphate in Damascus (661–750), Islam's third dynastic caliphate arose as a vast empire with Baghdad as its center and Basra as its major port city opening onto the Persian Gulf and the great sea routes of the Indian Ocean. Founded by the first Abbasid caliph, Baghdad was a planned city dubbed the City of Peace. As the empire's hub, Baghdad was a great metropolitan culture capital with commercial and cultural ties stretching across the African continent, far west to Spain, and far east to India, Southeast Asia, and China—arguably one among a number of modernities, including preeminently the Tang and Song Dynasties of China.[22] Under the Abbasids, the arts and sciences flourished, creating new knowledge and technologies that drew on a wide array of classical Greek and Roman texts and religious and secular works from many cultures, including Jewish and Christian ones. The most illustrious of the Abbasid caliphs was Harun al-Rashid, who figures centrally in *The Thousand and One Nights*, the great collection of Persian, Indian, and Arab oral tales compiled and first written down starting about 1000. In contrast to the warlike, nationalist epic tradition of *The Iliad* and *The Aeneid*, *The Thousand and One Nights* uses a frame tale of the clever and learned storyteller Scheherazade, whose stories frequently feature networks of merchants and travelers joining the caravans and wandering the bazaars of a vast commercial empire.

As the center of tremendous wealth and power, Baghdad was what André Gunder Frank calls a great "turntable" or "fulcral" city, a "crossroads" serving as a hub for the globe's other great cities and complex network of land and sea trade.[23] During the early Abbasid Caliphate, dramatic Arab and Persian navigational advances led to the opening of a direct sea route from the Persian Gulf, across the Indian Ocean, through the Strait of Malacca to China, including the great port city of Quanzhou, with its large Muslim community dating back to the early years of the Tang Dynasty, the same city I discussed at the end of chapter 3. Since the Chinese themselves had little interest in long ocean voyages during this period, the Arab traders quickly became the leading merchant middlemen, bringing ivory, pearls, incense, and spices to China (and ports along the way) and picking up Chinese silk, paper, ink, tea, and ceramics as prized luxury items in the Abbasid court centered in Baghdad. The Silk Road over the Asian land mass had been in existence since the beginning of the first millennium. But the relatively sudden advances that made longer seagoing voyages possible in the ninth century gave a particularly prominent role to the merchants of the vast Arab-Islamic Empire, a story reflected in *Shipwrecked: Tang Treasures and Monsoon Winds*, an account of the sixty thousand glazed Chinese ceramics and other treasures recovered from the shipwreck of an Arab merchant ship in the Java Sea.[24]

Basra's cobalt blue comes into the story of transcontinental trade in the second half of the eighth century, as told in a brilliant exhibit entitled "Iraq and China: Ceramics, Trade, and Innovation" and curated by Jessica Hallett at the Arthur M. Sackler Gallery in Washington, D.C., in 2005. Basra was not a particularly powerful center for ceramics until the Iraqi potters' own techniques for tin-glaze ceramics met up with the technologies for Tang Dynasty white stoneware and porcelain from China. As the Sackler Gallery exhibit brochure puts it, "With unusual swiftness and without apparent precedent, the humble character of Near Eastern pottery changed radically during the rule of the powerful Abbasid Empire. In less than forty years, Iraqi potters transformed common earthenware into a vehicle for complex multicolored designs."[25] The Tang potters had developed exquisitely thrown ceramics with a pearly-white glaze that was unlike anything in the Abbasid world. The Basra potters lacked the white clay, wheel skills, and firing technology of the more advanced Chinese potters and were unable to attain the translucence or purity of Tang porcelain or stoneware. But they improvised by combining their indigenous clays and unique tin-glazing technologies to produce a cloudy-white surface that approximated the hard, white ceramics of the Chinese.[26]

The Basra potters' indigenization of Tang ceramics involved even more radical improvisations, however. They applied bold designs in their signature glaze, an intense cobalt blue used only in Iraq, to the already-fired white surface, and fired the vessels again. This blue made a striking contrast with the milky-white surface, and the Basra potters often signed their distinctive blue-and-white pieces thrown in shapes borrowed from China. They also experimented with brightly colored glazes applied to the white surface, and they improvised further with the luster glaze that Iraqi potters had been the first to apply to earthenware pottery.

Luster glazes create a shiny, metallic surface produced by a mixture of silver and copper, a technology that was difficult, costly, and highly prized for its rich ambers, blues, and greens and for the golden sheen that some combinations produced. Lusterware itself represents an indigenization of foreign techniques, since the Iraqi potters adapted the process from the Egyptians, who had used the mixture of silver and copper on glass.[27]

The Basra designs, especially in the beginning, were often strikingly abstract, full of seemingly improvisational "optical excitement" and a "wild appearance," according to Alan Caiger-Smith. He calls these early designs "modern," "ingenious," "extravagant and sometimes dramatic" in their stylizations of shapes taken from local leaves, flowers, and vines. Later, the

Figure 5.1 Bowl, white-glazed earthenware with design in cobalt blue and green. Ninth century. Basra, Iraq.

Source: Freer Gallery of Art, Smithsonian Institution, Washington, D.C. Purchase, F2000.2.

potters created more representational forms—especially animals in motion in the vibrant blues, greens, and brown glazes that stood out so sharply against the white surface.[28]

These innovations accomplished in the short space of about forty years revolutionized ceramic art in the centuries that followed. First, they became a major new luxury item for Arab merchants to trade. Second, the Basra inventions were themselves indigenized as the process of traveling cultures evolved. But because the Iraqi luster technology was a closely guarded trade secret passed down orally by master potters, new improvisations developed slowly. With the decline of the Abbasids by the tenth century, the center of Islamic power moved to Cairo, and the Iraqi potters took their trade secrets to Egypt, where their influence continued to grow as their wares spread throughout the Mediterranean, to Persia, and eventually as far east as China. The intricately designed lusterware of Islamic Spain descends from Iraqi luster ceramics, as does Renaissance Italian *majolica*, known for its historical and religious subjects carefully drawn on the white surface of the tin glaze. The luster technology moved eastward as well, indigenized in Persia to produce the famous Kashan lusterware, often considered the most skilled and best designed of luster pottery. The traders brought the Iraqi ceramics as far east as China, too. By the fourteenth century, it was the cobalt-blue glaze that most interested the Chinese potters of the Yuan (Mongol) Dynasty (1271–1368). The Basra cobalt-blue glaze was reborn in the famous blue-and-white porcelain of Ming Dynasty China (1368–1644), a much-coveted item for trade that made its way back to Europe during the Qing Dynasty (1644–1911), eventually inspiring the blue-and-white Delft pottery of the Netherlands, Portugal's *azulejo* tiles, and the blue-willow-on-white of eighteenth-century England, the most copied china pattern of all time.[29]

The story of cobalt blue and Iraq-China ceramics is an instance—an allegory in the realm of the arts—of a wider societal phenomenon that I associate with particularized modernities. Happening in historically concentrated form, rapid changes in trade, markets, technologies of mobility, intercultural contact, and aesthetic practices produce sudden innovations in the uses of a glaze—in short, in the production of a "modern" art form that subsequently travels the globe. In terms of cultural practice, Basra ceramics involved the local articulation of ideas from elsewhere, a form of mediation in which local agencies transformed influences from outside until they become nativized in the vernacular of indigenous tradition in a process of circulation that I discussed in chapters 2 and 4. These origins from elsewhere were forgotten, particularly as a use of cobalt blue came to symbolize the distinctive character or "tradition" of different cultures, peoples, and nations: the Chinese, the Dutch, the English, and so forth.

The story of cobalt blue underlines how the cultures of European modernity are derivative, though not uniquely so, since the story of Iraq-China ceramics demonstrates how all cultures combine derivation with innovation on a global landscape of interculturalism and circulating modernities. At another level, the story of cobalt blue is an instance of Janet Abu-Lughod's narrative in *Before European Hegemony: The World System, AD 1250–1350*, which places the relatively backward European region within a world system dominated by West Asia, South and Southeast Asia, and

East Asia, as I discussed in chapter 3. The undeniably growing and ultimately hegemonic power of Europe from about the sixteenth through the twentieth centuries, she argues, is rooted in and develops out of the world system that preceded it.[30] But for my purposes in this chapter, the story of cobalt blue illustrates the utility of understanding modernism as the aesthetic dimension of modernity. The modernity of the Abbasid Caliphate in the ninth century produced its own modernism, one that emerged out of the convergence of major innovations and change across the domains of society, one that continued to circulate in newly indigenized forms through vast regions down through the centuries.

KABIR, TAMERLANE, AND RELIGIOUS MODERNITY IN NORTH INDIA

In the late fourteenth and fifteenth centuries, northern India was a vortex of rapid change during a period many call India's "early modernity."[31] With the Mongol Empire split into competing khanates in Persia, Russia, China, and Mongolia, another nomadic military conquest began under the leadership of Tamerlane (1336–1405), a nomadic Mongol-Turk from what is now Uzbekistan. From his capital in the golden city of Samarkand, Tamerlane invoked Genghis Khan as he rapidly spread his military rule across Eurasia, from Syria into western China, conquering as well the Delhi sultanate, along with much of northern India. Tamerlane's absolutist rule did not survive him, but his conquest brought enormous change to northern India, particularly in its complex religious configurations. Muslim armies had already pushed into the region before him, spreading Islam, but Tamerlane took religious conversion to a new level. As a devout Muslim calling himself the "Sword of Islam," Tamerlane encouraged or enforced wide-scale conversions to Islam, especially of lower-caste and out-caste Hindus. These conversions created considerable religious and cultural turmoil, in part because they appeared to provide a means for escaping the stigmas of caste (anticipating the related phenomenon of the "rice Christians" converting from Hinduism to Christianity in the nineteenth century). Muslim converts were allied with the rulers in religious terms but carried the taint of their former caste status; moreover, their new religion was monotheistic, at odds with the open syncretism of polytheistic Hindu religious practices.

As the great-great-grandfather of Babur, Tamerlane paved the way for the Mughal conquests coming from Persia across Afghanistan in the sixteenth century, leading to the establishment of the Mughal Empire (1526–1858). Delhi and the region in which it is located—now the state of Uttar Pradesh—became the thriving multicultural and multireligious center of the empire, rich in wealth, culture, and art. In the late fifteenth century, Guru Nanak founded Sikhism in the north, adapting aspects of Islam and Hinduism. In the sixteenth century, Akbar the Great (1542–1605), the grandson of Babur, united much of the subcontinent, greatly expanding the wealth and power of the Mughal Empire and developing a particular cosmopolitanism in which a multicultural blend of religion, knowledge, and the arts flourished. As Jonardon Ganeri writes in reference to the great explosion of new philosophical thought in Mughal India, "India in the seventeenth century, the century after Akbar, was in intellectual overdrive. Muslim, Jaina, and Hindu intellectuals produced work of tremendous vitality, and ideas circulated around South Asia, through the Persianate and Arabic worlds, and out to Europe and back." "Modernity," he writes about this cultural efflorescence, "was the alternative to irrelevance."[32]

The intercultural clashing and blending initiated by the Muslim incursions into India from the west not only linked India more firmly into the global system of the time but also gave India's modernity of the fifteenth through the seventeenth centuries a distinctive interreligious character that differed significantly from the conquests and religious wars of Europe during the same period.[33] In *Islam Translated*, Ronit Ricci characterizes the result of conversions in South and Southeast Asia as an "Arabic cosmopolis" especially rich in its "interconnected nodal points of material and cultural exchange" and its blend of oral and written stories, poetry, histories, treatises, and performances.[34]

Out of this context, specifically in the wake of Tamerlane's conquest and mass conversions, the phenomenon of Kabir arose in the early fifteenth century, providing an instance of a very different kind of modernism than that of the Tang's Du Fu or Basra's cobalt-blue glaze. Born most likely in Benares at the height of the religious turmoil Tamerlane's rule brought to northern India, Kabir (c. 1398–1448) was a poet/singer whose work reflects the religious instabilities and ambiguities of the time. He came from a low-caste family of weavers who had joined the massive conversions of the weaver caste to Islam in the decades of Tamerlane's rule before his birth. Large numbers of Muslim and Hindu weavers lived in Benares (now Vanarisi), the holy city on the Ganges still sacred to Hindus but also important to Muslims, Jains, and Buddhists and still a major center for weaving and its highly prized silk saris. Poor, most likely illiterate, and without formal education, Kabir survived as a cotton weaver, producing a large body of song/poems widely known in his lifetime and continuing to spread after his death. The early ambiguity about his actual name—Kabir versus Kamir—illuminates the religious and caste tensions among which he lived and performed. Vinay Dharwadker explains that Kabir (*al-Kabír*) means "the great" in Arabic and is one of the names of Allah in the Qur'an; Kamir, the name sometimes used in the earliest Kabir manuscripts, echoes Hindi-Urdu words rooted in the Farsi term *kam*, which means "low, deficient, less, mean, base, or despicable."[35] In turn, the name Kamir reverberates with *mlechchhas*, the Hindu caste name for Muslim weavers in Benares, a term meaning "outsiders, people of a foreign race or faith" that contrasts with the term *shúdras* (servants) used for the Hindu weavers (Dharwadker, 12–13, 8). "Everybody," Kabir sang in one poem, "reduces my caste to a laughing stock: // but it devotes itself to the Creator, / and I martyr myself to its cause" (Dharwadker, 8).

After Kabir's death, his fame spread even more widely, always under the name "Kabir," with his song/poems first appearing in written manuscripts in 1570 and 1582 and continuing as a living, still-changing improvisational tradition of both written and oral performance into the twenty-first century. Competing legends grew up about his life and work, making Kabir an "author" and celebrity even as his body of work expanded and diversified in both manuscript and oral forms. As Dharwadker argues, Kabir's corpus demonstrates the practice of a "community of authors," with authorship as an "aggregate affair" and texts "open to endless proliferation" yet exhibiting a "shared structure of ideas, images, arguments and dispositions" (60–61, 77). Over time, his song/poems became ever more multiregional, multilingual, and multireligious, expanding in size and heterogeneity as they circulated beyond their original emergence in Kabir's own lifetime.[36] Kabir—or more properly the phenomenon of "Kabir"—has been and still is variously known, adapted, deployed, reinvented, and performed for his particular blend of mysticism, metaphysics, philosophy, social politics, iconoclasm, poetry, and song.

Both Muslims and Hindus have claimed Kabir as their own for centuries, identifying as his burial site the side-by-side Hindu temple and Muslim mausoleum (now a Sufi shrine) in Maghar, a small town in the Benares region known for its Muslim weavers and to which legend has him retreat near the end of his life (Dharwadker, 3–4). Additionally, the Sikhs produced the first manuscript of his poems in 1570 and centrally incorporated his monotheistic mysticism into Sikhism. However, Kabir continuously attacks all institutionalized religions, makes fun of ritual practices and sacred texts, espouses a notion of a single unknowable god, and exhibits a personal religious sensibility allied with mysticism based in direct experience of the divine. This song/poem in Arvind Krishna Mehrotra's translation characteristically positions Kabir ambiguously apart from Hinduism and Islam:

> Listen carefully,
> Neither the Vedas
> Nor the Qur'an
> Will teach you this:
> Put the bit in its mouth,
> The saddle on its back,
> Your foot in the stirrup,
> And ride your wild runaway mind
> All the way to heaven.[37]

In his rejection of established religion and advocacy of mysticism, Kabir drew on a long tradition of *bhakti* poet-saints that began in the Tamil culture in southern India in the sixth century and gradually circulated through and indigenized in many parts of India. In his introduction to *Songs of Kabir*, Mehrotra suggests that *bhakti* achieved its fullest expression in northern India from the fifteenth through the seventeenth centuries, with Kabir as perhaps the best known and loved in the tradition. He notes that the *bhakti* movement originated in and remains part of "a devotional turn" in Hindu culture, with "its distinguishing feature . . . an inward love for the One Deity, in disregard of, and often in opposition to religious orthodoxies and social hierarchies" (xxi). *Bhakti* singer-saints often defied religious and family conventions if they stood in the way of this direct engagement with deity. In formal terms, "*bhakti* favored the informal over the formal, the spontaneous over the prescribed, and the vernacular over Sanskrit" (Mehrotra, xxi). The *bhakti* singer-poet was a "new kind of person or persona" who came into fashion, a "'person who flouts proprieties, refuses the education of a poet, insists that anyone can be a poet—for it is the Lord who sings through one.' This new person, the poet-saint, could be a king or a prime minister or a low-caste cobbler, tailor, barber, cotton-carder, boatman, or weaver.... The poet-singer could, of course, also be a woman" (Mehrotra, xxii). Jabanababi, a thirteenth-century maidservant and poet-saint, sang, for example, "god my darling / do me a favor and kill mother-in-law" (Mehrotra, xxi). According to A. K. Ramanujan, the *bhakti* poet-saints constituted a third gender, with men absorbing the feminine and women, the masculine.[38]

Kabir was both of the *bhakti* tradition and an innovator within it: he was one of a kind, his songs instantaneously recognizable for being the most outspoken and confrontational. "Friend, / You had one life, / And you blew it" opens one song/poem (Mehrotra, xxiii). "O pundit, your hairsplitting's / So much bullshit. I'm surprised / You still get away with it," begins another (Mehrotra, 26). "His is a collective voice that is so individual that it cannot be mistaken for anyone else's," Mehrotra writes (xxii–xxiii). Kabir's song/poems reinvent the *bhakti* devotional practice of opposition to established polytheistic Hinduism to challenge the institutionalized religious conventions of both Hindus and Muslims, the very groups who coexisted in a tug of war as a result of Tamerlane's recent conquest. As singer, he positions himself between the two opposing groups, offering a different way based on his particular combination of poetry, singing, and bodily intimacy with the divine:

> Were the Creator
> Concerned about caste,
> We'd arrive in the world
> With a caste mark on the forehead.
>
> If you say you're a Brahmin
> Born of a mother who's a Brahmin,

> Was there a special canal
> Through which you were born?
>
> And if you say you're a Turk
> And your mother's a Turk,
> Why weren't you circumcised
> Before birth?
>
> Nobody's lower-caste;
> The lower castes are everywhere.
> They're the ones
> Who don't have Rama on their lips,
>
> Kabir says.
>
> (Mehrotra, 28)

Similarly, Kabir adapts the *bhakti* convention of gender bending by combining it with religious, caste, sexual, and ethnic border crossings to characterize himself "without a place to call home," a place that allows for the experience of the divine within, as in this poem/song:

> Tell me, wise one,
> How did I become
> A woman from a man?
>
> I never got married,
> Was never pregnant,
> But gave birth to sons.
>
> I fucked young men,
> Too numerous to count,
> And stayed a virgin.
>
> In a Brahmin's house,
> I become a Brahmin's wife;
> In a yogi's, a lay yogini;

> In a Turk's, I read the *kalma*
> And do as Turkish women do;
> And yet I'm always alone
>
> Without a place to call home.
> Listen, saints, Kabir says,
> This is my body.
>
> I don't let
> My husband touch it
> Or anyone else.
>
> (Mehrotra, 50)

Kabir's "modern" sensibility—his awareness of the world split open, his search for the divine (whom he calls Rama), his self-reflexivity about his songs—constitute an aesthetic dimension of the particular modernity into which he was born, one in which competing and often warring religious concepts and discourse were central. He writes, for example:

> Unlettered, I go
> Through a world
> That's self-igniting,
> Self-destructing.
> I let it be.
>
> To each his own, Kabir says.
> I've thrown my lot in with Rama.
>
> (Mehrotra, 41)

Unlettered he may be, but he is also rhetorically complex, playful with words and images, and philosophically astute; he balances the power of language with the phenomenology of the mystic. Never simply devotional *cris de coeur*, his song/poems push the envelope of paradox, riddle, absurdity, contradiction, opposition, anaphorism, and syntactic parallelism. In this sense, he is most likely both *of* the *bhakti* tradition but also a supreme master of it (as Shakespeare was of Elizabethan drama and poetry). For example, in the song/poem that opens with the challenge "O pundit, your hairsplitting's / So much bullshit," he continues:

> If parroting the name
> Of Rama brought salvation,
> Then saying *sugarcane*
> Should sweeten the mouth,
> Saying *fire* burn the feet,
> Saying *water* slake thirst,
> And saying *food*
> Would be as good as a belch.
>
> If saying *money* made everyone rich,
> There'd be no beggars in the streets.
>
> My back is turned on the world,
> You hear me singing of Rama and you smile.
> One day, Kabir says,
> All bundled up,
> You'll be delivered to Deathville.

(Mehrotra, 26)

Talk is cheap, Kabir says, and hides the emptiness within words, even as his text unfolds in deliciously elegant renunciations of language in the service of divine song. Anglo-American modernist angst about the efficacy of language has a predecessor in Kabir's query:

> Except that it robs you of who you are,
> What can you say about speech?
> Inconceivable to live without
> And impossible to live with,
> Speech diminishes you.
> . . . .
> Strike a half-empty pot, and it'll make
> A loud sound; strike one that is full,
> Says Kabir, and hear the silence.

(Mehrotra, 90)

The improvisational, continually reinvented, vernacular, and communal dimensions of Kabir's oeuvre also make him useful for thinking expansively about the different modernisms that accompany multiple modernities. Kabir represents the fluidity of a "tradition" in tune with improvisational change even as he represents a certain kind of religious and poetic celebrity around whom centuries of legends have been created. Even though not a single Kabir text can be authenticated in the conventional sense, his song/poems continue to be produced under the sign of his name and personality. Through the centuries, numerous anthologies and translations of his work have been compiled, both within India for Indian consumption and abroad. He continues to exist and be performed in the vernaculars of India, while well-known writers like Tagore, Pound, Czeslaw Milosz, Robert Bly, and Robert Hass have also published translations. As Mukti Lakhi Mangharan notes, Shabnam Virmani has made four documentary films of contemporary performances of Kabir, each of which attests to his vibrant contemporary following.[39] Such oral performances, as well as the printed anthologies and translations, improvise with Kabir's corpus. Likening Kabir in print and performance to the blues, Mehrotra points out that different images are often substituted and many other changes made:

> For the singer, the *pada* was not something whose words had unalterably been fixed, to be slavishly followed while singing, but something that was provisional and fluid, a working draft, whose lines and images could be shifted around, or substituted by others, or deleted entirely. As with the blues, another example of "collective creation," the lines could be "altered, extended, abridged, and transposed."
>
> (Mehrotra, xxxi)

In his translations, Mehrotra participates in the improvisational fluidity of Kabir. He prefaces the song "O pundit, your hairsplitting's / So much bullshit" with an epigraph from Leadbelly: "It take a man that have the blues so to sing the blues" (Mehrotra, 26). He updates Kabir's language with references to "megaphone" and "chromosome" (21, 41), as Kabir performers regularly do, incorporating such things as engines, tickets, and trains into their Kabir songs. His epigraphs and notes juxtapose Kabir's song with writers as varied as Horace, Bhettrihari, Coleridge, Yeats, Pound, and

Cavafy and texts like the Ramayana and Rig Veda. As a contemporary "performer" in print of Kabir's corpus, Mehrotra reinvents Kabir in the deep time of an ever-evolving, cosmopolitan world literature.

Conventional Western notions of post-1500 aesthetic modernity associate it with the fixing of texts, the standardization of language, the authenticity of the author, and the rationalization of religion. In this context, Kabir is not modern: he represents "tradition," particularly the oral tradition rooted in folkways and communal life. But the more expansive concept of multiple and recurrent modernisms that I suggest in this book opens up the possibility of seeing Kabir's work as a form of aesthetic modernity—a modernism—that helped shape the fifteenth-century modernity of Tamerlane's empire with its multireligious ambiguities and that continues to participate in spawning new forms in the subsequent modernities of South Asia under the Mughals, the British, and in the postcolonial period.

CONCLUSION

As the aesthetic dimension of modernity, modernism gives form to the visionary, imaginary, phenomenological, emotional, mimetic, and symbolic modes of human meaning making caught up in the mobilities and fissures of accelerating change, in the networks of often clashing forces in the particular world system of its geohistorical emergence. I have argued against the definition of modernism as a particular period, movement, or style located initially in Europe, Britain, and the United States in the late nineteenth/early twentieth century. The retreat to this familiar and seemingly more manageable timeframe and landscape for modernism is insufficiently transhistorical and planetary; it recapitulates in the aesthetic domain the story of the West's invention of modernity and its diffusion to the Rest. It operates out of a nominal approach to definition, as I have argued in earlier chapters about modernity, and leads us to ask how any given non-Western aesthetic text or art resembles the work of such iconic figures as Picasso, Joyce, Woolf, or Eliot. This is precisely the conundrum in which Eric Hayot is caught. He wants, in the essay from which the epigraph is taken, to "denaturalize centrisms of all types," he wants to include China among the global modernisms," but he is unable to abandon "the temporal logic" that has structured the field of modernist studies. For him, China's modernism is inevitably an effect of a prior European modernism to which it relates in a state of "mimetic desire."[40]

Modernism, I suggest in contrast, is more usefully understood in relational terms, as the aesthetic expressivities in the cultural field of any given modernity. In such relational terms, we might ask how the aesthetic forms of a given modernity engage with (reflect, shape) the other dimensions of that modernity? How do its forms embody interactions of tradition and modernity? Since aesthetic forms always draw on older forms to some extent, what are the intertextualities of the new modernisms? How do the new and old clash and blend? How do they travel, transplant, and indigenize through time and across space? What are the meanings of modernism in the networks of the large-scale *longue durée* or the small-scale level of text or aesthetic object?

The very different poetries of Du Fu and Kabir and the invention of cobalt-blue glazes on white pots, I have shown, function as case studies to demonstrate the connection/disconnection between distinctive modernities and their modernisms *before* 1500. While each flourished in the context of empire, the imperial frameworks within which they worked were significantly different: the civil war of the An Lushan Rebellion, the vast commercial network of the Abbasids, and the postconquest period of Tamerlane's mass conversions. Small-scale analysis at the level of an aesthetic object in its immediate and different context provides a test case for the usefulness of moving beyond a conventional periodization for modernism to posit particular modernisms as the convention-breaking aesthetic dimension of multiple and recurrent modernities. I do not claim that *modernism* should be the main or sole framework for interpreting Du Fu, Kabir, or cobalt-blue glazes. Nonetheless, I suggest that my borrowing of these small-scale aesthetic innovations from their more conventional fields of scholarship has much to contribute to the question of how to think about the relationship between modernism and modernity in the *longue durée*. That has been my intention: to show the potential usefulness of linking modernism as an aesthetic to the modernity of which it is a part, within a spatio/temporal landscape of centuries across the globe. In the next chapter, I turn, with some relief, to the field of my own original specialization: the modernisms of the long twentieth century.

SIX
CIRCULATING MODERNISMS

Collages of Empire in Fictions of the Long Twentieth Century

> Empires—self-consciously maintaining the diversity of people they conquered and incorporated—have played a long and critical part in human history. For much of the last two millennia, empires and their rivalries, in regions or around the world, created contexts in which people formed connections—as ethnic or religious communities, in networks of migrants, settlers, slaves, and commercial agents.
>
> —Jane Burbank and Frederick Cooper, *Empires in World History*

> The awareness of modernity... offer[s] us the image of relations, similarities of situations or diverging directions, between what is us and what is other.
>
> —Édouard Glissant, *Poetics of Relation*

> To speak here of borrowing and adaptation is not adequate. There is in particular an intellectual, and perhaps moral, community of a remarkable kind, *affiliation* in the deepest and most interesting sense of the word.
>
> —Edward W. Said, "Traveling Theory Reconsidered."

Modernism, I hope to have established in the preceding chapters, is the aesthetic dimension of modernity. Multiple and recurrent modernities produce their own particular multiple and recurrent modernisms. Across the globe and through time, these modernisms are not only distinctive but also linked to other modernisms in vast relational networks. They constitute a multinodal world system of expressive/symbolic culture, one not set apart from but rather embedded within the other dimensions of the modernities of which they are a part—the realms of the political, economic, technological, cultural, and so forth. And as aesthetic articulations repeatedly read, viewed, and dialogued with, they have an afterlife or a new life with each iteration, with each new engagement—some more than others, of course. Like pebbles thrown into a pool, the bigger the stone, the wider its circles. Factors vary in what makes some bigger in effect than others; these particularities matter, whether at the scale of centuries or of the individual text or artifact. Whatever the scale, the story of these circulations constitutes what Glissant calls "the image of relations," what Said calls "affiliation," what Jahan Ramazani calls "enmeshment," and what Zygmunt Bauman terms the "matrix" of culture.[1] The planetary framework I have advocated throughout this book brings into heightened visibility such mobile, interlocking, yet distinctive modernisms.

In this chapter, I zoom in on the circulating modernist fictions produced in the matrix of empires in the long twentieth century, including their constitutive logics of race, gender, sexuality, class, and caste. This "long" century is the time when Western imperial hegemonies reach their height and then break apart in times marked by world wars, the formation of emergent non-Western nation-states, and the newest phase of globalization enabled by rapid technological change. In working with a transcontinental network of textual relations, I emphasize the modernities of colonialism and its legacies in part because others have so ably examined other aspects of rapid change in the twentieth century but more substantively because I regard the catastrophes of the century not simply as war between nation-states but as seismic conflict among and within global empires. This conflict among European, Russian, Ottoman, Chinese, Japanese, and American empires constituted a planetary geopolitics with deep effects among peoples they colonized, including not only the humiliations of colonialism but also intensified and at times creative contact among diverse peoples and cultures. I agree with Jane Burbank and Frederick Cooper in their insistence that the "modern" nation-state did not supplant the much older and ongoing civilizational structure based on empire but rather developed within and through those imperial structures (1–3). Instead of regarding colonial and postcolonial issues as an adjunct to the modernities of the Western metropole, I regard them as central and constitutive. "The great categories that came to define the modern age," Simon Gikandi writes, "were haunted, from the start, by the colonial question."[2] "Coloniality," Walter Mignolo writes in a similar vein, as I discussed in chapters 2 and 3, "is the hidden face of modernity and the very condition of possibility."[3] So too the long century's modernisms in their transcontinental relations.

Collage provides this chapter's central structure for examining circulating modernisms within the framework of modern empires. In collages, fragments set side by side lead the eye to move across the surface and to discover or invent some patterns of relation in color, shape, form, and meaning. As a medium going back centuries, collage burst into the modern art scene alongside cubism, echoing (whether consciously or not) their immediate precursors in the collages of late-nineteenth-century women's memorabilia and scrapbooks. Built on the principle of paratactic juxtaposition, collage in turn helped generate cinematic montage, with its principles of sharp cutting miming the Hegelian dialectic of thesis/antithesis/synthesis in the film theory of Sergei Eisenstein.[4] Collage and its echo in montage inspire the method of this chapter as I explore the circulation of these texts and as I travel back and forth between them, looking for the "image of relations, similarities of situations or diverging directions, between what is us and what is other," to invoke Glissant's *Poetics of Relation* again (199).

In adapting early-twentieth-century collage, however, I do so in the conviction that this form of aesthetic modernism anticipated the spatial turn that pervades the late-twentieth-century/early-twenty-first century modernities and modernisms and that undergirds the synchronic tropes of modernity in chapter 4. As Michel Foucault writes in "Of /Other Spaces," "We are in the epoch of juxtaposition, the epoch of side-by-side, of the dispersed. We are at a moment, I believe, when our experience of the world is less that of a long life developing through time than that of a network that connects points and intersects with its own skein."[5] The identification of intersecting networks effectively challenges the diffusionist and center/periphery models of modernity that have been so influential in discussions of global modernisms. The transnational turn in modernist studies will never be fulfilled if we maintain the story of the Western origins of modernism and its spread elsewhere. Like conventional notions of modernity critiqued in chapter 3, this story of modernism centers innovation in the West and belated derivation in the Rest; it dooms the artists, writers, and intellectuals of non-Western parts of the world, many of them colonized by or newly liberated from European and American empires, to reaction, to a perpetual writing back that obscures their own creative initiative. As significant as Homi K. Bhabha's concept of colonial mimicry has been for understanding the denaturalizing adaptations of the colonized, his notion does not in the end unseat these center/periphery and diffusionist models of cultural production.[6] Mimicry is a form of parody that remains caught within the system it deconstructs and is therefore insufficient for understanding global circulations of culture.

Collage, in contrast, potentially offers a fully contextualized agency to each piece within the larger cultural field; it also invites relational thinking as the eye travels from one creative agency to another seeking "similarities of situations or diverging directions." Collage facilitates what Glissant calls in *Poetics of Relation* the elimination of relational trajectories leading "from the Center toward the peripheries" or "from the peripheries to the Center." These eliminations in turn allow "the poet's word" to lead "from periphery to periphery . . . ; that is, it makes every periphery into a center; furthermore, it abolishes the very notion of center and periphery" (29).

In moving the scale of analysis to the level of aesthetic texts, this chapter collages four paired readings of Joseph Conrad's *Heart of Darkness* (1899) and Tayeb Salih's *Season of Migration to the North* (1966), E. M. Forster's *A Passage to India* (1924) and Arundhati Roy's *The God of Small Things* (1997), and Virginia Woolf's *A Room of One's Own* (1929) and related novels and short stories of Rabindranath Tagore and Swarnakumari Devi. These four distinct collages also reverberate as a whole, both for their engagements with twentieth-century empires and for their explorations of gender, sexuality, race, and caste as discrepant modern formations within imperial contexts. Additionally, they provide snapshots of the four strategies for a planetary modernist studies outlined in chapter 2: *re-vision*, as a return to the familiar texts of modernism to be read anew in a global framework; *recovery*, as an effort to expand the archives of modernism beyond the West; *circulation*, as a tracking of modernist mobilities through time and space; and *collage*, as a form of radical juxtaposition that produces new insight.

CIRCULATING MODERNISMS • 219

These readings posit a notion of mobile modernisms that highlight aesthetic agencies existing within a world system based in relational, multinodal networks of traveling creativities, where power is discrepant and modernities are uneven and divergent, to echo terms introduced in chapter 4. They draw heavily on Said's concept of "affiliation" in the context of "traveling theory," on Glissant's relational poetics of archipelagic modernities, and on Ramazani's model of circulating "enmeshments," all of which deserve a brief review. Said's notion of affiliation originates in his seminal essay "Traveling Theory" (1983), which emphasizes local creative agencies in the global circulation of symbolic/representational forms and ideas in the context of empire. He argues that as ideas travel from one culture to another, the "transplantation, transference, circulation, and commerce" of these ideas "is never unimpeded."[7] What interests him are the "conditions of acceptance or, as an inevitable part of acceptance, resistances" that confront "the transplanted theory or idea." In its new location, "the now full (or partly) accommodated (or incorporated) idea is to some extent transformed by its new uses, its new position in a new time and place" (227).

In "Traveling Theory Reconsidered" (1994), Said criticizes his earlier essay for not recognizing that such transplanted ideas can be more "radical" or "rebellious" than their original formulation. "Later versions of the theory cannot replicate its original power," he writes in summary of his earlier view, "because the situation has quieted down and changed, the theory is subdued, made into a relatively tame academic substitute for the real."[8] Rather than theories becoming diluted as they travel, Said argues for a kind of "affiliation" that is based not on "static, fixed" reproductions of the original idea but on the way in which travel and transplantation allow for "its fiery core" to be "reignited" (452). For Said, this is not an affiliation of genealogical lineage, mimicry, anonymous intertextuality, or unequals. Instead, his notion of affiliation presumes multiple creative agencies and centers that exist within the structures of colonialism and its legacies in the postcolonial world. As such, it has much to offer models of traveling, circulating fictions.

Where Said's theory of affiliation tends to be unidirectional—from colonizing center to colonial periphery as a site of "firey" agency, Glissant develops his poetics of relation out of his notion of archipelagic modernities—multinodal, multidirectional flows of relational representation—and the particular role of the symbolic and linguistic in the formation of world cultures. Writers located at different nodal points in the network of modernities create not in isolation but in linked relationship to creative producers elsewhere. Interactions at the symbolic level are not necessarily imitative, signs of a one-way influence, as the center/periphery or diffusionist models of modernity would have it. Nor do colonial or postcolonial texts exist solely in opposition to or reaction against those of the colonizers. Instead, the concept of global affiliations focuses attention on interculturalism at the level of representation. Such affiliations come out of and create a network of texts that exist in dialogic relationship without definitive origins or endpoints.

In *Transnational Poetics*, Ramazani adapts concepts of networks, enmeshment, and linkages from Glissant and from globalization theory more generally to understand what he calls the planetary circulations of poetry "in the context of a globalizing modernity" (10).[9] Influenced by anthropological concepts of traveling cultures and global flows, Ramazani is interested in the mobility of texts around the globe, their circulations that both resist the homogenizing tendencies of globalization and the purely nativist insistence on difference.[10] What modernity enables, he argues, is "poetry's transnational flows [that] can be seen as moving in multiple directions, or in leaps and loops, or in what creolization theorist Édouard Glissant styles as returns and detours (*le retour et le détour*)" (10). The Biafran poet Christopher Okigbo, for example, "indigenizes Western poetic forms to pay homage to the Igbo river goddess dwelling hear his home village" (9), and "Kamau Brathwaite describes West Indian writers as being given access for the first time to their local speech rhythms . . . through the detour of none other than T. S. Eliot's voice transmitted to Barbados by the British Council" (10). For Ramazani, the irony is that the Caribbean writer becomes "more 'indigenous' by virtue of becoming at the same time more 'modernist'" and open to the world (10). Nor does Ramazani see this symbolic/linguistic/textual circulation as constructing only the African or Caribbean poets. Ezra Pound, he notes, "discovers in haiku and other East Asian cultural forms possibilities for breaking through the impasse of European symbolism to an imagist poetics of the natural image" (10). Recognizing the overarching colonial/imperial contexts, Ramazani does not collapse the two circuits: "Brathwaite hears a recorded voice from the 'frozen Nawth' by way of a propaganda arm of the British Empire, while Pound's arrogation of minimalist Asian technique may not be innocent of American expansionism" (10).

The point for Ramazani is that in the aesthetic realm of modernity, the circulation of representational forms follows patterns of the global ecumene more generally, establishing a transnational poetics of continual movement, affiliations, and indigenizations. Quoting Revathi Krishnaswamy, Ramazani insists that the circuits of symbolic forms are not "unilinear . . . because movement between cultural/geographical areas always involves selection, interpretation, translation, mutation, and adaptation—processes designated by terms such as *indigenization* and *vernacularization*—with the receiving culture bringing its own cultural resources to bear, in dialectical fashion, upon cultural imports" (9–10).[11] The circuits Ramazani and Krishnaswamy identify recall the travels and indigenizations of modernity that I theorized in chapter 4.

Said's concept of intellectual affiliation, Glissant's multinodal poetics of relation, and Ramazani's transnational poetics of enmeshed, circulating networks offer a framework for this chapter's collaged readings of selected modernist fictions within the long twentieth century. In contrast to readings based in center/periphery and linear diffusionist models for transnational modernism, the readings assume an indeterminacy of origins, the ongoingness of mobile modernisms, and an affiliation of projects that indigenize ideas from elsewhere—transporting, translating, and transculturating them from context to context, from agency to agency. They track not only the mobile networks among the texts but also my own circulations among the texts to explore what comes newly into visibility through their juxtaposition. Addressing these two levels of circulation, I hope to show the creative agencies of affiliations that reinvigorate the fiery core of a transcontinental selection of modernist fictions in the long twentieth century. Repeatedly drawing on the insights of postcolonial studies, I emphasize throughout the significance of empire for these affiliations. But I also emphasize ways that gender, race, caste, and sexuality rupture narratives based on coloniality alone to suggest other forms of affiliation. As instances of divergent and uneven modernities *within* each society of the post/colonial, these forms of affiliation constitute another dimension of the "fiery core," one that resists simple binaries of imperial oppression and post/colonial resistance.

COLLAGE 1: HEARTS OF DARKNESS IN JOSEPH CONRAD AND TAYEB SALIH

As Simon Gikandi demonstrates compellingly in *Maps of Englishness*, early-twentieth-century British modernism develops relationally out of the British Empire, with the very concept of Englishness dependent on intercultural encounters within an imperial framework.[12] As modernist studies has increasingly absorbed the insights of postcolonial studies, Joseph Conrad has steadily become more central to literary histories of British modernism. *Heart of Darkness*, originating in the author's childhood fantasy of central Africa as a blank spot on the map and in his much later trip up the Congo River in 1890, has taken on allegorical force in the field for its aesthetics of irony and unreliable narration and for the indeterminacy of its politics on colonialism, race, and gender.[13] Published in 1899 at the very cusp of the century's turn, *Heart of Darkness* has been variously read as the epitome of imperial racism (Chinua Achebe), as ambiguously complicit with and critical of imperialism (Edward W. Said), and as a deconstructive text that unravels the very foundation of empire (Marianne DeKoven).[14] Whatever its meanings to differently located readers, *Heart of Darkness* has spawned numerous rewritings, re-visions, versionings, cultural translations, and intertextual dialogues by writers from across the globe, as Regelind Farn documents in *Colonial and Postcolonial Rewritings of* Heart of Darkness.[15]

HEART OF DARKNESS

This pervasive centrality of *Heart of Darkness* in twentieth-century literary history in general and modernist studies more specifically appears to establish the novel as an Ur-text for later writers, with Conrad as an initiator of discourse to which later writers are drawn charismatically to repeat or react against. The journeys of Kurtz and Marlow into the depths of the unnamed Congo, the revelation of the "darkness" at the heart of Belgian imperialism,[16] the muteness of the African *other* (subjected but never subjects), and the deception of the Intended, who is allowed to maintain her belief in the high idealism of her fiancé's endeavors, function as literary and historical ground upon which the later writers construct their own edifices of aesthetic modernity. To the extent that colonial and postcolonial writers create fictions that answer *Heart of Darkness*, they seem caught as its satellites, limited to the periphery of modernism's center. As such, this relationship appears to confirm the diffusionist model of modernity/modernism that I challenged in chapter 3. It also appears to support the notion of derivative belatedness that postcolonial theorists like Partha Chatterjee and Dipesh Chakrabarty lament and that R. Radhakrishnan calls the "curse of derivativeness," as discussed in chapter 3.

Such a view, however, ignores the fact that as an immigrant Pole and a seaman, Conrad is ambiguously British, formed in the wake of his imperial wanderings and migration as an exile from a Poland colonized by Russia. His homeland and language as a writer are adoptive, testament to his formation within a global matrix of colonial modernities through which he circulates. He is not so much a point of origin to which others must react as he is yet one more manifestation of a centuries-long tradition of travel writing, one particularly intense at the height of the British Empire, when its global hegemony seemed but was not in fact unassailable. His own identity as writer and the identities of his protagonists reflect a relational process of formation in which continual engagement with others far from "home" or in some way "foreign," *other*, or alien are constitutive of the self. In some sense, Conrad, like his avatar Marlow, is both lost and found in translation, a particularly modern dislocation.

Moreover, a reading of *Heart of Darkness* in conjunction with one of its most influential rewritings highlights the political ambiguities of the novel and demonstrates the invigorating affiliation that Said theorizes rather than the curse of derivativeness. Tayeb Salih's *Season of Migration to the North*, completed by the Sudan's leading writer during his exile in Beirut, is by now a postcolonial classic that appeared in Arabic in 1966 and then in English translation in 1969, with an ongoing globalized reading public in over thirty languages.[17] The representational strategies of both *Heart of Darkness* and *Season of Migration to the North* rely on rupture, self-reflexivity, multiperspectivity, jumbled chronology, simultaneity, ambiguity, and disruption of normative certainties. Both narrativize the psychodynamic processes of consciousness, memory, and desire—embodying or implying the mechanisms of repression and the symptomatic return of the repressed. Both use migratory motifs to narrate the world split open, the center that cannot hold. For both, the effects of empire are inseparable from issues of individual subjectivity, agency, and intimacy. And for both, the intersection of race and gender function as the linchpin that holds together the social order of the nation and its discontents. These parallels are not the product of imitation but rather Salih's affiliation with Conrad's project, one that translates *Heart of Darkness* into the heart of darkness within the postcolonial state and culture at the same time that it challenges Conrad's complicities with the imperialism he morally condemns.

The key to understanding the relational and affiliational poetics of *Heart of Darkness* and *Season of Migration to the North* lies in Conrad's continuously shifting relationship as the writer to his main narrator Marlow—at times, the two seem indistinguishable; at other times the ironic gap between them opens wide. Salih's novel exploits this irony, helping bring these moments into even sharper visibility. Readings of *Heart of Darkness* often overlook what Salih affiliates with and reinvents. In his critique of Conrad's politics, Said, for example, collapses the distinction between writer and protagonist(s):

> But Marlow and Kurtz are also creatures of their time and cannot take the next step, which would be to recognize that what they saw, disablingly and disparagingly, as a non-European "darkness" was in fact a non-European world *resisting* imperialism so as one day to regain sovereignty and independence, and not, as Conrad reductively says, to reestablish the darkness. Conrad's tragic limitation is that even though he could see clearly that on one level imperialism was essentially pure dominance and land-grabbing, he could not then conclude that imperialism had to end so that "natives" could lead lives free from European domination. As a creature of his time, Conrad could not grant the natives their freedom, despite his severe critique of the imperialism that enslaved them.[18]

From one perspective, I think Said is correct: Conrad did not see or at least made no attempt to represent the colonized Africans as full subjects with thoughts, feelings, and agencies in their own right—a lack upon which Chinua Achebe bases his attack on the novel's racism. In this sense, Salih's novel goes well beyond Conrad's because African subjectivities are its main focus, asserted in the face of British characters who repeatedly racialize and Orientalize the African ones. But at another level, Said (and Achebe) ignores the critical eye that Conrad casts upon his narrator and to some extent against himself.

Reminding us of the divergent modernities discussed in chapter 4, the power differentials existing *within* a given modernity, Marlow is the Englishman that Conrad himself could never be, though his identification with Marlow at times may well express his desire as an immigrant to Britain to assimilate fully, to be accepted as English. Marlow is part projection of Conrad's desires and part critique of what he emulates. Marlow's unreliability as narrator is, of course, well known and central to readings of the novel as modernist. Marlow's desires, failings, and blind spots are themselves focal points for Conrad's exploration of the colonizing subject as agent of empire. However, just as interesting and not as often examined are those enigmatic elements or moments in the novel when Marlow *almost* breaks through to an awareness of the humanity and subjectivity of the African *other*. At these moments, the novel's irony is at its height, as we readers recognize that Marlow is both shocked by these momentary recognitions and unable to act upon the insight they provide. They disrupt his colonial view of the world that is unable to acknowledge the other's subjectivity. Ignoring the lessons of these brief, epiphanic moments, Marlow confirms the colonial view at the novel's end by lying to the Intended, maintaining the fiction of the civilizing mission of imperialism that he knows to be false, because in the end he takes sides with Europe against the racial other.

One such enigma is the puzzling presence of the "harlequin" Russian, "the man of patches" who ambiguously guides Marlow to the site of ultimate "horror," the dying Kurtz, and possibly provides a carnivalesque rupture of colonial authority and the imperial narrative that associates blankness and savagery with the heart of Africa and the patina of civilization with Europe (98). This man "in motley" is Marlow's final guide into the heart of darkness, a sort of halfway native informant whose narrative provides the clues to Kurtz's descent. As such, he remains a mystery to Marlow, as to the reader: "there he was before me, in motley, as though he had absconded from a troupe of mimes, enthusiastic, fabulous. His very existence was improbable, inexplicable and altogether bewildering. He was an insoluble problem. It was inconceivable how he had existed, how he had succeeded in getting so far, how he managed to remain—why he did not instantly disappear" (100). Marlow describes him as Kurtz's "last disciple," shocked to discover how he served as go-between for the native Africans and the colonial agent (105). In one sense, the Russian's inexplicable presence gestures at the existence of another, ambiguously non-European imperial center, tsarist Russia, at the hands of which Conrad's own Polish family and nation had suffered. As such, his presence destabilizes even as it serves European colonialism in Africa. In another sense, however, the Russian may represent, as Urszula Horoszko argues, power relations within Eurasia in which both Poles and Russians occupied the "savage" slot in relation to the British and Europeans of northwestern Europe.[19] Whatever the Russian represents in the novel, the enigma of his presence shatters Marlow's imperial narrative, disrupting the binarist meanings he brings to the story by exhibiting the structure of divergent modernities.

Three scenes centered around reciprocal gazes between Marlow and black Africans punctuate Marlow's story to the men on board the *Nellie*, each scene challenging the ideology of civilized/savage upon which European imperialism was built. The first of these takes place at the Company's station on the coast, right after Marlow sees the chain-gang of six men with iron collars. Looking for shade, Marlow stumbles upon "black shapes crouched" where they had "withdrawn to die": "They were dying slowly—it was very clear. They were not enemies, they were not criminals, they were nothing earthly now, nothing but black shadows of disease and starvation" (58). Marlow doesn't see these shadows as men, as human. But a flicker of recognition of the other's humanity occurs, just for a moment:

> Then glancing down I saw a face near my hand. The black bones reclined at full length with one shoulder against the tree, and slowly the eyelids rose and the sunken eyes looked up at me, enormous and vacant, a kind of blind, white flicker in the depths of the orbs which died out slowly. The man seemed young—almost a boy—but you know with them it's hard to tell. I found nothing else to do but to offer him one of my good Swede's ship's biscuits I had in my pocket. The fingers closed slowly on it and held—there was no other movement and no other glance. He had tied a bit of white worsted round his neck—Why? Where did he get it? Was it a

badge—an ornament—a charm—a propitiatory act? Was there any idea at all connected with it?

(58–59)

Marlow, who had just told his listeners how tough he was, reveals how he came to see "the black bones" as a "man" through the agency of their shared gaze. The man's eyes are "vacant," scarcely human, but enough to compel Marlow's gesture of offering food and a recognition that the "white worsted round his neck" must have a reason—an idea—behind it, suggesting the man's human subjectivity. Marlow retreats quickly from the implications of his momentary insight into the man's humanity, describing another man as "one of these creatures [who] rose to his hands and knees and went off on all-fours towards the river to drink," lapping water out of his hands (59). Marlow recounts how he was "horror-struck" by the sight, anticipating Kurtz's final words, but, ironically, he doesn't recognize what Conrad reveals: that he, Marlow, is "the horror" for seeing the man as an animal, for retreating into the safety of the binaries of civilized/savage, human/animal, European/African, white/black.

Marlow's brief connection with the dying men at the Company station foreshadows the more extended experience of an uncanny reciprocal gaze shared by Marlow and his black helmsmen, as they journey up river and face a fierce attack from what Marlow repeatedly calls the "savages" on shore. As the black helmsmen dies while they look into each other's eyes, Marlow's assumption of the civilized/savage binary splits open, a different sensation of "horror" in which he recognizes the intelligent humanity and agency of the foreign and specifically black *other*. Initially, Marlow regards his helmsman as "the most unstable kind of fool I had ever seen," an "athletic black" who "thinks the world of himself" and whose "swagger" offends Marlow's sensibilities (89). But when the "fool-nigger" successfully defends the steamer from ambush and loses his life by his bravery, Marlow's sense of civilized superiority is shaken. The helmsman's "eyes shone with an amazing lustre" as Marlow stands in a pool of his blood. "He looked at me anxiously," Marlow remembers. "I had to make an effort to free my eyes from his gaze and attend to the steering" (91). As he dies, Marlow and the Manager stand over him while his "lustrous and inquiring glance enveloped us both" (91). Marlow can't get his dead helmsman out of his mind:

> No; I can't forget him. . . . Perhaps you will think it passing strange this regret for a savage who was no more account than a grain of sand in a black Sahara. Well, don't you see, he had done something. . . . He steered for me—I had to look after him, I worried about his deficiencies, and thus a subtle bond had been created, of which I only became aware when it was suddenly broken. And the intimate profundity of that look he gave me when he received his hurt remains to this day in my memory—like a claim of distant kinship affirmed in a supreme moment.
>
> (96)

The helmsman's lustrous gaze is the uncanny mark of his agency, the sign of his humanity, and the evidence of a kinship that Marlow both affirms and continually struggles to deny.

The power of these gazes between Marlow and the black Africans returns in the enigmatic and completely silent gazes Marlow exchanges with the two women who are devoted to Kurtz: the regal African woman, who mutely greets the steamer with dignity and knowledge, and Kurtz's betrothed, the Intended, who understands only Kurtz's ideal, not his reality. The two women are set up as opposites; both are in some sense figments of Marlow's masculine/colonial desire rather than fully embodied human subjects. In Marlow's account, they embody the polarities of empire in Africa: white/black, civilized/savage, wife-to-be/mistress, colonizer/colonized. Yet as women they remain linked as forever *other* to Marlow. His final account of the Intended compares the two women directly:

> She put out her arms, as if after a retreating figure, stretching them black and with clasped hands across the fading and narrow sheen of the window. . . . I shall see her too, a tragic and familiar Shade resembling in this gesture another one, tragic also and bedecked with powerless charms, stretching her brown arms over the glitter of the infernal stream, the stream of darkness.
>
> (125)

Marlow's account both affirms and ruptures these imperial binaries. While he contrasts the Intended's paleness with the African woman's darkness, his account of the two women shows more respect for the humanity of the

African woman, who is both uncannily strange and admirable to him as they share a reciprocal gaze. He recalls how the African woman greets the steamer, a figure to him of barbarism and irresistible power:

> And from right to left along the lighted shore moved a wild and gorgeous apparition of a woman. She walked with measured steps, draped in striped and fringed cloths, treading the earth proudly with a slight jingle and flash of barbarous ornaments. She carried her head high, her hair was done in the shape of a helmet. . . . She was savage and superb, wild-eyed and magnificent; there was something ominous and stately in her deliberate progress.
>
> (107)

As with his helmsman, the emotive power of the woman's face and the humanity of her gaze haunt Marlow, embodying yet throwing into doubt her strangeness: "Her face had a tragic and fierce aspect of wild sorrow and of dumb pain mingled with the fear of some struggling, half-shaped resolve. She stood looking at us without a stir and like the wilderness itself, with an air of brooding over an inscrutable purpose. . . . She looked at us all as if her life had depended upon the unswerving steadiness of her glance" (107).

Where he respects the humanity of the African woman (even as he reaffirms her barbarism), Marlow dishonors that of the Intended by lying to her about Kurtz's dying words, which he falsely reports to have been her name. As he recalls, her gaze is full of innocence, the desire to believe in Kurtz's high purpose and morality to the end: "This fair hair, this pale visage, this pure brow, seemed surrounded by an ashy halo from which the dark eyes looked out at me. Their glance was guileless, profound, confident, and trustful" (122). The Intended's gaze embodies for Marlow the purity and simplicity of Victorian womanhood, the spiritual home or center, sustained by empire and nurturing of it. Its guileless trust, however, is a mark not of subjectivity, as is the gaze of the African woman, but rather of a self that is founded upon a lie. Marlow pities the "civilized" white woman and can't help but admire the "barbarous" black woman, whose "tragic" gaze communicates her understanding of the truth the white woman supposedly could not bear to hear. The bond between the white agent of empire and the black woman who symbolizes Africa itself is a distant kinship that suppresses the agency and knowledge of the white woman in whose name the empire is defended.

The final irony of the text is that Marlow's lie to protect the European woman's innocence is in some sense a lie that reinforces his own sense of masculine superiority by maintaining his belief in feminine weakness and need for protection. As he tells his listeners in explaining his lie, "They—the women I mean—are out of it—should be out of it. We must help them stay in that beautiful world of their own lest ours gets worse" (93). For all his revelation of the "heart of darkness" at the center of European colonialism through the story of Kurtz, Marlow in the end sides with the ideology of Western civilization that rationalizes the patriarchal superiority of men over women and the European dominance of a colonized and feminized African continent. The ironic gap between Conrad and Marlow is at its widest as Marlow recounts how his defense of civilization is based on a lie.

SEASON OF MIGRATION TO THE NORTH

In its challenges to and affiliations with *Heart of Darkness*, *Season of Migration to the North* thematizes the enmeshing of both European and African modernities with colonialism and the seeming ruptures brought about by the end of European rule and the rise of new African nation-states like the Sudan. Where Conrad makes no attempt to represent the subjectivity of Africans, Salih centers his tale in their agencies during both colonial and postcolonial periods. But *Season* shares with *Heart of Darkness* the deconstruction of the familiar binaries of West/Rest, civilized/savage, and modernity/tradition by exploring the heart of darkness within the South as well as the North. Working even more extensively with categories of modernity than Conrad, *Season* shows North and South as imitative of the other; each, in other words, is engaged in mimetic encounters that intermix the modern and traditional as constitutive of modernity itself in its different locations. Women—specifically, attraction to them, violence against them, and women's own engagements with modernity—figure centrally in his complex staging of intercultural encounters.

As echo to *Heart of Darkness*, *Season of Migration to the North* reverses the journey of Kurtz from Europe to Africa. Mustafa Sa'eed is a brilliant

Sudanese prodigy who travels from the South to the North, early in the century, into the heart of the colonial metropolis—first to Khartoum, then to Cairo, and finally to London and Oxford. Like *Heart of Darkness*, Mustafa's tale is mostly told by one main narrator, who, like Marlow, becomes ever more clearly unreliable and heavily ironized. Even more than Conrad's novel, *Season* is a narrative of indeterminacy; of mysteries, lies, and truths; of mediating events through the perspectives of multiple embedded narrators; of complex tapestries with interlocking motifs and symbols; and of pervasive irony.[20] Stylistically speaking, Salih's novel shares more with the experimental narrative forms of Woolf and Faulkner than *Heart of Darkness*, which remains closer to the conventions of realism.[21] Written in classical Arabic, however, *Season* also blends these aesthetics of indeterminacy with echoes of the centuries-long conventions of the "high" culture of Arabic poetry and the "low" culture of the Arabic folk tradition.

Just as Kurtz exceeded expectations as a colonial agent, Mustafa is a great success in Britain. He acquires degrees and becomes the darling of the British left, writing books and advising ministers on economics and development in the Empire. In a love/hate relationship with the culture that exoticizes him, he turns into "the black Englishman," infected with the disease of those he lives among, much as Kurtz had "gone native" in the Congo. He seduces scores of white women, "modern" women whose Orientalist fantasies he exploits and exposes as a form of modern longing for a premodern desert Arab or black primitive prince. He hunts them like prey, driving two to suicide and murdering the last, his wife, the one he loves, in a sadomasochistic orgy.[22] In a fit of liberal guilt, the English court lets him off with a light sentence, buying into the myth of the colonized victim and denying him the dignity of free will and moral responsibility for his actions. In disgust, Mustafa migrates back to the Sudan, selecting a village at the bend of the Nile, where he appears out of nowhere one day to buy land, farm, marry a local woman, and find partial acceptance as the stranger with a hidden past he shares with no one, until he tells a part of his story to the nameless narrator. One day, after making sure his affairs are in order, he mysteriously disappears. The villagers assume he drowned in the seasonal flooding of the Nile, either by accident or suicide, but a tale also surfaces in Khartoum that he secretly returned to Britain. In the penultimate chapter of the novel, the narrator opens the secret room Mustafa had kept hidden from everyone. The room is a replica in the desert of a British gentleman's library, complete with hundreds of books and a fireplace over which hangs a portrait of his dead white wife Jean Morris. In shock and despair, the narrator goes swimming in the Nile, heading for the northern shore, and although he chooses to live rather than drown, the novel leaves us hanging, as unsure of his final fate as we are of Mustafa's.

In an interview, Salih explains Mustafa's state of mind in terms of sexualized postcolonial revenge. "In Europe," Salih notes,

> there is the idea of dominating us. That domination is associated with sex. Figuratively speaking, Europe raped Africa in a violent fashion. Mustafa Sa'eed, the hero of the novel, used to react to that domination with an opposite reaction, which had an element of revenge seeking. In his violent female conquests he wants to inflict on Europe the degradation which it had imposed upon his people. He wants to rape Europe in a metaphorical fashion.[23]

Many have assumed that Mustafa's views are Salih's own. But the novel ultimately refuses such simple binaries of North/South, colonizer/colonized, and modernity/tradition. Instead, Salih unveils the interplay of these oppositions in both Britain and the Sudan, exploding in particular the association of modernity with the West and tradition with Africa. Establishing an ironic distance between himself and both the narrator and Mustafa, Salih exposes the way "tradition" is always in a process of change and "modernity" is never as complete a rejection of the past as it seems, a phenomenon I discussed in chapter 4. North and South are not so much opposites as they are mutually constitutive, existing in conjunctural relationship, both *between* nations and *within* nations. The gender systems in both the North and the South as well as in the relation between them are the causal factor, narratively speaking, that explodes the illusion of absolute difference.

Salih indigenizes Conrad's trope of journey to the heart of otherness as a means of exposing the darkness at home. The steamer's progress up the Congo River in Conrad's tale exposes the hypocrisy of European (or at least Belgian) imperialism in the Congo; the journey north in Salih's novel uncovers not only the diseased traditionalism of the North but also the brutalizing tradition in the Sudanese village on the Nile. To understand the novel's affiliation with Conrad's project, we must be attuned to the novel's pervasive modernist irony, its subtle undermining of illusion in both North and South, and the role that gender fissures play in its exposure.

The novel's village is not what the narrator and Mustafa imagine it to be—a changeless, simple, gracious place. It represents instead a particular postcolonial modernity, fraught with contradictions. There are signs of change everywhere, represented symptomatically in the novel by the steady beat of the "puttering pumps" that have replaced the older waterwheels. Moreover, Mustafa's "rape" through seduction of white women in the North has its counterpart in a terrifying rape in the village, which is sanctioned by tradition. Mustafa's widow, Hosna, a thoroughly "modern" woman in the context of the village, has refused to accept any suitors for her hand and instead makes known her desire for the narrator. She even approaches the narrator's father and tells him to instruct his son to marry her. The narrator's mother is scandalized: "What an impudent hussy! That's modern women for you!" (123). Afraid of his own desire for Hosna, the narrator agrees to do what he profoundly disapproves of: approach Hosna on behalf of the old village lecher and close friend of his grandfather, Wad Rayyes, who is determined to marry Hosna. As the narrator's friend later tells him,

> The world hasn't changed as much as you think. . . . Some things have changed—pumps instead of water-wheels, iron ploughs instead of wooden ones, sending our daughters to school, radios, cars, learning to drink whisky and beer instead of arak and millet wine—yet even so everything's as it was. . . . Women belong to men and a man's a man even if he's decrepit.
>
> (99–101)

Modernization of waterwheels is one thing, but modern women must be resisted. The result is catastrophic, ripping apart the seemingly placid and changeless surface of the village to reveal the brutality within: the divergence of one modernity for men, another for women. Hosna is forcibly married and manages to fend off the attacks of her new husband until one night when villagers hear her screams and do nothing to interfere, only to discover the pair dead and covered in blood. Hosna does what she told the narrator she would do—kill Wad Rayyes if she is forced to marry him. Then she kills herself. The village, Salih reveals, is a site of partial modernization, a growing modernity that does not incorporate its girls and women, its family institutions. Rape is not just a metaphor for colonial exploitation and postcolonial revenge. Rape is also what happens when "women belong to men." Hosna's city ways—her modernity—arouse not only the narrator, who is afraid to act, but also the old man whose desire to possess her is an allegory for the resistance to modernity itself performed in the name of tradition. Lest one think of Hosna's action as a simple importation of Western ways into the village, the reaction of Wad Rayyes's elder wife to the story of his death is a chilling warning: "Good riddance!" she says, and at his funeral she "gave trilling cries of joy" (128). The roots of gender modernization in the village lie in the suffering of its women and their own longing for freedom from tyranny in the family.

Salih further deconstructs the binary of (European) North and (African) South by using the issue of racialized gender relations to expose the North/South power divide *within* the Sudan itself, a longstanding ethnic and religious divide that led to decades of civil war between the dominant Arab and Muslim North and the dominated "black" and Christian/animist South. In a chapter that reproduces a "traditional" scene of storytelling, Wad Rayyes regales the narrator's grandfather and his friends in the village with the story of his kidnapping "a young slave girl from down-river" whom he delights in raping over and over again (74). That friends laugh in pleasure at his bawdy tale just days before he rapes Hosna heightens the novel's ironic exposure of violence within the seemingly placid surface of village life and allegorizes the North/South divisions within the Sudan.

The puzzling coldness of Mustafa's mother toward Mustafa makes little sense within a purely British imperial postcolonial framework. As Mustafa tells the novel's main narrator, she remained a "stranger" to him, with a masklike face, leaving him completely free from a sense of family obligation (19, 21, 22–23). When he is offered a scholarship to study in Cairo, she gives him money, saying "'It's your life and you're free to do with it as you will'. . . . That was our farewell: no tears, no kisses, no fuss." "I was cold as a field of ice," he tells the narrator (23). Her coldness is reborn in his, which manifests in his relations with the white women in London. It isn't until much later in the novel that one of the subsidiary narrators mentions an aspect of her background that might explain her nontraditional behavior, marked as it is by a seemingly modern adherence to individual freedom: "It is said that his mother was a slave from the south, from the tribes of the Sandi or Baria" who married a man from the north, a man of the Ababda, "the tribe" who helped Kitchener's army recapture the Sudan (54). Here is another story of North/South relations and "migration to the north," but one that reflects the existence of African slavery, African complicity in European conquest, the exchange of women as the property of men, and the major division in the Sudan between the largely Arab/Muslim and better-off North and the black/Christian/animist and poorer South—a split that was at the root of the Sudan's bitter civil war and its twenty-first-century division into two countries.

Further complicating Salih's deconstruction of North/South, white/black, and male/female binaries is the way in which the main narrator's account of Hosna's sensuous warmth and perfumed sweetness recapitulates Mustafa's report of the odor, laughter, and embrace of the one woman who seemed genuinely to care for him: the white woman Mrs. Robinson, the wife of a colonial administrator in Cairo who befriends the lonely boy. She mothers him as his own mother could not, with a kindly warmth associated with her European odor, a smell that kindles his first inkling of adult desire, perhaps presaging his attraction to the exotic otherness of the white women in London whom he seduces. The ultimate irony is that the sadomasochistic relationship with his white wife becomes an obsessive love from which he cannot escape, even in the arms of Hosna. In terms of the postcolonial revenge plot, Mustafa's desire for the odor and body of exotic white women is a form of Anglophilia akin to his recapitulation of an English gentlemen's library in his secret room in the village—feminized and masculinized forms of a postcolonial dis-ease that the novel attempts to exorcise. But in terms of the novel's gender plot, Mustafa's desire for the white female body is rooted in his southern mother's enslavement by the Arab north within the racial/religious politics of postcolonial Sudan, an enslavement that led to her coldness toward him and his response to the warmer substitute mothering of the white, colonizing woman in Cairo. In the divergent modernities Salih inscribes, complex gender formations and cross-racial desire interrupt a purely colonial/postcolonial reading of the novel as Sudanese resistance to the British Empire.

This gender-induced swerve away from the postcolonial revenge plot intensifies in the story of the main narrator, the character who most parallels Marlow. Like Mustafa, the unnamed narrator is a figure of colonial modernity: he too went to England to study and then returned home. But unlike Mustafa, he lives and works for the postcolonial state in Khartoum, returning to the village to restore his connection to "tradition." He needs the village to remain "traditional" in order to be "modern" in the city, something that his childhood friend, the village's modernizer, resents. The narrator's nostalgia for the "simple," traditional life of the village parallels the phenomenon Dipesh Chakrabarty describes in *Habitations of Modernity*, in which he notes that Bengali men working in Calcutta often spent their summers in their village homes, which they represented in stories as sites of nostalgic longing and changelessness; after Partition, they were cut off from those villages, a rupture that only increased their desire and idealization of village life.[24] Salih's narrator, educated in England and working in Khartoum for the new nation-state, exhibits many of these same "modern" traits, not only in his romanticization of his village but also in his exoticization (indeed, Orientalization) of the Bedouin women he sees dancing in the desert in the much-discussed desert caravan sequence (108–115).

The attraction Mustafa cannot feel for Hosna comes alive in the narrator, who experiences with her—particularly in her odor—some of the intimacy Mustafa felt with Mrs. Robinson. But it is a longing upon which the narrator is reluctant to act, in part because he wants the village to remain in its traditional state, a desire that sets in motion the disaster of forced marriage, murder, and suicide. The narrator's "traditional" exoticization of Hosna contrasts with her attempt to act on her own desire as a "modern" woman. She made clear her desire to marry him, but he clings to unchanging traditional ways and cannot act on his desires, a reluctance that leads to catastrophe. She demonstrates ways in which tradition can be open to change; he represents a nostalgic desire for return. The novel's complex circuits of travel and desire between North and South disrupt the fixed binaries of a postcolonial geopolitics. Gender criss-crosses the North/South itineraries to complicate the narrative, calling into question a too-easy alignment of the North with cold and the South with warmth. Salih's disruptions of North and South, cold and warmth, unravel as well the oppositions between subject and *other*, colonizer and colonized, victimizer and victim, modernity and tradition.

In so doing, Salih indigenizes Conrad's project in *Heart of Darkness* to reveal the hypocrisy of European imperialism's so-called civilizing mission in Africa and the reality of its greed and bestiality. Salih, like Conrad, exposes the heart of darkness at home, centered in the Sudan's gender and ethnic/religious/racial differences. Beneath the hypocrisy of serene village life in Salih's novel lies the hidden brutality of the village's ambivalent relationship to modernity and its refusal to incorporate the security and freedom of its women in its future. The traditionalism of Salih's "modern" narrator, the postcolonial government agent from Khartoum who is too timid to support Hosna's bid for freedom, has its parallel in Marlow's gender traditionalism at the end of *Heart of Darkness* when he refuses to tell the Intended the truth about Kurtz's last words. In maintaining her illusions about Kurtz's idealism, Marlow performs the traditional role of the man who protects the delicate woman from the harsh realities of life and thus sustains his own need for masculine mastery. Irony in both novels unravels the overlapping oppositions between modernity/tradition, North/South, and man/woman. But Salih reinvigorates Conrad's irony by showing the violence at the heart of the illusions of tradition and traditionalism. Where the Intended is sustained (though marginalized) by traditionalism, Hosna is doomed to die for her modernity.

The juxtaposition of *Heart of Darkness* and *Season of Migration to the North* breaks down the conventional narrative of modernism as the invention of the West imitated by the Rest. It shows how a polycentric approach to modernity and modernism reveals the way that each site—in Britain and in the Sudan—is constructed through engagement with the other. Further, each site also exhibits a key feature of modernity explored in earlier chapters: the struggle between modernizing and traditionalizing forces for which gendered and racialized others and the violence done to them exposes, indeed explodes, the cultural narratives of both rational progress and nostalgic tradition. Like Said's notion of the colonial intensification of the colonizer's traveling theory in "Traveling Theory Reconsidered," Salih's modernist exposure of the violent traditionalisms at the heart of both North and South is not so much derivative of Conrad as it is a sharper and more explicit attack on the gender/race systems of both the colonizer and the colonized. Salih's affiliation with Conrad leads to an indigenization of his tale in which "its fiery core" (to echo Said again) has been reignited with a vengeance.

COLLAGE 2: DARKS OF HEARTNESS IN E. M. FORSTER AND ARUNDHATI ROY

Conrad's *Heart of Darkness* "travels" to and transplants into both E. M. Forster's *A Passage to India* (1924) and Arundhati Roy's *The God of Small Things* (1997), novels that narrate voyages outward and inward in the context of colonial modernity and its legacies in postcolonial India.[25] Forster's anatomy of British racisms in India, as well as his complicity with them, is less binarist than Conrad's, particularly as he details a spectrum of British inhumanities that run the gamut from Orientalist desire to blatantly dehumanizing racism. Moreover, he attempts, where Conrad does not, to represent the subjectivity of at least one Indian character, Dr. Aziz, if not arguably more. Roy extends the critique of imperialism into the arena of Indian psychopathology on the one hand and into its contemporary neoliberal form with the rise of multinational capital and the hegemony of American culture at the end of the twentieth century on the other. Each in its own way rewrites Conrad's novel, showing the kind of transnational enmeshment that Ramazani theorized. My analysis here, however, will circulate back and forth between *A Passage to India* and *The God of Small Things* to show how each novel engages with a traveling, transnational modernity in which the stories of race endorse the discourses of nation and empire while the rhetorics of gender, caste, and sexuality challenge them. Reading sections of each novel in light of the other helps bring into focus the "fiery core" of their rewriting of Conrad and their own visions of colonial/postcolonial modernities, as Said's theory of affiliation helps explain. Both narrativize the psychologically damaging effects of colonial and postcolonial race relations at the same time that they explore how race is mediated by other systems of power. What this "conversation" between novels shows is that across space, time, and the power relations of post/colonialism, Forster and Roy do not stand in fixed opposition to each other—the one reflecting the standpoint of the colonial power, the other expressing the resistance of the formerly colonized. Rather, like *Heart of Darkness* and *Season of Migration to the North*, their novels, read paratactically, disclose some unexpected lines of affiliation between them. In turn, these parallels bring into sharp visibility the networked, multinodal, and circulating aspects of modernity.

RACE RELATIONS IN *A PASSAGE TO INDIA*

In *The Rhetoric of English Empire*, Sara Suleri reads *A Passage to India* as an Orientalist fantasy of cross-cultural, erotic congress that reveals "the anus of imperialism" and the adolescent rhetoric of colonialism.[26] Yet the novel uses a form of irony familiar to the English novel of manners epitomized by Jane Austen to satirize a spectrum of British racist attitudes—from the outright assertion of English/white superiority among the Anglo-Indians, to the paternalism and ignorance of the seemingly more tolerant, to the ignorant curiosity of those who travel to see the "real India." One of the marks of the novel's modernist indeterminacy is its simultaneous critique of and participation in a colonial standpoint. As a liberal with scathing contempt for British racism yet a lingering Orientalist attachment to the British Empire, Forster understood that the jewel in Victoria's crown was shattering under the sheer weight of imperial bullying and blundering. Forster's residence in India in the employ of an Indian prince in 1921–1922 following the shocking events of the bloody Amritsar Massacre of 1919 and the accelerated rise of Indian nationalism had a deep influence on his rendering of imperial rule in India.[27] While the novel famously closes with the assertion that cross-racial friendship is not yet possible, it nonetheless presents an anatomy of the colonial racism that was endemic to the rise of the Raj and that was hastening its demise.

For all its ties to the realist tradition in the English novel of manners, however, *A Passage to India* goes well beyond satire in its depiction of colonial racism and its exploration of cross-cultural contacts and currents. Evident in Forster's naming of the three-part structure of the novel—"Mosque," "Caves," "Temple"—the novel's fusion of realism with symbolist, religious, and mystical dimensions creates a hybrid text that, while not akin to Joyce, Woolf, or Faulkner in formalist terms, nonetheless departs significantly from the conventions of realism and introduces an unsettlingly indeterminate dimension to the story of many passages to and within India.

As a particular marker of the novel's modernist dimension, a space of absence governs the narrative. What happened in the Marabar cave is unnarrated and unnarratable, left in the blank space between chapters 15 and 16, as Brenda Silver and many others have observed.[28] This gap operates as the narrative's pivotal point—everything before leads up to it; everything that happens afterward results from it. It is the narrative's "black hole," a source of enormous power into which traumas, forbidden desires, and crimes have been drawn and disappeared from view. Forster is not known as a writer who admired or read Freud, nor is he usually read as someone who anticipated the kind of revolutionary use of psychoanalysis evident in Fanon. Nonetheless, I would suggest that the novel's colonial modernity centers on that black hole. It represents the heart of colonial darkness that represses the psychopathology of race and that returns symptomatically in the paranoia, hysteria, and desire of cross-racial relations in the context of empire.

As Jenny Sharpe has shown in *Allegories of Empire*, Forster's plotting of colonial racial psychology revolves around the fear of racial pollution through sexual contact between "black" men and "white" women," a fear that had taken the form among the tiny but powerful population of Anglo-Indians of extreme paranoia, beginning especially with the Sepoy Rebellion of 1857 and then reawakened in the wake of the Amritsar Massacre of 1919. Stories of Indian men attacking white women circulated widely throughout the Raj and were used as the justification for the imposition of martial law.[29] Forster's psychological study of white paranoia takes an ironic form that has the effect of heightening his racial critique. The woman at the center of the paranoia seems the least likely candidate for it. Adela is an outsider to the Anglo-Indian culture of the Raj and most unsympathetic to the forms of racism she observes. As Dr. Aziz observes, Adela, like Mrs. Moore, "had no race-consciousness" (129). Nonetheless, it is Adela's accusation of assault that upends his life. Having set Mrs. Moore and Adela up as lacking "race-consciousness" in part 1, "Mosque," Forster smashes the illusion by having the plot of colonial paranoia return with a vengeance in part 2, "Caves." The elaborate trip to the Marabar Caves that Aziz arranges to fulfill Adela's desire to see the "real India" removes the veil of racial tolerance from the English women to reveal another kind of reality: the "real" of English racism, all the more virulent because originally unconscious prior to its powerful return. Mrs. Moore becomes unhinged in some sort of unspecified way, resulting in a profound and nihilist indifference to everyone. Like instances of trauma as theorized by Freud, her horror and despair set in after the experience itself, as a sort of secondary event signified by the symptomatic and hysterical echo that never leaves her head.

Mrs. Moore's hysterical symptom foreshadows Adela's pathological response. Of the many ways in which the cave episode can be read, the experience of the two "liberal" Englishwomen signifies their confrontation with the primitive and primeval *other*, for which an ancient formation in the Indian landscape serves as a convenient symbol. Racialized in the utter blackness inside the caves, "India" surrealistically externalizes and projects a darkness within English identity that the concept of Englishness suppresses. For the women, the caves embody what the anthropologist Michel-Rolph Trouillot calls "the savage slot" of Western consciousness, the repressed, dystopian side of white subjectivity.[30] Repressed beneath the Englishwomen's patina of racial tolerance and sensitivity is the fear of the racial *other* as an unacknowledged part of the self and as evidence of how the English concept of English racial superiority is based in utopian fantasy.

The effect of the caves on Adela makes even more explicit the relationship between "the savage slot" and racial paranoia in the colonial context. What the narrator calls Adela's "intellectualism" leaves her unprepared for the return of her own repressed racial and sexual fears. Having scorned the overt racism of the Anglo-Indians, she ironically ends up repeating the paranoia of the whole community as a form of repetition compulsion. Her disclaimers of the event—"He never actually touched me once" (193)—would lead to tears and "then she would break down utterly" (193), weeping as "the echo flourished, raging up and down like a nerve in the faculty of her hearing" (194). The crime becomes in the minds of all, including Adela's, what might have happened, not what didn't happen. Adela's hysteria snowballs into communal hysteria as the repressed script of blackman-rapes-white woman comes fully into play. As the choric voice of the community, the narrator reports: "Each felt that all he loved best in the world was at stake, demanded revenge, and was filled with a not unpleasing glow, in which the chilly and half-known features of Miss Quested vanished, and were replaced by all that is sweetest and warmest in the private life. 'But it's the women and children,' they repeated. . . " (183). The effect of this racial fear for which the purity of white womanhood serves as the touchstone is the justification of the Raj in the eyes of the community.

Adela's retraction in the midst of the trial functions as a kind of "talking cure" that releases her from the echo, from the symptom of her own hysteria (229, 239). The witness box is an unlikely scene of psychoanalytic transference, but for Adela, the act of having to retell what happened—rather, what didn't happen—in the cave allows her to move beyond the repetition compulsion of neurotic symptom into the act of remembering what has been repressed. In a series of "numerous curious conversations" with Fielding (238), Adela continues the talking cure, attempting to figure out why she behaved as she did, playing out the script of the frightened white woman who imagines an attack by a black man.

Exhibiting a characteristically modernist indeterminacy, the novel covertly suggests multiple overdeterminations for Adela's behavior, refusing to authorize any single cause and thus spawning differing critical interpretations that run the gamut from colonial racism to Anglo overintellectualism, sexual repression, hysterical neurosis, Orientalist homoeroticism, mysticism, misogyny, feminism, and so forth. For my purposes, Forster's examination of white paranoia and hysteria is especially interesting for the way he explores the role of eroticism in white colonial racism. Fear of the racial *other* is the flipside of desire for the racial *other*, Forster shows. Adela's experience in the cave, which leads to hysteria, is immediately preceded by her sad thoughts about her loveless marriage and her repressed desire for "the handsome little Oriental" (153), the sexualized *other* who fills "the savage slot" in Adela's imaginary as a projection of the *other* within herself that she has repressed and must repudiate by invoking the myth of the black rapist.

Forster's powerful critique of colonialist racism and the psychopathology it induces in the English does not, of course, free the novel from its own forms of colonial racism. At another level of the novel, Forster's position as a member of the British elite he criticizes bleeds into his portrait of Indians that remain in some ways forever a heterogeneous but nonetheless racialized *other*, at times all the more desirable because foreign (e.g., Aziz) and at other times just inscrutable (e.g., Godbole). Forster's discomfort with the Indian nationalist movement and his at-best ambivalent attitude toward the British Empire and Indian nationalism raise inevitable questions about the ways in which his novel perpetuates the racism that underlay the British Empire even as he attacked the racism that upheld it.

RACE RELATIONS IN *THE GOD OF SMALL THINGS*

Modernity in Roy's *The God of Small Things* centers in the shattering of the Raj at Independence in 1947 and the struggles of the new nation to make that independence real in the context of the ongoing aftereffects of colonialism. Like Forster, she is most interested in the psychological effects of colonial racism, but where he focused primarily on the racial paranoia of the English, she examines the psychopathology of racism in those who were colonized and their descendants, no doubt reflecting Fanon's psychoanalysis of internalized racism in *Black Skin, White Masks*.[31] In its ruptures of language, narrative chronology, and voice, the form of *The God of Small Things* is more akin to that of writers like Joyce, Woolf, and Faulkner than with the predominantly realist narrative of Forster. Repression of traumatic events and their symptomatic return govern the novel's reliance on a textual fabric of interlocking motifs and fragmentary memory to tell the story of what happened during the novel's two narrated time periods: the thirteen disastrous days in 1969 and the aftereffects of those events on one day in 1992. Echoing and rewriting *A Passage to India* and Conrad's *Heart of Darkness*, Roy explores colonial and postcolonial forms of Anglophobia and Anglophilia, adding to this concern with empire the meanings of American cultural hegemony and multinational corporations at the end of the twentieth century.[32]

The novel takes place in Kerala, an atypical Indian state on the southwestern coast. Twenty percent of the population are Syrian Christians whose conversion to Christianity goes back two thousand years. The catastrophes in 1969 bring about the collapse of the Syrian Christian Ipe family, initiated by the visit of Chacko Ipe's former English wife Margaret and daughter Sophie, whom he has never seen. Sophie's accidental death by drowning is entangled with the sudden affair of Ammu, Chacko's divorced sister, and Velutha, an Untouchable who has used the Gandhian "affirmative action" programs of the new nation to get an education and rise to the position of foreman over lower-caste workers in the Ipe family's Paradise Pickles and Preserves Factory. To cover up the disgrace of the affair, Ammu's aunt and mother charge Velutha with kidnapping Ammu's twins and raping Ammu, an accusation that leads the police to beat him nearly to death in front of the horrified eyes of the hiding twins. Estha, one of the twins, is convinced that he must lie about Velutha, whom he has loved for years as a surrogate father, in order to save his mother from prison. Velutha dies after watching Estha betray him, and Ammu is banished from the family home and later dies alone and in poverty. The twins are separated, leaving Chacko in charge of his mother's successful pickle factory, which he destroys by importing Western business practices before he eventually emigrates.

In 1992, Rahel, the other twin, returns from the United States to her decaying home in Kerala, finding her recently returned brother mute and shut off from life and her aunt obsessed with American TV shows. Like the children of Salman Rushdie's *Midnight's Children*, the twins are allegories of Indian's past and future. But unlike his children, the twins are emblems of pathological hysteria, reversing conventional gender patterns of traumatic effects: for twenty-three years, Estha has been obedient, silent, neat, housebound; Rahel has been rebellious, loud, messy, world traveling. Symptomatically opposites, they both remain frozen in past time, metonymically signaled by the motif of the child's watch, stuck at 2:15, that was lost at the site where they watched Velutha being beaten. With Rahel's return, they attend scenes from the great national epic of royal family strife, the Mahabharata, after which they lie down together, breaking another of the novel's many "Love Laws," leaving readers with an open question. Does the incest presage a decadent and ingrown paralysis (a frequent charge against the Syrian Christian elite) or a rebellious new beginning based in a transgression enacted for love that holds out the possibility of healing?

As avatar of a postcolonial love-hate relation with the former colonizers, Chacko informs the seven-year-old twins that the Ipes "were a *family* of Anglophiles. Pointed in the wrong direction, trapped outside their own history and unable to retrace their steps because their footprints had been swept away" (51). Chacko is himself a specimen of the germ he despises. He was a Rhodes Scholar whose degree from Oxford and acquisition of a white wife raised his status in the family and community. This family context explains the twins' sense of inferiority before the "clean white children" in *The Sound of Music* and their related belief that Sophie's whiteness made her the favored grandchild.

Echoing *A Passage to India*, Margaret and Sophie naïvely embark on their own passage to India, unaware of the internalized racism that awaits them, ignorant of the privileged position they occupy in the Ipe family's imaginary as a result of colonial racism. Margaret has something of Adela's curiosity about foreign India. "How marvelous!" she exclaims when Chacko explains that the cook raised Sophie's hands to her face and inhaled deeply as a "way of kissing you." "It's a sort of sniffing!" she continues and asks inappropriately, "Do Men and Women do it to each other too?" (170). Realizing her mistake, she blushes, not preventing, however, Ammu's cynical outburst: "Must we behave like some damn godforsaken tribe that's just been discovered?" (171). Like Adela, the contact zone between Margaret and India had led to an awakening: "Being with Chacko made Margaret Kochamma feel as though her soul had escaped from the narrow confines of her island country into the vast, extravagant spaces of his" (233).

After the death of Sophie, Margaret's behavior sharpens Roy's echoes of *A Passage to India*. Adela's unjustified accusation of Aziz reappears in Margaret's "irrational rage" at the twins, particularly Estha, whom "in her fevered mind" she blames for the accident and slaps in one of her moments of "sharp, steely slashes of hysteria" (249–250). Like Adela, she recants and apologizes, too late to help the one she accused, who had already been sent away. "I can't imagine what came over me," she wrote. "I can only put it down to the effect of the tranquilizers. I had no right to behave the way I did, and want you to know that I am ashamed and terribly, terribly sorry" (251). Like Forster, Roy points to the particular futility of English apology that cannot undo the harm done across racial lines in either a colonial or postcolonial context.

Chacko's metaphor for the inevitability of the racial chasm is to imagine the forces of history in architectural and spatial terms: "history was like an old house at night. With all the lamps lit. And ancestors whispering inside" (52). "To understand history," Chacko tells the twins, "we have to go inside and listen to what they're saying." This project is doomed to failure because the "post" in "postcolonial" is only an illusion that covers up the ongoing presence of the colonial past in the present:

"But we can't go in," Chacko explained, "because we've been locked out. And when we look in through the windows, all we see are shadows.

And when we try to listen, all we hear is a whispering. And we cannot understand the whispering, because our minds have been invaded by a war. A war that we have won and lost. The very worst sort of war. A war that captures dreams and re-dreams them. A war that has made us adore our conquerors and despise ourselves."

(52)

Chacko represents the view that the postcolonial condition of modernity provides no radical rupture from the colonial past but only a paralyzing return of the repressed. The twins literalize his metaphor by associating the "history house" with Akkara, the abandoned manor house of the rubber plantation across the river. The narrator blends the imaginary of Chacko and the twins to trope it repeatedly as the "History House," the "Heart of Darkness," and the site of the novel's most intense transgressions of the laws of touch, both loving and hateful.

The History House is a space that contains the palimpsestic layering of time within it, embedding Roy's scathing critique of racism in the context of colonial and postcolonial modernity. Here, in the colonial period, lived Kari Saipu, "The Black Sahib. The Englishman who had 'gone native.' Who spoke Malayalem and wore mundus. Ayemenem's own Kurtz. Ayemenem his private Heart of Darkness" (51). Roy weaves together echoes of Conrad and Forster to allegorize the postcolonial modernity of India. In 1959, the Anglo-Indian shot himself when the parents of his young lover took the boy away, leaving his cook and secretary to bicker about ownership of the house (an allusion, perhaps to Forster's racialized homosexuality). By 1969, the History House was abandoned, the site of the children's escapades, Ammu and Velutha's affair, and the police beating of Velutha. In 1992, when Rahel returns to Ayemenem, the History House has become the Heritage Hotel, a tourist site owned by a multinational chain of five-star hotels. Giving its franchise a "regional flavor," the Heritage Hotel packages the "real" India in bite-sized pieces: "So there it was then, History and Literature enlisted by commerce. Kurtz and Karl Marx joining palms to greet rich guests as they stepped off the boat" (120). Allegorizing the power of global forces of history to shape the lives of people in local places, the History House represents the structures of European imperialism and American economic and cultural hegemony that link Kerala—and by extension—all of India with the West in the twentieth century.

DOMESTIC AFFAIRS IN *THE GOD OF SMALL THINGS*

The collage of *The God of Small Things* and *A Passage to India* helps emphasize how each addresses the psychopathology of post/colonial racism on both sides of the racial divide. But it also brings more sharply into view additional affiliations between the fictional projects of the two novels, as well as with *Heart of Darkness*, Roy's other colonial intertext.[33] No doubt Roy's novel, like *Season of Migration to the North*, "writes back" to the Empire from the standpoint of postcolonial subjects. But even more radically, Roy's novel, like Salih's, identifies with the projects of her colonialist precursors. Like them, she forces readers "at home," in her case, India, to confront what she calls the "dark of heartness" within home itself—"home" as the space of intimacy and family, and "home" as nation. For all their own reification of colonial racism (Conrad more than Forster, in my view), *Passage to India* and *Heart of Darkness* turn the gaze of the English traveler back onto European imperialism itself, calling into question the ideology of empire and Western racial superiority that underlay the contact zones between Britain and India, Europe and Africa. But unlike them, Roy borrows their project—the critique of "home" by travel to the "other"—to move from considerations of race to explicit questions of gender, sexuality, and caste. In addition to attacking the racism of postcolonial relations between "West" and "East," Roy writes a political allegory of both Kerala and the nation to challenge Chacko's view that all India's current problems stem from British imperialism. The events of 1969 in the novel expose the violence of the state and the family based in reactionary Indian institutions of caste, sexuality, and gender that cling to past traditions, refuse an Indian modernity, and threaten to paralyze the future. In this regard, Roy's novel parallels Salih's *Season of Migration to the North*. Divergent modernities *within* the emergent nation-state demonstrate the mobilization of "tradition" that denies "modernity" to its women and outcasts.

Like *A Passage to India*, the plot of *The God of Small Things* turns around a false accusation of rape.[34] Roy borrows the emotional charge from the colonial racial plot that Forster used to heighten the significance of a false charge against the outcast Untouchable Velutha. Here, the accuser is the Ipe family itself, specifically Ammu's mother and aunt, who cry rape to cover their shame at Ammu's affair with an Untouchable. The Ipe family closes ranks to protect its reputation, preventing Ammu from telling the truth in time. Lies, secrets, and silence propel the cover-up, making the children's acts of forgetting and memory a kind of allegory for a nation that, in Roy's view, has not sufficiently "remembered" its own complicity in the suffering of its people.

Roy's rewriting of the false accusation rape plot—so resonant in the history of the Raj—forces attention to the violence of the caste system that Chacko ignores in his analysis of India's problems. In doing so, she addresses both the specific situation in Kerala and by extension political debates about India as a whole. In being touted as the miracle model for India and the developing world in general, Kerala does not come to terms with the suffering that its social conservatism causes for women and Dalits, Roy suggests. Kerala has the highest literacy rate for women in all of India, along with a generally better "safety net" and many other indicators of a higher status for women than other parts of the country. However, compared to the cosmopolitan cities of New Delhi, Mumbai, and Kolkata, Kerala is a gender backwater where women have little choice about marriage and property and where being divorced is a major family disgrace. Moreover, Kerala has the worst record in all India for land reform for the Dalits. The Communist Party, which has been elected to govern Kerala for most of the post-Independence period, won the loyalty of the lower-caste workers and unions by playing the "caste card" and blocking the advancement of the Dalits.[35]

The novel introduced Ammu and Chacko, sister and brother, in binary terms to highlight the double standard for men and women in socially conservative Kerala around issues of marriage, divorce, sexuality, education, caste, and property. Each chooses a mate instead of accepting a parentally arranged marriage, each marries outside the family religion, and each divorces and returns home. But the status of each is diametrically opposed. The family's money sends Chacko to Oxford, but Ammu's only escape from Kerala is to marry. Chacko's marriage to a white woman raises his status; Ammu's marriage to a Hindu lowers hers. Chacko's divorce is ignored, and his mother arranges a private entrance to the house so that "a Man's Needs" can be discreetly taken care of (160). Ammu, on the other hand, lives out a "modern" form of *sati*, like widows, a sexual status of living death. As for the caste laws, Chacko does not upset the family by having sex with lower-caste women from the factory, even in his own house (160). Ammu's breaking of the love laws governing touch brings punishment, exile in penury, and death, whereas Chacko takes over the family home and business and then opts to emigrate. Roy's exposure of the sexual double standard in Kerala charges the state with hypocrisy in touting its progressive stand on gender.

The inequities of the gender system mingle with the injustice of the caste system as the bodies of Ammu and Velutha ecstatically meet in the dangerous waters of the Menachal River, a scene not fully narrated until the final chapter of the novel. Roy's attack on the persistence of caste politics in Kerala begins in the irony of the Syrian Christian family's outraged response to the violation of the Hindu caste laws. As Christians, they should not share in the Hindu prohibition against touch. But as descendants of the original Brahmin converts, Syrian Christians in Kerala retain the aura of the upper castes and assume the prohibitions against caste pollution as their own. "Pappachi," we learn, "would not allow Paravans [Dalits] into the house. Nobody would. They were not allowed to touch anything that Touchables touched. Caste Hindus and Caste Christians" (71). Once Velutha and Ammu touched each other in all the forbidden ways, both families were scandalized as the fabric of tradition ruptured in their blasphemous break with the past.

Roy's exposure of Syrian Christian hypocrisy is matched by her scathing portrait of the caste politics of the Keralan Communist government. Comrade Pillai is a contemptible character, in bed with the Syrian Christian elite as well as the lower-caste unions in order to maintain his own power. He sells out Velutha, a rising member of his own party, to please both constituencies. His eventual success—evident in the striking prosperity of his family in the 1992 sections—rests upon the crime of his betrayal of Velutha to the police, who "in the Heart of Darkness . . . acted with economy, not frenzy. Efficiency , not anarchy. Responsibility, not hysteria . . . merely inoculating a community against an outbreak" (293).

Like Forster and Conrad, Roy tells a tale of many passages and travel in the contact zones of (neo)imperialism to encourage her readers "at home"—in this case, India—to look within the heart of its own civilization for the darkness within. Roy's anger at the West is evident enough in her more recent writings about the World Trade Center attacks and political activism both within and outside India.[36] But in *The God of Small Things*, she refuses to ignore the violence *within* the nation at the same time that she attacks the evils of colonialism and the multinational corporations of the global age. Reading Roy in the context of Forster highlights the way she borrows his racial plot in order to interrogate questions of gender and caste at home.

DOMESTIC AFFAIRS IN *A PASSAGE TO INDIA*

Returning to *A Passage to India* after reading *The God of Small Things* helps bring into focus how the issues of sexuality and gender that Roy explicitly explores exist in more covert forms in Forster's novel. Roy's narrativization of cultural paranoia about the pollution of forbidden touch suggests yet another partial affiliation between the colonial English and the postcolonial Indian writers. *A Passage to India* also contains a much less explicit story about forbidden touching, in this case cross-racial homosexuality. The taboo desire of intercaste eroticism acted out by Ammu and Velutha has an analogue in the unconsummated cross-gender homoeroticism thinly disguised in Forster's rendering of the "friendship" between Fielding and Aziz and in the more deeply suppressed story of Adela's desire for Aziz. In turn, this affiliation between novels of the 1920s and 1990s makes visible how the intimacies of sexuality and desire constitute one arena for the ruptures of enmeshed modernities.

For Suleri, Forster's use of the false rape accusation to attack British racism diverts attention from the "real" subject of the novel, the homoerotic eroticism of empire that covertly underlies the relationship between Aziz and Fielding, with cross-racial sex diluted into the more palatable question of cross-racial friendship. She regards the novel's homoeroticism as a symptom of imperialism and Forster's own racism, evident in his propensity to fall in love with "dark" men of the British colonies—first, his friend Syed Ross Masood, the man who inspired the characterization of Aziz and appeared in the novel's dedication; and then Mohammed el Adl, the Egyptian with whom Forster had his first consummated affair in Alexandria during World War I.[37] But read paratactically in the context of *The God of Small Things*, Forster's covert homosexual plot shares with Roy's project the insistence upon the multiple constituents of identity on both sides of the post/colonial racial divide. The complex intersections of race, sexuality, caste, and gender that Roy explicitly examines as constitutive of late-twentieth-century modernity (re)appear in Forster's novel in more repressed and displaced forms, a largely hidden dimension of the novel that exposes the effects of heterosexism in the modernity of the early twentieth century.

To explore this effect, I suggest that we regard Adela as Forster's fictionalized queer persona instead of reading her merely as a misogynistically imagined, sexually repressed female hysteric. In this context, Adela's accusation of rape and subsequent hysteria are vital parts of the repressed homoerotic plot and introduce issues of external and internalized homophobia. Evidence for such a reading lies in Forster's closeted homosexuality, the composition history of *Passage*, and the novel's intertextual relationship with the overtly homosexual narrative of *Maurice*.

Encouraged by Masood to write a novel about English–Indian relations, Forster first drafted part 1, "Mosque," of *Passage* before his trip to India in 1912–1913 and then set the novel aside until 1922. Right after his return from India in 1913, he visited Edward Carpenter, the well-known theorist of love between members of the "third sex," where an unexpected erotic touch led him to realize incontrovertibly his own homosexual orientation. The writing of *Maurice* followed quickly on the heels of this revelation in 1913, narrating the awakening of the upper-middle-class Maurice to homosexual desire and consummation through the touch of the charismatic gamekeeper. Short stories openly exploring homosexuality followed, but Forster refused to publish either *Maurice* or the stories in his own lifetime.[38] Perhaps silenced by the need for secrecy, Forster abandoned the novel form, turning instead to memoir and essay. Grief-stricken and paralyzed by the death of Mohammed el Adl, he returned to his drafts of *A Passage to India* in 1922, taking up the story with part 2, "Caves," and part 3, "Temple," but never again writing another novel.[39] Thereafter, Forster's closeted affairs were either with men of different races or different classes, men who filled the "savage slot" in the psychosexual circuits of forbidden desire. Transgression of sexual mores went hand in hand for Forster with crossing racial or class boundaries. The entanglements of race, class, sexuality, and self-censorship in the context of empire and British laws against homosexuality underwrite both *Maurice* and *A Passage to India*—not just as instances of Orientalist racism but also as explorations of internalized homophobia mediated by race or class.

Certain aspects of Adela's story resonate strongly with Forster's closeted homosexuality—namely, the uncanny erotic awakening Adela experiences in the accidental touch of hands during the car accident (87–88); Adela's preoccupation with love, marriage, and the physical beauty of Aziz's body just before she enters the cave (153); the echo as symptomatic hysteria and sign of repressed and forbidden desire; and her conclusion in her talks with Fielding that she hallucinated the touch in the cave after a period of nervous illness (238–243). The implication of cross-racial rape underneath Adela's accusation of an inappropriate touch and struggle over her field glasses takes on additional resonances in the context of Forster's hidden homosexuality. What Forster does is introduce the complications of race and colonialism into the etiology of hysteria that Freud postulated in *Dora*.[40] As an instance of queer displacement, Adela represents a case study for someone who imagines what she (he) desires and thereby creates social havoc and personal catastrophe in her (his) neurotic confusion of hallucination with reality. She figures in fictional form a displaced form of Forster's own repressed sexuality and cross-racial desire. She acts out, perhaps, his sense that catastrophe lurks in the open expression of these wishes and the consequent need for silence.

Forster's earlier drafts of the novel support such a reading. The gap between chapters 15 and 16 in the published novel—what happens in the Marabar cave—is the story of desire that dares not speak its name but did in fact do so in displaced form in earlier versions of the novel. In the earliest fragment, Forster planned a doomed love affair between Aziz and Janet, the English protagonist. As Forster's brief outline makes clear, the relationship breaks taboos of interracial sex, love, and marriage in colonial India. Each of the lovers has mixed feelings based on some combination of moral repugnance, pragmatic assessment of public consequences, and some concern about "purity of blood," a fear of pollution that itself picks up on India's caste system and Britain's racial imaginary. In this case, the impossibilities of interracial marriage substitute for homosexuality, and the fear of moral transgression takes the place of internalized homophobia.[41]

Forster's second and more substantial draft of *A Passage to India* changes the story of an affair into a tale of sexual assault. In this version, Forster directly narrates what happens in the cave, leaving ambiguous only the identity of the assailant, whom Adela assumes to be Aziz. The scene is a violent one, stopping just short of rape: Adela manages to fight off the attack with her field glasses. To quote in part:

> She struck out and he got hold of her other hand and forced her against the wall, he got both her hands in one of his, and then felt at her <dress> \breasts/. "Mrs. Moore," she yelled. "Ronny—don't let him, save me." The strap of her Field Glasses, tugged suddenly, was drawn across her throat. She understood—it was to be passed once round her neck, <it was to> she was to be throttled as far as necessary and then...[42]

The change from love to assault in the first two versions of the novel is itself a form of symptomatic condensation that resides in the textual and political unconscious of the published version of the novel. This change could signify how a desire that is forbidden expression through love can resort to a fantasy of rape to bring about what cannot be consciously chosen. Heterosexual rape fantasies in women are sometimes interpreted in this way: sexual repression can lead to dreams of "being taken" by force. Alternatively, the two early versions together suggest another kind of love, a form of sadomasochistic blending of eros and thanatos.

As the novel that stands between Forster's composition of the early and final versions of *Passage*, *Maurice* supports particularly the latter reading. A sadomasochistic mix of tenderness and incipient, phallic violence characterizes the first sexual meeting between Maurice and Scudder, the gamekeeper. Filled with an unnamed desire, Maurice stands at his window, saying "Come" into the darkness, a call that brings Scudder climbing up a ladder into Maurice's room: "The head and shoulders of a man rose up, paused, a gun was leant against the window sill very carefully, and someone he scarcely knew moved towards him and knelt beside him and whispered, 'sir, was you calling out for me?... Sir, I know.... I know,' and touched him."[43] The intimacy of Scudder's touch is nothing like the attack Adela faces in the second version of *Passage*, but the gun he carries symbolically links the homosexual phallus with violence. Maurice's fear of homosexuality has its parallel in Adela's terror of cross-racial, heterosexual attack. Like the final version of *Passage*, what happens next in *Maurice* is left unnarrated, in the gap between chapters. But unlike the published version of *Passage*, there is no ambiguity about what happened. *Maurice* is a utopic coming-out

Bildungsroman, a narrative rite de passage that ushers in fulfilled love. As such, Forster wouldn't allow its publication in his lifetime, accomplishing in its publication history the sexual repression that Maurice gives up. The published version of *A Passage to India*, in contrast, leaves Adela in a state of neurosis and sexual repression that brings about disaster for both Aziz and herself.

In moving from the story of homoerotic relations across class lines to the narrative of interracial relations in the colonial context, Forster engages in a complex transposition. He encodes the homoerotic story in his queer protagonist Adela, whose unresolved neurotic fear of and desire for black men stands in for Maurice's fear of his own homosexual desire for working-class men and perhaps Forster's own anxiety about his unfilled desire for Syed Ross Masood, his grief for Mohammed el Adl, and the needs and psychology of the closet. Though much less directly than Roy, Forster "echoes" Roy's project by bringing readers of colonial modernism "back home" to the homophobia and heterosexism that can paralyze desire and forbid love in Britain as well as its colonies.

Reading into the gap in Forster's novel—what happened in the cave—raises the question of how gaps function in Roy's novel. *The God of Small Things* is a novel whose narrative strategies depend upon elision, fragmentation, and displacement—the very symptomatology of hysteria produced by trauma according to Joseph Breuer and Freud in their *Studies in Hysteria*.[44] The readers must piece together into a coherent narrative the fragments of the twins' childhood perceptions and adult memories. But where Forster excised from the final version of the novel the secret events in the cave that drive the whole narrative, Roy finally fills the gaps in memory by directly narrating in the novel's concluding chapters the beating of Velutha, the twins' incest, and, most taboo of all, the ecstatic cross-caste touches of Velutha and Ammu. More attuned to early-twentieth-century experimentalist modernist narrative strategies, *The God of Small Things* is paradoxically less indeterminate than Forster's novel, which only hints at while hiding its subterranean desires.

Moving back and forth between *A Passage to India* and *The God of Small Things*, much as the eye travels among sections of a collage, brings to the surface "the fiery core" of how love and violence are enmeshed in the context of imperial and postimperial relations—not only by the state power of empire but also by what Roy calls "the love laws" of intimacy that must be policed and transgressed.[45] Where Suleri sees only "the anus of empire" in Forster's *A Passage to India*, Roy's novel helps us see where the two novels cross paths, however different their standpoints. Roy explores the lives destroyed through gender and caste prohibitions within the larger frames of empire and multinational corporations while Forster symptomatically examines the psychological costs of suppressed desire within the context of the Raj, when even friendship across racial lines, let alone erotic love, is not yet possible. Although the specifics of prohibition differ, the two novels affiliate especially around the issue of forbidden love to probe the intimate underbelly of empire and nation-state in the context of twentieth century modernities.

COLLAGE 3: SISTERS/BROTHERS IN VIRGINIA WOOLF, SWARNAKUMARI DEVI, AND RABINDRANATH TAGORE

The gender of imperial and post/colonial modernities circulates in and through the novels of Conrad and Salih, Forster and Roy, often rewriting the fictions of empire to examine the intimacies of power within the scene of the domestic as public and private spheres intersect.[46] In *Heart of Darkness*, the regal African woman and the innocent Intended as competing images in Marlow's psyche reveal the lie upon which European imperialism depends. In *A Passage to India*, Adela's neuroticism covers up forbidden desires across colonial lines. In tune with Said's concept of affiliation, *Season of Migration to the North* and *The God of Small Things* intensify the complications of gender in the earlier novels with a more explicitly feminist focus on the meanings of gender systems as the structures of race, caste, and empire experience the ruptures of their distinctive but interlocking modernities. Coming after their earlier intertexts, *Season* and *The God of Small Things* "reinvigorate" issues of gender rather than imitate or parody *Heart of Darkness* and *A Passage to India*.

But what about colonial gender relations in fictions that *precede* seminal feminist texts produced in the imperial West? How might the circulation of ideas about gender, and especially the lives of women, embody the earlier modernities of empire? What does a spotlight on gender reveal about the relational networks of imperial/colonial modernisms in the earliest era of the long twentieth century? This collage addresses these questions by juxtaposing Virginia Woolf's trope of Shakespeare's sister in *A Room of One's Own* with earlier manifestations of the trope produced in the modernizing colonies, especially in the fictions of Rabindranath Tagore and his largely forgotten sister, Swarnakumari Devi, an important writer and activist in her own right.

A spotlight on gender is especially telling because gender relations are an intense flashpoint for conflict during periods of rapid change, as the reaction of the villagers in *Season* to Hosna's "modern" ways reveals. Women—especially the bodies of women—are often the battleground between modernizing and traditionalizing forces as constitutive of a particular modernity, often intensely so in the context of empire, where women's bodies frequently stand in symbolically for both colonizing and colonized nations. Moreover, the ongoing debate about the origins of feminism and its transnational pathways represents a particular instance of the larger issue discussed in chapters 3 and 4 of diffusionism versus network theory as a framework for understanding transnational modernities and their modernisms.

For some, feminism is an invention of the West that spreads elsewhere, with its Western origins making it suspect in other parts of the world, particularly in the colonies and postcolonies of the West. Having roots in the explosion of women's writing and salons among the elites in seventeenth-century England and France, influenced by the revolutionary thought and abolitionism of the eighteenth century, feminism is conventionally understood as a constitutive part of Enlightenment modernity, breaking open the world of gender relations in Europe and North America in the late nineteenth and early twentieth centuries. Ann Ardis's *New Woman, New Novels: Feminism and Early Modernism* maps the "new woman" literary terrain out of which Woolf's first two novels, *The Voyage Out* and *Night and Day*, came.[47] Extended to the European colonies, the notion of women's rights as a key element of modernity all too often became a rationalization for colonialism, using women to justify the need for foreign rule by "civilizing" Western cultures, as the use of *sati* reform in India demonstrated, according to Uma Narayan, among others.[48] In defense of Wallerstein's world-systems theory of core/periphery, Tani E. Barlow argues that the Western "new woman" or "modern girl" trope spread throughout the colonies and semicolonies as part of the commodity logic of colonialism in the early twentieth century.[49] She describes the "'modern girl' phenomenon which erupted globally in the interwar years, 1919–41" as an "event" that was a "constituent part of what made colonialism a modernist project" (166). With her modern clothes, bobbed hair, cosmetics, and generally fashionable and somewhat risqué air, the West's trope of the "modern girl" swept East Asia in particular, conflating her image with modernity itself, thereby encapsulating the seductions and anxieties of colonialism. For many like Barlow, the issue of feminism in the colonies and postcolonies has been overdetermined by the economic, political, and cultural dominance of Western modernity in the tradition-bound but modernizing non-West.

For others, however, the unidirectional diffusionist model for the spread of feminism from the West to the Rest as part of modernity is misleading.[50] Shifting gender formations have surely been one of the symptomatic signs of any number of modernities—from the court women of the Tang dynasty adopting the somewhat freer clothing, horse riding, and other practices of Turkic women to the elite Indian women of the Raj seeking education and moving out of the *zenana*. Rather than seek a single origin for feminism and then its diffusion outward, others see various kinds of feminism both as indigenous and as part of global networks along which ideas and practices travel back and forth, changing as they encounter others in the context of world systems of modernizing forces. Countering the diffusionist model of modernity, single origins are impossible to locate in the mobile networks of traveling cultures and circulating modernities.

In *Dislocating Cultures*, Uma Narayan argues that traditionalizing forces in the colonies and postcolonies have used the diffusionist view of feminism to resist indigenous advocacy of some form of modernity for women:

> Many feminists from Third-World contexts confront voices that are eager to convert any feminist criticism they make of their culture into a mere symptom of their "lack of respect for their own culture," rooted in the "Westernization" that they seem to have caught like a disease. These voices emanate from disparate sources, from family members, and ironically enough, from other intellectuals whose own political perspectives are indebted to political theories such as Marxism and liberalism that have

"Western" origins. This tendency to cast feminism as an aping of "Westernized" political agendas seems commonplace in a number of Third-World contexts ... [provoking] criticism that portrays feminist activism as originating out of a Western, bourgeois, modernist perspective.

(6)

Narayan suggests about Indian feminism instead that "our feminist consciousness is not a hot-house bloom grown in the alien atmosphere of 'foreign' ideas, but has its roots much closer to home" (6)—indeed, in the very politics of home space in Indian family practices as she delineates them throughout the book. Fully aware of how British colonizers used the "civilizing" mission of eliminating *sati* to justify colonial rule, Narayan nonetheless argues for a comparative approach to violence against women in India, Britain, and the United States, challenging the notion of the Western origins of feminism through a recognition of the indigeneity, travels, and indigenizations of global feminisms.

Virginia Woolf's creation of the trope of Shakespeare's sister in *A Room of One's Own* to initiate a discussion of the conditions under which gifted women become writers provides a useful case in point for this debate about diffusionist versus network theories of transnational feminist modernisms. "A woman writing thinks back through her mothers," Woolf writes in *A Room of One's Own*, a maternal lineage that is purely English for Woolf, going back to writers like the "melancholy" Lady Winchelsea and the "crazy" Margaret Cavendish of the 1600s and earlier still to her fictionalization of Shakespeare's sister Judith.[51] "Let me imagine, since facts are so hard to come by," she writes, "what would have happened had Shakespeare had a wonderfully gifted sister, called Judith, let us say" (48). After spinning her tale of woe that ends in Judith's pregnancy and suicide, Woolf famously concludes:

> This may be true or it may be false—who can say?—but what is true in it, so it seemed to me, reviewing the story of Shakespeare's sister as I had made it, is that any woman born with a great gift in the sixteenth century would certainly have gone crazed, shot herself, or ended her days in some lonely cottage outside the village, half witch, half wizard, feared and mocked at.

(51)

Judith Shakespeare is a *figure of*—that is, an image of, a synecdoche for—the girl who might have become Shakespeare had her circumstances been different, openly suggesting a gendered rivalry conditioned by patriarchal formations. More specifically, "Shakespeare's sister" suggests a sibling contestation, an intragenerational competition of age peers much like the one Roy exposes in *The God of Small Things*. It's brother versus sister, not daughter against tyrannical father, and not the son or daughter repeating the patterns of oedipal or preoedipal desire, narrative structures that have long been staples of narrative theory, especially for *Bildung* and *Kunstler* plots. The triangularization of desire in reconfigurations of the family romance—father/mother/child—omits a sibling structure as a site of desire and competition.[52] It fails to suggest narratives of development that take place among siblings or by extension a larger extended family or even a group of companions in which peers jockey for attention and finite, often discriminatory resources. That Woolf bypasses the names of Shakespeare's actual sisters (Joan, Margaret, and Anne) and uses the name of his daughter Judith Shakespeare, the twin of his son Hamnet, emphasizes the significance of Woolf's interest in sister/brother relationships in theorizing women's writing as instances of an evolving modernity.

Woolf's fiction of "Shakespeare's sister" still travels the globe in texts that directly cite, adapt, indigenize, rewrite, and resist what she wrote out of the particular histories and cultures in which they appear.[53] As such, it would seem to confirm the notion of bourgeois Western origins for modernity's feminism. But the trope of the woman writer as gifted as a man, particularly in the brother-sister dyad, existed in the colonies well *before* it coalesced so brilliantly and influentially into the figure of Judith Shakespeare. These earlier instances of the trope—versions of it that appear in Ireland, South Africa, and India before Woolf creates Judith Shakespeare—challenge the diffusionist model of feminist modernity. They suggest as well that Said's "Traveling Theory Revised" does not go far enough in its revision because it still assumes the West, the site of colonial power, as the origin of ideas that get reinvigorated in the colonies. Traveling back in time to earlier instances of Woolf's trope sheds new light on the relational modernities of feminism in the colonial context. In the process, it helps bring into focus an approach to Woolf's trope that has been relatively unexplored, sibling rivalry between brothers and sisters in the context of colonizing and colonized modernities.

THE TROPE IN THE COLONIES: JAMES JOYCE AND OLIVE SCHREINER

As iconic as Shakespeare's sister has become, the trope of the woman writer as gifted as the man sprung up here and there, like mushrooms after the rain, in the colonies, *before* Woolf wrote it. Joyce, for example, embeds it into an allusive, epiphanic moment in the "Wandering Rocks" episode of *Ulysses*. Stephen, who has recently expounded his theory of Shakespeare in the library, bumps into his sister Dilly at the bookcarts. He sees her "high shoulders and shabby dress" and thinks "I told her of Paris," understanding in a flash that she was imitating him, the one the scant family resources sent to Paris for an education denied to her. He thinks: "My eyes they say she has. Do others see me so? Quick, far and daring. Shadow of my mind. . . . She is drowning. Agenbite. Save her."[54] She is his twin, "shadow of my mind," but without the education and family encouragement to develop it. He pities her, fears her fate, but he, this would-be Shakespeare, doesn't save her—she a sister of Shakespeare's sister, in Ireland, in the colonies, before Woolf dreams her up. She remains in *Ulysses* an implied story, thwarted by the uneven modernities of empire and gender, a story that Joyce leaves unnarrated as his interest in the feminine swerves away from the woman with the gift of her brother and toward the eternal feminine of Molly Bloom.[55]

Woolf read *Ulysses*, we know, leaving open the possibility that her Judith Shakespeare develops the implied, largely unnarrated story present in the image of Dilly and Stephen at the bookcarts.[56] But had she seen Shakespeare's sister as the South African writer Olive Schreiner (1855–1920) imagined her in *From Man to Man*, completed in 1920 and published in 1926? The novel features a pair of sisters, one bookish, the other beautiful—not rivals but representing differently gendered pathways through South African settler life. Ignoring her husband's unacknowledged children by their black servant, Rebekah sets up a room of her own avant la lettre, a tiny closet of a room off her children's bedroom in which she stashes her extensive library of books. There she retreats to read and write—diaries, stories, novels, essays, and scraps. Anticipating Doris Lessing's *The Golden Notebooks*, *From Man to Man* is a hybrid novel: part realist fiction, part tragedy, part journal, part polemic. One of Rebekah's notebook entries reflects:

> We have a Shakespeare; but what of the possible Shakespeares we might have had, who passed their life from youth upward brewing currant wine and making pastries for fat country squires to eat, with no glimpse of the freedom of life and action . . . stifled out without one line written, simply because, being of the weaker sex, life gave no room for action and grasp on life?[57]

In reading backward, from imperial center to the colonies, Schreiner's earlier version of Shakespeare's suffocated peer leaps off the page. Does Woolf pick up in *A Room of One's Own* the implied story where Schreiner left off, introducing more specifically the sibling rivalry? "I told you in the course of this paper," Woolf continues, "that Shakespeare had a sister; but do not look for her in Sir Sidney Lee's life of the poet. She died young—alas, she never wrote a word. . . . Now it is my belief that this poet who never wrote a word . . . lives in you and in me, and in many other women who are not here tonight, for they are washing up the dishes and putting the children to bed" (117).

I am not making an argument about influence, here—I prefer the mushroom analogy. There is no evidence that Woolf read Schreiner's second novel—no mention of it appears in her letters, diaries, or notebooks.[58] But I am suggesting that the feminist tropes about women's writing for which Woolf has become iconically world famous had sprung up earlier, in the colonies, as a result of the interlocking, circulating modernities of the nineteenth century.[59] These earlier manifestations of the trope suggest that the cultural narrative of feminism's origin in the imperial centers oversimplifies the more dialogic realities of transcontinental interaction during the formation of colonial modernities. Recovering Schreiner's forgotten woman Shakespeare and collaging it with Joyce's implied story of Dilly as Stephen/Shakespeare's sister leads to a re-vision of Woolf's iconic trope. Their tropes contain a common core of brother-sister rivalry in the arts, but each embodiment of it is thoroughly marked by its geohistorical location in London, Ireland, or South Africa.

TAGORE'S SISTER: SWARNAKUMARI DEVI

Colonial modernities produced indigenous Shakespeares who were both hybridized through interactions with the colonizing cultures and rooted in their own vernaculars and cosmopolitan traditions: Joyce (1882–1941) in the Irish Renaissance of the early twentieth century and Rabindranath Tagore (1861–1941) in the Bengal Renaissance of the nineteenth century. Winner of the Nobel Prize for his poetry in 1913, Tagore needs no recovery in India, where he was and remains a literary, aesthetic, and musical giant of India's colonial period. But in other locations, Tagore is little read outside of postcolonial studies and thus still needs recovery in the context of transnational literary and specifically modernist studies. Steeped in Sanskrit, emergent literary Bengali, and European literary traditions, Tagore was preminently a poet, but he also composed music (including what became the national anthems of India and Bangladesh), wrote songs (still among Bengal's favorites), exhibited his paintings around the world in the later years of his life, and published novels, short stories, essays, and reminiscences from the late 1870s through his death in 1941. In all media, Tagore was innovative, breaking with the aesthetic forms of his predecessors and contemporaries in India.

Tagore was the youngest of fourteen children in a remarkable, wealthy family that served as the center of the Bengal Renaissance and political/religious reform in Kolkata (Calcutta) for decades. Building on the family's historic connection with the East India Company, Tagore's grandfather acquired vast wealth in land, shipping, and commercial enterprises; more spiritually than commercially inclined, his father developed the Brahmo sect (a modern monotheistic reform movement within Hinduism) into a significant force. Members of the family were involved in the formation and development of the Indian National Congress, serving as key figures in the anticolonialist movement as well as reform efforts around women's education, child marriage, the status of widows, and the seclusion of women. His brother Satyendranath was the first Indian the British allowed into the civil service, and his insistence that his wife Jnanadanandini break seclusion, go riding with him in public, and accompany him to England was considered scandalous. Tagore's family embodied the contradictions of the colonial elite: aligned with, benefiting from, yet resisting British colonial modernity.[60]

The trope of Shakespeare's sister enables re-vision of Tagore's work in the light of a recovery of his sister. Tagore actually *had* a sister who wrote—a real one, not just a shadow of his mind, a trope, or an implied story. Five or six years older than her brother, Swarnakumari Devi (1855/56–1932) was Bengal's first substantial woman writer and a living example of the contradictory colonial modernity for elite Indian women.[61] Unlike her brothers, she was educated at home with her three sisters, and, in spite of her father's support of major reforms for women, she grew up in a household that observed the conventions of child marriage and women's seclusion to the inner quarters, the *zenana*. She was married at age eleven to Janakinath Ghosal, had four children, served as a voting delegate at the Indian National Congress, which her husband cofounded, and established feminist organizations advocating reform. In 1877, at age fifteen, she published anonymously her first novel, *Dipnirban* (*The Snuffing Out of the Light*), quickly becoming a literary sensation once her identity leaked out. Taking over the Tagore family magazine (founded in 1877), she edited *Bharati* for nearly thirty years (1885–1905; 1909–1915) with the assistance of her two daughters, "shaping the literary and cultural tastes of an entire generation of men and women," according to Rajul Sogani and Indira Gupta.[62] After Tagore, she was the most prolific of her siblings, including her better-known brothers. Over her lifetime, she published in Bengali some thirteen novels, two collections of short stories, two volumes of poetry, four plays, an opera, several farces, literature for children, travelogues, memoirs, and essays on scientific and reform issues. Like Tagore, she also composed music and songs, one of which was sung at his wedding in 1883. Significantly, in terms of family history, she published her volume of short stories before Tagore wrote any (he is often credited with inventing the Bengali short story), and she wrote the first opera in Bengali in 1879, a major influence on Tagore, whose first opera appeared later. The dedication of her first volume of poems in 1880 to Tagore hints at the competition between them:

> To my younger brother.
> Let me present these poems: carefully
> gleaned and strung
> To the most deserving person.
> But you are so playful. I hope you will not
> Snap and scatter these flowers for fun.[63]

Tagore's unsuccessful efforts to prevent the publication of Swarnakumari's translation of her novel *Kahake* (1898) as *The Unfinished Song* in England (1913) suggest that he too felt the competition. Ostensibly wanting to spare her the criticism of English reviewers, he writes to William Rothenstein in 1914: "She is one of those unfortunate beings who has more ambition than ability. But just enough talent to keep her alive for a short period. Her weakness has been taken advantage of by some unscrupulous literary agents in London and she has had stories translated and published. I have given her no encouragement but have not been successful in making her see things in the proper light."[64] In fact, *The Unfinished Song* received a positive review in London and went into a second edition in 1914, belying his need to keep her novel in the linguistic "seclusion" of Bengali. An ongoing, subterranean competition between older sister and younger brother reenacts the trope of Shakespeare's sister.[65]

As a nationalist, a feminist reformer, and an advocate of a new Bengali literature and culture that broke from older forms, Swarnakumari Devi also read extensively in English literature, as did her brother Rabindranath. For both, the Victorian novel, with its capacity to probe the subtleties of family and communal life, must have seemed ideally adaptable for representing the hybrid lives of the Bengal elite as they sought a modern prose form rooted in the life and language of Bengal. As Priya Joshi argues in *In Another Country: Colonialism, Culture, and the English Novel in India*, the novel develops as a form in India during the second half of the nineteenth century through uneven processes of indigenization that conjoined aspects of Indian literary culture—from the popular epics to conventionalized poetry—to the English novels from abroad, borrowing from both domestic plots and sensationalist fiction. Bankim Chandra Chatterjee (1838–1894) was the first and most prominent Indian to adapt the novel form into Bengali, suited to Indian interests and conventions.[66] Swarnakumari and Rabindranath, aware of Bankim Chandra's efforts, followed in his wake, developing a new, hybrid prose narrative form in Bengali, aesthetic forms that in their ruptures from the conventional embodied the colonial modernity of their time and place, constituting a specifically colonial modernism.

Whereas George Eliot appeared to writers like Virginia Woolf and Dorothy Richardson to be mired in a Victorian past they rejected, Eliot was among Swarnakumari Devi's favorite writers, in part because she enabled a new discourse for the elite Bengali context that opened up the possibilities of women's desire for both intellectual and sexual lives of their own. Significantly, George Eliot appears in contestation with Shakespeare, gratuitously, unnecessarily, in a full chapter of Swarnakumari Devi's *Kahake/ The Unfinished Song*. *The Unfinished Song* is a scandalous first-person narrative about Moni, a woman who narrates the interiority of her dreams and passions. Her full name, Mrinaline, just happens to be the name the Tagore family gave to Rabindranath's child-bride at their marriage in 1883.[67] Moni backs out of a public engagement she had made herself, refuses a marriage her father arranges, and insists on a love marriage of her own choice. In what Suzanne Keen calls a "narrative annex," Swarnakumari Devi devotes a whole chapter of the novel to a passionate debate about whether George Eliot's genius equals that of Shakespeare, with the pro-Eliot side argued by Moni's doctor, the man she loves, and the anti-Eliot side argued by her brother-in-law.[68] When the doctor asks, "Has any writer of the stronger sex been able to equal her?" the brother-in-law says, "I disagree with you. Do you mean to say she is as great as Shakespeare, for instance?" "Of course," he says. "Why not? I have not the slightest hesitation in pronouncing her as great in her sphere as Shakespeare was in his." "What a monstrous assertion," the brother-in-law snaps back. "It sounds almost like blasphemy. I never heard such a ridiculous comparison. She is no more a Shakespeare than you, my dear fellow, however cleverly she may have written her novels" (56–57). And the debate goes on for another page, reappearing once more later in the novel. It includes Moni's allusion to Dorothea and Maggie as "portraits of the author's own character" (56), a telling reference to Maggie Tulliver in *The Mill on the Floss*, whose intelligence and passion for learning outshines her dull-witted brother. As a narrative annex, this contestation over Shakespeare and Eliot is a tangential episode unnecessary to the unfolding courtship plot. Moni and the doctor have already recognized though not yet acknowledged their love for each other. The debate, however, confirms her feelings. It serves, in other words, as an emotional transition point that signals to the reader where her affections lie and why. In this respect, the trope functions according to the principles of Sanskrit narrative theory by drawing attention to emotional transition points rather than causal structures.[69]

Did Woolf know this novel? Possibly. It was published in English in two different translations, the second in England in Swarnakumari Devi's own translation in 1913. But there is no evidence that Woolf had even heard of Tagore's sister. Leonard Woolf even doubted that Woolf had ever read Tagore, though Tagore's *Reminiscences* (1917) appears in her diary on a short list of books she has at hand to read.[70] The significance of Swarnakumari Devi and Tagore for Woolf lies not in the circulation of their texts to Woolf's library but rather in the circulations between brother and sister as a prior instance of the trope that Woolf would reproduce in *A Room of One's Own* much later.

THE SISTER'S BROTHER: TAGORE'S FICTIONS OF SISTERS, BROTHERS, AND WRITING

As synecdoche of a colonial modernity among elite Bengalis, the trope of the woman writer as gifted as the man appears repeatedly with fascinating modulations in Tagore's innovative short stories and novellas written from the 1890s through the early twentieth century, a highly formative period for the development of his writing. While Swarnakumari Devi remained in Kolkata in the 1890s, living often in seclusion, Tagore's father sent his impractical son to East Bengal to manage the vast family estates for ten years (1890–1900), an experience unavailable to elite Bengali women of the period and one that provided Tagore with insight into the lives of rural people of all classes and genders far from the intellectual centers of the Bengal Renaissance.[71]

In his short stories, Tagore does not invoke Shakespeare or pose the debate about women writers the way Swarnakumari Devi, Schreiner, or Woolf do. Rather, the trope appears within the broader context of narratives about girls and women who resist but are often destroyed by the demands of the joint family structure, about the practice of child brides, and about the vulnerable position of child widows and widows in general.[72] Many of these female characters crave to learn, love to read, and sometimes find a way to write, often secretly and, for elite women, within the confines of the home's inner quarters, the *zenana*.[73] Tagore spun story after story out of the feminist issues his sister raised in her own fiction, the multidimensional, modern reform for which his family stood, and the lives he learned about in East Bengal. Often, the agonistic plots revolve around a contest of wills between a girl or woman and her age peers in the family—a brother, a husband, or in-laws of both sexes. Sometimes, the contestation involves writing, with Tagore narrativizing the trope of the woman as gifted as the man, but with a difference. Tagore's stories about male writers almost invariably mock the men, ironizing their literary and intellectual pretensions, making fun of their style and their egos.[74] For Tagore, the girl or woman writer is invariably bolder, truer, and *more* gifted than the man, and in this way more "modern" in both desire and aesthetic style.

Take, for example, "Khata" (1891), translated as "The Notebook" or "Exercise-Book," a short short story—almost fable-like in its simplicity, akin in its painful irony to stories of Chekov or Joyce in *Dubliners*.[75] The story is about little Uma, her older brother Govinda Lal, and her husband Pyari Mohan, all of whom write. The story opens starkly, almost manically, when Uma is seven, two years before her marriage: "Ever since she had learned to write, Uma created havoc in the household. She drew huge wobbly lines on the walls of every room in the house, immature letters of the alphabet in charcoal: 'Rain spatters, leaves patter.'"[76] Uma moves from walls to writing on the pages of her sister-in-law's romantic novel to scribbling all over an essay her brother has published challenging European scientists: "Gopal is a very good boy," she writes; "He eats whatever he is given," Gopal being the name for cowherd (44). Outraged, Govinda smacks her and takes away "her meager but precious writing materials" (44), then relents and gives her a notebook, in which she first copies poems and prose and then starts writing her own compositions.

Two years later, nine-year-old Uma is married to Pyari Mohan, Govinda's "fellow *littérateur*," about whom the narrator ironically observes, "Though not very old and with some education, his mind was impervious to new ideas. The village people therefore held him in high esteem" (45). Uma's mother warns her to "leave reading and writing alone," and Govinda tells her: "Look here, don't write on the walls there. It's not that kind of house. And remember to keep your pen away from Pyari Mohan's compositions" (46). Joshi, the family's maidservant, takes pity on Uma and secretly places the notebook among her possessions. Refused permission to visit her family ever again, Uma continues her notebook "scribbling" in secret. Discovering her secret from his sisters, Uma's husband ridicules her publicly. He is "greatly disturbed. If this kind of studying once took hold, novel- and play-reading could not be far behind, and soon it would be difficult to uphold domestic decorum" (48). He publishes an essay arguing that teaching women to read and write would unbalance the female principle in the home and end in the destruction of the family and widowhood for women. "No one," the narrator sardonically comments, "had yet been able to counter this theory" (48).

So far, the narrator's ironic tone keeps the story light, almost playful, though Uma's abandonment of her writing carries ominous undertones. But the tropic contest turns devastatingly grim when the sisters-in-law discover Uma writing in her notebook the sad song of a beggar-woman, a song about a Rani who yearns to embrace the mother from whom she was severed at marriage. Encapsulating the loyalties within the suffocating joint family, the sisters side with their brother, bringing him into the women's quarters where Uma is writing. He commands her to give him the notebook. The story ends as starkly as it began: "Uma never had a notebook again. The notebook of Pyrari Mohan, on the other hand, went on accumulating discerning dissertations and thorny theories. But there was no one to seize it from him, and destroy it for the benefit of mankind" (50).

Tagore's brilliant feminist fable, which has all the *condensare* of a poem, narrates two stories implied in the trope of the woman writer *more* gifted than the man—first, there is an implied contest between Uma and the two male writers; second, there is the story of Tagore's own developing modern poetics in the 1890s. Uma serves as a complex persona for Tagore himself, as the gifted girl or woman writing does in a number of his other stories. The giveaway is not only her inborn passion to write but also the phrase she writes all over the walls: "Rain spatters, leaves patter." At the beginning of *Reminiscences*, Tagore recounts one of his earliest memories as the day he realized the reverberations of poetic language, rhythm, and rhyme. "What constantly recurs to me," he writes, is " 'The rain patters, the leaf quivers,' " a phrase from the *Bengali Child's Primer* which was "for me the first poem of the Arch Poet."[77] Tagore did not face the prohibitions about writing that Uma experienced. But his bond with her as writer, against the pretentious writings of her brother and husband, is clear. Uma's last entry in her notebook is the song of the beggar-woman, an echo of Tagore's search in his prose of the 1890s for a literary language fed by, though not limited to, the oral traditions of the rural poor, especially of women, a search that resulted in his break with artificial conventions of elite writers. For Tagore—at least in his prose—the "modern" was vernacular.[78]

Tagore's novella, *Nashtanir/The Broken Nest* narrates more fully the implied story of his identification with Uma in "The Notebook" and also integrates these issues with Bengal's hybrid colonial modernity. Serialized in *Bharpati* in 1901, under Swarnakumari Devi's editorship, *The Broken Nest* later appeared in Bengali editions of Tagore's stories in 1909 and 1926 but was not translated into English until 1971.[79] The novella weaves two narrative lines together: the first, about the transgressive desires fostered by the joint family structure, child-bride practices, and the seclusion of women in upper-class Bengal; the second, about artistic development and narrative poetics in the Bengal Renaissance. The trope of the woman writer *more* gifted than the man is central to the way Tagore combines the narratives. And like "The Notebook," Tagore's identification is with the woman writer, who is both stifled by the family structure yet creative in a way that Tagore seeks for his own work.

The family story is ultimately a very sad one, filled with irony, ending with the protagonists living separate lives of quiet desperation. Bhupati, the kindly modern husband preoccupied with his English-language newspaper, loses his young wife Charulata (often called Charu) when she falls deeply in love with his younger "cousin-brother" Amal, a charming but somewhat vain and superficial young college student whom Bhupati encourages to tutor his lonely and bookish wife. When Charu's jealousy of Amal's attentions to her sister-in-law Manda surfaces, Amal abruptly accepts a marriage Bhupati has been attempting to arrange for him and sets off for England to avoid betraying his main family protector. Charu is devastated by this loss, and Bhupati's efforts to woo her back fail entirely. Bhupati also loses his newspaper after the embezzlement of his fortune by Charu's brother, whom he had naïvely trusted to run the business side of the magazine. He himself tries to write like Amal in an effort to ignite Charu's passion, but she refuses to recreate with her husband the world of secret writings she had with Amal. Brokenhearted, he leaves "the broken nest"; she remains caught in the *zenana* forever and alone.

Emphasizing the distinctive rather than imitative development of a colonial modernism, the triangles of the oedipal family romance have no place in *The Broken Nest*. Instead there is the hothouse atmosphere of crisscrossing desires, pleasures, jealousies, slights, insults, and secrets of a joint family of brothers, sisters, husbands, wives, and in-laws, with most of the action taking place in the women's quarters. This story builds on what Bankim Chandra Chatterji started in *The Poison Tree* (1872), but rather retreat from the perceived dangers of a modernizing Bengal, both Tagore and Swarnakumari Devi explore the explosive tensions between the traditionalizing and modernizing dimensions of Bengal's colonial modernity within the extended family, especially among siblings and age peers. Swarnakumari Devi's *The Uprooted Vine* (1892), first serialized in *Bharati* from 1889 to 1891, is a feminist rewriting of *The Poison Tree*'s more conservative views on the dangers of educating women, especially child widows; her version attacks the double standard that extends a full modernity to Bengali men but not make it available to their wives, daughters, and especially child widows. Tagore's *A Grain of Sand* (1903) rewrites both novels, depicting a claustrophobic world of illicit intimacies and thwarted lives, especially among its women, but presenting a more ambivalent view of the dazzling widow than his sister.[80] In *The Broken Nest*, Tagore focuses on the special relationship of a teasing intimacy allowed in the *zenana* between younger brothers and sisters-in-law that developed in upper-class Bengal society in conjunction with the practice of child-brides for older husbands.[81]

Tagore himself had such a relationship with Kadambari Devi, the child bride of his older brother Jyotirindranath, with whom he had an intensely close relationship that began after the death of his mother when he was thirteen. She was an avid reader, involved in play-acting and music, thoroughly immersed in the Bengal Renaissance, and vital for the family's journal *Bharati*. When Tagore's father suddenly arranged a marriage for the twenty-two-year-old Tagore to an eleven-year-old girl, Kadambari committed suicide shortly thereafter, a scandal the family quickly covered up, burning all her papers, thus leaving the reasons for her suicide open to conjecture and destroying what might have existed of her own creative efforts. Tagore was devastated by her loss and wrote about her often in his poetry. Late in life, images of the same woman haunt his paintings, and many, including Tagore, believe they represent Kadambari and the tremendous hold she maintained over his spirit.[82]

The biographical origins of Tagore's narrative in his relationship with Kadambari are widely accepted. However, I want to suggest that Tagore fictionalizes himself not only in the figure of Amal but also in that of Charulata, anticipating Forster's cross-gendered use of Adela as a persona. Amal, whose ironic name means "stainless," is a Joycean portrait-of-the-artist-as-a-young-man avant la lettre, a kind of self-caricature of Tagore as a young poet, whose first volume of poems in 1878 won him the name of the "Bengal Shelley."[83] But Charu's crazed grief at the loss of Amal parallels Tagore's distress at his loss of Kadambari. Even more centrally, Charu serves as *his* persona in the contest between her modern aesthetic style and that of Amal's stylized Bengali and Bhupati's journalistic English. In short, the trope for which Tagore supplies the implied story makes for a more complex set of transgendered identifications, anticipating Forster's disguised narrativization in *A Passage to India*.

The initially innocent and increasingly illicit intimacy between Charu and Amal develops as first Amal, and then Charu, become writers. As companions in their love of literature, music, and laughter, Charu and Amal dream of building a secret garden together, a plan that leads Charu to suggest that Amal write about the garden.[84] Diffident at first, Amal blossoms under Charu's continual urging and praise. Not content with an audience of one, Amal publishes his work and gains a following as one of the bright new figures on the Bengali literary scene, even being called the "Ruskin of Bengal" by one critic (36), a rubric that may echo Tagore's title as the "Bengal Shelley." Charu is both pleased and hurt by his success, realizing that "her exclusive enthusiasm and encouragement were no longer necessary to force him into writing" (33). "The mischief was done," she realizes, "the very day his writing made a name for him. . . . Now Amal did not consider her his equal. He had by-passed her. Now he was the writer, Charu the reader. There must be some solution for that" (46). The solution, Tagore implies, is that Charu must become a writer herself to win back Amal's attention, especially as he increasingly succumbs to the flattering manipulations of her sister-in-law Manda.

Tagore stages the contest between the conventional writing of Amal and the modern writing of Charu first in three private scenes of Charu writing and then in the public pages of the newspaper. In the first scene, Amal finds Charu writing, snatches the notebook over her protestations, and pronounces it "wonderful" (47). His praise, we discover, is beautifully ironic, because in the second scene of Charu writing, "Whatever she wrote became exactly like Amal's writing; when she compared it, she found that some parts were quoted word for word from him" (48). Finally, to escape "Amal's encircling influence she changed her subject matter": "Moon, cloud, *shephali* flowers, *bau-katha-kao* bird, all were discarded" (48). Instead, she turns to her childhood memories of the Kali temple in her village, her curiosities and fears about it, and the "ancient story long known in the village" about the resident deity (48–49). "Her opening section was flowery, in the style of Amal," the narrator tells us, "but her writing progressed with simple ease and was full of the speech, manner, intonation of the countryside" (49).

Charu's style, as the narrator describes it, is similar to the modern style Tagore himself had forged in his resistance to the elaborately stylized aesthetic conventions drawn from the Sanskrit tradition and put in the vernacular Bengali as the dominant poetics of the anti-Anglophile strand of the Bengal Renaissance of Tagore's youth.[85] As Mary Lago explains in her introduction to *The Broken Nest*, Bengali was not a literary language until the vernacular movement of the nineteenth century, often dubbed the Bengal Renaissance. Bengal's long literary tradition reflected the engagement with classical Sanskrit and the dominance of Persian, Bengal's language of government until 1834, when English replaced it.[86] The modernizing linguistic movements of the nineteenth century in Bengal either favored the "translation" of the classical conventions into Bengali (Amal's style) or the development of an English-language Indian culture in newspapers, magazines, and literature (Bhupati's choice). *The Broken Nest* enters these linguistic/stylistic debates through the contrasting writing modes of Amal, who writes in a Sankritized Bengali; Bhupati, whose name means "rootless" and who edits an English newspaper; and Charu, who writes in the vernacular of the countryside. For Tagore, what is truly "modern" is Charu's style, the one that breaks most radically with elite literary cultures, whether in Bengali or English.

The contest between Charu and Amal moves from the seclusion of the women's quarters to a very public stage when Bhupati declares, "Charu, you've become a writer," as he shows her a prominent literary magazine, in which her writing appears alongside Amal's, and then a newspaper article entitled "Current Bengali Literary Style," which directly sets the two writers against each other:

> The author had written a very stringent essay criticizing the extravagant prose of a group of modern writers. Amal and Manmatha Datta were among those whom the critic scathingly ridiculed. On the other hand he had high praise for the naturalness and simplicity of language, the ease and genuineness, the descriptive skill of the new writer, Srimati Charubala. He wrote: "The salvation of Amal and Company, if they wish to succeed, lies in imitation of this creative method; otherwise there is no doubt that they will be cast aside."
>
> (51)

Charu realizes with shock and a sense of betrayal not only that Amal broke his promise to "publish" their joint writings solely in their own secret journal but also that he didn't show these publications to her because, she assumes, he was angry about the article praising her and condemning him. Tagore has used the trope of the woman writer who is *more* talented than her brother as a cover to defend his own modern poetics, for which he was much attacked in the Bengal press. In short, Tagore embodies his new aesthetic in the figure of an imaginative, gifted, and passionate woman confined to the woman's quarters at a time when his own world had expanded tremendously by his nomadic life on a houseboat listening to the stories of people in the countryside who didn't or couldn't write.

Tagore's emphasis in *The Broken Nest* on Charu's desire for secrecy to be shared only with Amal—secret garden, secret writings, secret journal—resonates with the issue of women's seclusion, which was highly controversial among the reform-minded, modernizing, and nationalist Bengal elite at the end of the nineteenth century. Publication—submitting her work to the gaze of men who are not relatives—functions as a metaphor for Charu's potential emergence from seclusion into the public eye. As committed to the education of women as Tagore's father was, he and many others (including the conservative women of the Tagore family) maintained the importance of the seclusion of women in the *zenana* along with the practice of child brides for the older sons.[87] Swarnakumari Devi did not have the freedom of her brother to attend school outside the home or to wander the countryside of East Bengal. But she made sure her daughters did—Sarala Devi graduated from Bethune College in the early 1890s, having begun her career majoring in physics, "Just like the boys in the family," she said, and while Swarnakumari often observed seclusion, she also regularly left the women's quarters.[88] Her elder sister-in-law, Jnanadanandini Devi, refused to live in her father-in-law's joint family compound, and with the encouragement of her husband Satrendranath Tagore, she broke with purdah entirely, accompanied him to England, and reformed women's dress.[89] Seclusion in the Tagore family was breaking down intergenerationally at the time Tagore started writing prose. The publication of Charu's writing, against her will, reenacts that change, a modern rupture of family practice.

SIBLINGS, WOOLF'S WRITING, AND COMING OUT

The brother-sister entanglements of Swarnakumari Devi and Rabindranath Tagore in their writing careers bring into focus some new ways of regarding Woolf and the relationship of her writing to her family and her reading public, ways at which I only gesture here. Discovering Tagore's gifted sister and seeing the way Tagore repeatedly uses gifted but often thwarted girls and women as the persona for himself as a modern writer, I wonder if we have overlooked the significance of Woolf's brother-sister relationships for her writing and the way in which her anxieties about publication reenact issues of women's seclusion in the home. Woolf's need to free herself from the obsessive influence of her dead parents in order to write is well known. Around the time she invents the trope of Shakespeare's sister, she writes about her father in her diary on November 28, 1928: "He would have been 96, yes, today . . . but mercifully was not. His life would have entirely ended mine. What would have happened? No writing, no books;—inconceivable. I used to think of him & mother daily; but writing The Lighthouse laid them in my mind. . . . I believe this to be true—that I was obsessed by them both, unhealthily; & writing of them was a necessary act."[90] *To the Lighthouse*, published in the same year, reinvents her parents in the figures of Mr. and Mrs. Ramsay as a kind of writing cure that frees her from this parental obsession. In large joint family settings like the Tagores, parent-child intensities were more diffused, with intragenerational relations as likely, if not more likely, to be fraught. But thinking about the buried rivalry between the Tagore brother and sister leads me to ask if we have ignored Woolf's relations with her older brother Thoby Stephen, whom she also adored and whose death from typhoid in 1906 might have also freed her to write.

Like Swarnakumari Devi, Virginia had a "gifted" and "dominant" brother sent to public school and university while she was educated at home.[91] As Hermione Lee writes about his school years, "they would argue about Shakespeare, Thoby ruthlessly dominating her with his confident certainties, she feeling the need to oppose and resist his point of view and make her own judgments. They developed an amicably combative intellectual relationship."[92]

Are there patterns of talented brother-sister contestation in Woolf's narratives that could be seen anew, not in place of but in subterranean relationship to the oedipal/preoedipal plots that are admittedly so significant in her work? In "A Sketch of the Past," a journal written in the last years of Woolf's life, Thoby figures centrally in her recollections of the three "exceptional moments" that led to her discovery of her writing's ordering and compensatory power: "I was fighting with Thoby on the lawn. We were pummelling each other with our fists. Just as I raised my fist to hit him, I felt: why hurt another person? I dropped my hand instantly, and stood there, and let him beat me." The result, she remembers, is a feeling of "horror," of powerlessness that she later learned to counter by putting things into words: "It is only by putting things into words that I make it whole; this wholeness means that it has lost its power to hurt me" (71). As many have noted, Woolf's first experimental novel, *Jacob's Room* (1922), draws on the figure of Thoby in presenting the protagonist who haunts rather than dominates the narrative, all the more so in that this *Bildungsroman* ends in his absence as the aftermath of his death during World War I. How might this narrative of the different fates of men and women in war, of talent unfulfilled, be rethought in sibling terms? How much might Woolf's presence in the world of letters depend upon the absence of her highly gifted brother?[93]

Tagore's conflation of seclusion with issues of publication in *The Broken Nest* also fosters new insight into Woolf's intense dread—indeed, often relapse into mental illness—right before the publication of her books.[94] Publication, for Woolf, was something she eagerly sought but also feared; it represented an unveiling of her private self that made fully public her feminism, among other things. She particularly dreaded the judgment of the men of Bloomsbury—especially that of the members of the Apostles, the Cambridge group of which her dead brother Thoby had been a formative part. Like the women of the Tagore family, like Charu, emergence into the public sphere open to the gaze of men was an issue for Woolf, differently of course, but still an issue. The thrill and angst of exposure drive the last artist figure Woolf created before her suicide: Miss LaTrobe, the lesbian playwright of *Between the Acts*, who exposes her vision of Britain's imperial and familial histories for all to see, who holds the mirror up to the present age to unveil its worm of fascism within the British home.[95] Out of seclusion, out of the closet.

WOOLF, SATYAJIT RAY, AND THE CIRCULATIONS OF SHAKESPEARE'S SISTER

The pre-life of Woolf's trope of Shakespeare's sister in the colonies has a postcolonial afterlife in the circulations of both *The Broken Nest* and *A Room of One's Own*. Jessica Berman, the coordinator of the International Virginia Woolf Society Conference in 2000, collaged Woolf with Rabindranath Tagore by screening Satyajit Ray's 1964 film *Charulata* (*The Lonely Wife*) throughout the conference. Ray (1921–1992), India's leading art filmmaker best known for *The Apu Trilogy* (1956–1959), came from a prominent Bengali family interconnected with the Tagores for generations. Ray's grandfather was a photographer whose early-twentieth-century portrait of Tagore is often reproduced. Ray attended the university Tagore founded at Santiniketan; one of his favorite actresses, Sharmila Tagore, was Tagore's grand-niece; and Ray's adaptations of several Tagore stories and novels are well known.

At the Woolf conference, no commentary was necessary since the parallels between Charu's writing and the women's writing Woolf theorizes in *A Room of One's Own* lit up like light bulbs in our minds. The differences are of course fully evident, but Woolf and Ray share a perception of how the conditions in which the writer writes shapes what is possible, how men's and women's writing have been set up in competition, and how the "modern" and innovative might be produced through the vernacular style of women. This insight, produced by the circulation of text into film and then by an Indian movie being inserted into a Woolf conference thirty-six years later, was heightened in part by the changes that Ray made to *The Broken Nest* in his adaptation, changes that may or may not have been influenced by the worldwide circulations of *A Room of One's Own*.

Ray's "translation" of Tagore's text into filmic language is multidimensional and complex, especially in his visual techniques for rendering emotion.[96] But for my purposes, I want to highlight one major departure Ray makes from Tagore's plot, one that suppresses the implied story of emergence from seclusion I have emphasized. Like Tagore, Ray sequences the story by having Amal write first and then Charu deciding to write as well. Also like Tagore, Ray emphasizes the tropic contest between the two and highlights the different poetics that underlie their writing. The change he makes, however, is instructive. His Charu knows Amal's writing is silly, and she, not Amal as in Tagore's version, makes the decision to send out her own work for publication as part of a defiant competition with him. Where Tagore has Amal violate Charu's commitment to the "seclusion" of her writing, Ray makes Charu a fully "modern" woman in deciding to publish her own work, which she knows to be better than Amal's.

Tagore's subtle play with the overlapping themes of secrecy and seclusion is muted in Ray's film by Charu's deliberate and competitive act. The trope of the woman writer more gifted *and* more stifled than the man has lost some of Tagore's subtlety in the translation. Ray's change, however, sharpens the political message of Charu as an emergent, modern woman writer, making her own decision to enter the public sphere of publication. Comparing the Charu of Tagore and Ray recapitulates some of the political differences between Swarnakumari Devi and Tagore over the status of women evident in his patronizing letter about her desire to see her novel published in translation in England as well as in the stark political differences between their rewrites of Bankim Chandra's *The Poison Tree* in *The Uprooted Vine* and *A Grain of Sand*. The circulation of Woolf's trope of Shakespeare's sister among these Bengali writers and filmmaker emphasizes both the potency of the trope and the significance of its variations.

Shakespeare's sister as Woolf fictionalizes her is a figure of a gendered modernity that preexists *A Room of One's Own* in the colonies and that takes on a new life in the postcolony as Ray films her. As we readers circulate backward and forward in time and across space, the question of brother/sister relations in the context of both patriarchal and colonial formations brings into sharp focus some feminist dimensions of circulating modernisms. Setting aside vexed parent/child relationships, these narratives, read together, foreground intragenerational and sibling issues, especially as they might take form in large extended or joint families across gender lines. The changing patterns of family relations, the shifting expectations about women's seclusion, the challenge to divisions of family resources among brothers and sisters, the developing modernity of women who write and speak in public, the men who identify with or imaginatively inhabit the lives of women—all these issues and more circulate back and forth through Woolf's London, Tagore's Calcutta, and Ray's recreation of that colonial past. They also reappear in new form in the brother-sister tales of Ammu and Chacko and Rahel and Estha in *The God of Small Things*. Far from suggesting that the West invents feminism and spreads it to the Rest, this mobile collage attests to the complex network of circulating, affiliative, and enmeshed ideas that the gendered dimensions of modernity generated in the long twentieth century.

COLLAGE PATTERNS

The intent behind the collage structure of this chapter has been to break the chronological, diffusionist, unidirectional model of modernism by formulating alternative strategies for reading fictions of twentieth-century global modernisms.[97] Collage is based on a principle of paratactic juxtaposition for the meanings that become newly visible through reading separate things together. A collage is typically not read from left to right, in linear fashion, chronologically, but instead fosters circulations back and forth and identification of different networks of meaning. In turn, this mobile mode of reading anticipates the increasingly associative reading practices encouraged by the multiple platforms of digital media in the twenty-first century. To borrow from Said once again, collage fosters what he calls a *contrapuntal* reading—a "plurality of vision" that "gives rise to an awareness of simultaneous dimensions" and "an originality of vision."[98] To see contrapuntally is to see dialogically, multiply, and comparatively.

Collage fosters a form of comparative thought based not on using one element as the standard by which another is measured but rather on encounters that call for what Mary Layoun calls a "relational literacy" as part of the very "ground (political, historical, social) of modernity." Transnational comparison, she argues, involves "a listening to, speaking with, and inhabiting diverse communities in a diverse world." Comparison can be "the great jostling of differences" anchored in the "massive movements and dislocations of peoples in the modern period, the radical juxtaposition—in metropolitan cities or in colonial centers, for example—of different peoples and ideas and things that were hitherto not colliding with one another in quite the same close fashion." Comparison's utopian potential emerges out of a commitment "to the effort to cohabit with, listen to, and consider alternate stories of those who are different."[99] Such jostling and colliding are not always oppositional, I would add. They can produce, as R. Radhakrishnan theorizes, "reciprocal defamiliarization," with each element denaturalizing the other, bringing to the fore new ways of seeing.[100] And as Said and Ramazani suggest, they can uncover unexpected lines of affiliation, interconnection, resonance, and reinvigoration.

As a reading strategy in the context of colonial and postcolonial modernisms, comparative collages challenge the diffusionist strategy that identifies the imperial center first and then its effects elsewhere: first, modernism in London, Paris, New York, Berlin, etc.; then, modernism in Kolkata, Beijing, Cairo, Rio de Janeiro. This is precisely the binarist construction that posits the West as initiator of discourse with the Rest as its imitator, and it is precisely the trajectory that Glissant attacks in advocating an end to center/periphery frameworks of thought and the development of a relational poetics. What patterns, then, have the collages in this chapter suggested?

As constitutive dimensions of interlocking modernities, colonialism and its legacies in the long twentieth century have been undeniably brutal, a reality that Conrad and Forster represent as well as Salih and Roy. But in the aesthetic realm of the imagination, writers claim more freedom to represent a world that exceeds imperial power. By engaging with the modernities of which they are a part, modernist writers from colonizing cultures like Conrad and Forster go beyond their complicity in colonial modernity to expose its pathologies and inhumanities and to indigenize ideas from elsewhere. Similarly, modernist writers from the colonies and postcolonies like Salih, Roy, Tagore, and Swarnakumari Devi are not solely fixated on colonial brutality but represent heterogeneous figures who negotiate the complexities of colonial and postcolonial modernities differently and with varying degrees of success.

Rather than set up a fixed opposition between the British writers on the one hand and the Indian and Sudanese writers on the other, these collages resist such simple oppositions to show how each society contains within it some conflict between "tradition" and "modernity" as constitutive of its own modernities. Notions of colonial mimicry and belated imitation do not fully explain the post/colonial modernisms because they are based on inaccurate diffusionist and center/periphery models of imperial and post/colonial relations. Swarnakumari Devi's and Tagore's fictions of the woman writer as gifted as the man come *before*, not *after*, Woolf's fiction of Shakespeare's sister, thus challenging the notion that feminist modernity is exported from the West to the colonies. The novels of Salih and Roy attest to the ongoing circulation of Conrad's and Forster's novels, but postcolonial writers do not remain caught within the frameworks of their precursors. They create their own visions of modernity; they write against the ideological and material effects of colonial modernities, but they also affiliate with Conrad's and Forster's attacks on the structures of power within their own societies. As texts, they form a network of interrelated mobile modernisms in which new ideas circulate, affiliate, and reinvigorate.

These collages break open purely post/colonial logics to expose the fissures of modernity *within* each location as well as the relations between them. In particular, gender—combined with sexuality, race, caste, and class—provides a basis for affiliation among writers on different sides of the post/colonial divide. Taken together, these fictions all demonstrate that traditionalist resistance to modernizing gender and sexual relations is a feature of different modernities. The rebellions of girls and women, the expression of forbidden desires and sexualities, and the dismantling of caste relations all function to disclose the mobilities of threatening change in the midst of colonial and postcolonial modernities. Gender, sexuality, and caste in these texts serve as linchpins, as causal elements for narrative movement that contain both the utopic and dystopic potentialities of modernity.

Moreover, reading back and forth among the collages provides new insights about each text. Salih's narrative of the violence inherent in traditional village gender relations helps bring into sharper visibility the violence of Marlow's lie to the Intended as a constituent part of a colonizing ideology. Roy's intense focus on hidden cross-caste desire helps us see the homosexual desires buried in the political unconscious and compositional history of *A Passage to India*. Swarnakumari Devi's and Tagore's reinvention of the British courtship plot as a postmarriage plot in the context of elite Bengal's joint family structure suggests the brother-sister dynamics at work in Woolf's famous trope and her relations with her brother. *Heart of Darkness* and *Season of Migration to the North* share an obsessive narrativization of the gaze in cross-racial and cross-gender encounters, and *A Passage to India* and *The God of Small Things* both focus on the possibilities and problems of illicit touch across forbidden body borders. Tagore and Forster experiment with cross-gender personae that allow for their disguised self-revelations. Salih's heavily ironized portraits of both Mustafa and the narrator depend for their meaning on his identification with Hosna, the "modern" woman whom "tradition" kills. And so forth.

These collages, which juxtapose paired novels and circulate back and forth among fictions in each pair, perform a kind of networked global relationality, a mobility in the realm of the reader. As such, they engage in a kind of comparative work based in a recognition of the in/commensurability of the texts set in conversation. Rather than using one text (e.g., the British one) as the standard by which the others are measured, collage sets each text in its own context and uses comparison to see how each might defamiliarize or illuminate the other. Reading backward in time is as important as reading in chronological order. As such, these collages produce not a historical chronology of modernist texts in relation to one another but space for theorizing fluid networks of relational and mobile modernisms.

SEVEN
DIASPORIC MODERNISMS

Journeys "Home" in Long Poems of Aimé Césaire and
Theresa Hak Kyung Cha

> Migration is a central force in the constitution of modernity. . . . The metaphor of the journey, the figure of the stranger and the experience of displacement have been at the centre of many of the cultural representations of modernity.
>
> —Nikos Papastergiadis, *The Turbulence of Migration*

> We may speak of diasporas of hope, diasporas of terror, and diasporas of despair. But in every case, these diasporas bring the force of the imagination, as both memory and desire, into the lives of many ordinary people . . .
>
> —Arjun Appadurai, *Modernity at Large*

> Is home the place from where you have been displaced, or where you are now? Is home where your mother lives? . . . I am moved when I am asked the phenomenological question "Are you at home in the world?"
>
> —Madan Sarap, "Home and Identity"

Migration often accompanies the turbulence of modernity, as both cause and effect of the epistemological turmoil rendered in aesthetic forms. The journey of modernity, to echo Nikos Papastergiadis, invokes human mobilities as constitutive of the modern—movements from the physical and geopolitical to the psychological, philosophical, aesthetic, and spiritual. As such, diasporas reflect dislocations of both space and time—material movements that signal the far more profound psychological effects of displacement, often incorporating both the dystopic and utopic tendencies of modernity. For Edward W. Said, modernity in our times is "the age of the refugee, the displaced person, mass immigration.... The pathos of exile is in the loss of contact with the solidity and the satisfaction of earth: homecoming is out of the question."[1] For Azade Seyhan, diasporas create "the sentiment that neither a return to the homeland left behind nor being at home in the host country is an option."[2] For Arjun Appadurai, modernity engenders a form of diaspora, a phenomenology blending despair and hope, terror and the imagination, memory and desire. For Avtar Brah, such diasporas are paradoxical—as "journeys" that are "about settling down, about putting roots 'elsewhere.'"[3] For James Clifford, the discrepant modernities across the globe engender a "diaspora consciousness [that] lives loss and hope as a defining tension."[4]

Diasporas involve a personally felt experience of communal exile that simultaneously includes the sense of being cut off from the past and past home/lands and the necessity to forge new, often imaginary home/lands for the future. Consequently, memory and creativity are constitutive dimensions of diasporic modernities. In contrast to modernity's drive to "ruthless forgetting," as a way of asserting "the new," a psychodynamic discussed in chapters 1 and 2, diasporic modernity exhibits a "ruthless remembering" as a precondition of "the new." In "Imaginary Homelands," Salman Rushdie writes that the "exiles or emigrants or expatriates" are "haunted by some sense of loss, some urge to reclaim, to look back," desires that in turn lead them to "create fictions . . . imaginary homelands, Indias of the mind."[5] As Said observes, "what is true of all exile is not that home and love of home are lost, but that loss is inherent in the very existence of both" (185). This loss, for Said, becomes paradoxically the site for potential creativity. It is a *"contrapuntal"* experience, giving rise to a "life outside habitual order," one that is "nomadic, decentered," with an "unsettling force [that] erupts anew" (186). Diasporas epitomize, indeed intensify, the sensation of the world split open, of things falling apart. Whether lived in hope, despair, or a combination of the two, diasporas play out in microcosm the contradictions of modern experience. In doing so diasporas heighten the need to remember the past and the resultant drive to create for the future.[6]

I do not mean to suggest, of course, that there is a single phenomenology of modernity. Variations across and within times and places of different modernities most certainly exist and shape their accompanying modernisms. But I am struck by how the nomadic, exilic, or diasporic experience of modernity captures in intensified form some of the contradictions that inhere in the concept of modernity I have proposed in prior chapters. In particular, diaspora exhibits the paradox of modernity's conflicting, dialectically related dystopic and utopic effects. Throughout this book, I have rejected a singular value for modernity—whether good or bad, progressive or reactionary, liberating or enslaving, redemptive or viral. Instead, I have suggested that modernity in all its different and recurrent articulations typically combines the violence of dislocation and the regeneration of relocation, the despair of loss and the exhilaration of new agencies. The enslavement of millions in the Atlantic slave trade after 1500, for example, produced alienated, dislocated "modern subjects" avant la lettre, as Paul Gilroy argues in *The Black Atlantic*, but this African diaspora also unleashed untold creative energies in the arts that have continued to spread throughout the world, as I suggested in chapter 2. The shattering Mongol conquests of the thirteenth century left among its conquered peoples east and west a sense of historical trauma that still drives geopolitical relations today. Yet it also led to the Pax Mongolica, characterized by major innovations in all domains of society in the context of a vast, networked interlocking of different societies, as I discussed in chapter 3. Europe's imperial modernities obscured its own reliance on earlier non-European modernities for its discoveries, but its cultural presence in Asia and Africa played a dialogic role in the production of non-Western modernisms, as I explored in chapter 6. On the global map of multiple modernities, the contradictory pull between dystopic and utopic forces has been a pervasive, underlying pattern.

How does this broad-scale pattern manifest at the small-scale level of a poem? In this chapter, I turn to the diasporic modernism of two poets, Aimé Césaire and Theresa Hak Kyung Cha, both of whom echo but significantly transform the familiar tropes of exile present in the life and texts of early-twentieth-century modernists like James Joyce, T. S. Eliot,

H.D., and Ezra Pound, for whom exile was individual rather than communal and expressed the spirit of modern rebellion against the conventionalities of their homelands. Although similarly delineating desires for freedom, the diasporic modernism of Césaire and Cha, in contrast, are not so much in affiliation with American and Irish expatriates as they are redefining diasporic modernity along axes of traumatic memory and return. The tension between dystopic and utopic aspects of modernity drive the narratives of their two long poems: Césaire's *Cahier d'un retour au pays natal/Notebook of a Return to the Native Land* (1939) and Cha's *Dictée* (1982).[7] In pairing these texts, I answer Jahan Ramazani's call in *The Hybrid Muse* to pay attention to transnational poetry as well as fiction and to Françoise Lionnet and Shu-mei Shih's call in *Minor Transnationalism* to read non-Western writers in relation to each other.[8] I suggest that read contrapuntally, in a form of mobile collage that moves back and forth, these poems exhibit a diasporic consciousness that negotiates the opposition between nihilistic despair and creative regeneration through acts of creative memory and a return to beginnings as a necessity for the future. The poet-speakers of these poems demonstrate how the dislocations of their particular diasporic modernities become a potential site of creative agency. "The migrant, exile, or voyager," Seyhan writes, "not only crosses the threshold into another history and geography but also steps into the role of an itinerant cultural visionary." For "writers of the modern diaspora," dislocation produces a "third geography," an alternative "space of memory, of language, of translation," in short, "a terrain of writing" (15). "Memory marks a loss" of what can only "be retrieved in symbolic action," Seyhan explains (16). In the third geography of writing, Césaire and Cha work through the pangs of memory and symbolic representation to (re)experience the depths of past abjection as a necessary foundation for new beginnings and for the homecoming their poems provisionally achieve. Resonating with the differences gender makes in the fictions discussed in chapter 6, the differently gendered inflections of Césaire's and Cha's visionary journeys bring into focus yet another fissure in the competing pulls of their *nostoi*: the world split open *between* men and women, masculine and feminine. The diasporic modernities of their poems encapsulate the contradictory impulses, heterogeneities, and unevenness of modernity itself.

CÉSAIRE AND CHA: A CONTRAPUNTAL JUXTAPOSITION

Césaire and Cha[9] appear to have little in common and have seldom been read in the context of each other or of modernism—Césaire, because he writes from the Caribbean and is most often read through a postcolonial lens; Cha, because she is variously read within Korean, Asian American, feminist, or poststructuralist frameworks.[10] Geographically and temporally, Césaire's *Cahier/Notebook* and Cha's *Dictée* are at the periphery or outside the conventional boundaries of modernism. Yet read in juxtaposition, in what I have called in chapters 2 and 6 a comparative methodology of collage, these poems embody a diasporic modernism in which the need to return "home"—to perform a *nostos* through memory—constitutes the psychological journey that makes things new, a re-membering of the broken past to enable a hope for a regenerative future.

Aside from their affinities for French intellectual culture and language, Césaire and Cha are an odd couple. Born in Martinique in 1913 and educated in Paris during the 1930s, Césaire was the great theorist and poet of negritude, a pan-African and diasporic aesthetic and political movement celebrating blackness that began in the late 1930s and held enormous sway among a loose affiliation of black writers, politicians, and artists in the Caribbean, sub-Saharan Africa, and diasporic communities of Europe and the Americas well into the 1960s and 1970s. Césaire's *Cahier/Notebook* is his first significant publication and the place in which the term *negritude* first appears. The writing of the poem itself embodies the migratory subjectivity of a colonial writer moving back and forth between home and elsewhere. He began the poem in the summer of 1935 on Martinska, an island on the periphery of Europe off the Adriatic coast of Yugoslavia whose name might have reminded him of Martinique. In the summer of 1936, he worked again on the poem while in Martinique and kept returning to the poem from 1936 through 1939 while he worked on his thesis on the theme of the South in black American fiction for his Diplôme d'Etudes Supérieures in Paris. In 1939, he returned to Martinique for good and published his first version of *Cahier/Notebook* in the Parisian review *Voluntés*. During the war, he edited and frequently wrote for the Martinique journal *Tropiques*, mixing European modernism and Martinican negritude in the discourse of surrealism, an evasive form that allowed him to skirt the censorship of the

Vichy regime. Although his imagination and network ranged widely over the globe, Martinique would remain his nodal point for the production of a post/colonial discourse that wove together poetics and politics. His widely circulated *Discourse on Colonialism* (1955) is often read in tandem with *Cahier/Notebook* for its denunciation of Europe's barbarity and polemical rejection of all that its culture has stood for.[11]

Cha spent her formative years in South Korea, born in 1951 during the Korean War as the child of parents who had been refugees in Manchuria from Japanese imperialism and colonization of Korea. In 1962, her family moved to Hawaii and then to San Francisco in 1964, where she attended a convent school. After graduating from Berkeley with a background in comparative literature and art, she went to Paris in 1976 to study film theory and then returned to Berkeley for an MFA in art in 1977–1978. In the late 1970s or early 1980s, she visited Korea with her brother in the midst of massive student demonstrations, only to learn that she was a stranger at home.[12] As a performance artist, filmmaker, and editor of film theory much influenced by continental European philosophy and art, she published her collection *Apparatus* in 1980 and *Dictée* in 1982. Seven days after *Dictée*'s appearance, she was murdered by a stranger in the streets of New York City. At first ignored by readers seeking a more accessible and mimetic mirror for identity, the poem has lived on, acquiring a wider circle of critics, who tend to read the poem against a backdrop of the Korean and Asian diaspora, feminist theory, and poststructuralism.[13]

Césaire's *Cahier/Notebook*, written entirely in French (albeit not standard French),[14] is an emotionally intense, apocalyptic meditation on the meaning of the poet's homeland to the body and soul of blackness imaginatively conceived as originating in Africa and forcibly migrating to the New World. Located in time "at the end of the wee hours" and in space by an unnamed Antillean town "sprawled-flat" under "a cursed venereal sun" (35), the poet examines "home" most specifically as a Caribbean island in the Antilles and more generally as the Caribbean and the locations of the African diaspora itself. Oscillating between the extremes of self-loathing and affirmation, the poem has an implicit narrative drive: the poet's immersion in the old negritude of black enslavement and abjection, moving with teleological insistence toward the assertion of the new negritude of black dignity and freedom of spirit.[15] Written out of a colonial space and time, the poem imagines a postcolonial domain in which the poet's task is to confront unflinchingly the degradations of the past and present and to articulate the embrace of this past as the precondition for the birth of a newly fertile and communal soul. Mixing classical with dialect French, the poet's language is surreal, figuring the emotional and spiritual extremes of hate and love in images at times violent and ugly, at times tender and delicate, in tones of exaggeration and outrage, as well as moments of great lyricism.

The poet in *Cahier/Notebook* writes in multiple senses with a DuBoisian "double consciousness" that Nick Nesbitt associates with the poem's pervasive "antinomies."[16] Writing in his native French, the poet from the colony is always already in a state of linguistic exile, writing in a tongue that is both his own and not his own. Although Césaire's fluid mixing of hexagonal and Antillean French marks his distance from the French of the Académie Française, the poem's French invokes the diasporic language imposed by the Middle Passage and serves as a linguistic marker of the poet's abjection. Yet this French is also the tongue in which the poet sings lyrically about his emergence from that abjection into the new negritude. As much as he might condemn the whole cultural tradition of the West, including that of France, in the poem's prose companion, *Discourse on Colonialism*,[17] the poem's poetics testifies to the power of that aesthetic in its very form and figural textures, even as these are marshaled to defend the poet's "Leaving Europe utterly twisted with screams / the silent currents of despair" (59). Departing surely from the metropolitan locus of Baudelaire's *Les fleurs du mal*,[18] Césaire's *Cahier/Notebook* nonetheless harkens back to it as the poet immerses himself in a faraway regional/rural cesspool of decay in which he ultimately finds the flower of blackness. Using extremes of imagery to picture the violent and violated landscape of despair, Césaire draws on the French symbolists, much as Eliot did in externalizing the spiritual sterility he found in postwar London. Naturalism appears in the discourse of Césaire's "monstrous putrefactions" (47) and his memory encircled in "a belt of corpses" (59). While the underlying narrative of movement from death to rebirth is in some sense universal, the rich exaggerations of Césaire's figuration contribute to the poem's dreamlike surface, helping associate the poem with the surrealist movement to which he is often linked.[19]

Cha's *Dictée* is a multilingual, hybrid poem in ten sections, opening with a heterogeneous patchwork of invocations to beginnings, including a direct invocation to the poet's muse: "O Muse, tell me the story / Of all these things, O Goddess, daughter of Zeus / Beginning wherever you wish, tell even us" (7). This prologue leads to nine sections named after a modified version of the nine Greek muses, each linked with her creative domain— "Clio History," "Calliope Epic Poetry," "Urania Astronomy," "Melpomene Tragedy," "Erato Love Poetry," "Elitere Lyric Poetry," "Thalia Comedy," "Terpsichore Choral Dance," and "Polymnia Sacred Poetry."[20] Photographs, charts, maps, Chinese characters, calligraphy, manuscripts, etchings, film cuts, and letters frame the text, introduce each section, and punctuate the words on the page. As a whole, *Dictée* is insistently multimedial, weaving different forms of visual culture and disciplinary discourses in between the verbal parts of the text.

Inseparable from its nonlinear form, the poem moves back and forth through time and across space to explore in acts of memory the history of her family in exile, Japanese imperialism and Korean resistance, the Korean War, postwar U.S. hegemony, the repressive regimes and student rebellions in South Korea, her family's migration to the West, her return visit to Korea in the midst of civil strife, and the poet's struggle to achieve speech through the mechanisms of the body and writing. Although mostly in English, the poem contains long sections in French, a Korean inscription, and several pages of Chinese calligraphy. Multiple technologies of writing and typography appear: fonts in ordinary and italic print, typescript and handwritten manuscript, and print and handwritten (grass script) calligraphy. Supplementing these typographies are a Western chart on the physiology of speech and a Chinese medical chart on the body's points of energy flow (the *chi*, important for acupuncture).

Holding together the centrifugal pieces of the poem is the poet's search through the multimedial and multicultural shards of time and space to find the speech and writing that will bring her "home." This home is neither the actual geographical entity of Korea nor an idealized Korean homeland. Rather, "home" functions as the imagined "destination" of perpetual search. It is an imaginary home beyond a single place or history or tradition, but it is also a home with the specificities of many times, many places. As Brah writes, "On the one hand, 'home' is a mythic place of desire in the diasporic imagination. . . . On the other hand, home is also the lived experience of a locality" (192).

At the heart of this search for poetic *logos* is not one nation, one language, one racial essence, but rather a hybridic muse associated with the mother, the maternal body, and a matrilineage within and beyond the family.[21] Cha's matrilineal feminine parallels Césaire's negritude as the longed for basis of being in one sense but departs from his implicit racial essentialism in another. Rather than embodying the essence of the feminine, the various women pictured, narrated, and desired in Cha's poem are iconic and mythic figures of martyrdom and resistance, each fully located in her own body, race, cultural community, and nation. "Our destination," the poet writes in "Melpomene Tragedy," "is fixed on the perpetual motion of search. Fixed in its perpetual sense of exile" (81). In the final section, "Polymnia Sacred Poetry," the poet opens and closes the sacred hymn with a gesture at "home," as a place to look away from while enfolded in the mother's guiding presence. The closing lines of the poem end with the daughter's plea, "Lift me up mom to the window. . . . Lift me to the window" (179).

POETICS OF DISPLACEMENT AND RETURN

The ruptures of modernity and linguistic representation in Césaire's *Cahier/Notebook* and Cha's *Dictée*—as perhaps for many postcolonial modernist texts—are based on a poetics of loss and displacement, a feeling of homelessness and exile that is neither embraced as the precondition of freedom nor lamented as a wholeness once had and now lost. Rather, the sensation of dislocation is based on the longstanding effects of enslavement and colonialism and is endured as the constitutive center of their modernity. As Paul Gilroy argues in *The Black Atlantic*, coercive forms of enslavement, migration, and colonialism create the conditions of epistemological, spiritual, and physical rupture that are hallmarks of Western modernity—and often do so before or alongside such dislocations in the West rather than as the result of a later diffusion.[22] Expanding to a planetary landscape, Gilroy's focus on enslaved Africans in the New World as "the first truly modern people," the juxtaposition of Césaire and Cha reinforces the notion of a postcolonial modernism that is multilingual and multicultural as an effect, and often a painful one, of different colonialisms and not just Western ones.

Instead of abandoning tradition as the prisonhouse of the modern spirit, Césaire and Cha engage in multiple forms of return in their poems. This "return to the native land"—to echo Césaire's resonant title—reverses the direction of journey found in such English-language classics of Western modernism as Joyce's *A Portrait of the Artist as a Young Man* and *Ulysses*, Eliot's *The Waste Land*, Conrad's *Heart of Darkness*, Forster's *A Passage to India*, and Lawrence's *Sons and Lovers* or "The Woman Who Rode Away." Exile in the postcolonial modernism of Césaire and Cha is not a radical rupture from the obligations of nation and family to make it new, as it was for so many of the wandering moderns in Europe and the United States. Rather, exile for Césaire and Cha is a condition of dislocation enforced by history and a diasporic "geography of becoming" that makes a return to the old a precondition of the new.

The poems enact a *nostos* only partially accomplished in the imagination and through the agency of the poetic word, a homecoming that is fraught with self-loathing, the pain of muteness, the struggle for speech, and the drive for rebirth. I use the Greek term—*nostos*—for the topos of the return home to bring into play the associations of longing for home that underlie *The Odyssey*, so different from the topoi of conquest and nation building associated with epics like *The Iliad* and *The Aeneid*. To amend Pound's famous dictum that epics are poems containing history,[23] *Cahier/Notebook* and *Dictée* are long poems that reclaim the past of the dispossessed as the constitutive act that makes possible a different kind of future.

CÉSAIRE'S "*RETOUR*"

Césaire's *nostos* involves both a physical removal from a culture capital of European modernism and a spiritual descent into the heart of a colonially imposed darkness as preconditions for the rebirth of a new negritude. From center to periphery, from metropole to island town, from the urban to the land and sea, from the cosmopolitan to the unlettered—the poet's journey is a bitter but regenerative homecoming. The poem opens with the body's journey complete and the spirit's return just beginning. With jaundiced eye, the poet wanders the night through the broken town of ruin. "Unreal City," he might have said, invoking both Baudelaire's *Les fleurs du mal* and

Eliot's *The Waste Land*.²⁴ The poem contains no such direct citation, but the mood induced by this colonial-modernist *flânerie* is reminiscent of the earlier moderns. "At the end of the wee hours, this town sprawled-flat," the poet finds

> the hungry Antilles, the Antilles pitted with smallpox, the Antilles dynamited by alcohol; stranded in the mud of this bay, in the dust of this town sinisterly stranded.
>
>   At the end of the wee hours, the extreme, deceptive desolate bedsore on the wound of the waters; the martyrs who do not bear witness; the flowers of blood that fade and scatter in the empty wind like the screeches of babbling parrots; an aged life mendaciously smiling, its lips opened by vacated agonies; an aged poverty rotting under the sun, silently; an aged silence bursting with tepid pustules, the awful futility of our raison d'être.²⁵
>
> (35)

This landscape of despair, however, is decidedly not urban—it's hardly even human. The lines are filled with reference to land, sea, and the mud in between. Flowers and wind, waters and bay, parrots and sun bespeak an earthly presence that the modern city of concrete covers over. It's an "inert town" whose dehumanized crowds are a "throng detoured from its cry of hunger, of poverty, of revolt, of hatred, this throng so strangely chattering and mute" (35). Pustules of disease pock the refuse of rot under the "venereal sun."

  The poet's homecoming elicits an excess of extreme images, spilling out an initial contempt for his "*pays natal /* native land." The very earth and sea and sky are instances of abjection, traces of the colonized inhabitants who are homeless in the place of their birth. The pace and rhythm of insult accelerate as the poet's roving eye catches "the sleepy little nigger" who refuses to learn (37), the suicides with swallowed tongue and bursting belly floating bloated down the Capot River (37), "the panting of a deficient cowardice, the heave-holess enthusiasm of supernumerary sahibs, the greeds, the hysterias, the perversions, the clownings of poverty, the cripplings, the itchings, the hives, the tepid hammocks of degeneracy" (38–39). And so forth.

Echoing the poetics of surrealism, the external landscape of home delineated in such stark and visual detail externalizes the poet's interior psyche. The return to his native land brings the poet face to face with his own abjection as a black man ravaged by the psychic wounds of the African diaspora, the pathology induced as the effect of slavery and colonialism.[26] "My dignity wallows in puke…" the poet states at one point, wishing for "a leap beyond the sweet and greenish / treading of the waters of abjection!" (59, 61). Lest one think that this abjection is the flipside of Francophilia, the poet insists on his contempt for the Europe he has left behind:

> Leaving Europe utterly twisted with screams
> the silent currents of despair
> leaving timid Europe which
> collects and proudly overrates itself
> I summon this egotism beautiful
> and bold[27]
>
> (59)

The poet's "egotism beautiful / and bold" has nothing to do with Afrocentric fantasies of a glorious past—"I refuse to pass off my puffiness for authentic glory. / And I laugh at my former childish fantasies. / No, we've never been Amazons of the king of Dahomey, nor princes of Ghana with eight hundred camels, nor wise men in Timbuktu under Askia the Great" (61). The poet's home is not Africa and the glories of its past history but rather the Antilles, where "I may as well confess that we were at all times pretty mediocre dishwashers, shoeblacks without ambition, at best conscientious sorcerers and the only unquestionable record that we broke was that of endurance under the chicote" (61). The return to his native land from Europe is riven with irony because the home he returns to is itself the site of diaspora and diminished lives. Home for the black Antillean is simultaneously a location of belonging and the site of displacement, the trace of the removal from Africa as the homeland lost through slavery.

The poem exhibits no nostalgia for home, no romanticization of home. To idealize or celebrate his Antillean home in reaction against the colonial assumption of European superiority would be to deny the worst effects of that diaspora. Consequently, the poet's catalogue of abjections insists upon reimmersion into the heart of the degradation—material, psychological, spiritual—that colonialism has wrought. This degradation is the heart of darkness of communal diaspora, echoing only to turn upside-down the journey of Conrad's Marlow and anticipating Roy's articulation of the "dark of heartness" discussed in chapter 6. To discover the new negritude, Césaire's poet must "wallow in puke," treading in the waters of the negritude of old, the meanings of blackness created by enslavement and colonialism. For Césaire, the formation of an oppositional consciousness does not mean the mere reversal of how the colonial powers have defined the colonized. Instead, it involves a return to the native land as an epic descent into hell as the precondition of another kind of return, the return of new beginnings, new hope, new life. At the center of this newness is an epistemological transformation, a change in the poet's way of seeing what he sees: "By a sudden and beneficent inner revolution, I now ignore my repugnant ugliness" (61).

As an "inner revolution," the pathway to rebirth is not strictly linear in the poem—much less linear, in fact, that the underlying narrative of *The Waste Land*, for example. Rather, the poem oscillates between the moods and modes of self-loathing and self-assertion, abjection and resistance, with the regenerative discourses of rebirth and the vision of the new negritude gradually gaining dominance by the end of the poem. As befits the emphasis on "inner revolution," the poem's rhythm is epiphanic, moving back and forth between revelations of degradation and regeneration.

At the core of these epiphanic moments is the poet's insistence on the materiality and lasting effects of enslavement. The poem is punctuated by moments of sudden delineation—indeed, vivid visualizations or soundings—of oppression. In thinking of "We the vomit of slave ships," for example, the poet suddenly hears the sounds of the Middle Passage: "I hear coming up from the hold the enchained curses, the gasps of the dying, the noise of / someone thrown into the sea... the baying of a woman in labor... the scrape of fingernails seeking throats... the flouts of the whip... the seethings of vermin amid the weariness..." (61, 63; ellipses in original). Distinctions of time and space, history and geography, self and ancestors collapse into a single presence, a reperformance of the past in the present, a restaging of the catastrophic journey on the Antillean shore.

Equally at the core of these pivotal moments is the poet's claim to rootedness in the elemental land and sea air of his island home and "the archipelago arched with an anguished desire to negate itself" of which the Antilles are a part (47). In calling forth the spirit and light of his ancestors—"those who have invented neither powder nor compass / those who could harness neither steam nor electricity" (67)—the poet locates his new negritude:

> my negritude is neither tower nor cathedral
> it takes root in the red flesh of the soil
> it takes root in the ardent flesh of the sky
> it breaks through the opaque prostration with its upright
>   patience
>
> Eia for the royal Cailcedra!
> Eia for those who have never invented anything
> for those who have never explored anything
> for those who never conquered anything
>
> but yield, captivated, to the essence of all things
> ignorant of surfaces but captivated by the motion of all things
> indifferent to conquering, but playing the game of the world.[28]
>
> (67, 69)

CHA'S "ALLER/RETOUR"

Césaire's homecoming is materially and figuratively tied to his departure from Europe and his literal return to what "I call 'our house,' comically perched on minute cement paws, its coiffure of corrugated iron in the sun like a skin laid out to dry" (39), to the town of his youth, and to the island of enslavement and degradation.

Not so Cha. The poet left Korea as a child, returns only once in the course of the poem, and remains cut off throughout the poem from her native land, except for one visit, when she realizes anew her alienation from home. In some sense, her native home travels with her as a site of origin that lives in the imagination that perpetually reinvents its spiritual homeland through acts of memory, expressive speech, writing, and visualization. She is like Gloria Anzaldúa, who writes in *Borderlands/La Frontera—the New Mestiza*, "I am a turtle, wherever I go I carry 'home' on my back."[29] The structuring principle of the Greek muses signifies the role of memory in her homecoming since the daughters of Melpomene (whose name means *memory* in Greek) govern the arts of history, philosophy, poetry, and music.[30]

Like the Antilles of Césaire's poem, however, Cha's homeland is a location of continual dislocation, of colonization, forced migration, and martyrdom. The poem's opening graphic embodies the way in which the poet's original homeland is defined through involuntary removal and foreign imperialism. Preceding even the title page, the poem opens with a mottled photo in black and white of anonymous wall carvings. A well-known image in Korean history, it depicts Korean characters scrawled on the wall of a coal mine by a Korean forced into labor during the Japanese occupation of Korea early in the twentieth century. The only Korean script in the poem, it reads: "Mother, I miss you, I'm hungry, I want to go home to my native place."[31]

The laborer's words—presumably those of a man—lament the removal from both his mother and his motherland and thereby establish the motif of search for the mother that drives the poet. "*Every bird that migrates North for Spring and South for Winter becomes a metaphor for the longing of return. Destination. Homeland,*" the poet muses (80). The motif of "aller/retour"—to go/return—recurs especially in "Elitere Lyric Poetry," which contains sections titled "Aller/Retour," "Aller," and "Retour." This "aller/retour" resonates as a sort of postcolonial modernist *fort/da* throughout *Dictée*. Physically, spiritually, and aesthetically, the poet is perpetually forced to go and compelled to return through the agency of memory, writing, and speech.

As acts of memory, Cha's *nostos* in the poem begins with Clio, the muse of history, and takes fragmentary and multimedial form in a complex succession of severances from and within the homeland, each with its own story of separation and degradation. Unlike Césaire's triangular "milieu of becoming"—Africa, the Antilles, and France—Cha's postcolonial geography incorporates multiple locations of tyranny and oppression, sites both external and internal to Korea. Where Césaire's history operates on white/

black and West/African or Afro-Caribbean binaries, Cha's national history incorporates East/West, Japanese/Korean, North/South, and Cold War oppositions, making the identification of the national imaginary and its enemy much more difficult. She includes, for example, a historical document, a letter from the Koreans of Hawaii to President Roosevelt in 1905, appealing for help after noting that the Japanese takeover of Korea began with an invitation by the Korean government for an alliance to stop the incursions of imperial Russia in Asia (34–36). The story of Japan's brutal occupation of Korea for nearly forty years emerges in the narration of her family's forced exile in Manchuria and the resistance of the revolutionary Korean Yu Guan Soon, compared in the poem to Joan of Arc.

In "Melpomene Tragedy," the poet reflects on how Japan's defeat in World War II led not to Korean freedom, as her mother had hoped, but rather to other forms of national degradation and partition, particularly as Korea became the battleground for the Cold War and for the American fixation on its new enemy, communism in China and the Soviet Union. The motif of return is multilayered. In 1980, the poet returns to Korea for the first time in eighteen years, remembering both the Korean War and the South Korean violence against student demonstrators in 1960–1962, events that led her family to flee yet again. Resisting simple binaries of good and evil, right and wrong, she addresses the national "tragedy" as the fate of division within a global system of competing forces. In thinking about the martyrdom of the student demonstrators, for example, she counters with the story of her brother's shame—that when his mother begged him to stay home, he did not join the martyrs. Her silent address to a young government soldier she witnesses during the demonstrations in 1980 is oddly sympathetic, understanding the trap of unthinking patriotism in which he is caught: "You wear a beret in the 90 degree sun there is no shade at the main gate you are fixed you cannot move you dare not move. You are your post you are your vow in nomine patris you work your post you are your nation defending your country from subversive infiltration from your own countrymen" (86).

In the context of Korean history, the poet's "return" to her native land leads to her reflections on how history repeats itself in the economy of the same—the endless repetition of war, severance, and exile within landscapes that are regional, national, and global:

Our destination is fixed on the perpetual motion of search. Fixed in its perpetual exile. Here at my return in eighteen years, the war is not ended. We fight the same war. We are inside the same struggle seeking the same destination. We are severed in Two by an abstract enemy an invisible enemy under the title of liberators who have conveniently named the severance, Civil War. Cold War. Stalemate.

(81)

To break the cycle of this kind of repetitive return, the poet struggles for words to bring into being another kind of return, an imaginative recreation of the homeland that is not simply nationalist, patriotic, or chauvinist. Supplemented at every turn by images, language is the poet's predominant medium of memory and transformative vision.[32] The poem's paratactic and elusive qualities embody in poetic form a kind of linguistic stutter representing the poet's search for language and signifying the effects of colonialism and dislocation on speech itself. In "Terpsichore Choral Dance," for example, the poet writes at one point about her attempts to speak and write:

At times, starts again. Noise. Semblance of noise. Speech perhaps. Broken. One by one. At a time. Broken tongue. Pidgeon tongue. Semblance of speech. . . . Maimed. Accident. Stutters. Almost a name. Half a name. Almost a place. Starts. About to. Then stops. Exhale swallowed to a sudden arrest. Pauses. How vast this page. Stillness, the page. Without. Can do without rests. Pause. Without them. All. Stop start.

(158–159)

Embedded in the poem's title, "dictation" is the central trope for its multifaceted examination of language. In its French form, *dictée* condenses the historical, spatial, physiological, and linguistic conditions of search. As the poem's prologue suggests (with its paragraph in French, followed by a translation in English, including words in both languages for punctuation [1]), *dictée* is the term used in French pedagogy to refer to a particular type of exam, the requirement that students reproduce in writing what the teacher says orally.[33] This exercise stands in for many other forms or aspects of dictation in the poem: the tyranny of political and cultural dictation; the imposition of foreign tongues on colonized and exiled people, impelled to parrot back words, to speak the language of others; the cultural translation involved in moving from one language to another; the dissociation between the one who produces speech and the one who transcribes it onto the page; the catechism of Catholicism as a form of spiritual dictation; and the sense of the poet's body as a site upon which culture is written and through which culture speaks. Above all, *dictée* suggests the fraught relation between oral and written speech, a problematic at the heart of Derridean deconstruction, one that Cha rewrites to insist upon the interdependence of both, colored by a postcolonial poetics of dislocation. In the end, the poem itself is the poet's *dictée*, the poetic speech—oral, written, visual—that results from the poet's encounter with the nine muses invoked in the poem, what she calls at one point the "extended journey" (140) of memory, and the "homeland" of the spirit to which she ultimately returns through her writing. By writing, she reflects, she "could continue to live" (141). The poem itself signals the return.

THE GENDER OF RETURN IN *CAHIER/NOTEBOOK* AND *DICTÉE*

The poetics of dislocation and return in *Cahier/Notebook* and *Dictée* are gendered in ways that illuminate central thematics of loss and dispossession in diasporic modernism. Césaire and Cha both use the gendered body of colonial subjects to allegorize the story of national identity.[34] But they do so in strikingly different ways, a contrast that points up not only some differences between these two writers but also the way in which gender narratives can at times interrupt the discourse of nationalism and resist the reduction of identity to a single constituent such as race or nation. What this distinction highlights is the differing stances toward cultural or national chauvinism, "ethnic absolutism," and cultural hybridity that diasporic modernism can take. Césaire's gendering of diasporic modernism emphasizes the basis in "blood" of a people whereas Cha's gendering of the national story draws upon a syncretism of peoples, languages, and cultures.[35]

Césaire's central epiphany of renaissance—the birth of the new negritude—follows on the heels of a memory of seeing "One evening on the streetcar facing me, a nigger." To the recently returned poet, the large, poor, black workingman represents an extreme form of degradation, a projection of the poet's own self-loathing for his negritude and that of his people. I quote only in part from the lengthy and pivotal portrait:

> A nigger big as a pongo trying to make himself small on the streetcar bench. He was trying to leave behind, on this grimy bench, his gigantic legs and his trembling famished boxer hands. And everything had left him, was leaving him. His nose which looked like a drifting peninsula and even his negritude discolored as a result of untiring tawing. And the tawer was Poverty. A big unexpected lop-eared bat whose claw marks in his face had scabbed over into crusty islands. . . .
> He was a gangly nigger without rhythm or measure.
> A nigger whose eyes rolled a bloodshot weariness.
> A shameless nigger and his toes sneered in a rather stinking way at the bottom of the yawning lair of his shoes.
> Poverty, without any question, had knocked itself out to finish him off. . . .
> And the whole thing added up perfectly to a hideous nigger, a grouchy nigger, a melancholy nigger, a slouched nigger, his hands joined in prayer on a knobby stick. A nigger shrouded in an old threadbare coat. A comical and ugly nigger, with some women behind me sneering at him.
> He was COMICAL AND UGLY,
> COMICAL AND UGLY for sure. (63)

The poet's memory of this confrontation with negritude across class lines represents a post/colonial version of the *flâneur*'s modernist dissociation.[36] He fixates on the body of the black man and finds its hugeness, its evidence of menial labor, its poverty to be "COMICAL AND UGLY." Women sneer at this body. He too sneers at this emasculated huge blackness. But the fact that he introduces this memory as a confession of his own cowardice—"You must know the extent of my cowardice" (63)—suggests that he now understands his earlier mocking dissociation from the black man to be a sign of his own degradation and emasculinization: "My heroism, what a farce! / This town fits me to a t. / And my soul is lying down. Lying down like this town in its refuse and mud" (63). Confrontation with his own gendered blackness in the form of the poor black laborer represents his epic descent into hell and an identification with male blackness-as-abjection as the necessary precondition of renaissance.

The old negritude is reborn in the poet's imagination as the new negritude in a birth scene ecstatically charged with lyrical images of sea, island, flora, fauna, impregnation, and parturition celebrating an organic (not urban) island world and heavily dependent on the traditional binary of masculine/feminine. I quote in part from the lengthy epiphany that immediately precedes Césaire's announcement of the new negritude:

>But what strange pride suddenly illuminates me!
>let the hummingbird come
>let the sparrow hawk come
>
>....................
>let the lotus bearer of the world come
>the pearly upheaval of dolphins
>cracking the shell of the sea
>
>....................
>let the ovaries of the water come where the future stirs
>   its testicles
>
>....................
>Calm and lull oh my voice the child who does not know
>that the map of spring is always to be
>drawn again
>
>............................
>zinnias
>coryanthas
>will then pour into the rich extremity of my fatigue
>and you star please from your luminous foundation draw
>   lemurian being—of man's unfathomable
>sperm the yet undared form
>
>carried like an ore in woman's trembling belly![37]

(67)

The poet announces a reborn relationship to the body of blackness by invoking "Blood! Blood! all our blood aroused by the male heart of the sun" and "the femininity of the moon's oily body" (69). In accepting his race, he sees for himself and by extension for the black poet a special role based in a reborn manhood, one that prefigures the masculinism of the Black Arts movement of the 1960s, one that androgynously takes on the task of both creation and procreation of the race through the male stewardship of the word:

> Make me a steward of its blood
> make me trustee of its resentment
> make me into a man for the ending
> make me into a man for the beginning
> make me into a man of meditation
> but also make me into a man of germination[38]
>
> (71)

Like Césaire, Cha imagines the degradation of her homeland in bodily terms, but her image of abjection centers on violation of the female body, not emasculinization.[39] In a trope familiar to much postcolonial literature (by men as well as women), the woman's body figures as the geo-body of the nation—violated by invasion, driven into exile, riven by partition in the context of the Cold War, torn apart as one sector of society is set upon another under dictatorship, teetering between muteness and fragmentary speech.[40] Cha narrates the twentieth-century history of Korea allegorically, by focusing on its women, specifically the revolutionary martyr Yu Guan Soon (1903–1920) and then her own mother, and by imagining the nation as a motherland split in two, "She" and "HER." "Clio History" features Yu Guan Soon as Korea's Jeanne d'Arc, the only daughter in a family of sons and the one who led a massive rebellion against the Japanese occupation in 1919 (24–31). Her body, suffering multiple stab wounds to the chest after her arrest, stands in for the body of the nation, of the people, of the language and culture forbidden to its people.

Moving from the national martyrdom of Yu Guan Soon into the family sphere, the poem's next section, "Calliope Epic Poetry," continues the allegory of the nation through the personal suffering of her mother Yong Jung, born in exile in Manchuria, forced to speak Japanese and Chinese, uttering the mother tongue only in secret, in a whisper, singing the national anthem only "in your spirit-heart" (46). The body of speech itself tells the story of colonial abjection and prefigures the poet's own struggle with language. The merger of mother and daughter-poet becomes even more pronounced as the daughter tells the story of her mother's second exile. Sent far from home to teach in the Manchurian countryside in 1940, her mother longs for home, for her own mother. Protesting nothing, with little to eat, she becomes ill, a bodily collapse that acts out the spiritual exile of her people: "You cannot ask for more than millet and barley to eat. You take what is given to you. Always do. Always have. You. Your people" (49).

In writing to her own mother of her desire for home, Yong Jung prefigures the daughter-poet later writing of her homeland. Cha's imaginative recreation of her mother's writing home folds into an expression of the poet's own special task through the double meaning of the second person "you": "You write. You write you speak voices hidden masked you plant words to the moon you send word through the wind. Through the passing of seasons. By sky and by water the words are given birth given discretion. From one mouth to another, from one reading to the next the words are realized in their full meaning" (48). Reunion of Yong Jung with her mother represents the dream of an end to exile and the return to the motherland and mother tongue: "You take the train home. Mother. . . . You are home now your mother your home. Mother inseparable from which is her identity, her presence. . . . Mother, I dream you just to be able to see you. . . . Mother, my first sound. The first utter. The first concept" (49–50). This dream of reunion with mother/land is broken when the poet recalls that the defeat of the Japanese resulted in bitter partition and dictatorship rather than liberation:

Imaginary borders. Un imaginable boundaries.

Suffice more than that. SHE opposes Her.
SHE against her.

(87)

The tragedy in "Melpomene Tragedy" of the riven mother as the allegory of Korea leads into an exploration of intimacy and the private sphere in the next section, "Erato Love Poetry," a highly elusive and allusive sequence that interrupts the anti-imperial national narrative that has predominantly characterized the poem so far by foregrounding the issue of male dominance within the family, religion, nation, and transnational landscape. "Erato Love Poetry" interweaves the abjection of women within marriage and of women martyrs within the Church, specifically of Jeanne d'Arc and her own namesake, St. Thérèse of Liseux (1873–1897), the French Carmelite nun who came to be known as Little Flower or Saint Thérèse of the Child Jesus. Moving outside of an explicitly Korean frame, Cha bookends the section with a photo of St. Thérèse dressed as Jeanne d'Arc, an image she borrowed from St. Thérèse's autobiography, *Story of a Soul*,[41] and with a still from Carl Theodor Dreyer's silent-film classic, *La passion de Jeanne d'Arc* (1928).[42] In between these photos of religious and national martyrs, Cha interlaces on facing pages quotations from *Story of a Soul* with figures of a woman or composite women linked to the cinema and representing various dimensions of erotic thralldom and entrapment within marriage and within the scene of cinematic representation itself. Operating like the lens of a movie camera, the poet records the movements of a woman going into a movie theater, where she watches herself enter a foreign film with subtitles, to become the object of her own and our gaze. St. Thérèse's ecstatic but pained submission to Jesus is superimposed on Jeanne's martyrdom by the Church and on the woman's abjection in marriage, with a husband who dominates and betrays her.[43] All are love stories of sorts, stories of abjection whose patriarchal politics uncannily echo the national politics already told through the stories of Yu Guan Soon and Yong Jung.

St. Thérèse is a martyr in love with her own abjection to Jesus: "I am only a child, powerless and weak, and yet it is my weakness that gives me the boldness of offering myself as *VICTIM of your love, O Jesus!* . . . *Love has chosen me as a holocaust, me, a weak and imperfect creature.* . . . Like You, my Adorable Spouse, I would be scourged and crucified" (111, 117). This marriage to Jesus and identification with his martyrdom parallels a different sort of marriage, not the mystic union of spiritual lovers but the secular union of husband and wife told in the film. The woman, we learn, had no say in the marriage, an arrangement made for her with a stranger who then becomes unfaithful to her (102). "You only hear him taunting and humiliating her," Cha writes (102). She struggles in the film to speak, lacking the language, experiencing the muteness we have come to associate with the colonization of Korea. Just as Japan "owned" the body of Korea and Koreans, the husband possesses the body of the woman, and just as Yu Guan Soon resisted, so does the wife against the rule of her husband:

> It is the husband who touches. Not as husband. He touches her as he touches all the others. But he touches her with his rank. By his knowledge of his own rank. By the claim of his rank. Gratuity is her body her spirit. Her non-body her non-entity. His privilege possession his claim. Infallible is his owner-ship. Imbues with mockery at her refusal of him, but her very being that dares to name herself as if she possesses a will. Her own.
>
> (112)

The modified echo of Virginia Woolf's *A Room of One's Own*—"a will. [of] Her own"—helps emphasize the link between Cha's argument and that of Woolf's own in *Three Guineas*, which draws a connection between the fascism of the state and the patriarchy of the home.[44] Where Cha had initially used the body of women as allegory of the colonized state, she now uses the history of the nation to allegorize the story of marriage. Moreover, she moves away from nationalist chauvinism or the ethnic absolutism toward which Césaire's poem tends by linking the history of Korea with the story of two "marriages," that of St. Thérèse and of the woman/women in the film/s.

The poem's syncretist anticolonialism and antipatriarchalism come together in the poem's evocation of the Eleusinian mysteries. The severance of daughter from mother—a theme throughout Cha's allegory of nation—intensifies in the second half of the poem with the parallels drawn between Korea, her own family, and the story of Demeter and Persephone as a kind of archetypal tale of rape, loss, exile, and partial reunion. First appearing in the poet's reflections on the partition of Korea (88), Demeter reappears with the brief allusion to Eleusis in a lyric on the death of the gods and of memory (130) and then again in the poet's call for the daughter to "*Restore memory. Let the one who is diseuse, one who is daughter restore spring with her each appearance from beneath the earth*" (133). These fragments represent a paratactic *condensare* of the full Greek story and suggest analogues between family and nation centered on the rape of the daughter, the mourning of the mother, the death of all living things, and the return of life through the reunion of mother and daughter. However, Cha reverses the Eleusinian mysteries in which the mother Demeter brings her daughter Persephone back to the land of the living for six months each year. Instead, in Cha's poem, it is the daughter-poet who restores the mother to life. The daughter's poem is the ritual act of memory that accomplishes in a postcolonial context what the rituals of the Eleusinian mysteries produced in the ancient Mediterranean world.

Cha's excursion into Greek tradition brings her back "home" and lays the foundation for the telling of the folktale in which the daughter seeks medicines that can cure her ailing mother in the opening to the poem's final section (167–170). Again reversing the Eleusinian mysteries, Cha's tale features the daughter who hopes to cure the mother. Echoing the narrative and linguistic simplicity of folktales, Cha's story unfolds without the stutters, fragments, and resistance to coherent narrative that characterize most of *Dictée*. As Shu-mei Shih points out, the story alludes to the Korean myth of Princess Pali, who in one version descends to the underworld to seek an herb that will regenerate her mother's health. But significantly, Cha does not identify the tale as Korean, leaving its national allusion available only to those who know it.[45] Told without specific identification as to nation or people, the tale echoes with a difference the untranslated, unidentified inscription with which *Dictée* opens: the message in Korean script scrawled on the wall by a colonized Korean miner far from home: "Mother, I miss you, I'm hungry, I want to go home to my native place."

The simply told tale functions as both allegory for the colonized and severed nation of Korea and for a generalized representation of human exile, loss, and search for healing. But it does so by focusing on the relations of daughter and mother in which the daughter-poet heals the mother/land. "Polymnia Sacred Poetry" represents the poet's final return to a homeland of memory, an imaginative space where the daughter-poet can appeal to her mother as the precondition of poetic vision in the poem's final ode: "Lift me up mom to the window" (179). Like the birds going south in winter and north in summer, Cha's *aller/retour* contains the specific reference to the story of her own nation and people as well as a transnational and intercultural reach that weaves together the disparate traditions of the human family with a focus on the potentially healing bonds of mother and daughter.

CONCLUSION

In reading Césaire's *Cahier/Notebook* and Cha's *Dictée* contrapuntally in the context of modernism, I am going against the grain—against the more frequently examined peripheries in modernist studies, against the often national and/or racial boundaries in much postcolonial studies, and against the gender borders still common in feminist criticism. This pairing suggests some transcultural patterns in postcolonial modernism centered around issues of the journey, of migration and exile, of a diasporic consciousness caught up in both despair and new creation, of the search for the meanings of home. Attention to these patterns brings into focus the meanings of modernity outside the West and ultimately suggests ways to rethink the significance of diaspora not only for postcolonialism but also for modernism in general.

The post/colonial modernism that emerges from this contrapuntal reading strategy with Césaire and Cha is based on a diasporic poetics of dislocation and return that engenders an imaginative search for a homeland of the spirit, one in which the body of the poet and its analogue—the body of the nation and its people—are no longer sites of humiliation, abjection, self-loathing, shame, and violation. History, tradition, and memory are central constituents of "making it new," of making the body whole, of envisioning a future not just for the individual rebel but for the self as a member of a diasporic community. Gender—whether masculine/feminine or male/female—serves as apt allegory for communal humiliation and renaissance, providing sexual and familial models of pain and rebirth. Gender also introduces complicating narratives of difference *within* the nation and its people, signaling in the case of Césaire his retreat into the biologism of racialized manhood and in the case of Cha her blend of the locationally specific and the generally human patterns of *aller/retour* through the mother/daughter relation. And as Ramazani suggests in *The Hybrid Muse*, cultural hybridity is a central quality of post/colonial and diasporic poetics, whether it is unacknowledged as in Césaire's *Cahier/Notebook* or embraced as a poetic and political principle in Cha's *Dictée*.

The poet's struggle with language—such a familiar trope in early-twentieth-century Anglo-American modernist poetry, as in poetry generally—takes on additional dimensions in post/colonial, diasporic settings, where speech and writing are riven with the histories of forbidden languages, enforced multilingualism, and the reliance on the master's tongue. Within this context, the poet's task is to create a poetics that acknowledges the linguistic dislocations of history and that forges a new linguistic return to the "homeland." Césaire and Cha both "journey" to this homeland of the spirit through their struggles with language. They differ significantly as to whether that homeland is restricted to a single cultural group, but their sense of the poet's responsibility to the communal achieved through poetic language is strongly shared. Both experience viscerally the pain of their linguistic travels to a home/land rended in words. "We are / mumblers of words," Césaire writes in *Cahier/Notebook*, "words of fresh blood, words that are / tidal waves . . . / and blazes of flesh, / and blazes of cities" (57). In a multiple address to her mother, Korea, and a generalized reader, Cha reflects, "You are here I raise the voice. Particle bits of sound and noise gathered pick up lint, dust. They might scatter and become invisible. Speech morsels. Broken chips of stones. Not hollow not empty" (56).

The poems of Césaire and Cha are "speech morsels"—full of significance, "not hollow not empty." Read in collage on the small-scale level of individual poems and read across their temporal, spatial, racial, and gender differences, they exist as poetic agencies that foster a planetary understanding of twentieth-century modernities and their modernisms. In registering the pain, humiliation, and global relationalities wrought by conquest and dislocation, they belong to the archipelagic modernity Glissant theorizes. Yet they also embody Said's view that "exiles cross borders, break barriers of thought and experience" (185). They narrate in poetic terms modernity's turbulence, multiplicity, polycentrism, recurrence, and discrepance. And they show how diasporic exiles inhabit with particular intensity the dystopic/utopic contradictory core of modernity itself.

CONCLUSION
A DEBATE WITH MYSELF

Of those who debate I am the dialectic.
—The Bhagavadgita, translated by S. Radhakrishnan

Planetary Modernisms is not a manifesto, though it may at times read like one. My intent has been to provoke more debate, not close it off. The book is an effort in speculation, where the central task is how to move from a provincial Western perspective with a predetermined archive of modernism to a more expansive—indeed, planetary—perspective that opens doors for a cosmopolitan framework that resists homogenization and recognizes the heterogeneity of geohistorical patterns of different modernities and their modernisms in the *longue durée*.

As widely used terms, *modernity* and *modernism* mean many things, at times even opposite things. However, this diversity exists not only in the field of modernist studies but also as raucous debates I have with myself. Reading widely in the fields that invoke these terms, I have come across many powerful arguments that continually raise doubts about what I have suggested in these chapters. And so I resist here the convention of the conclusion as a flourish of big claims, insistent argumentation, and synthesis of prior chapters.

Instead, I return to the questions of definition and scope with which the book begins, and I end with "thirteen ways of looking at a blackbird," to adapt once again Wallace Stevens's poem as I did in chapter 2: thirteen debates I have with myself, thirteen bang/clashes with my internal voices arguing this way and that. Underlying these voices are the insecurities generated by the scope of this book's speculative provocations and the anxieties that have made this project a difficult one to complete.

DEBATE 1: SCALE

ON THE ONE HAND

The spatiotemporal scale of modernity/modernism around the world in the *longue durée* requires a knowledge archive of monstrous proportions, one beyond the expertise of any individual. The potential is enormous for superficiality, irresponsible interdisciplinarity, overreliance on the scholarship of others, and the loss of richly contextualized geohistorical and linguistic particularity. It's a staggering task to know enough to write convincingly about the Tang Dynasty on one page, the Mongol Empire on another, and early-twentieth-century Brazilian modernism on yet another, as chapter 3 attempts to do. Dipping into vast and complex fields to extract what might be resonant for another can produce arguments that would not convince the experts in any one of those fields. The necessary reliance on translation is a particular liability, for knowledge of the many languages required for in-depth understanding of cultural difference on a global scale is a near-impossibility.

Modernity/modernism is best studied in depth by those that have the historical, cultural, and linguistic knowledge to do justice to its complexity in one time/space. Franco Moretti's large-scale "distant reading" may work for a certain kind of statistically oriented sociology of literature,[1] but it is much less effective or reliable for theoretical analysis of concepts like modernity or modernism, let alone for aesthetic texts, objects, and performances that require extensive linguistic, cultural, and historical contextualization.

ON THE OTHER HAND

A scalar approach to modernism/modernity has the flexibility to zoom out and zoom in for different kinds of study—from the general and comparative to the particular and richly contexted, as the moves from parts 1 and 2 to part 3 in this book attempt to demonstrate. Large-scale approaches enable transformational thinking that can provide a framework for connecting the pathbreaking and diverse work being done today in the name of modernity/modernism. Large-scale work also fosters comparative thinking beyond the national paradigm and new theoretical concepts that can be useful for understanding the disparate phenomena under the global umbrella of modernity/modernism in the *longue durée*. Small-scale approaches can focus on areas of expertise at the same time that they are informed by the perspectives of large-scale work—for example, the studies of modernist fiction and poetry in the long twentieth century that probe the implications of global modernities for local literary texts in chapters 6 and 7.

Large-scale perspectives make visible the often unacknowledged assumptions that frame work on modernism/modernity, particularly Eurocentric ones. If modernist studies develops out of an entirely Western archive or out a diffusionist model of Western expansionism, the danger of parochialism and false universalisms is palpable. Good work on a purely Western archive can surely be done, but an insufficiently global perspective can often miss how Western modernity/modernism has been formed in relation to non-Western modernities/modernisms. Large-scale geohistories, comparative analysis, and judicious use of translation can shake up unacknowledged assumptions, undo prevailing center/periphery models, and facilitate a fundamental rethinking of what *modernity* might mean in the *longue durée* across the planet. This view helps break down the ideological compulsion for European or American exceptionalism that has been central to the formation of the metanarrative of Western modernity discussed in chapter 3.

While the knowledge of multiple languages is highly desirable, the reliance on translation and the lingua franca of English is not simply a liability. First, translation makes available what would otherwise be unavailable and thus widens the archive out of which generalizations about modernity/modernism are made. Second, the new translation studies emphasizes the creative space that opens up between the original and target languages, a space of difference where the negotiation between cultural distinctiveness embedded in language is a rich source of new understanding.[2] Third, the formation of lingua francas in the context of many vernaculars is nothing new; it's been a part of human history ever since the formation of the global ecumene. In fact, as I mentioned in chapter 2, Sheldon Pollock argues that lingua francas like Sanskrit and Latin actually enhanced the development of literate vernacular cultures.[3]

As for the impossibility of planetary archives, I reiterate the point I made in chapter 2—no one has to attempt to do it all. I offered four different ways of developing a doable planetary strategy: *re-vision*, the return to the conventional canon of modernism/modernity, asking new questions about local/global interrelations; *recovery*, the search for new archives outside the Western canon; *circulation*, the tracing of networks, linkages, and conjunctions on a transcontinental landscape; and *collage*, the juxtaposition of different archives or texts for comparative purposes. It is true that *Planetary Modernisms* develops each of these strategies, thus seeming to suggest that others must attempt this scope as well. But what I mean to suggest is that any one of these approaches is sufficient and doable.

More fundamentally, I defend the reliance on the scholarship of and conversations with others. The resistance to collaboratively produced knowledge in the humanities is breaking down in this century for many reasons, from the digital revolution to the budgetary constraints of funding higher education. The "laboratories" of the humanities are our libraries and websites; our collaborations begin in reading and communication—the wider and more diverse, the better. Future developments in the humanities are likely to produce collaborative teams of scholars working across disciplinary boundaries. The scope of *Planetary Modernisms* no doubt reflects the limitations of my expertise, but it also exemplifies how a planetary modernist studies might occupy the cutting edge of transformations in the humanities more generally. I have no doubt that others will go much further than I in the new modernities of the knowledge revolution.

DEBATE 2: EXPANSION AND EXPANSIONISM

ON THE ONE HAND

The expansion of the terms *modernity/modernism* to include any period of accelerating change and accompanying aesthetic expressions evacuates any usable meaning in the concepts. Categories are by nature delimiting—some phenomena reside within a circle of meaning (however porous the borders), others outside. Analysis is a mode of thought that requires categories with meanings that include particular limits. Such categories often function as a convenient shorthand for a commonly understood cluster of meanings. Expanding the concept of *modernity* developed in the post-1500 West to include so much of human history makes the term meaningless. Any term can be redefined willy-nilly, but such redefinitions remain idiosyncratic, not widely enough accepted to be useful. Ditto for *modernism*. If *modernism* is so inclusive as an aesthetic category that it can encompass such divergent texts as James Joyce's *Ulysses* and Monica Ali's *Brick Lane*, then it has little precision or usefulness. There's no intellectual payoff for globalizing the meanings of *modernity/modernism*.

Moreover, expanding the terms *modernity/modernism* to incorporate regions of the world outside the West and their arts, especially colonized or postcolonial societies, is expansionist, reproducing the logic of imperialism itself. The field of modernist studies swallows up other fields, especially postcolonial studies, claiming a privileged position for *modernism*, thereby marginalizing all over again the West's "Others."[4] Other histories and frameworks—e.g., those based on resistance—are far more fruitful for understanding post/colonial arts, literature, thought, and politics. Use of globalizing categories like planetary modernism reimposes hegemonic Western issues on other places in the world where people are likely to define their concerns in other ways, with other agendas. Within the academy, *modernism* increasingly names the field of twentieth-century studies (much as *romanticism* has done for its period). This expansionist move should be resisted because it marginalizes those aesthetic formations and practices that diverge significantly from the core meanings of *modernism*, particularly *high modernism*.

ON THE OTHER HAND

The horse is already out of the barn; the cat's out of the bag. Planetary expansion in modernist studies has long been underway, beginning as an effect of contemporary globalization and adapting the epistemological breakthroughs of postcolonial studies, diaspora studies, the new world literature, and world history. It may make more analytic sense to limit the meanings of *modernity/modernism*, but various forms of pluralization are already widely available. The numerous critiques of multiple modernity discourse are themselves evidence that concepts of pluralized modernities are widespread. Exciting new archives are being delineated and explored while new transnational methodologies foregrounding interculturalism, relationality, traveling cultures, multilingualism, translation, and comparison are developing across the disciplines and interdisciplines of modernist studies.

With geohistorically contextualized, small-scale readings of selected texts, chapters 5, 6, and 7 aim to demonstrate the intellectual payoff from expanded meanings of *modernity/modernism*. But they have been written in the company of a wide array of publications on transcontinental, transnational, and planetary modernities and modernisms cited throughout the book. Whether based in difference, circulation, or comparison, the new planetary modernist studies has already substantially recast the metanarrative of Western modernity/modernism. This geographical expansion of modernism is only one dimension of other expansions in the field—recognition of the multiple modernities and modernisms *within* the West. The incorporation of women writers and artists into modernism began in the 1970s, amid much resistance. Recognition of the Harlem Renaissance as inextricably interwoven with American modernism and pan-African modernities followed by the 1980s. Modernity within the West was pluralized to recognize the different forms modernity took for racialized groups, religious and sexual minorities, working-class and rural people, and so forth. As a result, the reliance on the aesthetic styles associated with aesthetic experimentalism began to diffuse. As Douglas Mao, Rebecca L. Walkowitz, and Andreas Huyssen have stressed, modernist studies has increasingly broken down high/low distinctions, unleashing a rash of studies on different modernisms based in popular and mass cultures and incorporating a variety of aesthetic styles, including realism.[5]

As for the charge of imperialist expansionism, I emphasize that consideration of *modernity/modernism* in non-Western parts of the world does not preclude other frameworks of analysis such as post/colonialism, neoliberalism, comparative literature, world literature, diaspora, race, gender, sexuality, formalism, genre, indigenous traditions, translation, and so forth. Planetary modernist studies is not hell-bent on a power grab, gobbling up other fields like territory to be ruled; it offers one among many categories within which the historical conditions and aesthetic expressions of non-Western societies can be interpreted.

Moreover, the category of modernity—and sometimes modernism—has considerable discursive currency in many parts of the non-West—it's variously debated, characterized, internalized, resisted, adapted, transformed, deployed, and so forth. In short, it's alive as an issue and a rhetoric outside the West; it's entangled with geopolitical, economic, and cultural questions of value and power. Consequently, attention to the global meanings and deployments of the categories *modernity/modernism* are fully justified. In short, we need to assume the agency of non-Western societies and cultural producers rather than pure victimization. Within the academy, the transformative broadening of the categories *modernity/modernism* with the use of non-Western and pre-1500 archives helps dissolve the ideological compulsion to put the West at the center of inquiry and as the measure of all others. Maintenance of the narrow categories of *modernity/modernism* in effect leaves Eurocentrism firmly in its dominant position in the academy. It is better to risk expansionism that to perpetuate the Eurocentric box.

DEBATE 3: WHAT IS NOT MODERN? NOT MODERNIST?

ON THE ONE HAND

"As the modernities proliferate," Frederick Cooper writes, "the capacity to distinguish modernity from anything else is diminished."[6] Categories are usable only if they exclude as well as include. The expansive definition of *modernity/modernism* doesn't exclude anything. What time/space is not modern? What aesthetic expression is not modernist? The assertion of global, multiple, and recurrent modernities in the *longue durée* effectively ends up designating all of human history as "modern." This relational approach fails to distinguish between "modernity" and the ongoing histories of successive global ecumenes or empires. Whether produced through conquest or commerce, systemic interculturalism, networks, and circulations are simply part of human history—not distinctive enough to characterize a particular formation called "modernity." In the face on such conflations, we need a distinctive historical period or project designated *modernity*, one that can be distinguished from other periods or projects. A nominal definition of *modernity*—even if agreement on what constitutes *modernity* is not achievable—is far more useful than a relational definition precisely because it provides a basis for deciding what is *modern* or *not modern*.

The expansive concept of modernism that includes diverse expressive styles engaging with modernity stretches the meaning of modernism beyond any use value. It turns into a chronological category that incorporates all expressive/creative forms that are produced within a certain geohistorical period. Modernism is thus reduced to chronology, a kind of time marker that carries little meaning. We need, for example, a distinction between modernism and the nonmodernist arts of the twentieth century. For *modernism* to include both the experimentalism of Woolf's *The Waves* and the realism of Mulk Raj Anand's *Untouchable* renders the term meaningless as an aesthetic category. We need a term that clearly signals a certain kind of experimentalism that characterizes a fractional but influential archive of aesthetic modernity concentrated in the first half of the twentieth century. Otherwise, the term becomes so broad that it excludes nothing outside its historical chronology.

ON THE OTHER HAND

Modernity delineated as I have done so in chapters 3 and 4 does not incorporate every period of human history. While the interaction of change with continuity does characterize all societies, the relational concept of modernity posits sharpened change, radical ruptures, accelerated mobilities—in short, an intensification of ongoing processes concentrated in a vortex that brings together all societal domains. I return to the metaphor of the combustion engine echoed from Garry Leonard in chapter 2—that modernity encapsulates the processes of pressure buildup-containment-explosion. In this sense, the relation between the *modern* and the *not modern* is rhythmic—from periods of explosive change to consolidation or relative quiescence, as the forces of rupture begin to build again.

In this context, the distinction between *modern* and *not modern* resides in the scale of observation. Acceleration and rupture are relative, not absolute categories and thus dependent on a spatial or temporal vantage point. In small-scale terms, for example, the modernities of the early twentieth and twenty-first centuries appear distinctive—the first, fostered by new technologies like the telephone, the steamship, the machine gun, the automobile, the airplane, the cinema, the atomic bomb; the second, created by the digital revolution. But in large-scale terms, from the perspective of centuries, these modernities appear as part of the same phenomena, distinctive from Europe's medieval, Renaissance, or industrial periods. This fluidity of scale helps explain why *modernity* can have explanatory power in application to such different geohistorical locations—from the early urbanization of the Indus Valley to a world historian, for example, to scholars of the Scottish Enlightenment, of Meiji Japan, or of post–World War II colonial struggles of liberation in Africa. What remains constant within the context of varying scales is the principle of heightened, intensified, and disorienting change, a vortex that spins across all societal dimensions.

DEBATE 4: POSTMODERNITY, POSTMODERNISM, AND THE CONTEMPORARY

ON THE ONE HAND

Planetary Modernisms hardly gives a nod to *postmodernism*, a term that has ongoing currency to describe the arts, literature, philosophy, and critical theory *after* modernism. Modernism remains a fundamental basis for the aesthetic styles and concerns of postmodernism—hence the *post* before *modernism* instead of a newly named movement or period. Postmodernism developed as a term in use by writers like John Barth and cultural critics like Linda Hutcheon, Brian McHale, Andreas Huyssen, Fredric Jameson, Ihab Hassan, and Marianne DeKoven to indicate an aesthetic tired of the grand despair and cosmic gestures of modernism, one more willing to draw on such qualities as playfulness, pastiche, popular culture, "little" narratives, and realism (though with a metafictional nod to artifice).[7] Jameson's *Postmodernism, or, The Cultural Logic of Late Capitalism* identifies wide-ranging effects on aesthetic forms resulting from the rise of multinational corporations and neoliberalism in an era of globalization. Following François Lyotard's influential *The Postmodern Condition* and

French poststructuralist theory more generally, social theory deploys the terms *postmodernity* and *postmodernism* to indicate the critique of Western humanism, structuralism, and the epistemology of transparent representation. From aesthetics to philosophy, politics, and economics, *postmodernism* is a useful term with explanatory power for the cultural production and thought of the second half of the twentieth century. To use the terms *modernity/modernism* to describe historical conditions and aesthetics of the post-1950 period is to refuse important distinctions between the two halves of the century and to extend *modernism* beyond its core period, a move that obscures the historical specificity of postmodern conditions and marginalizes the aesthetic practices that differ markedly from those of canonical modernists.

Planetary Modernisms also ignores the growing body of theory around the word *contemporary* as distinct from *modern*. Using *modernity* and *modernism* as foils for the recent past, the *contemporary* or *contemporaneity* signify what is the most recent, the "now," the still unfolding, in contrast to the *modern*, which has already happened and become institutionalized. In the visual arts, Terry Smith's *What Is Contemporary Art?* (2009) and *Contemporary Art: World Currents* (2011) argue for a "global shift from modern to contemporary art," in which "artists everywhere [since the 1980s] have embraced the contemporary world's teeming multiplicity, its proliferating differences, and its challenging complexities and new technologies."[8] The journal *Contemporary Literature* defines the contemporary as post–World War II literature; *Contemporary Women's Writing* engages with writing in the post-1970 era. The Literature Now series at Columbia University Press focuses on literatures of the present, presumably more recent than the "modern." Dates differ, but cultural, literary, and visual arts fields increasingly designate the *contemporary* as a recognizable period distinct from *modernism*.

ON THE OTHER HAND

The terms *postmodernism* and *the contemporary* imply that modernism itself is definitively over at the same time that the events of world and local histories suggest that modernity itself is anything but "over." The post–World War II era is not postmodern. Instead, new incarnations of modernity keep being reproduced in all sectors of society. With the end of colonial rule, newly constituted nation-states formed, confronting new issues of modernization in the face of self-rule and a geopolitical and economic world order in which the West remained dominant until the new rise of Asia and emergent economies in the twenty-first century. Rising powers like China and Iran claim the discourse of "alternative modernity" to justify their difference from the West. Modernity is a key category in the popular culture and social media in the uprisings of the Arab Spring and in countries as diverse as Turkey and Brazil. The digital revolution—and the financial and knowledge revolutions it enabled—signals another cycle of accelerated and transformational change across all societal domains, including the aesthetic. Massive waves of migration—from refugees to economic and political migrants—have brought intensified forms of interculturalism and new hybridities. Modernity's tendency to spawn bitter conflict between modernizers and traditionalists underlies more than fifty years of tension between the West and the non-West, complicated by the geopolitics of the Cold War, the heightened conflict between fundamentalist and secular discourses *within* all the major world religions (including Christianity), and the resurgence of imperial designs based on past histories across the Asian continent, as André Wink has argued.[9] One of the many lessons of 9/11 has surely been that battles over "modernity" are far from over, although the question of *whose* modernity is very much up in the air.

These geopolitical, cultural, technological, and philosophical conditions represent a new modernity, not a postmodernity. Modernity perpetually reinvents itself as the new contemporary. As chapter 4 discusses, the etymology of the term *modern* enfolds the meanings of the contemporary—the now, the present. To distinguish between the contemporary and the modern is to engage in a fixed and nominal process of periodization, opening up all the problems of periodization reviewed in chapter 3. "Modernity is now (and has been for some time) everywhere," Andreas Huyssen writes in departing for his earlier advocacy of postmodernism in *After the Great Divide* (1985); "the discourse of postmodernity seems only an episode (if a significant one) within a certain transformation of Western modernity itself." Globalization—and the "political and cultural developments of the 1990s," he notes—"have not been kind to the postmodernists' confident prediction that modernity was at an end."[10]

The concepts of multiple, recurrent, and polycentric modernities have more explanatory power for understanding the matrix of rapid change in the late twentieth-/early twenty-first centuries than an emphasis on "postness" in *postmodernity* or the distinctively "now" of *contemporaneity*. There is so much slippage in the meanings of postmodernity, poststructuralism, and modernity, as the review of theorists from Lyotard, James C. Scott, and David Harvey to Marshall Berman and Alice Jardine in chapter 1 demonstrates. Moreover, scholars in modernist studies still debate with no resolution in sight whether postmodernism is an extension of early-twentieth-century modernism or a break from it and whether it is a "period" or an aesthetic style that in some cases (like Gertrude Stein) chronologically preceded "modernism." Given this level of confusion, there is more analytic precision in affirming the multiplicity and recurrence of modernity and modernism.

DEBATE 5: TRADITION

ON THE ONE HAND

Tradition is *not* just the invention of modernity, as chapters 1, 2, and 4 claim. While ideological or nostalgic reconstructions of past traditions often characterize modernity, traditions also exist in the form of knowledge, values, and practices that are passed down from generation to generation. As Mark Salber Phillips writes in *Questions of Tradition*, *tradition* and *traditionalism* are not the same. Where *traditionalism* functions as a politics, often a particular politics of modernity, *tradition* can include both tacit practices and self-conscious transmissions based in continuity over time.[11] Such traditions, and the "traditional" societies that value them, emphasize continuity with the past instead of ruptures from it. This positive construction of tradition as distinct from modernity has particularly characterized theorizations of indigenous cultures, ways of knowing, and valuation of continuity and spirituality. In this context, traditional knowledge and epistemology operate as a form of resistance to the encroaching expansions of hegemonic modernities, as Linda T. Smith argues in *Decolonizing Methodology: Research and Indigenous Peoples*.[12] Affirmation or restoration of tradition can function as oppositional consciousness and decolonizing activism.

As for modernism, tradition sometimes functions as a foil for the modern, as when the impressionists, Cezanne, Picasso, and Braque broke with the conventions of realism in genre painting—changing the relationship of color and light, radically breaking the perspectival plane of the canvas, or creating the effects of simultaneity. But Cezanne's still lifes gain their intensity by riffing off centuries of still life paintings; Picasso's nudes depend upon the tradition of the nude in European painting for their shocking effects. Modernist writers often had a complex relation to aesthetic traditions of the past, even the immediate past. Although Marinetti's "Futurist Manifesto" rejected the past in its entirety, Pound's dictum "make it new" did not signify a complete rejection of tradition but rather a new reappropriation in the present. As Eliot explains in "Tradition and the Individual Talent," much modernist poetics did not envision abandonment of past traditions but rather an active/creative relation to them; indeed Pound's *Cantos*, H.D.'s *Trilogy*, and Joyce's *Ulysses* engage centrally with past literary, historical, religious, and aesthetic traditions from a strikingly global archive.[13] Breaking with the past for many modernists meant more specifically an ostensible rejection of the immediate past and then a revisionist blending of many traditions, frequently from non-Western parts of the world, as a way of engaging with the dislocations of modernity. In short, tradition in various forms remained a central component of early-twentieth-century European modernism.

ON THE OTHER HAND

I recognize that tradition can be an effective concept to describe forms of knowledge and practice passed down through time as well as the blending of the old with the new. But I agree with James Clifford, who calls in "Traditional Futures" for an end to the binary opposition of tradition/modernity, recognizing that this opposition itself typically posits tradition as unchanging and can be used to straitjacket peoples labeled "traditional." "The making, contesting, unmaking, and remaking of traditions," he writes in reorienting tradition to the future, "now appear as a permanent source of innovation and instability at all political levels and spatial scales."[14] In linguistic terms, vernacularism is also linked to tradition but can function as modern experimentalism, as it does with Tagore's early prose. Modernist writers like Zora Neale Hurston, for example, integrated into the novel form aspects of the oral tradition and ethnography—two important forms "tradition" can take.

I promoted the notion of tradition as the invention of modernity in part to insist on dismantling the conventional opposition between modernity and tradition, a binary that has had particularly pernicious effects in colonial and indigenous situations. Moreover, I suggest that tradition can function symptomatically as an idea consciously or unconsciously invented and deployed for ideological, oppositional, or purely creative purposes. Tradition often suppresses the history of its origin, presenting itself as essentially or timelessly present—as the instances of traditional foods noted in chapter 3 attest (the Irish potato, the Indian chili, the Italian tomato). "We often forget," Madan Sarap writes, "that tradition, too, is always being made and remade. Tradition is fluid, it is always being reconstituted. Tradition is about change—change that is not being acknowledged."[15]

As invented, tradition plays a particularly important role in the contradictory tensions produced by modernity, often spawning traditionalisms and attachment to an imagined past. As chapter 3 argues, modernity's rapid ruptures and mobilities produce a counterdesire for continuity and stability. Consequently, a symptomatic condition of modernity is conflict between those advocating "the modern" versus those defending "tradition." In this sense, tradition is not modernity's opposite but its symptom.

DEBATE 6: TERMINOLOGICAL ENTROPY

ON THE ONE HAND

The term *modernity* should be abandoned; it has outlived its usefulness as an analytic category. Perhaps, as Clifford suggests, "the two terms, modernity and tradition can be left behind."[16] As Frederick Cooper writes,

> The word *modernity* is now used to make so many different points that continued deployment of it may contribute more to confusion than to

clarity. . . . Modernity is evoked in public debate, and such uses demand attention. But modernity is not just a "native's category"; it is employed as an analytic category as well—defining a subject for scholarly inquiry—and that is where its value is in doubt.[17]

Attempting to achieve greater inclusiveness or clarity in the term is a hopeless cause; it is better to avoid the term altogether, aiming for analytic precision by using alternative words, phrases, arguments, and so forth, all of which can be particularized in appropriate time/space locations. Even within the context of Western modernity, use of the same term to cover such diverse historical phenomena as the seafaring "discoveries" of the 1400–1500s and Enlightenment rationalism is too big a stretch for a single word. Globalizing the term in the *longue durée* renders the term as an analytic tool practically useless. It is preferable to make whatever arguments need to be without recourse to a term that lacks precise or consensual meaning.

If used at all, the term *modernism* should focus primarily on the aesthetic, philosophical, and cultural rather than the historical conditions of modernity, especially since *modernity* has lost precise meaning. For sure, *modernism* needs some historical contextualization, but to insist that modernism is but one among many dimensions of modernity, a term with little consensual meaning, drags *modernism* into the definitional morass of *modernity*.

ON THE OTHER HAND

The term *modernity* has an electrical charge precisely because it has been so controversial, so undefinable, so multiplicitous. It has ongoing currency in a multitude of ways. It remains a critical issue in the current discourses of the world, entering discussions of globalization, revolutionary movements like the Arab Spring, transnational feminisms, and so forth. In the world of ideas, debates about *modernity* have increased, particularly as the currency of *postmodernism* ebbs. Whether embraced, redefined, or resisted, *modernization* as an issue remains current. *Modernity* sells books and provides jobs, as does *modernism*. Modernist studies as a field has grown exponentially, moving through the disciplines of the humanities and social sciences, generating discourses that the sciences and technology adapt as well. *Modernity* is in the Now, the Contemporary. It's also here to stay as a focus of inquiry about the past. The very fluidity and flexibility of *modernity* and *modernism* function linguistically to crystallize whole fields of debate. What's to be gained by dropping the terms? Any attempt to abandon the terms is doomed to fail in any case.

DEBATE 7: THE HERMENEUTIC CIRCLE

ON THE ONE HAND

The claim to establish a purely relational definition of *modernity/modernism* falls into a nominalism of its own that threatens to be just as circular as conventional meanings of the terms. Chapter 1 refuses to fix the definition of *modernity*, arguing instead that the interrogation of contradictory meanings itself constitutes the core tension of modernity. But chapters 2, 3, and 4 propose a definition of modernity that is at least partially nominal—that is, identified by a set of characteristics such as intensified acceleration, mobility, networks, and rapid change across all domains of society.[18] This set of characteristics is not as specific as the conventional ones (capitalism, nation-states, rationality, universalism, secularism, etc.), but it functions nonetheless in a nominal way.

Moreover, this definition emerges out of a predetermined archive, that of world history in the *longue durée* instead of just the post-1500 West. This expanded archive does as much to determine the definition of modernity as the more limited Western archive does. There's no getting around the hermeneutic circle of assuming the very characteristics that definitions set out to determine through observation. Given this circularity, it makes analytic sense to limit the definition of modernity to more workable limits. Ditto for *modernism*. The decision to generalize about modernism based on a global body of creative work in the *longue durée* predetermines a plurality of modernisms that differ dramatically. It makes analytic sense to begin with a more restricted spatio/temporal archive out of which more coherent generalizations about modernism can be formed.

Finally, this provisional definition of *modernism/modernity* has all the earmarks of my original training in early-twentieth-century Western modernism—the experimentalisms of Joyce and Woolf, Eliot and H.D. For all my attempts to be interdisciplinary and planetary in scope, the roots of my thinking in English literary studies of the early twentieth century are pervasively influential, as much as I have roamed far from those early intellectual sources into world history and global literatures and arts. Even the various experiments with academic discourse that the chapters (and this conclusion) attempt reflect a privileging of formalist experimentalism based in my beginnings in the study of what has come to be called "high modernism."

ON THE OTHER HAND

It is true that no definition can be purely relational. Even the definitions that emerge from the relational unit of *big/small* assumes that size is the issue at stake, an element of nominalism. For *modernity*, both relational and nominal definitions assume that some form of change is common to both approaches. But the more expansive concept of modernity that allows for its different manifestations in large-scale space/time is more relational than the restricted concept. In other words, the relational and nominal aspects of definition exist in different proportions.

It is also true that definition itself is a circular endeavor. What one chooses to observe predetermines to some extent the nature of the generalizations that emerge out of that observation. Chapter 3 draws on a global archive in the *longue durée*—including Tang Dynasty China, the Mongol Empire, and contemporary Shanghai; consequently, the notion of modernity that emerges from these examples is expansive. Like this conclusion presented in the form of a debate, *Planetary Modernisms* remains committed to the argument presented in chapter 1 that the contradictions of modernity themselves are repeated in the debates about it and that the definition of modernity and modernism should never be fixed. The disagreements are themselves epistemologically productive. Chapters 3 and 4 present predominantly relational definitions of *modernity* in recognition of the need for categories to have some form of consensual meaning, no matter how provisional and fluid. I invoked Gayatri Chakravorty Spivak's concept of "strategic essentialism" to justify my attempt to provide a framework of meanings for *modernity* that have explanatory power for a historical and geographical diversity of modernities.

As for the imprint of my original training in early-twentieth-century experimental literature, I am guilty as charged. The adaptation of these forms in a project dedicated to exploding the Eurocentric box is a fundamental irony, if not downright contradiction, of *Planetary Modernisms*. Yet I defend the significance of these representational experiments from the early twentieth century for the book's project as a whole because they were based so fundamentally on epistemology's entanglement with representation, as is my attempt to undo the ideological force of the metanarrative of Western modernity. In this sense, I repeat early-twentieth-century experimentalist unravelings of Enlightenment modernity in order to dismantle Eurocentric formulations of modernism/modernity more generally.

DEBATE 8: MODERNITY AS A WESTERN "IDEA"

ON THE ONE HAND

Modernity is itself a Western concept, developing philosophically and politically in the late seventeenth and eighteenth centuries and continuing through the present—from the seventeenth-century debates about the ancients versus the moderns, through Hegel, Weber, Foucault, Lyotard, Habermas, and many others. As an idea, *modernity* has an evolving and complex intellectual history that cannot be ignored. Its sheer weight as an idea in both the history of the West and the West's imperial projects argues against changing its range of meanings as they developed historically in the West. To broaden the term beyond the framework of that evolving debate is to eviscerate it of any precision.

While its meanings differ, there is nonetheless a framework of consensus across the disciplines that *modernity* develops in conjunction with such phenomena as the rise of capitalism, the formation of nation-states after the Treaty of Westphalia in 1648 (first in Europe and then elsewhere), European imperialism, secularism, the spread of print culture, the increasingly panoptical institutions and discourses governing everyday life, the growing hegemony of science, the ideology of individualism, and so forth. In the realm of ideas, *modernity* is widely associated (for good or bad) with the Enlightenment and universalist concepts like "freedom," "justice," "truth," "citizenship," and so forth. It is not really possible or even desirable to go against this extensive intellectual consensus about the meaning of *modernity*, an argument that Eric Hayot has forcefully made in *On Literary Worlds* and elsewhere.[19] Even challenges to Western modernity in defense of non-Western parts of the world are best done by burrowing from within, demonstrating the Eurocentrism of the Western idea from within Western frameworks. Focusing on non-Western modernities/modernisms is a recipe for being ignored by the modernist studies mainstream.

ON THE OTHER HAND

Modernity is not just an "idea," a set of meanings evolving within a particular intellectual tradition. For sure, one of modernity's many articulations exists in the realm of ideas, and the idea of modernity has indeed been powerful and pervasive since at least the Enlightenment period in the West. But the realm of ideas is only one arena of modernity's existence. More broadly understood, modernity is a geohistorical formation produced by a spectrum of forces, institutions, events, things, ideas, representations, and experiences in which the local and global are entangled.

To remain within the Western idea of *modernity* is to remain captured within its ideological formation. No doubt, one effect of poststructuralism emanating from France in the second half of the twentieth century has been ever more sophisticated ways of dismantling the universalisms and centrisms of Western intellectual thought from within. But there are limitations to this restriction. For one thing, the focus remains on *critique*, not discovery or even new ways of thinking. For another, it ends up reinforcing the very centrism it would displace because what the West has produced remains the center of attention. That this attention is critique does little to broaden the scope of understanding.

If the archive of ideas about modernity remains exclusively Western in the post-1500 period, then other concepts of the "modern" remain undiscoverable. Even the word *modern* in English goes back at least to the sixteenth century, but it draws from the earlier Latin *modernus*, as I discussed in chapter 4. Contact with non-European peoples was constitutively a part of the intellectual tradition that developed the Western idea of modernity, and the engagements with that Western idea by people outside the West—frequently the colonized—greatly expanded its meanings, as the fiction and poetry discussed in chapters 6 and 7 demonstrate.

Is the West alone in producing an idea of the *modern*? Only a comparative and transcontinental linguistic study in the *longue durée*, a project I encourage others more qualified than I to do, could discover whether cultures outside the West named something akin to the *modern* and what they meant by it. But there is no doubt that other societies demonstrated self-reflexive awareness of rapid change, disorienting transformations, and temporal distinctions between now versus then. As I discussed in chapter 3, the Mongol histories of Rashid al-Din and others exhibited a concept of the Mongol Empire as world encompassing and new. Whether this constitutes an "idea" of the "modern" in a Western intellectual sense can be debated. But an assertion that no other society had a concept of the modern without making an exhaustive, linguistically based study of societies outside the West is inherently flawed by its exclusively Western archive. We have to look to find. We ought to generalize based on what we find, not what we assume to begin with. *Planetary Modernisms* attempts to open the door to such new discoveries that others more qualified than I can make.

DEBATE 9: MODERNISM AS A WESTERN "PERIOD" IN THE ARTS, LITERATURE, AND PHILOSOPHY

ON THE ONE HAND

The *modernism* of modernist studies is a disciplinary term created to describe the loosely affiliated aesthetic movements that began in the nineteenth century and gained momentum in the early twentieth century around ruptures of Victorian and other nineteenth-century conventions of representation and with the disillusionment with Enlightenment ideals and notions of progress in the aftermath of World War I. In this context, there is a relatively broad consensus throughout the disciplines in the arts and literature that *modernism* is a recognizable period term implying certain aesthetic styles and philosophical leanings. The location of modernism is typically designated as the great culture capitals of Europe, Britain, and the United States. While there is increasing recognition that great cities in the colonized or semicolonized world were also producing modernist art, literature, and manifestos, modernism's center remains Western, with the rest of modernist production peripheral and largely reactive rather than innovative.

Although the periodization of modernism varies somewhat by national language, the heyday of modernism is usually understood to occur in the first half of the twentieth century, with World War II as a consensual endpoint for an aesthetic period that is now decidedly over.

In the histories of the arts, literature, and philosophy, the periodization of romanticism, realism, modernism, and postmodernism continues to have great explanatory power. To recognize that modernism has had a continuing influence after World War II is legitimate, but exploring the legacies of modernism among later writers and artists is not the same as positing modernism as open-ended and ongoing. To be useful, the concept of a period needs to be bookended, no matter how debatable the beginning and ending points might be. Modernism is and needs to be distinguished from the contemporary. To refuse periodization leaves us with no term to designate a period that most people today recognize as *modernism.*

ON THE OTHER HAND

Periodization, I argued in chapter 3, is a misleading and at times pernicious strategy because it suppresses its assumptions about spatial location, universalizes what might be appropriate for one region of the world, and functions ideologically in modernist studies to center the West and peripheralize the Rest. The conventional ending point for modernism is around 1945, just at the point when the movements for independence from European colonial powers are gaining momentum, as I discussed in chapters 2 and 3. Since colonialism was constitutive of European modernity, it reproduces the logic of colonialism to see modernism ending just as the postcolonial literatures and arts engage with the modernities of their independence.

I recognize the continuing force in modernist studies of the idea of modernism as an identifiable aesthetic style with an avant-garde approach to experimenting with conventions of representation. I myself, as I confessed in chapter 2, have found this idea very difficult to give up, perhaps because it was so foundational to my earliest training in modernist poetics. Yet the field has moved way beyond this early privileging of style by asserting the link between aesthetic modernism and the historical conditions of modernity of which it is a part. This connection, I argued in chapter 5, opens the door for a radical rethinking of global modernisms, with modernism becoming the aesthetic dimension of any given modernity—whatever its time and place. We look not for one particular style of avant-gardism but rather for the different forms in which writers and artists innovate, break with past conventions, and "make it new" in the context of the shattering or exhilarating modernities in which they live. *Planetary Modernisms* presents a mosaic of such innovators—from the potters of Basra and the woodblock artists of Edo, to the poetry of Du Fu, the performances of Kabir, and the fictions of Tagore and Swarnakumari Devi, Salih, and Roy. What holds these and others together is not a period, not a movement, and not a single aesthetic style. It is the urge to innovate in the midst of the accelerating changes of their particular modernities.

DEBATE 10: MODERNIZATION AS WESTERNIZATION

ON THE ONE HAND

Global ecumenes and empires before 1500—whether termed modernities or not—are irrelevant to post-1500 modernities. The rise of the West after 1500—its ideological, economic, political, and cultural power—is vast and undeniable. The global hegemony of Western modernity has been the major force shaping the societies of the non-Western world (and the peoples colonized within the West) since the end of the eighteenth century. The "project" of Western modernity has spread throughout the regions of the world it colonized to such a degree that modernization has been indistinguishable from Westernization. From capitalism to nationalism, from colonialism to development, from secularism to democracy, from human rights to feminism, and so forth—modernity has historically been associated for good and bad with the West and the West's imposition of its values and institutions on the Rest. Those colonized by Western countries, especially those newly liberated in the second half of the twentieth century, continue to struggle with the conflict between the power of Western modernity, the erosion of traditional cultures, and efforts to modernize on their own terms.

This association of modernization with Westernization has been as strong in the rest of the world as it has been in the West, especially among the colonized and formerly colonized. Whatever the facts in the context of *longue durée* world history, this *experience* of modernization as Westernization should not be discounted. To do so recapitulates the psychological humiliations of colonialism itself—that is, the refusal to grant subjectivity and agency to those with less power. As I have discussed in chapters 2, 3, and 6, this phenomenological dimension of modernization often involves the "curse" of derivativeness, a state of always already playing "catch up," or being destined to imitation instead of innovation. We should not add to this humiliation by ignoring how those in modernizing societies perceive their relationship to the West. I am haunted still by the student from Shanghai described in chapter 3. She firmly believed that the unbearably rapid modernization of Shanghai was Westernization. My attempts to dissuade her publicly displayed her ignorance, magnified my own knowledge, and in effect discounted how she understood what was happening in her own country.

Modernization in the aesthetic realm outside the dominant culture capitals of the West is also fraught with the ambivalence of belatedness and what Eric Hayot calls "mimetic desire," the dominance of Western modernity producing the need for non-Western artists and intellectuals to imitate Western modernity to catch up, to "be modern" at the same time that they explore their difference. Pascale Casanova's *The Republic of Letters* may be gallingly Gallocentric, proposing as it does that would-be modernist writers all over the world looked to Paris, the center of a vast network of literary peripheries. Even British and American modernists made the trek from London to Paris for its cosmopolitan vortex of manifesto avant-gardism and experimentalism, as Cyrena Pondrom documented in *The Road from Paris*.[20] Césaire's surrealism and Cha's poststructuralism, discussed in chapter 7, are telling proof for the defining influence of Western modernism on non-Western writers.

ON THE OTHER HAND

"Be careful that by modernization you don't mean Westernization," the world historians Stephen K. Sanderson and Thomas D. Hall warn.[21] The equation of "the West" with "the modern" in the post-1500 world overemphasizes the singularity of the West, ignoring the considerable power of other empires, including the Ottoman, the Chinese (until the early 1800s), the Russian, and the Japanese (after the 1850s), ignoring as well the influence on the West of earlier empires like those of the Abbasids, Mongols, and Mughals. While I understand the Shanghai student's deep angst, large-scale and rapid urbanization is hardly a Western invention. The formation of cities—where wealth accumulates through specialized labor, conquest, and participation in extensive market systems; where large concentrations of people live, often mingling with different cultures; where complex infrastructure is developed to ensure food, water, travel, sanitation, education, etc.—goes back at least to the Indus and Mesopotamian civilizations some four to five millennia ago. In chapter 3, I insisted that the equation of modernity with the West, no matter how compelling phenomenologically, is the product of an ideological metanarrative produced by the West to explain and rationalize its growing world dominance. Ideology has real effects—no denying that—but those effects do not make the metanarrative an accurate account of geohistories in the *longue durée*. They are part of the story we need to account for, not the story we should use to explain modernity.

The concept of modernization as Westernization assumes a unidirectional flow of power and influence, with innovative ideas all coming from the West and traveling to the Rest. Chapter 3 argues instead that the "rise of the West" is a chapter in the planetary *longue durée* that includes other dominant powers and many innovations imported into and adapted by Europe. At this scale of human history, Western modernity is itself belated. Europe's and then the United States' power and innovative practices follow those of Asia—and are currently being overtaken. Chapter 4 proposes a different approach to traveling modernities, one based on networks and systems, circulations, and relational formations. Whether in the realm of technology or aesthetics, the production of the modern arises in the context of intercultural interactions that are as likely to be violent as peaceful. Dominance, resistance, and asymmetrical power relations are always at issue; hybridity and reciprocal transculturations do not imply equality of the parties involved. The story that produces the West as modern and the Rest as traditional—either in the process of modernization or resisting modernization in the name of tradition—not only functions ideologically but is also misleading and inaccurate in the context of world history.

Modernization of aesthetics outside the West, I have shown in chapters 6 and 7, is a much more complicated story than the angst of belatedness and mimetic desire. Salih doesn't imitate Conrad or simply write back against *Heart of Darkness*. Instead he blends aspects of Arab aesthetic traditions in his reinvention of the novel as a form suited for postcolonial African literature. In Edward W. Said's terms, reviewed in chapter 6, Salih affiliates with Conrad's project as he reinvigorates its fiery core, radicalizes it, and otherwise engages contrapuntally with it. Woolf's influential trope of Shakespeare's sister has indeed traveled the globe as part of a diverse transnational feminist discourse, but the trope did not begin with her text any more than feminism did. It arose out of the transnational circulations of ideas about women and art, with potent expressions in the colonies before Woolf "invented" it. As chapter 7 shows, the diasporic modernism of Césaire and Cha reinvents—indeed reinvigorates—modernism's "make it new" with an emphasis on a return to the abjection of enslavement and partition as a precondition for regeneration through the poetic word. In the actual testing ground of literary modernism of the long twentieth century, modernization as Westernization has no explanatory power.

DEBATE 11: EMPIRE

ON THE ONE HAND

The planetary modernities in the *longue durée* delineated in *Planetary Modernisms* seem indistinguishable from empire. Is modernity inherently the result of widespread conquest and the rule of some by others? Does empire always bring with it some form of modernity? If so, is modernity always tied to violence and oppression? How then does modernity acquire its utopic dimensions? What is the relationship between the dystopic and utopic aspects of any given modernity? *Planetary Modernisms* continually invokes empire, but it fails to interrogate its meanings and only gestures at its effects. As Mary Lou Emery writes in her richly contextualized study of Caribbean modernism: "Friedman proposes a planetary modernism as an expansive and creative epistemological project that, in the most recent version of her argument [in 2010] extends to include the planet but avoids any discussion of political/economic forces and institutions."[22] Presumably, she means that my discussions of such aspects of modernity as networks, circulation, and aesthetics (and so forth) do not incorporate consideration of how institutional power works in and through these structures. Empire is everywhere present in *Planetary Modernisms* but insufficiently analyzed in the specificity of its political, economic, and cultural power.

ON THE OTHER HAND

In its efforts to rethink modernity, *Planetary Modernisms* deliberately pairs two of the most powerful and influential empires in human history to make the point that many qualities typically associated with European modernity appeared earlier in two very different yet decidedly imperial forms: the sedentary Tang Dynasty and the nomadic Mongol Empire. My bookshelves are filled with histories of different empires, from the so-called ancient period to the modern and neoliberal. These accounts confirm for me a key thesis of Jane Burbank and Frederick Cooper's *Empires in World History*—namely, that rather than being supplanted by the rise of the nation-state, empires have retained their pervasive global influence. The nation-states of post-Westphalian Europe and the emergent formerly colonized world exist as a form *within* the continuing transnational structures of empires—whether the Spanish or the Portuguese, the British or the French, the Ottoman or the Chinese, the German or the Russian. What they challenge is the common historical notion that European modernity—with its nation-state political structure—supplanted the imperial forms of human civilization that go back millennia.[23] Their *longue durée* and global framework differs markedly from Michael Hardt and Antonio Negri's *Empire*, which usefully associates Western modernity with its empires but fails to consider these empires in the context of non-Western or pre-1500 ones.[24] Empires, Burbank and Cooper conclude, exist in many types and evolve in different ways. But the attempt to expand and maintain power over diverse regions and peoples through conquest, incorporation, or political and economic dominance has an ancient and still contemporary history.

Planetary Modernisms expands on Burbank and Cooper's views by associating the many forms of modernity with the kinds of intensified conflict, interculturalism, networks, circulations, and technological, aesthetic, and intellectual innovation that imperial conquest, rule, and incorporation appear to establish. This is *not* to justify empire, *not* to whitewash the brutalities of empire, *not* to ignore the political, economic, and cultural power of empire. Rather, it is to insist that empires typically intensify the rate of rupture and accelerate change in ways that are both dystopic and utopic, both shattering and progressive, depending on the particularities of change and of location within the imperial system. Empires combine brutal humiliations and control; they also in many cases result in cultural, technological, governmental, and commercial flowering, like the Pax Mongolica that followed the swift killing machines of the Mongol conquest, or the Songhay Empire's "golden age" based on the rule of Askia the Great in Timbuktu, Goa, and Jenne. Think of the trains in India: a product of the British Raj; a means of increasing the mobility of people, ideas, and goods in different parts of the country and thus a key technology in building anticolonial resistance; an instrument of terror during Partition and its legacies in sectarian violence into the late twentieth century. Modernities morph over time, and key to these changes are factors of empire.

Chapters 5, 6, and 7 provide readings of modernisms produced in the thick of empire—from Du Fu and Kabir to writers from Asia, Africa, Britain, the Caribbean, and the United States in the long twentieth century. Empire in different forms is the primary condition of these writers' historical modernity, although gender, sexuality, race, caste, and religion enter the texts of these writers in significant ways. *Planetary Modernisms* refuses to separate the world of letters from the larger world in which it operates, as the world-system analysis of both Pascale Casanova and Franco Moretti do. In defining the modernism of these texts as the aesthetic dimension of specific modernities, these readings insist at every step on seeing how the writers register experiential and often individual responses to the colonial and postcolonial modernities that pervade their lives, narratives, and poetry.

DEBATE 12: GENDER AND . . .

ON THE ONE HAND

Why doesn't *Planetary Modernisms* systematically theorize gender's centrality to a rethinking of *modernism/modernity*? How might feminist theory enable a newly expansive approach? What, in turn, does the book add to feminist theory? I cut my academic teeth in modernist studies since the 1970s with a focus on gender and women's writing. Since publishing *Mappings: Feminism and the Cultural Geographies of Encounter* in 1998, I have written extensively on transnational feminist theory, especially in border, migration, and diaspora studies. Why hasn't this work become a central part of my retheorization of modernity and modernism, especially in parts 1 and 2 of the book?

Planetary Modernisms embodies an odd contradiction, one evident in its very structure. The theoretical chapters on large-scale modernities and their related modernisms—chapters 1 through 4—contain scarcely a word about gender unless it appears in an occasional example. Yet the chapters focusing on the smaller-scale fictions and poems of the long twentieth century foreground gender (along with the other identity categories that intersect gender, like race, caste, sexuality, and class) as central to the meanings of modernity articulated in selected texts by men as well as women. Race and other forms of "othering" appear as pervasive categories in discussions of imperial modernities. But the transnational readings of texts in chapters 6 and 7 repeatedly show gender and sexuality issues interrupting the binary politics of colonialism and race. Even the discussion of Kabir in chapter 5 looks at his transgender play in the context of his resistance to all orthodoxies. It's the pairing of the Intended and the African woman in *Heart of Darkness* that heightens the ironic distance between Conrad and Marlow, and though I didn't explore it, the uncanny bond Marlow feels with his dying helmsman borders on the same kind of homoerotic friendship in the context of empire that fascinates Forster. It's the fate of Hosna in Salih's *Season of Migration to the North* that provides the primary wedge between the North/South and modernity/tradition oppositions to suggest Salih's affiliation with Conrad's project to unveil the heart of darkness within. The matrix of gender, caste, and sexuality in Roy's *The God of Small Things* helps open up Forster's more covert and displaced explorations of related issues in the relationship of Adela and Aziz. The gender-inflected relationship and writings of the Tagore siblings suggest new ways of formulating Woolf's gendered modernism. Divergent treatments of gender in Césaire and Cha open up a gap in their shared diasporic modernisms.

Gender is front and center—everywhere—in chapters 6 and 7 and hardly anywhere in chapters 1 through 4. Why?

ON THE OTHER HAND

I don't know. I've thought a lot about this question. Feminist theory and criticism in modernist studies and beyond remain vital touchstones for the book, including such works as Rita Felski's *The Gender of Modernism* and Bonnie Kime Scott's *Gender in Modernism: New Geographies, Complex Intersections*.[25] *Planetary Modernism*'s theoretical approach to multiple and divergent modernities across time and through space owes greatly to the concept of "locational" feminism developed in *Mappings* and subsequent transnationalizing work. The book's theoretical efforts to displace Eurocentric metanarratives of world history represent an expansion of the familiar feminist critique of androcentrism and phallogocentrism: the refusal to use one mode of human existence as the universal standard by which all others are to be measured and deemed "other," deficient, lacking.

Without directly addressing gender in parts 1 and 2, the emphasis the book places on the keyword-images for modernity of *divergence*, *discrepance*, and *fissure* in chapter 4 comes implicitly out of feminist theory, particularly the concept of intersectionality: the assertion that different systems of power always articulate through one another and never alone. The intersections of such axes of difference as gender, race, sexuality, class, religion, caste, disability (and the proverbial so forth) inevitably create divergent and discrepant modernities.[26] Gender—like these other categories—can function as a fissure that cracks open a story of modernity based solely on colonialism, or economics, or technology. The continual reversion to the significance of gender in chapters 6 and 7 demonstrates one form of divergence in modernity and thereby the whole principle of modernity's unevenness.

Nonetheless, I accept the puzzle here. Feminist theory permeates the underlying assumptions of *Planetary Modernisms* yet peripheralizes gender in its theorization of modernity even as it locates gender at the very center of its readings of modernist texts. It's a fundamental contradiction, one that I invite others to resolve or pursue.

DEBATE 13: INSTITUTIONAL PRAGMATISM

ON THE ONE HAND

The geohistorical expansion of *modernity/modernism* into a seemingly endless plurality is impractical for the institutions of knowledge like the academy, professional organizations, publishing, libraries, and digital-based knowledge production. Rebecca L. Walkowitz, whose own work on modernism encompasses global aesthetic formations in the long twentieth century, posed this question to me in genuine puzzlement about to what extent we can formalize the new transnationalism in the our curriculum, teaching, and hiring practices.[27] As Kate Trumpener writes, "The traditional notion of period may be bankrupt, depleted, a mere placeholder for a truth we know to be more complicated. Yet it is hard to see just how to reorganize curricula, job descriptions, or library cataloguing systems using alternative templates. The academy could potentially become a kind of Babel, in which competing historical models simply jostled one another. Our current system provides us with convenient if crude sorting devices."[28] David James and Urmila Seshagiri argue openly for a return to modernism as a distinctive period and style in the early twentieth century.[29]

Students learning the field have to begin somewhere, and it is tempting to start off with the conventional definitions so ably articulated in such overviews as Pericles Lewis's *The Cambridge Introduction to Modernism* or Peter Nicholls's *Modernisms: A Literature Guide*.[30] The Anglo-American/European modernism of the early twentieth century serves as a foundational core for the pragmatic dimensions of higher education: syllabus formation, graduate student training, professionalization, conference organization, anthologies, and so forth. Similarly, the commonly understood nominal definition of modernity as a Western formation constitutes a necessary historical anchor for issues that have come to encompass the globe. Globalization of modernity/modernity is most effectively done once a foundation of its Western manifestations have been established. Information technology and library cataloguing systems require manageable categories that can be integrated into existing systems; incorporating all the potential global modernities/modernisms in the *longue durée* would jam the machinery of knowledge storage and retrieval. It's just not practical to begin with modernity/modernism on the whole globe and throughout history.

ON THE OTHER HAND

Maintaining a concept of "core" *modernity* or "canonical" *modernism* may be convenient, but it is fundamentally misleading and inhibits the expansions in the field that are already taking place. It dooms modernities/modernisms elsewhere and in other times to the status of perpetual "other," as add-ons with an inevitably secondary status. As challenging as it is for the institutional pragmatics of knowledge creation and dissemination, a transformation of the fundamental framework for *modernity/modernism* is necessary. The difficulties and ambiguities of expansion are themselves "teachable moments," providing a self-reflexive examination of how syllabi, anthologies, introductory volumes, book markets, websites, and cataloguing systems are put together.

All syllabi are selective; they never encompass the full diversity of the field, whatever its scale or scope. At issue is the principle of selection and what that framework teaches. A course on the twentieth-century modernist novel in English that incorporates the reverberating modernisms of Conrad's *Heart of Darkness*, Joyce's *A Portrait of the Artist as a Young Man*, Woolf's *The Waves*, Salih's *Season of Migration to the North*, Morrison's *Beloved*, and Roy's *The God of Small Things* (to pose one example grouping) provides extensive opportunities for cultural, political, and formalist analysis of aesthetic modernities in English (including translated novels like *Season* that have an extensive "life" in English). Such a course taught *before* students are exposed to the conventional Anglo-American canon of modernist novels would provide a foundation of a different sort, a more expansive one to which additional texts could be added with further study. To prepare students for the intensified globalization of the twenty-first century, teachers need to move beyond the national and trans-Atlantic paradigms for modernist studies into fully planetary frameworks.

The job market, departmental hiring, cataloguing systems, and the organization of professional societies are notoriously slow in keeping up with changes in any field. Interdisciplinarity—ideal for modernist studies—is difficult to institutionalize with the high level of specialization that has dominated the twentieth-century academy. These factors alone provide enormous incentive to emphasize the conventional understandings of modernity and the familiar canon of early-twentieth-century modernism. But as academics, we need to resist having the tail wag the dog. Institutionalization of any field of study should reflect the nature of the intellectual project, not the other way around. The pragmatics of the field need to keep up with the advances in knowledge. The book publishers and journals have already done so, regarding the transnational turn in modernist studies as a cutting edge in the field worthy of dissemination and justified by its marketability. The digital revolution—with its "big data" capacities, inventions of new methodologies of research, development of multiple platforms for presentation and dissemination of knowledge—represents an ideal opportunity for modernist studies to institutionalize the newest thinking in the field. As the academy reinvents itself in the twenty-first century, the institutions of modernist studies must change.

THE DEBATE: INTERMINABLE AND TERMINABLE

The debate inside my head and the world beyond it does not end with this book.[31] Indeed, the indeterminacy of this conclusion deliberately mirrors the contradictions inherent in modernity itself. It also testifies to the importance of the issues at stake in these and other debates about modernity. In a world perpetually riven with both local and global conflicts, in a world continually split open by transformational discoveries and new mobilities, modernity matters. People and societies aspire to and reject it, fight for and against it, die for and against it. As long as modernity matters across the planet, debating its meanings and effects matters. As long as artists, writers, and thinkers participate in the modernity of their place and times with their creative efforts, the multiple meanings of modernism matter.

The Babel of debate I have with myself, that scholars have with one another, and that societies have on a planetary landscape signifies vibrancy. It puts into play what the inventiveness of the humanities accomplishes—creating new frameworks for interpretation, raising questions, exploring the unexplored, recentering the forgotten or marginalized. In brief, the interminability of debate about modernity is a plus.

Yet *Planetary Modernisms* is not in the end a dispassionate mapping of differing positions on the landscape of debate about modernity. The book's aim to rethink modernity and modernism on a planetary scale, in the *longue durée*, and for the twenty-first century takes sides in the debate. Aware of the counterarguments, it nonetheless argues for more expansive and fluid geohistorical frameworks and against those who would narrow and fix the meanings of *modernity* and *modernism*. It does so out of a conviction that modernity understood as the invention of the West remains in a bubble of Eurocentric/Americentric belief that inhibits a genuinely planetary framework for understanding human engagement with modernity. The modernisms attached to this restricted view of modernity will interminably reproduce the metanarrative of the West as the world's center and the Rest as its periphery, whether for good or evil. *Planetary Modernisms* rejects an additive approach to global modernisms and promotes instead a transformational one, a fundamental rethinking on a planetary scale in the *longue durée* as a necessary framework to fulfill the transnational turn in modernist studies and to prepare ourselves to survive and thrive in the still-unfolding modernities of the twenty-first century.

NOTES

INTRODUCTION

1. William Butler Yeats, "The Second Coming," in *The Collected Poems of W. B. Yeats*, ed. Richard J. Finneran (New York: Macmillan, 1956), 284.
2. Arjun Appadurai, *Modernity at Large: Cultural Dimensions of Globalization* (Minneapolis: University of Minnesota Press, 1996).
3. Andreas Huyssen, "The High/Low in an Expanded Field," *Modernism/Modernity* 9, no. 3 (September 2002): 366. Huyssen's article is based on the keynote address that he gave at the Modernist Studies Association conference one month after 9/11.
4. Rita Felski, "New Cultural Theories of Modernity," in *Doing Time: Feminist Theory and Postmodern Culture* (New York: New York University Press, 2000), 55.
5. Douglas Mao and Rebecca L. Walkowitz, "The New Modernist Studies" *PMLA* 123, no. 3 (2008): 737–748.
6. Fredric Jameson, *A Singular Modernity: Essay on the Ontology of the Present* (London: Verso, 2002); Immanuel Wallerstein, *The Modern World-System: Capitalist Agriculture and the Origins of the European World-Economy in the Sixteenth Century* (New York: Academic Press, 1974); Gilles Deleuze and Félix Guattari, *Kafka: Toward a Minor Literature*, trans. Dana Colan (Minneapolis: University of Minnesota Press, 1986). See also Dilip Parameshwar Gaonkar, ed., *Alternative Modernities* (Durham, N.C.: Duke University Press, 2001).
7. "West" and "Western" are capitalized throughout *Planetary Modernisms* to emphasize their status as idea rather than as fixed geographical region. For ease of reading, however, the scare quotes have been subsequently removed. See extended discussion in chapter 3.
8. Shu-mei Shih, *The Lure of the Modern: Writing Modernism in Semicolonial China, 1917–1937* (Berkeley: University of California Press, 2001), 1; Ella Shohat and Robert Stam, *Unthinking Eurocentrism: Multiculturalism and the Media* (London: Routledge, 1994), esp. "The Myth of the West," 13–15.

9. Thomas S. Kuhn, *The Structure of Scientific Revolutions* (Chicago: University of Chicago Press, 1963). Max Weber's *The Protestant Ethic and the Spirit of Capitalism*, trans. Talcott Parsons (New York: Scribner's, 1958), influenced decades of social theory that assumes modernity to be uniquely or originally Western.
10. Paul Jay, *Global Matters: The Transnational Turn in Literary Studies* (Ithaca, N.Y.: Cornell University Press, 2010); see also the special issue on "Globalizing Literary Studies," *PMLA* 116, no.1 (January 2001).
11. Simon Gikandi, *Modernism in Limbo* (Ithaca, N.Y.: Cornell University Press, 1992); Priya Joshi, *In Another Country; Colonialism, Culture, and the English Novel in India* (New York: Columbia University Press, 2002); Fernando J. Rosenberg, *The Avant-Garde and Geopolitics in Latin America* (Pittsburgh, Penn.: University of Pittsburgh Press, 2006); Shih, *The Lure of the Modern*.
12. Peter Brooker and Andrew Thacker, eds., *Geographies of Modernism: Literatures, Cultures, Spaces* (London: Routledge, 2005); Laura Doyle and Laura Winkiel, eds., *Geomodernisms: Race, Modernism, Modernity* (Bloomington: Indiana University Press, 2005); Astradur Eysteinsson and Vivian Liska, eds., *Modernism* (Amsterdam: John Benjamins, 2007); Irena Ramalho Santos and António Sousa Ribeiro, eds., *Translocal Modernisms: International Perspectives* (Bern: Peter Lang, 2008); Peter Brooker, Andrzej Gąsiorek, and Deborah Longworth, eds., *The Oxford Handbook of Modernisms* (Oxford: Oxford University Press, 2010); Mark Wollaeger, ed., with Matt Eatough, *The Oxford Handbook of Global Modernisms* (Oxford: Oxford University Press, 2012); special issue on "Modernisms and Transnationalism," *Modernism/Modernity* 19, no. 3 (September 2006), ed. Cassandra Laity; Regina Gagnier, ed., *Literature Compass: The Global Circulation Project*; special issue on the Global Circulation Project's *Forum on Global Modernisms* 9, no. 9 (September 2012), ed. Laura Doyle and Regina Gagnier.
13. Jessica Berman, *Modernist Commitments: Ethics, Politics, and Transnational Modernism* (New York: Columbia University Press, 2011); Christopher GoGwilt, *The Passage of Literature: Genealogies of Modernism in Conrad, Rhys, and Pramoedya* (Oxford: Oxford University Press, 2011); Charles W. Pollard, *New World Modernisms: T. S. Eliot, Derek Walcott, and Kamau Brathwaite* (Charlottesville: University of Virginia Press, 2004); Jahan Ramazani, *A Transnational Poetics* (Chicago: University of Chicago Press, 2009); Gayle Rogers, *Modernism and the New Spain: Britain, Cosmopolitan Europe, and Literary History* (Oxford: Oxford University Press, 2012).
14. Edward W. Said, *Orientalism* (New York: Random House, 1978); Aimé Césaire, *Discourse on Colonialism* [1955], trans. Joan Pinkham (New York: Monthly Review, 1972); Frantz Fanon, *Black Skin, White Masks* [1952], trans. Charles Lam Markmann (New York: Grove, 1967); Gayatri Chakravorty Spivak, *In Other Worlds: Essays in Cultural Politics* (New York: Methuen, 1987); Rosalind C. Morris, ed., *Can the Subaltern Speak? The History of an Idea* (New York: Columbia University Press, 2010); Homi K. Bhabha, *The Location of Culture* (London: Routledge, 1994); Dipesh Chakrabarty, *Provincializing Europe: Postcolonial Thought and Historical Difference* (Princeton, N.J.: Princeton University Press, 2000); Anne McClintock, *Imperial Leather: Race, Gender, and Sexuality in the Colonial Context*

INTRODUCTION • 347

(London: Routledge, 1995); and R. Radhakrishnan, *Diasporic Mediations: Between Home and Location* (Minneapolis: University of Minnesota Press, 1996).

15. See for example Emily Apter, *The Translation Zone: A New Comparative Literature* (Princeton, N.J.: Princeton University Press, 2006) and *Against World Literature: On the Politics of Untranslatability* (London: Verso, 2013); David Damrosch, *What Is World Literature?* (Princeton, N.J.: Princeton University Press, 2003); Theo D'haen, David Damrosch, and Djelal Kadir, eds., *The Routledge Companion to World Literature* (London: Routledge, 2011); Wai Chee Dimock, *Through Other Continents: American Literature Across Deep Time* (Princeton, N.J.: Princeton University Press, 2006); Eric Hayot, *The Hypothetical Mandarin: Sympathy, Modernity, and Chinese Pain* (Oxford: Oxford University Press, 2009); Françoise Lionnet and Shu-mei Shih, eds., *Minor Transnationalism* (Durham, N.C.: Duke University Press, 2003); the journal *World Literature Today*, ed. Djelal Kadir; special issue on "What Counts as World Literature?" *Modern Language Quarterly* 74, no. 2 (June 2013), ed. Caroline Levine and B. Venkat Mani; Christopher Prendergast, ed., *Debating World Literature* (New York: Verso, 2004); Haun Saussy, ed., *Comparative Literature in an Age of Globalization* (Baltimore, Md.: Johns Hopkins University Press, 2006).

16. Appadurai, *Modernity at Large*; James Clifford, *Routes: Travel and Translation in the Late Twentieth Century* (Cambridge, Mass.: Harvard University Press, 1997); Renato Rosaldo, *Culture and Truth: The Remaking of Social Analysis* (Boston, Mass.: Beacon, 1993); and Anna L. Tsing, *Friction: An Ethnography of Global Connection* (Princeton, N.J.: Princeton University Press, 2004).

17. Throughout the book, I use the terms *planetary* and *planetarity* in an epistemological sense to imply a consciousness of the earth as planet, not restricted to geopolitical formations and potentially encompassing the nonhuman as well as the human; this use differs from Gayatri Chakravorty Spivak's "planetarity" in *Death of a Discipline* (New York: Columbia University Press, 2003), where she invokes the term as a utopian gesture of resistance against globalization's domination of the Global South. Terms such as *planet*, *planetary*, *globality*, *globalism*, *world*, *worldness*, *worlding*, and *worldliness* abound in cultural theory but without stable meanings; they are often utopic or dystopic, typically connoting a transnational consciousness or world system beyond the national paradigm, though seldom denying the continued significance of the nation-state. See for example Mary Louise Pratt, *Imperial Eyes: Travel Writing and Transculturation* (London: Routledge, 1992), 1–37; Paul Gilroy, *Postcolonial Melancholia* (New York: Columbia University Press, 2005), 29–57; Dimock, *Through Other Continents*; Edward W. Said, "Culture and the Vultures," *Times Higher Education Supplement* 24 (January 1992): 19; Bruce Robbins, "Comparative Cosmopolitans," in *Cosmopolitics: Thinking and Feeling Beyond the Nation*, ed. Pheng Cheah and Bruce Robbins (Minneapolis: University of Minnesota Press, 1998), 247; Franco Moretti, "Conjectures on World Literature," *New Left Review*, 2nd. ser. (January/February 2000): 54–68; Apter, *The Translation Zone*, 3–11, 85–93; Robin Morgan, "Planetary Feminism," in *Sisterhood Is Global* (New York: Feminist Press, 1996), 1–37; R. Radhakrishnan, "Worlding,

by Any Other Name," in *History, the Human, and the World Between* (Durham, N.C.: Duke University Press, 2008), 183–248; Aamir R. Mufti, "Global Comparison," *Critical Inquiry* 31 (Winter 2005), 487; Édouard Glissant, "The Unforeseeable Diversity of the World," trans. Haun Saussy, in *Beyond Dichotomies: Histories, Identities, Cultures, and the Challenge of Globalization*, ed. Elisabeth Mudimbe-Boyi (Albany, N.Y.: SUNY Press, 2002), 287–288, 295; Édouard Glissant, *Poétique de la relation* (Paris: Gallimard, 1990), 155–181 (in English: *Poetics of Relation*, trans. Betsy Wing [Ann Arbor: University of Michigan Press, 1997], 141–167).

18. Fernand Braudel, *The Mediterranean and the Mediterranean World in the Age of Phillip II*, trans. Siân Reynolds (New York: Harper and Row, 1972); Wallerstein, *The Modern World-System*. Subsequently, Wallerstein summarized his extensive oeuvre in *World-Systems Analysis: An Introduction* (Durham, N.C.: Duke University Press, 2004).

19. Janet L. Abu-Lughod, *Before European Hegemony: The World-System, AD 1250–1350* (Oxford: Oxford University Press, 1989); J. M. Blaut, *The Colonizer's Model of the World: Geographical Diffusionism and Eurocentric History* (New York: Guilford, 1983); *Civilization and World Systems: Studying World-Historical Change*, ed. Stephen K. Sanderson (London: Sage, 1995); André Gunder Frank, *ReOrient: Global Economy in the Asian Age* (Berkeley: University of California Press, 1998); John Hobson, *The Eastern Origins of Western Civilisation* (Cambridge: Cambridge University Press, 2004); Jane Burbank and Frederick Cooper, *Empires in World History: Power and the Politics of Difference* (Princeton, N.J.: Princeton University Press, 2010).

20. William H. McNeill, *The Rise of the West* (Chicago, Ill.: University of Chicago Press, 1963); "The Rise of the West after Twenty-Five Years" [1990], in Sanderson, ed., *Civilizations and World Systems*, 304–320, hereafter cited in the text.

21. Wallace Stevens, "Thirteen Ways of Looking at a Blackbird," in *The Collected Poems of Wallace Stevens* (New York: Vintage, 1990), 92–95.

22. William Butler Yeats, "Among School Children," in *The Collected Poems of W. B. Yeats* (New York: Macmillan, 1956), 14.

23. Portions of this work have been reformulated significantly in chapters 3, 6, and 7.

1. DEFINITIONAL EXCURSIONS

1. This chapter is based on "Definitional Excursions: The Meanings of *Modern/Modernity/Modernism*," which appeared in *Modernism/Modernity* 8, no. 3 (September 2001): 493–513; special thanks to Cassandra Laity and Rita Felski for their astute comments and support. Earlier versions were presented at the Modernist Studies Association (2000) and the University of Coimbra, Portugal (2000). The 2001 article was condensed from a longer version that subsequently appeared in Chinese translation in *China Scholarship* 2 (Fall 2002): 1–44. This chapter integrates portions from the version in *China Scholarship* and thus differs slightly from the 2001 version in *Modernism/Modernity*. I have not updated the citations, which represent the state of scholarship in modernist studies

1. DEFINITIONAL EXCURSIONS • 349

in the first part of this century; subsequent to the article's 2001 publication, modernist studies has changed dramatically, as I discuss in later chapters.

2. I echo here Ezra Pound's famous slogan in *Make It New* (London: Faber and Faber, 1934) and two influential early essays: Harry Levin's "What Was Modernism?" in *Refractions: Essays in Comparative Literature* (Oxford: Oxford University Press, 1965), 271–295; Maurice Beebe's "What Modernism Was," *Journal of Modern Literature* 3 (July 1974): 1065–1084.

3. Malcolm Bradbury and James McFarlane, eds., introduction to *Modernism: A Guide to European Literature, 1890–1930* (London: Penguin, 1976), 27.

4. Anthony Giddens, foreword to *NowHere: Space, Time, and Modernity*, ed. Roger Friedland and Deirdre Boden (Berkeley: University of California Press, 1994), xii.

5. Robert Casserio, *The Novel in England, 1900–1950* (New York: Twayne, 1999), 82.

6. T. J. Clark, *Farewell to an Idea: Episodes from a History of Modernism* (New Haven, Conn.: Yale University Press, 1999), 139.

7. Bradbury and McFarlane, *Modernism*, 26.

8. James C. Scott, *Seeing Like a State: How Certain Schemes to Improve the Human Condition Have Failed* (New Haven, Conn.: Yale University Press, 1998), 89–90.

9. Marshall Berman, *All That Is Solid Melts Into Air: The Experience of Modernity* [1981] (New York: Viking Penguin, 1988), 151.

10. Scott Lash and Jonathan Friedman, eds., "Introduction: Subjectivity and Modernity's Other," in *Modernity and Identity* (Oxford: Basil Blackwell, 1992), 1. But they also write, "modernity is a matter of movement, of *flux*, of *change*, of *unpredictability*" (1).

11. Alice Jardine, *Gynesis: Configurations of Woman and Modernity* (Ithaca, N.Y.: Cornell University Press, 1985), 25.

12. Jean-François Lyotard, *The Postmodern Condition: A Report on Knowledge*, trans. Geoff Bennington and Brian Massumi (Minneapolis: University of Minnesota Press, 1984), xxiii–xxiv.

13. Marianne DeKoven, *Rich and Strange: Gender, History, Modernism* (Princeton, N.J.: Princeton University Press, 1991), 6.

14. Ihab Hassan, *The Dismemberment of Orpheus: Toward a Postmodern Literature* [1971], 2nd ed. (Madison: University of Wisconsin Press, 1992), 267–268.

15. David Harvey, *The Condition of Postmodernity: An Enquiry Into the Origins of Social Change* (Oxford: Basil Blackwell, 1989), 10–12; hereafter cited in the text.

16. Harvey, *The Condition of Postmodernity*, 35. I end this chain of paratactic pairs with quotations from the same author to highlight the existence of unexamined and seemingly un-self-reflexive contradiction within the work of the same person.

17. In ways different from my own, others have noted contradictions in passing or in an attempt to resolve the conflict. See for example Rita Felski, *The Gender of Modernity* (Cambridge, Mass.: Harvard University Press, 1995), where her succinct summary (12–13) paves the way for her advocacy of a cultural studies approach to Western modernity from the Enlightenment to its breakup in the early twentieth century; Bernard Yack, *The Fetishism of Modernities: Epochal Self-Consciousness in Contemporary Social and Political*

Thought (Notre Dame, Ind.: Notre Dame University Press, 1997), where he reviews four distinct concepts of modernity in the West (philosophical, sociological, political, and aesthetic) and argues that for all their differences they share "an emphasis on innovation and challenge to traditional authority" (35, 1–40); Eric Rothstein, "Broaching a Cultural Logic of Modernity," *Modern Language Quarterly* 61, no. 2 (June 2000): 359–394, where he emphasizes the heterogeneous distributions of modernity within the modern; and Berman, *All That Is Solid Melts Into Air*, which resolves the contradictions by positing evolutionary stages of modernity over multiple centuries.

18. I do not examine the term *modernization* because there is more consensus about its basic meaning as the process that brings about *modernity* (however that may be defined); debate about the causes, effects, and politics of modernization of course abound.

19. The relation between the terms *modern/postmodern* and *modernism/postmodernism* is as contested as the meanings of the root words and beyond the scope of this chapter. Many social theorists use *postmodern* or *postmodernism* to refer to the rupture from Enlightenment modernity, regarding the aesthetic dismantlings of this modernity in the nineteenth and twentieth centuries as early harbingers of the change to come later and more broadly in the long twentieth century. What many others understand to be modernity and modernism are thus folded into postmodernism. See for example Lyotard, *The Postmodern Condition*; and Harvey, *The Condition of Postmodernity*. Because of the inconsistency in terminology, their critiques of societal modernism are often misunderstood to be attacks on aesthetic modernism as well. The difficulty in determining whether postmodernism represents an intensification of modernism or a radical rupture from it is compounded by these differing uses of the terms *modernity/modernism* and *postmodern/postmodernism*. Left unexplored is the possibility that the most significant break from modernity is just now in the making, through the knowledge revolution instituted by the computer and the related effects of accelerating globalization, as discussed in chapter 4.

20. See especially Freud's papers on technique, especially "The Dynamics of the Transference" and "Remembering, Repeating and Working-Through," in *The Standard Edition of the Psychological Works of Sigmund Freud*, trans. James Strachey (London: Hogarth Press, 1958), 12:97–108, 145–156. In *The Fetishism of Modernities*, Yack characterizes the postmodernists' attention to modernity as an "obsession" and a "fetishism" that leads to misleading totalizations of an epoch much at odds with their advocacy of *petits recits* and heterogeneity (esp. 1–16).

21. See especially Julia Kristeva, *Desire in Language*, trans. Thomas Gora, Alice Jardine, and Leon S. Roudiez (New York: Columbia University Press, 1980), 36–91; Fredric Jameson, *The Political Unconscious: Narrative as a Socially Symbolic Act* (Ithaca, N.Y.: Cornell University Press, 1981); Shoshana Felman, ed., *Literature and Psychoanalysis: The Question of Reading: Otherwise* (Baltimore, Md.: Johns Hopkins University Press, 1980), 94–207; and Shoshana Felman, *Lacan and the Adventure of Insight* (Cambridge, Mass.: Harvard University Press, 1987), 27–51.

22. I am indebted to Noel Carroll for bringing to my attention nominal and relational modes of definition in the discipline of philosophy. I have added to his observation the grammatical dimension, emphasizing the distinction between nouns and adjectives in definitions of *modern/modernity/modernism*.
23. Although some scholars invoke one mode rather than the other, many use both. See for example Anthony Giddens's nominal assertion in *Modernity and Self-Identity: Self and Society in the Late Modern Age* (Stanford, Calif.: Stanford University Press, 1991): "I use the term 'modernity' in a very general sense, to refer to the institutions and modes of behavior established first of all in post-feudal Europe, but which in the twentieth-century increasingly have become world-historical in their impact. 'Modernity' can be understood as roughly equivalent to 'the industrialised world,' so long as it is recognised that industrialism is not its only institutional dimension" (14–15). But in a relational mode, he writes, "Inherent in the idea of modernity is a contrast with tradition," in *The Consequences of Modernity* (Stanford, Calif.: Stanford University Press, 1990), 36.
24. As mentioned in the introduction, I use the capitalized terms "the West" and "Western" not in reference to a specific geographical region of the world but rather to what Shu-mei Shih calls "a symbolic construct" with ideological weight placing Europe (especially northern Europe) and the United States at the center. See Shih, *The Lure of the Modern: Writing Modernism in Semicolonial China, 1917–1937* (Berkeley: University of California Press, 2001), 1.
25. See for example, Giddens, *The Consequences of Modernity* and *Modernity and Self-Identity*; Harvey, *The Condition of Postmodernity*; Lyotard, *The Postmodern Condition*; Scott, *Seeing Like a State*; Yack, *The Fetishism of Modernities*; Jürgen Habermas, "Modernity Versus Postmodernity," *New German Critique* 22 (Winter 1981): 3–14, and *The Philosophical Discourse of Modernity* (Oxford: Oxford University Press, 1987); Arjun Appadurai, *Modernity at Large: Cultural Dimensions of Globalization* (Minneapolis: University of Minnesota Press, 1996); Stuart Hall, David Held, Con Hubert, and Kenneth Thompson, eds., *Model Modernity: An Introduction to Modern Societies* (Oxford: Basil Blackwell, 1996).
26. See for example Bradbury and McFarlane, eds., *Modernism*; and Richard Ellmann and Charles Feidelson, eds., *The Modern Tradition* (Oxford: Oxford University Press, 1965), collections that in spite of their exclusions maintain a seminal position in defining the meanings and canon of aesthetic modernism. For more recent definitional overviews, see Astradur Eysteinsson, *The Concept of Modernism* (Ithaca, N.Y.: Cornell University Press, 1990); Margot Norris, "Modernist Eruptions," in *The Columbia History of the American Novel*, ed. Emory Elliot (New York: Columbia University Press, 1991), 311–330; Marjorie Perloff, "Modernist Studies," in *Redrawing the Boundaries: The Transformation of English and American Literary Studies*, ed. Stephen Greenblatt and Giles Gunn (New York: Modern Language Publications, 1992), 154–178; Matei Calinescu, *Five Faces of Modernity*, 2nd ed. (Durham, N.C.: Duke University Press, 1987); Peter Nicholls, *Modernisms: A Literary Guide* (Berkeley: University of California Press, 1995; rev. ed., 2009);

Bonnie Kime Scott, ed., *The Gender of Modernism: A Critical Anthology* (Bloomington: Indiana University Press, 1990); Clark, *Farewell to an Idea*; and Jardine, *Gynesis*.

27. The association of modernism and modernity with Europe and the United States in the humanities not only excludes non-Western locations but also contains peripheries within "the West"—including, for example, margins based on gender, race, and geography, namely those of women, ethnic and racial minorities, and locations such as Spain, Portugal, the Balkans and Eastern Europe, Brazil, and the Caribbean. See for example Scott, *The Gender of Modernism*; DeKoven, *Rich and Strange*; Felski, *The Gender of Modernity*; Rachel Blau DuPlessis, *Genders, Races, and Religious Cultures in Modern American Poetry, 1908-1934* (Cambridge: Cambridge University Press, 2001); Joseph Allen Boone, *Libidinal Currents: Sexuality and the Shaping of Modernism* (Chicago: University of Chicago Press, 1998); Shari Benstock, *Women of the Left Bank: Paris, 1900-1940* (Austin: University of Texas Press, 1986); Sandra Gilbert and Susan Gubar, *No Man's Land: The Place of the Woman Writer in the Twentieth Century*, 3 vols. (New Haven, Conn.: Yale University Press, 1988-1994); Simon Gikandi, *Writing in Limbo: Modernism and Caribbean Literature* (Ithaca, N.Y.: Cornell University Press, 1992); Houston A. Baker Jr., *Modernism and the Harlem Renaissance* (Chicago: University of Chicago Press, 1987); Paul Gilroy, *The Black Atlantic: Modernity and Double Consciousness* (Cambridge, Mass.: Harvard University Press, 1993); Alice Gambrell, *Women Intellectuals, Modernism, and Difference: Transatlantic Culture, 1919-1945* (Cambridge: Cambridge University Press, 1997); Ned J. Davison, *The Concept of Modernism in Hispanic Criticism* (Boulder, Colo.: Pruett, 1966).
28. Marc Manganaro, ed., *Modernist Anthropology: From Fieldwork to Text* (Princeton, N.J.: Princeton University Press, 1990), esp. 3-50.
29. In developing a "scalar" model of modernity in "Broaching a Cultural Logic of Modernity," Eric Rothstein works with a relational mode in describing societies as "hot," "warm," or "cold" in reference to how intense or pervasive the phenomenon or phenomenology of rupture are in a given time and space. His relational approach to periodization takes into account the heterogeneity within any so-called period at the same time that some measure of nominal generalization is acknowledged.
30. Habermas, "Modernity Versus Postmodernity," 5.
31. See Pound, *Make It New*; Mina Loy, "Aphorisms on Futurism," in Scott, ed., *The Gender of Modernism*, 245. "Our Vortex," *Blast* 1 (1914), in *Blast 1*, ed. Wyndham Lewis (Santa Barbara, Calif.: Black Sparrow, 1981), 147; the error of "it's" for "its" is in the text. *Fire!*, ed. Wallace Thurman, 1, no. 1 (November 1926): 1.
32. Raymond Williams, *The Politics of Modernism: Against the New Conformists*, ed. Thomas Pinkney (London: Verso, 1989), esp. 32-36. The first essay in this collection, "When Was Modernism?" (31-36), alludes to and revises the earlier essays by Levin and Beebe cited in note 2.
33. Paul de Man, "Literary History and Literary Modernity," *Blindness and Insight* [1971] (Minneapolis: University of Minnesota Press, 1983), 147-148. See Felski, *The Gender of*

Modernity; Harvey, *The Condition of Postmodernity*, 36–38; and Yack, *The Fetishism of Modernities*, esp. 12–13, for variations on this argument.
34. See Rita Felski, *The Gender of Modernity* and "New Cultural Theories of Modernity," in *Doing Time: Feminist Theory and Postmodern Culture* (New York: New York University Press, 2000), in which she claims that the blend of aesthetics and sociology that characterizes cultural studies fosters consideration of not only elite culture but also the cultural practices of everyday life, popular and mass culture, and the voices of those often marginalized or regarded as sheer victims.
35. Toni Morrison, "Unspeakable Things Unspoken: The Afro-American Presence in American Literature," *Michigan Quarterly Review* 28 (Winter 1989): 1–34, esp. 8.
36. Giddens, *The Consequences of Modernity*, 174–175.
37. Sanjay Subrahmanyam, "Hearing Voices: Vignettes of Early Modernity in South Asia, 1400–1750," *Daedalus* 127, no. 3 (Summer 1998): 99–100. As part of the South Asian diaspora, Subrahmanyam has lived and worked in France, Britain, and the United States. For another attack on Western diffusionist models of modernity, see Charles S. Maier, "Consigning the Twentieth Century to History: Alternative Narratives for the Modern Era," *American Historical Review* 105, no. 3 (2000): 1–47.
38. I am indebted to Cyrena N. Pondrom's application of the notion of the hermeneutic circle to definitional issues in modernist studies (unpublished paper). For related critiques of the circularity of literary history, see for example Cary Nelson, *Repression and Recovery: Modern American Poetry and the Politics of Cultural Meaning, 1910–1945* (Madison: University of Wisconsin Press, 1989), 9–12; and Jameson, *The Political Unconscious*, 27–28.
39. Hugh Kenner, "The Making of the Modernist Canon," *Chicago Review* 34 (Spring 1984): 49–61.
40. Even by 2001, literary histories that incorporate black writers into the landscape of a diverse modernism had begun to increase, although some critics still segregated black modernism, and others discussed only white appropriations of black art forms. See for example Gilroy, *The Black Atlantic*; Baker, *Modernism and the Harlem Renaissance*; DuPlessis, *Genders, Races, and Religious Cultures in Modern American Poetry*; Boone, *Libidinal Currents*; Nelson, *Repression and Recovery*; Gambrell, *Women Intellectuals, Modernism, and Difference*; James De Jongh, *Vicious Modernism: Black Harlem and the Literary Imagination* (Cambridge: Cambridge University Press, 1990); Marianna Torgovnick, *Gone Primitive: Savage Intellectuals, Modern Lives* (Chicago: University of Chicago Press, 1990); Michael North, *The Dialect of Modernism: Race, Language, and Twentieth-Century Literature* (Oxford: Oxford University Press, 1994); Laura Doyle, *Bordering the Body: The Racial Matrix of Modern Fiction and Culture* (New York: Oxford University Press, 1994); and Susan Gubar, *Racechanges: White Skin, Black Face in American Culture* (Oxford: Oxford University Press, 1997).
41. Shmuel N. Eisenstadt and Wolfgang Schluchter, introduction to special issue on "Early Modernities," *Daedalus* 127, no. 3 (Summer 1998): 4–5. Hereafter cited in the text.

42. Björn Wittrock, "Early Modernities: Varieties and Transitions," *Daedalus* 127, no. 3 (Summer 1998): 19–20.
43. Jameson, *The Political Unconscious*, 28.
44. For discussion of these debates, see for example Michael Jacobsen and Ole Bruun, eds., *Human Rights and Asian Values: Contesting National Identities and Cultural Representations in Asia* (Richmond: Curzon, 2000); and Peter Van Ness, ed., *Debating Human Rights: Critical Essays from the United States and Asia* (London: Routledge, 1999). I am indebted to Edward Friedman for this point.
45. See for example Edward Friedman, "Asia as a Fount of Universal Human Rights," in Van Ness, ed., *Debating Human Rights*, 56–79; "Since There Is No East and There Is No West, How Could Either Be the Best?" in Jacobsen and Bruun, eds., *Human Rights and Asian Values*, 21–42; and "On Alien Western Democracy," in *Globalization and Democratization in Asia: The Construction of Identity*, ed. Catarina Kinnvall and Kristina Jönsson (London: Routledge, 2002), 53–72.
46. Edward W. Said, "Traveling Theory," in *The World, The Text, and the Critic* (Cambridge, Mass.: Harvard University Press, 1983), 226–47.
47. From Amiri Baraka (Leroi Jones), "Return of the Native," in *Black Magic: Saborage, Target Study, Black Art: Collected Poetry, 1961–1967* (New York: Bobbs-Merrill, 1969), 108. It is cited as epigraph in De Jongh's *Vicious Modernism*. Used courtesy of Chris Calhoun Agency.
48. See for example Nicholls's *Modernisms*; its plural title suggests heterogeneity, but its contents devote twelve chapters to Western, white, male modernism and one chapter entitled "At a Tangent: Other Modernisms," into which female modernism is herded. The 2009 edition includes a new chapter on African American Modernisms.

2. PLANETARITY

1. This chapter is a slightly modified version of "Planetarity: Musing Modernist Studies," *Modernism/Modernity* 17, no. 3 (September 2010): 471–499; the article is an expanded version of a keynote address written for the Modernist Studies Association Conference, Montréal, Canada, November 2009, and intended to address the conference theme—The Languages of Modernism—and location, with thanks to the conference organizers Allan Hepburn, Miranda Hickman, and Omri Moses. Versions of the multimedia paper were presented at the World Literature/s Conference, Madison, Wisconsin, December 2009; Institute for Research in the Humanities, University of Wisconsin–Madison, December 2009; Colgate University, January 2009; University of Miami, February 2009; and Loyola University of Chicago, September 2009. For challenges, encouragement, and suggestions I owe deep thanks to these audiences, to the students in my 2009 seminar on global modernisms, and to Susan D. Bernstein, Marina Camboni, Pamela L. Caughie, Michael Coyle, Wai Chee Dimock, Eric Hayot, Paul Jay, Cassandra Laity, B. Venkat Mani, Rob Nixon, Victoria Rosner, and Mark Wollaeger. Thanks to Anupam Basu and Elizabeth Schewe for assistance with images and permissions.

2. With thanks for their collaborations, scripts, and translations: Tejumola Olaniyan (Yoruba); Anupam Basu (Bengali); Guillermina De Ferrari (Spanish); Nicole Huang, Edward Friedman, and Daisy Yan Du (Chinese); Duaa Salemeh and Ammar Naji (Arabic); and B. Venkat Mani (Hindi). In the Montréal address, the audience saw and heard the statements in their original languages in an audiovisual presentation prepared by Anupam Basu.
3. See Marshall Berman, *All That Is Solid Melts Into Air: The Experience of Modernity* [1982] (New York: Penguin, 1988), titled after Karl Marx and Frederick Engels, *The Communist Manifesto*.
4. W. B. Yeats, "Among School Children," in *The Collected Poems of W. B. Yeats* (New York: Macmillan, 1956), 212–214.
5. Douglas Mao and Rebecca L. Walkowitz, "The New Modernist Studies," *PMLA* 123, no. 3 (2008): 737–748.
6. Jennifer Wicke, "Appreciation, Depreciation: Modernism's Speculative Bubble," *Modernism/Modernity* 8, no. 3 (September 2001): 389–404.
7. Pamela L. Caughie, introduction to *Disciplining Modernism*, ed. Pamela L. Caughie (New York: Palgrave Macmillan, 2010), 1–10.
8. Garry Leonard, "'The Famished Roar of Automobiles': Modernity, the Internal Combustion Engine, and Modernism," in *Disciplining Modernism*, ed. Pamela L. Caughie (New York: Palgrave Macmillan, 2010), 221–241.
9. Stephen Ross, "Uncanny Modernism; or, Analysis Interminable," in *Disciplining Modernism*, ed. Pamela L. Caughie (New York: Palgrave Macmillan, 2010), 33–52.
10. See Astradur Eysteinsson, *The Concept of Modernism* (Ithaca, N.Y.: Cornell University Press, 1990).
11. Malcolm Bradbury and James McFarlane, "The Name and Nature of Modernism," *Modernism: A Guide to European Literature, 1890–1930* (1976; New York: Penguin, 1991), 27.
12. Wallace Stevens, "Thirteen Ways of Looking at a Blackbird," in *The Collected Poems of Wallace Stevens* (New York: Vintage, 1990), 92–95.
13. Susan Stanford Friedman, "Periodizing Modernism: Postcolonial Modernities and the Space/Time Borders of Modernist Studies," *Modernism/Modernity* 12, no. 3 (September 2006): 425–44; "Paranoia, Pollution, and Sexuality: Affiliations between E. M. Forster's *A Passage to India* and Arundhati Roy's *The God of Small Things*," in *Geomodernism: Race, Modernism, Modernity*, ed. Laura Doyle and Laura Winkiel (Bloomington: Indiana University Press, 2005), 245–261.
14. Monica Ali, *Brick Lane* (New York: Scribner's, 2003); Nikos Papastergiadis, *The Turbulence of Migration: Globalization, Deterritorialization, and Hybridity* (Cambridge: Polity, 2000), 12.
15. Aamir R. Mufti, "Global Comparison," *Critical Inquiry* 31 (Winter 2005): 473.
16. Dipesh Chakrabarty, *Provincializaing Europe: Postcolonial Thought and Historical Difference* (Princeton, N.J.: Princeton University Press, 2000).
17. Mufti, "Global Comparison," 474. For this argument on European priority as an ideological construct rationalizing European imperialism, see also J. M. Blaut, *The Colonizer's*

Model of the World: Geographical Diffusionism and Eurocentric History (New York: Guilford, 1993); Friedman, "Periodizing Modernism," 429; Susan Stanford Friedman, "Unthinking Manifest Destiny: Muslim Modernities on Three Continents," in *Shades of the Planet: American Literature as World Literature*, ed. Wai Chee Dimock and Lawrence Buell (Princeton, N.J.: Princeton University Press, 2007), 62–100.

18. Anthony Giddens. *The Consequences of Modernity* (Stanford, Calif.: Stanford University Press, 1994). See also Stuart Hall and Bram Gieben's *Formations of Modernity*, a textbook summarizing the prevailing view (Cambridge: Polity, 1992).
19. Bruno Latour, *We Have Never Been Modern* [1991], trans. Catherine Porter (Cambridge, Mass.: Harvard University Press, 1993), 10.
20. Susan Stanford Friedman, "Definitional Excursions: The Meanings of *Modern/Modernity/Modernism*," *Modernism/Modernity* 8, no. 3 (September 2001): 504, 510; "Periodizing Modernity," 434–439.
21. For extended discussion, see Susan Stanford Friedman, "One Hand Clapping: Colonialism, Postcolonialism, and the Spatio/Temporal Boundaries of Modernism," in *Translocal Modernisms: International Perspectives*, ed. Irene Ramalho Santos and António Sousa Ribeiro (New York: Peter Lang, 2008), 11–40.
22. Comments during discussion of Susan Stanford Friedman, "Planetary Modernisms and the Modernities of Empire and New Nations," paper delivered at the conference on Meanings of Modern: South Asia Before and After Colonialism, Madison, Wisconsin, December 4–6, 2008.
23. Fredric Jameson, *A Singular Modernity: Essay on the Ontology of the Present* (London: Verso, 2002), 12. In spite of his belief "that the only satisfactory semantic meaning of modernity lies in its association with capitalism," his book analyzes the many "uses of the word 'modernity'" in the history of ideas and claims that he "rejects any presupposition that there is a correct use of the word," thus contradicting his own prescriptive and limited definition (13).
24. See for example Homi K. Bhabha, *The Location of Culture* (London: Routledge, 1993); special issue on "Multiple Modernities," *Daedalus* 129, no. 1 (Winter 2000), ed. S. N. Eisenstadt; special issue on "Early Modernities," *Daedalus* 127, no. 3 (Summer 1998), ed. Shumel N. Eisenstadt and Wolfgang Schluchter; Dilip Parameshwar Gaonkar, ed., *Alternative Modernities* (Durham, N.C.: Duke University Press, 2001); Mary Louise Pratt, "Modernity and Periphery: Toward a Global and Relational Analysis," in *Beyond Dichotomies: Histories, Identities, Cultures, and the Challenge of Globalization*, ed. Elisabeth Mudimbe-Boyi (Albany, N.Y.: SUNY Press, 2002), 21–48; R. Radhakrishnan, "Derivative Discourses and the Problem of Signification," *European Legacy* 7, no. 6 (2002): 783–795; Julios Ramos, *Divergent Modernities: Culture and Politics in Nineteenth-Century Latin America*, trans. John D. Blanco (Durham, N.C.: Duke University Press, 2001); Sanjay Subrahmanyam, "Hearing Voices: Vignettes of Early Modernity in South Asia, 1400–1750," *Daedalus* 127, no. 3 (1998), 75–104; Satya P. Mohanty, "Alternative Modernities and Medieval Indian Literature: The Oriya *Lakshmi Purana* as Radical Pedagogy," *Diacritics* 38, no. 3 (Fall 2008): 3–21.

25. My thanks to Jay Clayton for suggesting the term *recurrent* to describe my concept of modernity in the *longue durée*.
26. Wai Chee Dimock, *Through Other Continents: American Literature Across Deep Time* (Princeton, N.J.: Princeton University Press, 2006), 1–6.
27. Dilip Parameshwar Gaonkar, "On Alternative Modernities," in *Alternative Modernities*, ed. Dilip Parameshwar Gaonkar (Durham, N.C.: Duke University Press, 2001), 23.
28. Walter D. Mignolo, *Local Histories/Global Designs: Coloniality, Subaltern Knowledges, and Border Thinking* (Princeton, N.J.: Princeton University Press, 2000), 43.
29. Andreas Huyssen, "Geographies of Modernism in a Globalisizing World," in *Geographies of Modernism: Literatures, Cultures, Spaces*, ed. Peter Brooker and Andrew Thacker (London: Routledge, 2005), 7.
30. See Friedman, "Unthinking Manifest Destiny."
31. Paul Gilroy, *The Black Atlantic: Modernity and Double Consciousness* (Cambridge, Mass.: Harvard University Press, 1993), 221.
32. Édouard Glissant, *Poétique de la Relation* (Paris: Gallimard, 1990), 39 (in English: *Poetics of Relation*, trans. Betsy Wing [Ann Arbor: University of Michigan Press, 1997], 26).
33. André Gunder Frank, *ReOrient: Global Economy in the Asian Age* (Berkeley: University of California Press, 1998). See Blaut, *The Colonizer's View of the World*, and Stephen K. Sanderson, ed., *Civilizations and World Systems: Studying World-Historical Change* (London: Sage, 1995).
34. James Clifford, *Routes: Travel and Translation in the Late Twentieth Century* (Cambridge, Mass.: Harvard University Press, 1997). See also Anna L. Tsing, *Friction: An Ethnography of Global Connection* (Princeton, N.J.: Princeton University Press, 2004).
35. Jahan Ramazani, *A Transnational Poetics* (Chicago: University of Chicago Press, 2009), 16; *The Hybrid Muse: Postcolonial Poetry in English* (Chicago: University of Chicago Press, 2001).
36. Laura Doyle and Laura Winkiel, eds., *Geomodernisms: Race, Modernism, Modernity* (Bloomington: Indiana University Press, 2005), 430. See also Brooker and Thacker, *Geographies of Modernism*; Mark Wollaeger with Matt Eatough, ed., *The Oxford Handbook of Global Modernisms* (Oxford: Oxford University Press, 2012); Mary Ann Gillies, Helen Sword, and Steven Yao, eds., *Pacific Rim Modernisms* (Toronto: University of Toronto Press, 2009).
37. Melba Cuddy-Keane, "Modernism, Geopolitics, Globalization," *Modernism/Modernity* 10, no. 3 (September 2003): 544.
38. Peter Brooker and Andrew Thacker, introduction to *Geographies of Modernism: Literatures, Cultures, Spaces*, ed. Peter Brooker and Andrew Thacker (London: Routledge, 2005), 4.
39. Global Circulation Project, founded by Regenia Gagnier and supported by Wiley-Blackwell's Literature Compass. http://www.blackwell-compass.com/subject/literature/.
40. Édouard Glissant, "The Unforeseeable Diversity of the World," trans. Haun Saussy, in *Beyond Dichotomies: Histories, Identities, Cultures, and the Challenge of Globalization*, ed. Elisabeth Mudimbe-Boyi (Albany, N.Y.: SUNY Press, 2002), 290 (original French not available).

41. This chart appeared in "One Hand Clapping," in *Translocal Modernisms*, 24.
42. Ramazani, *A Transnational Poetics*, 11. See also Sally Price, *Primitive Art in Civilized Places* (Chicago: University of Chicago Press, 1989).
43. See for example William Rubin, "Modernist Primitivism: An Introduction," in *"Primitivism" in Twentieth-Century Art: Affinity of the Tribal and the Modern*, ed. William Rubin, vol. 1 (Boston, Mass.: Little, Brown, 1984); Christopher Green, ed., *Picasso's Les Demoiselles d'Avignon* (Cambridge: Cambridge University, 2001).
44. Simon Gikandi, "Picasso, Africa, and the Schemata of Difference," *Modernism/Modernity* 10, no. 3 (September 2003): 455–480.
45. Van Gogh's comment is quoted in Rubin, "Modernist Primitivism," 2.
46. For fuller discussion of the impact of African colonial modernities on Picasso and Japanese modernity on the impressionists, see Friedman, "One Hand Clapping," 29–34.
47. Langston Hughes, *Montage of a Dream Deferred* [1951], in *Collected Poems of Langston Hughes*, ed. Arnold Rampersad with David Roessel (New York: Vintage, 1994), 388; copyright © 1994 by the Estate of Langston Hughes, used by permission of Alfred A. Knopf, an imprint of the Knopf Doubleday Publishing Group, a division of Random House LLC. All rights reserved. See also Arnold Rampersad, "Langston Hughes and Approaches to Modernism in the Harlem Renaissance," in *The Harlem Renaissance Revaluations*, ed. Amrijit Singh, William S. Shiver, and Stanley Brodwin (New York: Garland, 1989), 49–71. For transnational approaches to Harlem Renaissance modernism, see Edward M. Pavlić, *Crossroads Modernism: Descent and Emergence in African-American Literary Culture* (Minneapolis: University of Minnesota Press, 2002); Brent Hayes Edwards, *The Practice of Diaspora: Literature, Translations, and the Rise of Black Internationalism* (Cambridge, Mass.: Harvard University Press, 2003); and the special issue, "In Conversation: The Harlem Renaissance and the New Modernist Studies," *Modernism/Modernity* 20, no. 3 (September 2013), ed. Adam McKible and Suzanne W. Churchill.
48. Tayeb Salih, *Season of Migration to the North* [1966], trans. Denys Johnson-Davies (Boulder, Colo.: Three Continents, 1997); Arundhati Roy, *The God of Small Things* (New York: Random House, 1997), 290. See Friedman, "Periodizing Modernism," 435–439; and "Paranoia, Pollution, and Sexuality."
49. Huyssen, "Geographies of Modernism in a Globalising World," 15, 13.
50. Mary Louise Pratt, "Modernity and Periphery," 40–43.
51. Glissant, *Poétique de la Relation*, 31 (*Poetics of Relation*, 19).
52. Glissant, "The Unforeseeable Diversity of the World," 287.
53. For other theorizations of multilingualism and polyglot languages (including Englishes), see Evelyn Nien-ming Ch'en, *Weird English* (Cambridge, Mass.: Harvard University Press, 2004); Marina Camboni, "Impure Lines: Multilingualism, Hybridity, and Cosmopolitanism in Contemporary Women's Poetry," *Contemporary Women's Writing* 1, no. 1 (December 2007): 34–44; John Marx, *The Modernist Novel and the Decline of Empire* (Cambridge: Cambridge University Press, 2005); Françoise Lionnet, "Continents and Archipelagoes: From *E Pluribus Unum* to Creolized Solidarities," *PMLA* 123, no. 5

(2008): 1503–1515; Stuart Hall, "The Local and the Global: Globalization and Ethnicity," in *Culture, Globalization and the World-System*, ed. Anthony King (Minneapolis: University of Minnesota Press, 1997), 19–40.
54. See Walter D. Mignolo, "Globalization, Civilization Processes, and the Relocation of Languages and Cultures," in *The Cultures of Globalization*, ed. Fredric Jameson and Masao Miyoshi (Durham, N.C.: Duke University Press, 1999), 32–53; Brian Stock, "Toward Interpretive Pluralism: Literary History and the History of Reading," *New Literary History* 39, no. 3 (Summer 2008): 389–413; David Bleich, "Globalization, Translation, and the University Tradition," *New Literary History* 39, no. 3 (Summer 2008): 497–517.
55. See Esther Allen's discussion of "English as an Invasive Species" in "Translation, Globalization, and English," and Simona Škrabec, "Literary Translation: The International Panorama," *Pen/IRL Report on the International Situation of Literary Translation*, ed. Esther Allen (2007), 1–48, http://www.centerforliterarytranslation.org/TranslationReport.
56. See Sheldon Pollock, "Cosmopolitan and Vernacular in History," in *Cosmopolitanism*, ed. Carol A. Breckenridge, Sheldon Pollock, Homi K. Bhabha, and Dipesh Chakrabarty (Durham, N.C.: Duke University Press, 2002), 15–53; Sheldon Pollock, *The Language of the Gods in the World of Men: Sanskrit, Culture, and Power in Premodern India* (Berkeley: University of California Press, 2006); Benedict Anderson, *Imagined Communities: Reflections on the Origins and Spread of Nationalism* [1983] (London: Verso, 2006), 47–82.
57. Muraski Shikidu, *The Tale of Genji*, trans. Edward G. Seidensticker (New York: Knopf, 1978).
58. Maria Rosa Menocal, *The Arabic Role in Medieval Literary History: A Forgotten Heritage* (Philadelphia: University of Pennsylvania Press, 1987), 91–114.
59. Mohanty, "Alternative Modernities and Medieval Indian Literature," 3–5.
60. Rabindranath Tagore, *The Broken Nest/Nashtanir* [1901], trans. Mary M. Lago and Supriya Sen (Columbia: University of Missouri Press, 1971).
61. Amit Chaudhuri, introduction to *The Picador Book of Modern Indian Literature*, ed. Amit Chaudhuri (London: Picador, 2001), xx.
62. Another set of reading strategies is implicit in Melba Cuddy-Keane's identification of "four strands of globalized thinking in modernist texts" aimed at locating what she calls the "critical, syncretic, cohabiting, and runaway modes" of globalized thinking ("Modernism, Geopolitics, Globalization," 545).
63. Simon Gikandi, *Maps of Englishness: Writing Identity in the Culture of Colonialism* (New York: Columbia University Press, 1996). See also Marx, *The Modernist Novel and the Decline of Empire*; Richard Begam and Michael Valdez Moses, eds., *Modernism and Colonialism: British and Irish Literature, 1899–1939* (Durham, N.C.: Duke University Press, 2007). Consideration of East Asia (especially China) in Western modernism is especially well developed; see Stephen G. Yao, *Translation and the Languages of Modernism: Gender, Politics, Language* (New York: Palgrave Macmillan, 2002); Zhaoming Qian, *Orientalism and Modernism: The Legacy of China in Pound and Williams* (Durham, N.C.:

Duke University Press, 1995), *The Modernist Response to Chinese Art: Pound, Moore, Stevens* (Charlottesville: University of Virginia Press, 2003), and *Ezra Pound and China* (Ann Arbor: University of Michigan Press, 2003); Robert Kern, *Orientalism, Modernism, and the American Poem* (Cambridge: Cambridge University Press, 2009); Christopher Bush, *Ideographic Modernism: China, Writing, Media* (Oxford: Oxford University Press, 2010); Eric Hayot, *Chinese Dreams: Pound, Brecht, Tel Quel* (Ann Arbor: University of Michigan Press, 2003) and *The Hypothetical Mandarin: Sympathy, Modernity, and Chinese Pain* (Oxford: Oxford University Press, 2009).

64. Dimock, *Through Other Continents*.
65. Pingali Suranna, *The Sound of the Kiss, or the Story That Must Never Be Told*, trans. Velcheru Narayana Rao and David Shulman (New York: Columbia University Press, 2002); Gurajada Apparao, *Girls for Sale: Kanyasulkam, a Play from Colonial India*, trans. Velcheru Narayan Rao (Bloomington: Indiana University Press, 2007).
66. See edited volumes listed in note 36. Recoveries of Latin American modernisms are particularly prevalent; see Fernando J. Rosenberg, *The Avant-Garde and Geopolitics in Latin America* (Pittsburgh: University of Pittsburgh Press, 2006); Vicky Unruh, *Latin American Vanguards: The Art of Contentious Encounters* (Berkeley: University of California Press, 1994); Cathy L. Jrade, *Modernismo: Modernity and the Development of Spanish American Literature* (Austin: University of Texas Press, 1998). For pre-1500 modernisms in India, see Suranna, *The Sound of the Kiss*, and Mohanty, "Alternative Modernities and Medieval Indian Literature," and for Indian modernisms from the late nineteenth and twentieth centuries, see Priya Joshi, *In Another Country: Colonialism, Culture, and the English Novel in India* (New York: Columbia University Press, 2002); Aparna Dharwadker, "Mohan Rakesh, Modernism, and the Postcolonial Present," *South Central Review* 25, no. 1 (Spring 2008): 136–162.
67. Virginia Woolf, "Time Passes," in *To the Lighthouse* [1927] (New York: Harcourt Brace Jovanovich, 1981), 125–143. See also Ursula K. Heise, *Sense of Place and Sense of Planet: The Environmental Imagination of the Global* (Oxford: Oxford University Press, 2008); Robert Nixon, *Slow Violence and the Environmentalism of the Poor* (Cambridge, Mass.: Harvard University Press, 2012); Lawrence Buell, *The Future of Environmental Criticism: Environmental Crisis and Literary Imagination* (Oxford: Blackwell, 2005); Tsing, *Friction*.
68. Heise, *Sense of Place and Sense of Planet*, 10, 6.
69. Glissant, *Poetics of Relation*, 146, hereafter identified in the text. Phrases from *Poétique de la Relation*, not quoted here, are from 160, 164, 165.

3. STORIES OF MODERNITY: PLANETARY SCALE IN THE *LONGUE DURÉE*

1. This chapter is adapted, woven, and newly configured from a series of linked essays I have written from 1999 to 2006, including (in order of writing) "Cultural Parataxis and Transnational Landscapes of Reading: Toward a Locational Modernist Studies,"

in *Modernism*, ed. Vivian Liska and Astradur Eysteinsson (Philadelphia: John Benjamins, 2007), 35–52; "One Hand Clapping: Colonialism, Postcolonialism, and the Spatio/Temporal Boundaries of Modernism," in *Translocal Modernisms: International Perspectives*, ed. Irene Ramalho Santos and António Sousa Ribeiro (Bern: Peter Lang, 2008), 11–40; "Periodizing Modernism: Postcolonial Modernities and the Space/Time Borders of Modernist Studies," *Modernism/Modernity* 13, no. 3 (September 2006): 425–444; "Unthinking Manifest Destiny: Muslim Modernities on Three Continents," in *Shades of the Planet: American Literature as World Literature*, ed. Wai Chee Dimock and Lawrence Buell (Princeton, N.J.: Princeton University Press, 2007), 39–61. Since the earliest of these, written in 1999 (which quixotically argues for a single category of modernism, with different locational and temporal formations), my thinking has evolved considerably as I read more, particularly in world history, and as I learned from others developing global approaches to pluralized modernities and modernisms.
2. Fredric Jameson, *The Political Unconscious: Narrative as Socially Symbolic Act* (Ithaca, N.Y.: Cornell University Press, 1981), 9; Susan Stanford Friedman, *Mappings: Feminism and the Cultural Geographies of Encounter* (Princeton, N.J.: Princeton University Press, 1998), 130–131; and "Periodizing Modernism," 426.
3. Dilip Parameshwar Gaonkar, "On Alternative Modernities," in *Alternative Modernities*, ed. Dilip Parameshwar Gaonkar (Durham, N.C.: Duke University Press, 2001), 15, 17; hereafter cited in the text. Abbas Milani, *Lost Wisdom: Rethinking Modernity in Iran* (Washington, D.C.: Mage, 2004), 20; Andreas Huyssen, "Geographies of Modernisms in a Globalising World," in *Geographies of Modernism: Literatures, Cultures, Spaces*, ed. Peter Brooks and Andrew Thacker (London: Routledge, 2005), 7. Gaonkar and Huyssen may be echoing Luce Irigaray's profound insights into the liberatory potential of breaking open the ideology of singularity: see Luce Irigaray, *This Sex Which Is Not One*, trans. Catherine Porter (Ithaca, N.Y.: Cornell University Press, 1985).
4. Michel Foucault, "Of Other Spaces" [1984], trans. Jay Miskowiec, *Diacritics* 16 (Spring 1986): 22.
5. Edward W. Soja, *Postmodern Geographies: The Reassertion of Space in Critical Social Theory* (London: Verso, 1989), 11. See also Fernando J. Rosenberg's critique of the emphasis on temporality in modernist studies and development of a non-nation-based spatialized analysis of Latin American avant-gardism in *The Avant-Garde and Geopolitics in Latin America* (Pittsburgh, Penn.: University of Pittsburgh Press, 2006), 12–48.
6. Douglas Mao and Rebecca L. Walkowitz, "The New Modernist Studies," *PMLA* 123, no. 3 (2008): 737–748. For discussion of the spatial turn in modernist studies in the context of geographical theory, see Andrew Thacker, *Moving Through Modernity: Space and Geography in Modernism* (Manchester: University of Manchester Press, 2003).
7. Peter Brooker, Andrzej Gąsiorek, Deborah Longworth, and Andrew Thacker, eds., *The Oxford Handbook of Modernisms* (Oxford: Oxford University Press, 2010); Mark Wollaeger, ed., with Matt Eatough, *The Oxford Handbook of Global Modernisms* (Oxford: Oxford University Press, 2012).

8. The distinction I maintain in this chapter between modernity as the broad-scale geohistorical phenomenon of which modernism is the specifically aesthetic dimension was introduced in chapter 2 and is explored more fully in chapter 5.
9. Eric Hayot, "Against Periodization; or, On Institutional Time," *New Literary History* 42, no. 4 (2011): 740. Katie Trumpener also challenges the institutional hold of conventional periodization in literary studies in job descriptions, syllabi, and library cataloguing: "In the Grid: Period and Experience," *PMLA* 127, no. 2 (March 2012): 349–356. For discussions of periodization, see also the special issue on "Periodization: Cutting Up the Past," *Modern Language Quarterly* 62, no. 4 (December 2001); "Theories and Methodologies: The Long and the Short: Problems of Periodization," *PMLA* 127, no. 2 (March 2012): 301–356; Kathleen Davis, *Periodization and Sovereignty: The Ideas of Feudalism and Secularization Governing the Politics of Time* (Philadelphia: University of Pennsylvania Press, 2008); and Morag Shiach, "Periodizing Modernism," in Wollaeger, ed., *The Oxford Handbook of Global Modernisms*, 25–47.
10. Like Mao and Walkowitz's "The New Modernist Studies," James and Seshagiri's essay "Metamodernism: Narratives of Continuity and Revolution" appears in the Theories and Methodologies section of *PMLA* 129, no. 1 (2014): 87–100. For overviews of modernism published after the "transnational turn" that reinstate the original Euro/American canon, see for example Christopher Butler, *Modernism: A Very Short Introduction* (Oxford: Oxford University Press, 2010); Michael Levenson, ed., *The Cambridge Companion to Modernism* (Cambridge: Cambridge University Press, 1999); Pericles Lewis, *The Cambridge Introduction to Modernism* (Cambridge: Cambridge University Press, 2007). The market appeal of introductions, companions, and handbooks for modernism no doubt reinforces the conservative return of the field to its geographically and temporally narrow origins.
11. Brooker et al., *The Oxford Handbook of Modernisms*.
12. The noun "world" often follows the adjectival period—as in the ancient world, the medieval world—thus illustrating the universalist assumption.
13. J. M. Blaut, *The Colonizer's Model of the World: Geographical Diffusionism and Eurocentric History* (New York: Guilford, 1993); hereafter cited in the text.
14. Marshall Brown, "Periods and Resistance," *Modern Language Quarterly* 62, no. 4 (December 2001): 309, 315.
15. Modernist Studies Association, http://msa.press.jhu.edu/; emphasis added. In contrast to the MSA's official mission statement, its annual conferences and its issues of *Modernism/Modernity* are much more inclusive.
16. Marshall Berman, *All That Is Solid Melts Into Air: The Experience of Modernity* [1982], rev. ed. (New York: Penguin, 1988); Malcolm Bradbury and James McFarlane, ed. *Modernism: A Guide to European Literature, 1890–1930* (New York: Penguin, 1976); Astradur Eysteinsson, *The Concept of Modernism* (Ithaca, N. Y.: Cornell University Press, 1990); Peter Nicholls, *Modernism: A Literary Guide*, rev. ed. (Berkeley: University of California Press, 2009); and Charles Baudelaire, "The Painter of Modern Life," in *Selected Writings on Art and Literature*, trans. R. E. Charvet (New York: Penguin, 1973), 403–405.

Modernism in Spanish has yet another periodization, as Cathy L. Jrade explores in *Modernismo: Modernity and the Development of Spanish American Literature* (Austin: University of Texas Press, 1998). Houston A. Baker Jr.'s pathbreaking book *Modernism and the Harlem Renaissance* (Chicago: University of Chicago Press, 1987) posited a distinctive and differently periodized modernity for African Americans and thus for their particular modernism.

17. The European Network for Avant-Garde and Modernism Studies (EAM), http://www.eam-europe.be/; emphasis added. The websites of the British Association for Modernist Studies (BAMS) and the Australian Modernist Studies Network (AMSN) avoid any reference to modernism's spatio/temporal borders, stating that BAMS "aims to bring together all those in the UK interested in modernism, and to connect outwards globally" (http://www.bams.ac.uk) and AMSN "aims to support and promote modernist studies throughout Australasia and to provide a forum for productive exchange between Australian scholars and the wider international community" (http://www.amsn.org.au).

18. Frantz Fanon, *Black Skins, White Masks: The Experiences of a Black Man in a White World* [1952], trans. Charles Lam Markmann (New York: Grove, 1967).

19. Edward W. Said, *Orientalism* (New York: Vintage, 1978). For postcolonial studies' impact on rethinking modernity, see also Partha Chatterjee, *The Partha Chatterjee Omnibus* (Oxford University Press, 1999); Chakrabarty, *Provincializing Europe*; and Walter D. Mignolo, *The Darker Side of Western Modernity: Global Futures, Decolonial Options (Latin America Otherwise)* (Durham, N. C.: Duke University Press, 2011).

20. Walter Mignolo, "The Many Faces of Cosmo-polis: Border Thinking and Critical Cosmopolitanism," in *Cosmopolitanism*, ed. Carol A. Breckenridge, Sheldon Pollock, Homi K. Bhabha, and Dipesh Chakrabarty (Durham, N. C.: Duke University Press, 2002), 158.

21. Anthony Giddens, *The Consequences of Modernity* (Stanford, Calif.: Stanford University Press, 1990); emphasis added. Hereafter cited in the text. Also see his *Modernity and Self-Identity: Self and Society in the Late Modern Age* (Stanford, Calif.: Stanford University Press, 1991). For a more recent example, see Dorothy Ross, who writes, "I take modernity to denote a stage of history characterized by national state formation, industrialization, and the rise of new ideas of reason, human agency, and historical progress." Dorothy Ross, "American Modernities, Past and Present," *American Historical Review* 116, no. 3 (June 2011): 702. The fact that Ross critiques the Eurocentrism of the linked concepts of American exceptionalism and modernity does not change her perpetuation of that conventional nominal approach to the definition of modernity.

22. Like much contemporary social theory on modernity, Giddens's work shows the pervasive influence of Max Weber, especially *The Protestant Ethic and the Spirit of Capitalism*, trans. Talcott Parsons (New York: Scribner's, 1950). See also Jürgen Habermas, *The Philosophical Discourse of Modernity: Twelve Lectures*, trans. Frederick G. Lawrence (Cambridge, Mass.: MIT Press, 1995); Zygmunt Bauman, *Modernity and Ambivalence* (Ithaca, N.Y.: Cornell University Press, 1991); James C. Scott, *Seeing Like a State: How Certain Schemes to Improve the Human Condition Have Failed* (New Haven, Conn.: Yale University Press, 1998).

23. For discussion of contestations in the discipline of history about periodization, see David Blackbourn, "'The Horologe of Time': Periodization in History," *PMLA* 177, no. 2 (2012): 301–307. The "Theories and Methodologies" section of this issue of *PMLA* focuses on "The Long and the Short: Problems of Periodization" (301–356). For other debate among historians about periodization in general and the periodization of modernity specifically, see the Forum on Modernity, *American Historical Review* 116, no. 3 (June 2001): 663–726.
24. See Susan Gilman's advocacy of the *longue durée* for an oceanic American Studies in "Oceans of *Longue Durées*," *PMLA* 127, no. 2 (March 2012): 328–334; to expanded spatio/temporal scales, she adds the linguistic scale. In her afterword to the *Oxford Handbook of Global Modernisms*, Laura Doyle invokes the *longue durée* going back to what she refers to as the "medieval" period linking especially Spain, North Africa, West Asia, and India (Wollaeger, *Oxford Handbook*, 669–696).
25. Eric Sheppard and Robert B. McMaster, *Scale and Geographical Inquiry: Nature, Society, and Method* (Oxford: Blackwell, 2004). For distinctions between scale in cartography and in human geography, see their "Introduction: Scale and Geographic Inquiry" (1–22) and "Scale and Geographic Inquiry: Contrasts, Intersections, and Boundaries" (256–267) as well as examples of each in their volumes. I am indebted to Nirvana Tanoukhi for directing me to Sheppard and McMaster, in her essay "The Scale of World Literature," in *Immanuel Wallerstein and the Problem of the World*, ed. David Palumbo-Liu, Bruce Robbins, and Nirvana Tanoukhi, (Durham, N.C.: Duke University Press, 2011), 78–98.
26. See especially Malcolm Bradbury, "The Cities of Modernism," in Bradbury and McFarlane, *Modernism*, 96–104.
27. James Joyce, *A Portrait of the Artist as a Young Man* [1916] (New York: 1968), 15–16. Adrienne Rich echoes Stephen's scalar sequence in "Notes Toward a Politics of Location," in *Blood, Bread, and Poetry: Selected Prose, 1979–1985* (New York: Norton, 1986), 210–232.
28. For advocates of the network model of human geography, see for example Peter J. Taylor, "Is There a Europe of Cities? World Cities and the Limits of Geographical Scale Analysis," in Sheppard and McMaster, *Scale and Geographical Inquiry*, 213–235; and Helga Leitner, "The Politics of Scale and Networks of Spatial Connectivity: Transnational Interurban Networks and the Rescaling of Political Governance in Europe," in Sheppard and McMaster, *Scale and Geographical Inquiry*, 236–255. For uses of geographical scale in literary studies, see especially Tanoukhi, "The Scale of World Literature," 78–100; Franco Moretti, "World-Systems Analysis, Evolutionary Theory, *Weltliteratur*," in Palumbo-Liu, Robbins, and Tanoukhi, eds., *Immanuel Wallerstein and the Problem of the World*, 67–77; and Shu-mei Shih, "Relational Comparison," in *Comparison: Theories, Approaches, Uses*, ed. Rita Felski and Susan Stanford Friedman (Baltimore, Md.: Johns Hopkins University Press, 2013), 73–98.
29. Immanuel Wallerstein, *The Modern World-System: Capitalist Agriculture and The Origins of the European World-Economy in the Sixteenth Century* (New York: Academic Press, 1974); and *World-Systems Analysis: An Introduction* (Durham, N.C.: Duke University Press, 2004), hereafter cited as *Introduction*. Wallerstein's "introduction" to decades of

his work both summarizes his theory and methods and addresses his critics. For discussions of Wallerstein's wide-ranging impact, see Palumbo-Liu, Robbins, and Tanoukhi, eds., *Immanuel Wallerstein and the Problem of the World*.

30. Pascale Casanova, *The World Republic of Letters*, trans. M. B. DeBevoise (Cambridge, Mass.: Harvard University Press, 2004); Franco Moretti, "Conjectures on World Literature," *New Left Review* 2nd ser. (January–February 2000): 54–68; and "World-Systems Analysis, Evolutionary Theory, *Weltliteratur*." See my critique of their adaptation of world-systems theory to literary history in "World Modernisms, World Literature, and Comparativity," in Wollaeger, *Oxford Handbook of Global Modernisms*, 499–525.

31. See for example Stephen K. Sanderson and Thomas D. Hall, "World Systems Approaches to World-Historical Change," in *Civilizations and World Systems: Studying World-Historical Change*, ed. Stephen K. Sanderson (London: Sage, 1995), 95–107; Victor Roudometof and Roland Robertson, "Globalization, World-System Theory, and the Comparative Study of Civilizations," in Sanderson, *Civilization and World Systems*, 273–298; André Gunder Frank, *ReOrient: Global Economy in the Asian Age* (Berkeley: University of California Press, 1998) and "The Modern World System Revisited," in Sanderson, *Civilization and World Systems*, 163–194.

32. Frank, "The Modern World System Revisited," in Sanderson, *Civilization and World Systems*, 183. Frank's essay, in which he significantly refuses the hyphen and its meaning in Wallerstein's concept of the world-system, contains the gist of his later book *ReOrient*.

33. Janet L. Abu-Lughod, *Before European Hegemony: The World System, AD 1250–1350* (Oxford: Oxford University Press, 1989); Blaut, *The Colonizer's Model of the World*; Wai Chee Dimock, *Through Other Continents: American Literature Across Deep Time* (Princeton, N.J.: Princeton University Press, 2006); Frank, *ReOrient*; John M. Hobson, *The Eastern Origins of Western Civilisation* (Cambridge: Cambridge University Press, 2004); Marshall G. S. Hodgson, *Rethinking World History: Essays on Europe, Islam, and World History*, ed. Edmund Burke, III (Cambridge: Cambridge University Press, 1993); George Makdisi, *The Rise of Humanism in Classical Islam and the Christian West: With Special Reference to Scholasticism* (Edinburgh: University of Edinburgh Press, 1990); Sanderson, *Civilizations and World Systems*; Milani, *Lost Wisdom*.

34. For an even longer *durée*, see the concept of "deep history," which integrates human civilization pre- and postwriting into a multimillennia approach to human physiology, evolution, and culture. See for example Andrew Shryock, *Deep History: The Architecture of Past and Present* (Berkeley: University of California Press, 2011).

35. Peasant and other women had no such privileges, and this period also saw the rise of concubinage and courtesans, models for the later Japanese geisha; see Mark Edward Lewis, *China's Cosmopolitan Empire: The Tang Dynasty* (Cambridge, Mass.: The Belknap Press of Harvard University Press, 2009), 180–189, hereafter cited in the text.

36. Mary M. Anderson, *Hidden Power: The Palace Eunuchs of Imperial China* (Amherst, N.Y.: Prometheus, 1990). See also Christopher Beckwith, *Empires of the Silk Road* (Princeton, N.J.: Princeton University Press, 2009); T. H. Barrett, *The Woman Who Discovered Printing* (New Haven, Conn.: Yale University Press, 2008).

37. On foreigners residing in China during the Tang Dynasty, Tang fascination with the exotic, and foreign influences in Tang arts and poetry, see Edward H. Schafer, *The Golden Peaches of Samarkand: A Study of T'ang Exotics* (Berkeley: University of California Press, 1963), esp. 14–39. Charles Benn, *China's Golden Age: Everyday Life in the Tang Dynasty* (Oxford: Oxford University Press, 2002), 40–43, also emphasizes the Tang openness to foreign knowledge, including Indian astronomy, astrology, and mathematics (especially the zero, trigonometry, and division of the circle into 360 degrees); Buddhism; and military prowess, reflected in the number of Tang generals who were foreign.
38. These changes are detailed at length in chapters 4–9 of Lewis's *China's Cosmopolitan Empire*, 85–271.
39. Hobson, *Eastern Origins of Western Civilisation*, 50–61.
40. Guanzhou's tourist information first acquainted me with the city's history. See also the following websites: http://travel.cnn.com/quanzhou-chinas-forgotten-historic-port-258149; http://www.pbs.org/wgbh/nova/sultan/archeology.html; http://www.archnet.org/library/sites/one-site.tcl?site_id=9143. Historians typically agree that the Ming Dynasty's policy of isolationism after the 1440s contributed greatly to China's decline and the rise of Europe on the global market; however, Ming China continued substantial illicit trade.
41. Lewis, *China's Cosmopolitan Empire*, 147; see also Benn, *China's Golden Age*, 40–41.
42. See for example Anatoly M. Khazanov, *Nomads and the Outside World*, rev. ed. (Madison: University of Wisconsin Press, 1994); Anatoly M. Khazanov and André Wink, eds., *Nomads in the Sedentary World* (London: Routledge, 2001); David W. Anthony, *The Horse, the Wheel, and Language: How Bronze-Age Riders from the Eurasian Steppes Shaped the Modern World* (Princeton, N.J.: Princeton University Press, 2007); Peter B. Golden, *Nomads and Sedentary Societies in Medieval Eurasia* (Washington, D.C.: American Historical Association, 1998). As an interesting side note on periodization, the terms "medieval," "early modern," and "modern" are variously used by these scholars to describe the periods of Eurasian conquest and empires.
43. For an account of these Eurasian steppe empires, see especially David Morgan, *The Mongols*, rev. ed. (Oxford: Blackwell, 2007); Anthony, *The Horse, the Wheel, and the Sedentary World*, 225–290; Jane Burback and Frederick Cooper, *Empires in World History: Power and the Politics of Difference* (Princeton, N.J.: Princeton University Press, 2010), 93–116; Jerry H. Bentley, *Old World Encounters: Cross-Cultural Contacts and Exchanges in Pre-Modern Times* (New York: Oxford University Press, 1993), 111–164.
44. Khazanov, "Nomads in the History of the Sedentary Worlds," in Khazanov and Wink, *Nomads in a Sedentary World*, 1–23.
45. Benn, *China's Golden Age*, 40–41; Schafer, *The Golden Peaches of Samarkand*, 60–73; Lewis, *China's Cosmopolitan Empire*, 145–178.
46. Genghis Khan is more properly known as Chingiz, Chingiss, or Tchingis Khan; I follow the more familiar English spelling. For the following review of the Mongol Empire, I draw especially on Jack Weatherford, *Genghis Khan and the Making of the Modern World*

3. STORIES OF MODERNITY • 367

(New York: Three Rivers, 2004); David Morgan, *The Mongols*; Burbank and Cooper, *Empires in World History*, 93–117; Timothy May, *The Mongol Conquests in World History* (London: Reaktion, 2012), especially its overview of Mongol historiography; Jean-Paul Roux, *Genghis Khan and the Mongol Empire*, trans. Toula Ballas (New York: Abrams, 2002); Bentley, *Old World Encounters*, 111–164; and Thomas T. Allsen, *Culture and Conquest in Mongol Eurasia* (Cambridge: Cambridge University Press, 2001), *Mongol Imperialism* (Berkeley: University of California Press, 1987), and *Commodity and Exchange in the Mongol Empire* (Cambridge: Cambridge University Press, 1997). See Morgan, *The Mongols*, 5–29, for an in-depth discussion of the varied historical sources used in discussions of the Mongol Empire. Citations from these books will hereafter be in the text.

47. Weatherford relies on a variety of sources as well as on field work in Mongolia, drawing most extensively on *The Secret History of the Mongols*, a Mongolian text written in Chinese characters borrowed from the Uighurs representing thirteenth-century Mongolian and not deciphered until the 1970s. A translation into English appeared in 1980, but on-site fieldwork conducted by Weatherford and Mongolian scholars has been necessary to unravel many aspects of the text (Weatherford, *Genghis Khan*, xxvii–xxx). See also Morgan's discussion of *The Secret History of the Mongols* in relation to the many Persian histories of the Mongols, preeminently that of the Jewish convert to Islam Rashid al-Din, Chinese sources, and European sources (Morgan, *The Mongols*, 5–29).

48. Periodization terms for the Mongol Empire differ. Weatherford openly invokes "modernity" in his title; Morgan in *The Mongols* prefers "medieval"; Allsen typically avoids characterizing the Mongols with such period terms but alludes to premodern, early modern, or modern times in addressing world history.

49. As Weatherford points out, the Mongols differed from the Persians, Chinese, and Europeans, whose rulers and armies used public displays of torture to inspire fear and for entertainment; the Mongols did not "torture, mutilate, or maim" those they conquered (115).

50. Scholars such as Janet Abu-Lughod (*Before European Hegemony*, 153–184) and André Gunder Frank (*ReOrient*, 255–256) point to the significance of the Mongol Empire in challenging Wallerstein's contention that the capitalist world-system begins about 1500 with the rise of the West. But in emphasizing trade, Abu-Lughod and Frank treat the Mongols mainly as conduits between the highly developed and rich cultures of China and India with the less developed and much poorer cultures of Europe.

51. Arthur Waldron, introduction to *The Mongol Period*, by Bertold Spuler, trans. F. R. C. Bagley (Princeton, N.J.: Princeton University Press, 1994), vii; quoted in May, *The Mongol Conquests in World History*, 8; emphasis added. For extended discussion of the Pax Mongolica, see May, *The Mongol Conquests in World History*, 109–129; Burbank and Cooper, *Empires in World History*, 104–111; Allsen, *Culture and Conquest in Mongol Eurasia*, 5, 83–188.

52. On Genghis Khan's Great Law, including relative equality before the law, religious freedom, and the refusal to establish a state religion, see Weatherford, *Genghis Khan*, 55–77;

Morgan, *The Mongols*, 83–87; Roux, *Genghis Khan*, 68; Burbank and Cooper, *Empires in World History*, 108–109. Since no copy of the Great Law has survived, although *The Secret History of the Mongols* and other sources allude to it as a written code, Morgan is cautious about its actual existence: "It is not feasible at this stage to state with certainty that the Great Yasa did not exist: only that the sources which have so far been used to demonstrate the proposition that it did do not show anything of the sort" (*The Mongols*, 87). But he does grant at the very least the existence of "unwritten Mongol customary law," an evolving practice that predated and postdated Genghis Khan (86).

53. For the administrative apparatus of the Mongol Empire (e.g., census, taxes, bureaucracy, military, professionals), see Allsen, *Mongol Imperialism*, 77–216.
54. For the innovations of Genghis Khan and subsequent rulers of the Mongol Empire, especially Khubilai Khan, see Weatherford, *Genghis Khan*, xxii–xxiii, 67–77, 218–240.
55. See Weatherford, *Genghis Khan*, 106; and Janet L. Abu-Lughod, *Before European Hegemony*, 333–334. Abu-Lughod notes that the Mongol Empire improved upon the Song Dynasty's invention of paper money by banning the use of gold and silver in trade.
56. Scholars debate endlessly whether the commercial practices of the world-system before 1500 can be described as "capitalism," with neo-Marxists like Wallerstein and conservatives like Huntington insistent upon reserving the term "capitalism" for the financial practices of the West after 1500. Weatherford doesn't enter this debate over terminology but points out that European feudalism emphasized an ideal of self-sufficiency for the manor, minimal trade in luxury goods for the elite, and the noninvolvement of rulers and aristocratic elites in trade; this he contrasts to the Mongol's emphasis on increased trade of all kinds of goods, the accumulation of wealth, and the close involvement of ruling elites in commercial activities (*Genghis Khan*, 225). See Blaut, *The Colonizer's Model of the World*, 152–178; and Frank, "Modern World System Revisited" for reviews of the debate about the term "capitalism."
57. This evidence of the Mongols' concept of their world rule belies Eric Hayot's assertion in *On Literary Worlds* (Oxford: Oxford University Press, 2012) that "no other modernity-like transformation before it [European modernity] had ever been able to locate its world-view so firmly in the specific spatial extension of the globe and of the cosmos," a "uniqueness" that "produces the historical consciousness of the modern world-view" (117). While the Mongols had no knowledge of the Americas, they operated within a concept of the "whole" world and cosmos.
58. In his extensive review of documentary sources for the Mongol Empire, Morgan explains that *The Secret History* is the "only substantial surviving Mongol work" about the empire from the perspective of the Mongols themselves; other historical documents were written by "the conquered or the hostile" (*The Mongols*, 9).
59. See also Allsen's chapter on Rashid al-Din and the production of histories on a massive scale, particularly in the Persian khanate, in *Culture and Conquest in Mongol Eurasia* (83–102).

3. STORIES OF MODERNITY • 369

60. See Weatherford, *Genghis Khan*, xxii; he believes Genghis Khan, who is known to have entered only one building in his lifetime (at the conquest of Bukhara), built more bridges than any man in history. Subsequent khans became significant builders, as for example Khubilai Khan, who initially built the Forbidden City in Beijing as the walled compound for the Mongol rulers (Weatherford, *Genghis Khan*, 198–199).
61. See Allsen's chart detailing the exchange of professional and artisanal classes "East" and "West" in *Culture and Conquest in Mongol Eurasia*, 6.
62. Blaut argues that disease even more than military technology accounted for the early European conquests in the Americas, with diseases to which the native populations had no immunity killing up to 75 percent of the population in the sixteenth century (*The Colonizer's Model of the World*, 184).
63. Morgan disputes the term religious tolerance to characterize the Mongols and prefers "indifference" (*The Mongols*, 37–38); however, Möngke's analogy of the hand as Rubruck reports it appears consistent with a religious tolerance that did not develop in Europe until after the brutal religious wars of the seventeenth century. See also May's chapter on "Religion and the Mongol Empire," in *The Mongol Conquests in World History*, 172–198; May also points out that "religious toleration appears as a longstanding tradition in Inner Asian empires, perhaps due to it so often being a crossroads for many religious systems" (172).
64. For information on the Roman Catholic and Spanish Inquisitions, see *The Catholic Encyclopedia*. For an account of the debate in Möngke Khan's court, see Weatherford, *Genghis Khan*, 171–174, for which he draws on Rubruck's travel writings reprinted in Dawson.
65. Doyle, afterword, in Wollaeger, *Oxford Handbook of Global Modernisms*, 672–675. See also Burbank and Cooper, *Empires in World History*.
66. William H. McNeill, *The Rise of the West* (Chicago: University of Chicago Press, 2003); Louis Auguste Paul Rougier, *The Genius of the West* (Los Angeles: Nash, 1971); J. M. Roberts, *The Triumph of the West* (Boston: Little, Brown, 1985); Eric L. Jones, *The European Miracle*, 3rd ed. (Cambridge: Cambridge University Press, 2003); and Ricardo Duchesne, *The Uniqueness of Western Civilization* (Leiden: Brill, 2011).
67. I invoke here the standard distinctions in narrative theory between the underlying structure of a narrative and its various discursive formations. See Dan Shen, "Story/Discourse," in *The Routledge Encyclopedia of Narrative Theory*, ed. David Herman, Manfred Jahn, and Marie Laure-Ryan (London: Routledge, 2005), 566–568; Seymour Chatman, *Story and Discourse: Narrative Structure in Fiction and Film* (Ithaca, N.Y.: Cornell University Press, 1978).
68. Wallerstein, *The Modern World-System*, 15.
69. Samuel Huntington, *The Clash of Civilizations and the Remaking of World Order* (New York: Simon and Schuster, 1996), 302.
70. Stuart Hall and Bram Gieben, eds., *Formations of Modernity* (Cambridge, Mass.: Polity, 1992), 277. As a sociology textbook, *Formations of Modernity* reproduces the story of modernity in reductionistically bland terms and from a seemingly neutral standpoint.

71. Martin Bernal, *The Black Athena: The Afroasiatic Roots of Classical Civilization*, vol. 1: *The Fabrication of Ancient Greece, 1785–1985* (New Brunswick, N.J.: Rutgers University Press, 1987).
72. The Modern Language Association, for example, has a Discussion Section called "West Asian Languages and Literatures." The term Coordinated Universal Time (UTC) took the place of Greenwich Mean Time in 1972, although Greenwich still functions as the reference point for global time. The Prime Meridian (zero degrees longitude) has been variously located since the end of the British Empire; the United States currently uses the International Reference Meridian.
73. Blaut, *The Colonizer's Model of the World*, 82–86; Hobson, *The Eastern Origins of Western Civilisation*, 11–19; Hodgson, *Rethinking World History*.
74. Samir Amin, *Eurocentrism* (New York: Monthly Review, 1988).
75. Blaut, *The Colonizer's Model of the World*, 59; hereafter cited in the text. Blaut devotes an extended chapter to this historiography, reviewing theories of European exceptionalism based on biology and race, the environment, rationality, technology, and society (including the state, religion, class, and the family) (50–151).
76. Hobson, *The Eastern Origins of World Civilisation*, 8. Hobson adds the binarisms of gender and race to Blaut's table of nineteenth-century diffusionist thought in binary form (17). Hobson does not reject diffusionism as a model for global influence, but he argues that the advanced economic, technological, and intellectual dimensions of the Orient "diffused" into Europe; he explains the eventual dominance of Europe by emphasizing European agency in adapting practices from the East.
77. Samuel Huntington, "The Clash of Civilizations?" *Foreign Affairs* 72, no. 3 (Summer 1993): 22–49; *The Clash of Civilizations and the Remaking of World Order*, hereafter cited in the text.
78. See Immanuel Wallerstein, "Eurocentrism and Its Avatars: The Dilemmas of Social Science," *New Left Review* 226 (November–December 1997): 93–108; hereafter cited in the text.
79. Stuart Hall and Bram Gieben, eds., *Unthinking Eurocentrism: Multiculturalism and the Media* (London: Routledge, 1994), 3.
80. My colleagues from Korea Jong-Im Lee and Yoon-Young Choi report that this housing trend in Hong Kong is also characteristic of Korea (personal communications, December 2011).
81. As of 2014, Abu Dhabi boasts the tallest skyscraper, but the competition continues.
82. See Friedman, "Unthinking Manifest Destiny," in Dimock and Buell, *Shades of the Planet*, 62–100.
83. Sanderson and Hall, "World System Approaches to World-Historical Change," in Sanderson, *Civilizations and World Systems*, 234.
84. Leslie Bary, "Oswald de Andrade's 'Cannibalist Manifesto,'" trans. Leslie Bary, *Latin American Literary Review* 19, no. 38 (July–December 1991): 38, 39, 40, 41; hereafter cited in the text.
85. Vicky Unruh, *Latin American Vanguards: The Art of Contentious Encounters* (Berkeley: University of California Press, 1994), 40.

86. John King, introduction to *The Cambridge Companion to Modern Latin American Culture* (Cambridge: Cambridge University Press, 2004), 2. See also Neil Whitehead's discussion of European imitation of New World cannibalism in culturally mimetic forms during the period of early contact in his "Monstrosity and Marvel: Symbolic Convergence and Mimetic Elaboration in Transcultural Representation," *Studies in Travel Writing* 1 (1997): 72–96.
87. Rosenberg, *The Avant-Garde and Geopolitics in Latin America*, 78.
88. Anna Lowenhaupt Tsing, "Transitions as Translations," in *Transitions, Environments, Translations: Feminisms in International Politics*, ed. Joan W. Scott, Cora Kaplan, and Debra Keates (London: Routledge, 1997), 255; hereafter cited in the text. Tsing summarizes an account she finds in Richard Grove, *Green Imperialism: Colonial Expansion, Tropical Island Edens, and the Origin of Environmentalism, 1600–1860* (Cambridge: Cambridge University Press, 1995).
89. Anna Lowenhaupt Tsing, *Friction: An Ethnography of Global Connection* (Princeton, N.J.: Princeton University Press, 2004), x–xi.
90. Fanon, *Black Skin, Black Masks*; Bhabha, *The Location of Culture*; Partha Chatterjee, *Nationalist Thought and the Colonial World: A Derivative Discourse?* (1986), in *The Partha Chatterjee Omnibus* (New Delhi: Oxford University Press, 1999), 1–181.
91. Partha Chatterjee, *A Possible India: Essays in Political Criticism* (1997), in *The Partha Chatterjee Omnibus*, 281.
92. Chatterjee, *Nationalist Thought and the Colonial World*, 65.
93. Chakrabarty, *Provincializing Europe*, 39.
94. R. Radhakrishnan, "Derivative Discourses and the Problem of Signification," *The European Legacy* 7, no. 6 (2002): 783–795; hereafter cited in the text.
95. See also Laura Doyle's discussion of the so-called belatedness of non-Western modernities, a view that ignores, she argues, how non-Western knowledges were crucial in the first place to the development of Western modernity (afterword, in Wollaeger, *The Oxford Handbook of Global Modernisms*, 675–680).

4. FIGURES OF MODERNITY: RELATIONAL KEYWORDS

1. Raymond Williams, *Keywords: A Vocabulary of Culture and Society* [1976], rev. ed. (New York: Oxford University Press, 1983); I first adapted his approach to the identification of keywords for modernism's traveling cultures, transculturation, and hybridization in "One Hand Clapping: Colonialism, Postcolonialism, and the Spatio/Temporal Boundaries of Modernism," in *Translocal Modernisms: International Perspectives*, ed. Irene Ramalho Santos and António Sousa Ribeiro (Bern: Peter Lang, 2006), 22–25, and condensed in chapter 2. For other keyword approaches to modernism, see Melba Cuddy-Keane, *Modernism: Keywords* (Oxford: Wiley-Blackwell, 2014), featuring historically oriented keywords such as *new woman*, *primitive*, and *shell shock*; and Eric Hayot and Rebecca L. Walkowitz, eds., *Keywords for Global Modernism* (New York: Columbia University Press, 2015).

372 • 4. FIGURES OF MODERNITY

2. *The Compact Oxford English Dictionary*, "Modern," "Modernism," "Modernity," "Modernize" (Oxford: Oxford University Press, 1971), 1:1828.
3. For discussions of in/commensurability in comparison, see Susan Stanford Friedman, "Why Not Compare?" *PMLA* 126, no. 3 (May 2011): 753–762; and "World Modernisms, World Literature, and Comparativity," in *The Oxford Handbook of Global Modernisms*, ed. Mark Wollaeger, with Matt Eatough (Oxford: Oxford University Press, 2012), 499–525; Natalie Melas, *All the Difference in the World: Postcoloniality and the Ends of Comparison* (Stanford, Calif.: Stanford University Press, 2007).
4. Fredric Jameson, *A Singular Modernity: Essay on the Ontology of the Present* (London: Verso, 2002); Immanuel Wallerstein, "Eurocentrism and Its Avatars: The Dilemmas of Social Science," *New Left Review* 226 (November–December 1997): 93–108.
5. To my knowledge, the notion of strategic essentialism first appears in Gayatri Chakravorty Spivak, "Subaltern Studies: Deconstructing Historiography," in *In Other Worlds: Essays in Cultural Politics* (London: Methuen, 1987), 205. It reappears importantly in her *The Postcolonial Critics: Interviews, Strategies, Dialogues* (London: Routledge, 1990), 11–12, 15.
6. Michel Foucault, "Of Other Spaces" [1984], trans. Jay Miskowiec, *Diacritics* 16, no. 1 (Spring 1986): 22.
7. Here and throughout the chapter, definitions, synonyms, and antonyms are culled from various dictionary and thesaurus resources, with the intent of being suggestive, not exhaustive or definitive.
8. Dilip Parameshwar Gaonkar, "On Alternative Modernities," in *Alternative Modernities*, ed. Dilip Parameshwar Gaonkar (Durham, N.C.: Duke University Press, 2001), 17; hereafter cited in the text.
9. Jameson, *A Singular Modernity*, 12–13; hereafter cited in the text.
10. Bruce Robbins, "Blaming the System," in *Immanuel Wallerstein and the Problem of the World: System, Scale, Culture*, ed. David Palumbo-Liu, Bruce Robbins, and Nirvana Tanoukhi (Durham, N.C.: Duke University Press, 2011), 52.
11. Timothy Mitchell, introduction to *Questions of Modernity*, ed. Timothy Mitchell (Minneapolis: University of Minnesota Press, 2000), xii.
12. Nirvana Tanoukhi, "The Scale of World Literature," in Palumbo-Liu et al., *Immanuel Wallerstein*, 89.
13. Frederick Cooper, *Colonialism in Question: Theory, Knowledge, History* (Berkeley: University of California Press, 2005), 114; see also his discussion of singular modernity, 113–114, 129. In the Forum on Modernity in the *American Historical Review* 116, no. 3 (June 2011), several historians critique the concepts of multiple, alternate, or early modernities. Dipesh Chakrabarty in "The Muddle of Modernity" argues that the concepts emerge from the "sentiment of egalitarianism," lacking historical specificity, but in his critique of Eurocentric periodization of modernity, he offers no substitutes (663–675). Carol Gluck in "The End of Elsewhere: Writing Modernity Now" argues for a concept of conjunctural, coproduced, and global modernity of the past three hundred years and rejects "alternative" and "multiple" modernities as misleading (676–677). As a

medievalist, Carol Symes in "When We Talk About Modernity" argues that modernity as a concept performs "epistemic violence" against all "un-Modern" societies in the past and present and is thus inherently imperialist (715–726).

14. Dipesh Chakrabarty, *Provincializing Europe: Postcolonial Thought and Historical Difference* (Princeton, N.J.: Princeton University Press, 2000), 89; hereafter cited in the text.

15. Peter Nicholls, *Modernisms: A Literature Guide* (Berkeley: University of California Press, 1995). Nicholls published a second edition (New York: Palgrave Macmillan, 2009), which includes a new chapter entitled "African American Modernism" but retains the chapter entitled "At a Tangent: Other Modernisms."

16. Gilles Deleuze and Félix Guattari, *Kafka: Toward a Minor Literature*, trans. Dana Colan (Minneapolis: University of Minnesota Press); Abdul R. JanMohamed and David Lloyd, eds., *The Nature and Context of Minority Discourse* (Oxford: Oxford University Press, 1990); Françoise Lionnet and Shu-mei Shih, eds. *Minor Transnationalism* (Durham, N.C.: Duke University Press, 2005), hereafter cited in the text.

17. Marshall Berman, *All That Is Solid Melts Into Air: The Experience of Modernity* [1982], 2nd ed. (New York: Penguin, 1988), 21. Berman's title alludes to Marx's phrase and discussion of modernity in *The Marx-Engels Reader*, ed. Robert C. Tucker, 2nd ed. (New York: Norton, 1978), 577–578.

18. Rabindranath Tagore, *The Home and the World* [1916] (New York: Penguin, 1985), 26.

19. Rita Felski, *Doing Time: Feminist Theory and Postmodern Culture* (New York: New York University Press, 2000), 69; hereafter cited in text.

20. Eric Hayot, "Chinese Modernism, Mimetic Desire, and European Time," in Wollaeger, ed., *The Oxford Handbook of Global Modernism*, 161–162.

21. Paul de Man, "Literary History and Literary Modernity," in *Blindness and Insight* (Minneapolis: University of Minnesota Press, 1983), 147–148.

22. On the invention of tradition, see Arjun Appadurai, *Modernity at Large* (Minneapolis: University of Minnesota Press, 1996), 44; Edward Shils, *Tradition* (Chicago: University of Chicago Press, 1981); and Eric Hobsbawm and Terrence Ranger, eds., *The Invention of Tradition* (Cambridge: Cambridge University Press, 1983). In *Questions of Tradition* (Toronto: University of Toronto Press, 2004), editors Mark Salber Phillips and Gordon Schochet challenge the purely constructionist view of tradition as invented and make a distinction between "tradition" as tacit custom and established folkways versus "traditionalism" as an ideological effect of modernity. See also James Clifford's dialectical understanding of tradition/modernity in "Traditional Futures," in *Questions of Tradition*, 152. For a different view, see Michael Valdez Moses, *The Novel and the Globalization of Culture* (New York: Oxford University Press, 1995); although he brings attention to the modernisms produced in the postcolonies, Moses finds in these texts a critique of Western modernity based in the authors' premodern and traditional cultural contexts (esp. xiv–xvi, 24–25, 107–92). Like many social theorists, Moses argues that modernization causes global homogenization, and he regards the premodern and the traditional in the Third World as forces of resistance to modernity's homogenization. Others, like Clifford in "Traditional Futures," Gaonkar in "On Alternative Modernities," and Victor

374 • 4. FIGURES OF MODERNITY

Roudeometof in "Globalization or Modernity?" (*Comparative Literature Review* no. 31 [1994]: 18–45) argue against this view, suggesting instead that globalization heightens the indigenizations of traveling cultures and the ensuing hybrid heterogeneity of local cultures.

23. Dipesh Chakrabarty, *Habitations of Modernity: Essays in the Wake of Subaltern Studies* (Chicago: University of Chicago Press, 2002), 127–128. See also his "Adda, Calcutta: Dwelling in Modernity" for discussion of the Bengali traditional practice of male chatting with intimate friends as a "modern" form of resistance to modernization, in Gaonkar, *Alternative Modernities*, 123–164.
24. See for example Leslie Marmon Silko, *Ceremony* (New York: Signet, 1977); Louise Erdrich, *Tracks* (New York: Harper Perennial, 1988); and Linda Hogan, *Solar Storms: A Novel* (New York: Scribner, 1995).
25. David McFadden, "Showcasing a Unique Culture," *Wisconsin State Journal* (August 19, 2012): T1–2.
26. In *On the Move: Mobility in the Modern Western World* (London: Routledge, 2006), Tim Cresswell argues for mobility as a constitutive component of modernity, but he considers modernity only in its Western formation (see esp. 1–24). For discussion of "the mobility paradigm" in social science, see John Urry, *Mobilities* (Malden, Mass.: Polity, 2007), 44–63; his approach is global but deals only with twentieth- and twenty-first-century mobilities, arguing that 1990 represents a major turning point.
27. Arjun Appadurai, *Modernity at Large: Cultural Dimensions of Globalization* (Minneapolis: University of Minnesota Press, 1996), 37; hereafter cited in the text.
28. Nikos Papastergiadis, *The Turbulence of Migration: Globalization, Deterritorialization, and Hybridity* (Cambridge: Polity, 2000), 12, 13, 15.
29. Stuart Hall and Bram Gieben, *Formations of Modernity*, 15–16.
30. Henry Adams, "The Dynamo and the Virgin" [1900], in *The Education of Henry Adams* (1918; Blacksburg, Va.: Wilder, 2009), 243–249.
31. Enda Duffy, *The Speed Handbook: Velocity, Pleasure, Modernism* (Durham, N.C.: Duke University Press, 2009), 10, 11. Although he does not emphasize speed, Andrew Thacker in *Moving Through Modernity: Space and Geography in Modernism* (Manchester: University of Manchester Press, 2003) emphasizes the new technologies of mobility in early-twentieth-century modernism.
32. Marian Aguiar, *Tracking Modernity: India's Railway and the Culture of Mobility* (Minneapolis: University of Minnesota Press, 2011).
33. Zygmunt Bauman, *Culture as Praxis* [1973], rev. ed. (London: Routledge, 1999), xxiii, xxx; hereafter cited in the text.
34. Kären Wigen, "Cartographies of Connection: Ocean Maps as Metaphors for Inter-Area History," in Palumbo-Liu et al., *Immanuel Wallerstein*, 138, 144.
35. George P. Landow, *Hypertext 3.0: Critical Theory and New Media in an Era of Globalization* [1992], 3rd ed. (Baltimore: Johns Hopkins University Press, 2006), 53–68.
36. Albert-László Barabási, *Linked: How Everything Is Connected to Everything Else and What It Means for Business, Science, and Everyday Life* (New York: Plume, 2002), 7.

4. FIGURES OF MODERNITY • 375

For an overview of social network theory in sociology and anthropology, see John Scott, *Social Network Analysis: A Handbook*, 2nd ed. (London: Sage, 2000).

37. Manuel Castells, *The Rise of the Network Society*, 2nd ed. (Oxford: Blackwell-Wiley, 2010). For a discussion of Castells in the context of network theory more generally, see Felix Stalder, *Manuel Castells* (Cambridge: Polity, 2006), esp. 169–181.

38. For Deleuzian/Guattarian network theory, see especially Gilles Deleuze and Félix Guattari, *A Thousand Plateaus: Capitalism and Schizophrenia*, trans. Brian Massumi (Minneapolis: University of Minnesota Press, 1987), 3–25. They stress that a rhizome is "unlike a structure" and is "composed not of units but of ... directions in motion." It "is made only of lines" and "operates by variation, expansion, conquest, capture, offshoots. ... In contrast to centered (even polycentric) systems with hierarchical modes of communication and preestablished paths, the rhizome is an acentered, nonhierarchical, nonsignifying system ... defined solely by a circulations of states" (21).

39. For the combination of systems and network theory in mathematics, sciences, and the social sciences, see John Urry's chapter on network theory in *Mobilities* (211–229).

40. See for example Niklas Luhmann, *Introduction to Systems Theory*, ed. Dirk Baeker, trans. Peter Gilgen (2002; Cambridge: Polity, 2013); Hans-Georg Moeller, *Luhmann Explained: From Souls to Systems* (Chicago: Open Court, 2006); William Rasch, *Niklas Luhmann's Modernity: The Paradoxes of Differentiation* (Stanford, Calif.: Stanford University Press, 2000).

41. For Bourdieu's concept of habitus, see especially "Structures, Habitus, Practices," in *The Logic of Practice* (52–79), where he defines the habitus at one point as a "system of dispositions" that have been "durably inculcated by the possibilities and impossibilities, freedoms and necessities, opportunities and prohibitions" that are "a product of history" (54–55). Since Bourdieu conceives of the habitus as a "system of structured, structuring dispositions" (52), his concept of cultural practice is somewhat closer to the Malinowskian concept of culture as system that Bauman critiques, but it shares with Bauman's view a spatialized concept of cultural dynamism and mobility.

42. Édouard Glissant, "Unforseeable Diversity of the World," in *Beyond Dichotomies: Histories, Identities, Cultures, and the Challenge of Globalization*, ed. Elisabeth Mudimbe-Boyi (Albany, N.Y.: SUNY Press, 2002), 287–295.

43. On the Caribbean, see also Urry, *Mobilities*, where he argues that "the modern Caribbean ... is the result of multiple, intersecting mobilities. Indeed it has been more deeply and continuously affected by migration than any other world region; the essence of Caribbean life is movement" (57).

44. See for example the section on oceanic studies in "Theories and Methodologies," *PMLA* 125, no. 3 (May 2010): 657–636; Ian Baucom, *Specters of the Atlantic: Finance Capital, Slavery, and the Philosophy of History* (Durham, N.C.: Duke University Press, 2005); Jerry H. Bentley, Renate Bridenthal, and Kären Wigen, eds., *Seascapes: Maritime Histories, Littoral Cultures, and Transoceanic Exchanges* (Honolulu: University of Hawaii Press, 2007); Paul Gilroy, *The Black Atlantic: Modernity and Double Consciousness* (Cambridge, Mass.: Harvard University Press, 1993); *Indian Ocean Studies: Cultural,*

Social, and Political Perspectives, ed. Shanti Moorthy and Ashraf Jamal (London: Routledge, 2009).

45. Basil Davidson, *Africa in History* [1966], rev. ed. (New York: Touchstone, 1995), 61–140. On Timbuktu as an intellectual/religious center with some 150 to 180 Qur'anic schools and vast libraries, see Brent D. Singleton, "African Bibliophiles: Books and Libraries in Medieval Timbuktu," *Libraries and Culture* 39, no. 1 (Winter 2004): 1–12.

46. David Wilkinson, "Central Civilization," in *Civilizations and World Systems: Studying World-Historical Change*, ed. Stephen K. Sanderson (London: Sage, 1995), 47–49.

47. James Clifford, "Traveling Cultures," in *Routes: Travel and Translation in the Late Twentieth Century* (Cambridge, Mass.: Harvard University, 1997), 17–46, 2. For hybridization as the ordinary process of cultural formation, see Renato Resaldo, *Culture and Truth: The Remaking of Social Analysis* (Boston: Beacon, 1993), 196–217. For an overview of travel theory, see Caren Kaplan, *Questions of Travel: Postmodern Discourses of Displacement* (Durham, N.C.: Duke University Press, 1996).

48. Mary Louise Pratt, *Imperial Eyes: Travel Writing and Transculturation* (London: Routledge, 1992); Walter Mignolo, *Local Histories/Global Designs: Coloniality, Subaltern Knowledges, and Border Thinking* (Princeton, N.J.: Princeton University Press, 2000).

49. Edward W. Said, "Traveling Theory," in *The World, the Text, and the Critic* (Cambridge, Mass.: Harvard University Press, 1983), 226–247; and "Traveling Theory Reconsidered," in *Reflections on Exile and Other Essays* (Cambridge, Mass.: Harvard University Press, 2002), 436–452.

50. David Damrosch, *What Is World Literature?* (Princeton, N.J.: Princeton University Press, 2003); Wai Chee Dimock, *Through Other Continents: American Literature Across Deep Time* (Princeton, N.J.: Princeton University Press, 2006); Jahan Ramazani, *A Transnational Poetics*; B. Venkat Mani, "Bibliomigrancy: Book-Series and the Making of World Literature," in *The Routledge Companion to World Literature*, ed. Theo D'haen, David Damrosch, and Djelal Kadir (New York: Routledge, 2011), 283–296; Rebecca L. Walkowitz, *Born Translated: The Contemporary Novel in an Age of World Literature* (New York: Columbia University Press, 2015).

51. See for example Jennifer Wicke, "Appreciation, Depreciation: Modernism's Speculative Bubble," *Modernism/Modernity* 8, no. 3 (September 2001): 389–404; and "The Bananas of Modernity," unpublished paper; Stewart Lee Allen, *The Devil's Cup: Coffee, the Driving Force in History* (London: Soho, 1999); Mike Sash, *Tulip Mania: The Story of the World's Most Coveted Flower and the Extraordinary Passions It Aroused* (New York: Three Rivers, 1999); Sidney W. Mintz, *Sweetness and Power: The Place of Sugar in Modern History* (New York: Penguin, 1985); Reay Tannahill, *Food in History* [1973], rev. ed. (New York: Broadway, 1995); Jack Turner, *Spice: The History of a Temptation* (New York: Vintage, 2004); Larry Zuckerman, *The Potato* (New York: North Point, 1998). On Europe's relatively sudden ability to compete strongly in the global markets after the conquest of the Americas (especially with its silver and gold) and the slave trade, see J. M. Blaut, *The Colonizer's Model of the World: Geographical Diffusionism and Eurocentric History* (New York: Guilford, 2003), 179–205; André Gunder Frank, *ReOrient: Global Economy in the Asian Age* (Berkeley: University of California Press, 1998), 277–320.

52. Zuckerman, *The Potato*, 6–7.
53. Toni Morrison, *Beloved* (New York: Random House, 1987), 193.
54. Tayeb Salih, *Season of Migration to the North* [1966], trans. Denys Johnson-Davies (Boulder, Colo.: Three Continents, 1997).
55. Julio Ramos, *Divergent Modernities: Culture and Politics in Nineteenth-Century Latin America*, trans. John D. Blanco (Durham, N.C.: Duke University Press, 2001).
56. José David Saldívar, foreword to *Divergent Modernities: Culture and Politics in Nineteenth-Century Latin America*, by Julio Ramos, trans. John D. Blanco (Durham, N.C.: Duke University Press, 2001), xi–xxxiv.
57. Fernando J. Rosenberg, *The Avant-Garde and Geopolitics in Latin America* (Pittsburgh, Penn.: University of Pittsburgh Press, 2006).
58. Laura Doyle, "Afterword: Modernist Studies and Inter-Imperiality in the Longue Durée," in *The Oxford Handbook of Global Modernisms*, ed. Mark Wollaeger, with Matt Eatough (Oxford: Oxford University Press, 2012), 674–675.
59. I am freely amending Foucault's influential, multifaceted neologism in "Of Other Spaces," 22–27, hereafter cited in the text. As a fairly recent neologism, synonyms and antonyms don't (yet) exist. See Thacker's discussion of heterotopias in modernism in *Moving Through Modernity*, 22–29.
60. Arundhati Roy, "The Greater Common Good," in *The Cost of Living* (New York: Modern Library, 1999), 15, 80.
61. "The Judgement of the Supreme Court of India," October 18, 2000, http://www.narmada.org/sardar-sarovar/sc.ruling/.
62. Ramachandra Guha, "The Arun Shourie of the Left," *The Hindu* (November 26, 2000); and "Perils of Extremism," *The Hindu* (December 17, 2000), http://www.narmada.org/debates/ramguha. Gail Omvedt, "An Open Letter to Arundhati Roy," http://www.narmada.org/debates/gail/gail.open.letter.html/.
63. Walter Benjamin, "Theses on the Philosophy of History," in *Illuminations: Essays and Reflections*, ed. Hannah Arendt (1950; New York: Schocken, 1968), 257–258.
64. Garry Leonard, "'The Famished Roar of Automobiles': Modernity, the Internal Combustion Engine, and Modernism," in *Disciplining Modernism*, ed. Pamela L. Caughie (New York: Palgrave Macmillan, 2010), 221–241.
65. Zygmunt Bauman, *Liquid Modernity* (Cambridge: Polity, 2000), 2.

5. MODERNITY'S MODERNISMS: AESTHETIC SCALE AND PRE-1500 MODERNISMS

1. In "Languages Other Than English," Gayatri Chakravorty Spivak warned against the conflation of modernism with modernity, suggesting that "modernism" should retain its association with a "named movement" located in the West (Conference on Comparative Modernisms, Medialities, Modernities, New York University/Fordham University/Modern Language Initiative, May 4–5, 2012). Katie Trumpener favors the narrow, period boundaries in "Modernist Geographies: The Provinces and the World," in The Global Circulation Project Forum on *Global Modernisms, Literature Compass* 9, no. 9

(September 2012): 623–630. See also David James and Urmila Seshagiri, "Metamodernism: Narratives of Continuity and Revolution," *PMLA* 129, no. 1 (2014): 87–100.
2. See for example Pericles Lewis, *The Cambridge Introduction to Modernism* (Cambridge, Mass.: Cambridge University Press, 2007), 3–10; Malcolm Bradbury and James McFarlane, eds., *Modernism: A Guide to European Literature, 1890–1930* [1976], 2nd ed. (New York: Penguin, 1991), esp. 24–28, 36, 48–50.
3. See for example Harry Levin, "What Was Modernism?" [1960], in *Refractions: Essays in Comparative Literature* (Oxford: Oxford University Press, 1966), 271–295; Maurice Beebe, "What Modernism Was," *Journal of Modern Literature* 3, no. 5 (July 1974): 1065–1084; Robert Martin Adams, "What Was Modernism?" *Hudson Review* 31, no. 1 (Spring 1978): 19–33; Patrick Zuk, "What Was Modernism?" *Journal of Music* 4, no. 5 (September–October 2004); Raymond Williams, "When Was Modernism?" *New Left Review* 1, no. 175 (May–June 1989), http://www.newleftreview.org.ezproxy.library.wisc.edu/I/175/raymond.williams/.
4. Malcolm Bradbury and James McFarlane, "The Name and Nature of Modernism," in Bradbury and McFarland, *Modernism*, 27.
5. Pascale Casanova, *The World Republic of Letters*, trans. M. B. DeBevoise (Cambridge, Mass.: Harvard University Press, 2004). Casanova relies heavily on a center/periphery model of a literary world-system, with occasional reference to Wallerstein. Franco Moretti's sociology of the novel in "Conjectures on World Literature" is more direct in invoking Wallerstein, but he also posits a literary world-system of "weak" and "strong" literatures operating generically without reference to the economic and geopolitical world-system (*New Left Review*, 2nd ser. [January–February 2000]: 54–68).
6. For the term "social philology" and the critical practice of reading it, see Rachel Blau DuPlessis, *Genders, Races, and Religious Cultures in Modern Poetry, 1908–1934* (Cambridge: Cambridge University Press, 2001).
7. Douglas Mao and Rebecca L. Walkowitz, "The New Modernist Studies," *PMLA* 123, no. 3 (2008): 737–748. In *Gender of Modernity* (Cambridge, Mass.: Harvard University Press, 1995), Rita Felski called for a distinction to be made between "modernism" and "modern" literature, reserving the term "modernism" for conventionally understood experimentalist work and using the term "modern" as the more general period term (22–29); however, modernist studies has expanded the meanings of modernism rather than adopting the term *modern* to encompass a variety of aesthetic styles.
8. Hayot, "Chinese Modernism, Mimetic Desire, and European Time," 151. Although Hayot is sympathetic to efforts to break the Eurocentric hold on the field, his discussions of modernism remain within what he calls "European time."
9. For new approaches in translation studies, see Lawrence Venuti, ed., *The Translation Series Reader* (New York: Routledge, 2000); Emily Apter, *The Translation Zone: A New Comparative Literature* (Princeton, N.J.: Princeton University Press, 2006) and *Against World Literature: On the Politics of Untranslatability* (London: Verso, 2013).
10. I allude to the debate on "distant" versus "close" reading in Franco Moretti, "Conjectures on World Literature"; and Gayatri Chakravorty Spivak, *Death of a Discipline* (New York: Columbia University Press, 2003).

11. Mark Edward Lewis, *China's Cosmopolitan Empire: The Tang Dynasty* (Cambridge, Mass.: Harvard University Press, 2009), 241–271; hereafter cited in the text. Li Bo and Du Fu are also commonly Romanized as Li Po and Tu Fu. For an earlier Tang poetry innovator writing during the reign of Empress Wu, see Richard M. W. Ho, *Ch'en Tzu-Ang: Innovator in T'ang Poetry* (London: School of Oriental and African Studies, 1993).
12. David Hinton, *The Selected Poems of Li Po*, trans. David Hinton (New York: New Directions, 1996), 126n41.
13. David Young, introduction to *The Clouds Float North: The Complete Poems of Yu Xuanji*, trans. David Young and Jiann I. Lin (Hanover, N.H.: Wesleyan University Press, 1998), xi.
14. See Jeanne Larsen, *Brocade River Poems: Selected Works of the Tang Dynasty Courtesan Xue Tao*, trans. Jeanne Larsen (Princeton, N.J.: Princeton University Press, 1987). For other Tang women poets, see Young and Lin, *The Clouds Float North*; Jeanne Larsen, *Willow, Wine, Mirror, Moon: Women's Poems from Tang China*, trans. Jeanne Larsen (Rochester, N.Y.: Boa, 2005); Christopher Kelen, Hilda Tam, Song Zijiang, Iris Fan, and Carol Ting, *Poem on a Plane Tree's Leaf: Women Poets of the Tang Dynasty, New Translations* (Virtual Artists Collection, 2011).
15. Ezra Pound's *Cathay* (1915) includes his translations of Li Bo, whom he calls after his Japanese name, Rihaku; see Ming Xie, *Ezra Pound and the Appropriation of Chinese Poetry: Cathay, Translation, and Imagism* (London: Routledge, 1998); Stephen G. Yao, *Translation and the Languages of Modernism: Gender, Politics, Language* (New York: Palgrave Macmillan, 2002).
16. David Young, *Five T'ang Poets*, trans. and introduced by David Young (Oberlin, Ohio: Oberlin College Press, 1990), 77, 79; used by permission; hereafter cited in the text.
17. David Hinton, *The Selected Poems of Tu Fu*, trans. David Hinton (London: Anvil, 1990), viii.
18. Eva Shan Chou, *Reconsidering Tu Fu: Literary Greatness and Cultural Context* (Cambridge: Cambridge University Press, 1995), 4, 2–11; used by permission, copyright © Cambridge University Press; hereafter identified in the text. Chou's readings continuously emphasize the impact of historical context. Although Li Bo is known for his focus on inner subjectivity, see his "War South of the Great Wall" and "Spending the Night Below Wu-Sung Mountain, in Old Mrs. Hsün's House" for examples of poems that blend war and suffering with the poet's feelings, in Hinton, *The Selected Poems of Li Po*, 58–59, 116.
19. Lewis (251) cites Stephen Owen, *The Great Age of Chinese Poetry: The High T'ang*, ed. and trans. Stephen Owen (New Haven, Conn.: Yale University Press, 1981), 201; used by permission, copyright © 1981 Yale University Press. For another powerful translation, see J. P. Seaton and James Cryer, *Bright Moon, Perching Bird: Poems by Li Po and Tu Fu* (Middletown, Conn.: Wesleyan University Press, 1987), 65. See in that volume Du Fu's "Golden Countryside" (51) and "Drinking Alone" (55) for poems conveying a similarly bleak sensibility alluding to societal chaos relieved only by the possibility of poetry.

20. Young, *Five T'ang Poets*, 85–87; Young's selection reproduces only a part of the poem.
21. This section is adapted from Susan Stanford Friedman, "Unthinking Manifest Destiny: Muslim Modernities on Three Continents," in *Shades of the Planet: American Literature as World Literature*, ed. Wai Chee Dimock and Lawrence Buell (Princeton, N.J.: Princeton University Press, 2007), 62–100.
22. For Baghdad during the Abbasid Caliphate, see Hugh Kennedy, *When Baghdad Ruled the Muslim World: The Rise and Fall of Islam's Greatest Dynasty* (Cambridge, Mass.: Da Capo, 2004); Albert Hourani, *A History of the Arab Peoples* (Cambridge, Mass.: Harvard University Press, 1991), esp. 33–36, 189–205; Fatima Mernissi, *Islam and Democracy: Fear of the Modern World* [1992], trans. Mary Jo Lakeland, 2nd ed. (New York: Basic Books, 2001), 6–7, 34–37.
23. André Gunder Frank, "The Modern World System Revisited: Rereading Braudel and Wallerstein," in *Civilizations and World Systems*, ed. Stephen K. Sanderson (Walnut Creek, Calif.: Altamira, 1995), 166.
24. Regina Krahl and John Guy, *Shipwrecked: Tang Treasures and Monsoon Winds* (Washington, D.C.: Smithsonian Books, 2011).
25. "Iraq and China: Ceramics, Trade, and Innovation" (Washington, D.C.: Smithsonian Institution, 2005), 1. See also Jessica Hallett, "Iraq and China; Trade and Innovation in the Early Abbasid Period," *TAOCI, Chine-Méditerranée: Routes and échanges del la céramique avant le XVIe siècle* 4 (December 2005): 21–29.
26. Hallett, "Iraq and China," 21; she cites evidence that communication between Basra and Chinese potters led to the adaptation of some Chinese wheel and shaping technologies (25). See also Alan Caiger-Smith, *Tin-Glaze Pottery in Europe and the Islamic World: The Tradition of One Thousand Years in Maiolica, Faience, and Delftware* (London: Faber and Faber, 1973); and *Lustre Pottery: Technique, Tradition and Innovation in Islam and the Western World* (London: Faber and Faber, 1985).
27. See Caiger-Smith, *Lustre Pottery*, 24–26; and Oliver Watson, *Persian Lustre Ware* (London: Faber and Faber, 1985).
28. Caiger-Smith, *Lustre Pottery*, 21–25; *Tin-Glaze Pottery*, 24, 25, 27.
29. "Iraq and China"; Caiger-Smith, *Tin-Glaze Pottery*, 28; *Lustre Pottery*, 51–154; and on the history of Spode's Willow, http://spodemuseumtrust.org/history-of-spode.html.
30. Janet L. Abu-Lughod, *Before European Hegemony: The World System, AD 1250–1350* (Oxford: Oxford University Press, 1989).
31. On India's "early modernity," see for example Sanjay Subrahmanyam, "Hearing Voices: Vignettes of Early Modernity in South Asia, 1400–1750," *Daedalus* 127, no. 3 (Summer 1998): 75–104.
32. Jonardon Ganeri, *The Lost Age of Reason: Philosophy in Early Modern India, 1450–1700* (Oxford: Oxford University Press, 2011).
33. For accounts of Tamerlane's empire, see Jane Burbank and Frederick Cooper, *Empires in World History: Power and the Politics of Difference* (Princeton, N.J.: Princeton University Press, 2010), 113–114, 172–173; John Darwin, *After Tamerlane: The Global History of Empire Since 1405* (New York: Bloomsbury, 2008), 4–6.

34. Ronit Ricci, *Islam Translated: Literature, Conversion, and the Arabic Cosmopolis of South and Southeast Asia* (Chicago: University of Chicago Press, 2011), 4; Ricci does not discuss Tamerlane's conversions in the north, focusing instead on southern India, Malaysia, and Indonesia.
35. Vinay Dharwadker, introduction to *Kabir: The Weaver's Songs*, trans. Vinay Dharwadker (London: Penguin, 2003), 13; hereafter identified in the text. For more discussion of the "two centuries Hindu-Muslim symbiosis" (67) in northern India, Kabir's biography, and his written/oral afterlife, see Charlotte Vaudeville, *A Weaver Named Kabir: Selected Verses with a Detailed Biographical and Historical Introduction* (Delhi: Oxford University Press, 1993).
36. Dharwadker identifies three major mediating strands of Kabir written/oral traditions, each with its own particular emphases and deployments: the "northern line," established by the Sikhs, who produced the first manuscript in 1570; the "western line" in Rajasthan, which used and expanded the manuscript of 1582; and the "eastern line" in the Benares region, which remained largely oral until it produced a manuscript in 1805 (27–41).
37. Arvind Krishna Mehrotra, *Songs of Kabir*, trans. Arvind Krishna Mehrotra (New York: NYRB, 2011), 14; used by permission, copyright © Arvind Krishna Mehrotra; hereafter cited in the text. One section Mehrotra calls "Against Pundits and Muezzins" is devoted to Kabir's attacks on established religions (19–34). Mehrotra reviews the many editions and translations of Kabir (xxi–xxix) and bases his translations, including numerous contemporary allusions, on "Parasnath Tiwari's landmark *Kabir-granthavali* of 1961" (xxix).
38. A. K. Ramanujan, "Men, Women, and Saints," in *The Collected Essays of A. K. Ramanujan*; cited in Mehrotra, *Songs of Kabir*, 51. See also Ramanujan's introduction to his *Speaking of Śiva* (London: Penguin, 1973) for an account of the *bhakti* tradition in Kannada and his translation of four Kannada *bhakti* poet-saints, including the woman Mahādēviyakka.
39. My thanks to Mukti Lakhi Mangharan for sending me the link to these films: http://www.kabirproject.org/thefilms.
40. Hayot, "Chinese Modernism," 155, 162–163. The same contradiction underlies Hayot's probing account of modernity in *On Literary Worlds* (Oxford: Oxford University Press, 2012); see especially 116–117, where he acknowledges the significance of the concept of multiple modernities through time but insists upon the uniqueness and totality of Western modernity before which any other instances must pale.

6. CIRCULATING MODERNISMS: COLLAGES OF EMPIRE IN FICTIONS OF THE LONG TWENTIETH CENTURY

1. Jahan Ramazani, *A Transnational Poetics* (Chicago: University of Chicago Press, 2009), 9; hereafter cited in the text. Zygmunt Bauman, *Culture as Praxis* [1970], rev. ed. (London: Sage, 1999), xx–xxix.

2. Simon Gikandi, *Maps of Englishness: Writing Identity in the Culture of Colonialism* (New York: Columbia University Press, 1996), 3.
3. Walter Mignolo, "The Many Faces of Cosmo-polis: Border Thinking and Critical Cosmopolitanism," in *Cosmopolitanism*, ed. Carol A. Breckenridge, Sheldon Pollock, Homi K. Bhabha, and Dipesh Chakrabarty (Durham, N.C.: Duke University Press, 2002), 158.
4. Sergei M. Eisenstein, "The Principles of Film Form," *Close Up* 8, no. 3 (September 1931): 167–181.
5. Michel Foucault, "Of Other Spaces," trans. Jay Miskowiec, *diacritics* 16, no. 1 (Spring 1986): 22.
6. Homi K. Bhabha, *The Location of Culture* (London: Routledge, 1994). Although Bhabha does not invoke Luce Irigaray, his analysis of mimicry parallels her earlier concept of parody as a means for deconstructing the politics of gender underlying Western philosophy; see her *Speculum of the Other Woman*, trans. Gillian C. Gill (Ithaca, N.Y.: Cornell University Press, 1985); and "The Power of Discourse and the Subordination of the Feminine," in *This Sex Which Is Not One*, trans. Catherine Porter (Ithaca, N.Y.: Cornell University Press, 1985), 68–86.
7. Edward W. Said, "Traveling Theory," in *The World, the Text, and the Critic* (Cambridge: Harvard University Press, 1983), 227; hereafter cited in the text.
8. Edward W. Said, "Traveling Theory Reconsidered" [1994], in *Reflections on Exile and Other Essays* (Cambridge, Mass.: Harvard University Press, 2002), 436; hereafter cited in the text.
9. Chapters 1 and 2 of *Transnational Poetics* present a powerful paradigm for reading twentieth-century poetry in English within a transnational frame that eludes the diffusionist and center/periphery models.
10. Clifford, "Traveling Cultures"; Arjun Appadurai, *Modernity at Large: Cultural Dimensions of Globalization* (Minneapolis: University of Minnesota Press, 1996), 27–65.
11. See Revanthi Krishnaswamy, "Connections, Conflicts, Complicities," in *The Postcolonial and the Global*, ed. Revathi Krishnaswamy and John C. Hawley (Minneapolis: University of Minnesota Press, 2008), 11. Much influenced by anthropologists such as James Clifford, Arjun Appadurai, Neil Whitehead, and Anna L. Tsing, I published a similar argument about cultural circulation, indigenization, and vernacularization (written in 2004, published in 2007, integrated into chapter 3) in "One Hand Clapping: Colonialism, Postcolonialism, and the Spatio/Temporal Boundaries of Modernism," in *Translocal Modernisms: International Perspectives*, ed. Irene Ramalho Santos and António Sousa Ribeiro (New York: Peter Lang, 2008), 11–40.
12. Readings in this section are adapted from Susan Stanford Friedman, "Cultural Parataxis and Transnational Landscapes of Reading: Toward a Locational Modernist Studies," in *Modernism*, ed. Astradur Eysteinsson and Vivian Liska (Amsterdam: John Benjamins, 2007), 35–52; and "Periodizing Modernism: Postcolonial Modernities and the Space/Time Borders of Modernist Studies," *Modernism/Modernity* 13, no. 3 (September 2006): 425–444.
13. Joseph Conrad, *Heart of Darkness* [1899], Norton Critical Edition, ed. Paul B. Armstrong (New York: Norton, 2006); hereafter cited in the text. In *A Personal Record* (1912),

Conrad recalls that at about nine years of age "while looking at a map of Africa of the time and putting my finger on the blank space then representing the unsolved mystery of that continent . . . I said to myself . . . 'When I grow up I shall go *there*'" (quoted in Armstrong, *Heart of Darkness*, 242). See "Conrad in the Congo" in Armstrong's edition for excerpts from Conrad's letters, "Congo Diary," and "Up-river Book" about his six-month stay in the Congo (242–273).

14. Chinua Achebe, "An Image of Africa: Racism in Conrad's *Heart of Darkness*," in Armstrong, *Heart of Darkness*, 336–348. Edward W. Said, "Two Visions in *Heart of Darkness*," in *Culture and Imperialism* (New York: Vintage, 1993), 19–31. Marianne DeKoven, *Rich and Strange: Gender, History, Modernism* (Princeton, N.J.: Princeton University Press, 1991), 85–138.

15. Regelind Farn, *Colonial and Postcolonial Rewritings of* Heart of Darkness: *A Century of Dialogue with Joseph Conrad* (Boca Raton, Fla.: Dissertation.com, 2005). As extensive as Farn's archive is, he misses Virginia Woolf's important recasting of Marlow's voyage upriver in her first novel, *The Voyage Out* [1915] (London: Vintage, 2000), which I discuss in some detail in "Cultural Parataxis and Transnational Landscapes of Reading," 35–52.

16. There is, of course, much critical debate about Conrad's views on colonialism. I read *Heart of Darkness* in the context of the widespread attacks at the time on the particular brutality of Belgian imperialism in the Congo, a huge, heavily populated, and resource-rich area that King Leopold of Belgium claimed as his personal property. His practice of cutting off the hands and feet of black Africans was bitterly satirized in Mark Twain's *King Leopold's Soliloquy* (1905). Attacks on Belgian imperialism did not always imply similar critiques of European, British, and American forms of imperialism in general; indeed, they sometimes represented hierarchies of value within the West itself, implying, for example, that the British Empire exercised its authority in a moral way, accepting the "white man's burden" to "civilize" the colonized rather than to brutalize them.

17. Tayeb Salih, *Season of Migration to the North* [1966], trans. Denys Johnson-Davies (Boulder, Colo.: Three Continents, 1997); hereafter cited in the text. Criticism on the novel has proliferated rapidly; although references to Salih's echoing of *Heart of Darkness* abound, Saree Makdisi is one of the very few to consider *Season* within the context of modernism, in "The Empire Renarrated: *Season of Migration to the North* and the Reinvention of the Present," *Critical Inquiry* 18 (Summer 1992): 804–820. For discussion of Salih's community of exiles and writers in Beirut, see Mona Takieddine Amyuni, introduction to *Season of Migration to the North, by Tayeb Salih: A Casebook* (Beirut: American University of Beirut, 1985); Philip Sadgrove, "Al-Tayyib Salih," *African Writers*, ed. Brian C. Cox (New York: Charles Scribner's, 1997), 2:733–744. For selected discussions of the novel, see especially Amyuni's *Casebook*, produced in Beirut; Ali Abdalla Abbas, "Notes on Tayeb Salih: *Season of Migration to the North* and *The Wedding of Zein*," *Sudan Notes and Records* 55 (1974): 46–60; John E. Davidson, "In Search of a Middle Point: The Origins of Oppression in Tayeb Salih's *Season of Migration to the North*," *Research in African Literatures* 20, no. 3 (Fall 1989): 385–400; Patricia Geesey, "Cultural

Hybridity and Contamination in Tayeb Salih's *Mawsim al-hijira ila al-Shamal (Season of Migration to the North),*" *Research in African Literatures* 28 (Fall 1997): 128–140; Brian Gibson, "An Island Unto Himself? Masculinity in *Season of Migration to the North,*" *Jouvert* 7, no. 1 (Autumn 2002); Barbara Harlow, "Othello's Season of Migration," *Edebiyat* 4, no. 2 (1979): 157–175; Wail S. Hassan, *Tayeb Salih: Ideology and the Craft of Fiction* (Syracuse, N.Y.: Syracuse University Press, 2003), 82–128; R. S. Krishnan, "Reinscribing Conrad: Tayeb Salih's *Season of Migration to the North,*" *International Fiction Review* 23, nos. 1–2 (1996): 7–15; Muhammed Siddiq, "The Process of Individuation in Al-Tayyeb Salih's Novel *Season of Migration to the North,*" *Journal of Arabic Literature* 9 (1978): 67–104; Gayatri Chakravorty Spivak, *Death of a Discipline* (New York: Columbia University Press, 2003), 54–66.

18. Edward W. Said, *Culture and Imperialism* (New York: Vintage, 1993), 30.
19. Urszula Horoszko, "Terror and Irony of Eastern Europe in Joseph Conrad's *Heart of Darkness,*" unpublished paper.
20. For the relation of the novel to *Heart of Darkness*, see especially Mohammad Shaheen, "Tayeb Salih and Conrad," *Comparative Literature Studies* 22, no. 1 (1985): 156–171; Krishnan, "Reinscribing Conrad"; Said, *Culture and Imperialism*, 30, 211–212; Hassan, *Tayeb Salih*, 82–90; and Spivak, *Death of a Discipline*, 54–66.
21. For discussion of *Season* and other contemporary Arab novels (especially by Lebanese writers) as part of an "Arab modernism," see Saree Makdisi, "'Postcolonial' Literature in a Neocolonial World: Modern Arabic Culture and the End of Modernity," *boundary 2* 22, no. 1 (1995): 104–105.
22. On Mustafa's hypermasculinity and its relationship to colonialism, see Gibson, "An Island Unto Himself?"; Wail S. Hassan, "Gender (and) Imperialism: Structures of Masculinity in Tayeb Salih's *Season of Migration to the North,*" *Men and Masculinities* 5, no. 3 (2003): 309–324; Spivak also briefly discusses gender, modernity, and tradition in *Season*, noting Salih's displacements of the familiar binary (*Death of a Discipline*, 54–66).
23. Constance E. Berkley and Osman Hassan Ahmed, eds., *Tayeb Salih Speaks: Four Interviews with the Sudanese Novelist*, trans. Berkley and Ahmed (Washington, D.C.: Embassy of the Democratic Republic of the Sudan, 1982), 15–16.
24. Dipesh Chakrabarty, *Habitations of Modernity: Essays in the Wake of Subaltern Studies* (Chicago: University of Chicago Press, 2002), 115–137.
25. This section is adapted from Susan Stanford Friedman, "Paranoia, Pollution, and Sexuality: Affiliations Between E. M. Forster's *A Passage to India* and Arundhati Roy's *The God of Small Things,*" in *Geomodernisms: Race, Modernism, Modernity*, ed. Laura Doyle and Laura Winkiel (Bloomington: Indiana University Press, 2005), 245–261.
26. Sara Suleri, *The Rhetoric of English Empire* (Chicago: University of Chicago Press, 1932), 132. On homoerotic Orientalism, see also Joseph Allen Boone, "Vacation Cruises; or, The Homoerotics of Orientalism," *PMLA* 110, no. 1 (January 1995): 89–107; for a more sympathetic treatment of Forster's liberalism, see Benita Parry, *Delusions and Discoveries: Studies on India in the British Imagination, 1880–1930* (London: Penguin, 1972), 260–320.

27. P. N. Furbank, *E. M. Forster: A Life* (New York: Harcourt Brace, 1981), 2:68–70.
28. E. M. Forster, *A Passage to India* [1924] (New York: Harcourt Brace and World, 1984), 183; hereafter cited in the text. For some discussions of the cave episode, see Brenda R. Silver, "Periphrasis, Power, and Rape in *A Passage to India*," *Novel* 22 (Fall 1988): 86–105; Jo Ann Hoeppner Moran, "E. M. Forster's *A Passage to India*: What Really Happened in the Caves," *Modern Fiction Studies* 34, no. 4 (Winter 1988): 596–604; Frances Restuccia, "'A Cave of My Own': The Sexual Politics of Indeterminacy," *Raritan* 2 (Fall 1989): 110–128; R. Radhakrishnan, "Why Compare?" in *Comparison: Theories, Approaches, Uses*, ed. Rita Felski and Susan Stanford Friedman (Baltimore, Md.: Johns Hopkins University Press, 2013), 29–33.
29. Jenny Sharpe, *Allegories of Empire: The Figure of Woman in the Colonial Text* (Minneapolis: University of Minnesota Press, 1993), 113–117.
30. Michel-Rolph Trouillot, "Anthropology and the Savage Slot: The Poetics and Politics of Otherness," in *Recapturing Anthropology: Working in the Present*, ed. Richard G. Fox (Santa Fe, N.M.: School of American Research Press, 1991), 17–44.
31. Frantz Fanon, *Black Skin, White Masks: The Experiences of a Black Man in a White World* [1952], trans. Charles Lam Markmann (New York: Grove, 1967).
32. Arundhati Roy, *The God of Small Things* (New York: Random House, 1997), hereafter cited in the text. For other discussions of Roy, see Alex Tickell, *Arundhati Roy's* The God of Small Things: *A Routledge Study Guide* (New York: Routledge, 2007); R. K. Dhwan, *Arundhati Roy: The Novelist Extraordinary* (New Delhi: Prestige, 1999); Amar Nath Prasad, *Arundhati Roy's* The God of Small Things: *A Critical Appraisal* (New Delhi: Sarup and Sons, 2004); Susan Stanford Friedman, "Feminism, State Fictions, and Violence: Gender, Geopolitics, and Transnationalism," *Communal/Plural* 9, no. 1 (2001): 112–129.
33. Roy's novel has many Indian intertexts as well, especially the *Mahabharata*, Mul Raj Anand's *Untouchable* [1940] (New York Penguin, 1986), and Salman Rushdie's *Midnight's Children* [1981] (New York: Random House, 2006).
34. For Roy's rewriting of Harper Lee's *To Kill a Mockingbird*, see Tracy Lemaster, "Influence and Intertextuality in Arundhati Roy and Harper Lee," *Modern Fiction Studies* 65, no. 4 (Winter 2010): 788–814.
35. See R. Franke, "The Kerala Model of Development: A Debate (Part I)," *Bulletin of Concerned Asian Scholars* 30, no. 3 (July–September 1998): 25–36.
36. Arundhati Roy, *The Cost of Living* (New York: Modern Library, 1999); *Power Politics*, 2nd ed. (Cambridge, Mass.: South End, 2001); *War Talk* (Cambridge, Mass.: South End, 2003).
37. Suleri, *The Rhetoric of English Empire*, 132–148. For Forster's relationships with Syed Ross Masood and Mohammed el Adl, see Furbank, *E. M. Forster: A Life*, 1:143–146, 167–169, 180–183, 193–197, 202–203, 246–247; Wendy Moffat, *A Great Unrecorded History: A New Life of E. M. Forster* (New York: Farrar, Strauss and Giroux, 2010), 88–91, 102–105, 151–180, 188–190.

38. For discussions of Forster's homosexuality, see especially Robert K. Martin and George Piggford, eds., *Queer Forster* (Chicago: University of Chicago Press, 1997); Elaine Freedgood, "E. M. Forster's Queer Nation: Taking the Closet to the Colony in *A Passage to India*," *Genders* 23 (1996): 123–144.
39. See Furbank, *E. M. Forster: A Life*, 1:255–260, 2:106–120; Forster, *The Manuscripts of* A Passage to India, correlated with Forster's final version by Oliver Stallybrass (New York: Homes and Meier, 1978); Robert L. Harrison, *The Manuscripts of* A Passage to India (diss. University of Texas, Austin, 1964); June Perry Levine, "An Analysis of the Manuscripts of *A Passage to India*," *PMLA* 85 (March 1975): 284–294.
40. Sigmund Freud, *Dora: An Analysis of a Case of Hysteria* [1904], ed. Philip Rieff (New York: Collier, 1961).
41. Forster, *Manuscripts*, 580. In the outline, the Englishwoman is assaulted in a cave but not by Aziz, with whom she is in love. See alternative discussions of the manuscript versions in Levine, "Analysis"; Harrison, "Manuscripts"; and Sharpe, *Allegories*, 113–117.
42. Forster, *Manuscripts*, 243. Ellipsis in the original.
43. E. M. Forster, *Maurice* (New York: Norton, 1972), 192. Ellipsis in the original.
44. Joseph Breuer and Sigmund Freud, *Studies in Hysteria* [1892] (New York: Avon, 1966).
45. For an anthropological study of cross-racial intimacy in the context of empire, see Ann Laura Stoler, *Carnal Knowledge and Imperial Power: Race and the Intimate in Colonial Rule* (Berkeley: University of California Press, 2002).
46. Readings in this section are adapted from Susan Stanford Friedman, "Towards a Transnational Turn in Narrative Theory: Literary Narratives, Traveling Tropes, and the Case of Virginia Woolf and the Tagores," *Narrative* 19, no. 1 (January 2011): 1–32.
47. Ann Ardis, *New Woman, New Novels: Feminism and Early Modernism* (New Brunswick, N.J.: Rutgers University Press, 1990); Virginia Woolf, *The Voyage Out* [1915] (London: Vintage, 2000); and *Night and Day* [1919] (London: Vintage, 2000).
48. Uma Narayan, *Dislocating Cultures: Identities, Traditions, and Third World Feminism* (London: Routledge, 1997), 6; hereafter cited in the text.
49. Tani E. Barlow, "What Is a Poem? The Event of Women and the Modern Girl as Problems in Global or World History," in *Immanuel Wallerstein and the Problem of the World: System, Scale, Culture*, ed. David Palumbo-Liu, Bruce Robbins, and Nirvana Tanoukhi (Durham, N.C.: Duke University Press, 2011), 159.
50. I review debates about transnational feminism in *Mappings: Feminism and the Cultural Geographies of Encounter* (Princeton, N.J.: Princeton University Press, 1998), 3–14, 107–131; see also Myra Marx Ferree and Aili Mari Tripp, eds., *Global Feminism: Transnational Women's Activism, Organizing, and Human Rights* (New York: NYU Press, 2006); Inderpal Grewal and Caren Kaplan, eds., *An Introduction to Women's Studies: Gender in a Transnational World* (New York: McGraw Hill, 2002); Chandra Talpade Mohanty, *Feminism Without Borders: Decolonizing Theory, Practicing Solidarity* (Durham, N.C.: Duke University Press, 2003); Valentine M. Moghadam, *Globalizing Women: Transnational Feminist Networks* (Baltimore, Md.: Johns Hopkins University Press, 2005).

51. Virginia Woolf, *A Room of One's Own* [1929] (New York: Harcourt Brace Jovanovich, 1957), 101; hereafter cited in the text.
52. For oedipal and preoedipal structures in narrative theory, see for example Peter Brooks, *Reading for the Plot: Design and Intention in Narrative* (New York: Knopf, 1984); Roland Barthes, "Introduction to the Structuralist Analysis of Narratives," in *A Barthes Reader*, ed. Susan Sontag (New York: Hill and Wang, 1982), 295; Teresa De Lauretis, *Alice Doesn't: Feminism, Semiotics, Cinema* (Bloomington: Indiana University Press, 1984); Marianne Hirsch, *The Mother-Daughter Plot: Narrative, Psychoanalysis, Feminism* (Bloomington: Indiana University Press, 1989); Rachel Blau DuPlessis, *Writing Beyond the Ending: Narrative Strategies of Twentieth-Century Women Writers* (Bloomington: Indiana University Press, 1985); Susan Winnett, "Coming Unstrung: Women, Men, Narrative, and Principles of Pleasure," in *Narrative Dynamics*, ed. Brian Richardson (Columbus: Ohio State University Press, 2002), 138–158; and Susan Stanford Friedman, "Lyric Subversion of Narrative in Women's Writing: Virginia Woolf and the Tyranny of Plot," in *Reading Narrative: Form, Ethics, Ideology*, ed. James Phelan (Columbus: Ohio State University Press, 1989), 162–185. Like Freud's theory of gender-differentiated psychosexual development, psychoanalytic narrative theory assumes triadic family structures based in father, mother, and child, without significant consideration of siblings or extended families.
53. See Susan Stanford Friedman, "Migration, Encounter, and Indigenization: New Ways of Thinking About Intertextuality in Women's Writing," in *European Intertexts: Women's Writing in English in a European Context*, ed. Patsy Stoneman, Vita Fortunati, and Eleonora Federici (Berlin: Peter Lang, 2005), 215–271, for discussion of indigenizations of Woolf's tropes from *A Room of One's Own* and "Professions for Women" (Shakespeare's sister, a room of one's own, and the angel in the house) in the work of Jyotirmoyee Devi, Alice Walker, Pamela Mordecai, Yuen Chiung-Chiung, and Maria Aurèlia Capmany. See also Brenda R. Silver's *Virginia Woolf Icon* (Chicago: University of Chicago, 1999) and Natalya Reinhold's *Woolf Across Cultures* (New York: Pace University Press, 2004).
54. James Joyce, *Ulysses* [1922], ed. Hans Walter Gabler (New York: Random House, 1986), 10:859–860, 865–866, 875–875.
55. See Susan Stanford Friedman, "Reading Joyce: Icon of Modernity? Champion of Alterity? Ventriloquist of Otherness?" in *Joycean Cultures/Culturing Joyce*, ed. Vincent J. Cheng, Kimberly J. Devlin, and Margot Norris (Newark: University of Delaware Press, 1998), 113–133, for a full discussion of Dilly and Stephen at the bookcarts and its significance for Joyce's treatment of gender in *Ulysses*.
56. Woolf began reading the episodes of *Ulysses* in 1918 as they appeared in *The Little Review*; she took notes on the novel in 1918 and 1919, explicitly refers to Joyce in "Modern Fiction," and uses her diary to work through her ambivalent response to *Ulysses*. See Hermione Lee, *Virginia Woolf* (New York: Vintage, 1996), 384–387, 397, 400, 433; Brenda R. Silver, *Virginia Woolf's Reading Notebooks* (Princeton, N.J.: Princeton University Press, 1983), 155–157.

57. Olive Schreiner, *From Man to Man* [1926] (London: Virago, 1982), 219. My thanks to Susan D. Bernstein for directing me to this passage in Schreiner's novel.
58. Woolf did, however, know *An African Farm*, and she reviewed the volume of Schreiner's letters that appeared in 1924, praising the "brilliance" of *An African Farm*, which reminded her of the Brontës, but ultimately dismissing her for her egotism and didacticism on "sex questions"; see Virginia Woolf, "Olive Schreiner," in *The Essays of Virginia Woolf, 1925–1930*, vol. 4, ed. Andrew McNeillie (London: Hogarth, 1994), 5. The hybrid form of *From Man to Man* looks ahead to Woolf's early drafts for what became *The Years* (1937); originally, she planned an "essay-novel" that would combine fiction and polemical essay, but dissatisfied with the blend of the didactic and the fictional, she split "The Partigers" into two texts that would become *The Years* and *Three Guineas*; see Mark Hussey, *Virginia Woolf A to Z: The Essential Reference to Her Life and Writing* (Oxford: Oxford University Press, 1995), 291–294.
59. Alison Booth points out (personal communication to author) that women writers in Britain had long faced the question of why there were no "women Shakespeares" as a challenge to their gender. Such anxieties surely migrated to the colonies along with settlers and then circulated back to Britain.
60. For histories of the Tagore family, see Krishna Dutta and Andrew Anderson, *Rabindranath Tagore: The Myriad-Minded Man* (London: I. B. Tauris, 2009), 1–46; Andrew Robinson, *The Art of Rabindranath Tagore* (London: Andre Deutsch, 1989), 17–42; Krishna Kripalani, *Rabindranath Tagore—A Biography* [1962], ed. Supriya Roy (New Delhi: UBS, 2008), 1–46; Uma Das Gupta, *Rabindranath Tagore: A Biography* (New Delhi: Oxford University Press, 2004), 1–9; and Chitra Deb, *Women of the Tagore Family*, trans. Amita Chowdhry and Sona Roy (New Delhi: Penguin, 2010).
61. For histories of her life, see "Swarnakumari Devi," in *Women Writing in India: 600 BC to the Present*, ed. Susie Tharu and L. Lalita, vol. 1, *600 BC to the Early Twentieth Century* (New York: Feminist Press, 1991), 235–238; Deb, *Women*, esp. 46–69, 173–174; Rajul Sogani and Indira Gupta, introduction to *The Uprooted Vine*, by Swarnakumari Debi, trans. Rajul Sogani and Indira Gupta (New Delhi: Oxford University Press, 2004); C. Vijayasree, introduction to *An Unfinished Song*, by Swarnakumari Devi Ghosal, ed. C. Vijayasree (New Delhi: Oxford University Press, 2008). On how to refer to or alphabetize her name (e.g., Swarnakumari, Tagore, Devi/Debi, or Ghosal), Anupam Basu explains (personal communication to author) that elite nineteenth-century women in Bengal who remained in seclusion would be known solely by their given names, not by their father's or husband's names; men as well as women were called only by their given names (i.e., Rabindranath, not Tagore). Devi or Debi was an honorific for married women, akin to Madame or Mrs. But as elite Bengali women began to emerge from seclusion, they variously used their husband's name or Devi/Debi as a surname; today, some Bengali women writers are alphabetized and alluded to in English as Devi or Debi as if this were a surname. I use Swarnakumari Devi, alphabetizing under Swarnakumari, except for her books published with her husband's surname, Ghosal.

62. Sogani and Gupta, introduction, viii.
63. Quoted in Tharu and Lalita, "Swarnakumari Devi," 237.
64. Quoted in Tharu and Lalita, "Swarnakumari Devi," 238.
65. Other translations of Swarnakumari Devi's work include *The Uprooted Vine*, hereafter cited in the text; *The Fatal Garland* (*Phuler Mala*) in *The Modern Review* in 1910; a collection of her short stories into English; the play *Dibya Kamal* into German (Sogani and Gupta, introduction, viii). The biographies of Tagore by Kripilani and Dutta and Anderson devote from one sentence to one paragraph to Swarnakumari Devi and contain nothing on the brother-sister relationship while extensively covering Tagore's relationship with his older brothers. The Tagore daughters are not included in William Radice's Tagore family tree in his introduction to *Selected Short Stories*, by Rabindranath Tagore, trans. William Radice, rev. ed. (London: Penguin, 2005), 324; nor does Radice mention Swarnakumari Devi in his substantial introduction to Tagore's life and work (1–28).
66. See the chapters on Bankim Chandra Chatterjee and another early woman writer, Krupa Satthianadhan, in Priya Joshi, *In Another Country: Colonialism, Culture, and the English Novel in India* (New York: Columbia University Press, 2002), 141–204.
67. Sogani and Gupta, introduction to *The Uprooted Vine*, xvii.
68. Suzanne Keen, *Victorian Renovations of the Novel: Narrative Annexes and the Boundaries of Representation* (Cambridge: Cambridge University Press, 1998).
69. For Sanskrit narrative theory, see *Routledge Encyclopedia of Narrative Theory*, ed. David Herman, Manfred Jahn, and Marie-Laure Ryan (London: Routledge, 2005), 15; Patrick Colm Hogan and Lalita Pandit, "Toward a Cognitive Science of Poetics: Anandavardhana, Abhinavagupta, and the Theory of Literature," in the special issue on "Comparative Poetics: Non-Western Traditions of Literary Theory," *College English* 23, no. 1 (February 1996): 164–178.
70. See Virginia Woolf, *The Diary of Virginia Woolf, 1915–1919*, vol.1, ed. Anne Olivier Bell (New York: Harcourt Brace Jovanovich, 1977), 165. In an entry dated November 8, 1930, of *The Diary of Virginia Woolf, 1925–1930*, vol. 3, ed. Anne Olivier Bell (New York: Harcourt Brace Jovanovich, 1980), Woolf notes Yeats's account of Tagore's notions about dreaming (329). Neither Swarnakumari Devi nor Tagore appears in Silver's *Virginia Woolf's Reading Notebooks*, Lee's biography, or any of the other standard biographies of Woolf.
71. Some fifty-nine of Tagore's more than ninety short stories were written during this decade, when he often lived on a houseboat going from village to village, mostly separated from his wife and children in Kolkata (Radice, introduction, 1–11; Dutta and Anderson, *Tagore*, 108–123).
72. See discussions of Tagore's identification with the plight of women in Mary M. Lago, introduction to *The Broken Nest*, by Rabindranath Tagore (Columbia: University of Missouri Press, 1971); Anita Desai, introduction to *Selected Short Stories*, by Rabindranath Tagore, trans. Rajul Sogani and Indira Gupta (New Delhi: Oxford University Press, 2004), 1–18; Joyaspree Mukerji, introduction to *She: Short Stories of Rabindranath Tagore*,

trans. Joyaspree Mukerji (New Delhi: UBS, 2004), ix–x; Sharmistha Mohanty, preface to *Rabindranath Tagore: Broken Nest and Other Stories*, trans. Sharmistha Mohanty (Chennai: Transquebar, 2009), x–xvii.

73. In addition to "The Notebook," *The Broken Nest*, and *The Home and the World*, see especially "The Postmaster," "Letter from a Wife," "Haimanti," "The Austere Wife," "Matchmaking," and "The Rejected Story" (variously collected in editions of Tagore's short stories translated into English).

74. See for example "The Postmaster," "Taraprasanna's Fame," "The Editor," "The Notebook," "Letter from a Wife," "Haimati," "The Rejected Story," and "Humbled Ego." The male writer in "Kabuliwallah" is a favored character, rare in Tagore's fiction.

75. Irony is pronounced throughout Tagore's short stories. Radice claims that "the great French and Russian masters" were not available to Tagore when he wrote his short stories (introduction, 28), but Lalita Pandit believes that writers like Chekov were widely available in Bengal in the late nineteenth century (personal communication to author). It is not clear how much Tagore's striking irony is individual to him, indigenous to Bengali intellectual culture, or indigenized from his exposure to European literature.

76. Dutta and Lago, translator's preface to Tagore, *Selected Short Stories*, 43; hereafter cited in the text.

77. Tagore, *Reminiscences* [1917] (London: Macmillan, 1961), 4.

78. For examples of Tagore's literary theory promoting Bengali literature based in vernacular speech and oral traditions instead of Sanskritized, highly artificial poetic Bengali, see "Baul Songs" and "Rural Literature" in Rabindranath Tagore, *Selected Writings on Literature and Language*, ed. Sukanta Chaudhuri (New Delhi: Oxford University Press, 2001), 42–50, 128–137. For discussions of Tagore's search in his prose style for direct speech instead of stylized conventions, see Mukerji, introduction, vii; Desai, introduction, 1; Dutta and Lago, translator's preface, 19; Lago, introduction to *Broken Nest*, 6–9, 15. For discussion of Tagore's essays on folk literature published in the 1890s, see Radice, introduction to *Selected Short Stories*, 15–16.

79. Rabindranath Tagore, *The Broken Nest* [1901], trans. Mary M. Lago and Supriya Sen (Columbia: University of Missouri Press, 1971), hereafter cited in the text; first published serially in 1901 as *Nastanir*; for publication history, see Lago, introduction, 1. Upon his return to Kolkata, Tagore began writing longer prose fiction narratives, including *The Broken Nest* (1901), *A Grain of Sand* (1903), *Gora* (1909), *Quartet* (1916), and *The Home and the World* (1916). With its intersections of nationalist and domestic narratives, *The Home and the World* has received the most critical attention. See for example Patrick Colm Hogan, *Empire and Poetic Voice: Cognitive and Cultural Studies of Literary Tradition and Colonialism* (Albany, N.Y. SUNY Press, 2004), 53–90; and Sangeeta Ray, *En-Gendering India: Woman and Nation in Colonial and Postcolonial Narratives* (Durham, N.C.: Duke University Press, 2000), 90–125.

80. Bankim Chandra Chatterji, *The Poison Tree*, trans. Marian Maddern and S. N. Mukherjee (New Delhi: Penguin, 1996); Rabindranath Tagore, *A Grain of Sand/Chokher Bali* [1903], trans. Sreejata Guha (New Delhi: Penguin, 2003).

81. See Lago, introduction, 10; Dutta and Anderson, *Tagore*, 82.
82. On Tagore's close relationship with Kadambari and its underlying eroticism, her suicide, his lifelong attachment to her, and his paintings most likely of her, see Dutta and Anderson, *Tagore*, 87–91; Kripalani, *Tagore*, 52–60, 117–119, 179, 276; and Deb, *Women*, 79–94. Kadambari was closely associated with the family's journal, *Bharati*, and at her death Tagore and his brother announced its demise. Instead, Swarnakarmi Devi took over its editorship in 1985, thus becoming linked with Kadambari (Kripalani, *Tagore*, 119). For many examples of Tagore's paintings said to be of Kadambari, see Robinson, *Art of Rabindranath Tagore*.
83. Dutta and Anderson, *Tagore*, 79.
84. Kadambari built a charming garden on the terrace connected to the inner quarters, where Tagore often spent hours in her company (Deb, *Women*, 82).
85. For discussion of another colonial writer whose "modern" style drew on vernacular oral traditions, see Edwige Tamalet Talbaryev's discussion of the Algerian Berber poet Jean El Mouhoub Amrouche in "Berber Poetry and the Issue of Derivation: Alternate Symbolist Trajectories," in *The Oxford Handbook of Global Modernisms*, ed. Mark Wollaeger, with Matt Eatough (Oxford: Oxford University Press, 2012), 81–109.
86. Lago, introduction, 1–3.
87. See Dutta and Anderson, *Tagore*, 36, 85; Kripalani, *Tagore*, 24–27.
88. Malavika Karlekar, *Re-Visioning the Past: Early Photography in Bengal, 1875–1915* (New Delhi: Oxford University Press, 2005), 119–120; the book contains a number of photos of Tagore family members.
89. Deb, *Women*, 31–46; Karlekar, *Re-Visioning the Past*, 94–95.
90. Woolf, *Diary*, 3:208.
91. For Woolf's well-known bitterness about the differential education of the boys and girls in the Stephens family, see especially Virginia Woolf, *A Sketch of the Past*, in *Moments of Being*, ed. Jeanne Schulkind, 2nd ed. (New York: Harcourt Brace Jovanovich, 1985), 125–126; hereafter cited in the text.
92. Lee, *Virginia Woolf*, 115; see also Quentin Bell, *Virginia Woolf: A Biography* (New York: Harcourt Brace Jovanovich, 1972), 1:27.
93. Virginia Woolf, *Jacob's Room* [1922] (London: Hogarth, 1990). See also Woolf's *Three Guineas* [1938] (New York: Harcourt, 2006), in which the sibling trope of brothers and sisters (often in direct competition and conflict) is more pervasive than tropes about the tyranny of fathers, especially 12, 18, 33, 37, 39–40, 53, 55, 60, 73, 80, 92–93, 94, 99, 101, 103–104, 106–107, 119, 123–129.
94. The nature and effects of Woolf's mental illness are complex and controversial, but fear of publication and reviews was one part of the story; see Lee, *Virginia Woolf*, 69–96, 182; Bell, *Virginia Woolf*, 2:28–29, 183–185.
95. Virginia Woolf, *Between the Acts* [1941] (London: Hogarth, 1990).
96. See Clinton B. Seely. "Translating between Media: Rabindranath Tagore and Satyajit Ray." *The Tagore Issue of Prabaas*. http://www.parabaas.com/rabindranath/articles/pClinton1.html/.

97. For other, particularly creative ways of reading twentieth-century modernisms comparatively without reproducing the diffusionist model, see Jessica Berman, *Modernist Commitments: Ethics, Politics, and Transnational Modernism* (New York: Columbia University Press, 2011); Jacob Edmond, *A Common Strangeness: Contemporary Poetry, Cross-Cultural Encounter, Comparative Literature* (New York: Fordham University Press, 2012); Christopher GoGwilt, *The Passage of Literature: Genealogies of Modernism in Conrad, Rhys, and Pramoedya* (Oxford: Oxford University Press, 2011); Gayle Rogers, *Modernism and the New Spain: Britain, Cosmopolitan Europe, and Literary History* (Oxford: Oxford University Press, 2012).
98. Edward W. Said, "Reflections on Exile," in *Reflections on Exile and Other Essays* (Cambridge, Mass.: Harvard University Press, 2002), 186; Said borrows the term from music to define exilic consciousness.
99. Mary Layoun, "Endings and Beginnings: Reimagining the Tasks and Spaces of Comparison," in *Comparison: Theories, Approaches, Uses*, ed. Rita Felski and Susan Stanford Friedman (Baltimore, Md.: Johns Hopkins University Press, 2013), 211–212, 234. For more on the politics and practices of comparison, see Felski and Friedman, *Comparison*; Susan Stanford Friedman, "World Modernisms, World Literature, and Comparativity," in *The Oxford Handbook of Global Modernisms*, ed. Mark Wollaeger, with Matt Eatough (Oxford: Oxford University Press, 2012), 499–525.
100. R. Radhakrishnan, *Theory in an Uneven World* (Oxford: Blackwell, 2003), 82.

7. DIASPORIC MODERNISMS: JOURNEYS "HOME" IN LONG POEMS OF AIMÉ CÉSAIRE AND THERESA HAK KYUNG CHA

1. Edward W. Said, "Reflections on Exile," in *Reflections on Exile and Other Essays* (Cambridge, Mass.: Harvard University Press, 2002), 174, 179; hereafter cited in the text.
2. Azade Seyhan, *Writing Outside the Nation* (Princeton, N.J.: Princeton University Press, 2001), 15; hereafter cited in the text.
3. Avtar Brah, *Cartographies of Diaspora: Contesting Identities* (London: Routledge, 1996), 182; hereafter cited in the text.
4. James Clifford, "Diasporas," in *Routes: Travel and Translation in the Late Twentieth Century* (Cambridge, Mass.: Harvard University Press, 1997), 257.
5. Salman Rushdie, "Imaginary Homelands," in *Imaginary Homelands: Essays and Criticism, 1981–1991* (London: Granta, 1991), 10.
6. For an overview of scholarship on migration and diaspora, including distinctions between these terms, see Susan Stanford Friedman, "Migrations, Diasporas, and Borders," in *Introduction to Scholarship in Modern Languages and Literatures*, ed. David G. Nicholls (New York: Modern Language Association), 260–293. On the relation of diaspora to a poetics of intimacy, see my "Bodies on the Move: A Poetics of Home and Diaspora," *Tulsa Studies in Women's Literature* 23, no. 2 (Fall 2004): 189–212.
7. Aimé Césaire, *Cahier d'un retour au pays natal/Notebook of a Return to the Native Land* [1939], in *Aimé Césaire: The Collected Poetry*, trans. Clayton Eshleman and Annette

Smith (Berkeley: University of California Press, 1982), 34–85, cited with permission, copyright © Regents of the University of California. Theresa Hak Kyung Cha, *Dictée* [1982] (Berkeley: Third Woman, 1995), cited with permission, Berkeley Art Museum and Pacific Film Archive. Hereafter, quotations will be identified in the text.

8. Jahan Ramazani, *The Hybrid Muse: Postcolonial Poetry in English* (Chicago: University of Chicago Press, 2001), 1–19; *Minor Transnationalism*, ed. Françoise Lionnet and Shu-mei Shih (Durham, N.C.: Duke University Press, 2005).

9. This reading is adapted from "Modernism in a Transnational Landscape: Spatial Poetics, Postcolonialism, and Gender in Césaire's *Cahier/Notebook* and Cha's *Dictée*," *Paideuma* 32, nos. 1, 2, 3 (Spring, Fall, Winter 2003): 39–74; since its publication, more discussions of Césaire and Cha have appeared, but none in combination. See for example the 2010 retrospective two years after Césaire's death, "Aimé Césaire: Poet, Politician, Intellectual," in Theories and Methodologies, *PMLA* 125, no. 3 (May 2010): 737–763; Josephine Nock-Hee Park, "'What of the Partition': *Dictée*'s Boundaries and the American Epic," *Contemporary Literature* 46, no. 2 (2005): 213–242; Timothy Yu, *Race and the Avant-Garde: Experimental and Asian American Poetry Since 1965* (Stanford, Calif.: Stanford University Press, 2009), 100–137.

10. A. James Arnold's *Modernism and Negritude: The Poetry and Poetics of Aimé Césaire* (Cambridge, Mass.: Harvard University Press, 1981) is an exception; for important critical studies of Caribbean literature in relation to modernism, see Simon Gikandi's *Modernism in Limbo: Modernism and Caribbean Literature* (Ithaca, N.Y.: Cornell University Press, 1992) and Charles W. Pollard, *New World Modernisms: T. S. Eliot, Derek Walcott, and Kamau Brathwaite* (Charlottesville: University of Virginia Press, 2004). For discussions of Cha in relation to postmodernism/poststructuralism, see for example Juliana M. Spahr, "Postmodernism, Readers, and Theresa Hak Kyung Cha's *Dictée*," *College Literature* 23, no. 3 (October 1996): 23–43; and Lisa Lowe, "Unfaithful to the Original: The Subject of *Dictée*," in *Writing Self Writing Nation: Essays on Theresa Hak Kyung Cha's* Dictée, ed. Elaine H. Kim and Norma Alarcón (Berkeley, Calif.: Third Woman, 1994), 35–72. See also Yu's extensive discussion of Cha's experimentalism in *Race and the Avant-Garde*, 100–137.

11. For information on Césaire's life and work, see Clayton Eshleman and Annette Smith, introduction to *Aimé Césaire: The Collected Poetry*, 1–31.

12. There is some ambiguity about the dates of Cha's visits to Korea. *Dictée* represents the return as a single visit in 1980, written, at least initially, in the form of a letter to her mother "eighteen years later," that is eighteen years since the family fled Korea in 1962 (80–89). The Online Archive of California's *Guide to the Theresa Hak Kyung Cha Collection, 1971–1991* notes that Cha returned twice to Korea during periods of massive unrest in 1979 and 1981, http://www.oac.cdlib.org/findaid/ark:/13030/tf238n986k/; in "Poised on the In-between: A Korean American's Reflections on Theresa Hak Kyung Cha's *Dictée*," Elaine H. Kim writes that Cha visited Korea several times between 1978 and 1981 (Kim and Alarcón, *Writing Self*, 29n22); and Shu-mei Shih mentions one return visit in 1980, which she discusses in some detail in "Nationalism and Korean American Women's Writing: Theresa Hak Kyung Cha's *Dictée*," in *Speaking the Other Self: American*

Women Writers, ed. Jeanne Campbell Reesman (Athens: University of Georgia Press, 1997), 152–153.

13. For this changing reception, see Kim and Alarcón, *Writing Self*; Shih, "Nationalism," 144–164; and Yu, *Race*, 100–123. For additional information about Cha's life and work, see Yi-Chun Tricia Lin, "Theresa Hak Kyung Cha," in *Asian American Novelists: A Bio-Bibliographical Critical Sourcebook*, ed. E. Nelson (Westport, Conn.: Greenwood, 2000), 34–37; *Guide to the Theresa Hak Kyung Cha Collection 1971–1991*, Online Archive of California. For discussion of *Apparatus* and Cha's interest in film, see John Cho, "Tracing the Vampire," *Hitting Critical Mass* 3, no.2 (Spring 1996): 87–113; Constance Lewallen, ed., *The Dream of the Audience: Theresa Hak Kyung Cha* (Berkeley: University of California Press, 2001).

14. Clayton Eshleman and Annette Smith's bilingual edition of Césaire's *Cahier* encourages the eye to travel back and forth from the French to the English. For the sake of simplicity, however, I will cite only the English translation, with full recognition of the limits of a monolingual analysis. For discussion of the poem's neologisms, paratactic syntax, and heterodox French, see James Clifford, "A Politics of Neologism: Aimé Césaire," in *The Predicament of Culture: Twentieth-Century Ethnography, Literature, and Art* (Cambridge, Mass.: Harvard University Press, 1988), 175–186.

15. For discussion of the three-part structure of the poem, see Thomas A. Hale, "Structural Dynamics in a Third World Classic: Aimé Césaire's *Cahier d'un retour au pays natal*," *Yale French Studies* 53 (1976): 15–23.

16. Nick Nesbitt, "Antinomies of Double Consciousness in Aimé Césaire's *Cahier d'un retour au pays natal*," *Mosaic* 33, no. 3 (September 2000): 107–138.

17. Aimé Césaire, *Discours sur le colonialisme* [1955]. Translated as *Discourse on Colonialism*, trans. Joan Pinkham (New York: Monthly Review Press, 1972).

18. Charles Baudelaire, *Les fleurs du mal* [1857]. Translated as *The Flowers of Evil*, trans. Richard Howard (Brighton: Harvester, 1982).

19. The variation in poetic line and the spirit of excess that governs the marvelous spew of words—all held together by the voice of the panoptic I of the poet blending with his people—also recalls Walt Whitman's bardic voice. For discussion of Césaire's extreme imagery, see Jean Khalfa, "Pustules, Spirals, Volcanoes: Some Images in Aimé Césaire's *Cahier d'un retour au pays natal*," *Wasafiri* 31 (Spring 2000): 43–51; Hedy Kalikoff, "Gender, Genre, and Geography in Aimé Césaire's *Cahier d'un retour au pays natal*," *Callaloo* 18, no. 2 (1995): 492–505; Hilary Okam, "Aspects of Imagery and Symbolism in the Poetry of Aimé Césaire," *Yale French Studies* 53 (1976): 175–196; and Arnold, *Modernism and Negritude*, 133–168. For generic issues in the poem, see Kara M. Rabbit, "Prose Poem, Anti-poème, Political Force: The Critical Function of Genre in Aimé Césaire's *Cahier d'un retour au pays natal*," *Romance Notes* 39, no. 1 (Fall 1998): 35–46; and Kalioff, "Gender." For the poem's hybridic qualities, see especially Clifford, "A Politics of Neologism."

20. Cha makes a few significant modifications in the conventional list of nine muses, the patrons of poetry, poetic inspiration, and prophecy in ancient Greek tradition. She omits Euterpe, the muse of flute playing; she associates Terpsichore solely with dance

instead of her usual connection to both lyric poetry and dance; and she adds the muse Elitere to the nine as the sole muse of lyric poetry. See *The New Larousse Encyclopedia of Mythology*, trans. Richard Aldington and Delano Ames (New York: Prometheus, 1968), 118–120, for conventional names, domains of poetry, attributes, and legends associated with the muses. See also Shelley Sunn Wong's discussion of Cha's changes to the Greek originals in "Unnaming the Same: Theresa Hak Kyung Cha's *Dictée*," in Kim and Alarcón, *Writing Self* (115, 137n2–3) and Yu's discussion of the poem's non-narrative movement through the muses, one that resists the mythic method of early-twentieth-century modernists like Joyce (*Race*, 124–135).

21. Critics are generally agreed that Cha destabilizes the very notion of identity and rejects a reductionist form of identity politics while at the same time insisting upon the specificities of Korean history and culture. See for example Elaine H. Kim, "Poised on the In-Between: A Korean American's Reflections on Theresa Hak Kyung Cha's *Dictée*," in Kim and Alarcón, *Writing Self*, 3–35; Lowe, "Unfaithful"; Spahr, "Postmodernism"; Shih, "Nationalism"; and Wong, who argues that for Cha, "Home, in this sense, neither is nor even can be a settled space" ("Unnaming," 109). Yu goes even further to argue that *Dictée*'s experimentalism, especially in the second half of the poem, locates "home" not in nation or Korean identity but in language, making her poetry more akin to that of experimentalists like Susan Howe and Charles Bernstein than to much Asian American poetry (*Race*, 136–137).

22. Paul Gilroy, *The Black Atlantic: Modernity and Double Consciousness* (Cambridge, Mass.: Harvard University Press, 1993), 221.

23. See especially Michael André Bernstein, *The Tale of the Tribe: Ezra Pound and the Modern Verse Epic* (Princeton, N.J.: Princeton University Press, 1980), 29–74.

24. Lines 60, 207, 375 in T. S. Eliot, *The Waste Land* [1922], Norton Critical Edition, ed. Michael North (New York: Norton, 2001), 7, 12, 18; Eliot's note directs readers to Baudelaire's "Fourmillante cité" in *Les fleurs du mal*.

25. *Cahier/Notebook* alternates between lines printed in prose paragraphs and those printed as short-line poetry. In citing the text, I have indicated line breaks with the slash (/) for the poetic lines. *Dictée* also combines varied lineation, with some sections having the short lines of a lyric, others looking like prose paragraphs, and still a third using short "prose" paragraphs that read like poetry. In quoting from *Dictée*, I use the same principle that I do with *Cahier/Notebook*.

26. In addition to surrealism, *Cahier/Notebook* anticipates Frantz Fanon's psychoanalysis of the pathologies of racism in *Black Skin, White Masks: The Experiences of a Black Man in a White World* [1952], trans. Charles Lam Markmann (New York: Grove, 1967), and parallels such narrative explorations of racially based psychic wounding as Nella Larsen's *Quicksand*, Richard Wright's *Native Son*, Ralph Ellison's *Invisible Man*, and Toni Morrison's *The Bluest Eye*.

27. In *Discourse on Colonialism*, Césaire somewhat reluctantly acknowledges the cultural hybridity that the poem exhibits but nonetheless denies in its embrace of negritude: "I admit that it is a good thing to place different civilizations in contact with each other;

that it is an excellent thing to blend different worlds; that whatever its own particular genius may be, a civilization that withdraws into itself atrophies; that for civilizations, exchange is oxygen" (33).
28. For discussion of the contradictions in Césaire's concept of the new negritude, as well as the difficulties of its realization, see Nesbitt, "Antinomies."
29. Gloria Anzaldúa, *Borderlands/La Frontera—the New Mestiza* (San Francisco, Calif.: Spinsters/Aunt Lute, 1987), 21.
30. Memory is a key component of return in Césaire's poem as well. For example, the poet's first turn away from self-loathing begins with the poem's first memory, the poet's sudden recollection of "our foolish and crazy stunts" in childhood and how this "joy of former times" leads him back to the house of his boyhood (39).
31. See Wong, "Unnaming," for this identification, translation, and discussion (107). See also Spahr, "Postmodernism," for a discussion of the controversy around the authenticity of this inscription.
32. For discussion of the language issues in the poem, see especially Lowe, "Unfaithful"; Eun Kyung Min, "Reading the Figure of Dictation in Theresa Hak Kyung Cha's *Dictée*," in *Other Sisterhoods: Literary Theory and U.S. Women of Color*, ed. Sandra Kumamoto Stanley (Urbana: University of Illinois Press, 1998), 309–324. L. Hyun Yi, "The 'Liberatory Voice' of Theresa Hak Kyung Cha's *Dictée*," in Kim and Alarcón, *Writing Self*, 73–102; Shih, "Nationalism," 154–156; and Yu, *Race*, 131–133.
33. For the significance of French dictation exercises in the poem, see Lowe, "Unfaithful," 38–42; Min, "Reading."
34. This is, of course, a common trope in postcolonial literature and theory. See for example Mary Layoun, "The Female Body and 'Transnational' Reproduction; or, Rape by Any Other Name?" in *Scattered Hegemonies: Postmodernity and Transnational Feminist Practices*, ed. Inderpal Grewal and Caren Kaplan (Minneapolis: University of Minnesota Press, 1994), 63–75; Lydia Liu, "The Female Body and Nationalist Discourse: The Field of Life and Death Revisited," in *Scattered Hegemonies*, 37–62; Nira Yuval-Davis, *Gender and Nation* (London: Sage, 1997); and Sangeeta Ray, *En-Gendering India: Woman and Nation in Colonial and Postcolonial Narratives* (Durham, N.C.: Duke University Press, 2001). For discussions of gender in *Dictée*, see Kim, "Poised"; Lowe, "Unfaithful"; Anita Choe, "A Novena of Rebirth," *Hitting Critical Mass: A Journal of Asian American Cultural Criticism* 3, no. 2 (Spring 1996): 75–84; Yi-Chun Tricia Lin, "Theresa Hak Kyung Cha," in *Asian American Novelists: A Bio-Bibliographical Critical Sourcebook*, ed. E. Nelson (Westport, Conn.: Greenwood, 2000), 34–37; Wong, "Unnaming"; and Shih, "Nationalism." With the exception of Shih's 1997 essay "Nationalism and Korean American Women's Writing" (which I did not see before the 2003 publication of my essay), none of the gender discussions of *Dictée* deals in a sustained way with the poem's heavy reliance on the stories of woman as national allegory or with Cha's overarching mother/daughter narrative.
35. "Ethnic absolutism" is Paul Gilroy's phrase in *The Black Atlantic*, a position of racial essentialism that he rejects in favor of a more historicized and geographically specific

concept of the black diaspora, one that acknowledges intercultural influences and hybridity. For other discussions of cultural hybridity, see for example Homi K. Bhabha, *The Location of Culture* (London: Routledge, 1994); Susan Stanford Friedman, *Mappings: Feminism and the Cultural Geographies of Encounter* (Princeton, N.J.: Princeton University Press, 1998), 82–93; and *Debating Cultural Hybridity: Multicultural Identities and the Politics of Anti-Racism*, ed. Pnina Werbner and Tariq Modood (London: Zed, 1997). Some critics of Césaire regard his concept of negritude as less essentialist, more historically based, than that of Senghor; see for example Clifford, "A Politics of Neologism"; and Kalikoff, "Gender."

36. See for example Peter Nicholls's discussion of ironic modernist dissociation prefigured in Baudelaire's poem "To a Red-haired Beggar Girl," which he reads as an instance of the poet-flâneur's aesthetic voyeurism (*Modernisms: A Literary Guide* [Berkeley: University of California Press, 1995], 1–23).

37. Conventionally gendered tropes abound in the poem, especially in this section that Césaire refers to at one point as "my virile prayer" (73). In imagining himself to be "the father, the brother," and "the lover of this unique people," the poet also addresses the island as a woman to be caressed and licked by his tongue and his words (75; see also 53–54). For discussions of gender in *Cahier/Notebook*, see Kalikoff, "Gender"; and Ronnie Scharfman, *Engagement and the Language of the Subject in the Poetry of Aimé Césaire* (Gainesville: University of Florida Press, 1979).

38. In "Gender, Genre, and Geography," Kalikoff argues that Césaire's use of masculine/feminine binaries are unstable in the poem, shifting from "phallic negritude," to reversals of conventional gender, to androgyny; she finds in this instability an assumption that masculinity is constructed, not "natural." However, she acknowledges that Césaire's negritude does not envision women in the position of the subject. See also Scharfman's discussion of Césaire's masculinist decolonization in Lacanian terms (*Engagement and the Language of the Subject*).

39. The memory of her brother's shame in not joining the student martyrs, as well as her thoughts about the soldier boy, are exceptions. Also, her father has a presence alongside her mother in significant ways; it is his calligraphy, for example, that she features in the poem, according to her note. These male presences emphasize one of the many ways in which the poem resists any form of essentialist identity, whether Korean or female.

40. For the concept of the nation's "geo-body," that is, the geographically bounded territory associated with a people's nation as "imagined community," see Thongchai Winichakul, *Siam Mapped: A History of the Geo-body of a Nation* (Honolulu: University of Hawai'i Press, 1994).

41. Thanks to Jong-Im Lee for identification of this photo in her chapter on *Dictée* in her dissertation, "National Allegory and the Nomadic Subject in *Ulysses*, *Midnight's Children*, and *Dictée*," Dissertation.com, 2011.

42. Whether deliberate or not, the still from Dreyer's *La passion de Jeanne d'Arc* (*Dictée*, 119) echoes the featuring of the film and that still in H.D., "Joan of Arc," *Close Up* 3 (July

1928): 15–23; and Adrienne Rich, "Cartographies of Silence," in *The Dream of a Common Language: Poems, 1974–1977* (New York: Norton, 1978), 16–20.

43. Cha's note identifies the quotations to be from St. Thérèse's *Story of a Soul*. I have not been able to identify the film or films that Cha describes in such detail (98–99, 100, 102, 103, 104, 106, 108, 110?, 112?, 114, 118). It or they may be a composite of films or her own fictionalization. References in the poem to film(s) include a French film whose title in translation begins *Portrait of . . .* (98) and a film entitled *Gertrude*, perhaps Carl Theodor Dreyer's last film, *Gertrud* (1966). The partial title, *Portrait of . . .* , may allude to Henry James's *The Portrait of a Lady* (or a film based on the novel), which also narrates a woman's entrapment within marriage. As either the same film or a different one, the poet focuses briefly on the image of a woman who touches another's mouth as she herself speaks, "On verra" (one will see) (99, 100); Cha may be citing the 1946 Jean Delannoy film, *La symphonie pastorale*, based on André Gide's novel featuring a blind girl named Gertrude, loved and destroyed by her adoptive father and his son. Both film and novel have been staples of French pedagogy in the United States. Shih and Choe both identify the woman in the film (*Dictée*, 110) as Korean, specifically Cha's mother in the context of Korean marriage practices (Shih, "Nationalism," 154; Choe, "Novena"). Jong-Im Lee reads the brief invocation of "Mother" (*Dictée*, 109) as an allusion to Cha's own mother nurturing both child and husband with her body ("National Allegory and the Nomadic Subject"). The ambiguity of the various women's national and individual identities in "Erato Love Poetry" seems deliberate, part of Cha's general dissociation from essentialist nationalism and embrace of a composite experience of women's abjection.

44. Virginia Woolf, *A Room of One's Own* [1929] (New York: Harcourt Brace Jovanovich, 1957); *Three Guineas* [1938] (New York: Harcourt, 2002).

45. In "Nationalism and Korean American Women's Writing," Shih notes that the Korean folktale of Princess Pali is often "invoked in shamanistic rituals of the dead," with the shaman asking Pali to "guide the deceased through the underworld"; a variant tradition has Pali descending to the underworld to "find a magic herb with which she restores her mother's health" (157). See also Jong-Im Lee's discussion in "National Allegory and the Nomadic Subject." In *Race and the Avant-Garde* Yu argues that Cha's lack of direct reference to Princess Pali in the text "abstracts" the tale, removing it altogether from its Korean context (135).

CONCLUSION. A DEBATE WITH MYSELF

1. Franco Moretti, "Conjectures on World Literature," *New Left Review*, 2nd ser. (January–February 2000): 54–68.
2. See Lawrence Venuti, ed., *The Translation Studies Reader* (London: Routledge, 2000).
3. Sheldon Pollock, "Cosmopolitan and Vernacular in History," in *Cosmopolitanism*, ed. Carol A. Breckenridge, Sheldon Pollock, Homi K. Bhabha, and Dipesh Chakrabarty (Durham, N.C.: Duke University Press, 2002), 15–53.

4. See especially Joseph Slaughter, "Against Modernism," paper presented at the Conference on Comparative Modernisms, Medialities, Modernities, New York University and Fordham University, May 2012; Stephen Ross, "Uncanny Modernism, or Analysis Interminable," in *Disciplining Modernism*, ed. Pamela L. Caughie (New York: Palgrave Macmillan, 2010), 33–52.
5. Douglas Mao and Rebecca L. Walkowitz, "The New Modernist Studies," *PMLA* 123, no. 3 (May 2008): 737–748; Andreas Huyssen, "High/Low in an Expanded Field," *Modernism/Modernity* 9, no. 3 (September 2002): 363–374.
6. Frederick Cooper, *Colonialism in Question: Theory, Knowledge, History* (Berkeley: University of California Press, 2005), 129.
7. John Barth, "The Literature of Exhaustion" [1967], in *The Friday Book: Essays and Other Nonfiction* (Baltimore, Md.: Johns Hopkins University Press, 1984), 193–206; Marianne DeKoven, *Utopia Limited: The Sixties and the Emergence of the Postmodern* (Durham, N.C.: Duke University Press, 2004); Fredric Jameson, *Postmodernism, or, The Cultural Logic of Late Capitalism* (Durham, N.C.: Duke University Press, 1990); Brian McHale, *Postmodernist Fiction* (New York: Methuen, 1987); Ihab Hassan, *The Dismemberment of Orpheus: Toward a Postmodern Literature* (Madison: University of Wisconsin Press, 1992); Linda Hutcheon, *A Poetics of Postmodernism: History, Theory, Fiction* (London: Routledge, 1988); Andreas Huyssen, *After the Great Divide: Modernism, Mass Culture, Postmodernism* (Bloomington: Indiana University Press, 1985).
8. Terry Smith, *Contemporary Art: World Currents* (London: Pearson, 2001), bookjacket; Terry Smith, *What Is Contemporary Art?* (Chicago: University of Chicago Press, 2009).
9. André Wink, "Re-Emerging Super-Powers: Turkey, Iran, India, and China," Lecture, University of Wisconsin–Madison, March 5, 2014.
10. Huyssen, "High/Low in an Expanded Field," 366, 365; the article is based on his keynote address at the Modernist Studies Association conference in October 2011, at which he argued that 9/11 confirmed his belief that modernity is ongoing worldwide.
11. Mark Salber Phillips, introduction to *Questions of Traditions*, ed. Mark Salber Phillips and Gordon Schochet (Toronto: University of Toronto Press, 2004), 3–29.
12. Linda T. Smith, *Decolonizing Methodology: Research and Indigenous Peoples* (New York: St. Martins Press, 1999). See also Walter Mignolo and Madina Tlostanova, *Learning to Unlearn: Decolonial Reflections from Eurasia and the Americas* (Columbus: Ohio University Press, 2012).
13. F. T. Marinetti, "The Founding and Manifesto of Futurism" [1909], in *Futurist Manifestos*, ed. Umbro Apollonio (London: Thames and Hudson, 1973), 19–23. Ezra Pound, *Make It New: Essays* (London: Faber and Faber, 1934). T. S. Eliot, "Tradition and the Individual Talent" [1917], in *Selected Essays, 1917–1932* (New York: Harcourt Brace, 1932), 3–11.
14. James Clifford, "Traditional Futures," in *Questions of Tradition*, ed. Mark Salber Phillips and Gordon Schochet (Toronto: University of Toronto Press, 2004), 158.
15. Madan Sarap, "Home and Identity," in *Travellers' Tales: Narratives of Home and Displacement*, ed. George Robertson, Melinda Mash, Lisa Tickner, Jon Bird, Barry Curtis, and Tim Putnam (London: Routledge, 1994), 97.

16. Clifford, "Traditional Futures," 157.
17. Frederick Cooper, "Modernity," in *Colonialism in Question: Theory, Knowledge, History* (Berkeley: University of California Press, 2005), 113.
18. For this observation, a challenge that plagues me still, I am indebted to an anonymous reader of my essay "Periodizing Modernism," *Modernism/Modernity* 13, no. 3 (September 2006): 425–444.
19. I am particularly indebted to conversations and personal communications with Eric Hayot for this debate. The force of his argument has been particularly hard to counter, especially in the face of his significant contributions to European–Chinese interactions and his *On Literary Worlds* (Oxford: Oxford University Press, 2012), 1–22.
20. Eric Hayot, "Chinese Modernism, Mimetic Desire, and European Time," in *The Oxford Handbook of Global Modernisms*, ed. Mark Wollaeger, with Matt Eatough (Oxford: Oxford University Press, 2012), 149–170; Pascale Casanova, *The Republic of Letters*, trans. M. B. DeBevoise (Cambridge, Mass.: Harvard University Press, 2004); Cyrena N. Pondrom, *The Road from Paris: French Influence on English Poetry, 1900–1920* (Cambridge: Cambridge University Press, 1974).
21. Stephen K. Sanderson and Thomas D. Hall, "World Systems Approaches to World-Historical Change," in *Civilizations and World Systems: Studying World-Historical Change*, ed. Stephen K. Sanderson (London: Sage, 1995), 234.
22. Mary Lou Emery, "Caribbean Modernism: Plantation to Planetary," in *The Oxford Handbook of Global Modernisms*, ed. Mark Wollaeger, with Matt Eatough (Oxford: Oxford University Press, 2012), 70n3.
23. Jane Burbank and Frederick Cooper, *Empires in World History: Power and the Politics of Difference* (Princeton, N.J.: Princeton University Press, 2010), 7–8.
24. Michael Hardt and Antonio Negri, *Empire* (Cambridge, Mass.: Harvard University Press, 2000); the book's Eurocentrism is also evident in the absence of Asia in its accounts of past and current imperial formations, especially the late-twentieth/early-twenty-first-century rise of Japan, China, and India.
25. Rita Felski, *The Gender of Modernity* (Cambridge, Mass.: Harvard University Press, 1995); Bonnie Kime Scott, ed., *Gender in Modernism: New Geographies, Complex Intersections* (Chicago: University of Illinois Press, 2007).
26. See for example Mary Hawkesworth, "Intersectionality," in *Feminist Inquiry: From Political Conviction to Methodological Innovation* (New Brunswick, N. J.: Rutgers University Press, 2006), 207–248.
27. Question posed after delivery of "Planetarity" to the Modernist Studies Association conference, Montreal, November 2009; see Rebecca L. Walkowitz, *Cosmopolitan Style: Modernism Beyond the Nation* (New York: Columbia University Press, 2006); and *Born Translated: The Contemporary Novel in an Age of World Literature* (New York: Columbia University Press, 2015). She also co-edits the Literature Now series for Columbia University Press.
28. Kate Trumpener, "In the Grid: Period and Experience," *PMLA* 127, no. 2 (March 2012): 354.

29. David James and Urmila Seshagiri, "Metamodernism: Narratives of Continuity and Revolution," *PMLA* 129, no. 1 (2014): 87–100; James co-edits the Literature Now series at Columbia University Press.
30. Pericles Lewis, *The Cambridge Introduction to Modernism* (Cambridge: Cambridge University Press, 2007); Peter Nicholls, *Modernisms: A Literary Guide* [1995], rev. ed. (Berkeley: University of California Press, 2009). Conventional overviews of modernity exist as well; see for example Stuart Hall, David Held, Don Hubert, and Kenneth Thompson, eds., *Modernity: An Introduction to Modern Societies* (Oxford: Blackwell, 1996); Anthony Giddens, *The Consequences of Modernity* (Stanford, Calif.: Stanford University Press, 1990).
31. I deliberately echo here Sigmund Freud's seminal late essay "Analysis Terminable and Interminable" (1937), adapting his idea of analysis without end and the perpetuation of a transferential logic with an unending compulsion to repeat; *The Standard Edition of the Psychological Works of Sigmund Freud*, trans. James Strachey (London: Hogarth, 1958), 23:209–254.

BIBLIOGRAPHY

Abbas, Ali Abdalla. "Notes on Tayeb Salih: *Season of Migration to the North* and *The Wedding of Zein.*" *Sudan Notes and Records* 55 (1974): 46–60.

Abu-Lughod, Janet L. *Before European Hegemony: The World System, AD 1250–1350*. Oxford: Oxford University Press, 1989.

Achebe, Chinua. "An Image of Africa: Racism in Conrad's *Heart of Darkness.*" In *Heart of Darkness*, by Joseph Conrad, Norton Critical Edition, ed. Paul B. Armstrong, 36–48. New York: Norton, 2006.

Henry Adams, "The Dynamo and the Virgin" [1900]. In *The Education of Henry Adams*, 243–249. 1918; Blacksburg, Va.: Wilder, 2009.

Adams, Robert Martin, "What Was Modernism?" *Hudson Review* 31, no. 1 (Spring 1978): 19–33.

Aguiar, Marian. *Tracking Modernity: India's Railway and the Culture of Mobility*. Minneapolis: University of Minnesota Press, 2011.

"Aimé Césaire: Poet, Politician, Intellectual." Theories and Methodologies. *PMLA* 125, no. 3 (May 2010): 737–763.

Ali, Monica. *Brick Lane*. New York: Scribner's, 2003.

Allen, Esther. "English as an Invasive Species." In "Translation, Globalization, and English," *Pen/IRL Report on the International Situation of Literary Translation*, ed. Esther Allen, 17–22. 2007.

Allen, Lee Stewart. *The Devil's Cup: Coffee, the Driving Force in History*. London: Soho, 1999.

Allsen, Thomas R. *Commodity and Exchange in the Mongol Empire*. Cambridge: Cambridge University Press, 1997.

——. *Culture and Conquest in Mongol Eurasia*. Cambridge: Cambridge University Press, 2001.

——. *Mongol Imperialism: The Policies of the Grand Qan Möngke in China, Russia, and the Islamic Lands, 1251–1259*. Berkeley: University of California Press, 1987.

Amin, Samir. *Eurocentrism*. New York: Monthly Review, 1988.

Amyuni, Takieddine Mona. Introduction to *Season of Migration to the North, by Tayeb Salih: A Casebook*. Beirut: American University of Beirut, 1985.

Anand, Mulk Raj. *Untouchable* [1940]. New York: Penguin, 1986.
Anderson, Benedict. *Imagined Communities: Reflections on the Origins and Spread of Nationalism.* 2nd ed. London: Verso, 2006.
Anderson, Mary M. *Hidden Power: The Palace Eunuchs of Imperial China.* Amherst, N.Y.: Prometheus, 1990.
Andrade, Oswald de. "Manifesto Antropófago" [1928]/"Cannibalist Manifesto." Trans. Leslie Bary. *Latin American Literary Review* 19, no. 38 (July–December 1991): 33–47.
Anthony, David W. *The Horse, the Wheel, and Language: How Bronze-Age Riders from the Eurasian Steppes Shaped the Modern World.* Princeton, N.J.: Princeton University Press, 2007.
Anzaldúa, Gloria. *Borderlands/La Frontera—the New Mestiza.* San Francisco: Aunt Lute, 1987.
Appadurai, Arjun. *Modernity at Large: Cultural Dimensions of Globalization.* Minneapolis: University of Minnesota Press, 1996.
Apparao, Gurajada. *Girls for Sale: Kanyasulkam, a Play from Colonial India.* Trans. Velcheru Narayan Rao. Bloomington: Indiana University Press, 2007.
Apter, Emily. *Against World Literature: On the Politics of Untranslatability.* London: Verso, 2013.
——. *The Translation Zone: A New Comparative Literature.* Princeton, N.J.: Princeton University Press, 2006.
Arnold, A. James. *Modernism and Negritude: The Poetry and Poetics of Aimé Césaire.* Cambridge, Mass.: Harvard University Press, 1981.
Baker, Houston A., Jr. *Modernism and the Harlem Renaissance.* Chicago: University of Chicago Press, 1987.
Barabási, Albert-László. *Linked: How Everything Is Connected to Everything Else and What It Means for Business, Science, and Everyday Life.* New York: Plume, 2003.
Baraka, Amiri (Leroi Jones). *Black Magic: Sabotage, Target Study, Black Art: Collected Poetry, 1961–1967.* New York: Bobbs-Merrill, 1969.
Barlow, Tani. E. "What Is a Poem? The Event of Women and the Modern Girl as Problems in Global or World History." In *Immanuel Wallerstein and the Problem of the World: System, Scale, Culture,* ed. David Palumbo-Liu, Bruce Robbins, and Nirvana Tanoukhi, 155–183. Durham, N.C.: Duke University Press, 2011.
Barrett, T. H. *The Woman Who Discovered Printing.* New Haven, Conn.: Yale University Press, 2008.
Barth, John. "The Literature of Exhaustion" [1967]. In *The Friday Book: Essays and Other Nonfiction,* 193–206. Baltimore, Md.: Johns Hopkins University Press, 1984.
Barthes, Roland. "Introduction to the Structuralist Analysis of Narratives" [1966]. In *A Barthes Reader,* ed. Susan Sontag, 251–295. New York: Hill and Wang, 1982.
Bary, Leslie. Introduction to "Oswald de Andrade's 'Cannibalist Manifesto.'" Trans. Leslie Bary. *Latin American Literary Review* 19, no. 38 (July–December 1991): 35–36.
Baucom, Ian. *Specters of the Atlantic: Finance Capital, Slavery, and the Philosophy of History.* Durham, N.C.: Duke University Press, 2005.
Baudelaire, Charles. *Les fleurs du mal* [1857]/*The Flowers of Evil.* Trans. Richard Howard. Brighton: Harvester, 1982.

——. "The Painter of Modern Life." In *Selected Writings on Art and Literature*. Trans. R. E. Charvet. 403–405. New York: Penguin, 1973.

Bauman, Zygmunt. *Culture as Praxis* [1973]. Rev. ed. London: Routledge, 1999.

——. *Liquid Modernity*. Cambridge: Polity, 2000.

Beebe, Maurice. "What Modernism Was." *Journal of Modern Literature* 3, no. 5 (July 1974): 1065–1084.

Begam, Richard, and Michael Valdez Moses, eds. *Modernism and Colonialism: British and Irish Literature, 1899–1939*. Durham, N.C.: Duke University Press, 2007.

Bell, Quentin. *Virginia Woolf: A Biography*. New York: Harcourt Brace Jovanovich, 1972.

Benjamin, Walter. "Theses on the Philosophy of History" [1950]. In *Illuminations: Essays and Reflections*, ed. Hannah Arendt, 253–264. New York: Schocken, 1968.

Benn, Charles. *China's Golden Age: Everyday Life in the Tang Dynasty*. Westport, Conn.: Greenwood, 2002.

Benstock, Shari. *Women of the Left Bank: Paris, 1900–1940*. Austin: University of Texas Press, 1986.

Bentley, Jerry H. *Old World Encounters: Cross-Cultural Contacts and Exchanges in Pre-Modern Times*. New York: Oxford University Press, 1993.

Bentley, Jerry H., Renate Bridenthal, and Kären Wigen, eds. *Seascapes: Maritime Histories, Littoral Cultures, and Transoceanic Exchanges*. Honolulu: University of Hawai'i Press, 2007.

Berkley, Constance E., and Osman Hassan Ahmed, ed. and trans. *Tayeb Salih Speaks: Four Interviews with the Sudanese Novelist*. Washington, D.C.: Embassy of the Democratic Republic of the Sudan, 1982.

Berman, Jessica. *Modernist Commitments: Ethics, Politics, and Transnational Modernism*. New York: Columbia University Press, 2011.

Berman, Marshall. *All That Is Solid Melts Into Air: The Experience of Modernity* [1982]. 2nd ed. New York: Penguin, 1988.

Bernstein, Michael André. *The Tale of the Tribe: Ezra Pound and the Modern Verse Epic*. Princeton, N.J.: Princeton University Press, 1980.

Bhabha, Homi K. *The Location of Culture*. London: Routledge, 1994.

Bhagavadgita. Trans. S. Radhakrishnan. New Delhi: HarperCollins Publishers India, 1948.

Blackbourn, David. "'The Horologe of Time': Periodization in History." *PMLA* 127, no. 2 (March 2012): 301–307.

Blaut, J. M. *The Colonizer's Model of the World: Geographical Diffusionism and Eurocentric History*. New York: Guilford, 1993.

Bleich, David. "Globalization, Translation, and the University Tradition." *New Literary History* 39, no. 3 (Summer 2008): 497–517.

Boone, Joseph Allen. *Libidinal Currents: Sexuality and the Shaping of Modernism*. Chicago: University of Chicago Press, 1998.

——. "Vacation Cruises; or, The Homoerotics of Empire." *PMLA* 110, no. 1 (January 1995): 89–107.

Bourdieu, Pierre. *The Field of Cultural Production: Essays on Art and Literature*, ed. Randal Johnson. New York: Columbia University Press, 1993.

———. "Structures, *Habitus*, Practices" [1980]. In *The Logic of Practice*. Trans. Richard Nice, 52–65. Stanford, Calif.: Stanford University Press, 1990.

Bradbury, Malcolm. "The Cities of Modernism." In *Modernism: A Guide to European Literature, 1890–1930*, ed. Malcolm Bradbury and James McFarlane, 96–104. New York: Penguin, 1991.

Bradbury, Malcolm, and James McFarlane. "The Name and Nature of Modernism." In *Modernism: A Guide to European Literature, 1890–1930*, 27–55. New York: Penguin, 1991.

Bradbury, Malcolm, and James McFarlane, eds. *Modernism: A Guide to European Literature, 1890–1930*. New York: Penguin, 1976.

Brah, Avtar. *Cartographies of Diaspora: Contesting Identities*. London: Routledge, 1996.

Braudel, Fernand. *The Mediterranean and the Mediterranean World in the Age of Phillip II*. Trans. Siân Reynolds (New York: Harper and Row, 1972).

Brooker, Peter, and Andrew Thacker. Introduction to *Geographies of Modernism: Literatures, Cultures, Spaces*, ed. Peter Brooker and Andrew Thacker, 1–5. London: Routledge, 2005.

Brooker, Peter, and Andrew Thacker, eds. *Geographies of Modernism: Literatures, Cultures, Spaces*. London: Routledge, 2005.

Brooker, Peter, Andrzej Gąsiorek, Deborah Longworth, and Andrew Thacker, eds. *The Oxford Handbook of Modernisms*. Oxford: Oxford University Press, 2011.

Brooks, Peter. *Reading for the Plot: Design and Intention in Narrative*. New York: Knopf, 1984.

Brown, Marshall. "Periods and Resistances." *Modern Language Quarterly* 62, no. 4 (December 2001): 309–316.

Buell, Lawrence. *The Future of Environmental Criticism: Environmental Crisis and Literary Imagination*. Oxford: Blackwell, 2005.

Burbank, Jane, and Frederick Cooper. *Empires in World History: Power and the Politics of Difference*. Princeton N.J.: Princeton University Press, 2010.

Bush, Christopher. *Ideographic Modernism: China, Writing, Media*. Oxford: Oxford University Press, 2010.

Butler, Christopher. *Modernism: A Very Short Introduction*. Oxford: Oxford University Press, 2010.

Calinescu, Matei. *Five Faces of Modernity*. Durham, N.C.: Duke University Press, 1987.

Caiger-Smith, Alan. *Lustre Pottery: Technique, Tradition, and Innovation in Islam and the Western World*. London: Faber and Faber, 1985.

———. *Tin-Glaze Pottery in Europe and the Islamic World: The Tradition of One Thousand Years in Maiolica, Faience, and Delftware*. London: Faber and Faber, 1973.

Camboni, Marina. "Impure Lines: Multilingualism, Hybridity, and Cosmopolitanism in Contemporary Women's Poetry." *Contemporary Women's Writing* 1, no. 1 (December 2007): 34–44.

Casanova, Pascale. *The World Republic of Letters* [1999]. Trans. M. B. DeBevoise. Cambridge, Mass.: Harvard University Press, 2004.

Caserio, Robert. *The Novel in England, 1900–1950*. New York: Twayne, 1999.

Caughie, Pamela L. Introduction to *Disciplining Modernism*, ed. Pamela L. Caughie, 1–10. New York: Palgrave Macmillan, 2010.

Césaire, Aimé. *Cahier d'un retour au pays natal* [1939]/*Notebook of a Return to the Native Land*. In *Aimé Césaire: The Collected Poetry*, trans. Clayton Eshleman and Annette Smith, 34–85. Berkeley: University of California Press, 1982.
———. *Discours sur le colonialisme* [1955]. *Discourse on Colonialism*. Trans. Joan Pinkham. New York: Monthly Review Press, 1972.
Cha, Theresa Hak Kyung. *Apparatus: Cinematographic Apparatus: Selected Writings*. New York: Tanam, 1980.
———. *Dictée* [1982]. Berkeley, Calif.: Third Woman, 1995.
Chakrabarty, Dipesh. *Habitations of Modernity: Essays in the Wake of Subaltern Studies*. Chicago: University of Chicago Press, 2002.
———. "The Muddle of Modernity." *American Historical Review* 116, no. 3 (June 2011): 663–675.
———. *Provincializing Europe: Postcolonial Thought and Historical Difference*. Princeton, N.J.: Princeton University Press, 2000.
Chatman, Seymour. *Story and Discourse: Narrative Structure in Fiction and Film*. Ithaca, N.Y.: Cornell University Press, 1978.
Chatterji, Bankim Chandra. *The Poison Tree* [1872]. Trans. Marian Maddern and S. N. Mukherjee. New Delhi: Penguin, 1996.
Chatterjee, Partha. "A Possible India: Essays in Political Criticism" [1997]. In *The Partha Chatterjee Omnibus*, 1–285. New Delhi: Oxford University Press, 1999.
———. "Nationalist Thought and the Colonial World: A Derivative Discourse?" [1986]. In *The Partha Chatterjee Omnibus*, 1–301. New Delhi: Oxford University Press, 1999.
Chaudhuri, Amit. Introduction to *The Picador Book of Modern Indian Literature*, ed. Amit Chaudhuri. London: Picador, 2001.
Ch'ien, Evelyn Nien-ming. *Weird English*. Cambridge, Mass.: Harvard University Press, 2004.
Chitra, Deb. *Women of the Tagore Family*. Trans. Amita Chowdhry and Sona Roy. New Delhi: Penguin, 2010.
Cho, John. "Tracing the Vampire." *Hitting Critical Mass: A Journal of Asian American Cultural Criticism* 3, no. 2 (Spring 1996): 87–113.
Choe, Anita. "A Novenna of Rebirth." *Hitting Critical Mass: A Journal of Asian American Cultural Criticism* 3, no. 2 (Spring 1996): 75–84.
Chou, Eva Shan. *Reconsidering Tu Fu: Literary Greatness and Cultural Context*. Cambridge: Cambridge University Press, 1995.
Clark, T. J. *Farewell to an Idea: Episodes from a History of Modernism*. New Haven, Conn.: Yale University Press, 1999.
Clifford, James. "Diasporas." In *Routes: Travel and Translation in the Late Twentieth Century*. 244–278. Cambridge, Mass.: Harvard University Press, 1997.
———. "A Politics of Neologism: Aimé Césaire." In *The Predicament of Culture: Twentieth-Century Ethnography, Literature, and Art*, 175–181. Cambridge, Mass.: Harvard University Press, 1988.
———. *The Predicament of Culture: Twentieth-Century Ethnography, Literature, and Art*. Cambridge, Mass.: Harvard University Press, 1988.

———. *Routes: Travel and Translation in the Late Twentieth Century*. Cambridge, Mass.: Harvard University Press, 1997.

———. "Traditional Futures." In *Questions of Tradition*, ed. Mark Salber Phillips and Gordon Schochet, 152–168. Toronto: University of Toronto Press, 2004.

———. "Traveling Cultures" [1992]. In *Routes: Travel and Translation in the Late Twentieth Century*, 17–46. Cambridge, Mass.: Harvard University Press, 1997.

Conrad, Joseph. *Heart of Darkness* [1899]. Ed. Paul B. Armstrong. 4th Norton Critical Edition: Authoritative Text, Backgrounds and Contexts, Criticism. 3–77. New York: Norton, 2006.

Cooper, Frederick. *Colonialism in Question: Theory, Knowledge, History*. Berkeley: University of California Press, 2005.

Cresswell, Tim. *On the Move: Mobility in the Western World*. London: Routledge, 2006.

Cuddy-Keane, Melba. *Modernism: Keywords*. Oxford: Wiley-Blackwell, 2014.

———. "Modernism, Geopolitics, Globalization." *Modernism/Modernity* 10, no. 3 (September 2003): 539–558.

Damrosch, David. *What Is World Literature?* Princeton, N.J.: Princeton University Press, 2003.

Darwin, John. *After Tamerlane: The Global History of Empire After 1405*. New York: Bloomsbury, 2008.

Davis, Kathleen. *Periodization and Sovereignty: The Ideas of Feudalism and Secularization Governing the Politics of Time*. Philadelphia: University of Pennsylvania Press, 2008.

Davidson, Basil. *Africa in History* [1966]. Rev. ed. New York: Touchstone, 1995.

Davidson, John E. "In Search of a Middle Point: The Origins of Oppression in Tayeb Salih's *Season of Migration to the North*." *Research in African Literatures* 20, no. 3 (Fall 1989): 385–400.

Davison, Ned J. *The Concept of Modernism in Hispanic Criticism*. Boulder, Colo.: Pruett, 1966.

De Jongh, James. *Vicious Modernism: Black Harlem and the Literary Imagination*. New York: Cambridge University Press, 1990.

DeKoven, Marianne. *Rich and Strange: Gender, History, Modernism*. Princeton, N.J.: Princeton University Press, 1991.

———. *Utopia Limited: The Sixties and the Emergence of the Postmodern*. Durham, N.C.: Duke University Press, 2004.

Deleuze, Gilles, and Félix Guattari. *Kafka: Toward a Minor Literature* [1975]. Trans. Dana Colan. Minneapolis: University of Minnesota Press, 1986.

———. *A Thousand Plateaus: Capitalism and Schizophrenia* [1980]. Trans. Brian Massumi. Minneapolis: University of Minnesota Press, 1987.

Desai, Anita. Introduction. In *Selected Short Stories*, by Rabindranath Tagore, trans. Rajul Sogani and Indira Gupta, 1–18. New Delhi: Oxford University Press, 2004.

De Lauretis, Teresa. *Alice Doesn't: Feminism, Semiotics, Cinema*. Bloomington: Indiana University Press, 1984.

De Man, Paul. "Literary History and Literary Modernity." In *Blindness and Insight*, 142–165. Minneapolis: University of Minnesota Press, 1983.

D'haen, Theo, David Damrosch, and Djelal Kadir, eds. *The Routledge Companion to World Literature*. London: Routledge, 2011.

Dharwadker, Aparna. "Mohan Rakesh, Modernism, and the Postcolonial Present." *South Central Review* 25, no. 1 (Spring 2008): 136–162.
Dharwadker, Vinay. Introduction to *Kabir: The Weaver's Songs*, trans. Vinay Dharwadker, 1–96. London: Penguin, 2003.
———. *Kabir: The Weaver's Songs*. Trans. Vinay Dharwadker. London: Penguin, 2003.
Dhwan, R. K. *Arundhati Roy: The Novelist Extraordinary*. New Delhi: Prestige, 1999.
Dimock, Wai Chee. *Through Other Continents: American Literature Across Deep Time*. Princeton, N.J.: Princeton University Press, 2006.
Doyle, Laura. "Afterword: Modernist Studies and Inter-Imperiality in the Longue Durée." In *The Oxford Handbook of Global Modernisms*, ed. Mark Wollaeger, with Matt Eatough, 669–96. Oxford: Oxford University Press, 2012.
———. *Bordering the Body: The Racial Matrix of Modern Fiction and Culture*. New York: Oxford University Press, 1994.
Doyle, Laura, and Laura Winkiel, eds. *Geomodernisms: Race, Modernism, Modernity*. Bloomington: Indiana University Press, 2005.
Doyle, Laura, and Regenia Gagnier, eds. Forum on *Global Modernisms*, *The Global Circulation Project*, Literature Compass 9, no. 9 (September 2012). http://literature-compass.com/global-circulation-project/.
Dreyer, Carl Theodor. *La passion de Jeanne d'Arc*. Film. 1928.
Duchesne, Ricardo. *The Uniqueness of Western Civilization*. Leiden: Brill, 2011.
DuPlessis, Rachel Blau. *Genders, Races, and Religious Cultures in Modern American Poetry, 1908–1934*. New York: Cambridge University Press, 2001.
———. *Writing Beyond the Ending: Narrative Strategies of Twentieth-Century Women Writers*. Bloomington: Indiana University Press, 1985.
Dutta, Krishna, and Andrew Anderson. *Rabindranath Tagore: The Myriad-Minded Man*. London: I. B. Tauris, 2009.
Dutta, Krishna, and Mary Lago. Preface to *Selected Short Stories*, by Rabindranath Tagore, trans. Krishna Dutta and Mary Lago, 19–24. London: Macmillan, 1991.
Edmond, Jacob. *A Common Strangeness: Contemporary Poetry, Cross-Cultural Encounter, Comparative Literature*. New York: Fordham University Press, 2012.
Edwards, Brent Hayes. *The Practice of Diaspora: Literature, Translations, and the Rise of Black Internationalism*. Cambridge, Mass.: Harvard University Press, 2003.
Eisenstadt, Shmuel N., ed. Special Issue on "Multiple Modernities." *Daedalus* 129, no. 1 (Winter 2000).
Eisenstadt, Shmuel N. and Wolfgang Schluchter, eds. Special Issue on "Early Modernities." *Daedalus* 127, no. 3 (Summer 1998).
Eisenstein, Sergei M. "The Principles of Film Form." *Close Up* 8, no. 3 (September 1931): 167–181.
Eliot, T. S. "Tradition and the Individual Talent." In *Selected Essays, 1917–1932*, 3–11. New York: Harcourt Brace, 1932.
———. *The Waste Land*. Norton Critical Ed., ed. Michael North. 1–26. New York: Norton, 2001.

Ellmann, Richard, and Charles Feidelson, eds. *The Modern Tradition*. New York: Oxford University Press, 1965.

Erdrich, Louise. *Tracks*. New York: Harper, 1988.

European Network for Avant-Garde and Modernism Studies. http://www.eam-europe.be/.

Eysteinsson, Astradur. *The Concept of Modernism*. Ithaca, N.Y.: Cornell University Press, 1990.

Eysteinsson, Astradur, and Vivian Liska, eds. *Modernism*. Amsterdam: John Benjamins, 2007.

Fanon, Frantz. *Black Skins, White Masks: The Experiences of a Black Man in a White World* [1952]. Trans. Charles Lam Markmann. New York: Grove, 1967.

Farn, Regelind. *Colonial and Postcolonial Rewritings of* Heart of Darkness: *A Century of Dialogue with Joseph Conrad*. Boca Raton, Fla.: Dissertation.com, 2005.

Felman, Shoshana. *Jacques Lacan and the Adventure of Insight*. Cambridge, Mass.: Harvard University Press, 1987.

Felman, Shoshana, ed. *Literature and Psychoanalysis: The Question of Reading: Otherwise*. Baltimore, Md.: Johns Hopkins University Press, 1980.

Felski, Rita. *Doing Time: Feminist Theory and Postmodern Culture*. New York: New York University Press, 2000.

———. *The Gender of Modernity*. Cambridge, Mass.: Harvard University Press, 1995.

———. "New Cultural Theories of Modernity." In *Doing Time: Feminist Theory and Postmodern Culture*, 55–76. New York: New York University Press, 2000.

Felski, Rita, and Susan Stanford Friedman, eds. *Comparison: Theories, Approaches, Uses*. Baltimore, Md.: Johns Hopkins University Press, 2013.

Fergusson, James. "Decomposing Modernity: History and Hierarchy After Development." In *Postcolonial Studies and Beyond*, ed. Ania Loomba, Suvir Kaul, Matti Bunzl, Antoinette Burton, and Jed Esty, 166–181. Durham, N.C.: Duke University Press, 2005.

Ferree, Myra Marx, and Aili Mari Tripp, eds. *Global Feminism: Transnational Women's Activism, Organizing, and Human Rights*. New York: New York University Press, 2006.

Fire! Ed. Wallace Thurman. 1, no. 1 (November 1926).

Forum on Modernity. *American Historical Review* 116, no. 3 (June 2011): 676–726.

Forster, E. M. *The Manuscripts of* A Passage to India. Correlated with Forster's final version by Oliver Stallybrass. New York: Homes and Meier, 1978.

———. *Maurice*. New York: Norton, 1971.

———. *A Passage to India* [1924]. New York: Harcourt Brace, 1984.

Foucault, Michel. "Of Other Spaces" [1984]. Trans. Jay Miskowiec. *diacritics* 16 (Spring 1986): 22–27.

Frank, André Gunder. "The Modern World System Revisited: Rereading Braudel and Wallerstein." In *Civilizations and World Systems*, ed. Stephen K. Sanderson, 149–180. Walnut Creek, Calif.: Altamira, 1995.

———. *ReOrient: Global Economy in the Asian Age*. Berkeley: University of California Press, 1998.

Franke, R. "The Kerala Model of Development: A Debate (Part I)." *Bulletin of Concerned Asian Scholars* 30, no. 3 (July–September 1998): 25–36.

Freedgood, Elaine. "E. M. Forster's Queer Nation: Taking the Closet to the Colony in *A Passage to India*." *Genders* 23 (1996): 123–144.

Freud, Sigmund. "Analysis Terminable and Interminable" [1937]. In *The Standard Edition of the Psychological Works of Sigmund Freud*. Trans. James Strachey, 23:209–254. London: Hogarth, 1958.

———. *Dora: An Analysis of a Case of Hysteria* [1904]. Ed. Philip Rieff. New York: Collier, 1961.

———. "The Dynamics of the Transference" [1912]. In *The Standard Edition of the Psychological Works of Sigmund Freud*. Trans. James Strachey, 12:97–109. London: Hogarth, 1958.

———. "Remembering, Repeating, and Working-Through" [1914]. In *The Standard Edition of the Psychological Works of Sigmund Freud*. Trans. James Strachey, 12:144–158. London: Hogarth, 1958.

Friedman, Edward. "Asia as a Fount of Universal Human Rights." In *Debating Human Rights: Critical Essays from the United States and Asia*, ed. Peter Van Ness, 56–79. London: Routledge, 1999.

———. "On Alien Western Democracy." *Globalization and Democratization in Asia: The Construction of Identity*, ed. Catarina Kinnvall and Kristina Jönsson, 53–72. London: Routledge, 2002.

———. "Since There Is No East and There Is No West, How Could Either Be the Best?" In *Human Rights and Asian Values: Contesting National Identities and Cultural Representations in Asia*, ed. Michael Jacobsen and Ole Bruun, 21–42. Richmond: Curzon, 2000.

Friedman, Susan Stanford. "Bodies on the Move: A Poetics of Home and Diaspora." *Tulsa Studies in Women's Literature* 23, no. 4 (2004): 189–212.

———. "Cultural Parataxis and Transnational Landscapes of Reading: Toward a Locational Modernist Studies." In *Modernism*, ed. Vivian Liska and Astradur Eysteinsson, 35–52. Philadelphia: John Benjamins, 2007.

———. "Definitional Excursions: The Meanings of *Modern/Modernity/Modernism*." *Modernism/Modernity* 8, no. 3 (September 2001): 493–513.

———. "Feminism, State Fictions, and Violence: Gender, Geopolitics, and Transnationalism." *Communal/Plural* 9, no. 1 (2001): 112–29.

———. "Lyric Subversion of Narrative in Women's Writing: Virginia Woolf and the Tyranny of Plot." In *Reading Narrative: Form, Ethics, Ideology*, ed. James Phelan, 162–185. Columbus: Ohio State University Press, 1989.

———. *Mappings: Feminism and the Cultural Geographies of Encounter*. Princeton, N.J.: Princeton University Press, 1998.

———. "Migration, Encounter, and Indigenization: New Ways of Thinking About Intertextuality in Women's Writing." In *European Intertexts: Women's Writing in English in a European Context*, ed. Patsy Stoneman, Vita Fortunati, and Eleonora Federici, 215–271. Berlin: Peter Lang, 2005.

———. "Migrations, Diasporas, and Borders." In *Introduction to Scholarship in Modern Languages and Literatures*, ed. David G. Nicholls, 260–293. New York: Modern Language Association.

———. "Modernism in a Transnational Landscape: Spatial Poetics, Postcolonialism, and Gender in Césaire's *Cahier/Notebook* and Cha's *Dictee*." *Paideuma* 32, no. 1/2/3 (Spring, Fall, Winter 2003): 39–74.

———. "One Hand Clapping: Colonialism, Postcolonialism, and the Spatio/Temporal Boundaries of Modernism." In *Translocal Modernisms: International Perspectives*, ed. Irene Ramalho Santos and António Sousa Ribeiro, 11–40. New York: Peter Lang, 2008.

———. "Paranoia, Pollution, and Sexuality: Affiliations Between E. M. Forster's *A Passage to India* and Arundhati Roy's *The God of Small Things*." In *Geomodernism: Race, Modernism, Modernity*, ed. Laura Doyle and Laura Winkiel, 245–261. Bloomington: Indiana University Press, 2005.

———. "Periodizing Modernism: Postcolonial Modernities and the Space/Time Borders of Modernist Studies." *Modernism/Modernity* 12, no. 3 (September 2006): 425–444.

———. "Planetary Modernisms and the Modernities of Empire and New Nations." Paper delivered at the Conference on Meanings of the Modern: South Asia Before and After Colonialism. Madison, Wisconsin, December 4–6, 2008.

———. "Reading Joyce: Icon of Modernity? Champion of Alterity? Ventriloquist of Otherness?" In *Joycean Cultures/Culturing Joyce*, ed. Vincent J. Cheng, Kimberly J. Devlin, and Margot Norris, 113–133. Newark: University of Delaware Press, 1998.

———. "Towards a Transnational Turn in Narrative Theory: Literary Narratives, Traveling Tropes, and the Case of Virginia Woolf and the Tagores." *Narrative* 19, no. 1 (January 2011): 1–32.

———. "Unthinking Manifest Destiny: Muslim Modernities on Three Continents." In *Shades of the Planet: American Literature as World Literature*, ed. Wai Chee Dimock and Lawrence Buell, 62–100. Princeton, N.J.: Princeton University Press, 2007.

———. "Why Not Compare?" *PMLA* 126, no. 3 (May 2011): 753–762.

———. "World Modernisms, World Literature, and Comparativity." In *The Oxford Handbook of Global Modernisms*, ed. Mark Wollaeger, with Matt Eatough, 499–525. Oxford: Oxford University Press, 2012.

Furbank, P. N. *E. M. Forster: A Life*. New York: Harcourt Brace, 1981.

Gagnier, Regenia, ed. *Literature Compass: The Global Circulation Project*. http://literature-compass.com/global-circulation-project/.

Gambrell, Alice. *Women Intellectuals, Modernism, and Difference: Transatlantic Culture, 1919–1945*. New York: Cambridge University Press, 1997.

Ganeri, Jonardon. *The Lost Age of Reason: Philosophy in Early Modern India, 1450–1700*. Oxford: Oxford University Press, 2011.

Gaonkar, Dilip Parameshwar. "On Alternative Modernities." In *Alternative Modernities*, ed. Dilip Parameshwar Gaonkar, 1–23. Durham, N.C.: Duke University Press, 2001.

Geesey, Patricia. "Cultural Hybridity and Contamination in Tayeb Salih's *Mawsim al-hijira ila al-Shamal (Season of Migration to the North)*." *Research in African Literatures* 28 (Fall 1997): 128–140.

Ghosal, Swarnakumai Debe. *An Unfinished Song/Kahake*. Ed. C. Vijayasree. New Delhi: Oxford University Press, 2008.

Gibson, Brian. "An Island Unto Himself? Masculinity in *Season of Migration to the North*." *Jouvert* 7, no. 1 (Autumn 2002). http://english.chass.ncsu.edu/jouvert/v7is1/gibson.htm.

Giddens, Anthony. *The Consequences of Modernity*. Stanford, Calif.: Stanford University Press, 1994.
——. Foreword to *NowHere: Space, Time and Modernity*, ed. Roger Friedland and Deirdre Boden, xi–xiii. Berkeley: University of California Press, 1994.
——. *Modernity and Self-Identity: Self and Society in the Late Modern Age*. Stanford, Calif.: Stanford University Press, 1991.
Gikandi, Simon. "Picasso, Africa, and the Schemata of Difference." *Modernism/Modernity* 10, no. 3 (September 2003): 455–480.
——. *Maps of Englishness: Writing Identity in the Culture of Colonialism*. New York: Columbia University Press, 1996.
——. *Writing in Limbo: Modernism and Caribbean Literature*. Ithaca, N.Y.: Cornell University Press, 1992.
Gilbert, Sandra, and Susan Gubar. *No Man's Land: The Place of the Woman Writer in the Twentieth Century*. 3 vols. New Haven, Conn.: Yale University Press, 1988–1994.
Gillies, Mary Ann, Helen Sword, and Steven Yao, eds. *Pacific Rim Modernisms*. Toronto: University of Toronto Press, 2009.
Gilman, Susan. "Oceans of Longue Durées." *PMLA* 127, no. 2 (March 2012): 328–334.
Gilroy, Paul. *The Black Atlantic: Modernity and Double Consciousness*. Cambridge, Mass.: Harvard University Press, 1993.
——. *Postcolonial Melancholia*. New York: Columbia University Press, 2005.
Glissant, Édouard. *Poétique de la relation*. Paris: Gallimard, 1990.
——. *Poetics of Relation*. Trans. Betsy Wing. Ann Arbor: University of Michigan Press, 1997.
——. "The Unforeseeable Diversity of the World." Trans. Haun Saussy. In *Beyond Dichotomies: Histories, Identities, Cultures, and the Challenge of Globalization*, ed. Elisabeth Mudimbe-Boyi, 278–295. Albany: State University of New York Press, 2002.
"Globalizing Literary Studies." Special Issue. *PMLA* 116, no. 1 (January 2001).
Gluck, Carol. "The End of Elsewhere: Writing Modernity Now." *American Historical Review* 116, no. 3 (June 2011): 676–687.
GoGwilt, Christopher. *The Passage of Literature: Genealogies of Modernism in Conrad, Rhys, and Pramoedya*. Oxford: Oxford University Press, 2011.
Golden, Peter B. *Nomads and Sedentary Societies in Medieval Eurasia*. Washington, D.C.: American Historical Association, 1998.
Green, Christopher, ed. *Picasso's Les demoiselles d'Avignon*. Cambridge: Cambridge University, 2001.
Grewal, Inderpal, and Caren Kaplan, eds. *An Introduction to Women's Studies: Gender in a Transnational World*. New York: McGraw Hill, 2002.
Grove, Richard. *Green Imperialism: Colonial Expansion, Tropical Island Edens, and the Origin of Environmentalism, 1600–1860*. Cambridge: Cambridge University Press, 1995.
Gubar, Susan. *Racechanges: White Skin, Black Face in American Culture*. New York: Oxford University Press, 1997.
Guha, Ramachandra. "The Arun Shourie of the Left," *The Hindu* (November 26, 2000). http://www.narmada.org/debates/ramguha/.

———. "Perils of Extremism." *The Hindu* (December 17, 2000). http://www.narmada.org/debates/ramguha/.
Gupta, Uma Das. *Rabindranath Tagore: A Biography.* New Delhi: Oxford University Press, 2004.
Guide to the Theresa Hak Kyung Cha Collection, 1971–1991. Berkeley Art Museum/Pacific Film Archive. Online Archive of California. http://www.oac.cdlib.org/findaid/ark:/13030/tf238n986k/.
H.D. (Hilda Doolittle). "Joan of Arc." *Close Up* 3 (July 1928): 15–23.
Habermas, Jürgen. "Modernity Versus Postmodernity." *New German Critique* 22 (Winter 1981): 3–14.
———. *The Philosophical Discourse of Modernity.* New York: Oxford University Press, 1987.
Hale, Thomas A. "Structural Dynamics in a Third World Classic: Aimé Césaire's *Cahier d'un retour au pays natal.*" *Yale French Studies* 53 (1976): 163–174.
Hall, Stuart. "The Local and the Global: Globalization and Ethnicity." In *Culture, Globalization, and the World-System*, ed. Anthony King, 19–44. Minneapolis: University of Minnesota Press, 1997.
Hall, Stuart, ed. *Model Modernity: An Introduction to Modern Societies.* Malden, Mass.: Basil Blackwell, 1996.
Hall, Stuart, and Bram Gieben, eds. *Formations of Modernity.* Cambridge: Polity, 1992.
Hall, Stuart, David Held, Don Hubert, and Kenneth Thompson, eds. *Modernity: An Introduction to Modern Societies.* Oxford: Blackwell, 1996.
Hallett, Jessica. "Iraq and China; Trade and Innovation in the Early Abbasid Period." *TAOCI, Chine-Méditerranée, routes et échanges de la céramique avant le XVIe siècle* 4 (December 2005): 21–29.
Hardt, Michael, and Antonio Negri. *Empire.* Cambridge, Mass.: Harvard University Press, 2000.
Harlow, Barbara. "Othello's Season of Migration." *Edebiyat* 4, no. 2 (1979): 157–175.
Harrison, Robert L. "The Manuscripts of *A Passage to India*," Austin, Tex. Diss. University of Texas, Austin, 1964.
Harvey, David. *The Condition of Postmodernity: An Enquiry Into the Origins of Social Change.* Oxford: Basil Blackwell, 1989.
Hassan, Ihab. *The Dismemberment of Orpheus: Toward a Postmodern Literature.* Madison: University of Wisconsin Press, 1992.
Hassan, Wail S. "Gender (and) Imperialism: Structures of Masculinity in Tayeb Salih's *Season of Migration to the North.*" *Men and Masculinities* 5, no. 3 (2003): 309–324.
———. *Tayeb Salih: Ideology and the Craft of Fiction.* Syracuse, N.Y.: Syracuse University Press, 2003.
Hayot, Eric. "Against Periodization; or, On Institutional Time." *New Literary History* 42, no. 4 (Autumn 2011): 739–756.
———. *Chinese Dreams: Pound, Brecht, Tel Quel.* Ann Arbor: University of Michigan Press, 2003.
———. "Chinese Modernism, Mimetic Desire, and European Time." In *The Oxford Handbook of Global Modernisms*, ed. Mark Wollaeger, with Matt Eatough, 149–170. Oxford: Oxford University Press, 2012.

———. *The Hypothetical Mandarin: Sympathy, Modernity, and Chinese Pain*. Oxford: Oxford University Press, 2009.

———. "Immigrating Fictions: Unfailing Mediation in *Dictée* and *Becoming Madame Mao*." *Contemporary Literature* 47, no. 4 (Winter 2006): 601–635.

———. *On Literary Worlds*. Oxford: Oxford University Press, 2012.

Hayot, Eric, and Rebecca L. Walkowitz. *A New Vocabulary for Global Modernism*. New York: Columbia University Press, 2015.

Heise, Ursula K. *Sense of Place and Sense of Planet: The Environmental Imagination of the Global*. Oxford: Oxford University Press, 2008.

Herman, David, Manfred Jahn, and Marie-Laure Ryan, eds. *Routledge Encyclopedia of Narrative Theory*. London: Routledge, 2005.

Hinton, David. *The Selected Poems of Li Po*. Trans. David Hinton. New York: New Directions, 1996.

———. *The Selected Poems of Tu Fu*. Trans. David Hinton. London: Anvil Press Poetry, 1990.

Hirsch, Marianne. *The Mother-Daughter Plot: Narrative, Psychoanalysis, Feminism*. Bloomington: Indiana University Press, 1989.

Ho, Richard M. W. *Ch'en Tzu-Ang: Innovator in T'ang Poetry*. London: School of Oriental and African Studies, 1993.

Hobson, John H. *The Eastern Origins of Western Civilisation*. Cambridge: Cambridge University Press, 2004.

Hobsbawm, Eric, and Terrence Ranger, eds. *The Invention of Tradition*. Cambridge: Cambridge University Press, 1983.

Hodgson, Marshall G. S. *Rethinking World History*. Cambridge: Cambridge University Press, 1993.

Hogan, Linda. *Solar Storms: A Novel*. New York: Scribner, 1995.

Hogan, Patrick Colm. *Empire and Poetic Voice: Cognitive and Cultural Studies of Literary Tradition and Colonialism*. Albany, N.Y.: SUNY Press, 2004.

Hogan, Patrick Colm, and Lalita Pandit. "Toward a Cognitive Science of Poetics: Anandavardhana, Abhinavagupta, and the Theory of Literature." Special Issue on "Comparative Poetics: Non-Western Traditions of Literary Theory." *College English* 23, no. 1 (February 1996): 164–178.

Horoszko, Urszula. "Terror and Irony of Eastern Europe in Joseph Conrad's *Heart of Darkness*." Unpublished paper.

Hourani, Albert. *A History of the Arab Peoples*. Cambridge, Mass.: Harvard University Press, 1991.

Hughes, Langston. *Montage of a Dream Deferred* [1951]. In *Collected Poems of Langston Hughes*, ed. Arnold Rampersad, 387–429. New York: Vintage, 1994.

Huntington, Samuel. "The Clash of Civilizations?" *Foreign Affairs* 72, no. 3 (Summer 1993): 22–49.

———. *The Clash of Civilizations and the Remaking of World Order*. New York: Simon and Schuster, 1996.

Hussey, Mark. *Virginia Woolf A to Z: The Essential Reference to Her Life and Writing*. Oxford: Oxford University Press, 1995.

Hutcheon, Linda. *A Poetics of Postmodernism: History, Theory, Fiction*. London: Routledge, 1988.

Huyssen, Andreas. *After the Great Divide: Modernism, Mass Culture, Postmodernism*. Bloomington: Indiana University Press, 1986.

———. "Geographies of Modernism in a Globalising World." In *Geographies of Modernism: Literatures, Cultures, Spaces*, ed. Peter Brooker and Andrew Thacker, 6–18. London: Routledge, 2005.

———. "High/Low in an Expanded Field." *Modernism/Modernity* 9, no. 3 (September 2002): 363–374.

———. Introduction. Special Issue on "Modernism After Postmodernity." *New German Critique* 33, no. 3 (Fall 2006): 1–5.

Irigaray, Luce. *Speculum of the Other Woman* [1974]. Trans. Gillian C. Gill. Ithaca, N.Y.: Cornell University Press, 1985.

———. "The Power of Discourse and the Subordination of the Feminine." In *This Sex Which Is Not One* [1977]. Trans. Catherine Porter. Ithaca, N.Y.: Cornell University Press, 1985.

Jacobsen, Michael, and Ole Bruun, eds. *Human Rights and Asian Values: Contesting National Identities and Cultural Representations in Asia*. Richmond: Curzon, 2000.

James, David, and Urmila Seshagiri. "Metamodernism: Narratives of Continuity and Revolution." *PMLA* 129, no. 1 (2014): 87–100.

Jameson, Fredric. *The Political Unconscious: Narrative as a Socially Symbolic Act*. Ithaca, N.Y.: Cornell University Press, 1981.

———. *Postmodernism; or, The Cultural Logic of Late Capitalism*. Durham, N.C.: Duke University Press, 1990.

———. *A Singular Modernity: Essay on the Ontology of the Present*. London: Verso, 2002.

JanMohamed, Abdul R., and David Lloyd, eds. *The Nature and Context of Minority Discourse*. Oxford: Oxford University Press, 1990.

Jardine, Alice. *Gynesis: Configurations of Woman and Modernity*. Ithaca, N.Y.: Cornell University Press, 1985.

Jay, Paul. *Global Matters: The Transnational Turn in Literary Studies*. Ithaca, N.Y.: Cornell University Press, 2010.

Jones, Eric L. *The European Miracle: Environments, Economies, and Geopolitics in the History of Europe and Asia*. 3rd ed. Cambridge: Cambridge University Press, 2003.

Joshi, Priya. *In Another Country: Colonialism, Culture, and the English Novel in India*. New York: Columbia University Press, 2002.

Joyce, James. *A Portrait of the Artist as a Young Man* [1916]. New York: Penguin, 1968.

———. *Ulysses* [1922]. Ed. Hans Walter Gabler. New York: Random House, 1986.

Jrade, Cathy L. *Modernismo: Modernity and the Development of Spanish American Literature*. Austin: University of Texas Press, 1998.

"Judgement of the Supreme Court of India." October 18, 2000. http://www.narmada.org/sardar-sarovar/sc.ruling/.

Kabir. *Songs of Kabir*. Trans. Arvind Krishna Mehrotra. New York: NYRB, 2011.

Kalikoff, Hedy. "Gender, Genre, and Geography in Aimé Césaire's *Cahier d'un retour au pays natal*." *Callaloo* 18, no. 2 (1995): 492–505.

Kang, L. Hyun Yi. "The 'Liberatory Voice' of Theresa Hak Kyung Cha's *Dictée*." In *Writing Self Writing Nation: Essays on Theresa Hak Kyung Cha's* Dictée, ed. Elaine H. Kim and Norma Alarcón, 73–102. Berkeley, Calif.: Third Woman, 1994.

Kaplan, Karen. *Questions of Travel: Postmodern Discourses of Displacement*. Durham, N.C.: Duke University Press, 1996.

Karlekar, Malavika. *Re-Visioning the Past: Early Photography in Bengal, 1875–1915*. New Delhi: Oxford University Press, 2005.

Keen, Suzanne. *Victorian Renovations of the Novel: Narrative Annexes and the Boundaries of Representation*. Cambridge: Cambridge University Press, 1998.

Kennedy, Hugh. *When Baghdad Ruled the Muslim World: The Rise and Fall of Islam's Greatest Dynasty*. Cambridge, Mass.: Da Capo, 2004.

Kenner, Hugh. "The Making of the Modernist Canon." *Chicago Review* 34, no. 2 (Spring 1984): 49–61.

Kern, Robert. *Orientalism, Modernism, and the American Poem*. Cambridge: Cambridge University Press, 2009.

Khalfa, Jean. "Pustules, Spirals, Volcanoes: Some Images in Aimé Césaire's *Cahier d'un retour au pays natal*." *Wasafiri* 31 (Spring 2000): 43–51.

Khazanov, Anatoly M. *Nomads and the Outside World*. Madison: University of Wisconsin Press, 1994.

——. "Nomads in the History of the Sedentary Worlds." In *Nomads in the Sedentary World*, ed. Anatoly M. Khazanov and André Wink, 1–23. London: Routledge, 2001.

Khazanov, Anatoly M., and André Wink, eds. *Nomads in the Sedentary World*. London: Routledge, 2001.

Kim, Elaine H. "Poised on the In-Between: A Korean American's Reflections on Theresa Hak Kyung Cha's *Dictée*." In *Writing Self Writing Nation: Essays on Theresa Hak Kyung Cha's* Dictée, ed. Elaine H. Kim and Norma Alarcón, 3–35. Berkeley, Calif.: Third Woman, 1994.

Kim, Elaine H., and Norma Alarcón, eds. *Writing Self, Writing Nation: Essays on Theresa Hak Kyung Cha's* Dictée. Berkeley, Calif.: University of California Press, 1994.

King, John. Introduction to *The Cambridge Companion to Modern Latin American Culture*, ed. John King, 1–4. Cambridge: Cambridge University Press, 2004.

Krahl, Regina, and John Guy, *Shipwrecked: Tang Treasures and Monsoon Winds*. Washington, D.C.: Smithsonian Books, 2011.

Kripilani, Krishna. *Rabindranath Tagore—A Biography* [1962]. Ed. Supriya Roy. New Delhi: UBS, 2008.

Krishnaswamy, Revathi. "Connections, Conflicts, Complicities." In *The Postcolonial and the Global*, ed. Revathi Krishnaswamy and John C. Hawley, 2–21. Minneapolis: University of Minnesota Press, 2008.

Krishnan, R. S. "Reinscribing Conrad: Tayeb Salih's *Season of Migration to the North*." *International Fiction Review* 23, nos. 1–2 (1996): 7–15.

Kristeva, Julia. *Desire in Language*. Trans. Thomas Gora, Alice Jardine, and Leon S. Roudiez. New York: Columbia University Press, 1980.

Kuhn, Thomas S. *The Structure of Scientific Revolutions*. Chicago: University of Chicago Press, 1963.

Lago, Mary M. Introduction to *The Broken Nest*, by Rabindranath Tagore, trans. Mary M. Lago and Supriya Sen, 1–18. Columbia: University of Missouri Press, 1971.

Laity, Cassandra, ed. Special Issue on "Modernism and Transnationalisms." *Modernism/Modernity* 13, no. 3 (September 2006).

Landes, David S. *The Wealth and Poverty of Nations: Why Some Are So Rich and Some So Poor*. New York: Norton, 1998.

Landow, George P. *Hypertext 3.0: Critical Theory and New Media in an Era of Globalization* [1992]. 3rd ed. Baltimore, Md.: Johns Hopkins University Press, 2006.

Lash, Scott, and Jonathan Friedman, eds. "Subjectivity and Modernity's Other." Introduction to *Modernity and Identity*, 1–30. Oxford: Basil Blackwell, 1992.

Latour, Bruno. *We Have Never Been Modern* [1991]. Trans. Catherine Porter. Cambridge, Mass: Harvard University Press, 1993.

Layoun, Mary. "Endings and Beginnings: Reimagining the Tasks and Spaces of Comparison." In *Comparison: Theories, Approaches, Uses*, ed. Rita Felski and Susan Stanford Friedman, 210–234. Baltimore, Md.: Johns Hopkins University Press, 2013.

——. "The Female Body and 'Transnational' Reproduction; or, Rape by Any Other Name?" In *Scattered Hegemonies: Postmodernity and Transnational Feminist Practices*, ed. Inderpal Grewal and Caren Kaplan, 63–75. Minneapolis: University of Minnesota Press, 1994.

Lee, Hermione. *Virginia Woolf*. New York: Vintage, 1996.

Lee, Jong-Im. "National Allegory and the Nomadic Subject in *Ulysses*, *Midnight's Children*, and *Dictée*." Madison, Dissertation.com, 2011.

Leitner, Helga. "The Politics of Scale and Networks of Spatial Connectivity: Transnational Interurban Networks and the Rescaling of Political Governance in Europe." In *Scale and Geographical Inquiry*, ed. Eric Sheppard and Robert B. McMaster, 236–255. Oxford: Basil Blackwell, 2004.

Leonard, Garry. "'The Famished Roar of Automobiles': Modernity, the Internal Combustion Engine, and Modernism." In *Disciplining Modernism*, ed. Pamela L. Caughie, 221–241. New York: Palgrave Macmillan, 2010.

Levenson, Michael, ed. *The Cambridge Companion to Modernism*. Cambridge: Cambridge University Press, 1999.

Levin, Harry. "What Was Modernism?" [1960]. In *Refractions: Essays in Comparative Literature*, ed. Harry Levin, 271–295. Oxford: Oxford University Press, 1966.

Levine, Caroline, and B. Venkat Mani, eds. Special Issue on "What Counts as World Literature?" *Modern Language Quarterly: A Journal of Literary History* 74, no. 2 (June 2013).

Levine, June Perry. "An Analysis of the Manuscripts of *A Passage to India*." *PMLA* 85 (March 1975): 284–294.

Lewallen, Constance, ed. *The Dream of the Audience: Theresa Hak Kyung Cha (1951–1982)*. Berkeley: University of California Press, 2001.

Lewis, Mark Edward. *China's Cosmopolitan Empire: The Tang Dynasty*. Cambridge, Mass.: The Belknap Press of Harvard University Press, 2009.

Lewis, Pericles. *The Cambridge Introduction to Modernism*. Cambridge: Cambridge University Press, 2007.

Lewis, Wyndham, ed. *Blast 1* [1914]. Santa Barbara, Calif.: Black Sparrow, 1981.

Lin, Yi-Chun Tricia. "Theresa Hak Kyung Cha." In *Asian American Novelists: A Bio-Bibliographical Critical Sourcebook*, ed. E. Nelson, 34–37. Westport, Conn.: Greenwood, 2000.

Lionnet, Françoise. "Continents and Archipelagoes: From *E Pluribus Unum* to Creolized Solidarities." *PMLA* 123, no. 5 (2008): 1503–1515.

Lionnet, Françoise, and Shu-mei Shih, eds. *Minor Transnationalism*. Durham, N.C.: Duke University Press, 2005.

Liu, Lydia. "The Female Body and Nationalist Discourse: *The Field of Life and Death* Revisited." In *Scattered Hegemonies: Postmodernity and Transnational Feminist Practices*, ed. Inderpal Grewal and Caren Kaplan, 37–62. Minneapolis: University of Minnesota Press, 1994.

Lowe, Lisa. "Unfaithful to the Original: The Subject of *Dictée*." In *Writing Self Writing Nation: Essays on Theresa Hak Kyung Cha's Dictée*, ed. Elaine H. Kim and Norma Alarcón, 35–72. Berkeley, Calif.: Third Woman, 1994.

Loy, Mina. "Aphorisms on Futurism." In *The Gender of Modernism*, ed. Bonnie Kime Scott, 245. Bloomington: Indiana University Press, 1990.

Luhmann, Niklas. *Introduction to Systems Theory* [2002]. Ed. Dirk Baeker, trans. Peter Gilgen. Cambridge: Polity, 2013.

Lyotard, Jean-François. *The Postmodern Condition: A Report on Knowledge*. Trans. Geoff Bennington and Brian Massumi. Minneapolis: University of Minnesota Press, 1984.

McClintock, Anne. *Imperial Leather: Race, Gender, and Sexuality in the Colonial Context*. London: Routledge, 1995.

McKible, Adam, and Suzanne W. Churchill, eds. Special Issue: "In Conversation: The Harlem Renaissance and the New Modernist Studies." *Modernism/Modernity* 20, no. 3 (September 2013).

McHale, Brian. *Postmodernist Fiction*. New York: Methuen, 1987.

McNeill, William H. *The Rise of the West*. Chicago: University of Chicago Press, 1963.

——. "*The Rise of the West* After Twenty-Five Years." In *Civilizations and World Systems: Studying World-Historical Change*, ed. Stephen K. Sanderson, 303–320. London: Sage, 1995.

Ma, Huan [Ying Yai Shenglan]. *The Overall Survey of the Ocean's Shores*. Trans. Feng Chengjun. Cambridge: Hakluyt Society of the University Press of Cambridge, 1970.

Maier, Charles S. "Consigning the Twentieth Century to History: Alternative Narratives for the Modern Era." *American Historical Review* 105, no. 3 (2000): 1–47.

Makdisi, Saree. "The Empire Renarrated: *Season of Migration to the North* and the Reinvention of the Present." *Critical Inquiry* 18 (Summer 1992): 804–820.

——. "'Postcolonial' Literature in a Neocolonial World: Modern Arabic Culture and the End of Modernity." *boundary 2* 22, no. 1 (1995): 104–105.

Manganaro, Marc, ed. *Modernist Anthropology: From Fieldwork to Text*. Princeton, N.J.: Princeton University Press, 1990.

Mani, B. Venkat. "Bibliomigrancy: Book-Series and the Making of World Literature." In *The Routledge Companion to World Literature*, ed. Theo D'haen, David Damrosch, and Djelal Kadir, 283–296. New York: Routledge, 2011.

Mao, Douglas, and Rebecca L. Walkowitz. "The New Modernist Studies." *PMLA* 123, no. 3 (2008): 737–748.

Martin, Robert K., and George Piggford, eds. *Queer Forster*. Chicago: University of Chicago Press, 1997.

Marx, John. *The Modernist Novel and the Decline of Empire*. Cambridge: Cambridge University Press, 2005.

May, Timothy. *The Mongol Conquests in World History*. London: Reaktion, 2012.

Mehrotra, Arvind Krishna. Introduction to *Songs of Kabir*, trans. Arvind Krishna Mehrotra, xix–xxxii. New York: NYRB, 2011.

Melas, Natalie. *All the Difference in the World: Postcoloniality and the Ends of Comparison*. Stanford, Calif.: Stanford University Press, 2007.

Menocal, Maria Rosa. *The Arabic Role in Medieval Literary History: A Forgotten Heritage*. Philadelphia: University of Pennsylvania Press, 1987.

Mernissi, Fatima. *Islam and Democracy: Fear of the Modern World* [1992]. Trans. Mary Jo Lakeland. 2nd ed. New York: Basic Books, 2001.

Mignolo, Walter D. *The Darker Side of Western Modernity: Global Futures, Decolonial Options (Latin America Otherwise)*. Durham, N.C.: Duke University Press, 2011.

——. "Globalization, Civilization Processes, and the Relocation of Languages and Cultures." In *The Cultures of Globalization*, ed. Fredric Jameson and Masao Miyoshi, 32–53. Durham, N.C.: Duke University Press, 1999.

——. *Local Histories/Global Designs: Coloniality, Subaltern Knowledges, and Border Thinking*. Princeton, N.J.: Princeton University Press, 2000.

——. "The Many Faces of Cosmo-polis: Border Thinking and Critical Cosmopolitanism." In *Cosmopolitanism*, ed. Carol A. Breckenridge, Sheldon Pollock, Homi K. Bhabha, and Dipesh Chakrabarty, 158–188. Durham, N.C.: Duke University Press, 2002.

Mignolo, Walter, and Madina Tlostanova. *Learning to Unlearn: Decolonial Reflections from Eurasia and the Americas*. Columbus: Ohio University Press, 2012.

Milani, Abbas. *Lost Wisdom: Rethinking Modernity in Iran*. Washington, D.C.: Mage, 2004.

Min, Eun Lyung. "Reading the Figure of Dictation in Theresa Hak Kyung Cha's *Dictée*." In *Other Sisterhoods: Literary Theory and U.S. Women of Color*, ed. Sandra Kumanoto Stanley, 309–324. Urbana: University of Illinois Press, 1998.

Mintz, Sidney W. *Sweetness and Power: The Place of Sugar in Modern History*. New York: Penguin, 1985.

Mitchell, Timothy. Introduction to *Questions of Modernity*, ed. Timothy Mitchell, xi–xxvii. Minneapolis: University of Minnesota Press, 2000.

"Modernism After Postmodernity." Special Issue, *New German Critique* 33, no. 3 (Fall 2006).

Moeller, Hans-Georg. *Luhmann Explained: From Souls to Systems*. Chicago: Open Court, 2006.
Moffat, Wendy. *A Great Unrecorded History: A New Life of E. M. Forster*. New York: Farrar, Strauss and Giroux, 2010.
Moghadam, Valentine M. *Globalizing Women: Transnational Feminist Networks*. Baltimore, Md.: Johns Hopkins University Press, 2005.
Mohanty, Chandra Talpade: *Feminism Without Borders: Decolonizing Theory, Practicing Solidarity*. Durham, N.C.: Duke University Press, 2003.
Mohanty, Satya P. "Alternative Modernities and Medieval Indian Literature: The Oriya *Lakshmi Purana* as Radical Pedagogy." *diacritics* 38, no. 3 (Fall 2008): 3–21.
Mohanty, Sharmistha. Preface to *Rabindranath Tagore: Broken Nest and Other Stories*, trans. Sharmistha Mohanty, x–xvii. Chennai: Transquebar, 2009.
Moorthy, Shanti, and Ashraf Jamal, eds. *Indian Ocean Studies: Cultural, Social, and Political Perspectives*. London: Routledge, 2009.
Moran, Jo Ann Hoeppner, "E. M. Forster's *A Passage to India*: What Really Happened in the Caves." *Modern Fiction Studies* 34, no. 4 (Winter 1988): 596–604.
Morgan, David. *The Mongols*. Rev. ed. Oxford: Basil Blackwell, 2007.
Morgan, Robin. "Planetary Feminism." In *Sisterhood Is Global*, ed. Robin Morgan, 1–37. New York: Feminist Press, 1996.
Moretti, Franco. "Conjectures on World Literature." *New Left Review*, 2nd ser. (January–February 2000): 54–68.
Morrison, Toni. *Beloved*. New York: Random House, 1987.
——. "Unspeakable Things Unspoken: The Afro-American Presence in American Literature." *Michigan Quarterly Review* 28 (Winter 1989): 1–34.
Moses, Michael Valdez. *The Novel and the Globalization of Culture*. New York: Oxford University Press, 1995.
Mufti, Aamir R. "Global Comparison." *Critical Inquiry* 31 (Winter 2005): 472–489.
Mukerji, Joyasree. Introduction to *She: Short Stories of Rabindranath Tagore*, trans. Joyasree Mukerji, i–xi. New Delhi, 2004.
Narayan, Uma. *Dislocating Cultures: Identities, Traditions, and Third World Feminism*. London: Routledge, 1997.
Nelson, Cary. *Repression and Recovery: Modern American Poetry and the Politics of Cultural Meaning, 1910–1945*. Madison: University of Wisconsin Press, 1989.
Nesbitt, Nick. "Antinomies of Double Consciousness in Aimé Césaire's *Cahier d'un retour au pays natal*." *Mosaic* 33, no. 3 (September 2000): 107–138.
New Larousse Encyclopedia of Mythology. Trans. Richard Aldington and Delano Ames. New York: Prometheus, 1968.
Nicholls, Peter. *Modernisms: A Literary Guide* [1995]. Rev. ed. New York: Macmillan, 2009.
Nixon, Robert. *Slow Violence and the Environmentalism of the Poor*. Cambridge, Mass.: Harvard University Press, 2010.
Norris, Margot. "Modernist Eruptions." In *The Columbia History of the American Novel*, ed. Emory Elliot, 311–330. New York: Columbia University Press, 1991.

North, Michael. *The Dialect of Modernism: Race, Language, and Twentieth-Century Literature.* New York: Oxford University Press, 1994.
Oceanic Studies. "Theories and Methodologies." *PMLA* 125, no. 3 (May 2010): 657–736.
Okam, Hilary. "Aspects of Imagery and Symbolism in the Poetry of Aimé Césaire." *Yale French Studies* 53 (1976): 175–196.
Omvedt, Gail. "An Open Letter to Arundhati Roy." June 1999. www.marvada.org/debates/gail/gail.open.letter.html/.
Online Archive of California. *Guide to the Theresa Hak Kyung Cha Collection 1971–1991.* http://www.oac.cdlib.org/findaid/ark:/13030/tf238n986k/.
Owen, Stephen, ed. *The Great Age of Chinese Poetry: The High T'ang.* New Haven, Conn.: Yale University Press, 1981.
Papastergiadis, Nikos. *The Turbulence of Migration: Globalization, Deterritorialization, and Hybridity.* Cambridge: Polity, 2000.
Josephine Nock-Hee Park, "'What of the Partition': *Dictée*'s Boundaries and the American Epic." *Contemporary Literature* 46, no. 2 (2005): 213–242.
Parry, Benita. *Delusions and Discoveries: Studies in India in the British Imagination, 1880–1930.* London: Penguin, 1972.
Pavlić, Edward M. *Crossroads Modernism: Descent and Emergence in African-American Literary Culture.* Minneapolis: University of Minnesota Press, 2002.
Perloff, Marjorie. "Modernist Studies." In *Redrawing the Boundaries: The Transformation of English and American Literary Studies,* ed. Stephen Greenblatt and Giles Gunn, 154–178. New York: Modern Language Publications, 1992.
Prendergast, Christopher, ed. *Debating World Literature.* London: Verso, 2004.
Phillips, Mark Salber, and Gordon Schochet, eds. *Questions of Tradition.* Toronto: University of Toronto Press, 2004.
Pollard, Charles W. *New World Modernisms: T. S. Eliot, Derek Walcott, and Kamau Brathwaite.* Charlottesville: University of Virginia Press, 2004.
Pollock, Sheldon. "Cosmopolitan and Vernacular in History." In *Cosmopolitanism,* ed. Carol A. Breckenridge, Sheldon Pollock, Homi K. Bhabha, and Dipesh Chakrabarty, 15–53. Durham, N.C.: Duke University Press, 2002.
———. *The Language of the Gods in the World of Men: Sanskrit, Culture, and Power in Premodern India.* Berkeley: University of California Press, 2006.
Pondrom, Cyrena N. *The Road from Paris: French Influence on English Poetry, 1900–1920.* Cambridge: Cambridge University Press, 1974.
Pound, Ezra. *Cathay, for the Most Part from the Chinese of Rihaku* [1915]. Forgotten Books, 2010. http://www.forgottenbooks.org/.
———. *Make It New.* London: Faber and Faber, 1934.
Prasad, Amar Nath. *Arundhati Roy's* The God of Small Things: *A Critical Appraisal.* New Delhi: Sarup and Sons, 2004.
Pratt, Mary Louise. *Imperial Eyes: Travel Writing and Transculturation.* London: Routledge, 1992.

———. "Modernity and Periphery: Toward a Global and Relational Analysis." In *Beyond Dichotomies: Histories, Identities, Cultures, and the Challenge of Globalization*, ed. Elisabeth Mudimbe-Boyi, 21–48. Albany, N.Y.: SUNY Press, 2002.
Price, Sally. *Primitive Art in Civilized Places*. Chicago: University of Chicago Press, 1989.
Qian, Zhaoming. *Orientalism and Modernism: The Legacy of China in Pound and Williams*. Durham, N.C.: Duke University Press, 1995.
———. *The Modernist Response to Chinese Art: Pound, Moore, Stevens*. Charlottesville: University of Virginia Press, 2003.
———. *Ezra Pound and China*. Ann Arbor: University of Michigan Press, 2003.
Rabbit, Kara M. "Prose Poem, *Anti-poème*, Political Force: The Critical Function of Genre in Aimé Césaire's *Cahier d'un retour au pays natal*." *Romance Notes* 39, no. 1 (Fall 1998): 35–46.
Radice, William. Introduction to *Selected Short Stories*, by Rabindranath Tagore. Trans. William Radice, 1–30. Rev. ed. London: Penguin, 2005.
Radhakrishnan, R. "Derivative Discourses and the Problem of Signification." *European Legacy* 7, no. 6 (2002): 783–795.
———. *Diasporic Mediations: Between Home and Location*. Minneapolis: University of Minnesota Press, 1996.
———. *Theory in an Uneven World*. Oxford: Blackwell, 2003.
———. "Why Compare?" In *Comparison: Theories, Approaches, Uses*, ed. Rita Felski and Susan Stanford Friedman, 15–33. Baltimore, Md.: Johns Hopkins University Press, 2013.
———. "Worlding by Any Other Name." In *History, the Human, and the World Between*, 183–248. Durham, N.C.: Duke University Press, 2008.
Ramanujan, A. K. *Speaking of Śiva*. Trans. A. K. Ramanujan. London: Penguin, 1973.
Ramazani, Jahan. *The Hybrid Muse: Postcolonial Poetry in English*. Chicago: University of Chicago Press, 2001.
———. *A Transnational Poetics*. Chicago: University of Chicago Press, 2009.
Ramos, Julio. *Divergent Modernities: Culture and Politics in Nineteenth-Century Latin America*. Trans. John D. Blanco. Durham, N.C.: Duke University Press, 2001.
Rampersad, Arnold. "Langston Hughes and Approaches to Modernism in the Harlem Renaissance." In *The Harlem Renaissance Revaluations*, ed. Amrijit Singh, William S. Shiver, and Stanley Brodwin, 49–71. New York: Garland, 1989.
Rasch, William. *Niklas Luhmann's Modernity: The Paradoxes of Differentiation*. Stanford, Calif.: Stanford University Press, 2000.
Ray, Sangeeta. *En-Gendering India: Woman and Nation in Colonial and Postcolonial Narratives*. Durham, N.C.: Duke University Press, 2001.
Ray, Satyajit. *Charulata (The Lonely Wife)*. Film. 1964.
Reinhold, Natalya, ed. *Woolf Across Cultures*. New York: Pace University Press, 2004.
Restuccia, Frances. "'A Cave of My Own': The Sexual Politics of Indeterminacy." *Raritan* 2 (Fall 1989): 110–128.
Ricci, Ronit. *Islam Translated: Literature, Conversion, and the Arabic Cosmopolis of South and Southeast Asia*. Chicago: University of Chicago Press, 2011.

Rich, Adrienne. "Notes Toward a Politics of Location." In *Blood, Bread, and Poetry: Selected Prose, 1979-1985*, 210-232. New York: Norton, 1986.
———. *On Lies, Secrets, and Silence: Selected Prose, 1966-1978*. New York: Norton, 1979.
Robbins, Bruce. "Blaming the System." In *Immanuel Wallerstein and the Problem of the World: System, Scale, Culture*, ed. David Palumbo-Liu, Bruce Robbins, and Nirvana Tanoukhi, 41-66. Durham, N.C.: Duke University Press, 2011.
———. "Comparative Cosmopolitans." In *Cosmopolitics: Thinking and Feeling Beyond the Nation*, ed. Pheng Cheah and Bruce Robbins, 246-264. Minneapolis: University of Minnesota Press, 1998.
Roberts, J. M. *The Triumph of the West*. Boston: Little, Brown, 1985.
Robinson, Andrew. *The Art of Rabindranath Tagore*. London: Andre Deutsch, 1989.
Rogers, Gayle. *Modernism and the New Spain: Britain, Cosmopolitan Europe, and Literary History*. Oxford: Oxford University Press, 2012.
Rosaldo, Renato. *Culture and Truth: The Remaking of Social Analysis*. Boston: Beacon, 1993.
Rosenberg, Fernando J. *The Avant-Garde and Geopolitics in Latin America*. Pittsburgh, Penn.: University of Pittsburgh Press, 2006.
Ross, Dorothy. "American Modernities, Past and Present." *American Historical Review* 116, no. 3 (June 2011): 702-714.
Ross, Stephen. "Uncanny Modernism; or, Analysis Interminable." In *Disciplining Modernism*, ed. Pamela L. Caughie, 33-52. New York: Palgrave Macmillan, 2010.
Rothstein, Eric. "Broaching a Cultural Login of Modernity." *Modern Language Quarterly* 61, no. 2 (June 2000): 359-394.
Rougier, Louis Auguste Paul. *The Genius of the West*. Los Angeles: Nash, 1971.
Roudometof, Victor, "Globalization or Modernity?" *Comparative Literature Review* 34 (1994): 18-45.
Roudometof, Victor, and Roland Robertson. "Globalization, World-System Theory, and the Comparative Study of Civilizations." In *Civilizations and World Systems: Studying World-Historical Change*, ed. Stephen K. Sanderson, 273-298. London: Sage, 1995.
Roux, Jean-Paul. *Genghis Khan and the Mongol Empire*. Trans. Toula Ballas. New York: Abrams, 2002.
Roy, Arundhati. *The Cost of Living*. New York: Modern Library, 1999.
———. *The God of Small Things*. New York: Random House, 1997.
———. *Power Politics*. 2nd ed. Cambridge, Mass.: South End, 2001.
———. *War Talk*. Cambridge, Mass.: South End, 2003.
Rubin, William. "Modernist Primitivism: An Introduction." In *"Primitivism" in Twentieth-Century Art: Affinity of the Tribal and the Modern*, ed. William Rubin, 1:1-84. Boston: Little, Brown, 1984.
Rushdie, Salman. "Imaginary Homelands." 1982. In *Imaginary Homelands: Essays and Criticism, 1981-1991*, 9-21. London: Granta, 1991.
———. *Midnight's Children*. 1981. New York: Random House, 2006.
Sadgrove, Philip. "Al-Tayyib Salih." In *African Writers*, ed. Brian C. Cox, 2:733-744. New York: Charles Scribner's, 1997.

Said, Edward W. *Culture and Imperialism*. New York: Vintage, 1993.
——. "Culture and the Vultures." *Times Higher Education Supplement* 24 (January 1992): 15.
——. *Orientalism*. New York: Random House, 1978.
——. "Reflections on Exile." In *Reflections on Exile and Other Essays*, 173–186. Cambridge: Harvard University Press, 2002.
——. "Traveling Theory." In *The World, the Text, and the Critic*, 226–247. Cambridge, Mass.: Harvard University Press, 1983.
——. "Traveling Theory Reconsidered" [1994]. In *Reflections on Exile and Other Essays*, 436–452. Cambridge, Mass.: Harvard University Press, 2002.
Saldívar, José David. Foreword to *Divergent Modernities: Culture and Politics in Nineteenth-Century Latin America*, by Julio Ramos, trans. John D. Blanco, xi–xxxiv. Durham, N.C.: Duke University Press, 2001.
Salih, Tayeb. *Season of Migration to the North* [first Arabic publication: 1966]. Trans. Denys Johnson-Davies [first English translation: 1969]. Boulder, Colo.: Three Continents, 1997.
Sanderson, Stephen K., ed. *Civilizations and World Systems: Studying World-Historical Change*. London: Sage, 1995.
Sanderson, Stephen K., and Thomas D. Hall, "World Systems Approaches to World-Historical Change." In *Civilizations and World Systems: Studying World Historical Change*, ed. Stephen K. Sanderson, 95–107. London: Sage, 1995.
Santos, Irene Ramalho, and António Sousa Ribeiro, eds. *Translocal Modernisms: International Perspectives*. Bern: Peter Lang, 2008.
Sarup, Madan. "Home and Identity." In *Travellers' Tales: Narratives of Home and Displacement*, ed. George Roberston, Melinda Mash, Lisa Tickner, Jon Bird, Barry Curtis, and Tom Putnam, 93–105. London: Routledge, 1994.
Sash, Mike. *Tulip Mania: The Story of the World's Most Coveted Flower and the Extraordinary Passions It Aroused*. New York: Three Rivers, 1999.
Saussy, Haun, ed. *Comparative Literature in an Age of Globalization*. Baltimore, Md.: Johns Hopkins University Press, 2006.
Schafer, Edward H. *The Golden Peaches of Samarkand: A Study of T'ang Exotics*. Berkeley: University of California Press, 1963.
Scharfman, Ronnie. *"Engagement" and the Language of the Subject in the Poetry of Aimé Césaire*. Gainesville: University of Florida Press, 1979.
Schreiner, Olive. *From Man to Man* [1926]. London: Virago, 1982.
Scott, Bonnie Kime, ed. *Gender in Modernism: New Geographies, Complex Intersections*. Urbana: University of Illinois Press, 2007.
——. Introduction to *The Gender of Modernism: A Critical Anthology*, ed. Bonnie Kime Scott, 1–18. Bloomington: Indiana University Press, 1990.
Scott, James C. *Seeing Like a State: How Certain Schemes to Improve the Human Condition Have Failed*. New Haven, Conn.: Yale University Press, 1998.
Scott, John. *Social Network Analysis: A Handbook*. 2nd ed. London: Sage, 2000.
Seaton, J. P., and James Cryer. *Bright Moon, Perching Bird: Poems of Li Po and Tu Fu*. Trans. J. P. Seaton and James Cryer. Middletown, Conn.: Wesleyan University Press, 1987.

Seely, Clinton B. "Translating Between Media: Rabindranath Tagore and Satyajit Ray." *The Tagore Issue of Parabaas*. http://www.parabaas.com/rabindranath/articles/pClinton1.html.
Seyhan, Azade. *Writing Outside the Nation*. Princeton, N.J.: Princeton University Press, 2001.
Shaheen, Mohammad. "Tayeb Salih and Conrad." *Comparative Literature Studies* 22, no. 1 (1985): 156–171.
Sharpe, Jenny. *Allegories of Empire: The Figure of Woman in the Colonial Text*. Minneapolis: University of Minnesota Press, 1993.
Shen, Dan. "Story/Discourse." In *The Routledge Encyclopedia of Narrative Theory*, ed. David Herman, Manfred Jahn, and Marie Laure-Ryan, 566–568. London: Routledge, 2005.
Sheppard, Eric, and Robert B. McMaster, eds. *Scale and Geographical Inquiry: Nature, Society, and Method*. Oxford: Blackwell, 2004.
Shih, Shu-mei. "Comparison as Relation." In *Comparison: Theories, Approaches, Uses*, ed. Rita Felski and Susan Stanford Friedman, 78–98. Baltimore, Md.: Johns Hopkins University Press, 2013.
——. "Nationalism and Korean American Women's Writing: Theresa Hak Kyung Cha's *Dictée*." In *Speaking the Other Self: American Women Writers*, ed. Jeanne Campbell Reesman, 144–162. Athens: University of Georgia Press, 1997.
——. *The Lure of the Modern: Writing Modernism in Semicolonial China, 1917–1933*. Berkeley: University of California Press, 2001.
Shikidu, Muraski. *The Tale of Genji*. Trans. Edward G. Seidensticker. New York: Knopf, 1978.
Shils, Edward. *Tradition*. Chicago: University of Chicago Press, 1981.
Shohat, Ella, and Robert Stam. *Unthinking Eurocentrism*. London: Routledge, 1994.
Shyrock, Andrew, ed. *Deep History: The Architecture of Past and Present*. Berkeley: University of California Press, 2011.
Siddiq, Muhammed. "The Process of Individuation in Al-Tayyeb Salih's Novel *Season of Migration to the North*." *Journal of Arabic Literature* 9 (1978): 67–104.
Silko, Leslie Marmon. *Ceremony*. New York: Signet, 1977.
Silver, Brenda R., "Periphrasis, Power, and Rape in *A Passage to India*," *Novel* 22 (Fall 1988): 86–105.
——. *Virginia Woolf Icon*. Chicago: University of Chicago Press, 1999.
——. *Virginia Woolf's Reading Notebooks*. Princeton, N.J.: Princeton University Press, 1983.
Singleton, Brent D. "African Bibliophiles: Books and Libraries in Medieval Timbuktu." *Libraries & Culture* 39, no. 1 (Winter 2004): 1–12.
Škrabec, Simona. "Literary Translation: The International Panorama." In *To Be Translated or Not to Be: Pen/IRL Report on the International Situation of Literary Translation*, ed. Esther Allen, 35–48. Barcelona: Institut Ramon Llull, 2007. http://www.peninternational.org/wpcontent/uploads/2011/04/Translation-report_OK-2.pdf.
Slaughter, Joseph, "Against Modernism." Conference on Comparative Modernisms, Medialities, Modernities. New York University/Fordham University/Modern Language Initiative, May 4–5, 2012.
Smith, Linda T. *Decolonizing Methodology: Research and Indigenous Peoples*. New York: St. Martins, 1999.

Smith, Terry. *Contemporary Art: World Currents*. London: Pearson, 2011.
———. *What Is Contemporary Art?* Pittsburgh, Penn.: Pittsburgh University Press, 2009.
Sogani, Rajul, and Indira Gupta. Introduction to *The Uprooted Vine*, by Swarnakumari Debi. Trans. Rajul Sogani and Indira Gupta, vii–xiv. New Delhi: Oxford University Press, 2004.
Soja, Edward. *Postmodern Geographies: The Reassertion of Space in Critical Social Theory*. London: Verso, 1989.
Spahr, Juliana M. "Postmodernism, Readers, and Theresa Hak Kyung Cha's *Dictée*." *College Literature* 23, no. 3 (October 1996): 23–43.
Spivak, Gayatri Chakravorty. *Can the Subaltern Speak? The History of an Idea*. Ed. Rosalind C. Morris. New York: Columbia University Press, 2010.
———. *Death of a Discipline*. New York: Columbia University Press, 2003.
———. *In Other Worlds: Essays in Cultural Politics*. London: Methuen, 1987.
———. "Subaltern Studies: Deconstructing Historiography." In *In Other Worlds: Essays in Cultural Politics*, 197–221. London: Methuen, 1987.
———. "Languages Other Than English." Conference on Comparative Modernisms, Medialities, Modernities. Fordham University/New York University/Modern Language Initiative, May 4–5, 2012.
Stadler, Felix. *Manuel Castells*. Cambridge: Polity, 2006.
Stevens, Wallace. "Thirteen Ways of Looking at a Blackbird." In *The Collected Poems of Wallace Stevens*, 92–95. New York: Vintage, 1990.
Stock, Brian. "Toward Interpretive Pluralism: Literary History and the History of Reading." *New Literary History* 39, no. 3 (Summer 2008): 389–413.
Stoler, Ann Laura. *Carnal Knowledge and Imperial Power: Race and the Intimate in Colonial Rule*. Berkeley: University of California Press, 2002.
Subrahmanyam, Sanjay. "Hearing Voices: Vignettes of Early Modernity in South Asia, 1400–1750." *Daedalus* 127, no. 3 (Summer 1998): 75–100.
Suleri, Sara. *The Rhetoric of British Empire*. Chicago: University of Chicago Press, 1992.
Suranna, Pingali. *The Sound of the Kiss, or the Story That Must Never Be Told*. Trans. Velcheru Narayana Rao and David Shulman. New York: Columbia University Press, 2002.
Swarnakumari Debi. *The Unfinished Song/Kahake* [1898]. Ed. C. Vijayasree. New Delhi: Oxford University Press, 2008.
———. *The Uprooted Vine/Snehalata ba Palita* [1892]. Trans. Rajul Sogani and Indira Gupta. New Delhi: Oxford University Press, 2004.
Symes, Carol. "When We Talk About Modernity." *American Historical Review* 116, no. 3 (June 2011): 715–726.
Tagore, Rabindranath. *The Broken Nest/Nashtanir* [1901]. Trans. Mary M. Lago and Supriya Sen. Columbia: University of Missouri Press, 1971.
———. *A Grain of Sand/Chokher Bali* [1903]. Trans. Sreejata Guha. New Delhi: Penguin, 2003.
———. *Gora*. [1909]. Trans. Sujit Mukherjee. New Delhi: Sahitya Akademi, 2010.
———. *The Home and the World/Ghare Baire* [1916]. Trans. Surendranath Tagore. London: Macmillan, 1985.
———. *Quartet/Chaturanga* [1916]. Trans. Kaiser Haq. Oxford: Heinemann, 1993.

———. *Rabindranath Tagore: Broken Nest and Other Stories*. Trans. Sharmistha Mohanty. Chennai: Tranquebar, 2009.

———. *Reminiscences* [1917]. London: Macmillan, 1961.

———. *Selected Short Stories*. Trans. Krishna Dutta and Mary Lago. London: Macmillan, 1991.

———. *Selected Short Stories*. Trans. William Radice. Rev. ed. London: Penguin, 2005.

———. *Selected Writings on Literature and Language*. Ed. Sukanta Chaudhuri. New Delhi: Oxford University Press, 2001.

———. *She: Short Stories of Rabindranath Tagore*. Trans. Joyaspree Mukerji. New Delhi: UBS, 2004.

Tannahill, Reay. *Food in History* [1973]. Rev. ed. New York: Broadway, 1995.

Tanoukhi, Nirvana. "The Scale of World Literature." In *Immanuel Wallerstein and the Problem of the World*, ed. David Palumbo-Liu, Bruce Robbins, and Nirvana Tanoukhi, 78–98. Durham, N.C.: Duke University Press, 2011.

Taylor, Peter J. "Is There a Europe of Cities? World Cities and the Limits of Geographical Scale Analysis." In *Scale and Geographical Inquiry: Nature, Society, and Method*, ed. Eric Sheppard and Robert B. McMaster, 213–235.Oxford: Blackwell, 2004.

Talbayev, Edwige Tamalet, "Berber Poetry and the Issue of Derivation: Alternate Symbolist Trajectories." In *The Oxford Handbook of Global Modernisms*, ed. Mark Wollaeger, with Matt Eatough, 81–109. Oxford: Oxford University Press, 2012.

Thacker, Andrew. *Moving Through Modernity: Space and Geography in Modernism*. Manchester: University of Manchester Press, 2003.

Tharu, Susie, and K. Lalita. "Swarnakumari Devi." In *Women Writing in India: 600 BC to the Present*, vol. 1: *600 BC to the Early Twentieth Century*, ed. Susie Tharu and K. Lalita, 235–238. New York: Feminist Press, 1991.

Tickell, Alex, ed. *Arundhati Roy's* The God of Small Things: *A Routledge Study Guide*. New York: Routledge, 2007.

Torgovnick, Marianna. *Gone Primitive: Savage Intellectuals, Modern Lives*. Chicago: University of Chicago Press, 1990.

Trouillot, Michel-Rolph. "Anthropology and the Savage Slot: The Poetics and Politics of Otherness." In *Recapturing Anthropology: Working in the Present*, ed. Richard G. Fox, 17–44. Santa Fe, N.M.: School of American Research Press, 1991.

Trumpener, Katie. "In the Grid: Period and Experience." *PMLA* 127, no. 2 (March 2012): 349–356.

———. "Modernist Geographies: The Provinces and the World." The Global Circulation Project on *Global Modernisms. Literature Compass* 9, no. 9 (September 2012): 623–630.

Tsing, Anna Lowenhaupt. *Friction: An Ethnography of Global Connection*. Princeton, N.J.: Princeton University Press, 2004.

———. "Transitions as Translations." In *Transitions, Environments, Translations: Feminisms in International Politics*, ed. Joan W. Scott, Cora Kaplan, and Debra Keates, 253–272. London: Routledge, 1997.

Tucker, Robert C., ed. *The Marx-Engels Reader*. 2nd. ed. New York: Norton, 1978.

Turner, Jack. *Spice: The History of a Temptation*. New York: Vintage, 2004.

Twentieth-Century Literature. Special Issue: "After Postmodernism." 53, no. 3 (2007).
Unruh, Vicky. *Latin American Vanguards: The Art of Contentious Encounters*. Berkeley: University of California Press, 1994.
Urry, John. *Mobilities*. Malden, Mass.: Polity, 2007.
Van Ness, Peter. *Debating Human Rights: Critical Essays from the United States and Asia*. Peter London: Rutledge, 1999.
Vaudeville, Charlotte. *A Weaver Named Kabir: Selected Verses with Detailed Biographical and Historical Introduction*. Delhi: Oxford University Press, 1993.
Venuti, Lawrence, ed. *The Translation Studies Reader*. London: Routledge, 2000.
Viviano, Frank. "China's Great Armada." *National Geographic* 208, no. 1 (July 2005): 28–53.
Waldron, Arthur. Introduction to *The Mongol Period*, by Bertold Spuler. Trans. F. R. C. Bagley. Princeton, N.J.: Princeton University Press, 1994.
Walkowitz, Rebecca L. *Born Translated: The Contemporary Novel in an Age of World Literature*. New York: Columbia University Press, 2015.
——. "Close Reading in an Age of Global Writing." *Modern Language Quarterly* 74, no. 2 (2013): 171–195.
——. *Cosmopolitan Style: Modernism Beyond the Nation*. New York: Columbia University Press, 2006.
Wallerstein, Immanuel. "Eurocentrism and Its Avatars: The Dilemmas of Social Science." *New Left Review* 226 (November–December 1997): 93–108.
——. *The Modern World-System: Capitalist Agriculture and the Origins of the European World-Economy in the Sixteenth Century*. New York: Academic Press, 1974.
——. *World-Systems Analysis: An Introduction*. Durham, N.C.: Duke University Press, 2004.
Watson, Oliver. *Persian Lustre Ware*. London: Faber and Faber, 1985.
Weatherford, Jack. *Genghis Khan and the Making of the Modern World*. New York: Three Rivers, 2004.
Weber, Max. *The Protestant Ethic and the Spirit of Capitalism*. Trans. Talcott Parsons. New York: Scribner's, 1958.
Werbner, Pnina, and Tariq Modood, eds. *Debating Cultural Hybridity: Multicultural Identities and the Politics of Anti-Racism*. London: Zed, 1997.
Whitehead, Neil. "Monstrosity and Marvel: Symbolic Convergence and Mimetic Elaboration in Transcultural Representation." *Studies in Travel Writing* 1 (1997): 72–96.
Wicke, Jennifer. "Appreciation, Depreciation: Modernism's Speculative Bubble." *Modernism/Modernity* 8, no. 3 (September 2001): 389–404.
——. "The Bananas of Modernity." Unpublished paper.
Wigen, Kären. "Cartographies of Connection: Ocean Maps as Metaphors for Inter-Area History." In *Immanuel Wallerstein and the Problem of the World*, ed. David Palumbo-Liu, Bruce Robbins, and Nirvana Tanoukhi, 138–186. Durham, N.C.: Duke University Press, 2011.
Wilkinson, David. "Central Civilizations." In *Civilizations and World Systems: Studying World-Historical Change*, ed. Stephen Sanderson, 31–59. London: Sage, 1995.
Williams, Raymond. *Keywords: A Vocabulary of Culture and Society* [1976]. Rev. ed. New York: Oxford University Press, 1983.

———. *The Politics of Modernism: Against the New Conformists.* New York: Verso, 1989.

———. "When Was Modernism?" *New Left Review* 1, no. 175 (May–June 1989). http://www.newleftreview.org.ezproxy.library.wisc.edu/I/175/raymond.williams/.

Wink, André. "Re-Emerging Super-Powers: Turkey, Iran, India, and China." Lecture, University of Wisconsin–Madison, March 5, 2014.

Winnett, Susan. "Coming Unstrung: Women, Men, Narrative, and Principles of Pleasure." In *Narrative Dynamics*, ed. Brian Richardson, 138–158. Columbus: Ohio State University Press, 2002.

Wollaeger, Mark, with Matt Eatough, eds. *The Oxford Handbook of Global Modernisms.* Oxford: Oxford University Press, 2012.

Wong, Shelley Sunn. "Unnaming the Same: Theresa Hak Kyung Cha's *Dictée*," in *Writing Self Writing Nation: Essays on Theresa Hak Kyung Cha's* Dictée, ed. Elaine H. Kim and Norma Alarcón, 103–142. Berkeley, Calif.: Third Woman, 1994.

Woodside, Alexander. *Lost Modernities: China, Vietnam, Korea, and the Hazards of World History.* Cambridge, Mass.: Harvard University Press, 2006.

Woolf, Virginia. *Between the Acts* [1941]. London: Hogarth, 1990.

———. *The Diary of Virginia Woolf, 1915–1919.* Vol. 1. Ed. Anne Olivier Bell. New York: Harcourt Brace Jovanovich, 1977.

———. *The Diary of Virginia Woolf, 1925–1930.* Vol. 3. Ed. Anne Olivier Bell. New York: Harcourt Brace Jovanovich, 1980.

———. *Jacob's Room* [1922]. London: Hogarth, 1990.

———. *Night and Day* [1919]. London: Vintage, 2000.

———. "Olive Schreiner." In *The Essays of Virginia Woolf, 1925–1930*, ed. Andrew McNeillie, 4:4–6. London: Hogarth, 1994.

———. *A Room of One's Own* [1929]. New York: Harcourt Brace Jovanovich, 1957.

———. *A Sketch of the Past.* In *Moments of Being*, ed. Jeanne Schulkind, 61–160. 2nd ed. New York: Harcourt Brace Jovanovich, 1985.

———. *To the Lighthouse* [1927]. New York: Harcourt Brace Jovanovich, 1981.

———. *The Voyage Out* [1915]. London: Vintage, 2000.

———. *The Years* [1937]. London: Hogarth, 1990.

———. *Three Guineas* [1938]. Ed. Jane Marcus. New York: Harcourt, 2006.

Yack, Bernard. *The Fetishism of Modernities: Epochal Self-Consciousness in Contemporary Social and Political Thought.* Notre Dame, Ind.: Notre Dame University Press, 1997.

Yao, Stephen G. *Translation and the Languages of Modernism: Gender, Politics, Language.* New York: Palgrave Macmillan, 2002.

Yeats, W. B. "Among School Children." In *The Collected Poems of W. B. Yeats*, ed. Richard J. Finneran, 212–214. New York: Macmillan, 1956.

———. "The Second Coming." In *The Collected Poems of W. B. Yeats*, ed. Richard J. Finneran, 284–287. New York: Macmillan, 1956.

Young, David, ed. *Five T'ang Poets.* Trans. David Young. Oberlin, Ohio: Oberlin College Press, 1990.

Young, Robert J. C. *Colonial Desire: Hybridity in Theory, Culture, and Race*. London: Routledge, 1995.

Yu, Timothy. *Race and the Avant-Garde: Experimental and Asian American Poetry Since 1965*. Stanford, Calif.: Stanford University Press, 2009.

Zuckerman, Larry. *The Potato*. New York: North Point, 1998.

Zuk, Patrick. "What Was Modernism?" *Journal of Music* 5, no. 5 (September–October 2004): 18–23.

INDEX

Abbasid Caliphate, 5, 61, 190, 199–204
Abu-Lughod, Janet, 9, 98, 99, 125, 203–4
acceleration, 158–62; with aesthetics, 314–15; digital revolution and, 321; relative nature of, 318–19; technology and, 161
Adl, Mohammed el, 250, 254
aesthetics, 4–6, 30–32, 183–214; Abbasid Caliphate and, 199–204; acceleration with, 314–15; avant-garde and, 332; cobalt blue glaze and, 199–204; Du Fu and, 191–98; Eurocentrism and, 190; of high culture, 51; high modernism and, 184–87; in India, 204–13; innovation and, 186–88, 191–95; Kabir and, 204–13; metonym and, 41; multiple modernities and, 185–86; postmodernism and, 319, 350n19; recurrent modernities and, 185–86; re-vision of, 11; sociology and, 353n34; Tamerlane, 204–13; Tang Dynasty and, 191–98; "the West" and, 189–91; Westernization and, 335
affiliation, 216, 219, 237–38, 250, 255
Afghanistan, 157
Africa: art of, 65–66, 66, 67; Enlightenment and, 62; enslavement and, 47, 62; jazz from, 62; polycentricity and, 59. *See also Heart of Darkness*; *Season of Migration to the North*; Songhay Empire

African Americans, 173–74; Harlem Renaissance of, 40–41, 316
After the Great Divide (Huyssen), 321
Age of Discoveries, 119, 137
Aguiar, Marian, 160
Akbar the Great, 205
Al-Andalus, 5, 61, 74–75
Ali, Monica, 53–54; divergence and, 315
Allegories of Empire (Sharpe), 240
All That Is Solid Melts Into Air (Berman), 32
alternative modernities, 59, 147–52, 321
Alternative Modernities (Gaonkar), 148–50
Amin, Samir, 125
Amritsar Massacre, 239
AMSN. *See* Australian Modernist Studies Network
Anand, Mulk Raj, 77, 188, 318
anarchy, 32
Anderson, Mary, 102–3
Anderson, Sherwood, 41
Andrade, Oswald de, 136–37, 174
androcentrism, 339
Angel of History, 178
An Lushan Rebellion, 194, 196, 198
anthropomorphism, 22
anxiety, 49–52, 75
Anzaldúa, Gloria, 297
"Aphorisms on Futurism" (Loy), 34

"Apollo and his raven on a white-ground bowl," 54
Appadurai, Arjun, 7, 62, 159, 283, 284
Apparao, Gurajada, 77
Apparatus (Cha), 288
Apter, Emily, 6, 73
Apu Trilogy, The (Ray), 276
Arab Spring, 2, 321, 325
Arab world: humanism in, 48, 99–100. *See also* Islam
archipelagos, 166, 219–20, 296
Ardis, Ann, 256
Armenian Genocide, 175
Arthur M. Sackler Gallery, 200–201
Askia the Great, 167, 337
Aswan Dam, 177
Ataturk, 175
Atlan Debter ("Golden Book"), 114
Austen, Jane, 239
Australian Modernist Studies Network (AMSN), 363n17
Autobiography of an Ex-Coloured Man (Johnson), 96
avant-garde, 31, 32, 37; aesthetics and, 332; derision of, 34–35; institutionalization of, 35; in Latin America, 71–72; periodization and, 89
Avant-Garde and Geopolitics in Latin America, The (Rosenberg), 6

Babur, 205
Bacon, Francis, 116
Bande Martaram (Hail Mother), 156
Barabási, Albert-Lázló, 163
Baraka, Amiri, 44–45
Barlow, Tani E., 256–57
Barth, John, 319
Basra, ceramics of, 199–204, 202
Bath, The (Cassatt), 69
Baudelaire, Charles, 4, 32, 289; Césaire and, 292–93; Eurocentrism and, 55; Gaonkar and, 151; "The Painter of Modern Life"

by, 89; periodization and, 89. *See also Les fleurs du mal*
Bauhaus, 30, 184
Bauman, Zygmunt, 160, 165, 216
Beckman-Harned, Selena, 52
Before European Hegemony: The World System, AD 1250–1350 (Abu-Lughod), 98, 125, 203–4
Beloved (Morrison), 172–73, 341
Bengali Child's Primer (Tagore), 268
Bengal Renaissance, 48, 95, 186, 272
Benjamin, Walter, 178, 184
Berman, Jessica, 6, 183, 276
Berman, Marshall, 22–23, 32, 322; enmeshment and, 155; on periodization, 89
Bernal, Martin, 122
Bhabha, Homi K., 6, 382n6; circulation and, 169; colonial mimicry and, 140, 150, 218; *The Location of Culture* by, 169
Bhagavadgita, 311
bhakti, 207–10
Bharati, 263, 269
bibliomigrancy, 169
Bildungsroman, 189, 259, 275
binary, 38–40, 279–80; diffusionism and, 370n76; Eurocentrism and, 126–27; gender and, 370n76; racism and, 370n76; of Self-Other, 64
Black Atlantic, The (Gilroy), 166–67, 285, 291
"Blackbirds" (Sherman), 76
Blackbirds Fly (Simmons), 69
Blackbirds of 1928, 72
Blackbird V (Graver), 57
black box, of Eurocentrism, 92–93
Black Skin, White Masks (Fanon), 243
Blaut, J. M., 9, 98; European exceptionalism and, 125–26; periodization and, 87–88; tunnel history and, 88; "the West" and, 121, 122
Bly, Robert, 212
Boating Party The (Cassatt), 67, 68

Borderlands/La Frontera—the New Mestiza (Anzaldúa), 297
Bourdieu, Pierre, 1, 2, 165, 375n41
Bradbury, Malcolm, 21, 22, 51, 95, 185; on periodization, 89
Brah, Avtar, 284
Brathwaite, Kamau, 220–21
Braudel, Fernand, 8, 94, 97
Breuer, Joseph, 254
Brick Lane (Ali), 53–54, 315
Broken Nest, The/Nashtanir (Tagore), 75, 269–74
Brooker, Peter, 63
Brown, Marshall, 88
Buddhism, 103; in Mongol Empire, 110
Burbank, Jane, 9, 111, 216–17, 337; *Empires in World History* by, 107–8, 118, 215, 336
bureaucracies, 56; in Mongol Empire, 112–13; periodization and, 93
Byron, Lord, 193

Cahier d'un retour au pays natal/Notebook of a Return to the Native Land (Césaire), 286, 287, 288–89, 395n26; colonialism and, 291, 293–95; gender in, 300–308; language and, 288, 289, 309; negritude and, 291, 295–96, 300–303; poetics of displacement of, 291–92
Caiger-Smith, Alan, 201–2
Cambridge Introduction to Modernism, The (Lewis), 340
cannibalization, 136–37
canon formation, 38
canonical modernism, 88, 341
Cantos, The (Pound), 74, 184, 193, 323
capitalism, 38, 56; Mongol Empire and, 367n50, 368n56; periodization and, 93; polycentricity and, 59; unequal exchange of, 97; Wallerstein and, 98; in "the West," 127; Westernization and, 333
Carpenter, Edward, 251
cartographic scale, 95

"Cartographies of Connection" (Wigen), 163
Casanova, Pascale, 98, 185, 333, 337
Caserio, Robert, 21
Cassatt, Mary, 67, *68*, 69
Castells, Manuel, 163
Cather, Willa, 57
Catholic Church, 116–17
Caughie, Pamela L., 49
census, in Mongol Empire, 113
ceramics, of Basra, 199–204, *202*
Césaire, Aimé, 6, 12, 77, 395n26; Cha and, 283–309; contrapuntal juxtaposition and, 287–91; diaspora and, 283–309; *Discourse on Colonialism* by, 288, 395n27; gender and, 339; negritude and, 291, 295–96, 300–303; poetics of displacement by, 291–92; surrealism and, 287–88, 289, 294. *See also Cahier d'un retour au pays natal/Notebook of a Return to the Native Land*
Cha, Theresa Hak Kyung, 12, 77, 333–34, 335, 393n12, 395n21; *Apparatus* by, 288; Césaire and, 283–309; contrapuntal juxtaposition and, 287–91; diaspora and, 283–309; Eleusinian mysteries and, 306–7; film and, 288, 305–6; gender and, 300–308, 339; Greek muses and, 289–90; Korea and, 290, 296–98, 303, 305, 306, 307–8; poetics of displacement by, 291–92. *See also Dictée*
Chakrabarty, Dipesh, 6, 140, 157, 223; Eurocentrism and, 54; *Provincializing Europe* by, 149
Charulata (*The Lonely Wife*) (Ray), 276
Chatterjee, Bankim Chandra, 157, 264, 277
Chatterjee, Partha, 140, 223
Chaucer, 74
Chaudhuri, Amit, 75
Chekov, Anton, 267
Chengde Imperial Palace Stele, 73, *73*
Childe Harold (Byron), 193

China, 48; Abbasid Empire and, 200; alternative modernities and, 321; Chengde Imperial Palace Stele in, *73*; cobalt blue glaze in, 203; economic dominance of, 99, 122–23; Great Mosque in, *104*, 104–5; gunpowder in, 105, 115; Industrial Revolution in, 103, 106; Islam in, *104*, 104–5; An Lushan Rebellion in, 194, 196, 198; Ming Dynasty of, 203; nomads in, 105–19; periodization in, 105; Qing Dynasty of, 73, *73*, 203; Song Dynasty of, 101–5, 192; Three Gorges Dam in, 177; urbanization in, 105–6; "the West" and, 133–36, *134*; Yuan Dynasty of, 107, 116, 203. *See also* Tang Dynasty

China's Cosmopolitan Empire: The Tang Dynasty (Lewis), 103, 191

Chinese Exclusion Acts, 174

"Chinese Modernism, Mimetic Desire, and European Time" (Hayot), 183

Chinua Achebe, 222, 224

Chou, Eva Shan, 194, 196

Christianity: Catholic Church, 116–17; in Mongol Empire, 110, 117; postmodernism and, 321. *See also God of Small Things, The*

chuanqi (transmissions of the remarkable), 192

circle, 40–41; debate on, 326–28; hermeneutic, 326–28, 353n38; of meaning, 315

circulation, 11, 62–67, 77, 167–72, 314, 317; collage and, 215–81; of commodities, 170

Civil War, U.S., 173

Clash of Civilizations and the Remaking of World Order, The (Huntington), 129–30

Clifford, James, 7, 62, 169, 323–24; on diaspora, 284

"Climbing Yueh-yang Tower" (Chou), 194

cobalt blue, 199–204

cold societies, 352n29

Cold War, 321

collage, 11, 15, 77, 217–18, 278–81, 314; circulation and, 215–81; Conrad and, 222–30; Devi and, 255–78; gender and, 255–78; *The God of Small Things* and, 238–55; *Heart of Darkness* and, 222–30; *A Passage to India* and, 238–55; patterns, 278–81; Ray and, 276–78; Salih and, 230–38; *Season of Migration to the North* and, 230–38; Tagore and, 255–78; Woolf and, 255–78

Collection of Histories (Din), 114

Colonial and Postcolonial Rewritings of Heart of Darkness (Farn), 222

colonialism, 61–62, 216–17; Conrad and, 383n16; contact zones and, 169; disease and, 369n62; of Europe, 47, 61, 125–26, 328; feminism and, 257; gender and, 340; *Heart of Darkness* and, 222–30; language and, 74; periodization of, 90, 91, 331; polycentricity and, 59; Westernization and, 333. *See also Cahier d'un retour au pays natal/Notebook of a Return to the Native Land; Dictée; God of Small Things, The; Passage to India, A; Season of Migration to the North*

colonial mimicry, 140, 150, 218

comfort zone, 49–52

commodification, 49

comparison, 278–81, 313. *See also* collage; contrapuntalism; paratactic juxtaposition

"Comparison as Relation" (Shu-mei Shih), 183

compass, of Mongol Empire, 116

Condition of Postmodernity, The (Harvey), 32

Confucianism, 103

conjuncture, 39, 130, 153, 154–58, 232

Conrad, Joseph, 12, 53, 71, 77, 78, 186–87, 188, 218, 222–30, 237–38, 292, 335, 341; Césaire and, 295; colonialism and, 383n16; gender and, 338; Salih and, 237; *The Secret Agent* by, 187. *See also Heart of Darkness*

Consequences of Modernity, The (Giddens), 92–93
contact, 167–72
contact zones, 169; Glissant and, 63
contemporary, the, 15–16, 58, 319–22
Contemporary Art: World Currents (Smith), 320
Contemporary Literature, 320
Contemporary Women's Writing, 320
contrapuntalism, 98, 278, 287–91
Cooper, Frederick, 9, 111, 148, 216–17, 317, 324–25, 337; *Empires in World History* by, 107–8, 118, 215, 336
Coordinated Universal Time (UTC), 370n72
courte durée (short span), 94
creolization, 63, 163, 166; Glissant and, 73; "Thirteen Ways of Looking at a Blackbird" and, 77
cubism, 52, 65–70, 217
Cuddy-Keane, Melba, 63
cultural globalization, 63
cultural matrix, 57–58, 165, 216
cultural modernity, 148, 151
Culture as Praxis (Bauman), 160, 165
curse of derivativeness, 223

Dada, 184
Damrosch, David, 6, 169
dams, 177–78
Dante, 74
Das, Balaram, 75
Decolonizing Methodology: Research and Indigenous Peoples (Smith), 322–23
Dedalus, Stephen, 86, 189
deep history, 87, 365n34
deep time, 60, 76, 87, 98
"Definitional Excursions: The Meanings of *Modern/Modernity/Modernis*" (Friedman), 348n1
DeKoven, Marianne, 23–24, 222, 319
Deleuze, Gilles, 151, 152, 163
Delft pottery, 199, 203

de Man, Paul, 35–36, 156
democracy, 333
derivativeness, curse of, 140–41, 223
Desani, G. V., 187
developmentalism, 55
Devi, Kadambari, 270–71, 391n82
Devi, Swarnakumari, 12, 332, 389n65; collage and, 255–78; *Dipnirban* by, 263; gender and, 261–66; *Kahake* by, 264, 265; *The Unfinished Song* by, 264, 265; *The Uprooted Vine* by, 277; Woolf and, 275
Dharwadker, Vinay, 206, 381n36
diaspora, 283–309; Césaire and, 283–309; Cha and, 283–309; hybridity and, 396n35; Mongol Empire and, 285
Dictée (Cha), 77, 286, 287, 288, 289–90, 297–300; colonialism in, 303–4, 306–7; gender in, 300–308; poetics of displacement of, 291–92
"DIE in the Past / LIVE in the Future" (Loy), 34
diffusionism: binary and, 370n76; Eurocentrism and, 126–27; feminism and, 257
digital revolution, 2, 321
Dimock, Wai Chee, 6, 60, 76, 98, 169
Din, Rashid al-, *109*, 114, 330
Dipnirban (The Snuffing Out of Light) (Devi,), 263
Disciplining Modernism (Caughie), 49
disconnection, 188–89
Discourse on Colonialism (Césaire), 288, 395n27
discrepance, 60, 147, 153, 172–75, 339
disease, 173; colonization and, 369n62; from Europe, 116; from "the West," 130
Dislocating Cultures (Narayan), 257–58
distant reading, 312
divergence, 44, 153, 172–75; Ali and, 315; *Brick Lane* and, 315; gender and, 339; *Heart of Darkness* and, 225; Joyce and, 315; *Ulysses* and, 315

Divergent Modernities: Culture and Politics in Nineteenth-Century Latin America (Ramos), 174
domestic affairs: in *The God of Small Things*, 247–50; in *A Passage to India*, 250–55
Doyle, Laura, 63, 118–19, 174–75; *longue durée* and, 364n24
Dreyer, Carl Theodor, 305
Dubliners (Joyce), 267
Duchesne, Ricardo, 119
Duffy, Enda, 160
Du Fu, 12, 332, 337; aesthetics and, 191–98
Duncan, Isadora, 184
DuPlessis, Rachel Blau, 185
dystopia, 4, 118, 175–78, 241

EAM. *See* European Network for Avant-Garde and Modernism Studies
"Early Modernities," 42
Eastern Origins of Western Civilisation, The (Hobson), 99–100, 103
Eatough, Matt, 85
eco-cosmopolitanism, 78–79
Egypt, 177
Eisenstadt, Shmuel N., 42
Eisenstein, Sergei, 217
Eliot, George, 264–65
Eliot, T. S., 195, 220; Césaire and, 293, 295; diaspora and, 286; expatriate internationalism and, 40; experimentalism of, 327; "Tradition and the Individual Talent" by, 323; *The Waste Land* by, 4, 74, 184, 292, 293, 295
Emery, Mary Lou, 336
Empire (Hardt and Negri), 336–37
empires: debate on, 335–38; *Heart of Darkness* and, 222–30; nation-states and, 118–19. *See also specific empires*
Empires in World History (Burbank and Cooper), 107–8, 118, 215, 336
Enlightenment, 22, 35, 119, 176–77, 325, 329; Africa and, 62; humanism of, 30; metonym and, 41; periodization of, 88; postmodernism and, 350n19; rationalism of, 325
enmeshment, 216, 219, 230; Berman and, 155; networks and, 162; Ramazani and, 143, 220–21
enslavement, 47, 62
Erdrich, Louise, 157
essentialism, strategic, 146, 328, 372n5
ethnic absolutism, 300, 306, 396n35
Eurocentrism, 3, 9–10, 32, 54–55; aesthetics and, 190; as belief system, 126; binary and, 39, 126–27; black box of, 92–93; diffusionism and, 126–27; expansion and, 317; periodization and, 93; periphery and, 126–27; relational and, 127–28
Eurocentrism (Amin), 125
"Eurocentrism and Its Avatars" (Wallerstein), 130
Europe: Age of Discoveries of, 119, 137; colonialism of, 47, 61, 125–26, 328; disease from, 116; enslavement by, 47; exceptionalism of, 9, 54, 120, 125, 127–28; feudalism in, 30, 110, 368n56; high modernism in, 50; humanities in, 352n27; nation-states of, 97; printing in, 328. *See also* Enlightenment
European Miracle, The (Jones), 119
European Network for Avant-Garde and Modernism Studies (EAM), 89, 363n17
"Exercise-Book" (Tagore), 267–69
exile. *See* diaspora
expansion, 48–49; debate on, 314–17; Eurocentrism and, 317; globalization and, 315; of world-system, 97–98
expatriate internationalism, 40
experimentalism, 53, 71–72, 187, 327. *See also* aesthetics; innovation
Eysteinsson, Astradur, 89

Fanon, Frantz, 6, 395n26; colonialism and, 140; indigenization and, 90;

psychoanalysis and, 90, 243; racism and, 243
Farn, Regelind, 222
Faulkner, William, 40, 41, 53
Felman, Shoshana, 28
Felski, Rita, 1, 2, 156, 339
feminism, 256–76, 339–40; colonialism and, 257; Devi and, 264; diffusionism and, 257; in India, 258; "the West" and, 256–57; Westernization and, 334
fetishism, 350n20
feudalism, 30, 110, 368n56
Fielding, Henry, 144
Field of Cultural Production, The (Bourdieu), 1
fissure, 172–75; gender and, 339
Fitzgerald, F. Scott, 41
Flowering Plum Tree (van Gogh), 68
Foreign Affairs, 129
Formations of Modernity (Hall and Gieben), 120–21, 143
Forster, E. M., 12, 14, 77, 187, 188, 218, 238–55, 292; gender and, 339; homosexuality and, 250–55; *Maurice* by, 251, 253–54. *See also Passage to India, A*
Foucault, Michel, 84, 146, 163, 217; on heterotopia, 177
Frank, André Gunder, 9, 62, 99, 165–66, 200; on Wallerstein, 98; "the West" and, 121
French Revolution, 22
Freud, Sigmund, 184, 254; early ridicule of, 35
Friction: An Ethnography of Global Connection (Tsing), 139
From Man to Man (Schreiner), 260–61
fulcral cities, 165–66
"Futurist Manifesto" (Marinetti), 323

Gagnier, Regenia, 63
Ganeri, Jonardon, 205
Gaonkar, Dilip Parameshwar, 60, 83, 84, 90, 147–51

gender: binary and, 370n76; Césaire and, 300–308; Cha and, 300–308, 339; collage and, 255–78; debate on, 338–40; Devi and, 261–66; in *Dictée*, 300–308; in *Notebook of a Return to the Native Land*, 300–308; parody and, 382n6; Ray and, 276–78; *Season of Migration to the North* and, 233–37, 256, 339; Tagore and, 262–66, 262–74, 339; in *Ulysses*, 260–61; Woolf and, 274–78, 339. *See also* feminism
Gender in Modernism: New Geographies, Complex Intersections (Scott), 339
Gender of Modernism, The (Felski), 339
Genghis Khan and the Making of the Modern World (Weatherford), 107
Genius of "the West," The (Rougier), 119
geo-body, 303, 397n40
Geographies of Modernism, 6
"Geographies of Modernism in a Globalizing World" (Huyssen), 83
geography, 84, 94–96, 122–24
geohistory, 84
Geomodernisms, 6, 63
Giddens, Anthony, 21, 38, 55–56, 57; black box of, 92–93; industrialization and, 351n23
Gieben, Bram, 120–21, 143, 159–60
Gikandi, Simon, 217, 222; African art and, 66; *Maps of Englishness* by, 76; *Writing in Limbo: Modernism and Caribbean Literature* by, 6
Gilroy, Paul, 62, 396n35; *The Black Atlantic* by, 166–67, 285, 291
Girls for Sale/Kanyasulkam (Apparao), 77
Glissant, Édouard, 159, 163, 166, 219–20, 279; contact zones and, 63; creolization and, 63, 73; language and, 72–73; planetary consciousness and, 72; poetics of, 80; *Poetics of Relation* by, 143, 152, 215, 217, 218; polycentricity and, 62; relational and, 79; worldness of, 72, 79

Global Circulation Project, 63
globalization, 1, 5; commodification and, 49; cultural, 63; expansion and, 315; indigenization and, 373n22; *longue durée* and, 325; postmodernism and, 321, 350n19; Ramazani and, 220–21; recurrent modernities, 59; relational and, 56; "the West" and, 341
Global Matters: The Transnational Turn in Literary Studies (Jay), 5
Global North, 123
Global South, 123, 132
God of Small Things, The (Roy), 53, 78, 188, 218, 238–55, 341; caste and, 248–50; colonialism and, 243–46; domestic affairs in, 247–50; gender and, 247–50, 339; racism and, 243–46
GoGwilt, Christopher, 6
"Golden Book" (*Atlan Debter*), 114
Golden Horde, of Russia, 107
Golden Notebooks, The (Lessing), 260
Gora (Tagore), 96, 189
Grain of Sand, A (Tagore), 277
Grand Canal (China), 101, 167
Graver, Mark, 57
Great Migration, U.S., 41
Great Mongol Nation (Yeke Mongol Ulus), 107
Great Mosque, in China, *104*, 104–5
Great Yasa, 110
Green Imperialism: Colonial Expansion, Tropical Island Edens, and the Origin of Environmentalism (Grove), 137–38
Greenwich Mean Time, 122, 127, 370n72
Greenwich Prime Meridian, 122, 127, 370n72
Grove, Richard, 137–38
Guardian of the Blackbirds, 79
Guattari, Félix, 151, 152, 163
gunpowder: in China, 105, 115; in Mongol Empire, 115, 116

Habermas, Jürgen, 22, 34, 176; binary and, 39
habitus, 165, 375n41
Hail Mother (*Bande Martaram*), 156
Hall, Stuart, 120–21, 143, 159–60
Hall, Thomas D., 136, 334
Hallett, Jessica, 200–201
Hardt, Michael, 336–37
Harlem Renaissance, 40–41, 316
Harvey, David, 25, 32, 322; binary and, 39
Hass, Robert, 212
Hassan, Ihab, 24, 319
Hayot, Eric, 6, 85, 156, 189–90, 333; "Chinese Modernism, Mimetic Desire, and European Time" by, 183; *On Literary Worlds* by, 329; multiple modernities and, 381n40
H.D., 4, 193; diaspora and, 287; experimentalism of, 327; *HERmione* by, 189; *Trilogy* by, 323
Heart of Darkness (Conrad), 71, 78, 96, 187, 218, 292, 341; collage and, 222–30; gender and, 338; *Season of Migration to the North* and, 237–38
Hegel, Georg Wilhelm Friedrich, 30
Heise, Ursula K., 78–79
Heisenberg, Werner, 51
heritage (*turath*), 48
hermeneutic circle, 40–41, 326–28, 353n38
HERmione (H.D.), 189
heterogeneity, 147, 206, 311; Nicholls and, 354n48; periodization and, 352n29
heterotopia, 11, 175–78
Hidden Power (Anderson, M.), 102–3
high culture, 51
high modernism, 22, 327; aesthetics and, 184–87; in Europe, 50; re-vision and, 76; in U.S., 50
Hinduism, 204–13
Hinton, David, 192, 194
Hiroshige, Utagawa, 68
History of the Mongols (Juzwani), 114

History of the World Conqueror (Jawayni), 114
Hobson, John M., 9, 98, 99–100, 103, 123; Eurocentrism and, 127; "the West" and, 121, 122
Hodgson, Marshall G. S., 98, 125
Hogan, Linda, 157
"Home and Identity" (Sarap), 283
Home and the World, The (Tagore), 155–56, 189
homosexuality, in *A Passage to India*, 250–54
Hoover Dam, 177
horizontal expansion, 48–49
horizontal spatialization, 95–96
Horoszko, Urszula, 226
hot societies, 352n29
Hughes, Langston, 70–71
humanism, 22; in Arab world, 48, 99–100; of Enlightenment, 30; Eurocentrism and, 55
humanities, 30–31, 352n27
Huntington, Samuel, 120, 129–30
Hurston, Zora Neale, 324
Hutcheon, Linda, 319
Huyssen, Andreas, 2, 61, 71, 83, 84, 316, 319; postmodernism and, 321
hybridity, 57, 107, 166; diaspora and, 396n35
Hybrid Muse, The (Ramazani), 286

ijtihad, 48
"Imaginary Homelands" (Rushdie), 284
imagism, 4
imperialism. *See* colonialism
In Another Country: Colonialism, Culture, and English Novel in India (Joshi), 6, 264
India, 48, 157; economic dominance of, 99; feminism in, 258; Hinduism in, 204–13; Islam in, 204–13; Kabir in, 204–13; Mughal Empire in, 61, 204–13; Narmada dam project in, 177–78; Orissa in, 75; polycentricity and, 59; religion in, 204–13; Renaissance in, 95; Tamerlane in, 204–13. *See also* Bengal Renaissance; *God of Small Things, The*; *Passage to India, A*; Rabindranath Tagore; Swarnakumari Devi
indigenization, 7, 74, 170–71, 221; globalization and, 373n22; psychoanalysis and, 90; Salih and, 237
individualism, 57
industrialization, 22, 319, 351n23
Industrial Revolution, 119; in China, 103, 106; in Netherlands, 161; periodization of, 88
Information Revolution, 163
innovation, 32, 66–72, 103, 200–203; aesthetics and, 186–88, 191–95
Inquisition, of Catholic Church, 116–17
institutional pragmatism, 5, 340–42
interculturalism, 63, 166–68, 203, 321
interdisciplinarity, 31–32, 89, 312, 327
internalization: of racism, 243; "the West" and, 133–36
International Reference Meridian, 370n72
Iran, 321
"Iraq and China: Ceramics, Trade, and Innovation" (exhibit), 200–201
Irigaray, Luce, 382n6
irony, 235, 239, 267, 294; of Tagore, 390n75
Islam: Abbasid Caliphate and, 190, 199–204; in China, 104, 104–5; in India, 204–13; in Mongol Empire, 110
Islam Translated (Ricci), 205
Israel, 123

Jacob's Room (Woolf), 275
Jamaica, 157
James, David, 86, 340
James, Henry, 28, 186–87
Jameson, Fredric, 28, 84, 85; *Postmodernisms, or, The Cultural Logic of Late Capitalism* by, 319; *A Singular Modernity* by, 59, 147–48

JanMohamed, Abdul R., 151
Japan: Cha and, 298; Ukiyo-e of, 66–67; in "the West," 122
Jardine, Alice, 23, 322
Jawayni, 114
Jay, Paul, 5
jazz, 62
Jazz Age, 41
Jeanne d'Arc, 303, 305
Johnson, James Weldon, 96
Jones, Eric L., 119, 125
Joshi, Priya, 6, 264
Joyce, James, 4, 53, 74, 96, 187, 188, 260–61, 292, 341, 387n56; diaspora and, 286; divergence and, 315; *Dubliners* by, 267; early ridicule of, 35; expatriate internationalism and, 40; experimentalism of, 327; *A Portrait of the Artist as a Young Man* by, 96, 189, 292, 341; tradition and, 323. See also *Ulysses*
Judaism, 110
Juzwani, 114

Kabir, 204–13, 332, 337, 381n36
Kadir, Djelal, 6
Kahake (Devi), 264, 265
Kalapurnodaymau/The Sound of the Kiss, 76–77
Kant, Immanuel, 22, 30
Kanyasulkam/Girls for Sale (Apparao), 77
Kenner, Hugh, 40
keywords, 143–80; relational, 143–46
Keywords (Williams), 143
Khan, Genghis, 107, 110, 111, 113, 114, 115, 366n46; Tamerlane and, 204
Khan, Hulegu, *113*
Khan, Khubilai, 107, 112, 114, 116
Khan, Möngke, 111, 117
Khan, Ogodei, 107, 113, 114
Khanate, Il-, 107
"Khata" (Tagore), 267–69
Khazanov, Anatoly, 106

Kim (Kipling), 96
King, John, 137
Kipling, Rudyard, 96
knowledge revolution, 163; in Mongol Empire, 115
Korea. See Cha, Theresa Hak Kyung
Krisnaswamy, Revathi, 221
Kristeva, Julia, 28
Kuhn, Thomas, 4
Künstlerroman, 189, 259

Landow, George P., 163
language, 72–75; colonialism and, 74; lingua franca, 72, 74, 77, 313–14; periodization and, 89; translation of, 73–74; vernacular and, 74–75, 221, 268–69, 271–73
"Languages Other Than English" (Spivak), 377n1
La passion de Jeanne d'Arc (Dreyer), 305
Lash, Scott, and Jonathan Friedman, 23
Latin America, 48, 174; avant-garde in, 71–72; colonialism in, 61; "the West" and, 136–37
Latour, Bruno, 56, 80
Lawrence, D. H., 187, 189, 292
Layoun, Mary, 279
Lee, Hermione, 275
Leonard, Garry, 49, 55, 318
Leopold (King), 383n16
Les demoiselles d'Avignon (Picasso), 4, 65, *65, 66, 67,* 95
Les fleurs du mal (Baudelaire), 4, 289; Césaire and, 292–93; periodization and, 89
Lessing, Doris, 260
le retour et le détour, 220
Lewis, Mark Edward, 103, 105, 191–93
Lewis, Pericles, 340; on periodization, 89
Li Bo, 191–98, 379n18
lingua franca, 72, 74, 77, 313–14
linkages: networks and, 162; Ramazani and, 220–21

Linnaeus, 138–39
Lionnet, Françoise, 6, 151–52, 286
literacy: in Mongol Empire, 112; relational, 279
Literary Compass: The Global Circulation Project, 6, 63
Lloyd, David, 151
Location of Culture, The (Bhabha), 169
Locke, John, 30, 41
Lonely Wife, The (*Charulata*) (Ray), 276
longue durée, 4, 8–9, 57, 311; Braudel and, 8–9, 94, 97; colonialism and, 61; deep time and, 76; Doyle and, 364n24; empires and, 335; before 1500, 96–119; globalization and, 325; multiple modernities in, 317; networks in, 167; periodization and, 87; planetary scale in, 83–142; recurrent modernities, 59; recurrent modernities in, 317; scale in, 312, 313; technology and, 160; vernacular and, 74–75, 268–69, 271–73; Wallerstein and, 97–98; "the West" and, 119; Westernization and, 333, 334
Lost Wisdom: Rethinking Modernity in Iran (Milani), 83
Louis IX (king), 117
low-caste (*sudra*), 75
Loy, Mina, 34
Luhmann, Niklas, 164–65
Lure of the Modern, The: Writing Modernism in Semicolonial China, 1917-1937 (Shih), 6
Lyotard, François, 23, 319–20, 322

machine à habiter, 22
magic realism, 71–72
Mahabharata, 188, 244
Mailer, Norman, 57
majolica, 203
Makdisi, George, 98, 99–100
Make It New (Pound), 34, 156
Malinowski, Bronisław, 31

Manganaro, Marc, 31
Mangharan, Mukti Lakhi, 212
Mani, B. Venkat, 169
manifest destiny, 173
manifesto, 2, 28, 136–37, 174, 311, 323
"Manifesto Antropófago" (Andrade), 136–37, 174
"Manifesto da Poesia Pau-Brasil" (Andrade), 136
Mao, Douglas, 187, 316; expansion and, 49; transnational turn and, 3, 84
Mappings: Feminism and the Cultural Geographies of Encounter (Friedman), 13, 338
Maps of Englishness (Gikandi), 76, 222
Marco Polo, 104, 107, 116
Marinetti, E. T., 4, 323
Maroons, 157
Márquez, Gabriel García, 71–72
Marti, José, 174
Marx, Karl, 125, 126, 155
Marxism, 22, 126
Masood, Syed Ross, 250, 251, 254
matrix, 57–58, 216; cultural, 165, 216; networks and, 162; postmodernism and, 322
Maurice (Forster), 251, 253–54
Mbuya mask, 66
McClintock, Anne, 6
McFarlane, James, 51, 95, 185; on periodization, 89
McHale, Brian, 319
McKean, Erin, 62
McMaster, Robert B., 94–95
McNeill, William H., 9–10, 119, 128–29
Mediterranean and the Mediterranean World in the Age of Phillip II, The (Braudel), 8, 94
Mehrotra, Arvind Krishna, 207–8, 212–13
Melville, Herman, 188, 190
Menocal, Maria Rosa, 75
Mercator projection, 123, *124*, 127

meritocracy, in Mongol Empire, 111
métissage, 48
metonym, 41–43
Mexican-American War of 1848, 173
Midnight: Mother and Sleepy Child (Kitagawa Utamaro), 69
Midnight's Children (Rushdie), 244
Mignolo, Walter D., 61, 169; on colonialism, 91
Milani, Abbas, 83, 84
Mill on the Floss, The (Eliot, G.), 265
Milosz, Czeslaw, 212
Milton, John, 57
mimetic desire, 333
mimicry, 41, 382n6; colonial, 140, 150, 218
Ming Dynasty, 203
minor modernities, 4, 151–52
Minor Transnationalism (Lionnet and Shih), 151, 286
misrecognition, with relational, 56
Mitchell, Timothy, 148
Moby-Dick (Melville), 188, 190
Modernism (Bradbury and McFarlane), 51, 95, 185
Modernism (journal), 6
"Modernism, Geopolitics, Globalization" (Cuddy-Keane), 63
Modernism and the New Spain (Rogers), 6
Modernism/Modernity (journal), 6, 14, 27, 51, 348n1, 354n1
Modernisms: A Literary Guide (Nicholls), 151, 340
Modernist Commitments (Berman), 6, 183
Modernist Studies Association (MSA), 50–51, 75, 90; periodization by, 89
Modernity at Large (Appadurai), 159, 283
"Modernity Versus Postmodernity" (Habermas), 34
Modern World-System, The (Wallerstein), 8, 120
Mohammed (Prophet), 105
Mohanty, Satya P., 57, 75

Mongol Empire, 105–19, *108*, *109*, *113*, 166, 312, 330, 336, 337; bureaucracies in, 112–13; capitalism and, 367n50, 368n56; census in, 113; Christianity in, 110, 117; compass of, 116; diaspora and, 285; gunpowder in, 115, 116; G. Khan of, 107, 110, 111, 113, 115, 204, 366n46; knowledge revolution in, 115; literacy in, 112; meritocracy in, 111; Pax Mongolica of, 110, 159, 285, 337; periodization for, 367n48; printing in, 112, 116; religion and, 110, 117–18, 369n63; Renaissance and, 116; shares in, 112; torture and, 367n49; universal education in, 112; world rule by, 368n57
Mongols, The (Morgan), 109
Montage of a Dream Deferred (Hughes), 70–71
Moretti, Franco, 98, 312, 337
Morgan, David, 109, 114, 368n58
Morris, Meaghan, 140
Morrison, Toni, 38, 172–74, 341
Moses, Michael Valdez, 373n22
Mowatt, Ken, 53
Mrs. Dalloway (Woolf), 53
MSA. See Modernist Studies Association
Mufti, Aamir, 54–55
Mughal Empire, 61, 204–13
multinodal, 153, 219, 239
multiple modernities, 44, 59–60, 146–54; aesthetics and, 185–86; gender and, 339; Hayot and, 381n40; Jameson and, 147–48; in *longue durée*, 317; periodization and, 85; postmodernism and, 322
"Multiple Modernities," 42
Murasaki, Lady, 74
Muslim Empire, 61
Muwashshahāt, 74–75

Naked and the Dead, The (Mailer), 57
Nanak, Guru, 205
Narayan, Uma, 256, 257–58

INDEX • 445

Narmada dam project, in India, 177–78
Nashtanir/The Broken Nest (Tagore), 75, 269–74
Nasir ad-Din Tusi, 113
nationalism, 333
nation-states, 38, 56; empires and, 118–19; periodization and, 93; world-system and, 97–99
native land/*pays antal*, 293
Nature and Context of Minority Discourse, The (JanMohamed and Lloyd), 151
Negri, Antonio, 336–37
negritude, 288–89, 291, 292, 295, 300–303, 396n28
Neolithic Revolution, 105–6
Netherlands, 161, 199, 203
networks, 62–69, 77, 162–67, *164*, 317; in *longue durée*, 167; periphery and, 217
"New Cultural Theories of Modernity" (Felski), 1
New Negro, 184, 187
New Woman, 184, 187, 256–57
New Woman, New Novels: Feminism and Early Modernism (Ardis), 256
New World Modernisms (Pollard), 6
Nicholls, Peter, 89, 151, 340, 354n48
Nietzsche, Friedrich, 36, 156, 184
Night and Day (Woolf), 256
9/11, 1
nomads, in China, 105–19
nominal, 29–37, 55–57, 91–93, 144–46, 180, 213, 326–28
nostos, 286, 287, 292, 297
"Notebook, The" (Tagore), 267–69
Notebook of a Return to the Native Land (Césaire). *See Cahier d'un retour au pays natal*

objective correlative, 195
oceanic studies, 166–67
"Of Other Spaces" (Foucault), 84, 146, 177, 217

Okigbo, Christopher, 220
Omvedt, Gail, 178
"On Alternative Modernities" (Gaonkar), 83
On Literary Worlds (Hayot), 329
O Pioneers! (Cather), 57
Orientalism (Said), 6, 90
Orissa, 75
Ottoman Empire, 175
Owen, Stephen, 195
Oxford Handbook of Global Modernisms, The, 6, 85, 174–75
Oxford Handbook of Modernisms, The, 6, 86

"Painter of Modern Life, The" (Baudelaire), 89
Papastergiadis, Nikos, 53, 159, 283
paper currency, in Mongol Empire, 111
Paradise Lost (Milton), 57
paratactic juxtaposition, 217, 278
parataxis, 21–27
parody, 25, 77; gender and, 382n6; mimicry as, 218
Passage of Literature, The (GoGwilt), 6
Passage to India, A (Forster), 14, 218, 292; collage and, 238–55; domestic affairs in, 250–55; homosexuality in, 250–55; racism in, 239–43
Pax Mongolica, 110, 159, 285, 337
pays natal/native land, 293
periodization, 31, 84–93; bookends of, 88–89; in China, 105; circle and, 40; colonialism and, 331; geographic boundaries to, 87–88; heterogeneity and, 352n29; logic of, 86; *longue durée* and, 87; for Mongol Empire, 367n48; of postmodernism, 87–88; relational and, 91–93; transnational turn and, 93
periphery: Eurocentrism and, 126–27; networks and, 217; scale and, 313
Persia, 107
Peters projection, 123, *124*
petits recits, 350n20

phallogocentrism, 339
phenomenology, 57
Phillips, Mark Salber, 322
Picasso, Pablo: *Les demoiselles d'Avignon* by, 4, 65, 65, 66, 67, 95; primitivism of, 41; tradition and, 323
Pilgrimage (Richardson), 189
pivot cities, 165–66
Planet, The (Spafford), 78
planetarity, 8, 78–80, 347–48n17
"Planetarity: Musing Modernist Studies" (Friedman), 354n1
planetary consciousness, 72, 79–80
planetary scale: before 1500, 96–119; in *longue durée*, 83–142; periodization and, 84–93; spatialization and, 84–93
Plum Estate, Kameido (Utagawa Hiroshige), 68
pluralization, 44, 147, 152, 316
PMLA, 48–49
Poe, Edgar Allan, 28
poetics: of displacement, 291–92; of Glissant, 80; "Thirteen Ways of Looking at a Blackbird" and, 69–72; transnational, 169
Poetics of Relation (Glissant), 143, 152, 215, 217, 218
Poison Tree, The (Chandra), 277
political unconscious, 28
Pollard, Charles W., 6
Pollock, Sheldon, 314
polycentricity, 153, 164–65; networks and, 162; postmodernism and, 322; technology and, 161–62; "Thirteen Ways of Looking at a Blackbird" and, 59–60
Pondrom, Cyrena, 333, 353n38
popular culture, 321
Portrait of the Artist as a Young Man, A (Joyce), 96, 189, 292, 341
postcolonialism, 5–6, 12–13, 90–91, 181–88, 222–55, 315–17. *See also* colonialism
Postmodern Condition, The (Lyotard), 319–20

postmodernism, 2, 24, 26, 32, 34–35; aesthetics and, 319, 350n19; debate on, 319–22; globalization and, 321; periodization of, 87–88
Postmodernisms, or, The Cultural Logic of Late Capitalism (Jameson), 319
poststructuralism, 320
Pound, Ezra, 156, 192, 292; *The Cantos* by, 74, 184, 193, 323; diaspora and, 287; expatriate internationalism and, 40; Kabir and, 212; *Make It New* by, 34, 156; tradition and, 323
Pratt, Mary Louise, 71–72, 169
primitivism, 30, 41
printing: in Europe, 328; in Mongol Empire, 112, 116
Provincializing Europe (Chakrabarty), 149
psychoanalysis, 27–28, 395n26; indigenization and, 90

Qing Dynasty, 73, 73; cobalt blue glaze in, 203
Questions of Tradition (Phillips), 322

racism: binary and, 370n76; in *The God of Small Things*, 243–46; internalization of, 243; in *A Passage to India*, 239–43. *See also Heart of Darkness*
Radhakrishnan, R., 6, 140–41, 150, 223, 279, 311
Ramanujan, A. K., 208
Ramayana, 213
Ramazani, Jahan, 65, 169, 216, 219; *The Hybrid Muse* by, 286; *A Transnational Poetics* by, 6, 62–63, 143, 220–21
Ramos, Julio, 174
Rao, V. Narayana, 76–77
Rashid, Harun al-, 200
rationalism: of Arab world, 48; of Enlightenment, 325
Ray, Satyajit, 276–78
realism, 316; aesthetics and, 53; magic, 71–72

reciprocal defamiliarization, 279
Reconsidering Tu Fu: Literary Greatness and Cultural Context (Chou), 194
Reconstruction (in U.S.), 173
recovery, 11, 76–77, 314
recurrent modernities, 59, 153; aesthetics and, 185–86; in *longue durée*, 317; postmodernism and, 322; technology and, 161–62
relational, 327, 351n23; Eurocentrism and, 127–28; Glissant and, 79; keywords for, 143–46; periodization and, 91–93; scale and, 352n29; "Thirteen Ways of Looking at a Blackbird" and, 55–57; tradition and, 56, 156–58
relational literacy, 279
religion: Buddhism, 103, 110; Confucianism, 103; Hinduism, 204–13; in India, 204–13; Judaism, 110; Mongol Empire and, 110, 117–18, 369n63; postmodernism and, 321; Sikhism, 205, 207; Spanish Inquisition and, 117; Taoism, 103. *See also* Christianity; Islam
Reminiscences (Tagore), 266
Renaissance: of Bengal, 48, 95, 186, 272; of Harlem, 40–41, 316; Mongol Empire and, 116; periodization of, 88; scale and, 319
ReOrient: Global Economy in the Asian Age (Frank), 99
Republic of Letters, The (Casanova), 185, 333
Resaldo, Renato, 7
Rethinking World History (Hodgson), 125
re-vision, 11, 76, 314
Rhetoric of English Empire, The (Suleri), 239
rhizome, 152, 163–64, 375n38; networks and, 162
Rhys, Jean, 77
Ricci, Ronit, 205
Richardson, Dorothy, 189, 264
Rig Veda, 213
Rise of Humanism in Classical Islam and Christian West, The (Makdisi), 99–100
Rise of "the West," The (McNeill), 9–10, 119, 128
Rite of Spring, The (Stravinsky), 4
Road from Paris, The (Pondrom), 333
Robbins, Bruce, 148
Roberts, J. M., 119
Rogers, Gayle, 6
Roman Empire, 61
romanticism, 5, 22, 24, 184, 315
Room of One's Own, A (Woolf), 218, 256, 258–59, 266, 276–77; Cha and, 306
Rosenberg, Fernando J., 6, 137, 174
Rosetta Stone, 73, 73
Ross, Stephen, 49
Rothenstein, William, 264
Rothstein, Eric, 352n29
Rougier, Louis, 119
Rousseau, Jean-Jacques, metonym and, 41
route, 167–72
Roux, Jean-Paul, 114
Roy, Arundhati, 12, 53, 71, 78, 187–88, 218, 238–55, 332, 341; Césaire and, 295; gender and, 339; on Narmada dam projects, 177–78. *See also God of Small Things, The*
rupture, 35, 37, 57, 154–58; colonialism and, 61–62; postmodernism and, 350n19; relative nature of, 318–19; Rothstein and, 352n29
Rushdie, Salman, 187, 188, 244, 284
Russia, Golden Horde of, 107
ruthless forgetting, 36, 56

Said, Edward W., 44, 169, 222, 224, 278, 335; on diaspora, 283; *Orientalism* by, 6, 90; "Traveling Theory" by, 219; "Traveling Theory Reconsidered" by, 215, 219, 237–38, 259
Saldívar, José David, 174
Salih, Tayeb, 12, 53, 71, 77, 78, 90, 173, 187, 218, 223, 332, 335, 341; collage and, 230–38; gender and, 339. *See also Season of Migration to the North*
Sanderson, Stephen K., 9, 136, 334

Sarap, Madan, 283, 324
Saussy, Haun, 6
scale, 8–9, 93–96; aesthetics and, 183, 189; cartographic, 95; debate on, 312–14; in *longue durée*, 312, 313; periphery and, 313; relational and, 318–19, 352n29; technology and, 319; translation and, 313–14. *See also* planetary scale
Scale and Geographical Inquiry (McMaster), 94–95
Scheherazade (fictional character), 200
Schluchter, Wolfgang, 42
Schreiner, Olive, 260–61; Woolf and, 388n58
Scott, Bonnie Kime, 164, *164*, 339
Scott, James C., 20, 22, 322
Scottish Enlightenment, 319
Season of Migration to the North (Salih), 53, 78, 90, 173, 218, 223, 247, 341; collage and, 230–38; gender and, 233–37, 256, 339; *Heart of Darkness* and, 237–38
"Second Coming, The" (Yeats), 32
Secret Agent, The (Conrad), 187
Secret History of the Mongols, The, 114, 367n47, 368n58
secularism, 91, 119, 328; Westernization and, 333
Self-Other, 64
Seshagiri, Urmila, 86, 340
Seyhan, Azade, 284, 286
shares, in Mongol Empire, 112
Sharpe, Jenny, 240
Shelley, Lynnette, 55
Sherman, Whitney, 76
Shipwrecked: Tang Treasures and Monsoon Winds, 200
Shohat, Ella, 3, 131–32
short span (*courte durée*), 94
Shu-mei Shih, 3, 151–53, 189; Cha and, 307; "Comparison as Relation" by, 183; *The Lure of the Modern: Writing Modernism in Semicolonial China, 1917–1937* by, 6; *Minor Transnationalism* by, 151, 286

Sikhism, 205, 207
Silko, Leslie Marmon, 157
Silk Road of the Sea, 104–5
Simmons, Lynn, 69
Singular Modernity, A (Jameson), 59, 147–48
Sketch of the Past, A (Woolf), 275
slavery, 47, 62, 172–73, 234–35, 272–73, 296
Smith, Linda T., 322–23
Smith, Terry, 320
Snuffing Out of Light, The (Dipnirban) (Devi), 263
social media, 321
social philology, 185
social sciences, 31
sociology, 353n34
Soja, Edward W., 84
Song Dynasty, 101–5, 192
Songhay Empire, 5, 167, 337
Songs of Kabir (Mehrotra), 207–8
Sons and Lovers (Lawrence), 189, 292
Sound of the Kiss, The (Kalapurnodaymau), 76–77
Sower, The (van Gogh), 68
Spafford, Michael, 78
Spanish Inquisition, 117
spatialization, 84–93, 147; human geography and, 95–96; "the West" and, 122–23, 125–26
speed, 158–62
Speed Handbook, The: Velocity, Pleasure, Modernism (Duffy), 160
Spivak, Gayatri Chakravorty, 6, 146, 327–28, 377n1
"Spring Prospect" (Du Fu), 196
Stam, Robert, 3, 131–32
Stein, Gertrude, 184, 322; *Tender Buttons* by, 4
Stevens, Wallace, 11, 52–79, 311–12
Story of a Soul (Thérèse of Liseux), 305
strategic essentialism, 146, 328, 372n5
Stravinsky, Igor, 4, 30, 184
Studies in Hysteria (Breuer and Freud), 254

Subrahmanyam, Sanjay, 39, 353n37
sudra (low-caste), 75
Suite of Ten (Cassatt), 67
Suleri, Sara, 239, 250
Suranna, Pingali, 76–77
surrealism, 333–34
Swift, Jonathan, 144
Sword of Islam. *See* Tamerlane
symbolic construct, 3
systems, 162–67, *164*

Tagore, Rabindranath, 75, 157, 332, 389n71; *Bengali Child's Primer* by, 268; *The Broken Nest/Nashtanir* by, 75, 269–74; collage and, 255–78; Devi, K., and, 270–71, 391n82; "Exercise-Book" by, 267–69; gender and, 262–66, 339; *Gora* by, 96, 189; *A Grain of Sand* by, 277; *The Home and the World* by, 155–56, 189; irony of, 390n75; Kabir and, 212; "Khata" by, 267–69; "The Notebook" by, 267–69; Ray and, 277; *Reminiscences* by, 266; tradition and, 324; Woolf and, 275–76; Yeats and, 389n70
Tale of Genji, The (Murasaki), 74
Taliban, 157
Tamerlane, 204–13
Tang Dynasty, 5, 9, 11, 12, 39–40, 61, 101–5, *102*, 190, 312, 336; aesthetics and, 191–98; feminism and, 257
Tanoukhi, Nirvana, 148
Taoism, 103
Tchingis Qaghan. *See* Genghis Khan
technology: acceleration and, 161; *longue durée* and, 160; polycentricity and, 161–62; recurrent modernities and, 161–62; scale and, 319
temporal expansion, 48–49
Temujin, 107, 114. *See also* Genghis Khan
Tender Buttons (Stein), 4
textual unconscious, 28
Thacker, Andrew, 63

Thérèse of Liseux, Saint, 305–6
"Theses on the Philosophy of History" (Benjamin), 178
Thirteen Blackbirds (Beckman-Harned), 52
"Thirteen Ways of Looking at a Blackbird" (Stevens), 11, 52–79, 311–12
Thousand and One Nights, The, 200
Thousand Plateaus, A (Deleuze and Guattari), 152
Three Gorges Dam, 177
Three Ravens (Shelley), 55
Timbuktu, 61, 167, 337
torture, 367n49
To the Lighthouse (Woolf), 78, 274
Tracking Modernity: India's Railway and the Culture of Mobility (Aguiar), 160
tradition, 33–34, 237–38, 340; collage and, 280; debate on, 322–24; Kabir and, 212; relational and, 56, 156–58
"Traditional Futures" (Clifford), 323–24
"Tradition and the Individual Talent" (Eliot), 323
transformational innovations, 103, 321
translation: of languages, 73–74; reliance on, 191; scale and, 313–14; "the West" and, 137–39
Translation Zone, The (Apter), 73
Translocal Modernisms, 6
transmissions of the remarkable (*chuanqi*), 192
transnationalism, 2, 5
transnational poetics, 169
Transnational Poetics, A (Ramazani), 6, 62–63, 143, 220–21
transnational turn, 3, 84, 86; periodization and, 93
transplantation, 169
"Traveling Theory" (Said), 219
"Traveling Theory Reconsidered" (Said), 215, 219, 237–38, 259
Trilogy (H.D.), 323
Triumph of "the West," The (Roberts), 119

Tropiques, 288
Trumpener, Kate, 340
Tsing, Anna L., 7, 137–39
turath (heritage), 48
Turbulence of Migration, The (Papastergiadis), 159, 283
Turkey, 175
Turn of the Screw, The (James), 28

Ukiyo-e, 66–67
Ulysses (Joyce), 4, 53, 74, 187, 292; divergence and, 315; gender in, 260–61; tradition and, 323; Woolf and, 387n56
uncertainty principle, 51
Unfinished Song, The (Devi), 264, 265
Uniqueness of Western Civilization, The (Duchesne), 119
United States, 173–74; Civil War of, 173; high modernism in, 50; Hoover Dam in, 177; humanities in, 352n27; Reconstruction of, 173
universal education, in Mongol Empire, 112
universal law, in Mongol Empire, 110
Unruh, Vicky, 136
Unthinking Eurocentrism (Shohat and Stam), 3
Untouchable (Anand), 318
Uprooted Vine, The (Devi), 277
urbanism, 51, 165–66; in China, 105–6, 133–35; in "the West," 136
U.S. *See* United States
Utamaro, Kitagawa, 67, 69
UTC. *See* Coordinated Universal Time
utopia, 4, 61, 117–18, 140–41, 175–78, 241

van Gogh, Vincent, 67, *68*
velocity, 158–62
vernacular, 74–75, 221, 268–69, 271–73
vertical expansion, 48–49
vertical spatialization, 95–96
Virmani, Shabnam, 212
Voluntés, 287

vortex, 57, 154–58
Voyage Out (Woolf), 256

Waldron, Arthur, 110
Walkowitz, Rebecca L., 187, 316, 340; circulation and, 169; expansion and, 49; transnational turn and, 3, 84
Wallerstein, Immanuel, 96–98, 120, 125, 127–28, 131, 165, 256–57, 378n5; "Eurocentrism and Its Avatars" by, 130; Global South and, 132; *The Modern World-System* by, 8, 120; on "the West," 130; *World-Systems Analysis: An Introduction* by, 98, 127–28
Waste Land, The (Eliot), 4, 74, 184, 292, 293, 295
Waves The (Woolf), 341
Weatherford, Jack, 107, 109–10, 115, 367n47
Weber, Max, 4, 125
"Wegyat Legend, Raven Stealing the Sun" (Mowatt), 53
We Have Never Been Modern (Latour), 80
"West, the," 3, 83, 119–26, *127*, 345n7; aesthetics and, 189–91; cannibalization and, 136–37; capitalism in, 127; China and, 133–36, *134*; debate on, 328–35; disease from, 130; feminism and, 256–57; globalization and, 341; internalization and, 133–36; Japan in, 122; Latin America and, 136–37; metanarrative of, 119–32; narrative point of view of, 128–31; spatialization and, 122–23, 125–26; translation and, 137–39; urbanization in, 136. *See also* Europe; United States
Westernization, 133–36, 332–35
Westphalia, Treaty of, 328
What Is Contemporary Art? (Smith), 320
Wicke, Jennifer, 49
Wigen, Kären, 163
Wilkinson, David, 168–69
William of Rubruck, 117
Williams, Raymond, 35, 40, 63, 143

Wink, André, 321
Winkiel, Laura, 63
Wittrock, Björn, 42
Wollaeger, Mark, 85
Woman and Man Playing Polo, 102
"Woman Who Rode Away, The" (Lawrence), 292
Woolf, Virginia, 12, 40, 78, 187, 188, 341; Cha and, 306; collage and, 255–78; Devi and, 266; G. Eliot and, 264; experimentalism of, 327; gender and, 274–78, 339; *Jacob's Room* by, 275; *To the Lighthouse* by, 78, 274; mental illness of, 391n93; *Mrs. Dalloway* by, 53; *Night and Day* by, 256; Ray and, 276–78; *A Room of One's Own* by, 218, 256, 258–59, 266, 276–77, 306; Schreiner and, 261, 388n58; *A Sketch of the Past* by, 275; *Ulysses* and, 260, 387n56; *Voyage Out* by, 256
World History, 9–10, 48, 88, 93–94, 96–101, 315–16, 332–34

worldness, 72, 79
world-system, 97–99, 99, 165, 256–57, 378n5
World-Systems Analysis: An Introduction (Wallerstein), 98, 127–28
World War I, 175, 187, 198, 250
World War II, 6, 35, 122, 298
Writing in Limbo: Modernism and Caribbean Literature (Gikandi), 6
Wu Zetian, 102–3

Xue Tao, 192

Yeats, W. B., 32, 48, 389n70
Yeke Mongol Ulus (Great Mongol Nation), 107
Yong Jung, 304–5
Young, David, 193–94, 196–98
Yuan Dynasty, 107, 116; cobalt blue glaze in, 203
Yu Guan Soon, 298, 303, 306

GPSR Authorized Representative: Easy Access System Europe, Mustamäe tee
50, 10621 Tallinn, Estonia, gpsr.requests@easproject.com